Business Foundations

A Changing World

eleventh edition

O.C. Ferrell
Auburn University

Geoffrey A. Hirt
DePaul University

Linda Ferrell
Auburn University

Mc
Graw
Hill
Education

BUSINESS FOUNDATIONS: A CHANGING WORLD, ELEVENTH EDITION

Published by McGraw-Hill Education, 2 Penn Plaza, New York, NY 10121. Copyright © 2018 by McGraw-Hill Education. All rights reserved. Printed in the United States of America. Previous editions © 2016, 2014, and 2011. No part of this publication may be reproduced or distributed in any form or by any means, or stored in a database or retrieval system, without the prior written consent of McGraw-Hill Education, including, but not limited to, in any network or other electronic storage or transmission, or broadcast for distance learning.

Some ancillaries, including electronic and print components, may not be available to customers outside the United States.

This book is printed on acid-free paper.

1 2 3 4 5 6 7 8 9 LWI 21 20 19 18 17

ISBN 978-1-259-68523-1
MHID 1-259-68523-3

Chief Product Officer, SVP Products & Markets:
  G. Scott Virkler
Vice President, General Manager, Products &
  Markets: Michael Ryan
Managing Director: Susan Gouijnstook
Director: Michael Ablassmeir
Brand Manager: Anke Weekes
Director, Product Development: Meghan Campbell
Product Developer: Gabriela G. Velasco
Freelance Product Developer: Shannon LeMay-Finn,
  Piper Editorial
Director of Marketing: Robin Lucan
Marketing Manager: Michael Gedatus
Market Development Manager: Nicole Young
Director of Digital Content: Kristy Dekat
Lead Digital Product Analyst: Sankha Basu
Director, Content Design & Delivery: Terri Schiesl
Program Manager: Mary Conzachi
Content Project Managers: Sheila M. Frank (Core),
  Evan Roberts (Assessment)

Buyer: Sandy Ludovissy
Design: Debra Kubiak
Content Licensing Specialists: Shawntel Schmitt
  (Image), Deanna Dausener (Text)
Cover Image: © eiyuwzhangjie/123RF
Compositor: SPi Global
Typeface: 10.25/12 STIX MathJax Main
Printer: LSC Communications
Icons: Green earth © beboy/Shutterstock.com; green
pushpin © Olivier Le Moal/Shutterstock.com; paper
people in circle © sheff/Shutterstock.com; jigsaw
puzzle piece © ALMAGAMI/Shutterstock.com;
magnifying glass © Kae Deezign/Shutterstock.com;
web, mobile, brochure © MIKHAIL GRACHIKOV/
Shutterstock.com; standing out from the crowd ©
Rusian Grechka/Shutterstock.com; empty scale ©
Design Pics/PunchStock; stones on beach © Ilya
Terentyev/Getty Images; businessman on stairs © Tom
Merton / age fotostock

All credits appearing on page are considered to be an extension of the copyright page.

Library of Congress Cataloging-in-Publication Data

Names: Ferrell, O. C., author. | Hirt, Geoffrey A., author. | Ferrell, Linda,
  author. | Ferrell, O. C. Business.
Title: Business foundations : a changing world / O.C. Ferrell, University of
  New Mexico, Geoffrey A. Hirt, DePaul University, Linda Ferrell, University
  of New Mexico.
Description: Eleventh Edition. | Dubuque : McGraw-Hill Education, 2017. |
  Revised edition of Business, [2016]
Identifiers: LCCN 2016041137 | ISBN 9781259685231 (alk. paper)
Subjects: LCSH: Business. | Management—United States.
Classification: LCC HF1008 .F47 2017 | DDC 658—dc23 LC record available at https://lccn.loc.
gov/2016041137

The Internet addresses listed in the text were accurate at the time of publication. The inclusion of a website does not indicate an endorsement by the authors or McGraw-Hill Education, and McGraw-Hill Education does not guarantee the accuracy of the information presented at these sites.

mheducation.com/highered

Dedication

To James Ferrell

To Linda Hirt

To George Ferrell

Authors

O.C. FERRELL

O.C. Ferrell is the James T. Pursell, Sr. Eminent Scholar in Ethics and Director of the Center for Ethical Organizational Cultures in the Raymond J. Harbert College of Business, Auburn University. He was formerly Distinguished Professor of Leadership and Business Ethics at Belmont University. He has also been on the faculties of the University of Wyoming, Colorado State University, University of Memphis, Texas A&M University, Illinois State University, and Southern Illinois University. He received his PhD in marketing from Louisiana State University.

Dr. Ferrell is president-elect of the Academy of Marketing Science. He is past president of the Academic Council of the American Marketing Association and chaired the American Marketing Association Ethics Committee. Under his leadership, the committee developed the AMA Code of Ethics and the AMA Code of Ethics for Marketing on the Internet. In addition, he is a former member of the Academy of Marketing Science Board of Governors and is a Society of Marketing Advances and Southwestern Marketing Association Fellow and an Academy of Marketing Science Distinguished Fellow. He has served for nine years as the vice president of publications for the Academy of Marketing Science. In 2010, he received a Lifetime Achievement Award from the Macromarketing Society and a special award for service to doctoral students from the Southeast Doctoral Consortium. He received the Harold Berkman Lifetime Service Award from the Academy of Marketing Science and, more recently, the Cutco Vector Distinguished Marketing Educator Award from the Academy of Marketing Science.

Dr. Ferrell has been involved in entrepreneurial engagements, co-founding Print Avenue in 1981, providing a solution-based printing company. He has been a consultant and served as an expert witness in legal cases related to marketing and business ethics litigation. He has conducted training for a number of global firms, including General Motors. His involvement with direct selling companies includes serving on the Academic Advisory Committee and as a fellow for the Direct Selling Education Foundation.

Dr. Ferrell is the co-author of 20 books and more than 100 published articles and papers. His articles have been published in the *Journal of Marketing Research, Journal of Marketing, Journal of Business Ethics, Journal of Business Research, Journal of the Academy of Marketing Science, AMS Review,* and the *Journal of Public Policy & Marketing,* as well as other journals.

GEOFFREY A. HIRT

Geoffrey A. Hirt of DePaul University previously taught at Texas Christian University and Illinois State University, where he was chairman of the Department of Finance and Law. At DePaul, he was chairman of the Finance Department from 1987 to 1997 and held the title of Mesirow Financial Fellow. He developed the

MBA program in Hong Kong and served as director of international initiatives for the College of Business, supervising overseas programs in Hong Kong, Prague, and Bahrain and was awarded the Spirit of St. Vincent DePaul award for his contributions to the university. Dr. Hirt directed the Chartered Financial Analysts (CFA) study program for the Investment Analysts Society of Chicago from 1987 to 2003. He has been a visiting professor at the University of Urbino in Italy, where he still maintains a relationship with the economics department. He received his PhD in finance from the University of Illinois at Champaign-Urbana, his MBA at Miami University of Ohio, and his BA from Ohio Wesleyan University.

Dr. Hirt is currently on the Dean's Advisory Board and Executive Committee of DePaul's School of Music. The Tyree Foundation funds innovative education programs in Chicago, and Dr. Hirt also serves on the Grant Committee. Dr. Hirt is past president and a current member of the Midwest Finance Association, a former editor of the *Journal of Financial Education*, and also a member of the Financial Management Association. He belongs to the Pacific Pension Institute, an organization of public pension funds, private equity firms, and international organizations such as the Asian Development Bank, the IMF, and the European Bank for Reconstruction and Development.

Dr. Hirt is widely known for his textbook *Foundations of Financial Management*, published by McGraw-Hill/Irwin. This book, in its sixteenth edition, has been used in more than 31 countries and translated into more than 14 different languages. Additionally, Dr. Hirt is well known for his textbook *Fundamentals of Investment Management*, also published by McGraw-Hill/Irwin and now in its tenth edition. Dr. Hirt enjoys golf, swimming, music, and traveling with his wife, who is a pianist and opera coach.

LINDA FERRELL

Linda Ferrell is Professor and Chair of the Marketing Department in the Raymond J. Harbert College of Business, Auburn University. She was formerly Distinguished Professor of Leadership and Business Ethics at Belmont University. She completed her PhD in business administration, with a concentration in management, at the University of Memphis. She has taught at the University of Tampa, Colorado State University, University of Northern Colorado, University of Memphis, University of Wyoming, and the University of New Mexico. She has also team-taught classes at Thammasat University in Bangkok, Thailand.

Her work experience as an account executive for McDonald's and Pizza Hut's advertising agencies supports her teaching of advertising, marketing management, marketing ethics, and marketing principles. She has published in the *Journal of Public Policy & Marketing, Journal of Business Research, Journal of the Academy of Marketing Science, Journal of Business Ethics, AMS Review, Journal of Academic Ethics, Journal of Marketing Education, Marketing Education Review, Journal of Teaching Business Ethics, Marketing Management Journal,* and *Case Research Journal,* and she is coauthor of *Business Ethics: Ethical Decision Making and Cases* (eleventh edition), *Management* (third edition), and *Business and Society* (sixth edition).

Dr. Ferrell is the immediate past president of the Academy of Marketing Science and a past president for the Marketing Management Association. She is a member of the NASBA Center for the Public Trust Board, on the Mannatech Board of Directors, and on the college advisory board for Cutco/Vector. She is also on the Board, Executive Committee, and Academic Advisory Committee of the Direct Selling Education Foundation. She has served as an expert witness in cases related to advertising, business ethics, and consumer protection.

Welcome

The eleventh edition represents a complete and comprehensive revision. This is because so many events and changes in the environment relate to the foundational concepts in business. This means that an introduction to business product has to provide adequate coverage of dynamic changes in the economy as they relate to business decisions. We have listened to your feedback and incorporated needed changes in content, boxes, cases, exercises, support, online resources and other features.

This is our fourth edition with a chapter on digital marketing and social networking in business. Since launching this chapter in the eighth edition, this dynamic area continues to change the face of business. Entrepreneurs and small businesses have to be able to increase sales and reduce costs by using social networking to communicate and develop relationships with customers. The sharing, or "gig," economy is transforming entrepreneurial opportunities for employees. For example, the number of independent contractors in our economy has increased from slightly over 5 percent to almost 16 percent of the workforce. The Internet is providing opportunities for peer-to-peer relationships for companies such as Uber, Lyft, TaskRabbit, as well as health care services like Dose. Because this area is a moving target, we have made substantial changes to the eleventh edition of Chapter 13, Digital Marketing and Social Networking. Digital marketing has helped many entrepreneurs launch successful businesses.

Throughout the product, we recognize the importance of sustainability and "green" business. By using the philosophy *reduce, reuse, and recycle,* we believe every business can be more profitable and contribute to a better world through green initiatives. There is a new "Going Green" box in each chapter that covers these environmental changes. Our "Entrepreneurship in Action" boxes also discuss many innovations and opportunities to use sustainability for business success. Sustainability is not only a goal of many businesses, but it is also providing career opportunities for many of our students.

We have been careful to continue our coverage of global business, ethics and social responsibility, and information technology as they relate to the foundations important in an introduction to business course. Our co-author team has a diversity of expertise in these important areas. O.C. Ferrell and Linda Ferrell have been recognized as leaders in business ethics education, and their insights are reflected in every chapter and in the "Consider Ethics and Social Responsibility" boxes. In addition, the website, http://danielsethics.mgt.unm.edu/ provides free resources such as PowerPoints and cases that can be used in the classroom. Geoff Hirt has a strong background in global business development, especially world financial markets and trade relationships.

The foundational areas of introduction to business, entrepreneurship, small business management, marketing, accounting, and finance have been completely revised. Examples have been provided to which students can easily relate. An understanding of core functional areas of business is presented so students get a holistic view of the world of business. Box examples related to "Responding to Business Challenges," "Entrepreneurship in Action," "Going Green," and "Consider Ethics and Social Responsibility" help provide real-world examples in these areas.

Our goal is to make sure that the content and teaching package for this book are of the highest quality possible. We wish to seize this opportunity to gain your trust, and we appreciate any feedback to help us continually improve these materials. We hope that the real beneficiary of all of our work will be well-informed students who appreciate the role of business in society and take advantage of the opportunity to play a significant role in improving our world. In this new edition, we have additional content to help our students understand how our free enterprise system operates and how we fit into the global competitive environment. This course is an opportunity for students to understand how they can create their own success and improve their quality of life.

O.C. Ferrell

Geoffrey A. Hirt

Linda Ferrell

Focused, Exciting, Applicable, Happening

Business Foundations: A Changing World, eleventh edition, offers faculty and students a **focused** resource that is **exciting, applicable,** and **happening**! What sets this learning program apart from the competition? An unrivaled mixture of exciting content and resources blended with application focused text and activities, and fresh topics and examples that show students what is happening in the world of business today!

Our product contains all of the essentials that most students should learn in a semester. *Business Foundations* has, since its inception, delivered a focused presentation of the essential material needed to teach introduction to business. An unrivaled mixture of exciting content and resources, application-focused content and activities, and fresh topics and examples that show students what is happening in the world of business today set this text apart!

Focused!

It's easy for students taking their first steps into business to become overwhelmed. Longer products try to solve this problem by chopping out examples or topics to make ad hoc shorter editions. *Business Foundations* carefully builds just the right mix of coverage and applications to give your students a firm grounding in business principles. Where other products have you sprinting through the semester to get everything in, Ferrell/Hirt/Ferrell allows you the breathing space to explore topics and incorporate other activities that are important to you and your students. The exceptional resources and the *Active Classroom Resource Manual* support you in this effort every step of the way.

Exciting

It's exciting to see students succeed! It's exciting to see more As and Bs in a course without grade inflation. Ferrell/Hirt/Ferrell makes these results possible for your course with its integrated learning package that is proven effective, tailored to each individual student, and easy to use.

Applicable

When students see how content applies to them, their life, their career, and the world around them, they are more engaged in the course. *Business Foundations* helps students maximize their learning efforts by setting clear objectives; delivering interesting cases and examples; focusing on core issues; and providing engaging activities to apply concepts, build skills, and solve problems.

Happening!

Because it isn't tied to the revision cycle of a larger book, *Business Foundations* inherits no outdated or irrelevant examples or coverage. Everything in the eleventh edition reflects the very latest developments in the business world—from the recent recession, high unemployment rates, and the financial instability in Europe to the growth of digital marketing and social networking. In addition, ethics continues to be a key issue, and Ferrell/Hirt/Ferrell use "Consider Ethics and Social Responsibility" boxes to instill in students the importance of ethical conduct in business. To ensure you always know what's happening, join the author-led Facebook group page supporting this text.

McGraw-Hill Connect®
Learn Without Limits

Connect is a teaching and learning platform that is proven to deliver better results for students and instructors.

Connect empowers students by continually adapting to deliver precisely what they need, when they need it, and how they need it, so your class time is more engaging and effective.

73% of instructors who use Connect require it; instructor satisfaction increases by 28% when Connect is required.

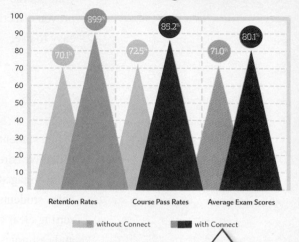

Connect's Impact on Retention Rates, Pass Rates, and Average Exam Scores

without Connect | with Connect

Using **Connect** improves retention rates by **19.8%**, passing rates by **12.7%**, and exam scores by **9.1%**.

Analytics

Connect Insight®

Connect Insight is Connect's new one-of-a-kind visual analytics dashboard—now available for both instructors and students—that provides at-a-glance information regarding student performance, which is immediately actionable. By presenting assignment, assessment, and topical performance results together with a time metric that is easily visible for aggregate or individual results, Connect Insight gives the user the ability to take a just-in-time approach to teaching and learning, which was never before available. Connect Insight presents data that empowers students and helps instructors improve class performance in a way that is efficient and effective.

Impact on Final Course Grade Distribution

	without Connect		with Connect
A	22.9%		31.0%
B	27.4%		34.3%
C	22.9%		18.7%
D	11.5%		6.1%
F	15.4%		9.9%

Students can view their results for any Connect course.

Mobile

Connect's new, intuitive mobile interface gives students and instructors flexible and convenient, anytime–anywhere access to all components of the Connect platform.

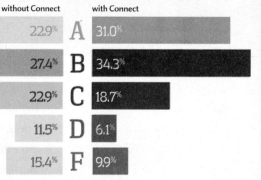

Adaptive

THE **ADAPTIVE** READING EXPERIENCE DESIGNED TO TRANSFORM THE WAY STUDENTS READ

More students earn **A's** and **B's** when they use McGraw-Hill Education **Adaptive** products.

SmartBook®

Proven to help students improve grades and study more efficiently, SmartBook contains the same content within the print book, but actively tailors that content to the needs of the individual. SmartBook's adaptive technology provides precise, personalized instruction on what the student should do next, guiding the student to master and remember key concepts, targeting gaps in knowledge and offering customized feedback, and driving the student toward comprehension and retention of the subject matter. Available on tablets, SmartBook puts learning at the student's fingertips—anywhere, anytime.

Over **8 billion questions** have been answered, making McGraw-Hill Education products more intelligent, reliable, and precise.

STUDENTS WANT ISMARTBOOK®

95% of students reported **SmartBook** to be a more effective way of reading material.

100% of students want to use the Practice Quiz feature available within **SmartBook** to help them study.

100% of students reported having reliable access to off-campus wifi.

90% of students say they would purchase **SmartBook** over print alone.

95% of students reported that **SmartBook** would impact their study skills in a positive way.

Mc Graw Hill Education

*Findings based on 2015 focus group results administered by McGraw-Hill Education

www.mheducation.com

New to This Edition

As always, when revising this material for the current edition, all examples, figures, and statistics have been updated to incorporate any recent developments that affect the world of business. Additionally, content was updated to ensure the most pertinent topical coverage is provided. We now provide bonus chapters in the text—Bonus Chapter A, The Legal and Regulatory Environment, and Bonus Chapter B, Personal and Financial Planning—to meet market demands. In addition, we have added a new online Appendix C, which provides the basics of risk management. Both insurable and noninsurable risk are covered in this appendix.

Here are the highlights for each chapter:

Chapter 1: The Dynamics of Business and Economics
- New boxed features describing real-world business issues
- New material on standard of living
- A new section on "The Importance of the American Economy"

Chapter 2: Business Ethics and Social Responsibility
- New boxed features describing issues in business ethics and social responsibility
- New examples of ethical issues facing today's businesses
- New *See for Yourself Videocase*—Warby Parker

Chapter 3: Business in a Borderless World
- New boxed features describing issues in international business
- New *See for Yourself Videocase*—Electra Bikes

Chapter 4: Options for Organizing Business
- New boxed features describing real-world business issues
- New definition of a master limited partnership
- New information on nonprofit organization

Chapter 5: Small Business, Entrepreneurship, and Franchising
- New boxed features describing current business issues
- New section on the sharing economy
- New material on nonstore retailing
- New information on incubators

Chapter 6: The Nature of Management
- New boxed features describing current business issues
- Staffing has been removed as a function of management, and the information on staffing has been moved toward the introduction
- New definition of brainstorming
- New information on participative decision making
- New *See for Yourself Videocase*—Panera Bread

Chapter 7: Organization, Teamwork, and Communication
- New boxed features describing current business issues
- A new objective on organizational culture
- New figure describing desired attitudes and behaviors associated with corporate culture

- New "Did You Know?" feature
- Information on formal communication has been placed in a table
- New *See for Yourself Videocase*—Hot Topic

Chapter 8: Managing Service and Manufacturing Operations
- New boxed features describing current business operational issues
- New material on the role of drones in operations
- New information on ISO 19600 related to compliance

Chapter 9: Motivating the Workforce
- New boxed features describing current business issues
- New section on goal-setting theory
- Updated information on best places for businesses and careers
- Definition of reinforcement theory

Chapter 10: Managing Human Resources
- New boxed features describing current HR issues
- A new "Did You Know?" feature
- New information on micropreneurs
- New information on exit interviews
- New material on mentoring employees
- New figure on recruiters' use of social networking in the recruitment process

Chapter 11: Customer-Driven Marketing
- New boxed features describing current marketing issues
- New material on marketing analytics
- New information on benefit segmentation
- New material on B2B marketing
- New *See for Yourself Videocase*—Marriott

Chapter 12: Dimensions of Marketing Strategy
- New boxed features describing current marketing issues
- New definition of merchant wholesalers
- Direct selling and direct marketing added as key terms
- New *See for Yourself Videocase*—Spirit Airlines

Chapter 13: Digital Marketing and Social Networking
- New boxed features describing current digital marketing issues
- New information on illicit activities conducted on the Internet
- New information on virtual gaming

Chapter 14: Accounting and Financial Statements
- New boxed features describing current accounting issues
- New information on the financial information and ratios of Microsoft
- Financial ratio comparisons of Microsoft and Google

Chapter 15: Money and the Financial System
- New boxed features describing current financial issues
- New material on reward cards
- New *See for Yourself Videocase*—State Farm

Chapter 16: Financial Management and Securities Markets
- New boxed features describing current financial issues
- New *See for Yourself Videocase*—Tom and Eddie's

Acknowledgments

The eleventh edition of *Business Foundations: A Changing World* would not have been possible without the commitment, dedication, and patience of Jennifer Sawayda and Julian Mathias. Jennifer Sawayda provided oversight for editing and developing text content, cases, boxes, and the supplements. Julian Mathias assisted in developing many of the boxes in this edition. Anke Weekes, Executive Brand Manager, provided leadership and creativity in planning and implementing all aspects of the eleventh edition. Gabriela G. Velasco, Product Developer, did an outstanding job of coordinating all aspects of the development and production process. Sheila Frank was the Content Project Manager. Evan Roberts managed the technical aspects of Connect. Others important in this edition include Michael Gedatus (Senior Marketing Manager) and Debra Kubiak (Designer). Michael Hartline developed the Personal Career Plan in Appendix B. Vickie Bajtelsmit developed Bonus Chapter B on personal financial planning. Eric Sandberg of Interactive Learning assisted in developing the interactive exercises. Many others have assisted us with their helpful comments, recommendations, and support throughout this and previous editions. Thank you for all of your insight and feedback. We'd like to express our sincere thanks to the reviewers who helped us shape the eleventh edition. Your time and thoughtful feedback has helped us greatly make this another great revision:

Vondra Armstrong
Pulaski Tech College

Gene Blackmun
Rio Hondo College

Susan Blumen
Montgomery College

Glenn Doolittle
Santa Ana College

Cheryl Fetterman
Cape Fear Community College

Anthony D. Fontes III
Bunker Hill Community College

John P. Guess
Delgado Community College

Paul Harvey
University of New Hampshire

Timothy D. Hovet
Lane Community College

Donald C. Hurwitz
Austin Community College

Kathleen Kerstetter
Kalamazoo Valley Community College

Jeffrey Lavake
University of Wisconsin–Oshkosh

Chad T. Lewis
Everett Community College

Terry Lowe
Illinois State University

Theresa Mastrianni
Kingsborough Community College

Mark McLean
Delgado Community College

Kimberly Mencken
Baylor University

Suzanne Murray
Piedmont Technical College

James Patterson
Paradise Valley Community College

Vincent Quan
Fashion Institute Technology

David Reiman
Monroe County Community College

Yalonda Ross Davis
Grand Valley State University

Brief Contents

Contents

Part 4

Creating the Human Resource Advantage   265

Part 5

Marketing: Developing Relationships 329

Cyndy Ruszkowski
Illinois State University

George Valcho
Bossier Parish Community College

Edith Strickland
Tallahassee Community College

Gunnar Voltz
Northern Arizona University–Flagstaff

Rodney Thirion
Pikes Peak Community College

Ruth White
Bowling Green State University

Allen D. Truell
Ball State University

Elisabeth Wicker
Bossier Parish Community College

Brenda Anthony, *Tallahassee Community College*
NaRita Gail Anderson, *University of Central Oklahoma*
Phyllis Alderdice, *Jefferson Community College*
Vondra Armstrong, *Pulaski Tech College*
John Bajkowski, *American Association of Individual Investors*
Gene Baker, *University of North Florida*
Lia Barone, *Norwalk Community College*
Ellen Benowitz, *Mercer County Community College*
Stephanie Bibb, *Chicago State University*
Barbara Boyington, *Monmouth–Ocean County Small Business Development Center*
Suzanne Bradford, *Angelina College*
Alka Bramhandkar, *Ithaca College*
Dennis Brode, *Sinclair Community College*
Harvey S. Bronstein, *Oakland Community College*
Colin Brooks, *University of New Orleans*
Eric Brooks, *Orange County Community College*
Nicky Buenger, *Texas A&M University*
Anthony Buono, *Bentley College*
Tricia Burns, *Boise State University*
Diana Carmel, *Golden West College*
William Chittenden, *Texas State University*
Michael Cicero, *Highline Community College*
Margaret Clark, *Cincinnati State Tech & Community College*
Mark Lee Clark, *Collin College*
Debbie Collins, *Anne Arundel Community College–Arnold*
Karen Collins, *Lehigh University*
Katherine Conway, *Borough of Manhattan Community College*
Rex Cutshall, *Indiana University*
Dana D'Angelo, *Drexel University*
Laurie Dahlin, *Worcester State College*
Deshaun H. Davis, *Northern Virginia Community College*
Peter Dawson, *Collin County Community College–Plano*
John DeNisco, *Buffalo State College*
Tom Diamante, *Corporate Consulting Associates, Inc.*
Joyce Domke, *DePaul University*
Michael Drafke, *College of DuPage*
John Eagan, *Erie Community College/City Campus SUNY*
Glenda Eckert, *Oklahoma State University*

Thomas Enerva, *University of Maine–Fort Kent*
Robert Ericksen, *Business Growth Center*
Donna Everett, *Santa Rosa Junior College*
Joe Farinella, *University of North Carolina–Wilmington*
Bob Farris, *Mt. San Antonio College*
Gil Feiertag, *Columbus State Community College*
James Ferrell, *R. G. Taylor, P.C.*
Art Fischer, *Pittsburg State University*
Jackie Flom, *University of Toledo*
Jennifer Friestad, *Anoka–Ramsey Community College*
Chris Gilbert, *Tacoma Community College/University of Washington*
Ross Gittell, *University of New Hampshire*
Connie Golden, *Lakeland Community College*
Terri Gonzales-Kreisman, *Phoenix College*
Kris Gossett, *Ivy Tech Community College of Indiana*
Carol Gottuso, *Metropolitan Community College*
Bob Grau, *Cuyahoga Community College–Western Campus*
Gary Grau, *Northeast State Tech Community College*
Jack K. Gray, *Attorney-at-Law, Houston, Texas*
Catherine Green, *University of Memphis*
Claudia Green, *Pace University*
Maurice P. Greene, *Monroe College*
Phil Greenwood, *University of Wisconsin–Madison*
David Gribbin, *East Georgia College*
Selina Andrea Griswold, *University of Toledo*
Peggy Hager, *Winthrop University*
Michael Hartline, *Florida State University*
Neil Herndon, *University of Missouri*
James Hoffman, *Borough of Manhattan Community College*
MaryAnne Holcomb, *Antelope Valley College*
Joseph Hrebenak, *Community College of Allegheny County–Allegheny Campus*
Stephen Huntley, *Florida Community College*
Rebecca Hurtz, *State Farm Insurance Co.*
Scott Inks, *Ball State University*
Steven Jennings, *Highland Community College*
Carol Jones, *Cuyahoga Community College–Eastern Campus*

Sandra Kana, *Mid-Michigan Community College*

Norm Karl, *Johnson County Community College*

Janice Karlan, *LaGuardia Community College*

Eileen Kearney, *Montgomery County Community College*

Craig Kelley, *California State University–Sacramento*

Susan Kendall, *Arapahoe Community College*

Ina Midkiff Kennedy, *Austin Community College*

Arbrie King, *Baton Rouge Community College*

John Knappenberger, *Mesa State College*

Gail Knell, *Cape Cod Community College*

Anthony Koh, *University of Toledo*

Regina Korossy, *Pepperdine University*

Velvet Landingham, *Kent State University–Geauga*

Daniel LeClair, *AACSB*

Richard Lewis, *East Texas Baptist College*

Corinn Linton, *Valencia Community College*

Corrine Livesay, *Mississippi College*

Thomas Lloyd, *Westmoreland Community College*

Terry Loe, *Kennerow University*

Kent Lutz, *University of Cincinnati*

Scott Lyman, *Winthrop University*

Dorinda Lynn, *Pensacola Junior College*

Isabelle Maignan, *ING*

Larry Martin, *Community College of Southern Nevada–West Charles*

Therese Maskulka, *Youngstown State University*

Kristina Mazurak, *Albertson College of Idaho*

Debbie Thorne McAlister, *Texas State University–San Marcos*

John McDonough, *Menlo College*

Tom McInish, *University of Memphis*

Noel McDeon, *Florida Community College*

Chris Mcnamara, *Fingers Lake Community College*

Mary Meredith, *University of Louisiana at Lafayette*

Michelle Meyer, *Joliet Junior College*

George Milne, *University of Massachusetts–Amherst*

Daniel Montez, *South Texas College*

Glynna Morse, *Augusta College*

Stephanie Narvell, *Wilmington College–New Castle*

Fred Nerone, *International College of Naples*

Laura Nicholson, *Northern Oklahoma College*

Stef Nicovich, *Lynchburg College*

Michael Nugent, *SUNY–Stony Brook University New York*

Mark Nygren, *Brigham Young University–Idaho*

Lauren Paisley, *Genesee Community College*

Wes Payne, *Southwest Tennessee Community College*

Dyan Pease, *Sacramento City College*

Constantine G. Petrides, *Borough of Manhattan Community College*

John Pharr, *Cedar Valley College*

Shirley Polejewski, *University of St. Thomas*

Daniel Powroznik, *Chesapeake College*

Krista Price, *Heald College*

Larry Prober, *Rider University*

Michael Quinn, *Penn State University*

Stephen Pruitt, *University of Missouri–Kansas City*

Victoria Rabb, *College of the Desert*

Gregory J. Rapp, *Portland Community College*

Tom Reading, *Ivy Tech State College*

Delores Reha, *Fullerton College*

Susan Roach, *Georgia Southern University*

Dave Robinson, *University of California–Berkeley*

Carol Rowey, *Surry Community College*

Marsha Rule, *Florida Public Utilities Commission*

Carol A. Rustad, *Sylvan Learning*

Martin St. John, *Westmoreland Community College*

Don Sandlin, *East Los Angeles College*

Nick Sarantakes, *Austin Community College*

Andy Saucedo, *Dona Ana Community College–Las Cruces*

Dana Schubert, *Colorado Springs Zoo*

Marianne Sebok, *Community College of Southern Nevada–West Charles*

Jeffery L. Seglin, *Seglin Associates*

Daniel Sherrell, *University of Memphis*

Morgan Shepherd, *University of Colorado Elaine Simmons, Guilford Technical Community College*

Greg Simpson, *Blinn College*

Nicholas Siropolis, *Cuyahoga Community College*

Robyn Smith, *Pouder Valley Hospital*

Kurt Stanberry, *University of Houston Downtown*

Cheryl Stansfield, *North Hennepin Community College*

Ron Stolle, *Kent State University–Kent*

Jeff Strom, *Virginia Western Community College*

Lisa Strusowski, *Tallahassee Community College*

Scott Taylor, *Moberly Area Community College*

Wayne Taylor, *Trinity Valley Community College*

Ray Tewell, *American River College*

Evelyn Thrasher, *University of Massachusetts–Dartmouth*

Steve Tilley, *Gainesville College*

Amy Thomas, *Roger Williams University*

Kristin Trask, *Butler Community College*

Ted Valvoda, *Lakeland Community College*

Sue Vondram, *Loyola University*

Elizabeth Wark, *Springfield College*

Emma Watson, *Arizona State University–West*

Frederik Williams, *North Texas State University*

Richard Williams, *Santa Clara University*

Pat Wright, *University of South Carolina*

Lawrence Yax, *Pensacola Junior College–Warrington*

Bruce Yuille, *Cornell University–Ithaca*

PART 1

Business in a Changing World

1

The Dynamics of Business and Economics

Chapter Outline

Learning Objectives

After reading this chapter, you will be able to:

LO 1-1   Define basic concepts such as business, product, and profit.

LO 1-2   Identify the main participants and activities of business and explain why studying business is important.

LO 1-3   Define economics and compare the four types of economic systems.

LO 1-4   Describe the role of supply, demand, and competition in a free-enterprise system.

LO 1-5   Specify why and how the health of the economy is measured.

LO 1-6   Trace the evolution of the American economy and discuss the role of the entrepreneur in the economy.

LO 1-7   Evaluate a small-business owner's situation and propose a course of action.

Enter the World of Business ⊖——————————

Dollar Shave Club Cuts through the Competition

For Dollar Shave Club (DSC), it's all about finding a better and more convenient way to meet the demand for razor blades. The idea for the firm emerged from a conversation entrepreneur Michael Dubin was having with co-founder Mark Levine about the annoyances of shaving. They found it inconvenient and costly to have to purchase multiple brand-name blades each month. This conversation resulted in the concept for a subscription-based service. Consumers who become members of DSC are mailed razor blades for as little as $1 per month.

The razor blade market is an example of monopolistic competition. The market is relatively easy to enter because the products are low tech, low cost, and easy to manufacture. Still, it is dominated by a few major brands, most notably Gillette and Schick. Gillette has 60 percent of the retail market. This meant that in order to compete against Gillette, DSC had to find a way to differentiate its product offering from rivals'. For DSC, the answer was not so much in the razor blade, but in the convenience and price savings offered to the consumer. Customers are paying for the service of having razor blades delivered to their door without the hassle or expense of purchasing them in a store. It also differentiates its business through its promotional techniques, most notably its humorously crafted, low-cost videos released on YouTube.

Gillette has taken notice. It has created its own shave club where consumers can order online. Other online competitors to DSC have also cropped up, including 800Razors LLC and Harry's Razor Co. For DSC to compete effectively, it is looking for further ways to "own the men's bathroom" with innovative products that meet customer needs. In 2016 Unilever purchased DSC for $1 billion.[1]

Introduction

We begin our study of business in this chapter by examining the fundamentals of business and economics. First, we introduce the nature of business, including its goals, activities, and participants. Next, we describe the basics of economics and apply them to the U.S. economy. Finally, we establish a framework for studying business in this text.

LO 1-1

Define basic concepts such as business, product, and profit.

business
individuals or organizations who try to earn a profit by providing products that satisfy people's needs.

product
a good or service with tangible and intangible characteristics that provide satisfaction and benefits.

profit
the difference between what it costs to make and sell a product and what a customer pays for it.

nonprofit organizations
organizations that may provide goods or services but do not have the fundamental purpose of earning profits.

The Nature of Business

A **business** tries to earn a profit by providing products that satisfy people's needs. The outcomes of its efforts are **products** that have both tangible and intangible characteristics that provide satisfaction and benefits. When you purchase a product, you are buying the benefits and satisfaction you think the product will provide. A Subway sandwich, for example, may be purchased to satisfy hunger, while a Honda Accord may be purchased to satisfy the need for transportation and the desire to present a certain image.

Most people associate the word *product* with tangible goods—an automobile, smartphone, coat, or some other tangible item. However, a product can also be a service, which occurs when people or machines provide or process something of value to customers. Dry cleaning, a checkup by a doctor, a movie or sports event—these are examples of services. Some services, such as Instagram, a mobile photo management and sharing application, do not charge a fee for use but obtain revenue from ads on their sites. A product can also be an idea. Accountants and attorneys, for example, generate ideas for solving problems.

The Goal of Business

The primary goal of all businesses is to earn a **profit,** the difference between what it costs to make and sell a product and what a customer pays for it. If a company spends $8.00 to manufacture, finance, promote, and distribute a product that it sells for $10.00, the business earns a profit of $2.00 on each product sold. Businesses have the right to keep and use their profits as they choose—within legal limits—because profit is the reward for the risks they take in providing products. Earning profits contributes to society by creating resources that support our social institutions and government. Businesses that create profits, pay taxes, and create jobs are the foundation of our economy. In addition, profits must be earned in a responsible manner. Not all organizations are businesses, however. **Nonprofit organizations**—such as National Public Radio (NPR), Habitat for Humanity, and other charities and social causes—do not have the fundamental purpose of earning profits, although they may provide goods or services and engage in fund raising. They also utilize skills related to management, marketing, and finance. Profits earned by businesses support nonprofit organizations through donations from employees.

To earn a profit, a person or organization needs management skills to plan, organize, and control the activities of the business and to find and develop employees so that it can make products consumers will buy. A business also needs marketing expertise to learn what products consumers need and want and to develop, manufacture, price, promote, and distribute those products. Additionally, a business needs financial resources and skills to fund, maintain, and expand its operations. Other challenges for businesspeople include abiding by laws and government regulations; acting in an ethical and socially responsible manner; and adapting to economic, technological, political, and social changes. Even nonprofit organizations engage in management, marketing, and finance activities to help reach their goals.

To achieve and maintain profitability, businesses have found that they must produce quality products, operate efficiently, and be socially responsible and ethical in dealing with customers, employees, investors, government regulators, and the community. Because these groups have a stake in the success and outcomes of a business, they are sometimes called **stakeholders.** Many businesses, for example, are concerned about how the production and distribution of their products affect the environment. New fuel requirements are forcing automakers to invest in smaller, lightweight cars. During times of low fuel prices, consumers tend to prefer bigger SUVs and trucks, putting more of a strain on automakers to meet environmental requirements as well as consumer demands.[2] Others are concerned with promoting science, engineering, and mathematics careers among women. Traditionally, these careers have been male dominated. The

Sustainability is a growing concern among both consumers and businesses. Walmart has invested in solar panels at some of its stores to decrease its energy usage.

© Thomas Cooper/Stringer/Getty Images

Association for Women in Science focuses on helping women reach their full potential in these underrepresented fields.[3] Other companies, such as Home Depot, have a long history of supporting natural disaster victims, relief efforts, and recovery.

stakeholders
groups that have a stake in the success and outcomes of a business.

The People and Activities of Business

Identify the main participants and activities of business and explain why studying business is important.

Figure 1-1 shows the people and activities involved in business. At the center of the figure are owners, employees, and customers; the outer circle includes the primary business activities—management, marketing, and finance. Owners have to put up resources—money or credit—to start a business. Employees are responsible for the work that goes on within a business. Owners can manage the business themselves or hire employees to accomplish this task. The president and CEO of Procter & Gamble, David S. Taylor, does not own P&G but is an employee who is responsible for managing all the other employees in a way that earns a profit for investors, who are the real owners. Finally, and most importantly, a business's major role is to satisfy the customers who buy its goods or services. Note also that people and forces beyond an organization's control—such as legal and regulatory forces, the economy, competition, technology, the political environment, and ethical and social concerns—all have an impact on the daily operations of businesses. You will learn more about these participants in business activities throughout this book. Next, we will examine the major activities of business.

Management.   Notice that in Figure 1-1, management and employees are in the same segment of the circle. This is because management involves developing plans, coordinating employees' actions to achieve the firm's goals, organizing people to work efficiently, and motivating them to achieve the business's goals. Management involves the functions of planning, organizing, leading, and controlling. Effective managers who are skilled in these functions display effective leadership, decision making, and implementation of work tasks. Management is also concerned with acquiring, developing, and using resources (including people) effectively and efficiently. For instance, managers at Hewlett-Packard made the strategic decision to split into two companies. Years of declining sales and corporate scandals convinced them that the firm needed to be smaller and more flexible to compete.[4]

FIGURE 1-1
Overview of the Business
World

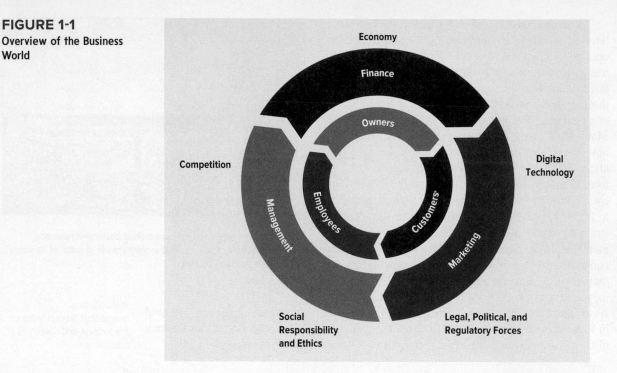

FIGURE 1-1
Overview of the Business World

Operations is another element of management. Managers must oversee the firm's operations to ensure that resources are successfully transformed into goods and services. Although most people associate operations with the development of goods, operations management applies just as strongly to services. Managers at the Ritz-Carlton, for instance, are concerned with transforming resources such as employee actions and hotel amenities into a quality customer service experience. In essence, managers plan, organize, staff, and control the tasks required to carry out the work of the company or nonprofit organization. We take a closer look at management activities in Parts 3 and 4 of this text.

Marketing.   Marketing and consumers are in the same segment of Figure 1-1 because the focus of all marketing activities is satisfying customers. Marketing includes all the activities designed to provide goods and services that satisfy consumers' needs and wants. Marketers gather information and conduct research to determine what customers want. Using information gathered from marketing research, marketers plan and develop products and make decisions about how much to charge for their products and when and where to make them available. They also analyze the marketing environment to see if products need to be modified. Marketing focuses on the four P's—product, price, place (or distribution), and promotion—also known as the marketing mix. Product management involves such key management decisions as product adoption or deletion, branding, and product positioning. Selecting the right price for the product is essential to the organization as it relates directly to profitability. Distribution is an important management concern because it involves making sure products are available to consumers in the right place at the right time. Marketers use promotion—advertising, personal selling, sales promotion (coupons, games, sweepstakes, movie tie-ins), and publicity—to communicate the benefits and advantages of their products to consumers and increase sales. We will examine marketing activities in Part 5 of this text.

The Aflac duck ad uses humor in its advertising to promote the insurance company.

© Chance Yeh/Contributor/Getty Images

Finance.   Owners and finance are in the same part of Figure 1-1 because, although management and marketing have to deal with financial considerations, it is the primary responsibility of the owners to provide financial resources for the operation of the business. Moreover, the owners have the most to lose if the business fails to make a profit. Finance refers to all activities concerned with obtaining money and using it effectively. People who work as accountants, stockbrokers, investment advisors, or bankers are all part of the financial world. Owners sometimes have to borrow money from banks to get started or attract additional investors who become partners or stockholders. Owners of small businesses in particular often rely on bank loans for funding. Part 6 of this text discusses financial management.

Why Study Business?

Studying business can help you develop skills and acquire knowledge to prepare for your future career, regardless of whether you plan to work for a multinational *Fortune* 500 firm, start your own business, work for a government agency, or manage or volunteer at a nonprofit organization. The field of business offers a variety of interesting and challenging career opportunities throughout the world, such as marketing, human resources management, information technology, finance, production and operations, wholesaling and retailing, and many more.

   Studying business can also help you better understand the many business activities that are necessary to provide satisfying goods and services—and that these activities carry a price tag. For example, if you buy a new DVD or Blu-ray disc, about half of the price goes toward activities related to distribution and the retailer's expenses and profit margins. The production (pressing) of the disc represents about $1, or a small percentage of its price. Most businesses charge a reasonable price for their products to ensure that they cover their production costs, pay their employees, provide their owners with a return on their investment, and perhaps give something back to their local communities and societies. Bill Daniels founded Cablevision, building his first cable TV system in Casper, Wyoming, in 1953, and is now considered "the father of cable television." Prior to Daniels' passing in 2000, he had established a foundation that currently has funding significantly over $1 billion and supports a diversity of causes from education to business ethics. During his career, Daniels created the Young Americans Bank, where children could create bank accounts and learn about financial responsibility, and this remains the world's only charter bank for young people. He named the Daniels College of Business through a donation of $20 million to the University of Denver. During his life, he affected many individuals and organizations, and his business success has allowed his legacy to be one of giving and impacting communities throughout the United States.[5] Most of the profits he earned in business continue to support nonprofit organizations and society. Thus, learning about business can help you become a well-informed consumer and member of society.

Business activities help generate the profits that are essential not only to individual businesses and local economies but also to the health of the global economy. Without profits, businesses find it difficult, if not impossible, to buy more raw materials, hire more employees, attract more capital, and create additional products that in turn make more profits and fuel the world economy. Understanding how our free-enterprise economic system allocates resources and provides incentives for industry and the workplace is important to everyone.

LO 1-3

Define economics and compare the four types of economic systems.

economics
the study of how resources are distributed for the production of goods and services within a social system.

natural resources
land, forests, minerals, water, and other things that are not made by people.

human resources
the physical and mental abilities that people use to produce goods and services; also called labor.

financial resources (capital)
the funds used to acquire the natural and human resources needed to provide products; also called capital.

economic system
a description of how a particular society distributes its resources to produce goods and services.

The Economic Foundations of Business

To continue our introduction to business, it is useful to explore the economic environment in which business is conducted. In this section, we examine economic systems, the free-enterprise system, the concepts of supply and demand, and the role of competition. These concepts play important roles in determining how businesses operate in a particular society.

Economics is the study of how resources are distributed for the production of goods and services within a social system. You are already familiar with the types of resources available. Land, forests, minerals, water, and other things that are not made by people are **natural resources. Human resources,** or labor, refer to the physical and mental abilities that people use to produce goods and services. **Financial resources,** or **capital,** are the funds used to acquire the natural and human resources needed to provide products. These resources are related to the *factors of production,* consisting of land, labor, capital, and enterprise used to produce goods and services. The firm can also have intangible resources such as a good reputation for quality products or being socially responsible. The goal is to turn the factors of production and intangible resources into a competitive advantage.

Economic Systems

An **economic system** describes how a particular society distributes its resources to produce goods and services. A central issue of economics is how to fulfill an unlimited demand for goods and services in a world with a limited supply of resources. Different economic systems attempt to resolve this central issue in numerous ways, as we shall see.

Although economic systems handle the distribution of resources in different ways, all economic systems must address three important issues:

1. What goods and services, and how much of each, will satisfy consumers' needs?
2. How will goods and services be produced, who will produce them, and with what resources will they be produced?
3. How are the goods and services to be distributed to consumers?

Communism, socialism, and capitalism, the basic economic systems found in the world today (Table 1-1), have fundamental differences in the way they address these issues. The factors of production in command economies are controlled by government planning. In many cases, the government owns or controls the production of goods and services. Communism and socialism are, therefore, considered command economies.

Communism.   Karl Marx (1818–1883) first described **communism** as a society in which the people, without regard to class, own all the nation's resources. In his ideal political-economic system, everyone contributes according to ability and receives benefits according to need. In a communist economy, the people (through the government) own and operate all businesses and factors of production. Central government planning determines what goods and services satisfy citizens' needs, how the goods and services are produced, and how they are distributed. However, no true communist economy exists today that satisfies Marx's ideal.

China has a communist economic system and is one of the largest economies in the world.

© Blend Images LLC

communism
first described by Karl Marx as a society in which the people, without regard to class, own all the nation's resources.

TABLE 1-1
Comparison of Communism, Socialism, and Capitalism

	Communism	Socialism	Capitalism
Business ownership	Most businesses are owned and operated by the government.	The government owns and operates some major industries; individuals own small businesses.	Individuals own and operate all businesses.
Competition	Government controls competition and the economy.	Restricted in major industries; encouraged in small business.	Encouraged by market forces and government regulations.
Profits	Excess income goes to the government. The government supports social and economic institutions.	Profits earned by small businesses may be reinvested in the business; profits from government-owned industries go to the government.	Individuals and businesses are free to keep profits after paying taxes.
Product availability and price	Consumers have a limited choice of goods and services; prices are usually high.	Consumers have some choice of goods and services; prices are determined by supply and demand.	Consumers have a wide choice of goods and services; prices are determined by supply and demand.
Employment options	Little choice in choosing a career; most people work for government-owned industries or farms.	More choice of careers; many people work in government jobs.	Unlimited choice of careers.

On paper, communism appears to be efficient and equitable, producing less of a gap between rich and poor. In practice, however, communist economies have been marked by low standards of living, critical shortages of consumer goods, high prices, corruption, and little freedom. Russia, Poland, Hungary, and other eastern European nations have turned away from communism and toward economic systems governed by supply and demand rather than by central planning. However, their experiments with alternative economic systems have been fraught with difficulty and hardship. Countries such as Venezuela have tried to incorporate communist economic principles. Even Cuba is experiencing changes to its predominately communist system. Massive government layoffs required many Cubans to turn toward the private sector, opening up more opportunities for entrepreneurship. The U.S. government has reestablished diplomatic relations with Cuba. Americans have more opportunities to visit Cuba than they have had for the past 50 years. Similarly, China has become the first communist country to make strong economic gains by adopting capitalist approaches to business. Economic prosperity has advanced in China with the government claiming to ensure market openness, equality, and fairness through state capitalism.[6] As a result of economic challenges, communism is declining and its future as an economic system is uncertain.

Socialism.   Socialism is an economic system in which the government owns and operates basic industries—postal service, telephone, utilities, transportation, health care, banking, and some manufacturing—but individuals own most businesses. For example, in France the postal service industry La Poste is fully owned by the French government and makes a profit. Central planning determines what basic goods and services are produced, how they are produced, and how they are distributed. Individuals and small businesses provide other goods and services based on consumer demand and the availability of resources. Citizens are dependent on the government for many goods and services.

Most socialist nations, such as Sweden, India, and Israel, are democratic and recognize basic individual freedoms. Citizens can vote for political offices, but central government planners usually make decisions about what is best for the nation. People are free to go into the occupation of their choice, but they often work in government-operated organizations. Socialists believe their system permits a higher standard of living than other economic systems, but the difference often applies to the nation as a whole rather than to its individual citizens. Socialist economies profess egalitarianism—equal distribution of income and social services. They believe their economies are more stable than those of other nations. Although this may be true, taxes and unemployment are generally higher in socialist countries. Perhaps as a result, many socialist countries have also experienced economic difficulties.

socialism
an economic system in which the government owns and operates basic industries but individuals own most businesses.

The Federal Trade Commission enforces antitrust laws and monitors businesses to ensure fair competition.

© Paul J. Richards/AFP/Getty Images

Capitalism.   Capitalism, or free enterprise, is an economic system in which individuals own and operate the majority of businesses that provide goods and services. Competition, supply, and demand determine which goods and services are produced, how they are produced, and how they are distributed. The United States, Canada, Japan, and Australia are examples of economic systems based on capitalism.

There are two forms of capitalism: pure capitalism and modified capitalism. In pure capitalism, also called a free-market system, all economic decisions are made without government intervention. This economic system was first described by Adam Smith in *The Wealth of Nations* (1776). Smith, often called the father of capitalism, believed that the "invisible hand of competition" best regulates the economy. He argued that competition should determine what goods and services people need. Smith's system is also called *laissez-faire* ("let it be") *capitalism* because the government does not interfere in business.

Modified capitalism differs from pure capitalism in that the government intervenes and regulates business to some extent. One of the ways in which the United States and Canadian governments regulate business is through laws. Laws such as the Federal Trade Commission Act, which created the Federal Trade Commission to enforce antitrust laws, illustrate the importance of the government's role in the economy. In the most recent recession, the government provided loans and took ownership positions in banks such as Citigroup, AIG (an insurance company), and General Motors. These actions were thought necessary to keep these firms from going out of business and creating a financial disaster for the economy.

Mixed Economies.   No country practices a pure form of communism, socialism, or capitalism, although most tend to favor one system over the others. Most nations operate as mixed economies, which have elements from more than one economic system. In socialist Sweden, most businesses are owned and operated by private individuals. In capitalist United States, an independent federal agency operates the postal service and another independent agency operates the Tennessee Valley Authority, an electric utility. In Great Britain and Mexico, the governments are attempting to sell many state-run businesses to private individuals and companies. In Germany, the Deutsche Post is privatized and trades on the stock market. In once-communist Russia, Hungary, Poland, and other eastern European nations, capitalist ideas have been implemented, including private ownership of businesses.

Countries such as China and Russia have used state capitalism to advance the economy. State capitalism tries to integrate the powers of the state with the advantages of capitalism. It is led by the government but uses capitalistic tools such as listing state-owned companies on the stock market and embracing globalization.[7] State capitalism includes some of the world's largest companies such as Russia's Gazprom, which is the largest natural gas company. China's ability to make huge investments to the point of creating entirely new industries puts many private industries at a disadvantage.[8]

The Free-Enterprise System

Many economies—including those of the United States, Canada, and Japan—are based on free enterprise, and many communist and socialist countries, such as China and Russia, are applying more principles of free enterprise to their own economic systems. Free enterprise provides an opportunity for a business to succeed or fail on the basis of market demand. In a free-enterprise system, companies that can efficiently manufacture and sell products that consumers desire will probably succeed. Inefficient businesses and those that sell products that do not offer needed benefits

capitalism (free enterprise)
an economic system in which individuals own and operate the majority of businesses that provide goods and services.

free-market system
pure capitalism, in which all economic decisions are made without government intervention.

mixed economies
economies made up of elements from more than one economic system.

will likely fail as consumers take their business to firms that have more competitive products.

A number of basic individual and business rights must exist for free enterprise to work. These rights are the goals of many countries that have recently embraced free enterprise.

1. Individuals must have the right to own property and to pass this property on to their heirs. This right motivates people to work hard and save to buy property.

2. Individuals and businesses must have the right to earn profits and to use the profits as they wish, within the constraints of their society's laws, principles, and values.

3. Individuals and businesses must have the right to make decisions that determine the way the business operates. Although there is government regulation, the philosophy in countries like the United States and Australia is to permit maximum freedom within a set of rules of fairness.

4. Individuals must have the right to choose what career to pursue, where to live, what goods and services to purchase, and more. Businesses must have the right to choose where to locate, what goods and services to produce, what resources to use in the production process, and so on.

Without these rights, businesses cannot function effectively because they are not motivated to succeed. Thus, these rights make possible the open exchange of goods and services. In the countries that favor free enterprise, such as the United States, citizens have the freedom to make many decisions about the employment they choose and create their own productivity systems. Many entrepreneurs are more productive in free-enterprise societies because personal and financial incentives are available that can aid in entrepreneurial success. For many entrepreneurs, their work becomes a part of their system of goals, values, and lifestyle. Consider the panelists ("sharks") on the ABC program *Shark Tank*. Panelists on *Shark Tank* give entrepreneurs a chance to receive funding to realize their dreams by deciding whether to invest in their projects. They include Barbara Corcoran, who built one of New York's largest real estate companies; Mark Cuban, founder of Broadcast.com and MicroSolutions; and Daymond John, founder of clothing company FUBU.[9]

The Forces of Supply and Demand

In the United States and in other free-enterprise systems, the distribution of resources and products is determined by supply and demand. **Demand** is the number of goods and services that consumers are willing to buy at different prices at a specific time. From your own experience, you probably recognize that consumers are usually willing to buy more of an item as its price falls because they want to save money. Consider handmade rugs, for example. Consumers may be willing to buy six rugs at $350 each, four at $500 each, but only two at $650 each. The relationship between the price and the number of rugs consumers are willing to buy can be shown graphically with a *demand curve* (see Figure 1-2).

Supply is the number of products that businesses are willing to sell at different prices at a specific time. In general, because the potential for profits is higher, businesses are willing to supply more of a good or service at higher prices. For example, a company that sells rugs may be willing to sell six at $650 each, four at $500 each, but just two at $350 each. The relationship between the price of rugs and the quantity the company is willing to supply can be shown graphically with a *supply curve* (see Figure 1-2).

---

demand
the number of goods and services that consumers are willing to buy at different prices at a specific time.

supply
the number of products—goods and services—that businesses are willing to sell at different prices at a specific time.

LO 1-4

Describe the role of supply, demand, and competition in a free-enterprise system.

Need help understanding supply and demand? Visit your Connect ebook video tab for a brief animated explanation.

In Figure 1-2, the supply and demand curves intersect at the point where supply and demand are equal. The price at which the number of products that businesses are willing to supply equals the amount of products that consumers are willing to buy at a specific point in time is the **equilibrium price.** In our rug example, the company is willing to supply four rugs at $500 each, and consumers are willing to buy four rugs at $500 each. Therefore, $500 is the equilibrium price for a rug at that point in time, and most rug companies will price their rugs at $500. As you might imagine, a business that charges more than $500 (or whatever the current equilibrium price is) for its rugs will not sell many and might not earn a profit. On the other hand, a business that charges less than $500 accepts a lower profit per rug than could be made at the equilibrium price.

An entrepreneur presents her idea for a new product. Entrepreneurs are more productive in free-enterprise systems.

© JGI/Jamie Grill/Blend Images LLC

If the cost of making rugs goes up, businesses will not offer as many at the old price. Changing the price alters the supply curve, and a new equilibrium price results. This is an ongoing process, with supply and demand constantly changing in response to changes in economic conditions, availability of resources, and degree of competition. For example, the price of oil can change rapidly and has been between $35 and $145 a barrel over the last five years. Prices for goods and services vary according to these changes in supply and demand. Supply and demand is the force that drives the distribution of resources (goods and services, labor, and money) in a free-enterprise economy.

equilibrium price
the price at which the number of products that businesses are willing to supply equals the amount of products that consumers are willing to buy at a specific point in time.

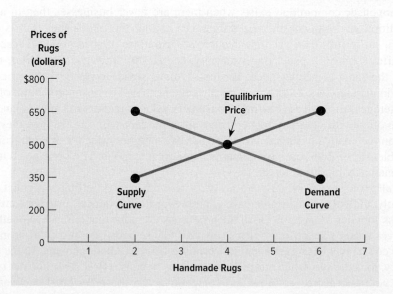

FIGURE 1-2
Equilibrium Price of Handmade Rugs

Critics of supply and demand say the system does not distribute resources equally. The forces of supply and demand prevent sellers who have to sell at higher prices (because their costs are high) and buyers who cannot afford to buy goods at the equilibrium price from participating in the market. According to critics, the wealthy can afford to buy more than they need, but the poor may be unable to buy enough of what they need to survive.

The Nature of Competition

competition
the rivalry among businesses for consumers' dollars

Competition, the rivalry among businesses for consumers' dollars, is another vital element in free enterprise. According to Adam Smith, competition fosters efficiency and low prices by forcing producers to offer the best products at the most reasonable price; those who fail to do so are not able to stay in business. Thus, competition should improve the quality of the goods and services available or reduce prices. Competition allows for open markets and provides opportunities for both individuals and businesses to successfully compete. Entrepreneurs can discover new technology, ways to lower prices, as well as methods for providing better distribution or services. Founder Jeff Bezos of Amazon.com is a prime example. He created an Internet bookstore at the height of the dot-com era in the 1990s. By avoiding building as well as other brick-and-mortar costs, Amazon was able to offer products at competitive prices and continued to succeed even after the dot-com bubble burst. Today, Amazon competes against such retail giants as Walmart in a number of industries, including entertainment, food, and consumer products. Its success in online retail has prompted rivals such as Barnes & Noble to open their own online stores to complement their brick-and-mortar locations.

Within a free-enterprise system, there are four types of competitive environments: pure competition, monopolistic competition, oligopoly, and monopoly.

pure competition
the market structure that exists when there are many small businesses selling one standardized product.

Pure competition exists when there are many small businesses selling one standardized product, such as agricultural commodities like wheat, corn, and cotton. No one business sells enough of the product to influence the product's price. And, because there is no difference in the products, prices are determined solely by the forces of supply and demand.

monopolistic competition
the market structure that exists when there are fewer businesses than in a pure-competition environment and the differences among the goods they sell are small.

Monopolistic competition exists when there are fewer businesses than in a pure-competition environment and the differences among the goods they sell is small. Aspirin, soft drinks, and vacuum cleaners are examples of such goods. These products differ slightly in packaging, warranty, name, and other characteristics, but all satisfy the same consumer need. Businesses have some power over the price they charge in monopolistic competition because they can make consumers aware of product differences through advertising. Consumers value some features more than others and are often willing to pay higher prices for a product with the features they want. For example, many consumers are willing to pay a higher price for organic fruits and vegetables rather than receive a bargain on nonorganic foods. The same holds true for non-genetically modified foods.

oligopoly
the market structure that exists when there are very few businesses selling a product.

An **oligopoly** exists when there are very few businesses selling a product. In an oligopoly, individual businesses have control over their products' price because each business supplies a large portion of the products sold in the marketplace. Nonetheless, the prices charged by different firms stay fairly close because a price cut or increase by one company will trigger a similar response from another company. In the airline industry, for example, when one airline cuts fares to boost sales, other airlines quickly follow with rate decreases to remain competitive. On the other hand, airlines often

Going Green

Whole Foods's Dilemma: It's Too Easy Being Green

Competition in the organic food industry is intensifying, and Whole Foods is feeling the heat. Much of its competition is coming not from other natural foods retailers but from traditional grocery chains selling more organic foods at discounted prices. Sales of organic food in the United States account for approximately $40 billion in purchases. These opportunities are encouraging even more competitors to enter the market.

Traditional supermarkets such as Walmart and Kroger have expanded their organic food offerings to capture the increased consumer demand for natural and organic food. This proliferation of organic food choices at traditional grocery stores has eaten into Whole Foods's bottom line. Walmart currently sells Wild Oats Marketplace–branded organic foods for similar prices to conventionally grown name-brand products. Kroger markets its own discount natural and organic food products under its Simple Truth brand. Both companies leverage their tremendous supplier buying power to offer consumers more

organic choices and undercut retailers like Whole Foods and Trader Joe's on price. In response, Whole Foods is launching its 365 by Whole Foods stores that will focus more on selling its 365 brand at lower prices. As more stores enter the market, Whole Foods must continue finding ways to differentiate itself in an industry characterized by intense monopolistic competition.[10]

Discussion Questions

1. How can Whole Foods compete better with the influx of organic foods sold at traditional grocery stores?
2. If Whole Foods launches a lower-priced 365 by Whole Foods store, will it be effective in competing against stores such as Walmart and Kroger?
3. Why should a company that operates in a monopolistic competitive environment constantly be on the lookout for ways to differentiate itself from the competition?

---

raise prices at the same time. Oligopolies exist when it is expensive for new firms to enter the marketplace. Not just anyone can acquire enough financial capital to build an automobile production facility or purchase enough airplanes and related resources to build an airline.

When there is one business providing a product in a given market, a **monopoly** exists. Utility companies that supply electricity, natural gas, and water are monopolies. The government permits such monopolies because the cost of creating the good or supplying the service is so great that new producers cannot compete for sales. Government-granted monopolies are subject to government-regulated prices. Some monopolies exist because of technological developments that are protected by patent laws. Patent laws grant the developer of new technology a period of time (usually 20 years) during which no other producer can use the same technology without the agreement of the original developer. The United States granted its first patent in 1790. Now its patent office receives hundreds of thousands of patent applications a year, although China has surpassed the United States in patent applications.[11] This monopoly allows the developer to recover research, development, and production expenses and to earn a reasonable profit. An example of this type of monopoly is the dry-copier process developed by Xerox. Xerox's patents have expired, however, and many imitators have forced market prices to decline.

monopoly
the market structure that exists when there is only one business providing a product in a given market.

Economic Cycles and Productivity

Expansion and Contraction.   Economies are not stagnant; they expand and contract. **Economic expansion** occurs when an economy is growing and people are spending more money. Their purchases stimulate the production of goods and services, which in turn stimulates employment. The standard of living rises because more people are

economic expansion
the situation that occurs when an economy is growing and people are spending more money; their purchases stimulate the production of goods and services, which in turn stimulates employment.

inflation
a condition characterized by a continuing rise in prices

economic contraction
a slowdown of the economy characterized by a decline in spending and during which businesses cut back on production and lay off workers.

recession
a decline in production, employment, and income.

unemployment
the condition in which a percentage of the population wants to work but is unable to find jobs.

employed and have money to spend. Rapid expansions of the economy, however, may result in **inflation,** a continuing rise in prices. Inflation can be harmful if individuals' incomes do not increase at the same pace as rising prices, reducing their buying power. The worst case of hyperinflation occurred in Hungary in 1946. At one point, prices were doubling every 15.6 hours. One of the most recent cases of hyperinflation occurred in Zimbabwe.[12] Zimbabwe suffered from hyperinflation so severe that its inflation percentage rate rose into the hundreds of millions. With the elimination of the Zimbabwean dollar and certain price controls, the inflation rate began to decrease, but not before the country's economy was virtually decimated.[13]

Economic contraction occurs when spending declines. Businesses cut back on production and lay off workers, and the economy as a whole slows down. Contractions of the economy lead to **recession**—a decline in production, employment, and income. Recessions are often characterized by rising levels of **unemployment,** which is measured as the percentage of the population that wants to work but is unable to find jobs. Figure 1-3 shows the overall unemployment rate in the civilian labor force over the past 75 years. Rising unemployment levels tend to stifle demand for goods and services, which can have the effect of forcing prices downward, a condition known as *deflation.* Deflation poses a serious economic problem because price decreases could result in consumers delaying purchases. If consumers wait for lower prices, the economy could fall into a recession. The European Union faced the dangers of deflation in 2015. France experienced major deflation, an occurrence that spelled trouble for the rest of the Eurozone as France is the union's second largest economy.[14]

The United States has experienced numerous recessions, the most recent ones occurring in 1990–1991, 2002–2003, and 2008–2011. The most recent recession (or economic slowdown) was caused by the collapse in housing prices and consumers' inability to stay current on their mortgage and credit card payments. This caused a crisis in the banking industry, with the government bailing out banks to keep them from failing. This in turn caused a slowdown in spending on consumer goods and an increase in employment. Unemployment reached 10 percent of the labor force. Don't forget that

FIGURE 1-3   Annual Average Unemployment Rate, Civilian Labor Force, 16 Years and Over

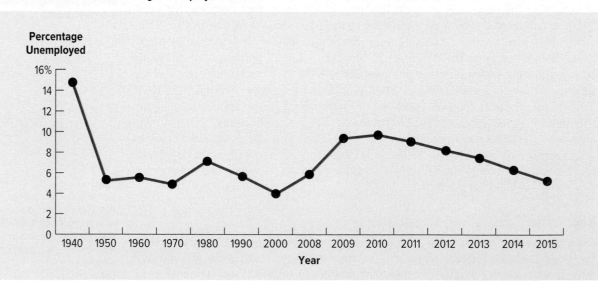

Sources: Bureau of Labor Statistics, "Labor Force Statistics from the Current Population Survey," http://data.bls.gov/timeseries/LNSI4000000 (accessed February 22, 2016).

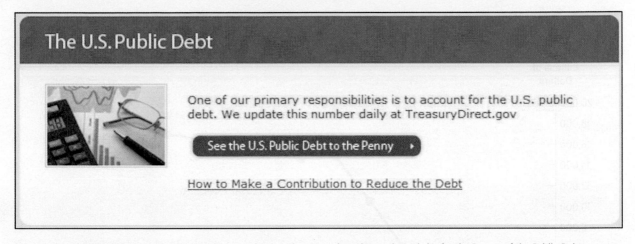

The U.S. Public Debt

One of our primary responsibilities is to account for the U.S. public debt. We update this number daily at TreasuryDirect.gov

See the U.S. Public Debt to the Penny ›

How to Make a Contribution to Reduce the Debt

You can see what the U.S. government currently owes—down to the penny—by going to the website for the Bureau of the Public Debt, www.publicdebt.treas.gov/

personal consumption makes up almost 70 percent of gross domestic product, so consumer behavior is extremely important for economic activity. A severe recession may turn into a **depression,** in which unemployment is very high, consumer spending is low, and business output is sharply reduced, such as what occurred in the United States in the early 1930s. The most recent recession is often called the Great Recession because it was the longest and most severe economic decline since the Great Depression.

Economies expand and contract in response to changes in consumer, business, and government spending. War also can affect an economy, sometimes stimulating it (as in the United States during World Wars I and II) and sometimes stifling it (as during the Vietnam, Persian Gulf, and Iraq wars). Although fluctuations in the economy are inevitable and to a certain extent predictable, their effects—inflation and unemployment—disrupt lives and thus governments try to minimize them.

Measuring the Economy.   Countries measure the state of their economies to determine whether they are expanding or contracting and whether corrective action is necessary to minimize the fluctuations. One commonly used measure is **gross domestic product (GDP)**—the sum of all goods and services produced in a country during a year. GDP measures only those goods and services made within a country and therefore does not include profits from companies' overseas operations; it does include profits earned by foreign companies within the country being measured. However, it does not take into account the concept of GDP in relation to population (GDP per capita). Figure 1-4 shows the increase in GDP over several years, while Table 1-2 compares a number of economic statistics for a sampling of countries.

Another important indicator of a nation's economic health is the relationship between its spending and income (from taxes). When a nation spends more than it takes in from taxes, it has a **budget deficit.** In the 1990s, the U.S. government eliminated its long-standing budget deficit by balancing the money spent for social, defense, and other programs with the amount of money taken in from taxes.

In recent years, however, the budget deficit has reemerged and grown to record levels, partly due to defense spending in the aftermath of the terrorist attacks of September 11, 2001. Massive government stimulus spending during the most recent recession also increased the national debt. Because many Americans do not want their

depression
a condition of the economy in which unemployment is very high, consumer spending is low, and business output is sharply reduced.

LO 1-5

Specify why and how the health of the economy is measured.

gross domestic product (GDP)
the sum of all goods and services produced in a country during a year.

budget deficit
the condition in which a nation spends more than it takes in from taxes.

FIGURE 1-4
Growth in U.S. Gross Domestic Product

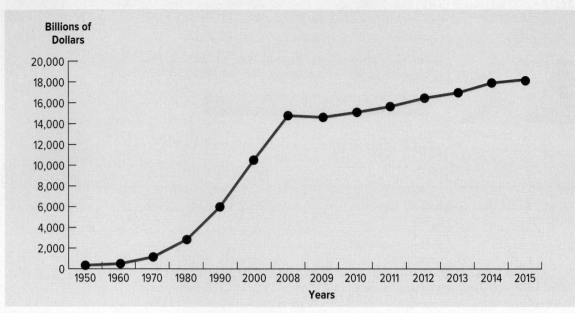

Source: U.S. Department of Commerce Bureau of Economic Analysis, "National Economic Accounts," www.bea.gov/national/index.htm#gdp (accessed February 22, 2016).

TABLE 1-2
Economic Indicators of
Different Countries

Country	GDP (in billions of dollars)	GDP per Capita	Unemployment Rate (%)	Inflation Rate (%)
Argentina	585.6	22,400	7.6	27.6
Australia	1,620	65,400	6.2	1.9
Brazil	1,903.9	15,800	6.4	10.6
Canada	1,592	45,900	6.9	1.2
China	11,383	14,300	4.2	1.5
France	2,464.8	41,400	9.9	0.1
Germany	3,467.8	47,400	4.8	0.2
India	2,288.7	6,300	7.1	5.6
Israel	305.7	34,300	5.6	−0.6
Japan	4,412.6	38,200	3.3	0.7
Mexico	1,291	18,500	4.5	2.7
Russia	1,178.9	23,700	5.4	15.4
South Africa	323.8	13,400	25.9	4.8
United Kingdom	2,761	41,200	5.4	0.1
United States	18,558.1	56,300	5.2	0.2

Source: CIA, The World Fact Book, https://www.cia.gov/library/publications/the-world-factbook/rankorder/rankorderguide.html
(accessed February 22, 2016; International Monetary Fund, http://www.imf.org/external/index.htm (accessed July 1, 2016).

Unit of Measure	Description
Trade balance	The difference between our exports and our imports. If the balance is negative, as it has been since the mid-1980s, it is called a trade deficit and is generally viewed as unhealthy for our economy.
Consumer Price Index	Measures changes in prices of goods and services purchased for consumption by typical urban households.
Per capita income	Indicates the income level of "average" Americans. Useful in determining how much "average" consumers spend and how much money Americans are earning.
Unemployment rate	Indicates how many working-age Americans are not working who otherwise want to work.
Inflation	Monitors price increases in consumer goods and services over specified periods of time. Used to determine if costs of goods and services are exceeding worker compensation over time.
Worker productivity	The amount of goods and services produced for each hour worked.

TABLE 1-3
How Do We Evaluate Our Nation's Economy?

taxes increased and Congress has difficulty agreeing on appropriate tax rates, it is difficult to increase taxes and reduce the deficit. Like consumers and businesses, when the government needs money, it borrows from the public, banks, and even foreign investors. In 2015, the national debt (the amount of money the nation owes its lenders) exceeded $19 trillion, a new high.[15] This figure is especially worrisome because, to reduce the debt to a manageable level, the government either has to increase its revenues (raise taxes) or reduce spending on social, defense, and legal programs, neither of which is politically popular. The size of the national debt and little agreement on how to reduce the deficit caused the credit rating of the U.S. debt to go down. The national debt figure changes daily and can be seen at the Department of the Treasury, Bureau of the Public Debt, website. Table 1-3 describes some of the other ways we evaluate our nation's economy.

The American Economy

As we said previously, the United States is a mixed economy with a foundation based on capitalism. The answers to the three basic economic issues are determined primarily by competition and the forces of supply and demand, although the federal government does intervene in economic decisions to a certain extent. For instance, the federal government exerts oversight over the airline industry to make sure airlines remain economically viable as well as for safety and security purposes.

Standard of living refers to the level of wealth and material comfort that people have available to them. The United States, Germany, Australia, and Norway all have a high standard of living, meaning that most of their citizens are able to afford basic necessities and some degree of comfort. These nations are often characterized by a high GDP per capita. However, a higher GDP per capita does not automatically translate into a higher standard of living. Costs of goods and services is also a factor. The European Union and Japan, for instance, tend to have higher costs of living than in the United States. Higher prices mean that it costs more to obtain a certain level of comfort than it does in other countries. Countries with low standards of living are usually characterized by poverty, higher unemployment, and lower education rates.

LO 1-6

Trace the evolution of the American economy and discuss the role of the entrepreneur in the economy.

standard of living
refers to the level of wealth and material comfort that people have available to them.

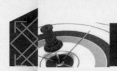

Responding to Business Challenges

Uber Swerves around Regulatory Obstacles

Thanks to Uber, consumers have more transportation options. Uber operates via a mobile phone app that connects drivers—everyday people with cars—with passengers who want to get somewhere. The passenger's credit card is automatically charged, and the driver gets a commission. Uber has operations in 300 cities worldwide.

Taxi companies argue that the ride-sharing model should be held to the same rules as taxis. Global governments have begun limiting Uber from operating until they can determine how to regulate it. In France, an attempt was made to ban an Uber service because drivers do not have to be licensed. Calls for Uber regulations occur when a driver commits a crime, even when not driving for Uber at the time. Uber is likely to encounter more difficulties in socialist or communist countries, where the government maintains more control.

However, it is also facing challenges on its home front. Although the United States is a free-market economy, the government still regulates the operation of businesses. Portland, Oregon, as well as other cities, would like to regulate Uber. Portland allowed Uber to operate but is likely to place limitations on its operations. The taxi industry claimed Uber puts them at a competitive disadvantage because of its advantage on saving costs on licensing, insurance, and other fees. Regulators are considering regulations that will deal with obstacles necessary to level the competitive playing field.[16]

Discussion Questions

1. Why is Uber likely to encounter challenges as it expands, particularly in countries that have more socialist or communist economies?
2. Why is Uber facing challenges in certain U.S. cities despite its free-market economy?
3. Do you think more regulation should be passed to level the playing field between Uber and the taxi industry?

To understand the current state of the American economy and its effect on business practices, it is helpful to examine its history and the roles of the entrepreneur and the government.

The Importance of the American Economy

open economy
an economy in which economic activities occur between the country and the international community.

The American economy is an **open economy,** or an economy in which economic activities occur between the country and the international community. As an open economy, the United States is a major player in international trade. Open economies tend to grow faster than economies that do not engage in international trade. This is because international trade is positively related to efficiency and productivity. Companies in the United States have greater access to a wider range of resources and knowledge, including technology. In today's global environment, the ability to harness technology is critical toward increased innovation.[17] In contrast, research indicates a negative relationship between regulatory actions and innovation in firms, suggesting that too much regulation hinders business activities and their contribution to the American economy.[18]

When looking at the American economy, growth in GDP and jobs are the two primary factors economists consider. A positive relationship exists between a country's employment rate and economic growth. A nation's output depends on the amount of labor used in the production process, so there is also a positive correlation between output and employment. In general, as the labor force and productivity increase, so does GDP. Profitable companies tend to hire more workers than those that are unprofitable. Therefore, companies that hire employees not only improve their profitability but also drive the economic well-being of the American economy.[19]

Government public policy also drives the economy through job creation. In order for any nation to ensure the social and economic health of the country, there must be a tax base to provide for the public interest. The vast majority of taxes come from

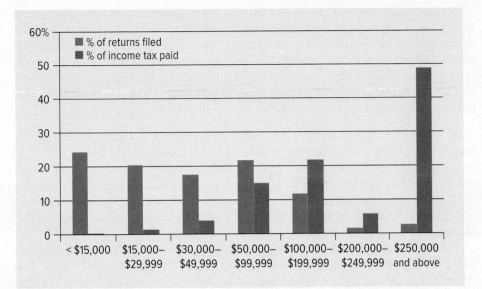

FIGURE 1-5

Individual Income Tax Statistics by Income Group

Source: Internal Revenue Service

individuals. It is estimated that the U.S. government obtains $1.4 trillion in individual income taxes. Figure 1-5 shows the distribution of returns and income taxes paid by individuals based on their gross income. Those who earn more than $250,000 pay an average tax rate of 25.6 percent and pay 48.9 percent of individual income taxes. Consumers earning less than $50,000 comprise the majority of individual tax returns filed but pay 6.2 percent of total taxes.[20]

Businesses are also an important form of tax revenue. Those that are classified as sole proprietorships, partnerships, and S corporations (discussed further in the chapter titled, Options for Organizing Business) pay taxes according to the individual income tax code. Corporations are taxed differently. Approximately 10.6 percent of the government's total revenues comes from corporate income taxes.[21] The United States has one of the highest corporate tax rates in the world. Its combined federal and state statutory corporate tax rate averages approximately 39 percent.[22] For this reason, many American companies have sought to reduce their tax rates through activities such as tax inversions, in which they locate their headquarters in a country with a lower tax rate, allowing them to save millions in taxes. For example, Burger King acquired Tim Hortons and became domiciled in Canada. Now that Burger King is under Canadian tax law, it pays U.S. taxes at the same rate, but its earnings in Canada and Ireland are taxed at the rate where they do business rather than the higher U.S. tax rate. The federal government is attempting to close loopholes that allow for tax inversions for the purposes of avoiding taxes.

A Brief History of the American Economy

The Early Economy.   Before the colonization of North America, Native Americans lived as hunter/gatherers and farmers, with some trade among tribes. The colonists who came later operated primarily as an *agricultural economy*. People were self-sufficient and produced everything they needed at home, including food, clothing, and furniture. Abundant natural resources and a moderate climate nourished industries such as farming, fishing, shipping, and fur trading. A few manufactured goods and money for the colonies' burgeoning industries came from England and other countries.

As the nation expanded slowly toward the West, people found natural resources such as coal, copper, and iron ore and used them to produce goods such as horseshoes, farm implements, and kitchen utensils. Farm families who produced surplus goods sold or traded them for things they could not produce themselves, such as fine furniture and window glass. Some families also spent time turning raw materials into clothes and household goods. Because these goods were produced at home, this system was called the domestic system.

The Industrial Revolution. The 19th century and the Industrial Revolution brought the development of new technology and factories. The factory brought together all the resources needed to make a product—materials, machines, and workers. Work in factories became specialized as workers focused on one or two tasks. As work became more efficient, productivity increased, making more goods available at lower prices. Railroads brought major changes, allowing farmers to send their surplus crops and goods all over the nation for barter or for sale.

Factories began to spring up along the railways to manufacture farm equipment and a variety of other goods to be shipped by rail. Samuel Slater set up the first American textile factory after he memorized the plans for an English factory and emigrated to the United States. Eli Whitney revolutionized the cotton industry with his cotton gin. Francis Cabot Lowell's factory organized all the steps in manufacturing cotton cloth for maximum efficiency and productivity. John Deere's farm equipment increased farm production and reduced the number of farmers required to feed the young nation. Farmers began to move to cities to find jobs in factories and a higher standard of living. Henry Ford developed the assembly-line system to produce automobiles. Workers focused on one part of an automobile and then pushed it to the next stage until it rolled off the assembly line as a finished automobile. Ford's assembly line could manufacture many automobiles efficiently, and the price of his cars was $200, making them affordable to many Americans.

The Manufacturing and Marketing Economies. Industrialization brought increased prosperity, and the United States gradually became a *manufacturing economy*—one devoted to manufacturing goods and providing services rather than producing agricultural products. The assembly line was applied to more industries, increasing the variety of goods available to the consumer. Businesses became more concerned with the needs of the consumer and entered the *marketing economy*. Expensive goods such as cars and appliances could be purchased on a time-payment plan. Companies conducted research to find out what products consumers needed and wanted. Advertising made consumers aware of products and important information about features, prices, and other competitive advantages.

Because these developments occurred in a free-enterprise system, consumers determined what goods and services were produced. They did this by purchasing the products they liked at prices they were willing to pay. The United States prospered, and American citizens had one of the highest standards of living in the world.

The Service and New Digital Economy. After World War II, with the increased standard of living, Americans had more money and more time. They began to pay others to perform services that made their lives easier. Beginning in the 1960s, more and more women entered the workforce. The United States began experiencing major shifts in the population. The U.S. population grew 9.7 percent in the past decade to about 319 million. This is the slowest pace of growth since the Great Depression, with the South leading the population gains. The United States is undergoing a baby bust, with record lows in the country's fertility rate.[23] While the birth rate in the United States is declining, new immigrants help with population gains.[24] The profile of the family is also changing: Today there are more single-parent families and individuals living alone, and in two-parent families, both parents often work.

One result of this trend is that time-pressed Americans are increasingly paying others to do tasks they used to do at home, like cooking, laundry, landscaping, and child care. These trends have gradually

DID YOU KNOW? Approximately 57 percent of adult women are engaged in the workforce.[25]

changed the United States to a *service economy*—one devoted to the production of services that make life easier for busy consumers. Businesses increased their demand for services, especially in the areas of finance and information technology. Service industries such as restaurants, banking, health care, child care, auto repair, leisure-related industries, and even education are growing rapidly and may account for as much as 80 percent of the U.S. economy. These trends continue with advanced technology contributing to new service products based on technology and digital media that provide smartphones, social networking, and virtual worlds. This has led to the growth of e-commerce, or transactions involving goods and services over the Internet. E-commerce has led to firms that would have been unheard of a few decades ago, such as eBay, Facebook, and Amazon.com. Figure 1-6 shows the type of technology devices owned by U.S. consumers. More about the digital world, business, and new online social media can be found in the chapter titled, Digital Marketing and Social Networking.

The Role of the Entrepreneur

An **entrepreneur** is an individual who risks his or her wealth, time, and effort to develop for profit an innovative product or way of doing something. Heidi Ganahl is a true American entrepreneur. She took the unusual concept of a day care center for dogs and turned it into a successful $85 million franchise operation. Her business Camp Bow Wow—which offers boarding, playtime, grooming, and other services for dogs—has since expanded to 152 locations. Eventually, the company caught the eye of animal health care business VCA. It purchased Ganahl's business for an undisclosed sum.[26]

entrepreneur
an individual who risks his or her wealth, time, and effort to develop for profit an innovative product or way of doing something.

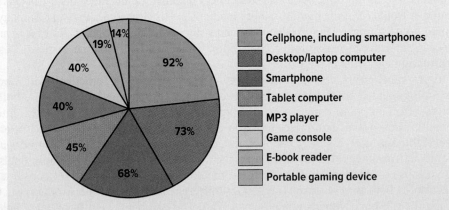

FIGURE 1-6
Technology Device Ownership

Source: Pew Research Center survey conducted March 17–April 12, 2015. Smartphone data based on Pew Research survey conducted June 10–July 12, 2015. Trend data are from previous Pew Research surveys.

- Cellphone, including smartphones
- Desktop/laptop computer
- Smartphone
- Tablet computer
- MP3 player
- Game console
- E-book reader
- Portable gaming device

92%
73%
68%
45%
40%
40%
19%
14%

Will Pizza Studio Slice Up the Competition?

Pizza Studio

Founders: Samit Varma and Ron Biskin

Founded: 2012, in Calabasas, California

Success: Pizza Studio seems to be thriving, netting $11.5 million in sales after only two years.

Currently, fast-food restaurants like Pizza Hut dominate the pizza market. The competition in the industry is immense and includes delivery pizza chains Papa John's and Domino's. However, this fact did not stop partners Samit Varma and Ron Biskin from entering the industry. They knew that in order to succeed, they would need a creative idea that would change competition in the pizza industry. Pizza Studio was born.

Pizza Studio offers customers a completely customized build-your-own-pizza experience. Customers can pick their crust, sauce, toppings, and cheeses. Pizza Studio prices its 11-inch pizzas competitively at $7.99. How does it offer such customized pizzas at such competitive prices? Varma and Biskin keep the chain running efficiently. For instance, a conveyer belt sends the prepared pies through a convection oven. Employees work in teams and are motivated through incentives such as stock option plans. The chain is doing so well that it would like to have hundreds of locations. However, as with all successful ideas, competitors are not far behind.[27]

Discussion Questions

1. How does Pizza Studio compete against similar restaurants in such a saturated market?
2. Is cutting costs and lowering the price of pizza enough to be successful in this industry?
3. Will Pizza Studio be effective in changing the pizza industry?

The free-enterprise system provides the conditions necessary for entrepreneurs like Ganahl to succeed. In the past, entrepreneurs were often inventors who brought all the factors of production together to produce a new product. Thomas Edison, whose inventions include the record player and lightbulb, was an early American entrepreneur. Henry Ford was one of the first persons to develop mass assembly methods in the automobile industry. Other entrepreneurs, so-called captains of industry, invested in the country's growth. John D. Rockefeller built Standard Oil out of the fledgling oil industry, and Andrew Carnegie invested in railroads and founded the United States Steel Corporation. Andrew Mellon built the Aluminum Company of America and Gulf Oil. J. P. Morgan started financial institutions to fund the business activities of other entrepreneurs. Although these entrepreneurs were born in another century, their legacy to the American economy lives on in the companies they started, many of which still operate today. Consider the history of Eli Lilly. Colonel Eli Lilly in Indianapolis, Indiana, was continually frustrated with the quality of pharmaceutical products sold at the time. As a pharmaceutical chemist, he decided to start his own firm that would offer the highest-quality medicines. His firm, Eli Lilly and Company, would go on to make landmark achievements, including being one of the first pharmaceutical firms to mass-produce penicillin. Today, Eli Lilly is one of the largest pharmaceutical firms in the world.[28]

Entrepreneurs are constantly changing American business practices with new technology and innovative management techniques. Bill Gates, for example, built Microsoft, a software company whose products include Word and Windows, into a multibillion-dollar enterprise. Frederick Smith had an idea to deliver packages overnight, and now his FedEx Company plays an important role in getting documents and packages delivered all over the world for businesses and individuals. Steve Jobs co-founded Apple and turned the company into a successful consumer electronics firm that revolutionized many different industries, with products such as the iPod, iPhone, Mac computers, and iPad. The company went from near bankruptcy in the 1990s to become one of the most valuable brands in the entire world.

Entrepreneurs have been associated with such uniquely American concepts as Dell Computers, Ben & Jerry's, Levi's, McDonald's, Dr Pepper, Apple, Google, Facebook, and Walmart. Walmart, founded by entrepreneur Sam Walton, was the first retailer to reach $100 billion in sales in one year and now routinely passes that mark, with more than $482 billion in 2015.[29] We will examine the importance of entrepreneurship further in Chapter 5.

The Role of Government in the American Economy

The American economic system is best described as modified capitalism because the government regulates business to preserve competition and protect consumers and employees. Federal, state, and local governments intervene in the economy with laws and regulations designed to promote competition and to protect consumers, employees, and the environment. Many of these laws are discussed in Bonus Chapter A.

Additionally, government agencies such as the U.S. Department of Commerce measure the health of the economy (GDP, productivity, etc.) and, when necessary, take steps to minimize the disruptive effects of economic fluctuations and reduce unemployment. When the economy is contracting and unemployment is rising, the federal government through the Federal Reserve Board (see Chapter 15) tries to spur growth so that consumers will spend more money and businesses will hire more employees. To accomplish this, it may reduce interest rates or increase its own spending for goods and services. When the economy expands so fast that inflation results, the government may intervene to reduce inflation by slowing down economic growth. This can be accomplished by raising interest rates to discourage spending by businesses and consumers. Techniques used to control the economy are discussed in Chapter 15.

Google Wallet is a mobile payments system that allows users to store their credit card or debit card information. When checking out at stores, users can bring up the app and use the information to pay for their purchases.

© PC Plus Magazine/Getty Images

The Role of Ethics and Social Responsibility in Business

In the past few years, you may have read about a number of scandals at a number of well-known corporations, including Volkswagen, Pfizer, General Motors, and even leading banks such as Bank of America and Citigroup. In many cases, misconduct by individuals within these firms had an adverse effect on current and retired employees, investors, and others associated with these firms. In some cases, individuals went to jail for their actions. These scandals undermined public confidence in corporate America and sparked a new debate about ethics in business. Business ethics generally refers to the standards and principles used by society to define appropriate and inappropriate conduct in the workplace. In many cases, these standards have been codified as laws prohibiting actions deemed unacceptable.

Many companies engage in socially responsible behavior to give back to their communities. Home Depot partners with Habitat for Humanity to build homes for disadvantaged families.

© Ariel Skelley/Getty Images

Society is increasingly demanding that businesspeople behave socially responsibly toward their stakeholders, including customers, employees, investors, government regulators, communities, and the natural environment. Diversity in the workforce is not only socially responsible but also highly beneficial to the financial performance of companies. According to a McKinsey consulting firm study, organizations that have diverse leadership are more likely to report higher financial returns. This study defined diversity as women and minorities. Diversity creates increased employee satisfaction and improved decision making.[30] When actions are heavily criticized, a balance is usually required to support and protect various stakeholders.

While one view is that ethics and social responsibility are a good supplement to business activities, there is an alternative viewpoint. Research has shown that ethical behavior can not only enhance a company's reputation but can also drive profits.[31] The ethical and socially responsible conduct of companies such as Whole Foods, Starbucks, and the hotel chain Marriott provides evidence that good ethics is good business. There is growing recognition that the long-term value of conducting business in an ethical and socially responsible manner that considers the interests of all stakeholders creates superior financial performance.[32]

To promote socially responsible and ethical behavior while achieving organizational goals, businesses can monitor changes and trends in society's values. Businesses should determine what society wants and attempt to predict the long-term effects of their decisions. While it requires an effort to address the interests of all stakeholders, businesses can prioritize and attempt to balance conflicting demands. The goal is to develop a solid reputation of trust and avoid misconduct to develop effective workplace ethics.

Can You Learn Business in a Classroom?

Obviously, the answer is yes, or there would be no purpose for this textbook! To be successful in business, you need knowledge, skills, experience, and good judgment. The topics covered in this chapter and throughout this book provide some of the knowledge you need to understand the world of business. The opening vignette at the beginning of each chapter, boxes, examples within each chapter, and the case at the end of each chapter describe experiences to help you develop good business judgment. The "Build Your Skills" exercise at the end of each chapter and the "Solve the Dilemma" box will help you develop skills that may be useful in your future career. However, good judgment is based on knowledge and experience plus personal insight and understanding. Therefore, you need more courses in business, along with some practical experience in the business world, to help you develop the special insight necessary to put your personal stamp on knowledge as you apply it. The challenge in business is in the area of judgment, and judgment does not develop from memorizing an introductory business textbook. If you are observant in your daily experiences as an employee, as a student, and as a consumer, you will improve your ability to make good business judgments.

Whether you choose to work at an organization or become an entrepreneur, you will be required to know the basic concepts and principles in this book. It should be exciting to think about your opportunities and the challenges of creating a successful career. Our society needs a strong economic foundation to help people develop a desired standard of living. Our world economy is becoming more digital

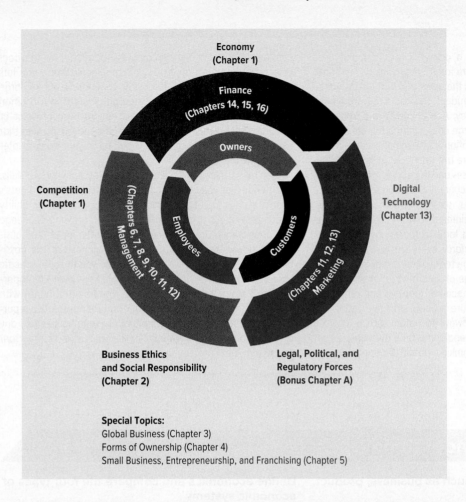

FIGURE 1-7
The Organization of This Book

and competitive, requiring new skills and job positions. Individuals like yourself can become leaders in business, nonprofits, and government to create a better life.

Figure 1-7 is an overview of how the chapters in this book are linked together and how the chapters relate to the participants, the activities, and the environmental factors found in the business world. The topics presented in the chapters that follow are those that will give you the best opportunity to begin the process of understanding the world of business.

When most people think of a career in business, they see themselves entering the door to large companies and multinationals that they read about in the news and that are discussed in class. In a national survey, students indicated they would like to work for Google, Walt Disney, Apple, and Ernst & Young. In fact, most jobs are not with large corporations, but are in small companies, nonprofit organizations, government, and even as self-employed individuals. There are nearly 27 million individuals who own their own businesses and have no employees. With more than 75 percent of the economy based on services, there are jobs available in industries, such as health care, finance, education, hospitality, entertainment, and transportation. The world is changing quickly and large corporations replace the equivalent of their entire workforce every four years.

The fast pace of technology today means that you have to be prepared to take advantage of emerging job opportunities and markets. You must also become adaptive and recognize that business is becoming more global, with job opportunities around the world. If you want to obtain such a job, you shouldn't miss a chance to spend some time overseas. To get you started on the path to thinking about job opportunities, consider all of the changes in business today that might affect your possible long-term track and that could bring you lots of success. You may want to stay completely out of large organizations and corporations and put yourself in a position for an entrepreneurial role as a self-employed contractor or small-business owner. However, there are many who feel that experience in larger businesses is helpful to your success later as an entrepreneur.

You're on the road to learning the key knowledge, skills, and trends that you can use to be a star in business. Business's impact on our society, especially in the area of sustainability and improvement of the environment, is a growing challenge and opportunity. Green businesses and green jobs in the business world are provided to give you a glimpse at the possibilities. Along the way, we will introduce you to some specific careers and offer advice on developing your own job opportunities. Research indicates that you won't be that happy with your job unless you enjoy your work and feel that it has a purpose. Because you spend most of your waking hours every day at work, you need to seriously think about what is important to you in a job.[33]

Review Your Understanding

Define basic concepts such as business, product, and profit.

A business is an organization or individual that seeks a profit by providing products that satisfy people's needs. A product is a good, service, or idea that has both tangible and intangible characteristics that provide satisfaction and benefits. Profit, the basic goal of business, is the difference between what it costs to make and sell a product and what a customer pays for it.

Identify the main participants and activities of business and explain why studying business is important.

The three main participants in business are owners, employees, and customers, but others—government regulators, suppliers, social groups, etc.—are also important. Management involves planning, organizing, and controlling the tasks required to carry out the work of the company. Marketing refers to those activities—research, product development, promotion, pricing, and distribution—designed to provide goods and services that satisfy customers. Finance refers to activities concerned with funding a business and using its funds effectively. Studying business can help you prepare for a career and become a better consumer.

Define economics and compare the four types of economic systems.

Economics is the study of how resources are distributed for the production of goods and services within a social system; an economic system describes how a particular society distributes its resources. Communism is an economic system in which the people, without regard to class, own all the nation's resources. In a socialist system, the government owns and operates basic industries, but individuals own most businesses. Under capitalism, individuals own and operate the majority of businesses that provide goods and services. Mixed economies have elements from more than one economic system; most countries have mixed economies.

Describe the role of supply, demand, and competition in a free-enterprise system.

In a free-enterprise system, individuals own and operate the majority of businesses, and the distribution of resources is determined by competition, supply, and demand. Demand is the number of goods and services that consumers are willing to buy at different prices at a specific time. Supply is the number of goods or services that businesses are willing to sell at different prices at a specific time. The price at which the supply of a product equals demand at a specific point in time is the equilibrium price. Competition is the rivalry among businesses to convince consumers to buy goods or services. Four types of competitive environments are pure competition, monopolistic competition, oligopoly, and monopoly. These economic concepts determine how businesses may operate in a particular society and, often, how much they can charge for their products.

Specify why and how the health of the economy is measured.

A country measures the state of its economy to determine whether it is expanding or contracting and whether the country needs to take steps to minimize fluctuations. One commonly used measure is gross domestic product (GDP), the sum of all goods and services produced in a country during a year. A budget deficit occurs when a nation spends more than it takes in from taxes.

Trace the evolution of the American economy and discuss the role of the entrepreneur in the economy.

The American economy is an open economy that engages in significant international trade. Government public policy helps drive the economy through job creation, requiring a tax base to provide for the public interest. Much of the government's revenue comes from individual income taxes, but corporations pay a high corporate tax in the United States.

The American economy has evolved through several stages: the early economy, the Industrial Revolution, the manufacturing economy, the marketing economy, and the service and Internet-based economy of today. Entrepreneurs play an important role because they risk their time, wealth, and efforts to develop new goods, services, and ideas that fuel the growth of the American economy.

Evaluate a small-business owner's situation and propose a course of action.

"Solve the Dilemma" at the end of this chapter presents a problem for the owner of the firm. Should you, as the owner, raise prices, expand operations, or form a venture with a larger company to deal with demand? You should be able to apply your newfound understanding of the relationship between supply and demand to assess the situation and reach a decision about how to proceed.

Revisit the World of Business

Revisit the World of Business Questions

- Why is it necessary for Dollar Shave Club to differentiate its product to compete?
- Do you think CEO Michael Dubin is a good entrepreneur?
- Why do consumers choose to become a member of Dollar Shave Club?

Learn the Terms

budget deficit 17
business 4
capitalism (free enterprise) 11
communism 9
competition 14
demand 12
depression 17
economic contraction 16
economic expansion 15
economic system 8
economics 8
entrepreneur 23

equilibrium price 13
financial resources 8
free-market system 11
gross domestic product (GDP) 17
human resources 8
inflation 16
mixed economies 11
monopolistic competition 14
monopoly 15
natural resources 8
nonprofit organizations 4
oligopoly 14

open economy 20
product 4
profit 4
pure competition 14
recession 16
socialism 10
stakeholders 5
standard of living 19
supply 12
unemployment 16

Check Your Progress

1. What is the fundamental goal of business? Do all organizations share this goal?

2. Name the forms a product may take and give some examples of each.

3. Who are the main participants of business? What are the main activities? What other factors have an impact on the conduct of business in the United States?

4. What are four types of economic systems? Can you provide an example of a country using each type?

5. Explain the terms *supply, demand, equilibrium price,* and *competition.* How do these forces interact in the American economy?

6. List the four types of competitive environments and provide an example of a product of each environment.

7. List and define the various measures governments may use to gauge the state of their economies. If unemployment is high, will the growth of GDP be great or small?

8. Why are fluctuations in the economy harmful?

9. How did the Industrial Revolution influence the growth of the American economy? Why do we apply the term *service economy* to the United States today?

10. Explain the federal government's role in the American economy.

Get Involved

1. Discuss the economic changes occurring in Russia and eastern European countries, which once operated as communist economic systems. Why are these changes occurring? What do you think the result will be?

2. Why is it important for the government to measure the economy? What kinds of actions might it take to control the economy's growth?

3. Is the American economy currently expanding or contracting? Defend your answer with the latest statistics on GDP, inflation, unemployment, and so on. How is the federal government responding?

Build Your Skills

The Forces of Supply and Demand

Background

WagWumps are a new children's toy with the potential to be a highly successful product. WagWumps are cute and furry, and their eyes glow in the dark. Each family set consists of a mother, a father, and two children. Wee-Toys' manufacturing costs are about $6 per set, with $3 representing marketing and distribution costs. The wholesale price of a WagWump family for a retailer is $15.75, and the toy carries a suggested retail price of $26.99.

Task

Assume you are a decision maker at a retailer, such as Target or Walmart, that must determine the price the stores in your district should charge customers for the WagWump family set. From the information provided, you know that the SRP (suggested retail price) is $26.99 per set and that your company can purchase the toy set from your wholesaler for $15.75 each. Based on the following assumptions, plot your company's supply curve on the graph provided in Figure I-8 and label it "supply curve."

Quantity	Price
3,000	$16.99
5,000	21.99
7,000	26.99

Using the following assumptions, plot your customers' demand curve on Figure I-8 and label it "demand curve."

Quantity	Price
10,000	$16.99
6,000	21.99
2,000	26.99

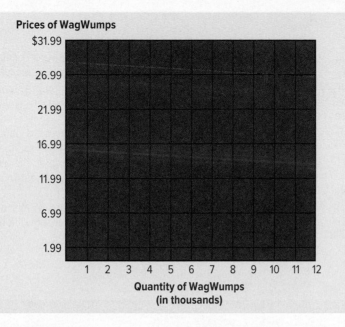

Prices of WagWumps

Quantity of WagWumps (in thousands)

FIGURE 1-8

Equilibrium Price of WagWumps

For this specific time, determine the point at which the quantity of toys your company is willing to supply equals the quantity of toys the customers in your sales district are willing to buy and label that point "equilibrium price."

Solve the Dilemma

Mrs. Acres Homemade Pies

Shelly Acres, whose grandmother gave her a family recipe for making pies, loved to cook, and she decided to start a business she called Mrs. Acres Homemade Pies. The company produces specialty pies and sells them in local supermarkets and select family restaurants. In each of the first six months, Shelly and three part-time employees sold 2,000 pies for $4.50 each, netting $1.50 profit per pie. The pies were quite successful and Shelly could not keep up with demand. The company's success results from a quality product and productive employees who are motivated by incentives and who enjoy being part of a successful new business.

To meet demand, Shelly expanded operations, borrowing money and increasing staff to four full-time employees. Production and sales increased to 8,000 pies per month, and profits soared to $12,000 per month. However, demand for Mrs. Acres Homemade Pies continues to accelerate beyond what Shelly can supply. She has several options: (1) maintain current production levels and raise prices; (2) expand the facility and staff while maintaining the current price; or (3) contract the production of the pies to a national restaurant chain, giving Shelly a percentage of profits with minimal involvement.

LO 1-7

Evaluate a small-business owner's situation and propose a course of action.

Discussion Questions

1. Explain and demonstrate the relationship between supply and demand for Mrs. Acres Homemade Pies.

2. What challenges does Shelly face as she considers the three options?

3. What would you do in Shelly's position?

Build Your Business Plan

The Dynamics of Business and Economics

Have you ever thought about owning your business? If you have, how did your idea come about? Is it your experience with this particular field? Or might it be an idea that evolved from your desires for a particular good or service not being offered in your community? For example, perhaps you and your friends have yearned for a place to go have coffee, relax, and talk. Now is an opportunity to create the cafe bar you have been thinking of!

Whether you consider yourself a visionary or a practical thinker, think about your community. What needs are not being met? While it is tempting to suggest a new restaurant (maybe even one near campus), easier-to-implement business plans can range from a lawn care business or a designated driver business to a placement service agency for teenagers.

Once you have an idea for a business plan, think about how profitable this idea might be. Is there sufficient demand for this business? How large is the market for this particular business? What about competitors? How many are there?

To learn about your industry, you should do a thorough search of your initial ideas of a product on the Internet.

See for Yourself Videocase

Redbox Succeeds by Identifying Market Need

Redbox's tell-tale bright red kiosks in stores and fast-food restaurants across the country have become an image of what a good business model can accomplish. The company's ability to offer customers a convenient and inexpensive DVD rental option has allowed it to succeed despite the wide-spread growth of streaming services such as Netflix and Amazon. However, the firm acknowledges the future of streaming, and Redbox has allegedly been discussing the launch of a new streaming service called "Redbox Variety." As one of the top rental companies in the United States, Redbox is a true entrepreneurial success story.

Building Redbox into a successful firm was not easy, however. It was fraught with challenges. Like most successful companies, Redbox started out by identifying a need. It recognized that consumers could not often find the movies they wanted in convenient locations. Like all good ideas, Redbox required funding to get started. This proved to be a major difficulty. Realizing that customers did not want to pay much for renting movies, Redbox decided to charge only one dollar. Yet the kiosks, which contain more than 800 components, required a large amount of capital. The combination of the capital-intensive nature of the business and the low prices was not an attractive recipe for venture capital funding.

However, Redbox was certain that demand for its product offerings would exceed the costs. The company finally found a partner in the more established Outerwall, formerly known as Coinstar, which already had partnerships with many different retailers. The alliance opened the way for Redbox to begin installing kiosks at the front of stores.

Redbox did not immediately expand across the country. Instead, it took a cautious approach toward its business model. It began by focusing its efforts on making one kiosk profitable, then replicating this way of thinking regionally and nationally. In this way, Redbox was able to test its concept without taking the risk of widespread failure.

Even though it was expanding, it was some time before Redbox was able to earn a profit. Like all entrepreneurs, the founders of Redbox had to take many risks if they wanted the company to succeed. "The risks for starting Redbox were significant," said Marc Achler, vice president of new business, strategy, and innovation. "The first couple years we had some red ink. It took us a while before we turned profitable." Yet with persistence and continual relationship building with retailers, Redbox has been able to secure more than 50 percent of the physical DVD-rental market.

One way that Redbox has been able to secure such a large share of the market is by meeting the needs of a variety of stakeholders. Redbox views its customers as its first priority and has developed its kiosks and database to meet their needs. For instance, customers can reserve movies online and pick them up at their nearest kiosk. If a kiosk happens to be out of a particular movie, customers can search the Redbox database to locate the movie at a nearby kiosk. This combination of convenience and low prices has attracted customers who desire a simplified process to renting movies.

Additionally, Redbox has created a process that also benefits the needs of its retail partners. Redbox kiosks help attract consumers to the store, where they may purchase additional products. Customers must come back the next day to return their movie, where they may once again purchase more products from the retailer. In this way, Redbox creates a win-win situation for both itself and its partners.

This is not to say that everything is easy for Redbox. For instance, it must continually safeguard against allowing underage children to rent inappropriate (rated-R) movies. And while Redbox has approached this changing and dynamic marketplace proactively, it must continue to do so in order to maintain its competitive position. With an increasing interest in streaming, Redbox has seen sales decline in recent years. Its first attempt to develop a streaming service with Verizon was unable to compete with Netflix and was discontinued. However, Redbox refuses to give up. It continues to look for other opportunities to gain advantages against the competition.[33]

Discussion Questions

1. Why are consumers so willing to rent from Redbox?
2. How was Redbox able to overcome some of its earliest challenges?
3. What are some recommendations for ways that Redbox can maintain its high market share?

You can find the related video in the Video Library in Connect. Ask your instructor how you can access Connect.

Team Exercise

Major economic systems, including capitalism, socialism, and communism, as well as mixed economies, were discussed in this chapter. Assuming that you want an economic system that is best for the majority, not just a few members of society, defend one of the economic systems as the best system. Form groups and try to reach agreement on one economic system. Defend why you support the system that you advance.

Endnotes

1. Serena Ng and Paul Ziobro, "Razor Sales Move Online, Away from Gillette," *The Wall Street Journal,* June 23, 2015, p. B1; "How YouTube Crashed Our Website—And Why We Loved It," *Inc.,* July/August 2015, pp. 98–100; Adam Lashinsky, "The Cutting Edge of Care,"*Fortune,* March 15, 2015, pp. 61–62; Dollar Shave Club website, http://www.dollarshaveclub.com/ (accessed July 14, 2015); Paresh Dave, "Up to 2 Million Members, Dollar Shave Club Worth $615 Million, Investors Say," *Los Angeles Times,* June 22, 2015, http://www.latimes.com/business/technology/la-fi-tn-dollar-shave-club-investment-20150622-story.html (accessed July 14, 2015); "Meet the 2015 CNBC Disruptor 50 Companies," *CNBC,* May 12, 2015, http://www.cnbc.com/2015/05/12/dollar-shave-club-disruptor-50.html (accessed July 14, 2015); Penny Morgan, "P&G's Gillette Files a Lawsuit against Dollar Shave Club," *Market Realist,* December 22, 2015, http://marketrealist.com/2015/12/pg-files-patent-infringement-suit-dollar-shave-club/ (accessed February 24, 2016).

2. Josh Mitchell, "Americans Are Buying Less-Efficient Cars as Gasoline Prices Dive," *The Wall Street Journal,* January 6, 2015, http://blogs.wsj.com/economics/2015/01/06/americans-are-buying-less-efficient-cars-as-gasoline-prices-dive/ (accessed February 22, 2016).

3. Association for Women in Science, "Who We Are," http://www.awis.org/?WhoWeAre (accessed February 22, 2016).

4. Robert McMillan, "Hewlett-Packard Officially Files to Split," *The Wall Street Journal,* July 1, 2015, http://www.wsj.com/articles/hewlett-packard-officially-files-to-split-1435783640 (accessed February 22, 2016).

5. "About Bill Daniels," www.danielsfund.org/About-Us/About-Bill-Daniels.asp (accessed February 22, 2016).

6. James T. Areddy and Craig Karmin, "China Stocks Once Frothy, Fall by Half in Six Months," *The Wall Street Journal,* April 16, 2008, pp. 1, 7.

7. "Special Report: The Visible Hand," *The Economist,* January 21, 2012, pp. 3–5.

8. "Special Report: The World in Their Hands," *The Economist,* January 21, 2012, pp. 15–17.

9. "The Shark Tank," *ABC,* http://abc.go.com/shows/shark-tank/bios (accessed April 2, 2014).

10. Annie Gasparro, "Whole Foods Sales Sour After Price Scandal," *The Wall Street Journal,* July 30, 2015, p. B1; Leslie Patton and Craig Giammona, "Whole Foods or Walmart?" *Bloomberg Businessweek,* May 18–24, 2015, pp. 21–22; Organic Trade Association, U.S. Consumers across the Country Devour Record Amount of Organic in 2014," *Organic Trade Association,* April 15, 2015, http://www.ota.com/news/press-releases/18061 (accessed August 25, 2015); Elizabeth A. Harris and Stephanie Strom, "Walmart to Sell Organic Food, Undercutting Big Brands," *The New York Times,* April 10, 2014, http://www.nytimes.com/2014/04/10/

business/walmart-to-offer-organic-line-of-food-at-cut-rate-prices.html?_r=0 (accessed August 25, 2015); Craig Giammona and Leslie Patton, "Whole Foods New Millennial-Focused Chain Will Be Called 365," *Bloomberg,* June 11, 2015, http://www.bloomberg.com/news/articles/2015-06-11/whole-foods-new-millennial-focused-chain-will-be-called-365 (accessed August 25, 2015).

11. World International Property Organization, *World Intellectual Property Indicators,* 2014, http://www.wipo.int/edocs/pubdocs/en/wipo_pub_941_2014.pdf (accessed February 22, 2016).

12. Paul Toscano, "The Worst Hyperinflation Situations of All Time," *CNBC,* February 14, 2011, http://www.cnbc.com/id/41532451 (accessed February 22, 2016).

13. "Zimbabwe," *CIA—The World Factbook,* https://www.cia.gov/library/publications/the-world-factbook/geos/zi.html (accessed February 22, 2016).

14. Ambrose Evans-Pritchard, "France Is 'Sliding into a Deflationary Vortex,'" *Business Insider,* December 12, 2014, http://www.businessinsider.com/france-is-sliding-into-a-deflationary-vortex-2014-12 (accessed February 22, 2016).

15. Stephan Dinan, "Federal Debt Hits $19 Trillion; New Record Set," *Washington Times,* February 1, 2016, http://www.washingtontimes.com/news/2016/feb/1/federal-debt-hits-19-trillion-new-record-set/ (accessed February 22, 2016).

16. Douglas MacMillan, "The Fiercest Rivalry in Tech: Uber vs. Lyft," *The Wall Street Journal,* August 12, 2014, p. B1; Trevor Hughes, "Passengers Flock to Upstart Car Services," *USA Today,* July 10, 2014, p. 5B; James Nash, "The Company Cities Love to Hate," *Bloomberg Businessweek,* July 3, 2014, pp. 31–33; Sam Schechner, "Uber Tries to Thwart Ban in French Court," *The Wall Street Journal,* November 29–30, 2014, p. B4; Joanna Sugden, Aditi Malhotra, and Douglas MacMillan, "Uber Under Attack around Globe," *The Wall Street Journal,* December 10, 2014, pp. B1, B4; Karen Weise, "How Uber Rolls," *Bloomberg Businessweek,* June 29–July 5, 2015, pp. 54–59.

17. World Trade Organization, "The WTO can . . . stimulate economic growth and employment," https://www.wto.org/english/thewto_e/whatis_e/10thi_e/10thi03_e.htm (accessed February 22, 2016).

18. Economist staff, "The Criminalisation of American Business," August 30-September 5, 2014, *Economist,* 21–24; Tracy Gonzalez-Padron, G. Tomas M. Hult, and O.C. Ferrell, "Stakeholder Marketing Relationships to Social Responsibility and Firm Performance," Working paper, 2015.

19. Ryan C. Fuhrmann, "Okuns Law: Economic Growth and Unemployment," *Investopedia,* 2016, http://www.investopedia.com/articles/economics/12/okuns-law.asp (accessed February 22, 2016); World Trade Organization,

"The WTO can . . . stimulate economic growth and employment," https://www.wto.org/english/thewto_e/whatis_e/10thi_e/10thi03_e.htm (accessed February 22, 2016).

20. Drew Desilver, "High-income Americans pay most income taxes, but enough to be "fair"?" *Pew Research Center,* March 24, 2015, http://www.pewresearch.org/fact-tank/2015/03/24/high-income-americans-pay-most-income-taxes-but-enough-to-be-fair/ (accessed February 22, 2016).

21. Ibid.

22. Martin Sullivan, "The Truth About Corporate Tax Rates," *Forbes,* March 25, 2015, http://www.forbes.com/sites/taxanalysts/2015/03/25/the-truth-about-corporate-tax-rates/#d18280620a54 (accessed February 22, 2016).

23. Neil Shah, "Baby Bust Threatens Growth," *The Wall Street Journal,* December 4, 2014, p. A3.

24. U.S. Census Bureau, "State & County Quick Facts," http://quickfacts.census.gov/qfd/states/00000.html (accessed February 22, 2016); Haya El Nasser, Gregory Korte, and Paul Overberg, "308.7 Million," *USA Today,* December 22, 2010, p. 1A.

25. U.S. Department of Labor, "Data & Statistics," http://www.dol.gov/wb/stats/stats_data.htm (accessed February 22, 2016).

26. Dinah Eng and Heidi Ganahl, "Finding Her 'Wow' in Camp Bow Wow," *Fortune,* March 15, 2015, pp. 41–42.

27. Karsten Strauss, "Reinventing the Pizza," *Forbes,* January 19, 2015, pp. 40–44; Richard Gorelick, "Pizza Studio Opening in Charles Villages," *The Baltimore Sun,* March 3, 2015, http://www.baltimoresun.com/entertainment/dining/baltimore-diner-blog/bal-pizza-studio-20150303-story.html (accessed July 6, 2015); Harrison Smith, "Free Food Alert: Pizza Studio Opens with a Lunch/Dinner Getaway," *Washingtonian,* April 23, 2015, http://www.washingtonian.com/blogs/bestbites/deals-and-bargains/free-pizza-in-dupont-circle-today.php (accessed July 6, 2015); Sarah Theebom, "Pizza Studio Is the Chipotle of the Pizza World," *First We Feast,* January 6, 2015, http://firstwefeast.com/eat/pizza-studio-is-the-chipotle-of-the-pizza-world/ (accessed July 6, 2015).

28. Eli Lilly, "Heritage," www.lilly.com/about/heritage/Pages/heritage.aspx (accessed February 23, 2016).

29. Walmart, "Corporate and Financial Facts," 2016, http://news.walmart.com/walmart-facts/corporate-financial-fact-sheet (accessed February 23, 2016); Anthony Bianco and Wendy Zellner, "Is Wal-Mart Too Powerful?" *BusinessWeek,* October 6, 2003, pp. 100–110.

30. Joann S. Lublin, "New Report Finds a Diversity Dividend at Work," *The Wall Street Journal,* January 20, 2015, http://blogs.wsj.com/atwork/2015/01/20/new-report-finds-a-diversity-dividend-at-work/ (accessed February 22, 2016).

31. "The 2011 Worlds Most Ethical Companies," *Ethisphere,* 2011, Q1, pp. 31–43.

32. Isabelle Maignon, Tracy L. Gonzalez-Padron, G. Tomas M. Hult, and O. C. Ferrell, "Stakeholder Orientation: Development and Testing of a Framework for Socially Responsible Marketing," *Journal of Strategic Marketing,* 19, no. 4 (July 2011), pp. 313–338.

33. Small Business Administration Office of Advocacy, *Frequently Asked Questions,* 2012, www.sba.gov/sites/ default/files/FAQ_Sept_2012.pdf (accessed February 23, 2016); Joel Holland, "Save the World, Make a Million," *Entrepreneur,* April 2010, http://www.entrepreneur.com/ article/205556 (accessed February 23, 2016); iContact, www.icontact.com (accessed February 23, 2016); Leigh Buchanan, "The U.S. Now Has 27 Million Entrepreneurs," *Inc.,* http://www.inc.com/leigh-buchanan/ us-entrepreneurship-reaches-record-highs.html (accessed February 23, 2016).

2

Business Ethics and Social Responsibility

© Aaron Roeth Photography

Learning Objectives

After reading this chapter, you will be able to:

LO 2-1 Define business ethics and social responsibility and examine their importance.

LO 2-2 Detect some of the ethical issues that may arise in business.

LO 2-3 Specify how businesses can promote ethical behavior.

LO 2-4 Explain the four dimensions of social responsibility.

LO 2-5 Debate an organization's social responsibilities to owners, employees, consumers, the environment, and the community.

LO 2-6 Evaluate the ethics of a business's decision.

Enter the World of Business ⊖━━━━━━━━

Mars M & Ms: Less Sugar for Your Sweet Tooth

Mars Inc. wants people to watch their sugar intake. This is surprising for a company specializing in chocolates such as M&Ms and Snickers. The company diverges from most of the big food manufacturers by supporting a government proposal to include measurements for added sugar on food labels. Currently, the Food and Drug Administration (FDA) does not set a recommended daily sugar allowance, and manufacturers are not required to include added sugar information on food packaging. Added sugar is sugar not naturally found in foods. Thus, it is challenging for consumers to know how much sugar they are actually consuming.

However, identifying the amount of added sugar in foods may soon get easier. The World Health Organization and some food companies are searching for ways to encourage less excessive sugar consumption, attributed to obesity and chronic health problems like diabetes. Recognizing the formidable health risk that excess sugar can cause, the FDA has proposed that food labels include the amount of added sugar. Naturally, this proposal has led to opposition from major food manufacturers.

Mars, on the other hand, not only supports the FDA's proposal but also supports additional recommendations that daily sugar consumption should not exceed 10 percent of an individual's diet. Mars Inc. recognizes the harmful impact of too much candy, and it feels it has a social responsibility to educate consumers about the dangers of excess sugar consumption. In this way, Mars hopes to maximize its positive impact on society. Mars Inc. demonstrates corporate citizenship by prioritizing the health challenges of perhaps its most important stakeholder—the customer.[1]

Introduction

Any organization, including nonprofits, has to manage the ethical behavior of employees and participants in the overall operations of the organization. Firms that are highly ethical tend to be more profitable with more satisfied employees and customers.[2] Therefore, there are no conflicts between profits and ethics—in fact, unethical conduct is more likely to lower profits than raise them. For instance, Volkswagen stock plummeted after news was released that it had installed defeat devices in its diesel vehicles to purposefully fool government emissions tests. Wrongdoing by some businesses has focused public attention and government involvement on encouraging more acceptable business conduct. Any organizational decision may be judged as right or wrong, ethical or unethical, legal or illegal.

In this chapter, we take a look at the role of ethics and social responsibility in business decision making. First, we define business ethics and examine why it is important to understand ethics' role in business. Next, we explore a number of business ethics issues to help you learn to recognize such issues when they arise. Finally, we consider steps businesses can take to improve ethical behavior in their organizations. The second half of the chapter focuses on social responsibility and unemployment. We describe some important issues and detail how companies have responded to them.

LO 2-1

Define business ethics and social responsibility and examine their importance.

business ethics
principles and standards that determine acceptable conduct in business.

Business Ethics and Social Responsibility

In this chapter, we define **business ethics** as the principles and standards that determine acceptable conduct in business organizations. Personal ethics, on the other hand, relates to an individual's values, principles, and standards of conduct. The acceptability of behavior in business is determined by not only the organization, but also stakeholders such as customers, competitors, government regulators, interest groups, and the public, as well as each individual's personal principles and values. The publicity and debate surrounding highly visible legal and ethical issues at a number of well-known firms, including JPMorgan Chase, Target, and Volkswagen, highlight the need for businesses to integrate ethics and responsibility into all business decisions. For instance, Target was criticized for not having appropriate internal controls in place to prevent the theft of millions of its customers' credit and debit card accounts. High-risk trading at JPMorgan Chase led to massive losses that affected the company's reputation and resulted in fines. Most unethical activities within organizations are supported by an organizational culture that encourages employees to bend the rules. On the other hand, trust in business is the glue that holds relationships together. In Figure 2-1, you can see that trust in banks is lower than in other industries, except for government and media. While business overall has over a 50 percent trust rate, a significant portion of the population does not trust business.

Organizations that exhibit a high ethical culture encourage employees to act with integrity and adhere to business values. Many experts agree that ethical leadership, ethical values, and compliance are important in creating good business ethics. To truly create an ethical culture, however, managers must show a strong commitment to ethics and compliance. This "tone at the top" requires top managers to acknowledge their own role in supporting ethics and compliance, create strong relationships with the general counsel and the ethics and compliance department, clearly communicate company expectations for ethical behavior to all employees, educate all managers and supervisors in the business about the company's ethics policies, and train managers and employees on what to do if an ethics crisis occurs.[3]

Entrepreneurship in Action

Beautycounter Is Lathered Up about Social Responsibility

Beautycounter
Founders: Gregg Renfrew
Founded: 2013, in Santa Monica, California
Success: In the first two years, Beautycounter grew 550 percent with 5,000 independent consultants.

It all started when the documentary "An Inconvenient Truth" inspired entrepreneur Gregg Renfrew to replace products in her house that could be harmful to humans or the environment. Yet, when it came to her beauty products, she was at a loss. Her beauty products contained toxic chemicals, but thus far, all alternative nontoxic beauty products were of lower quality.

This prompted Renfrew to partner with a team to develop nontoxic beauty products without sacrificing performance. Although it took time, they successfully developed beauty products with nontoxic materials, as well as the company's "never" list.

The "never" list is a list of chemicals Beautycounter promises to never use, such as animal fat and formaldehyde. This includes products banned in other countries even if not in the United States. Renfrew employs a direct selling model and also sells products through the company website, Gwyneth Paltrow's Goop.com, and J.Crew. To reinforce the safety and environmental friendliness of the products, Beautycounter received B (benefit) corporation certification, or third-party certification, that it strives for the highest standards of accountability and transparency.[4]

Discussion Questions

1. How did concern for social responsibility and sustainability lead Gregg Renfrew to start her own company?
2. How is Beautycounter transparent with its customers about the ingredients of its products?
3. As society becomes more health conscious, will Beautycounter be able to maintain its competitive advantage?

Businesses should not only make a profit but also consider the social implications of their activities. Walmart, for instance, donated $1.4 billion in cash and in-kind donations to philanthropic causes throughout the world, and its associates volunteered 1.5 million hours in their communities.[5] However, profits permit businesses to contribute to society. The firms that are more well known for their strong social contributions tend to be those that are more profitable. We define **social responsibility** as a business's obligation to maximize its positive impact and minimize its negative impact on society. Although many people use the terms *social responsibility* and *ethics* interchangeably, they do not mean the same thing. Business ethics relates to

social responsibility
a business's obligation to maximize its positive impact and minimize its negative impact on society.

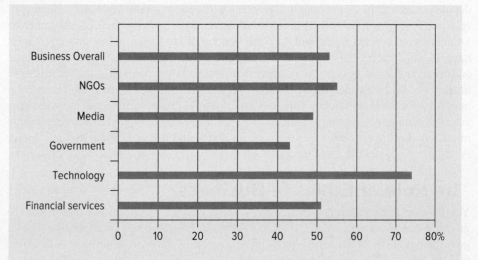

FIGURE 2-1
Global Trust in Different Institutions

Source: Edelman Trust Barometer, "2016 Edelman Trust Barometer," http://www.edelman.com/insights/intellectual-property/2016-edelman-trust-barometer/global-results/ (accessed February 23, 2016).

TABLE 2-1 Timeline of Ethical and Socially Responsible Activities

1960s	1970s	1980s	1990s	2000s
• Social issues	• Business ethics	• Standards for ethical conduct	• Corporate ethics programs	• Transparency in financial markets
• Consumer Bill of Rights	• Social responsibility	• Financial misconduct	• Regulation to support business ethics	• Corporate misconduct
• Disadvantaged consumer	• Diversity	• Self-regulation	• Health issues	• Intellectual property
• Environmental issues	• Bribery	• Codes of conduct	• Safe working conditions	• Regulation of accounting and finance
• Product safety	• Discrimination	• Ethics training	• Detecting misconduct	• Executive compensation
	• Identifying ethical issues			• Identity theft

an *individual's* or a *work group's* decisions that society evaluates as right or wrong, whereas social responsibility is a broader concept that concerns the impact of the *entire business's* activities on society. From an ethical perspective, for example, we may be concerned about a health care organization overcharging the government for Medicare services. From a social responsibility perspective, we might be concerned about the impact that this overcharging will have on the ability of the health care system to provide adequate services for all citizens.[6]

The most basic ethical and social responsibility concerns have been codified by laws and regulations that encourage businesses to conform to society's standards, values, and attitudes. For example, after accounting scandals at a number of well-known firms in the early 2000s shook public confidence in the integrity of corporate America, the reputations of every U.S. company suffered regardless of their association with the scandals.[7] To help restore confidence in corporations and markets, Congress passed the Sarbanes-Oxley Act, which criminalized securities fraud and stiffened penalties for corporate fraud. After the financial crisis occurred in the most recent recession, the Dodd-Frank Act was passed to reform the financial industry and offer consumers protection against complex and/or deceptive financial products. At a minimum, managers are expected to obey all laws and regulations. Most legal issues arise as choices that society deems unethical, irresponsible, or otherwise unacceptable. However, all actions deemed unethical by society are not necessarily illegal, and both legal and ethical concerns change over time (see Table 2-1). More recently, identity theft has become the number-one consumer complaint with the Federal Trade Commission, and companies have an ethical responsibility to protect customer data. Business law refers to the laws and regulations that govern the conduct of business. Many problems and conflicts in business could be avoided if owners, managers, and employees knew more about business law and the legal system. Business ethics, social responsibility, and laws together act as a compliance system, requiring that businesses and employees act responsibly in society. In this chapter, we explore ethics and social responsibility; Bonus Chapter A addresses business law, including the Sarbanes-Oxley Act and the Dodd-Frank Act.

The Role of Ethics in Business

You have only to pick up *The Wall Street Journal* or *USA Today* to see examples of the growing concern about legal and ethical issues in business. For example, the federal government accused Bristol-Myers Squibb of bribing state-owned hospitals in China to gain prescription sales. The company paid $14 million to settle the allegations.[8]

Regardless of what an individual believes about a particular action, if society judges it to be unethical or wrong, whether correctly or not, that judgment directly affects the organization's ability to achieve its business goals.[9]

Well-publicized incidents of unethical and illegal activity—ranging from accounting fraud to using the Internet to steal another person's credit card number, from deceptive advertising of food and diet products to unfair competitive practices in the computer software industry—strengthen the public's perceptions that ethical standards and the level of trust in business need to be raised. On the other hand, it is worth noting that the mass media frequently reports about firms that engage in misconduct related to bribery, fraud, and unsafe products. However, the good ethical conduct of the vast majority of firms is not reported as often. Therefore, the public often gets the impression that misconduct is more widespread than it is in reality.

It will likely take a long time for Volkswagen to recover from its environmental scandal. VW had installed defeat devices in its diesel vehicles to cheat government emissions tests.
© McPhoto/Weber/Alamy Stock Photo

Often, misconduct starts as ethical conflicts but evolves into legal disputes when cooperative conflict resolution cannot be accomplished. Headline-grabbing scandals like those associated with executive compensation and benefits packages create ethical concerns. Compensation for board members is another rising concern. In less than a decade, compensation for non-executive directors increased 50 percent, even though many work as directors part-time. The median pay of Standard & Poor's (S&P) 500 board members is $255,000 a year, although some companies such as Berkshire Hathaway only pay their board members $2,700 a year, and Amazon pays its board members nothing. It is feared that compensation over a certain amount affects directors' objectivity and duty to their firms.[10]

However, it is important to understand that business ethics goes beyond legal issues. Ethical conduct builds trust among individuals and in business relationships, which validates and promotes confidence in business relationships. Establishing trust and confidence is much more difficult in organizations that have reputations for acting unethically. If you were to discover, for example, that a manager had misled you about company benefits when you were hired, your trust and confidence in that company would probably diminish. And if you learned that a colleague had lied to you about something, you probably would not trust or rely on that person in the future.

Ethical issues are not limited to for-profit organizations either. Ethical issues include all areas of organizational activities. In government, several politicians and some high-ranking officials have faced disciplinary actions over ethical indiscretions. For instance, former New Mexico secretary of state Dianna Duran pled guilty to money laundering and embezzlement while in office to pay for gambling debts.[11] Even sports can be subject to ethical lapses. A major bribery scandal was discovered among high-ranking soccer officials in the Fédération Internationale de Football Association (FIFA), soccer's governing body. The officials were accused of bribery and racketeering in a corruption scandal that spanned years.[12] Whether made in science, politics, sports, or business, most decisions are judged as right or wrong, ethical or unethical. Negative judgments can affect an organization's ability to build relationships with customers and suppliers, attract investors, and retain employees.[13]

Although we will not tell you in this chapter what you ought to do, others—your superiors, co-workers, and family—will make judgments about the ethics of your actions and decisions. Learning how to recognize and resolve ethical issues is a key step in evaluating ethical decisions in business.

Recognizing Ethical Issues in Business

LO 2-2

Detect some of the ethical issues that may arise in business.

ethical issue
an identifiable problem, situation, or opportunity that requires a person to choose from among several actions that may be evaluated as right or wrong, ethical or unethical.

Recognizing ethical issues is the most important step in understanding business ethics. An **ethical issue** is an identifiable problem, situation, or opportunity that requires a person to choose from among several actions that may be evaluated as right or wrong, ethical or unethical. Learning how to choose from alternatives and make a decision requires not only good personal values, but also knowledge competence in the business area of concern. Employees also need to know when to rely on their organizations' policies and codes of ethics or have discussions with co-workers or managers on appropriate conduct. Ethical decision making is not always easy because there are always gray areas that create dilemmas, no matter how decisions are made. For instance, should an employee report on a co-worker engaging in time theft? Should a salesperson omit facts about a product's poor safety record in his presentation to a customer? Such questions require the decision maker to evaluate the ethics of his or her choice and decide whether to ask for guidance.

bribes
payments, gifts, or special favors intended to influence the outcome of a decision.

Many business issues seem straightforward and easy to resolve on the surface, but are in reality very complex. A person often needs several years of experience in business to understand what is acceptable or ethical. For example, it is considered improper to give or accept **bribes,** which are payments, gifts, or special favors intended to influence the outcome of a decision. A bribe benefits an individual or a company at the expense of other stakeholders. Companies that do business overseas should be aware that bribes are a significant ethical issue and are, in fact, illegal in many countries. In the United States, the Foreign Corrupt Practices Act imposes heavy penalties on companies found guilty of bribery.

Ethics is also related to the culture in which a business operates. In the United States, for example, it would be inappropriate for a businessperson to bring an elaborately wrapped gift to a prospective client on their first meeting—the gift could be viewed as a bribe. In Japan, however, it is considered impolite *not* to bring a gift. Experience with the culture in which a business operates is critical to understanding what is ethical or unethical. On the other hand, firms must also abide by the values and policies of global business.

To help you understand ethical issues that perplex businesspeople today, we will take a brief look at some of them in this section. Ethical issues can be more complex now than in the past. The vast number of news-format investigative programs has increased consumer and employee awareness of organizational misconduct. In addition, the multitude of cable channels and Internet resources has improved the awareness of ethical problems among the general public.

One of the principal causes of unethical behavior in organizations is rewards for overly aggressive financial or business objectives. It is not possible to discuss every issue, of course. However, a discussion

Ralph Lauren reported that its subsidiary had bribed foreign officials in Argentina. Because it took quick action to address the misconduct, the company did not face charges.

© NCI WENN Photos/Newscom

of a few issues can help you begin to recognize the ethical problems with which businesspersons must deal. Many ethical issues in business can be categorized in the context of their relation with abusive and intimidating behavior, conflicts of interest, fairness and honesty, communications, misuse of company resources, and business associations. The Global Business Ethics Survey found that workers witness many instances of ethical misconduct in their organizations and sometimes feel pressured to compromise standards (see Table 2-2).

Misuse of Company Time.   Theft of time is a common area of misconduct observed in the workplace.[14] One example of misusing time in the workplace is by engaging in activities that are not necessary for the job. For instance, many employees spend an average of one hour each day using social networking sites or watching YouTube. In this case, the employee is misusing not only time but also company resources by using the company's computer and Internet access for personal use.[15] Time theft costs can be difficult to measure but are estimated to cost companies hundreds of billions of dollars annually. It is widely believed that the average employee "steals" 4.5 hours a week with late arrivals, leaving early, long lunch breaks, inappropriate sick days, excessive socializing, and engaging in personal activities such as online shopping and watching sports while on the job. All of these activities add up to lost productivity and profits for the employer—and relate to ethical issues in the area of time theft.

Abusive and Intimidating Behavior.   Abusive or intimidating behavior is the most common ethical problem for employees. These concepts can mean anything from physical threats, false accusations, profanity, insults, yelling, harshness, and unreasonableness to ignoring someone or simply being annoying; and the meaning of these words can differ by person—you probably have some ideas of your own. Abusive behavior can be placed on a continuum from a minor distraction to a disruption of the workplace. For example, what one person may define as yelling might be another's definition of normal speech. Civility in our society is a concern, and the workplace is no exception. The productivity level of many organizations has been diminished by the time spent unraveling abusive relationships.

Abusive behavior is difficult to assess and manage because of diversity in culture and lifestyle. What does it mean to speak profanely? Is profanity only related to

Misconduct Facts	Percentages
Observed misconduct	30%
Abusive behavior	22%
Lying to stakeholders	22%
Conflict of interest	19%
Pressure to compromise standards	22%
Report observed misconduct	76%
Experience retaliation for reporting	53%

TABLE 2-2
Organizational Misconduct in the United States

Source: Ethics and Compliance Initiative, 2016 Global Business Ethics Survey™: Measuring Risk and Promoting Workplace Integrity (Arlington, VA: Ethics and Compliance Initiative, 2016), p. 43.

Abusive behavior such as bullying can lead to low morale, higher turnover, and increased absenteeism.

© Orange Line Media/Cutcaster

specific words or other such terms that are common in today's business world? If you are using words that are normal in your language but that others consider to be profanity, have you just insulted, abused, or disrespected them?

Within the concept of abusive behavior, intent should be a consideration. If the employee was trying to convey a compliment but the comment was considered abusive, then it was probably a mistake. The way a word is said (voice inflection) can be important. Add to this the fact that we now live in a multicultural environment—doing business and working with many different cultural groups—and the businessperson soon realizes the depth of the ethical and legal issues that may arise. There are problems of word meanings by age and within cultures. For example, an expression such as "Did you guys hook up last night" can have various meanings, including some that could be considered offensive in a work environment.

Bullying is associated with a hostile workplace when a person or group is targeted and is threatened, harassed, belittled, verbally abused, or overly criticized. Bullying may create what some consider a hostile environment, a term generally associated with sexual harassment. Although sexual harassment has legal recourse, bullying has little legal recourse at this time. Bullying is a widespread problem in the United States and can cause psychological damage that can result in health-endangering consequences to the target. Surveys reveal that bullying in the workplace is on the rise.[16] As Table 2-3 indicates, bullying can use a mix of verbal, nonverbal, and manipulative threatening expressions to damage workplace productivity. One may wonder why workers tolerate such activities. The problem is that 72 percent of bullies outrank their victims.[17]

TABLE 2-3
Actions Associated with Bullies

I. Spreading rumors to damage others
2. Blocking others' communication in the workplace
3. Flaunting status or authority to take advantage of others
4. Discrediting others' ideas and opinions
5. Using e-mail to demean others
6. Failing to communicate or return communication
7. Insults, yelling, and shouting
8. Using terminology to discriminate by gender, race, or age
9. Using eye or body language to hurt others or their reputation
IO. Taking credit for others' work or ideas

Source: © O. C. Ferrell, 2017.

Misuse of Company Resources.   Misuse of company resources has been identified by the Ethics Resource Center as a leading issue in observed misconduct in organizations. Issues might include spending an excessive amount of time on personal e-mails, submitting personal expenses on company expense reports, or using the company copier for personal use. An executive at Blue Shield of California was fired for allegedly charging more than $100,000 on his company credit card that he used for personal expenses.[18] While serious resource abuse can result in firing, some abuse can have legal repercussions. An Apple store employee was arrested for allegedly re-coding American Express and Visa gift cards and then using them to fraudulently purchase nearly $1 million in Apple gift cards.[19]

The most common way that employees abuse resources is by using company computers for personal use. Typical examples of using a computer for personal use include shopping on the Internet, downloading music, doing personal banking, surfing the Internet for entertainment purposes, or visiting Facebook. Some companies have chosen to block certain sites such as YouTube or Pandora from employees. However, other companies choose to take a more flexible approach. For example, many have instituted policies that allow for some personal computer use as long as the use does not detract significantly from the workday.

No matter what approach a business chooses to take, it must have policies in place to prevent company resource abuse. Because misuse of company resources is such a widespread problem, many companies, like Coca-Cola, have implemented official policies delineating acceptable use of company resources. Coca-Cola's policy states that company assets should not be used for personal benefit but does allow employees some freedom in this area. The policy specifies that it is acceptable for employees to make the occasional personal phone call or e-mail, but they should use common sense to know when these activities become excessive.[20] This kind of policy is in line with that of many companies, particularly large ones that can easily lose millions of dollars and thousands of hours of productivity to these activities.

Conflict of Interest.   A conflict of interest, one of the most common ethical issues identified by employees, exists when a person must choose whether to advance his or her own personal interests or those of others. For example, a manager in a corporation is supposed to ensure that the company is profitable so that its stockholder-owners receive a return on their investment. In other words, the manager has a responsibility to investors. If she instead makes decisions that give her more power or money but do not help the company, then she has a conflict of interest—she is acting to benefit herself at the expense of her company and is not fulfilling her responsibilities as an employee. To avoid conflicts of interest, employees must be able to separate their personal financial interests from their business dealings. Conflict of interest has long been a serious problem in the financial industry. Asset management firm BlackRock paid $12 million to the U.S. Securities and Exchange Commission for not disclosing that its fund manager had a major interest in a firm in which he deposited clients' money.[21] Conflict of interest can be particularly problematic in the finance industry because bad decisions can result in significant financial losses.

Insider trading is an example of a conflict of interest. Insider trading is the buying or selling of stocks by insiders who possess material that is still not public. The Justice Department has taken an aggressive stance toward insider trading. However, the courts have restricted the scope of insider-trading prosecutions, which has caused previous insider-trading convictions to be overturned.[22] Bribery can also be a conflict of interest. While bribery is an increasing issue in many countries, it is more prevalent in

TABLE 2-4
Least Corrupt Countries

Rank	Country
1.	Denmark
2.	Finland
3.	Sweden
4.	New Zealand
5.	Netherlands/Norway
7.	Switzerland
8.	Singapore
9.	Canada
10.	Germany/Luxembourg/United Kingdom
13.	Australia/Iceland
15.	Belgium
16.	Austria/United States

Corruption Perceptions Index (CPI) score relates to perceptions of the degree of public sector corruption as seen by businesspeople and country analysts and ranges between 0 (highly corrupt) and 10 (very clean).

Source: Rachel Beddow (Ed.), Corruptions Perceptions Index 2015 (Transparency International, 2016).

some countries than in others. Transparency International has developed a Corruption Perceptions Index (Table 2-4). Note that there are 15 countries perceived as less corrupt than the United States. The five countries rated by Transparency International as most corrupt include South Sudan, Sudan, Afghanistan, North Korea, and Somalia.[23]

Fairness and Honesty

Fairness and honesty are at the heart of business ethics and relate to the general values of decision makers. At a minimum, businesspersons are expected to follow all applicable laws and regulations. But beyond obeying the law, they are expected not to harm customers, employees, clients, or competitors knowingly through deception, misrepresentation, coercion, or discrimination. Honesty and fairness can relate to how the employees use the resources of the organization. In contrast, dishonesty is usually associated with a lack of integrity, lack of disclosure, and lying. One common example of dishonesty is theft of office supplies. Although the majority of office supply thefts involve small things such as pencils or Post-it Notes, some workers admit to stealing more expensive items or equipment such as computers or software. Employees should be aware of policies on stealing items and recognize how these decisions relate to ethical behavior.

One aspect of fairness relates to competition. Although numerous laws have been passed to foster competition and make monopolistic practices illegal, companies sometimes gain control over markets by using questionable practices that harm competition. For instance, the European Commission started an antitrust investigation into Google's practices to determine whether it was engaging in anticompetitive behavior. Several companies, including Microsoft, claimed that Google promoted its own search results over those of competitors in spite of their relevance. Because Google holds 90 percent of the search engine market in Europe, the controversy over how it is using its dominant position to remain ahead of competitors is not likely to

Misuse of company time through the use of personal social media is very costly to businesses.

© Jane Williams/Alamy

die down. The European Union's Parliament has called for the breakup of Google to separate its search engine business from its other services.[24] In many cases, the alleged misconduct not only can have monetary and legal implications, but can also threaten reputation, investor confidence, and customer loyalty. At the minimum, a business found guilty of anticompetitive practices will be forced to stop such conduct. However, many companies end up paying millions in penalties to settle allegations.[25]

Another aspect of fairness and honesty relates to disclosure of potential harm caused by product use. For instance, the FDA has become increasingly concerned about food safety rules after a contamination crisis involving Blue Bell ice cream caused three deaths. The agency adopted new rules that now requires food manufacturers to create and enforce detailed plans meant to prevent foodborne illness and contamination.[26]

Dishonesty has become a significant problem in the United States. In a survey of new students at Harvard, 23 percent admitted to cheating on schoolwork before attending Harvard, and 9 percent revealed that they had cheated on exams. If today's students are tomorrow's leaders, there is likely to be a correlation between acceptable behavior today and tomorrow. This adds to the argument that the leaders of today must be prepared for the ethical risks associated with this downward trend.[27]

Communications.   Communications is another area in which ethical concerns may arise. False and misleading advertising, as well as deceptive personal-selling tactics, anger consumers and can lead to the failure of a business. Truthfulness about product

TurnItIn is an Internet service that allows teachers to determine if their students have plagiarized content.

© Bloomberg/Contributor/Getty Images

safety and quality is also important to consumers. General Motors, Toyota, and Honda all faced fines for product quality issues and for not issuing recalls in a timely manner. In many of these situations, the companies were found to be slow on issuing recalls or making them well known, which resulted in accidents in some cases.

Some companies fail to provide enough information for consumers about differences or similarities between products. For example, driven by high prices for medicines, many consumers are turning to Canadian, Mexican, and overseas Internet sources for drugs to treat a variety of illnesses and conditions. However, research suggests that a significant percentage of these imported pharmaceuticals may not actually contain the labeled drug, and the counterfeit drugs could even be harmful to those who take them.[28]

Another important aspect of communications that may raise ethical concerns relates to product labeling. This becomes an even greater concern with potentially harmful products like cigarettes. The FDA warned three cigarette manufacturers against using "additive-free" or "natural" on their labeling out of concern that consumers would associate these terms as meaning that their products were healthier.[29] However, labeling of other products raises ethical questions when it threatens basic rights, such as freedom of speech and expression. This is the heart of

Russian tennis champion Maria Sharapova tested positive for a drug that had been banned, causing Nike to suspend its relationship with Sharapova.

© Cal Sport Media/Alamy Stock Photo

the controversy surrounding the movement to require warning labels on movies and videogames, rating their content, language, and appropriate audience age. Although people in the entertainment industry claim that such labeling violates their First Amendment right to freedom of expression, other consumers—particularly parents—believe that labeling is needed to protect children from harmful influences. Internet regulation, particularly that designed to protect children and the elderly, is on the forefront in consumer protection legislation. Because of the debate surrounding the acceptability of these business activities, they remain major ethical issues.

Business Relationships.   The behavior of businesspersons toward customers, suppliers, and others in their workplace may also generate ethical concerns. Ethical behavior within a business involves keeping company secrets, meeting obligations and responsibilities, and avoiding undue pressure that may force others to act unethically.

Managers in particular, because of the authority of their position, have the opportunity to influence employees' actions. For example, a manager might influence employees to use pirated computer software to save costs. The use of illegal software puts the employee and the company at legal risk, but employees may feel pressured to do so by their superior's authority. The National Business Ethics Survey found that employees who feel pressured to compromise ethical standards view top and middle managers as the greatest source of such pressure.[30]

It is the responsibility of managers to create a work environment that helps the organization achieve its objectives and fulfill its responsibilities. However, the methods that managers use to enforce these responsibilities should not compromise employee rights. Organizational pressures may encourage a person to engage in activities that he or she might otherwise view as unethical, such as invading others' privacy or stealing a competitor's secrets. The firm may provide only vague or lax supervision on ethical issues, creating the opportunity for misconduct. Managers who offer no ethical direction to employees create many opportunities for manipulation, dishonesty, and conflicts of interest.

Plagiarism—taking someone else's work and presenting it as your own without mentioning the source—is another ethical issue. As a student, you may be familiar with plagiarism in school—for example, copying someone else's term paper or quoting from a published work or Internet source without acknowledging it. In business, an ethical issue arises when an employee copies reports or takes the work or ideas of others and presents it as his or her own. A manager attempting to take credit for a subordinate's ideas is engaging in another type of plagiarism.

plagiarism
the act of taking someone else's work and presenting it as your own without mentioning the source.

Making Decisions about Ethical Issues

It can be difficult to recognize specific ethical issues in practice. Managers, for example, tend to be more concerned about issues that affect those close to them, as well as issues that have immediate rather than long-term consequences. Thus, the perceived importance of an ethical issue substantially affects choices. However, only a few issues receive scrutiny, and most receive no attention at all.[31] Managers make intuitive decisions sometimes without recognizing the embedded ethical issue.

Table 2-5 lists some questions you may want to ask yourself and others when trying to determine whether an action is ethical. Open discussion of ethical issues does not eliminate ethical problems, but it does promote both trust and learning in an organization.[32] When people feel that they cannot discuss what they are doing with their co-workers or superiors, there is a good chance that an ethical issue exists. Once a person has recognized an ethical issue and can openly discuss it with others, he or she has begun the process of resolving that issue.

TABLE 2-5
Questions to Consider in
Determining Whether an
Action Is Ethical

Are there any potential legal restrictions or violations that could result from the action?
Does your company have a specific code of ethics or policy on the action?
Is this activity customary in your industry? Are there any industry trade groups that provide guidelines or codes of conduct that address this issue?
Would this activity be accepted by your co-workers? Will your decision or action withstand open discussion with co-workers and managers and survive untarnished?
How does this activity fit with your own beliefs and values?

LO 2-3
Specify how businesses can
promote ethical behavior.

Improving Ethical Behavior in Business

Understanding how people make ethical choices and what prompts a person to act unethically may result in better ethical decisions. Ethical decisions in an organization are influenced by three key factors: individual moral standards and values, the influence of managers and co-workers, and the opportunity to engage in misconduct (Figure 2-2). While you have great control over your personal ethics outside the workplace, your co-workers and superiors exert significant control over your choices at work through authority and example. In fact, the activities and examples set by co-workers, along with rules and policies established by the firm, are critical in gaining consistent ethical compliance in an organization. If the company fails to provide good examples and direction for appropriate conduct, confusion and conflict will develop and result in the opportunity for misconduct. If your boss or co-workers leave work early, you may be tempted to do so as well. If you see co-workers engaged in personal activities such as shopping online or if they ignore the misconduct of others, then you may be more likely to do so also. Having sound personal values is important because you will be responsible for your own conduct.

Because ethical issues often emerge from conflict, it is useful to examine the causes of ethical conflict. Business managers and employees often experience some tension between their own ethical beliefs and their obligations to the organizations in which they work. Many employees utilize different ethical standards at work than they do at home. This conflict increases when employees feel that their company is encouraging unethical conduct or exerting pressure on them to engage in it.

It is difficult for employees to determine what conduct is acceptable within a company if the firm does not have established ethics policies and standards. And without such policies and standards, employees may base decisions on how their peers and superiors behave. Professional **codes of ethics** are formalized rules and standards that describe what the company expects of its employees. Codes of ethics do not have to be so detailed that they take into account every situation, but they should provide guidelines and principles that can help employees achieve organizational objectives and address risks in an acceptable and ethical way. The development of a code of ethics should include not only a firm's executives and board of directors, but also legal staff and employees from all areas of a firm.[33] Table 2-6 lists why a code of ethics is important.

codes of ethics
formalized rules and
standards that describe what
a company expects of its
employees.

FIGURE 2-2
Three Factors That
Influence Business Ethics

Individual Standards and Values		Managers' and Co-workers' Influence		Opportunity: Codes and Compliance Requirements		Ethical/Unethical Choices in Business
	+		+		=	

Come Fly with Me: Or Not?

Pet owners are willing to pay extra to ensure the comfort of their animals. However, this is causing trouble on flights as pets are increasingly riding in the cabin with owners. Many passengers have pet allergies and are finding themselves close to animals on their flights. Although they can call the airline beforehand and make special arrangements for major pet allergies, not many do so. Pets often get unruly on flights as well. In one instance, a pit bull riding in first class ran into the cockpit during takeoff, startling the pilots and causing a delay.

Pet owners are also receiving inconsistent treatment. In some incidents, such as an animal having an accident in its carrier, pet owners and their pets are removed from the flight. In other cases, they are not. Treatment of unruly pets can vary based on the airline and passenger.

Lax federal regulations and hefty pet fees are major reasons airlines might not be willing to remove certain pets from a flight. For instance, American Airlines is charging an extra $125 for first-class passengers to place their pets in a ventilated compartment during takeoffs and landings. The pets can then sit in their owners' laps during the flight.

Safety is also a concern for both passengers and pets. Currently, only one firm provides safety equipment for pets flying in the cabin.[34]

Discussion Questions

1. How are stakeholders affected by allowing some passengers to bring pets on board?
2. Because pets supply some passengers with emotional support, could airlines be criticized for denying passengers access to their pets while traveling?
3. Is it fair that some passengers with pets are treated differently than others?

Codes of ethics, policies on ethics, and ethics training programs advance ethical behavior because they prescribe which activities are acceptable and which are not, and they limit the opportunity for misconduct by providing punishments for violations of the rules and standards. This creates compliance requirements to establish uniform behavior among all employees. Codes and policies on ethics encourage the creation of an ethical culture in the company. According to the National Business Ethics Survey (NBES), employees in organizations that have written codes of conduct and ethics training, ethics offices or hotlines, and systems for reporting are more likely to report misconduct when they observe it. The survey found that a company's ethical culture is the greatest determinant of future misconduct.[35]

The enforcement of ethical codes and policies through rewards and punishments increases the acceptance of ethical standards by employees. For instance, Texas

• Alerts employees about important issues and risks to address.
• Provides values such as integrity, transparency, honesty, and fairness that gives the foundation for building an ethical culture.
• Gives guidance to employees when facing gray or ambiguous situations or ethical issues that they have never faced before.
• Alerts employees to systems for reporting or places to go for advice when facing an ethical issue.
• Helps establish uniform ethical conduct and values that provides a shared approach to dealing with ethical decisions.
• Serves as an important document for communicating to the public, suppliers, and regulatory authorities about the company's values and compliance.
• Provides the foundation for evaluation and improvement of ethical decision making.

TABLE 2-6
Why a Code of Ethics Is Important

Instruments has a strong code of ethics and a culture of corporate citizenship that encourages employee participation. Every year, the firm releases an ethics and citizenship report and exercises transparency by making it easily accessible through its website. Texas Instruments posts periodic updates on its citizenship activities throughout the year, and a brochure featuring its values and ethical expectations can also be downloaded from its websites.[36]

One of the most important components of an ethics program is a means through which employees can report observed misconduct anonymously. Although the risk of retaliation is still a major factor in whether an employee will report illegal conduct, the Global Business Ethics Survey found that whistleblowing has increased in the past few years. Approximately 76 percent of respondents said they reported misconduct when they observed it.[37] **Whistleblowing** occurs when an employee exposes an employer's wrongdoing to outsiders, such as the media or government regulatory agencies. However, more companies are establishing programs to encourage employees to report illegal or unethical practices internally so that they can take steps to remedy problems before they result in legal action or generate negative publicity. Unfortunately, whistleblowers are often treated negatively in organizations. The government, therefore, tries to encourage employees to report observed misconduct. Congress has also taken steps to close a legislative loophole in whistleblowing legislation that has led to the dismissal of many whistleblowers. In 2010, Congress passed the Dodd-Frank Act, which includes a "whistleblower bounty program." The Securities and Exchange Commission can now award whistleblowers between 10 and 30 percent of monetary sanctions over $1 million. The hope is that incentives will encourage more people to come forward with information regarding corporate misconduct.

The current trend is to move away from legally based ethical initiatives in organizations to cultural- or integrity-based initiatives that make ethics a part of core organizational values. Organizations recognize that effective business ethics programs are good for business performance. Firms that develop higher levels of trust function more efficiently and effectively and avoid damaged company reputations and product images. Organizational ethics initiatives have been supportive of many positive and diverse organizational objectives, such as profitability, hiring, employee satisfaction, and customer loyalty.[38] Conversely, lack of organizational ethics initiatives and the absence of workplace values such as honesty, trust, and integrity can have a negative impact on organizational objectives and employee retention. According to one study, three of the most common factors that executives give for why turnover increases are employee loss of trust in the company, a lack of transparency among company leaders, and unfair employee treatment.[39]

whistleblowing
the act of an employee exposing an employer's wrongdoing to outsiders, such as the media or government regulatory agencies.

The Nature of Social Responsibility

LO 2-4

Explain the four dimensions of social responsibility.

For our purposes, we classify four stages of social responsibility: financial, legal compliance, ethics, and philanthropy (Table 2-7). Another way of categorizing these four dimensions of social responsibility include economic, legal, ethical, and voluntary (including philanthropic).[40] Earning profits is the economic foundation, and complying with the law is the next step. However, a business whose *sole* objective is to maximize profits is not likely to consider its social responsibility, although its activities will probably be legal. (We looked at ethical responsibilities in the first half of this chapter.) Voluntary responsibilities are additional activities that may not be required but which promote human welfare or goodwill. Legal and economic concerns have long been acknowledged in business, and voluntary and ethical issues are being addressed by most firms.

Stages	Examples
Stage 1: Financial Viability	Starbucks offers investors a healthy return on investment, including paying dividends.
Stage 2: Compliance with Legal and Regulatory Requirements	Starbucks specifies in its code of conduct that payments made to foreign government officials must be lawful according to the laws of the United States and the foreign country.
Stage 3: Ethics, Principles, and Values	Starbucks offers health care benefits to part-time employees and supports coffee growers by offering them fair prices.
Stage 4: Philanthropic Activities	Starbucks created the Starbucks College Achievement Plan that offers eligible employees full tuition to earn a bachelor's degree in partnership with Arizona State University.

TABLE 2-7
Social Responsibility Requirements

Corporate citizenship is the extent to which businesses meet the legal, ethical, economic, and voluntary responsibilities placed on them by their various stakeholders. It involves the activities and organizational processes adopted by businesses to meet their social responsibilities. A commitment to corporate citizenship by a firm indicates a strategic focus on fulfilling the social responsibilities expected of it by its stakeholders. For example, CVS demonstrated corporate citizenship by eliminating tobacco products from its pharmacies. Although this cost the firm $2 billion in sales, CVS believed it was contradictory to market itself as a health care services business while still selling a dangerous product.[41] Corporate citizenship involves action and measurement of the extent to which a firm embraces the corporate citizenship philosophy and then follows through by implementing citizenship and social responsibility initiatives. One of the major corporate citizenship issues is the focus on preserving the environment. The majority of people agree that climate change is a global emergency, but there is no agreement on how to solve the problem.[42] Another example of a corporate citizenship issue might be animal rights—an issue that is important to many stakeholders. As the organic and local foods movements grow and become more profitable, more and more stakeholders are calling for more humane practices in factory farms as well.[43] Large factory farms are where most Americans get their meat, but some businesses are looking at more animal-friendly options in response to public outcry.

Part of the answer to the climate change crisis is alternative energy such as solar, wind, bio-fuels, and hydro applications. The drive for alternative fuels such as ethanol from corn has added new issues such as food price increases and food shortages. More than 2 billion consumers earn less than $2 a day in wages. Sharply increased food costs have led to riots and government policies to restrict trade in basic commodities such as rice, corn, and soybeans.[44]

To respond to these developments, most companies are introducing eco-friendly products and marketing efforts. Lighting giant Philips is investigating ways to use its LED lights for horticultural purposes. It is investing in vertical city farming, in which vegetables are grown in stacked layers under LED lighting. The company hopes this breakthrough will increase the yields of locally produced, fresh produce.[45] In one survey, 53 percent of respondents claimed they have boycotted or refused to purchase

corporate citizenship
the extent to which businesses meet the legal, ethical, economic, and voluntary responsibilities placed on them by their stakeholders.

connect
Need help understanding social responsibility? Visit your Connect ebook video tab for a brief animated explanation.

a company's products because it behaved socially irresponsibly.[46] This is because many businesses are promoting themselves as green-conscious and concerned about the environment without actually making the necessary commitments to environmental health.

The Ethisphere Institute selects an annual list of the world's most ethical companies based on the following criteria: corporate citizenship and responsibility; corporate governance; innovation that contributes to the public well-being; industry leadership; executive leadership and tone from the top; legal, regulatory, and reputation track record; and internal systems and ethics/compliance program.[47] Table 2-8 shows 26 from that list.

Although the concept of social responsibility is receiving more and more attention, it is still not universally accepted. Table 2-9 lists some of the arguments for and against social responsibility.

Social Responsibility Issues

LO 2-5

Debate an organization's social responsibilities to owners, employees, consumers, the environment, and the community.

As with ethics, managers consider social responsibility on a daily basis. Among the many social issues that managers must consider are their firms' relations with stakeholders, including owners and stockholders, employees, consumers, regulators, communities, and environmental advocates. For example, Denise Morrison, CEO of Campbell Soup, believes that businesses must take their leadership roles and commitment to social responsibility seriously.[48]

Social responsibility is a dynamic area with issues changing constantly in response to society's demands. There is much evidence that social responsibility is associated with improved business performance. Consumers are refusing to buy from businesses that receive publicity about misconduct. A number of studies have found a direct relationship between social responsibility and profitability, as well as a link that exists

TABLE 2-8
A Selection of the World's Most Ethical Companies

L'Oreal	Hasbro
Starbucks Coffee Company	Hospital Corporation of America (HCA)
Marks and Spencer	Xerox Corporation
3M Company	General Electric
T-Mobile US Inc.	Cummins Inc.
PepsiCo	Ford Motor Company
ManpowerGroup	LinkedIn Corporation
Colgate-Palmolive Company	Levi Strauss & Co.
International Paper Co.	Texas Instruments
VISA Inc.	Waste Management
UPS	Kellogg Company
Accenture	Aflac Incorporated
Wyndham Worldwide	Dell Inc.

Source: Ethisphere Institute, "World's Most Ethical Companies—Honorees," http://worldsmostethicalcompanies.ethisphere.com/honorees/ (accessed March 14, 2016).

TABLE 2-9
The Arguments For
and Against Social
Responsibility

For:
1. Social responsibility rests on stakeholder engagement and results in benefits to society and improved firm performance.
2. Businesses are responsible because they have the financial and technical resources to address sustainability, health, and education.
3. As members of society, businesses and their employees should support society through taxes and contributions to social causes.
4. Socially responsible decision making by businesses can prevent increased government regulation.
5. Social responsibility is necessary to ensure economic survival: If businesses want educated and healthy employees, customers with money to spend, and suppliers with quality goods and services in years to come, they must take steps to help solve the social and environmental problems that exist today.

Against:
1. It sidetracks managers from the primary goal of business—earning profit. The responsibility of business to society is to earn profits and create jobs.
2. Participation in social programs gives businesses greater power, perhaps at the expense of concerned stakeholders.
3. Does business have the expertise needed to assess and make decisions about social and economic issues?
4. Social problems are the responsibility of the government agencies and officials, who can be held accountable by voters.
5. Creation of nonprofits and contributions to them are the best ways to implement social responsibility.

between employee commitment and customer loyalty—two major concerns of any firm trying to increase profits.[49] This section highlights a few of the many social responsibility issues that managers face; as managers become aware of and work toward the solution of current social problems, new ones will certainly emerge.

Relations with Owners and Stockholders.   Businesses must first be responsible to their owners, who are primarily concerned with earning a profit or a return on their investment in a company. In a small business, this responsibility is fairly easy to fulfill because the owner(s) personally manages the business or knows the managers well. In larger businesses, particularly corporations owned by thousands of stockholders, ensuring responsibility becomes a more difficult task.

A business's obligations to its owners and investors, as well as to the financial community at large, include maintaining proper accounting procedures, providing all relevant information to investors about the current and projected performance of the firm, and protecting the owners' rights and investments. In short, the business must maximize the owners' investments in the firm.

Employee Relations.   Another issue of importance to a business is its responsibilities to employees. Without employees, a business cannot carry out its goals. Employees expect businesses to provide a safe workplace, pay them adequately for their work, and keep them informed of what is happening in their company. They want employers to listen to their grievances and treat them fairly. Many firms have begun implementing extended parental leave for families with new babies. Credit Suisse announced it was giving its U.S. employees up to 20 weeks off after having a child. Facebook also extended its parental leave for up to four months. These types of benefits are becoming increasingly important as firms strive to attract top-quality employees.[50]

Congress has passed several laws regulating safety in the workplace, many of which are enforced by the Occupational Safety and Health Administration (OSHA). Labor unions have also made significant contributions to achieving safety in the workplace and improving wages and benefits. Most organizations now recognize that the safety and satisfaction of their employees are critical ingredients in their success, and many strive to go beyond what is legally expected of them. Healthy, satisfied employees also supply more than just labor to their employers. Employers are beginning to realize the importance of obtaining input from even the lowest-level employees to help the company reach its objectives.

A major social responsibility for business is providing equal opportunities for all employees regardless of their sex, age, race, religion, or nationality. Diversity is also helpful to a firm financially. Firms with gender-diverse leadership are 15 percent more likely to report financial returns higher than the industry average, while those with ethnic-diverse leadership are 35 percent more likely.[51] Despite these benefits, women and minorities have been slighted in the past in terms of education, employment, and advancement opportunities; additionally, many of their needs have not been addressed by business. Discrimination still occurs in business. The Equal Employment Opportunity Commission (EEOC) filed a lawsuit against United Airlines for imposing restrictions that could limit employment for disabled individuals. This violated the Americans with Disabilities Act. United Airlines paid more than $1 million to settle the suit and changed its policies.[52] Women, who continue to bear most child-rearing responsibilities, often experience conflict between those responsibilities and their duties as employees. Consequently, day care has become a major employment issue for women, and more companies are providing day care facilities as part of their effort to recruit and advance women in the workforce. In addition, companies are considering alternative scheduling such as flex-time and job sharing to accommodate employee concerns. Telecommuting has grown significantly over the past 5 to 10 years as well. Many Americans today believe business has a social obligation to provide special opportunities for women and minorities to improve their standing in society.

Consumer Relations.   A critical issue in business today is business's responsibility to customers, who look to business to provide them with satisfying, safe products and to respect their rights as consumers. The activities that independent individuals, groups, and organizations undertake to protect their rights as consumers are known as **consumerism.** To achieve their objectives, consumers and their advocates write letters to companies, lobby government agencies, make public service announcements, and boycott companies whose activities they deem irresponsible.

Many of the desires of those involved in the consumer movement have a foundation in John F. Kennedy's 1962 consumer bill of rights, which highlighted four rights. The *right to safety* means that a business must not knowingly sell anything that could result in personal injury or harm to consumers. Defective or dangerous products erode public confidence in the ability of business to serve society. They also result in expensive litigation that ultimately increases the cost of products for all consumers. The right to safety also means businesses must provide a safe place for consumers to shop.

consumerism
the activities that independent individuals, groups, and organizations undertake to protect their rights as consumers.

The *right to be informed* gives consumers the freedom to review complete information about a product before they buy it. This means that detailed information about ingredients, risks, and instructions for use are to be printed on labels and packages. When companies mislead consumers about the benefits of their products, then they infringe on consumers' rights to be informed. AT&T was fined $100 million for selling data plans it marketed as unlimited without informing customers their data speeds would be capped when they reached a certain limit.[53] The *right to choose* ensures that consumers have access to a variety of goods and services at competitive prices. The assurance of both satisfactory quality and service at a fair price is also a part of the consumer's right to choose. The *right to be heard* assures consumers that their interests will receive full and sympathetic consideration when the government formulates policy. It also ensures the fair treatment of consumers who voice complaints about a purchased product.

Many companies including craft brewer New Belgium Brewing are looking into alternative energy sources such as wind power.

© Sergio Pitamitz/Getty Images

The role of the Federal Trade Commission's Bureau of Consumer Protection exists to protect consumers against unfair, deceptive, or fraudulent practices. The bureau, which enforces a variety of consumer protection laws, is divided into five divisions. The Division of Enforcement monitors legal compliance and investigates violations of laws, including unfulfilled holiday delivery promises by online shopping sites, employment opportunities fraud, scholarship scams, misleading advertising for health care products, and more.

Sustainability Issues.   Most people probably associate the term *environment* with nature, including wildlife, trees, oceans, and mountains. Until the 20th century, people generally thought of the environment solely in terms of how these resources could be harnessed to satisfy their needs for food, shelter, transportation, and recreation. As the earth's population swelled throughout the 20th century, however, humans began to use more and more of these resources and, with technological advancements, to do so with ever-greater efficiency. Although these conditions have resulted in a much-improved standard of living, they come with a cost. Plant and animal species, along with wildlife habitats, are disappearing at an accelerated rate, while pollution has rendered the atmosphere of some cities a gloomy haze. How to deal with these issues has become a major concern for business and society in the 21st century.

Although the scope of the word *sustainability* is broad, in this book we discuss the term from a strategic business perspective. Thus, we define **sustainability** as conducting activities in such a way as to provide for the long-term well-being of the natural environment, including all biological entities. Sustainability involves the interaction among nature and individuals, organizations, and business strategies and includes the assessment and improvement of business strategies, economic sectors, work practices, technologies, and lifestyles, so that they maintain the health of the natural environment. In recent years, business has played a significant role in adapting, using, and maintaining the quality of sustainability.

Environmental protection emerged as a major issue in the 20th century in the face of increasing evidence that pollution, uncontrolled use of natural resources, and population growth were putting increasing pressure on the long-term sustainability

sustainability
conducting activities in a way that allows for the long-term well-being of the natural environment, including all biological entities; involves the assessment and improvement of business strategies, economic sectors, work practices, technologies, and lifestyles so that they maintain the health of the natural environment.

of these resources. Governments around the globe responded with environmental protection laws during the 1970s. In recent years, companies have been increasingly incorporating these issues into their overall business strategies. Some nonprofit organizations have stepped forward to provide leadership in gaining the cooperation of diverse groups in responsible environmental activities. For example, the Coalition for Environmentally Responsible Economies (CERES)—a union of businesses, consumer groups, environmentalists, and other stakeholders—has established a set of goals for environmental performance.

In the following section, we examine some of the most significant sustainability and environmental health issues facing business and society today, including pollution and alternative energy.

Pollution.   A major issue in the area of environmental responsibility is pollution. Water pollution results from dumping toxic chemicals and raw sewage into rivers and oceans, oil spills, and the burial of industrial waste in the ground where it may filter into underground water supplies. Fertilizers and insecticides used in farming and grounds maintenance also run off into water supplies with each rainfall. Water pollution problems are especially notable in heavily industrialized areas. Medical waste—such as used syringes, vials of blood, and HIV-contaminated materials—has turned up on beaches in New York, New Jersey, and Massachusetts, as well as other places. Society is demanding that water supplies be clean and healthful to reduce the potential danger from these substances.

Air pollution is usually the result of smoke and other pollutants emitted by manufacturing facilities, as well as carbon monoxide and hydrocarbons emitted by motor vehicles. In addition to the health risks posed by air pollution, when some chemical compounds emitted by manufacturing facilities react with air and rain, acid rain results. Acid rain has contributed to the deaths of many forests and lakes in North America as well as in Europe. Air pollution may also contribute to global warming; as carbon dioxide collects in the earth's atmosphere, it traps the sun's heat and prevents the earth's surface from cooling. It is indisputable that the global surface temperature has been increasing over the past 35 years. Worldwide passenger vehicle ownership has been growing due to rapid industrialization and consumer purchasing power in China, India, and other developing countries with large populations. The most important way to contain climate change is to control carbon emissions. The move to green sustainable building practices could reduce the consumption of resources in building construction 46 percent by 2050.[54] The 2007 U.S. Federal Energy bill raised average fuel economy (CAFE) standards to 35 mpg for cars by 2020, while Europe has the goal of a 40 mpg standard by the same deadline. This becomes problematic when gas prices decrease because consumer demand for SUVs and trucks tend to rise significantly. Some utilities charge more for electricity in peak demand periods, which encourages behavioral changes that reduce consumption.

More and more consumers are recognizing the need to protect the planet. Figure 2-3 shows consumers' likelihood to personally address social responsibility and environmental issues. Although most consumers admit that sustainable products are important and that they bear responsibility for properly using and disposing of the product, many admit that they fail to do this.

Land pollution is tied directly to water pollution because many of the chemicals and toxic wastes that are dumped on the land eventually work their way into the water supply. A study conducted by the Environmental Protection Agency found residues of prescription drugs, soaps, and other contaminants in virtually every waterway in

Going Green

Cloud Computing at Amazon: Green or Red?

Amazon has been given a red warning light on its environmental sustainability. A big reason is because Amazon has not disclosed information on the energy consumption of its cloud-computing platform, Amazon Web Services (AWS). AWS powers the most cloud-computing systems worldwide, providing services to organizations including Netflix, Vine, Pinterest, and Yahoo's Tumblr. Cloud computing requires a large amount of power from server farms, resulting in massive uses of energy.

As we consume more of the planet's resources, stakeholders increasingly view sustainability as an ethical responsibility of business. Businesses are being held accountable for their energy usage, prompting many to invest in renewable forms of energy to reduce their environmental impact. Amazon has also pledged its commitment to renewable energy. In fact, the firm claims that although it does not release information on energy consumption for its AWS, its cloud computing infrastructure is actually more energy-efficient than other data centers.

The activist environmental group Greenpeace questions these claims, as well as some of the businesses that use AWS. Nineteen AWS clients signed a letter calling for Amazon to be more transparent on its energy consumption. Conversely, rivals Facebook, Google, and Microsoft have released environmental information on their cloud computing systems. Amazon continues to maintain that it is expanding its green energy usage, including investing in ways to use wind power for its data centers.[55]

Discussion Questions

1. Is energy usage at AWS an ethical issue?
2. From a social responsibility perspective, who are Amazon's most important stakeholders as they relate to AWS energy usage?
3. From a societal and political perspective, will Google have a competitive advantage if Amazon continues refusing to release information about its AWS energy consumption?

---

the United States. Effects of these pollutants on humans and wildlife are uncertain, but there is some evidence to suggest that fish and other water-dwellers are starting to suffer serious effects. Land pollution results from the dumping of residential and industrial waste, strip mining, forest fires, and poor forest conservation. In Brazil and other South American countries, rain forests are being destroyed to make way for farms and ranches, at a cost of the extinction of the many animals and plants (some endangered species) that call the rain forest home. For example, in Brazil trees were

FIGURE 2-3   Consumer Likelihood to Personally Address Social Responsibility Issues

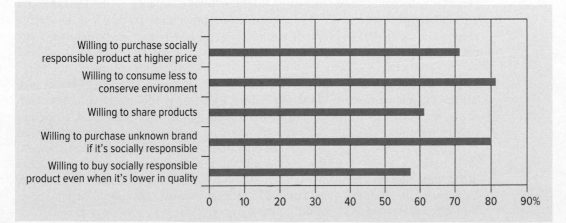

Online survey conducted by Cone Communications and Ebiquity of 9,709 adults in nine of the largest countries in the world by GDP.

Source: Cone Communications and Ebiquity, "2015 Cone Communications/Ebiquity Global CSR Study," http://www.conecomm.com/stuff/contentmgr/files/0/2482ff 6f22fe4753488d3fe37e948e3d/files/global_pdf_2015.pdf (accessed February 23, 2016).

Electric vehicles are growing in popularity.

© hans engbers/Alamy

cleared over an area spanning seven times the territory of New York City. Brazil has committed to zero percent illegal deforestation by 2030.[56] Large-scale deforestation also depletes the oxygen supply available to humans and other animals.

Related to the problem of land pollution is the larger issue of how to dispose of waste in an environmentally responsible manner. Americans use approximately 100 billion plastic bags per year.[57] California became the first state to institute a statewide ban on stores being able to give out free plastic bags. However, opposition from the plastics industry delayed the ban.[58] Many other countries are also in the process of phasing out lightweight plastic bags.

Alternative Energy.   With ongoing plans to reduce global carbon emissions, countries and companies alike are looking toward alternative energy sources. Traditional fossil fuels are problematic because of their emissions, but also because stores have been greatly depleted. Foreign fossil fuels are often imported from politically and economically unstable regions, often making it unsafe to conduct business there. However, the United States is becoming an energy powerhouse with its ability to drill for natural gas in large shale reserves. This is allowing the United States to move forward on its goals to reach energy independence. On the other hand, concerns over how these drilling methods are affecting the environment make this a controversial topic.

The U.S. government has begun to recognize the need to look toward alternative forms of energy as a source of fuel and electricity. There have been many different ideas as to which form of alternative energy would best suit the United States' energy needs. These sources include wind power, solar power, nuclear power, biofuels, electric cars, and hydro- and geothermal power. As of yet, no "best" form of alternative fuel has been selected to replace gasoline. Additionally, there are numerous challenges with the economic viability of alternative energy sources. For instance, wind and solar power cost significantly more than traditional energy. Alternative energy will likely require government subsidies to make any significant strides. However, the news for solar power might be getting brighter. Solar companies in the United States are beginning to rebound. Electric cars are also gaining importance. Most automobile companies such as BMW, General Motors, Nissan, and Toyota are introducing electric cars to help with sustainability.

Response to Environmental Issues.   Partly in response to federal legislation such as the National Environmental Policy Act of 1969 and partly due to consumer concerns, businesses are responding to environmental issues. Many small and large companies, including Walt Disney Company, Chevron, and Scott Paper, have created an executive position—a vice president of environmental affairs—to help them achieve their business goals in an environmentally responsible manner. Some companies are finding that environmental consciousness can save them money. For example, PepsiCo claims it saved more than $375 million in costs through its sustainability initiatives over a five-year period.[59]

Many firms are trying to eliminate wasteful practices, the emission of pollutants, and/or the use of harmful chemicals from their manufacturing processes. Other companies are seeking ways to improve their products. Utility providers, for example, are increasingly supplementing their services with alternative energy sources, including solar, wind, and geothermal power. Environmentalists are concerned that some companies are merely *greenwashing,* or "creating a positive association with environmental issues for an unsuitable product, service, or practice."

In many places, local utility customers can even elect to purchase electricity from green sources—primarily wind power—for a few extra dollars a month. Austin Energy of Austin, Texas, has an award-winning GreenChoice program that includes many small and large

businesses among its customers. The city has a community goal of having 35 percent of its electricity for Austin Energy customers come from renewable energy sources by 2020.[61] Indeed, a growing number of businesses and consumers are choosing green power sources where available. New Belgium Brewing Company, the fourth-largest craft brewer in the United States, is the first all-wind-powered brewery in the country. Many businesses have turned to *recycling,* the reprocessing of materials—aluminum, paper, glass, and some plastic—for reuse. Such efforts to make products, packaging, and processes more environmentally friendly have been labeled "green" business or marketing by the public and media. For example, lumber products at The Home Depot may carry a seal from the Forest Stewardship Council to indicate that they were harvested from sustainable forests using environmentally friendly methods.[62]

It is important to recognize that, with current technology, environmental responsibility requires trade-offs. Society must weigh the huge costs of limiting or eliminating pollution against the health threat posed by the pollution. Environmental responsibility imposes costs on both business and the public. Although people certainly do not want oil fouling beautiful waterways and killing wildlife, they insist on low-cost, readily available gasoline and heating oil. People do not want to contribute to the growing garbage-disposal problem, but they often refuse to pay more for "green" products packaged in an environmentally friendly manner, to recycle as much of their own waste as possible, or to permit the building of additional waste-disposal facilities (the "not in my backyard," or NIMBY, syndrome). Managers must coordinate environmental goals with other social and economic ones.

Community Relations.   A final, yet very significant, issue for businesses concerns their responsibilities to the general welfare of the communities and societies in which they operate. Many businesses simply want to make their communities better places for everyone to live and work. The most common way that businesses exercise their community responsibility is through donations to local and national charitable organizations. For example, General Electric employees hold fundraising efforts to raise money for the United Way.[63] Colorado Springs–based business ShelfGenie, which designs, builds, and customizes shelving systems for cabinets, works with the nonprofit organization Homes for Our Troops to provide homes customized for disabled veterans.[64]

Unemployment

After realizing that the current pool of prospective employees lacks many basic skills necessary to work, many companies have become concerned about the quality of education in the United States. Unemployment has become a significant problem since the onset of the financial crisis in 2008. In the years following, unemployment reached as high as 10 percent in the United States. Although it has fallen to about 5 percent since then, unemployment is still a significant issue.[65]

Thousands of jobs were lost after Blockbuster shuttered its stores.

© Julie Edwards/Alamy

Although most would argue that unemployment is an economic issue, it also carries ethical implications. Protests often occur in areas where unemployment is high, particularly when there seems to be a large gap between rich and poor. In Tunisia, high rates of unemployment among the younger generation caused unemployed citizens to arrange protests. Unemployment has worsened in the country since the former president was ousted. Approximately 62 percent of Tunisian graduates remain unemployed.[66]

Factory closures are another ethical issue because factories usually employ hundreds of workers. Sometimes it is necessary to close a plant due to economic reasons. However, factory closures not only affect individual employees, but their communities as well. After years of withstanding closures, even as other factories around it closed, a factory in the small town of Hanover, Illinois, shuttered its doors and transferred to Mexico. Several of the factory workers felt betrayed, and about 100 lost their jobs. Factory closures also have repercussions on other businesses in the area because more unemployed people mean fewer sales.[67]

Another criticism levied against companies involves hiring standards. Some employers have been accused of having unreasonable hiring standards that most applicants cannot meet, often leaving these jobs unfilled. Critics have accused companies of not wanting to take the time to train employees.[68] Employers, however, believe there is a significant lack of skills needed among job applicants. A survey of employers conducted in Indiana revealed that 39 percent reported leaving positions unfilled because the applicants were not qualified.[69] With more companies requiring specialized knowledge and a strong educational background, jobs are becoming increasingly competitive among those looking for employment.

On the other hand, several businesses are working to reduce unemployment. After becoming frustrated with high unemployment rates, Starbucks founder and CEO Howard Schultz partnered with a national network of community lenders called Opportunity Network to develop Create Jobs for USA. The program provided funding for community businesses with the intent to reduce unemployment in their areas. Starbucks initially donated $5 million to the initiative. Other companies made significant contributions, including Banana Republic, Citi, Google Offers, and MasterCard. During the three years the initiative ran, it received donations of $15.2 million that it provided to community development financial institutions. These institutions were able to generate more funding from these donations that helped to create or maintain over 5,000 jobs.[70]

Additionally, businesses are beginning to take more responsibility for the hardcore unemployed. These are people who have never had a job or who have been unemployed for a long period of time. Some are mentally or physically handicapped; some are homeless. Organizations such as the National Alliance of Businessmen fund programs to train the hard-core unemployed so that they can find jobs and support themselves. Such commitment enhances self-esteem and helps people become productive members of society.

So You Want a Job in Business Ethics and Social Responsibility

In the words of Kermit the Frog, "It's not easy being green." It may not be easy, but green business opportunities abound. A popular catch phrase, "Green is the new black," indicates how fashionable green business is becoming. Consumers are more in tune with and concerned about green products, policies, and behaviors by companies than ever before. Companies are looking for new hires to help them see their business creatively and bring insights to all aspects of business operations. The International Renewable Energy Industry estimates that the number of jobs in the renewable energy job market could rise to 24 million by 2030. Green business strategies not only give a firm a commercial advantage in the marketplace, but help lead the way toward a greener world. The fight to reduce our carbon footprint in an attempt against climate change has opened up opportunities for renewable energy, recycling, conservation, and increasing overall efficiency in the way resources are used. New businesses that focus on hydro, wind, and solar power are on the rise and will need talented businesspeople to lead them. Carbon emissions' trading is gaining popularity as large corporations and individuals alike seek to lower their footprints. A job in this growing field could be similar to that of a stock trader, or you could lead the search for carbon-efficient companies in which to invest.

In the ethics arena, current trends in business governance strongly support the development of ethics and compliance departments to help guide organizational integrity. This alone is a billion-dollar business, and there are jobs in developing organizational ethics programs, developing company policies, and training employees and management. An entry-level position might be as a communication specialist or trainer for programs in a business ethics department. Eventually there's an opportunity to become an ethics officer that would have typical responsibilities of meeting with employees, the board of directors, and top management to discuss and provide advice about ethics issues in the industry, developing and distributing a code of ethics, creating and maintaining an anonymous, confidential service to answer questions about ethical issues, taking actions on possible ethics code violations, and reviewing and modifying the code of ethics of the organization.

There are also opportunities to help with initiatives to help companies relate social responsibility to stakeholder interests and needs. These jobs could involve coordinating and implementing philanthropic programs that give back to others important to the organization or developing a community volunteering program for employees. In addition to the human relations function, most companies develop programs to assist employees and their families to improve their quality of life. Companies have found that the healthier and happier employees are the more productive they will be in the workforce.

Social responsibility, ethics, and sustainable business practices are not a trend; they are good for business and the bottom line. New industries are being created and old ones are adapting to the new market demands, opening up many varied job opportunities that will lead not only to a paycheck, but also to the satisfaction of making the world a better place.[71]

Review Your Understanding

Define business ethics and social responsibility and examine their importance.

Business ethics refers to principles and standards that define acceptable business conduct. Acceptable business behavior is defined by customers, competitors, government regulators, interest groups, the public, and each individual's personal moral principles and values. Social responsibility is the obligation an organization assumes to maximize its positive impact and minimize its negative impact on society. Socially responsible businesses win the trust and respect of their employees, customers, and society, and, in the long run, increase profits. Ethics is important in business because it builds trust and confidence in business relationships. Unethical actions may result in negative publicity, declining sales, and even legal action.

Detect some of the ethical issues that may arise in business.

An ethical issue is an identifiable problem, situation, or opportunity requiring a person or organization to choose from among several actions that must be evaluated as right or wrong. Ethical issues can be categorized in the context of their relation with conflicts of interest, fairness and honesty, communications, and business associations.

Specify how businesses can promote ethical behavior by employees.

Businesses can promote ethical behavior by employees by limiting their opportunity to engage in misconduct. Formal codes of ethics, ethical policies, and ethics training programs reduce the incidence of unethical behavior by informing employees what is expected of them and providing punishments for those who fail to comply.

Explain the four dimensions of social responsibility.

The four dimensions of social responsibility are economic or financial viability (being profitable), legal (obeying the law), ethical (doing what is right, just, and fair), and philanthropic, or voluntary (being a good corporate citizen).

Debate an organization's social responsibilities to owners, employees, consumers, the environment, and the community.

Businesses must maintain proper accounting procedures, provide all relevant information about the performance of the firm to investors, and protect the owners' rights and investments.

In relations with employees, businesses are expected to provide a safe workplace, pay employees adequately for their work, and treat them fairly. Consumerism refers to the activities undertaken by independent individuals, groups, and organizations to protect their rights as consumers. Increasingly, society expects businesses to take greater responsibility for the environment, especially with regard to animal rights, as well as water, air, land, and noise pollution. Many businesses engage in activities to make the communities in which they operate better places for everyone to live and work.

Evaluate the ethics of a business's decision.

The "Solve the Dilemma" feature later at the end of this chapter presents an ethical dilemma at Checkers Pizza. Using the material presented in this chapter, you should be able to analyze the ethical issues present in the dilemma, evaluate Barnard's plan, and develop a course of action for the firm.

Revisit the World of Business

1. Which stakeholders are likely to benefit from Mars Inc.'s decision to support the labeling of added sugar? Which stakeholders will likely see disadvantages?

2. Does Mars Inc. have a social responsibility to help curb excess sugar consumption among its customers even if it might cause it to sell less candy?

3. Will labeling the amount of sugar in candy curb excess sugar consumption?

Learn the Terms

bribes 42
business ethics 38
codes of ethics 50
consumerism 56

corporate citizenship 53
ethical issue 42
plagiarism 49
social responsibility 39

sustainability 57
whistleblowing 52

Check Your Progress

1. Define business ethics. Who determines whether a business activity is ethical? Is unethical conduct always illegal?

2. Distinguish between ethics and social responsibility.

3. Why has ethics become so important in business?

4. What is an ethical issue? What are some of the ethical issues named in your text? Why are they ethical issues?

5. What is a code of ethics? How can one reduce unethical behavior in business?

6. List and discuss the arguments for and against social responsibility by business (Table 2-9). Can you think of any additional arguments (for or against)?

7. What responsibilities does a business have toward its employees?

8. What responsibilities does business have with regard to the environment? What steps have been taken by some responsible businesses to minimize the negative impact of their activities on the environment?

9. What are a business's responsibilities toward the community in which it operates?

Get Involved

I. Discuss some recent examples of businesses engaging in unethical practices. Classify these practices as issues of conflict of interest, fairness and honesty, communications, or business relationships. Why do you think the businesses chose to behave unethically? What actions might the businesses have taken?

2. Discuss with your class some possible methods of improving ethical standards in business. Do you think that business should regulate its own activities or that the federal government should establish and enforce ethical standards? How do you think businesspeople feel?

3. Find some examples of socially responsible businesses in newspapers or business journals. Explain why you believe their actions are socially responsible. Why do you think the companies chose to act as they did?

Build Your Skills

Making Decisions about Ethical Issues

Background

The merger of Lockheed and Martin Marietta created Lockheed Martin, the number-one company in the defense industry—an industry that includes such companies as Raytheon and Northrop Grumman.

You and the rest of the class are managers at Lockheed Martin Corporation, Orlando, Florida. You are getting ready to do the group exercise in an ethics training session. The training instructor announces you will be playing *Gray Matters: The Ethics Game.* You are told that *Gray Matters,* which was prepared for your company's employees, is also played at 41 universities, including Harvard University, and at 65 other companies. Although there are 55 scenarios in *Gray Matters,* you will have time during this session to complete only the four scenarios that your group draws from the stack of cards.[72]

Task

Form into groups of four to six managers and appoint a group leader who will lead a discussion of the case, obtain a consensus answer to the case, and be the one to report the group's answers to the instructor. You will have five minutes to reach each decision, after which time, the instructor will give the point values and rationale for each choice. Then you will have five minutes for the next case, etc., until all four cases have been completed. Keep track of your group's score for each case; the winning team will be the group scoring the most points.

Since this game is designed to reflect life, you may believe that some cases lack clarity or that some of your choices are not as precise as you would have liked. Also, some cases have only one solution, while others have more than one solution. Each choice is assessed to reflect which answer is the most correct. **Your group's task is to select only one option in each case.**

4

Mini-Case

For several months now, one of your colleagues has been slacking off, and you are getting stuck doing the work. You think it is unfair. What do you do?

Potential Answers

A. Recognize this as an opportunity for you to demonstrate how capable you are.

B. Go to your supervisor and complain about this unfair workload.

C. Discuss the problem with your colleague in an attempt to solve the problem without involving others.

D. Discuss the problem with the human resources department.

7

Mini-Case

You are aware that a fellow employee uses drugs on the job. Another friend encourages you to confront the person instead of informing the supervisor. What do you do?

Potential Answers

A. You speak to the alleged user and encourage him to get help.

B. You elect to tell your supervisor that you suspect an employee is using drugs on the job.

C. You confront the alleged user and tell him either to quit using drugs or you will "turn him in."

D. Report the matter to employee assistance.

36
Mini-Case
You work for a company that has implemented a policy of a smoke-free environment. You discover employees smoking in the restrooms of the building. You also smoke and don't like having to go outside to do it. What do you do?
Potential Answers
A. You ignore the situation.
B. You confront the employees and ask them to stop.
C. You join them, but only occasionally.
D. You contact your ethics or human resources representative and ask him or her to handle the situation.

40
Mini-Case
Your co-worker is copying company-purchased software and taking it home. You know a certain program costs $400, and you have been saving for a while to buy it. What do you do?
Potential Answers
A. You figure you can copy it too because nothing has ever happened to your co-worker.
B. You tell your co-worker he can't legally do this.
C. You report the matter to the ethics office.
D. You mention this to your supervisor.

Solve the Dilemma

Customer Privacy

Checkers Pizza was one of the first to offer home delivery service, with overwhelming success. However, the major pizza chains soon followed suit, taking away Checkers's competitive edge. Jon Barnard, Checkers's founder and co-owner, needed a new gimmick to beat the competition. He decided to develop a computerized information database that would make Checkers the most efficient competitor and provide insight into consumer buying behavior at the same time. Under the system, telephone customers were asked their phone number; if they had ordered from Checkers before, their address and previous order information came up on the computer screen.

After successfully testing the new system, Barnard put the computerized order network in place in all Checkers outlets. After three months of success, he decided to give an award to the family that ate the most Checkers pizza. Through the tracking system, the company identified the biggest customer, who had ordered a pizza every weekday for the past three months (63 pizzas). The company put together a program to surprise the family with an award, free-food certificates, and a news story announcing the award. As Barnard began to plan for the event, however, he began to think that maybe the family might not want all the attention and publicity.

LO 2-6

Evaluate the ethics of a business's decision.

Discussion Questions

1. What are some of the ethical issues in giving customers an award for consumption behavior without notifying them first?

2. Do you see this as a potential violation of privacy? Explain.

3. How would you handle the situation if you were Barnard?

Build Your Business Plan

Business Ethics and Social Responsibility

Think about which industry you are considering competing in with your good/service. Is there any kind of questionable practices in the way the product has been traditionally sold? Produced? Advertised? Have there been any recent accusations regarding safety within the industry? What about any environmental concerns?

For example, if you are thinking of opening a lawn care business, you need to be thinking about what possible effects the chemicals you are using will have on the client and the environment. You have a responsibility to keep your customers safe and healthy. You also have the social responsibility to let the community know of any damaging effect you may be directly or indirectly responsible for.

See for Yourself Videocase

Warby Parker: An Affordable World Vision

Eyewear firm Warby Parker is known for more than just its affordable glasses. It has adopted a business model that helps advance entrepreneurship opportunities and economic development across the world. In 2008, co-founders Neil Blumenthal, David Gilboa, and three classmates embarked upon a plan to make glasses that would be affordable for the masses. The idea was developed for Wharton's business plan competition. Not only did their idea not win the competition, it did not even make it to the final round. Their plans for a company that sold glasses at a more affordable price seemed like a flop.

Fast track nearly a decade later, and Warby Parker has sold well over 1 million pairs of glasses. The premise behind the startup was simple. Blumenthal and Gilboa realized that one company had a near-monopoly over the optical industry, giving it the power to set steep prices. Blumenthal believed that by designing and manufacturing glasses in-house and selling them on the Internet, the company would be able to save on costs that it could then pass on to consumers. Warby Parker's unique business model enables the firm to sell designer-style eyeglasses for as little as $95 each.

From the get-go, the founders wanted to create a different kind of company centered on integrity. Blumenthal had previously worked with the nonprofit Visionspring, a charity that provides quality eyeglasses to those in need in developing countries. They decided to adopt a unique business model in which the organization would partner with Visionspring to provide one pair of eyeglasses to someone in need for every pair of eyeglasses sold. Every month, Warby Parker tallies the number of eyeglasses sold and makes a donation to Visionspring. The donation covers the costs of sourcing glasses. At Warby Parker, this initiative is not simply philanthropy; rather, it has been incorporated into the firm's business model as a critical component of its operations.

On the surface, donating eyewear might not seem like it directly affects economic development. However, the founder of Visionspring, Jack Kassalow, describes just how important eyewear is for people who have vision impairment problems that could be solved with a pair of eyeglasses. "Vision is critical for work. If you can't see, you can't work. Vision is critical to learn. If you can't see, you can't learn. And [it's] critical as well to human security. If you can't see, it's hard to be safe as you move about the world," Kassawlow says.

However, Warby Parker and Visionspring are careful not to simply donate the glasses. While this might help individuals with their sight, it would miss out on the opportunity to encourage economic growth. Instead, Visionspring trains local women to be entrepreneurs and sell the glasses to tradespeople for $4 each. This model provides jobs for women and enables them to earn wages that they can then spend improving their communities. As for the tradespeople who purchase the glasses, it is estimated that their productivity increases by 35 percent and their earning power by 20 percent.

Warby Parker is living proof that a company can be socially responsible and profitable. Although it started out as an online-only firm, Warby Parker has since opened 27 retail locations and is valued at $1.2 billion. Throughout its growth, Warby Parker has maintained a strong focus on the customer. For instance, it allows customers to try out five pairs of glasses for five days at no cost. Kasselow comments on how Warby Parker has been able to develop a highly efficient business model that is fair to both customers and those in developing nations. "The price is incredibly fair. But because they are able to be as efficient as they are in their supply chain, they're also able to bring it to market in a way that they can become a profitable company and scale their idea to provide affordable glasses to hopefully hundreds of millions of people, not only in the U.S. but all around the world," he says.[73]

Discussion Questions

1. Describe Warby Parker's ethical vision in selling eyeglasses.

2. How does Warby Parker integrate social responsibility into its business?

3. Why does Warby Parker charge $4 to those in need of eyeglasses in developing countries?

You can find the related video in the Video Library in Connect. Ask your instructor how you can access Connect.

Team Exercise

Sam Walton, founder of Walmart, had an early strategy for growing his business related to pricing. The "Opening Price Point" strategy used by Walton involved offering the introductory product in a product line at the lowest point in the market. For example, a minimally equipped microwave oven would sell for less than anyone else in town could sell the same unit. The strategy was that if consumers saw a product, such as the microwave, and saw it as a good value, they would assume that all of the microwaves were good values. Walton also noted that most people don't buy the entry-level product; they want more features and capabilities and often trade up.

Form teams and assign the role of defending this strategy or casting this strategy as an unethical act. Present your thoughts on either side of the issue.

Endnotes

1. Annie Gasparro, "M & M Maker Wants Labels for Sugar," *The Wall Street Journal,* May 8, 2015, p. B1; NBC News, "Candy Maker Mars Inc. Supports Eating Less Sugar," *NBC News,* May 8, 2015, http://www.nbcnews.com/news/us-news/kansas-man-accused-torturing-autistic-15-year-old-n435651 (accessed September 29, 2015); Ben Rooney, "M & Ms Candy Maker Says: Dont Eat Too Many," *CNN Money,* May 5, 2015, http://money.cnn.com/2015/05/08/news/mars-candy-m-and-m-sugar/ (accessed September 29, 2015).

2. Jacquelyn Smith, "The World's Most Ethical Companies," *Forbes,* March 6, 2013, http://www.forbes.com/sites/jacquelynsmith/2013/03/06/the-worlds-most-ethical-companies-in-2013/ (accessed February 5, 2015).

3. Kimberly Blanton, "Creating a Culture of Compliance," *CFO,* July/August 2011, pp. 19–21.

4. Sheila Marikar, "Selling Less Is More," *Inc.,* July/August 2015, p. 38; Christina Anderson, "Beautycounter Reveals Truth about Your Cosmetics . . . And It May Scare You (VIDEO)," *The Huffington Post,* May 1, 2013, http://www.huffingtonpost.com/2013/05/01/beauty-counter-video_n_3193424.html (accessed July 24, 2015); "Beautycounter Promotes Its Environmentally Themed Products," *The New York Times,* July 3, 2013, http://www.nytimes.com/2013/07/04/fashion/beautycounter-promotes-its-environmentally-themed-products.html?_r=0 (accessed July 24, 2015); Andrea Tortora, "Beautycounter: Safer Products Changing Lives," *Direct Selling News,* February 1, 2015, http://directsellingnews.com/index.php/view/beautycounter_safer_products_changing_lives#.VbKVCbNViko (accessed July 24, 2015); Beautycounter, "Beautycounter Is a B Corp," http://www.beautycounter.com/know-everything/beautycounter-is-proud-to-be-b-corp/ (accessed July 24, 2015).

5. Walmart, "Walmart and the Walmart Foundation Publish FY2015 Giving Report," 2016, http://news.walmart.com/news-archive/2015/12/18/walmart-and-the-walmart-foundation-publish-fy2015-giving-report (accessed March 2, 2016).

6. Kate Pickert, "Medicare Fraud Horror: Cancer Doctor Indicted for Billing Unnecessary Chemo," *Time,* August 15, 2013, http://nation.time.com/2013/08/15/medicare-fraud-horror-cancer-doctor-indicted-for-billing-unnecessary-chemo/ (accessed February 24, 2014).

7. Ronald Alsop, "Corporate Scandals Hit Home," *The Wall Street Journal,* February 19, 2004, http://online.wsj.com/news/articles/SB107715182807433462 (accessed February 26, 2016).

8. Roger Yu, "Bristol-Myers Fined $14M over Bribe Claims," *USA Today,* October 6, 2015, p. 3B.

9. O. C. Ferrell, John Fraedrich, and Linda Ferrell, *Business Ethics: Ethical Decision Making and Cases,* 8th ed. (Mason, OH: South-Western Cengage Learning, 2011), p. 7.

10. Theo Francis, "Corporate Directors' Pay Rachets Higher as Risks Grow," *The Wall Street Journal,* February 23, 2016, http://www.wsj.com/articles/corporate-directors-pay-ratchets-higher-as-risks-grow-1456279452 (accessed February 24, 2016).

11. Fernanda Santos, "New Mexico Secretary of State, Dianna Duran, Pleads Guilty to Fraud," *The New York Times,* October 23, 2015, http://www.nytimes.com/2015/10/24/us/new-mexico-secretary-of-state-dianna-duran-pleads-guilty-to-fraud.html (accessed February 24, 2016).

12. Rob Ledonne, "The 12 Biggest Sports Scandals of 2015," *Rolling Stone,* December 16, 2015, http://www.rollingstone.com/sports/lists/the-12-biggest-sports-scandals-of-2015-20151216 (accessed February 24, 2016); Matthew Futterman, "The FIFA Bribery Scandal's Miami Connection," *Wall Street Journal,* December 7, 2015, http://www.wsj.com/articles/the-fifa-bribery-scandals-miami-connection-1449532787 (accessed February 24, 2016).

13. Ferrell, Fraedrich, and Ferrell, *Business Ethics.*

14. Ethics Resource Center, *2011 National Business Ethics Survey®: Ethics in Transition* (Arlington, VA: Ethics Resource Center, 2012).

15. Bobby White, "The New Workplace Rules: No Video Watching," *The New York Times,* March 3, 2008, p. B1.

16. Shana Lebowitz, "What's Behind a Rise in Workplace Bullying?" *USA Today,* October 8, 2013, www.usatoday.com/story/news/health/2013/10/08/hostile-workplace-less-productive/2945833/ (accessed February 25, 2014).

17. Carolyn Kinsey Goman, "Is Your Boss a Bully?" *Forbes,* April 6, 2014, http://www.forbes.com/sites/carolkinseygoman/2014/04/06/is-your-boss-a-bully/ (accessed February 23, 2016).

18. Chad Terhune, "In Suit, Blue Shield Cites Extravagant Spending by Fired Executive," *Los Angeles Times,* April 24, 2015, http://www.latimes.com/business/la-fi-blue-shield-sharknado-20150425-story.html (accessed February 24, 2016).

19. NBC New York, "Apple Store Worker Charged with Using Bogus Credit Cards to Buy Nearly $1 Million in Apple Gift Cards," October 20, 2015, http://www.nbcnewyork.com/news/local/Apple-Worker-Arrest-Theft-Gift-Card-Fake-Credit-Information-Ruben-Profit-334735951.html (accessed February 24, 2016); Gregg Keizer, "Apple Employee Arrested, Charged with Buying $1M in Company Gift Cards with Fake Plastic," *Computerworld,* October 21, 2015, http://www.computerworld.com/article/2996000/technology-law-regulation/apple-employee-arrested-charged-with-buying-1m-in-company-gift-cards-with-fake-plastic.html (accessed February 24, 2016).

20. Coca-Cola Company, *Code of Business Conduct: Acting Around the Globe,* April 2009, p. 13, https://www.coca-colacompany.com/content/dam/journey/us/en/private/fileassets/pdf/2013/04/code-of-business-conduct-france-english.pdf (accessed April 22, 2016).

21. Reuters, "BlackRock to Pay $12 Million in SEC Conflict of Interest Case," *Fortune,* April 20, 2015, http://fortune.com/2015/04/20/blackrock-to-pay-12-million-in-sec-conflict-of-interest-case/ (accessed February 24, 2016).

22. Aruna Viswanatha, "Decision Foils Insider Cases," *The Wall Street Journal,* April 4–5, 2015, p. B2.

23. *Corruption Perceptions Index 2013.* Copyright Transparency International 2013. For more information, visit http://cpi.transparency.org/cpi2013/results/ (accessed February 21, 2014).

24. Holly Ellyatt, "EU Lawmakers Vote to Break Up Google," *CNBC,* November 27, 2014, http://www.cnbc.com/id/102222045#. (accessed February 23, 2016).

25. Federal Trade Commission, "Nations Largest Pool Products Distributor Settles FTC Charges of Anticompetitive Tactics," November 21, 2011, www.ftc.gov/news-events/press-releases/2011/11/nations-largest-pool-products-distributor-settles-ftc-charges (accessed April 7, 2014).

26. Jesse Newman, "FDA Tightens Its Food-Safety Rules," *The Wall Street Journal,* September 11, 2015, p. B3.

27. Sean Coughlan, "Harvard Students Take Pledge Not to Cheat," *BBC,* November 11, 2015, http://www.bbc.com/news/business-34769435 (accessed February 24, 2016).

28. "Campaign Warns about Drugs from Canada," *CNN,* February 5, 2004, www.cnn.com; Gardiner Harris and Monica Davey, "FDA Begins Push to End Drug Imports," *The New York Times,* January 23, 2004, p. C1.

29. Rachel Abrams, "F.D.A. Warns 3 Tobacco Makers about Language Used on Labels," *The New York Times,* August 27, 2015, http://www.nytimes.com/2015/08/28/business/fda-warns-3-tobacco-makers-about-language-used-on-labels.html (accessed February 24, 2016).

30. Ethics Resource Center, *2005 National Business Ethics Survey* (Washington, DC: Ethics Resource Center, 2005), p. 43.

31. Thomas M. Jones, "Ethical Decision Making by Individuals in Organizations: An Issue-Contingent Model," *Academy of Management Review* 2 (April 1991), pp. 371–73.

32. Sir Adrian Cadbury, "Ethical Managers Make Their Own Rules," *Harvard Business Review* 65 (September–October 1987), p. 72.

33. Ferrell, Fraedrich, and Ferrell, *Business Ethics,* pp. 174–75.

34. Christopher Elliott, "The Fur Is Flying," *USA Today,* August 3, 2015, p. 3B; Mary Forgione, "Youre Not the Only One Who Can Fly First Class; Now Your Dog or Cat Can Too," *Los Angeles Times,* August 18, 2015, http://www.latimes.com/travel/california/la-trb-american-airlines-pet-kennels-first-class-20150817-htmlstory.html (accessed August 20, 2015); Jim Dobson, "First Class Dogs: Luxury Travel with Mans Best Friend," *Forbes,* November 19, 2014, http://www.forbes.com/sites/jimdobson/2014/11/19/first-class-dogs-luxury-travel-with-mans-best-friend/ (accessed August 20, 2015).

35. Ethics Resource Center, *2009 National Business Ethics Survey* (Washington, DC: Ethics Resource Center, 2009), p. 41.

36. Texas Instruments, "Texas Instruments Rated One of the World's Most Ethical Companies by Ethisphere Institute," March 6, 2013, http://newscenter.ti.com/2013-03-06-Texas-Instruments-rated-one-of-the-Worlds-Most-Ethical-Companies-by-Ethisphere-Institute (accessed February 24, 2016).

37. Ethics and Compliance Initiative, *2016 Global Business Ethics Survey™: Measuring Risk and Promoting Workplace Integrity* (Arlington, VA: Ethics and Compliance Initiative, 2016), p. 43.

38. Ferrell, Fraedrich, and Ferrell, *Business Ethics,* p. 13.

39. "Trust in the Workplace: 2010 Ethics & Workplace Survey," Deloitte LLP (n.d.), www.deloitte.com/assets/Dcom-UnitedStates/Local%20 Assets/Documents/us_2010_Ethics_and_Workplace_Survey_ report_071910.pdf (accessed April 7, 2014).

40. Archie B. Carroll, "The Pyramid of Corporate Social Responsibility: Toward the Moral Management of Organizational Stakeholders," *Business Horizons* 34 (July/August 1991), p. 42.

41. Kelly Kennedy, "Pharmacies Look to Snuff Tobacco Sales," *USA Today,* February 6, 2014, p. 1A.

42. Bryan Walsh, "Why Green Is the New Red, White and Blue," *Time,* April 28, 2008, p. 46.

43. Adam Shriver, "Not Grass-Fed, But at Least Pain-Free," *The New York Times,* February 18, 2010, www.nytimes.com/2010/02/19/opinion/19shriver.html (accessed February 25, 2010)

44. Alan Beattie, "Countries Rush to Restrict Trade in Basic Foods," *Financial Times,* April 2, 2008, p. 1.

45. Corrine Iozzio, "A Farm on Every Street Corner," *Fast Company,* April 2015, p. 68; Philips, "Philips Commercializing City Farming Solutions Based on LED 'Light' Recipes that Improve Crop Yield and Quality," 2016, http://www.lighting.philips.com/main/products/horticulture/

press-releases/Philips-commercializing-city-farming-solutions-based-on-LED-light-recipes.html (accessed February 24, 2016).

46. Cone Communications and Ebiquity, "2015 Cone Communications/Ebiquity Global CSR Study," http://www.conecomm.com/stuff/contentmgr/files/0/2482ff6f22fe4753488d3fe37e948e3d/files/global_pdf_2015.pdf (accessed February 23, 2016).

47. "2014 Worlds Most Ethical Companies—Honorees," *Ethisphere*, http://ethisphere.com/worlds-most-ethical/wme-honorees/ (accessed April 7, 2014).

48. Ucilia Wang, "Campbell Soup CEO: 'You Can Lead the Change or Be a Victim of Change,'" *The Guardian*, October 25, 2013, http://www.theguardian.com/sustainable-business/campbell-soup-ceo-business-social-responsibility (accessed February 23, 2016).

49. Ferrell, Fraedrich, and Ferrell, *Business Ethics*, pp. 13–19.

50. Rachel Emma Silverstein, "Wall Street Perk: Parental Leave," *The Wall Street Journal*, December 1, 2015, p. C3; David Cohen, "Facebook Offers All Employees 4 Months' Parental Leave," December 1, 2015, http://www.adweek.com/socialtimes/four-months-parental-leave/630794 (accessed February 24, 2016).

51. Joann S. Lublin, "Study Links Diverse Leadership With Firms Financial Gains," *The Wall Street Journal*, January 20, 2015, http://www.wsj.com/articles/study-links-diverse-leadership-with-firms-financial-gains-1421792018 (accessed February 23, 2016).

52. U.S. Equal Employment Opportunity Commission, "United Airlines to Pay over $1 Million to Settle EEOC Disability Lawsuit," June 11, 2015, http://www.eeoc.gov/eeoc/newsroom/release/6-11-15.cfm (accessed February 24, 2016).

53. Gautham Nagesh and Thomas Gryta, "'Unlimited' Plan Draws $100 Million Fine for AT& T," *The Wall Street Journal*, June 18, 2015, pp. A1, A6.

54. Tania Goklany, "How Green Buildings Can Reduce Your Carbon Footprint," NDTV.com, July 30, 2015, http://sites.ndtv.com/breathe-clean/how-green-buildings-can-reduce-your-carbon-footprint-2 (accessed February 24, 2016).

55. Robert McMillan, "Customers Urge Amazon to Come Clean on Energy," *The Wall Street Journal*, June 4, 2015, p. B4; Heather Clancy, "Amazon, Microsoft, Google Fuel Up Renewable Energy Pledges," *Forbes*, November 21, 2014, http://www.forbes.com/sites/heatherclancy/2014/11/21/amazon-microsoft-google-fuel-up-renewable-energy-pledges/ (accessed July 28, 2015); Aaron Gell, "Amazon FLUNKS New Energy Report—Facebook and Apple Get A," *Business Insider*, April 2, 2014, http://www.businessinsider.com/greenpeace-cloud-computing-report-2014-4 (accessed July 28, 2015).

56. Jonathan Watts, "Amazon Deforestation Report Is Major Setback for Brazil Ahead of Climate Talks," *The Guardian*, November 27, 2015, http://www.theguardian.com/world/2015/nov/27/amazon-deforestation-report-brazil-paris-climate-talks (accessed February 24, 2016).

57. Janet Larsen and Savina Venkova, "Plan B Updates," April 22, 2014, http://www.earth-policy.org/plan_b_updates/2014/update122 (accessed February 23, 2016).

58. Richard Gonzales, "California Plastic Bag Referendum Could Spark Environmental Showdown," *NPR*, March 25, 2015, http://www.npr.org/2015/03/24/395119079/california-plastic-bag-referendum-could-spark-environmental-showdown (accessed February 24, 2016).

59. PR Newswire, "PepsiCo Sustainability Initiatives Delivered More Than $375 Million in Estimated Cost Savings Since 2010," *PepsiCo*, September 24, 2015, http://www.pepsico.com/live/pressrelease/pepsico-sustainability-initiatives-delivered-more-than-375-million-in-estimated-09242015 (accessed April 22, 2016).

60. Katherine Noyes, "Can 'Urban Mining' Solve the Worlds e-Waste Problem?" *Fortune*, June 26, 2014, http://fortune.com/2014/06/26/blueoak-urban-mining-ewaste/ (accessed February 23, 2016).

61. "GreenChoice Program Details," Austin Energy, http://austinenergy.com/wps/wcm/connect/d6b29f5f-052c-4aeb-b52d-73e4dd0265b7/updatedProgramDetails.pdf?MOD=AJPERES (accessed February 24, 2016).

62. "Certification," Home Depot, https://corporate.homedepot.com/CorporateResponsibility/Environment/WoodPurchasing/Pages/Certification.aspx (accessed February 25, 2016).

63. GE Foundation, "United Way," www.gefoundation.com/employee-programs/united-way/ (accessed February 24, 2016).

64. All Business Editors, "11 Heartwarming Ways Real Small Businesses Are Giving Back for the Holidays," *all Business*, http://www.allbusiness.com/slideshow/11-heartwarming-ways-real-small-businesses-are-giving-back-for-the-holidays-16739378-1.html/9 (accessed December 16, 2015).

65. Bureau of Labor Statistics, "Labor Force Statistics from the Current Population Survey, http://data.bls.gov/timeseries/LNS14000000 (accessed February 24, 2016).

66. "Tunisia Protest: Clashes as Demonstrations Spread," *BBC*, January 21, 2016, ttp://www.bbc.com/news/world-africa-35377580 (accessed February 25, 2016).

67. Chad Broughton, "Just Another Factory Closing," *The Atlantic*, September 23, 2015, http://www.theatlantic.com/business/archive/2015/09/factory-closure-private-equity/406264/ (accessed February 25, 2016).

68. Peter Cappelli, "The Skills Gap Myth: Why Companies Can't Find Good People," *Time*, June 4, 2012, http://business.time.com/2012/06/04/the-skills-gap-myth-why-companies-cant-find-good-people/ (accessed February 25, 2016).

69. Peter Cappelli, "Why Companies Aren't Getting the Employees They Need," *The Wall Street Journal*, October 24, 2011, pp. R1, R6.

70. "Create Jobs for USA Supporters," http://createjobsforusa.org/ supporters (accessed February 25, 2016); "Starbucks and Opportunity Finance Network: Taking Action to Reduce Unemployment in America," *Huffington Post,* February 5, 2013, www.huffingtonpost.com/create-jobs-for-usa/starbucks-and-opportunity_b_2622773.html (accessed February 25, 2016); Opportunity Finance Network, "Overview: Create Jobs for USA," 2016, http://ofn.org/create-jobs-usa (accessed February 25, 2016).

71. "Who Really Pays for CSR Initiatives," *Environmental Leader,* February 15, 2008, www.environmentalleader.com/ 2008/02/15/who-really-pays-for-csr-initiatives/ (accessed February 25, 2016); "Global Fund," www.joinred.com/ globalfund (accessed April 7, 2014); Reena Jana, "The Business of Going Green," *BusinessWeek Online,* June 22, 2007, www.businessweek.com/stories/2007-06-22/ the-business-benefits-of-going-greenbusinessweek-business-news-stock-market-and-financial-advice (accessed February 25, 2016); Emma Howard, "Green Jobs Boom: Meet the Frontline of the New Solar Economy," *The Guardian,* February 1, 2016, http://www.theguardian.com/global-development-professionals-network/2016/feb/01/solar-economy-renewable-energy-asia-africa (accessed February 25, 2016).

72. Permission granted by the author of *Gray Matters,* George Sammet Jr., Vice President, Lockheed Martin Corporation, Orlando, Florida, to use these portions of *Gray Matters: The Ethics Game* © 1992.

73. McGraw-Hill video, http://www.viddler.com/embed/93 938820/?f=1&autoplay=0&player=full&disablebrand ing=0 (accessed April 11, 2016); Douglas MacMillan, "Warby Parker Adds Storefronts to Its Sales Strategy," *The Wall Street Journal,*November 17, 2014, http://online.wsj.com/articles/warby-parker-adds-storefronts-to-its-sales-strategy-1416251866 (accessed November 17, 2014); Warby Parker, "Buy a Pair, Give a Pair," https://www.warbyparker.com/buy-a-pair-give-a-pair (accessed November 17, 2014); "5 Minutes with Neil Blumenthal," *Delta Sky,* September 2014, p. 30; Warby Parker website, https://www.warbyparker.com/ (accessed April 11, 2016); Jessica Pressler, "20/30 Vision," *New York Magazine,*August 11, 2013, http://nymag.com/news/features/warby-parker-2013-8/ (accessed October 14, 2014); David Zax, "Fast Talk: How Warby Parker's Cofounders Disrupted the Eyewear Industry and Stayed Friends," *Fast Company,*February 22, 2012, http://www.fastcompany.com/1818215/fast-talk-how-warby-parkers-cofounders-disrupted-eyewear-industry-and-stayed-friends (accessed October 14, 2014); Marcus Wohlsen, "Is Warby Parker Too Good to Last?" *Wired,*June 25, 2015, http://www.wired.com/2014/06/warby-parkers-quest-to-prove-not-sucking-is-the-ultimate-innovation/ (accessed October 14, 2014); Max Chafkin, "Warby Parker Sees the Future of Retail," *Fast Company,*February 17, 2015, http://www.fastcompany.com/3041334/most-innovative-companies-2015/warby-parker-sees-the-future-of-retail (accessed April 11, 2016); Chase Peterson-Withorn, "Warby Parker CEO Is Building a Brand that Gives Back," *Forbes,*September 8, 2014, http://www.forbes.com/sites/chasewithorn/2014/09/08/warby-parker-ceo-is-building-a-brand-that-gives-back/#c830c2069d3b (accessed April 11, 2016); L. V. Anderson, "Spectacular Advice," *Slate,*http://www.slate.com/articles/business/the_ladder/2016/03/career_and_productivity_advice_from_warby_parker_co_founder_and_co_ceo_dave.html (accessed April 11, 2016).

© McGraw-Hill Education/Barry Barker

3 Business in a Borderless World

Learning Objectives

After reading this chapter, you will be able to:

LO 3-1 Explore some of the factors within the international trade environment that influence business.

LO 3-2 Investigate some of the economic, legal, political, social, cultural, and technological barriers to international business.

LO 3-3 Specify some of the agreements, alliances, and organizations that may encourage trade across international boundaries.

LO 3-4 Summarize the different levels of organizational involvement in international trade.

LO 3-5 Contrast two basic strategies used in international business.

LO 3-6 Assess the opportunities and problems facing a small business that is considering expanding into international markets.

Enter the World of Business ⊖────────

Global Menu Customization: Squid Ink Burgers

Squid ink burgers and pizza with prawn toppings are not your typical fast-food fare in the United States. But in countries like Japan, they are in high demand. While fast-food restaurants pride themselves on being consistent throughout the nation, they often change their offerings when going abroad to appeal to local tastes. For instance, because India's Hindu population views cows as sacred, McDonald's offers a number of chicken alternatives such as its Chicken Maharaja Mac.

Changing or reinventing menu items is costly, but for those that succeed, it can be highly profitable. Take Domino's, for example. When expanding into India, the company reinvented everything down to its flour. It wanted to find the best way to appeal to local tastes and yet maintain its Western edge. The process took the chain eight months to get the product and price exactly right. Cultural tastes were considered during this time. For instance, dine-in areas were expanded as the typical Indian family sees eating out as a family event. Because of Domino's careful research, it now sells more pizzas in India than it does in the United States.

In sub-Saharan Africa, on the other hand, consumers prefer to pick up or have their pizzas delivered. Pizza Hut learned this the hard way and failed to catch on. Now it is entering the market once more, this time using more customized marketing tools such as local signage, popular food ingredients, and offerings such as French fries that are more affordable for local consumers. Although fast-food restaurants are increasingly becoming globalized, it is still important for them to customize their offerings to different cultural tastes.[1]

Introduction

Consumers around the world can drink Coca-Cola and Pepsi, eat at McDonald's and Pizza Hut, buy an Apple phone made in China, and watch CNN and MTV on Samsung televisions. It may surprise you that German automaker BMW has manufacturing facilities in Mexico and South Africa that export many of their cars to the United States. In fact, one-third of all 3-series sold in the United States are built in South Africa.[3] The products you consume today are just as likely to have been made in China, India, or Germany as in the United States.[4] Likewise, consumers in other countries buy Western electrical equipment, clothing, rock music, cosmetics, and toiletries, as well as computers, robots, and household goods.

Many U.S. firms are finding that international markets provide tremendous opportunities for growth. Accessing these markets can promote innovation while intensifying global competition spurs companies to market better and less expensive products. Today, the more than 7 billion people that inhabit the earth comprise one tremendous marketplace.

In this chapter, we explore business in this exciting global marketplace. First, we look at the nature of international business, including barriers and promoters of trade across international boundaries. Next, we consider the levels of organizational involvement in international business. Finally, we briefly discuss strategies for trading across national borders.

international business the buying, selling, and trading of goods and services across national boundaries.

LO 3-1

Explore some of the factors within the international trade environment that influence business.

The Role of International Business

International business refers to the buying, selling, and trading of goods and services across national boundaries. Falling political barriers and new technology are making it possible for more and more companies to sell their products overseas as well as at home. And, as differences among nations continue to narrow, the trend toward the globalization of business is becoming increasingly important. Starbucks serves millions of global customers at more than 21,000 locations in 65 countries.[5] The Internet and the ease by which mobile applications can be developed provides many companies with easier entry to access global markets than opening brick-and-mortar stores.[6] Amazon.com, an online retailer, has distribution centers from Nevada to Germany that fill millions of orders a day and ship them to customers in every corner of the world. China has become Apple's largest market outside of the United States and has doubled its revenue in the country year after year.[7] Indeed, most of the world's population and two-thirds of its total purchasing power are outside the United States.

When McDonald's sells a Big Mac in Moscow, Sony sells a television in Detroit, or a small Swiss medical supply company sells a shipment of orthopedic devices to a hospital in Monterrey, Mexico, the sale affects the economies of the countries involved.

American companies such as McDonald's have become widely popular in China. This restaurant in Beijing features elements from the Chinese culture as well as from American culture.

© China/Alamy

The U.S. market, with 316 million consumers, makes up only 5 percent of the more than 7 billion people elsewhere in the world to whom global companies must consider marketing.[8] Global marketing requires balancing your global brand with the needs of local consumers.[9] To begin our study of international business, we must first consider some economic issues: why nations trade, exporting and importing, and the balance of trade.

Why Nations Trade

Nations and businesses engage in international trade to obtain raw materials and goods that are otherwise unavailable to them or are available elsewhere at a lower price than that at which they themselves can produce. A nation, or individuals and organizations from a nation, sell surplus materials

Many companies choose to outsource manufacturing to factories in Asia due to lower costs of labor.

© Qilai Shen/Bloomberg via Getty Images

and goods to acquire funds to buy the goods, services, and ideas its people need. Poland, for example, began trading with Western nations in order to acquire new technology and techniques. Poland has taken these lessons and revitalized its formerly communist economy. It was the only EU country to avoid an economic recession during the financial crisis.[10] Which goods and services a nation sells depends on what resources it has available.

Some nations have a monopoly on the production of a particular resource or product. Such a monopoly, or **absolute advantage,** exists when a country is the only source of an item, the only producer of an item, or the most efficient producer of an item. An example would be an African mining company that possesses the only mine where a specialty diamond can be found. Russia has an absolute advantage in yuksporite, a rare and useful mineral that can be found only in Russia.

Most international trade is based on **comparative advantage,** which occurs when a country specializes in products that it can supply more efficiently or at a lower cost than it can produce other items. Hawaii has a comparative advantage in producing pineapples and Kona coffee because of the climate. France has a comparative advantage in making wine because of its agricultural capabilities, reputation, and the experience of its vintners. The United States, having adopted new technological methods in hydraulic fracturing, has created a comparative advantage in the mining and exporting of natural gas.[11] Other countries, particularly India and Ireland, are also gaining a comparative advantage over the United States in the provision of some services, such as call-center operations, engineering, and software programming. As a result, U.S. companies are increasingly **outsourcing,** or transferring manufacturing and other tasks to countries where labor and supplies are less expensive. Outsourcing has become a controversial practice in the United States because many jobs have moved overseas where those tasks can be accomplished for lower costs.

Trade between Countries

To obtain needed goods and services and the funds to pay for them, nations trade by exporting and importing. **Exporting** is the sale of goods and services to foreign markets. The United States exported more than $2.2 trillion in goods and services in 2015.[12] U.S. businesses export many goods and services, particularly

absolute advantage
a monopoly that exists when a country is the only source of an item, the only producer of an item, or the most efficient producer of an item.

comparative advantage
the basis of most international trade, when a country specializes in products that it can supply more efficiently or at a lower cost than it can produce other items.

outsourcing
the transferring of manufacturing or other tasks—such as data processing—to countries where labor and supplies are less expensive.

exporting
the sale of goods and services to foreign markets.

TABLE 3-1
U.S. Trade Deficit,
1980–2015 (in billions of
dollars)

	1990	2000	2010	2011	2012	2013	2014	2015
Exports	535.2	1,075.3	1,853.6	2,127	2,219	2,279.9	2,343.2	2,230.3
Imports	616.1	1,447.8	2,348.3	2,675.6	2,755.8	2,758.3	2,851.5	2,761.8
Trade surplus/ deficit	−80.9	−372.5	−494.7	−548.6	−536.8	−478.4	−508.3	−531.5

Sources: U.S. Bureau of the Census, Foreign Trade Division, U.S. Trade in Goods and Services—Balance of Payments (BOP) Basis, February 5, 2016, www.census.gov/foreign-trade/statistics/historical/gands.pdf (accessed February 27, 2014).

FIGURE 3-1
U.S. Exports to China
(millions of U.S. dollars)

Source: United States Census Bureau,
"Trade in Goods with China," https://
www.census.gov/foreign-trade/
balance/c5700.html (accessed
February 26, 2016).

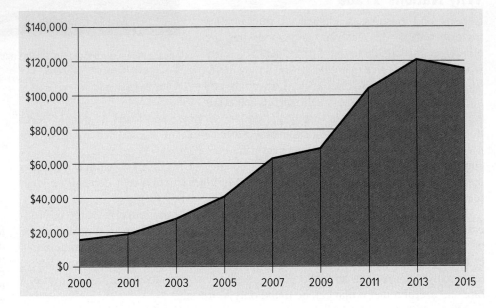

importing
the purchase of goods and
services from foreign sources.

Need help
understanding
balance of trade?
Visit your Connect
ebook video tab
for a brief animated
explanation.

balance of trade
the difference in value
between a nation's exports
and its imports.

agricultural, entertainment (movies, television shows, etc.), and technological products. **Importing** is the purchase of goods and services from foreign sources. Many of the goods you buy in the United States are likely to be imports or to have some imported components. Sometimes, you may not even realize they are imports. The United States imported more than $2.7 trillion in goods and services in 2015.[13]

Balance of Trade

You have probably read or heard about the fact that the United States has a trade deficit, but what is a trade deficit? A nation's **balance of trade** is the difference in value between its exports and imports. Because the United States (and some other nations as well) imports more products than it exports, it has a negative balance of trade, or **trade deficit.** Table 3-1 shows the trade deficit for the United States. In 2015, the United States had a trade deficit of more than $531 billion.[14] The trade deficit fluctuates according to such factors as the health of the United States and other economies, productivity, perceived quality, and exchange rates. As Figure 3-1 indicates, U.S. exports to China have been rapidly increasing but not fast enough to offset the imports from China. Trade deficits are harmful because they can mean the failure of businesses, the loss of jobs, and a lowered standard of living.

Trade Deficit	Trade Surplus
1. China	Hong Kong
2. Japan	United Arab Emirates
3. Germany	Netherlands
4. Mexico	Switzerland
5. Saudi Arabia	Belgium
6. Canada	Brazil
7. India	Australia
8. Ireland	Panama
9. South Korea	Singapore
10. Italy	Argentina

TABLE 3-2
Top 10 Countries with which the United States has Trade Deficits/Surpluses

Sources: "Top Ten Countries with which the U.S. has a Trade Deficit," April 2013, www.census.gov/foreign-trade/top/dst/current/deficit.html (accessed February 29, 2016); "Top Ten Countries with which the U.S. has a Trade Surplus," April 2013, www.census.gov/foreign-trade/top/dst/current/surplus.html (accessed February 29, 2016)

Of course, when a nation exports more goods than it imports, it has a favorable balance of trade, or trade surplus. Until about 1970, the United States had a trade surplus due to an abundance of natural resources and the relative efficiency of its manufacturing systems. Table 3-2 shows the top 10 countries with which the United States has a trade deficit and a trade surplus.

The difference between the flow of money into and out of a country is called its **balance of payments.** A country's balance of trade, foreign investments, foreign aid, loans, military expenditures, and money spent by tourists comprise its balance of payments. As you might expect, a country with a trade surplus generally has a favorable balance of payments because it is receiving more money from trade with foreign countries than it is paying out. When a country has a trade deficit, more money flows out of the country than into it. If more money flows out of the country than into it from tourism and other sources, the country may experience declining production and higher unemployment, because there is less money available for spending.

trade deficit
a nation's negative balance of trade, which exists when that country imports more products than it exports.

balance of payments
the difference between the flow of money into and out of a country.

International Trade Barriers

Completely free trade seldom exists. When a company decides to do business outside its own country, it will encounter a number of barriers to international trade. Any firm considering international business must research the other country's economic, legal, political, social, cultural, and technological background. Such research will help the company choose an appropriate level of involvement and operating strategies, as we will see later in this chapter.

Economic Barriers

When looking at doing business in another country, managers must consider a number of basic economic factors, such as economic development, infrastructure, and exchange rates.

LO 3-2

Investigate some of the economic, legal, political, social, cultural, and technological barriers to international business.

Economic Development.   When considering doing business abroad, U.S. businesspeople need to recognize that they cannot take for granted that other countries offer the same things as are found in *industrialized nations*—economically advanced countries such as the United States, Japan, Great Britain, and Canada. Many countries in Africa, Asia, and South America, for example, are in general poorer and less economically advanced than those in North America and Europe; they are often called *less-developed countries* (LDCs). LDCs are characterized by low per-capita income (income generated by the nation's production of goods and services divided by the population), which means that consumers are less likely to purchase nonessential products. Nonetheless, LDCs represent a potentially huge and profitable market for many businesses because they may be buying technology to improve their infrastructures, and much of the population may desire consumer products. For example, automobile manufacturers are looking toward LDCs as a way to expand their customer base. The rising middle class has caused many consumers in India and China to desire their own vehicles. The automobile market in China is now larger than the market in the United States.

A country's level of development is determined in part by its **infrastructure,** the physical facilities that support its economic activities, such as railroads, highways, ports, airfields, utilities and power plants, schools, hospitals, communication systems, and commercial distribution systems. When doing business in LDCs, for example, a business may need to compensate for rudimentary distribution and communication systems, or even a lack of technology.

infrastructure
the physical facilities that support a country's economic activities, such as railroads, highways, ports, airfields, utilities and power plants, schools, hospitals, communication systems, and commercial distribution systems.

exchange rate
the ratio at which one nation's currency can be exchanged for another nation's currency.

Exchange Rates.   The ratio at which one nation's currency can be exchanged for another nation's currency is the **exchange rate.** Exchange rates vary daily and can be found in newspapers and through many sites on the Internet. Familiarity with exchange rates is important because they affect the cost of imports and exports. When the value of the U.S. dollar declines relative to other currencies, such as the euro, the price of imports becomes more economical for U.S. consumers. For example, if the exchange rate for the dollar moves from $1.50 per euro to $1.25 per euro, then imports from Europe will be less expensive. On the other hand, U.S. exports become relatively inexpensive for international markets—in this example, the European Union (EU). The U.S. dollar is most frequently used in international trade, with 81 percent of trade finance conducted in U.S. dollars.[15]

China has started to reduce its trading limits, allowing its currency—the yuan—to fluctuate more in line with the market.

© John Woodworth/Getty Images

Occasionally, a government may intentionally alter the value of its currency through fiscal policy. Devaluation decreases the value of currency in relation to other currencies. If the U.S. government were to devalue the dollar, it would lower the cost of American goods abroad and make trips to the United States less expensive for foreign tourists. Thus, devaluation encourages the sale of domestic goods and tourism. On the other hand, when Switzerland's central bank let the value of the Swiss franc rise by 30 percent against the euro in 2015, it resulted in increasing the costs of exports. This made everything exported from Switzerland more expensive, including tourism. However, Swiss brands including expensive watches were offered at large discounts if bought using Swiss francs.[16] Revaluation, as in the Swiss example, increases the value of a currency in relation to other currencies, but occurs rarely.

Entrepreneurship in Action

Tracking Counterfeit Drugs

MPedigree Network

Founder: Bright Simons

Founded: 2007, in Accra, Ghana

Success: MPedigree won the Global Security Challenge Award and has since expanded its client base to Nigeria, India, and Egypt.

Counterfeit drugs are a huge problem in Africa, contributing to thousands of deaths annually. Enter Bright Simons, a talented entrepreneur who had developed a tracking software. Simons hoped to use the code to verify the authenticity of organic crops and help African farmers. However, when this idea did not pan out, Simons realized he could use his code to track down counterfeit medicines.

Calling his business MPedigree Network, Simons sells his tracking technology to drug manufacturers. Manufacturers who purchase the software use it to label individual packs of medicine with 12-digit codes, hidden behind a scratch-off label on the outside of the container. When consumers examine the medicines, they can call or text in the code to see if it corresponds to a legitimate product.

MPedigree's product has garnered a lot of interest. For instance, the codes were included on 50 million packs of antimalarial drugs in Nigeria. Simons sees this as just the beginning. He hopes to increase the breadth of MPedigree's offerings by adding business consulting and marketing analysis services, positioning MPedigree to operate in both the consumer and business sectors.[17]

Discussion Questions

1. Why do you think MPedigree was more successful in the pharmaceutical rather than produce industry?
2. Who do you think is MPedigree's target market?
3. How could Bright Simons use consumer information obtained from MPedigree coding technology to consult with global businesses?

Ethical, Legal, and Political Barriers

A company that decides to enter the international marketplace must contend with potentially complex relationships among the different laws of its own nation, international laws, and the laws of the nation with which it will be trading; various trade restrictions imposed on international trade; changing political climates; and different ethical values. Legal and ethical requirements for successful business are increasing globally. For instance, India has strict limitations for foreign retailers. For many years, India required foreign retailers operating in the country to locally source their merchandise within five years after their original investment. However, to attract more investment in the country, India loosened some of its rules regarding foreign investment. Among the changes, the government ruled that foreign retailers now have five years from the date of opening their first store before they must meet local-sourcing requirements. India is not the only country that is hesitant about foreign companies operating through the Internet.[18] Internet legislation in other countries is causing some companies to pause out of concern. The European Union, for instance, is adopting a number of regulations that dictate how companies can use the online information they collect about users.

Laws and Regulations. The United States has a number of laws and regulations that govern the activities of U.S. firms engaged in international trade. For example, the Webb-Pomerene Export Trade Act of 1918 exempts American firms from antitrust laws if those firms are acting together to enter international trade. This law allows selected U.S. firms to form monopolies to compete with foreign monopolistic organizations, although they are not allowed to limit free trade and competition within the United States or to use unfair methods of competition in international trade. The United States also has a variety of friendship, commerce, and navigation treaties with other nations. These treaties allow business to be transacted between citizens of the specified countries. Ireland is an up-and-coming example of a country that attracts American foreign investment. Corporate tax rates that are among the lowest in Europe, low wages, and sufficient infrastructure are just a few of the reasons investors are attracted to Ireland. This has led many U.S. firms—including Eaton and Burger King—to undergo tax inversions, which occurs when companies relocate their headquarters to countries with a lower tax rate. For instance, Caterpillar avoided $2.4 billion in U.S. taxes by diverting its profits to Switzerland. Tax inversions have been heavily criticized by U.S. lawmakers, who see these companies as using tax loopholes to avoid taxes. Ireland is passing legislation closing certain loopholes in their own tax systems, a change that could put a damper on corporate tax inversions.[19]

Once outside U.S. borders, businesspeople are likely to find that the laws of other nations differ from those of the United States. Many of the legal rights that Americans take for granted do not exist in other countries, and a firm doing business abroad must understand and obey the laws of the host country. Some countries have strict laws limiting the amount of local currency that can be taken out of the country and the amount of currency that can be brought in; others limit how foreign companies can operate within the country. In Mexico, for example, foreigners cannot directly own property in what is known as the "Restricted Zone." The Restricted Zone includes land within 100 kilometers of Mexico's international borders along with land within 50 kilometers of Mexico's oceans and beaches.[20]

Some countries have copyright and patent laws that are less strict than those of the United States, and some countries fail to honor U.S. laws. Because copying is a tradition in China and Vietnam and laws protecting copyrights and intellectual property are weak and minimally enforced, those countries are flooded with counterfeit videos, movies, CDs, computer software, furniture, and clothing. Companies are angry because the counterfeits harm not only their sales, but also their reputations if the knock-offs are of poor quality. Such counterfeiting is not limited to China or Vietnam. It is estimated that nearly half of all software installed on personal computers worldwide is not properly licensed.[21] In countries where these activities occur, laws against them may not be sufficiently enforced if counterfeiting is deemed illegal. Thus, businesses engaging in foreign trade may have to take extra steps to protect their products because local laws may be insufficient to do so.

Tariffs and Trade Restrictions.   Tariffs and other trade restrictions are part of a country's legal structure but may be established or removed for political reasons. An **import tariff** is a tax levied by a nation on goods imported into the country. A *fixed tariff* is a specific amount of money levied on each unit of a product brought into the country, while an *ad valorem tariff* is based on the value of the item. Most countries allow citizens traveling abroad to bring home a certain amount of merchandise without paying an import tariff. A U.S. citizen may bring $200 worth of merchandise into the United States duty free. After that, U.S. citizens must pay an ad valorem tariff based on the cost of the item and the country of origin. Thus, identical items purchased in different countries might have different tariffs.

Countries sometimes levy tariffs for political reasons, as when they impose sanctions against other countries to protest their actions. However, import tariffs are more commonly imposed to protect domestic products by raising the price of imported ones. Such protective tariffs have become controversial, as Americans become increasingly concerned over the U.S. trade deficit. Protective tariffs allow more expensive domestic goods to compete with foreign ones. For example, the United States has imposed tariffs on steel imported into the United States because imports have caused

import tariff
a tax levied by a nation on goods imported into the country.

many local steelworks to crash.[22] Other markets can produce steel more cheaply than the United States. Many people and special interest groups in the United States, such as unions, would like to see tariffs placed on Chinese steel, which is significantly less expensive, in order to protect remaining U.S. steel production. The United States has also imposed tariffs on imported sugar for almost two centuries. The EU levies tariffs on many products, including some seafood imports.

Critics of protective tariffs argue that their use inhibits free trade and competition. Supporters of protective tariffs say they insulate domestic industries, particularly new ones, against well-established foreign competitors. Once an industry matures, however, its advocates may be reluctant to let go of the tariff that protected it. Tariffs also help when, because of low labor costs and other advantages, foreign competitors can afford to sell their products at prices lower than those charged by domestic companies. Some Americans argue that tariffs should be used to keep domestic wages high and unemployment low.

Exchange controls restrict the amount of currency that can be bought or sold. Some countries control their foreign trade by forcing businesspeople to buy and sell foreign products through a central bank. If John Deere, for example, receives payments for its tractors in a foreign currency, it may be required to sell the currency to that nation's central bank. When foreign currency is in short supply, as it is in many LDCs, the government uses foreign currency to purchase necessities and capital goods and produces other products locally, thus limiting its need for foreign imports.

Due to the U.S. embargo against Cuba, many Cubans drive older automobiles.

© Henri Conodul/Iconotec.com

A **quota** limits the number of units of a particular product that can be imported into a country. A quota may be established by voluntary agreement or by government decree. The United States imposes quotas on certain goods, such as garments produced in Vietnam and China. Quotas are designed to protect the industries and jobs of the country imposing the quota.

An **embargo** prohibits trade in a particular product. Embargoes are generally directed at specific goods or countries and may be established for political, economic, health, or religious reasons. The United States currently maintains a trade embargo with Cuba. However, President Obama reestablished trade and diplomatic relations between Cuba and the United States. It is much easier to travel to Cuba, and U.S. citizens can bring back $100 worth of Cuban cigars and rum. The government has also approved the building of a U.S. factory in Cuba, the first time in more than 50 years.[23] It may be surprising to know that U.S. farmers export hundreds of millions of dollars' worth of commodities to Cuba each year, based on a 2000 law that provided permission for some trade to the embargoed country.[24] Health embargoes prevent the importing of various pharmaceuticals, animals, plants, and agricultural products. Muslim

exchange controls
regulations that restrict the amount of currency that can be bought or sold.

quota
a restriction on the number of units of a particular product that can be imported into a country.

embargo
a prohibition on trade in a particular product.

Political instability in many nations has led to an influx of refugees. The potential for political turmoil is a substantial risk businesses face when expanding overseas.

Cpl. Tammy K. Hineline/US Marine Corps/DoD

nations forbid the importation of alcoholic beverages on religious grounds.

One common reason for setting quotas or tariffs is to prohibit **dumping,** which occurs when a country or business sells products at less than what it costs to produce them. For example, China accused the European Union and Japan of dumping its stainless steel tubes, thus harming China's domestic industry.[25] A company may dump its products for several reasons. Dumping permits quick entry into a market. Sometimes, dumping occurs when the domestic market for a firm's product is too small to support an efficient level of production. In other cases, technologically obsolete products that are no longer salable in the country of origin are dumped overseas. Dumping is relatively difficult to prove, but even the suspicion of dumping can lead to the imposition of quotas or tariffs. China instituted anti-dumping duties on EU and Japanese imports.[26]

dumping
the act of a country or business selling products at less than what it costs to produce them.

Political Barriers.   Unlike legal issues, political considerations are seldom written down and often change rapidly. Nations that have been subject to economic sanctions for political reasons in recent years include Cuba, Iran, Syria, and North Korea. While these were dramatic events, political considerations affect international business daily as governments enact tariffs, embargoes, or other types of trade restrictions in response to political events.

Businesses engaged in international trade must consider the relative instability of countries such as Iraq, Ukraine, and Venezuela. Political unrest in countries such as Pakistan, Somalia, and the Democratic Republic of the Congo may create a hostile or even dangerous environment for foreign businesses. Natural disasters can cripple a country's government, making the region even more unstable. Even a developed country such as Japan had its social, economic, and political institutions stressed by the 2011 earthquake and tsunamis. Finally, a sudden change in power can result in a regime that is hostile to foreign investment. Some businesses have been forced out of a country altogether, as when Hugo Chavez conducted a socialist revolution in Venezuela to force out or take over American oil companies. Whether they like it or not, companies are often involved directly or indirectly in international politics.

cartel
a group of firms or nations that agrees to act as a monopoly and not compete with each other, in order to generate a competitive advantage in world markets.

Political concerns may lead a group of nations to form a **cartel,** a group of firms or nations that agrees to act as a monopoly and not compete with each other, to generate a competitive advantage in world markets. Probably the most famous cartel is OPEC, the Organization of Petroleum Exporting Countries, founded in the 1960s to increase the price of petroleum throughout the world and to maintain high prices. By working to ensure stable oil prices, OPEC hopes to enhance the economies of its member nations.

Social and Cultural Barriers

Most businesspeople engaged in international trade underestimate the importance of social and cultural differences; but these differences can derail an important transaction. Tiffany & Co. learned that more attentive customer service was necessary in order to succeed in Japan, and bold marketing and advertising served as the recipe for success in China.[27] And in Europe, Starbucks took the unprecedented step of allowing its locations to be franchised in order to reach smaller markets that are unfamiliar. This way

Starbucks reduced some of the cultural and social risks involved in entering such markets.[28] Unfortunately, cultural norms are rarely written down, and what is written down may well be inaccurate.

Cultural differences include differences in spoken and written language. Although it is certainly possible to translate words from one language to another, the true meaning is sometimes misinterpreted or lost. Consider some translations that went awry in foreign markets:

- Scandinavian vacuum manufacturer Electrolux used the following in an American campaign: "Nothing sucks like an Electrolux."
- The Coca-Cola name in China was first read as "Ke-kou-ke-la," meaning "bite the wax tadpole."
- In Italy, a campaign for Schweppes Tonic Water translated the name into Schweppes Toilet Water.[29]

Translators cannot just translate slogans, advertising campaigns, and website language; they must know the cultural differences that could affect a company's success.

Differences in body language and personal space also affect international trade. Body language is non-verbal, usually unconscious communication through gestures, posture, and facial expression. Personal space is the distance at which one person feels comfortable talking to another. Americans tend to stand a moderate distance away from the person with whom they are speaking. Arab businessmen tend to stand face-to-face with the object of their conversation. Additionally, gestures vary from culture to culture, and gestures considered acceptable in American society—pointing, for example—may be considered rude in others. Table 3-3 shows some of

Sociocultural differences can create challenges for businesses who want to invest in other countries.

© John Lund/Blend Images LLC

TABLE 3-3
Cultural Behavioral Differences

Region	Gestures Viewed as Rude or Unacceptable
Japan, Hong Kong, Middle East	Summoning with the index finger
Middle and Far East	Pointing with index finger
Thailand, Japan, France	Sitting with soles of shoes showing
Brazil, Germany	Forming a circle with fingers (the "O.K." sign in the United States)
Japan	Winking means "I love you"
Buddhist countries	Patting someone on the head

Source: Adapted from Judie Haynes, "Communicating with Gestures," EverythingESL (n.d.), www.everythingesl.net/inservices/body_language.php (accessed February 29, 2016).

the behaviors considered rude or unacceptable in other countries. Such cultural differences may generate uncomfortable feelings or misunderstandings when businesspeople of different countries negotiate with each other.

Family roles also influence marketing activities. Many countries do not allow children to be used in advertising, for example. Advertising that features people in nontraditional social roles may or may not be successful either. Companies should also guard against marketing that could be perceived as reinforcing negative stereotypes. Coca-Cola was forced to pull an online advertisement and issue an apology after releasing a Christmas ad showing fair-skinned people arriving at an indigenous village in Mexico bearing gifts of sodas and a Christmas tree. Mexican activists claimed the advertisement reinforced negative stereotypes of indigenous people and called for the government's anti-discrimination commission to issue sanctions against the company.[30]

The people of other nations quite often have a different perception of time as well. Americans value promptness; a business meeting scheduled for a specific time seldom starts more than a few minutes late. In Mexico and Spain, however, it is not unusual for a meeting to be delayed half an hour or more. Such a late start might produce resentment in an American negotiating in Spain for the first time.

Companies engaged in foreign trade must observe the national and religious holidays and local customs of the host country. In many Islamic countries, for example, workers expect to take a break at certain times of the day to observe religious rites. Companies also must monitor their advertising to guard against offending customers. In Thailand and many other countries, public displays of affection between the sexes are unacceptable in advertising messages; in many Middle Eastern nations, it is unacceptable to show the soles of one's feet.[31] In Russia, smiling is considered appropriate only in private settings, not in business.

With the exception of the United States, most nations use the metric system. This lack of uniformity creates problems for both buyers and sellers in the international marketplace. American sellers, for instance, must package goods destined for foreign markets in liters or meters, and Japanese sellers must convert to the English system if they plan to sell a product in the United States. Tools also must be calibrated in the correct system if they are to function correctly. Hyundai and Honda service technicians need metric tools to make repairs on those cars.

The literature dealing with international business is filled with accounts of sometimes humorous but often costly mistakes that occurred because of a lack of understanding of the social and cultural differences between buyers and sellers. Such problems cannot always be avoided, but they can be minimized through research on the cultural and social differences of the host country.

Technological Barriers

Many countries lack the technological infrastructure found in the United States, and some marketers are viewing such barriers as opportunities. For instance, marketers are targeting many countries such as India and China and some African countries where there are few private phone lines. Citizens of these countries are turning instead to wireless communication through cell phones. Technological advances are creating additional global marketing opportunities. Along with opportunities, changing technologies also create new challenges and competition. The U.S. market share of the personal computer market is dropping as new competitors emerge that are challenging U.S. PC makers. In fact, out of the top five global PC companies—Lenovo,

Hewlett-Packard, Dell, Asus, and Acer Group—three are from Asian countries. On the other hand, Apple Inc.'s iPad and other tablet computer makers have significantly eroded the market share of traditional personal computers, placing the industry in the maturity stage of the product life cycle.[32]

Trade Agreements, Alliances, and Organizations

LO 3-3

Specify some of the agreements, alliances, and organizations that may encourage trade across international boundaries.

Although these economic, political, legal, and sociocultural issues may seem like daunting barriers to international trade, there are also organizations and agreements—such as the General Agreement on Tariffs and Trade, the World Bank, and the International Monetary Fund—that foster international trade and can help companies get involved in and succeed in global markets. Various regional trade agreements, such as the North American Free Trade Agreement and the EU, also promote trade among member nations by eliminating tariffs and trade restrictions. In this section, we'll look briefly at these agreements and organizations.

General Agreement on Tariffs and Trade

During the Great Depression of the 1930s, nations established so many protective tariffs covering so many products that international trade became virtually impossible. By the end of World War II, there was considerable international momentum to liberalize trade and minimize the effects of tariffs. The **General Agreement on Tariffs and Trade (GATT),** originally signed by 23 nations in 1947, provided a forum for tariff negotiations and a place where international trade problems could be discussed and resolved. More than 100 nations abided by its rules. GATT sponsored rounds of negotiations aimed at reducing trade restrictions. The most recent round, the Uruguay Round (1988–1994), further reduced trade barriers for most products and provided new rules to prevent dumping.

The **World Trade Organization (WTO),** an international organization dealing with the rules of trade between nations, was created in 1995 by the Uruguay Round. Key to the World Trade Organization are the WTO agreements, which are the legal ground rules for international commerce. The agreements were negotiated and signed by most of the world's trading nations and ratified by their parliaments. The goal is to help producers of goods and services and exporters and importers conduct their business. In addition to administering the WTO trade agreements, the WTO presents a forum for trade negotiations, monitors national trade policies, provides technical assistance and training for developing countries, and cooperates with other international organizations. Based in Geneva, Switzerland, the WTO has also adopted a leadership role in negotiating trade disputes among nations.[33] For example, the WTO ruled that China's anti-dumping measures taken against Japan and the EU violated trade rules because China had not adequately proven that the imports of the stainless steel tubes had harmed China's domestic industry.[34]

The North American Free Trade Agreement

The **North American Free Trade Agreement (NAFTA),** which went into effect on January 1, 1994, effectively merged Canada, the United States, and Mexico into one market of nearly 470 million consumers. NAFTA virtually eliminated all tariffs on goods produced and traded among Canada, Mexico, and the United States to create a free trade area. The estimated annual output for this trade alliance is

General Agreement on Tariffs and Trade (GATT) a trade agreement, originally signed by 23 nations in 1947, that provided a forum for tariff negotiations and a place where international trade problems could be discussed and resolved.

World Trade Organization (WTO) international organization dealing with the rules of trade between nations.

North American Free Trade Agreement (NAFTA) agreement that eliminates most tariffs and trade restrictions on agricultural and manufactured products to encourage trade among Canada, the United States, and Mexico.

NAFTA, which went into effect on January I, 1994, has increased trade among Mexico, the United States, and Canada.

© scibak/Getty Images

about $17 trillion.[35] NAFTA makes it easier for U.S. businesses to invest in Mexico and Canada; provides protection for intellectual property (of special interest to high-technology and entertainment industries); expands trade by requiring equal treatment of U.S. firms in both countries; and simplifies country-of-origin rules, hindering Japan's use of Mexico as a staging ground for further penetration into U.S. markets.

Canada's nearly 35 million consumers are relatively affluent, with a per capita GDP of $45,000.[36] Trade between the United States and Canada totals approximately $575 billion.[37] In fact, Canada is the single largest trading partner of the United States. NAFTA has also increased trade between Canada and Mexico. Mexico is Canada's fifth largest export market and third largest import market.[38]

With a per capita GDP of $18,000, Mexico's nearly 121 million consumers are less affluent than Canadian consumers.[39] However, trade with the United States and Mexico has tripled since NAFTA was initiated. Mexico purchases more than $236 billion in U.S. products.[40] Millions of Americans cite their heritage as Mexican, making them the most populous Hispanic group in the country. These individuals often have close ties to relatives in Mexico and assist in Mexican–U.S. economic development and trade. Mexico is on a course of a market economy, rule of law, respect for human rights, and responsible public policies. There is also a commitment to the environment and sustainable human development. Many U.S. companies have taken advantage of Mexico's low labor costs and proximity to the United States to set up production facilities, sometimes called *maquiladoras*. Mexico is also attracting major technological industries, including electronics, software, and aerospace. Investors see many growth opportunities in Mexico, particularly in light of recent reforms. For instance, Mexico passed legislation to open up its state-controlled oil reserves to foreign companies. Additionally, if the United States does well economically, Mexico—its biggest customer—is also likely to do well.[41]

However, there is great disparity within Mexico. The country's southern states cannot seem to catch up with the more affluent northern states on almost any socioeconomic indicator. The disparities are growing, as can be seen comparing the south to the northern industrial capital of Monterrey, which is beginning to seem like south Texas.[42] Drug gang wars threaten the economic stability of Mexico, especially in the northern states close to the U.S. border. However, this situation is improving as the economy is growing and violence is decreasing.

Despite its benefits, NAFTA has been controversial, and disputes continue to arise over the implementation of the trade agreement. While many Americans feared the agreement would erase jobs in the United States, Mexicans have been disappointed that the agreement failed to create more jobs. Moreover, Mexico's rising standard of living has increased the cost of doing business there; many hundreds of *maquiladoras* have closed their doors and transferred work to China and other nations where labor costs are cheaper. Indeed, China has become the United States' second-largest importer.[43] On the other hand, high transportation costs, intellectual property theft, quality failures, and the difficulty management often incurs in controlling a business so far away and under a communist regime are now causing some manufacturers to reconsider opting for Mexican factories over China, even going so far as to relocate from China back to Mexico.[44]

Although NAFTA has been controversial, it has become a positive factor for U.S. firms wishing to engage in international marketing. Because licensing requirements have been relaxed under the pact, smaller businesses that previously could not afford to invest in Mexico and Canada will be able to do business in those markets without having to locate there. NAFTA's long phase-in period provided time for adjustment by those firms affected by reduced tariffs on imports. Furthermore, increased competition should lead to a more efficient market, and the long-term prospects of including most countries in the Western Hemisphere in the alliance promise additional opportunities for U.S. marketers.

The European Union

The **European Union (EU)**, also called the *European Community* or *Common Market,* was established in 1958 to promote trade among its members, which initially included Belgium, France, Italy, West Germany, Luxembourg, and the Netherlands.

East and West Germany united in 1991, and by 1995 the United Kingdom, Spain, Denmark, Greece, Portugal, Ireland, Austria, Finland, and Sweden had joined as well. The Czech Republic, Estonia, Hungary, Latvia, Lithuania, Poland, Slovakia, and Slovenia joined in 2004. In 2007, Bulgaria and Romania also became members, Cyprus and Malta joined in 2008, and Croatia joined in 2013, which brought total membership to 28. Macedonia, Albania, Serbia, and Turkey are candidate countries that hope to join the EU in the near future.[45] Until 1993, each nation functioned as a separate market, but at that time members officially unified into one of the largest single world markets, which today has nearly half a billion consumers with a GDP of more than $19 trillion.[46]

To facilitate free trade among members, the EU is working toward standardization of business regulations and requirements, import duties, and value-added taxes; the elimination of customs checks; and the creation of a standardized currency for use by all members. Many European nations (Austria, Belgium, Finland, France, Germany, Greece, Ireland, Italy, Luxembourg, the Netherlands, Portugal, Spain, and Slovenia) link their exchange rates to a common currency, the *euro;* however, some EU members such as the United Kingdom have rejected use of the euro in their countries. Although the common currency requires many marketers to modify their pricing strategies and will subject them to increased competition, the use of a single currency frees companies that sell goods among European countries from the nuisance of dealing with complex exchange rates.[47] The long-term goals are to eliminate all trade barriers within the EU, improve the economic efficiency of the EU nations, and stimulate economic growth, thus making the union's economy more competitive in global markets, particularly against Japan and other Pacific Rim nations, and North America. However, several disputes and debates still divide the member nations, and many barriers to completely free trade remain. Consequently, it may take many years before the EU is truly one deregulated market.

The EU has also enacted some of the world's strictest laws concerning antitrust issues, which have had unexpected consequences for some non-European firms. For instance, the European Union passed a law that established for Internet users the "right to be forgotten." Under the law, Internet users in the EU can request that

European Union (EU)
a union of European nations established in 1958 to promote trade among its members; one of the largest single markets today.

Going Green

The Fight over GMOs in Europe

Genetically modified (GM) crops continue to face legal and social barriers within the European Union (EU). The EU currently approves the cultivation of only one type of GM corn, created by biotech company Monsanto. However, new regulation might enable the adoption of GM crops in Europe as it would allow individual member states to ban or accept GM crops. Although the EU has determined that many varieties of GM crops are safe, France and Germany intend to utilize new opt-out rules to continue banning the import and export of all GM food. France already bans the cultivation of Monsanto's GM corn over concerns that it may negatively impact the environment.

Monsanto refutes claims that its GM corn is unsafe, citing scientific evidence and a long track record of its crops being safely cultivated and consumed. Consequently, many farmers in Europe rely on GM crops for animal feed, which only serves to intensify the debate further. Aside from restricting international agricultural trade, GM food bans may increase costs to farmers who would need to find new suppliers. The disagreement over GM food safety will likely continue, with individual European countries deciding whether to ban or allow GM foods. Ultimately, the degree of impact this will have on future agricultural trade and cultivation is unknown.[48]

Discussion Questions

1. Why do some countries oppose the cultivation and trading of GM food?
2. What are some possible advantages to allowing individual member states of the EU determine whether to accept or ban GM food? What are the disadvantages?
3. Has the EU discovered any safety concerns regarding GM food? If not, why do you think it is allowing member states to make their own decisions?

Internet search engines such as Google and Bing remove links involving personal information that does not hold a public interest. This is the first time such a rule has been implemented, and supporters believe this ruling should be applied worldwide. The European Parliament is also encouraging the breakup of Google's search engine business from its other businesses.[49]

The prosperity of the EU has suffered in recent years. EU members experienced a severe economic crisis in 2010 that required steep bailouts from the International Monetary Fund (IMF). The first country to come to the forefront was Greece, which had so much debt that it risked default. With an increase in Greek bond yields and credit risks—along with a severe deficit and other negative economic factors—the country's economy plummeted. Because Greece uses the euro as its currency, the massive downturn decreased the euro's value. This had a profound effect on other countries in the euro zone. (The euro zone refers collectively to European member countries that have adopted the euro as their form of currency.) Ireland and Portugal were particularly vulnerable because they had some of the region's largest deficits.[50] Ireland began experiencing problems similar to Greece, including a debt crisis, failing economic health, and rising bond yields.[51] Both Ireland and Portugal required bailout packages. In 2012, Spain and Cyprus also requested bailouts.

Greece continues to struggle even after the initial bailout because it did not have enough funds to repay its bondholders. Greece was forced to default. A default by one nation in the EU negatively affects the rest of the members by making them appear riskier as well.[52] The United Kingdom appears to have lost faith in the EU and has voted to exit the trade bloc by a narrow margin.[53] Germany, on the other hand,

The Asia-Pacific Economic Cooperation (APEC) is a forum for 21 Pacific Rim member economies that promotes free trade throughout the region.

© hans engbers/Shutterstock

has largely avoided the economic woes plaguing other countries. Germany has many exporting companies and has a smaller budget deficit and smaller household debt, which has enabled it to weather the crisis better than other EU members.[54]

Asia-Pacific Economic Cooperation

The **Asia-Pacific Economic Cooperation (APEC),** established in 1989, promotes open trade and economic and technical cooperation among member economies, which initially included Australia, Brunei Darussalam, Canada, Indonesia, Japan, South Korea, Malaysia, New Zealand, the Philippines, Singapore, Thailand, and the United States. Since then, the alliance has grown to include Chile; China; Hong Kong, China; Mexico; Papua New Guinea; Peru; Russia; Chinese Taipei; and Vietnam. The 21-member alliance represents approximately 2.8 billion people, 47 percent of world trade, and 57 percent of world GDP.[55] APEC differs from other international trade alliances in its commitment to facilitating business and its practice of allowing the business/private sector to participate in a wide range of APEC activities.[56]

Companies of the APEC have become increasingly competitive and sophisticated in global business in the past three decades. The Japanese and South Koreans, in particular, have made tremendous inroads on world markets for automobiles, cameras, and audio and video equipment. Products from Samsung, Sony, Canon, Toyota, Daewoo, Mitsubishi, Suzuki, and Lenovo are sold all over the world and have set standards of quality by which other products are often judged. The People's Republic of China, a country of more than 1.3 billion people, has launched a program of economic reform to stimulate its economy by privatizing many industries, restructuring its banking system, and increasing public spending on infrastructure (including railways and telecommunications). For many years, China was a manufacturing powerhouse. However, in recent years growth has slowed from its height of 10 percent down to 6.5 percent.[57] China's export market has consistently outpaced its import growth in recent years and its GDP is the world's second-largest economy, behind the United States. In fact, China has overtaken the United States as the world's largest trader.[58]

Increased industrialization has also caused China to become the world's largest emitter of greenhouse gases. China has overtaken the United States to become the world's largest oil importer.[59] On the other hand, China has also begun a quest to become a world leader in green initiatives and renewable energy. This is an increasingly important quest as the country becomes more polluted.

Another risk area for China is the fact that the government owns or has stakes in so many enterprises. On the one hand, China's system of state-directed capitalism has benefited the country because reforms and decisions can be made more quickly. On the other hand, state-backed companies lack many of the competitors that private industries have. Remember that competition often spurs innovation and lowers costs. If China's firms lack sufficient competition, their costs may very likely increase.[60] China's growing debt liabilities have also caused concern among foreign investors.[61]

Less visible Pacific Rim regions, such as Thailand, Singapore, Taiwan, Vietnam, and Hong Kong, have also become major manufacturing and financial centers. Vietnam, with one of the world's most open economies, has bypassed its communist government with private firms moving ahead despite bureaucracy, corruption, and poor infrastructure. In a country of 88 million, Vietnamese firms now compete internationally due to an agricultural miracle, making the country one of the world's main providers of farm produce. As China's labor costs continue to grow, more businesses are turning toward Vietnam to open factories.[62]

Asia-Pacific Economic Cooperation (APEC)
an international trade alliance that promotes open trade and economic and technical cooperation among member nations.

Bananas are a major export in Tahiti.

© Keith Levit/Alamy

Association of Southeast Asian Nations

The **Association of Southeast Asian Nations (ASEAN),** established in 1967, promotes trade and economic integration among member nations in Southeast Asia, including Malaysia, the Philippines, Singapore, Thailand, Brunei Darussalam, Vietnam, Laos, Indonesia, Myanmar, and Cambodia.[63] The 10-member alliance represents 600 million people with a GDP of $2.4 trillion.[64] ASEAN's goals include the promotion of free trade, peace, and collaboration between its members.[65]

However, ASEAN is facing challenges in becoming a unified trade bloc. Unlike members of the EU, the economic systems of ASEAN members are quite different, with political systems including democracies (Philippines and Malaysia), constitutional monarchies (Cambodia), and communism (Vietnam).[66] Major conflicts have also occurred between member-nations. In Thailand the military staged a coup and placed the country under martial law, a change that not only impacted Thailand but also ASEAN as a whole.[67]

Despite these challenges, ASEAN plans to increase economic integration in 2015, but unlike the EU, it will not have a common currency or fully free labor flows between member-nations. In this way, ASEAN plans to avoid some of the pitfalls that occurred among nations in the EU during the latest worldwide recession.[68]

Association of Southeast Asian Nations (ASEAN)
a trade alliance that promotes trade and economic integration among member nations in Southeast Asia.

World Bank

World Bank
an organization established by the industrialized nations in 1946 to loan money to underdeveloped and developing countries; formally known as the International Bank for Reconstruction and Development.

The **World Bank,** more formally known as the International Bank for Reconstruction and Development, was established by the industrialized nations, including the United States, in 1946 to loan money to underdeveloped and developing countries.

It loans its own funds or borrows funds from member countries to finance projects ranging from road and factory construction to the building of medical and educational facilities. The World Bank and other multilateral development banks (banks with international support that provide loans to developing countries) are the largest source of advice and assistance for developing nations. The International Development Association and the International Finance Corporation are associated with the World Bank and provide loans to private businesses and member countries.

International Monetary Fund

International Monetary Fund (IMF)
organization established in 1947 to promote trade among member nations by eliminating trade barriers and fostering financial cooperation.

The **International Monetary Fund (IMF)** was established in 1947 to promote trade among member nations by eliminating trade barriers and fostering financial cooperation. It also makes short-term loans to member countries that have balance-of-payment deficits and provides foreign currencies to member nations. The IMF tries to avoid financial crises and panics by alerting the international community about countries that will not be able to repay their debts. The IMF's Internet site provides additional information about the organization, including news releases, frequently asked questions, and members.

The IMF is the closest thing the world has to an international central bank. If countries get into financial trouble, they can borrow from the World Bank. However, the global economic crisis created many challenges for the IMF as it was forced to significantly increase its loans to both emerging economies and more developed nations. The usefulness of the IMF for developed countries is limited because these countries use private markets as a major source of capital.[69] Yet the European debt crisis changed this somewhat. Portugal, Ireland, Greece, and Spain (often referred to with the acronym PIGS) required billions of dollars in bailouts from the IMF to keep their economies afloat.

Getting Involved in International Business

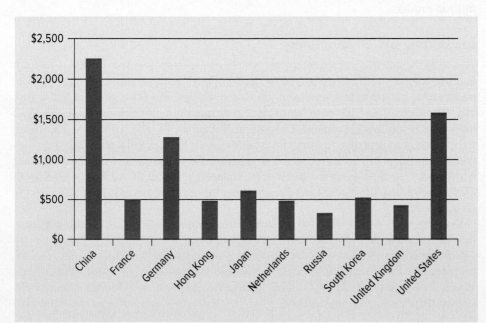

Businesses may get involved in international trade at many levels—from a small Kenyan firm that occasionally exports African crafts to a huge multinational corporation such as Shell Oil that sells products around the globe. The degree of commitment of resources and effort required increases according to the level at which a business involves itself in international trade. This section examines exporting and importing, trading companies, licensing and franchising, contract manufacturing, joint ventures, direct investment, and multinational corporations.

LO 3-4

Summarize the different levels of organizational involvement in international trade.

Exporting and Importing

Many companies first get involved in international trade when they import goods from other countries for resale in their own businesses. For example, a grocery store chain may import bananas from Honduras and coffee from Colombia. A business may get involved in exporting when it is called upon to supply a foreign company with a particular product. Such exporting enables enterprises of all sizes to participate in international business. Exporting to other countries becomes a necessity for established countries that seek to grow continually. Products often have higher sales growth potential in foreign countries than they have in the parent country. For instance, General Motors and YUM Brands! sell more of their products in China than in the United States. Walmart experienced large sales growth in international markets. Figure 3-2 shows some of the world's largest exporting countries.

FIGURE 3-2
Top Exporting Countries (in billions of $)

Source: Central Intelligence Agency, "Country Comparison::Exports," https://www.cia.gov/library/publications/the-world-factbook/rankorder/2078rank.html (accessed February 29, 2016).

countertrade agreements
foreign trade agreements that involve bartering products for other products instead of for currency.

Exporting sometimes takes place through **countertrade agreements,** which involve bartering products for other products instead of for currency. Such arrangements are fairly common in international trade, especially between Western companies and eastern European nations. An estimated 40 percent or more of all international trade agreements contain countertrade provisions.

Although a company may export its wares overseas directly or import goods directly from their manufacturer, many choose to deal with an intermediary, commonly called an *export agent.* Export agents seldom produce goods themselves; instead, they usually handle international transactions for other firms. Export agents either purchase products outright or take them on consignment. If they purchase them outright, they generally mark up the price they have paid and attempt to sell the product in the international marketplace. They are also responsible for storage and transportation.

An advantage of trading through an agent instead of directly is that the company does not have to deal with foreign currencies or the red tape (paying tariffs and handling paperwork) of international business. A major disadvantage is that, because the export agent must make a profit, either the price of the product must be increased or the domestic company must provide a larger discount than it would in a domestic transaction.

Trading Companies

trading company
a firm that buys goods in one country and sells them to buyers in another country.

A **trading company** buys goods in one country and sells them to buyers in another country. Trading companies handle all activities required to move products from one country to another, including consulting, marketing research, advertising, insurance, product research and design, warehousing, and foreign exchange services to companies interested in selling their products in foreign markets. Trading companies are similar to export agents, but their role in international trade is larger. By linking sellers and buyers of goods in different countries, trading companies promote international trade. WTSC offers a 24-hour-per-day online world trade system that connects 20 million companies in 245 countries, offering more than 60 million products.[70]

Licensing and Franchising

licensing
a trade agreement in which one company—the licensor—allows another company—the licensee—to use its company name, products, patents, brands, trademarks, raw materials, and/or production processes in exchange for a fee or royalty.

Licensing is a trade arrangement in which one company—the *licensor*—allows another company—the *licensee*—to use its company name, products, patents, brands, trademarks, raw materials, and/or production processes in exchange for a fee or royalty. The Coca-Cola Company and PepsiCo frequently use licensing as a means to market their soft drinks, apparel, and other merchandise in other countries. Licensing is an attractive alternative to direct investment when the political stability of a foreign country is in doubt or when resources are unavailable for direct investment. Licensing is especially advantageous for small manufacturers wanting to launch a well-known brand internationally. Yoplait is a French yogurt that is licensed for production in the United States.

franchising
a form of licensing in which a company—the franchiser—agrees to provide a franchisee a name, logo, methods of operation, advertising, products, and other elements associated with a franchiser's business in return for a financial commitment and the agreement to conduct business in accordance with the franchiser's standard of operations.

Franchising is a form of licensing in which a company—the *franchiser*—agrees to provide a *franchisee* the name, logo, methods of operation, advertising, products, and other elements associated with the franchiser's business, in return for a financial commitment and the agreement to conduct business in accordance with the franchiser's standard of operations. Wendy's, McDonald's, H&R Block, and Holiday Inn are well-known franchisers with international visibility. Table 3-4 lists some of the top global franchises.

Franchise	Country	Ranking
McDonald's	United States	1
Subway	United States	2
InterContinental Hotels and Resorts	United Kingdom	8
Carrefour	France	16
DIA	Spain	19
Kumon	Japan	40
Tim Horton's	Canada	42
H&R Block	Canada	66
Cartridge World	Australia	78
Husse	United States	96

TABLE 3-4
Top Global Franchises

Source: "Top 100 Global Franchises—Rankings," Franchise Direct, www.franchisedirect.com/top100globalfranchises/rankings/ (accessed February 29, 2016).

Licensing and franchising enable a company to enter the international marketplace without spending large sums of money abroad or hiring or transferring personnel to handle overseas affairs. They also minimize problems associated with shipping costs, tariffs, and trade restrictions, and they allow the firm to establish goodwill for its products in a foreign market, which will help the company if it decides to produce or market its products directly in the foreign country at some future date. However, if the licensee (or franchisee) does not maintain high standards of quality, the product's image may be hurt; therefore, it is important for the licensor to monitor its products overseas and to enforce its quality standards.

Contract Manufacturing

Contract manufacturing occurs when a company hires a foreign company to produce a specified volume of the firm's product to specification; the final product carries the domestic firm's name. Spalding, for example, relies on contract manufacturing for its sports equipment; Reebok uses Korean contract manufacturers to manufacture many of its athletic shoes.

contract manufacturing
the hiring of a foreign company to produce a specified volume of the initiating company's product to specification; the final product carries the domestic firm's name.

Outsourcing

Earlier, we defined outsourcing as transferring manufacturing or other tasks (such as information technology operations) to companies in countries where labor and supplies are less expensive. Many U.S. firms have outsourced tasks to India, Ireland, Mexico, and the Philippines, where there are many well-educated workers and significantly lower labor costs. Services, such as taxes or customer service, can also be outsourced.

Although outsourcing has become politically controversial in recent years amid concerns over jobs lost to overseas workers, foreign companies transfer tasks and jobs to U.S. companies—sometimes called *insourcing*—far more often than U.S. companies outsource tasks and jobs abroad.[71] However, some firms are bringing their outsourced jobs back after concerns that foreign workers were not adding enough value. Companies such as General Electric and Caterpillar are returning to the United

Disney has opened to theme parks in China, one in Shanghai and the other in Hong Kong.

© Xinhua/Alamy Stock Photo

offshoring
the relocation of business processes by a company or subsidiary to another country. Offshoring is different than outsourcing because the company retains control of the offshored processes.

joint venture
a partnership established for a specific project or for a limited time.

strategic alliance
a partnership formed to create competitive advantage on a worldwide basis.

direct investment
the ownership of overseas facilities.

States due to increasing labor costs in places such as China, the expense of shipping products across the ocean, and fears of fraud or intellectual property theft. Companies from other countries have also been moving some of their production to the United States; Caterpillar and Ford bought production of some of its excavators and medium-duty commercial trucks back to the United States.[72]

Offshoring

Offshoring is the relocation of a business process by a company, or a subsidiary, to another country. Offshoring is different than outsourcing: the company retains control of the process because it is not subcontracting to a different company. Companies may choose to offshore for a number of reasons, ranging from lower wages, skilled labor, or taking advantage of time zone differences in order to offer services around the clock. Some banks have chosen not to outsource because of concerns about data security in other countries. These institutions may instead engage in offshoring, which allows a company more control over international operations because the offshore office is an extension of the company. Shell, for example, opened a delivery center in India and moved its global IT jobs to that area.[73]

Joint Ventures and Alliances

Many countries, particularly LDCs, do not permit direct investment by foreign companies or individuals. A company may also lack sufficient resources or expertise to operate in another country. In such cases, a company that wants to do business in another country may set up a **joint venture** by finding a local partner (occasionally, the host nation itself) to share the costs and operation of the business. Qualcomm formed a joint venture with Chinese chip maker Semiconductor Manufacturing International Corporation to produce semiconductors. Qualcomm hopes this joint venture will help it to gain a foothold in selling chips in the Chinese market.[74]

In some industries, such as automobiles and computers, strategic alliances are becoming the predominant means of competing. A **strategic alliance** is a partnership formed to create competitive advantage on a worldwide basis. In such industries, international competition is so fierce and the costs of competing on a global basis are so high that few firms have the resources to go it alone, so they collaborate with other companies. An example of a strategic alliance is the partnership between LinkedIn and accounting firm Ernst & Young. The companies hope to use their combined expertise to assist other companies in using technology, social networking, and sales effectively.[75]

Direct Investment

Companies that want more control and are willing to invest considerable resources in international business may consider **direct investment,** the ownership of overseas facilities. Direct investment may involve the development and operation of new facilities—such as when Starbucks opens a new coffee shop in Japan—or the purchase of all or part of an existing operation in a foreign country. UPS invested in tech startup Ally Commerce Inc. to give it greater access to online sales.[76]

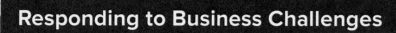

Disney China: It's a Big World after All

Disney entered unfamiliar territory when it began work on Shanghai Disneyland. The new $5.5 billion resort features six distinct Disney-themed lands, two hotels, and areas for shopping and dining. As part of its multinational strategy, Disney incorporated Chinese heritage into the design of the resort, resulting in unique attributes not found in other Disney parks. In addition to the first ever pirate-themed park, Shanghai Disneyland features an area where Chinese zodiac animals are represented by Disney and Pixar characters. The park also includes Tomorrowland, a setting with Chinese-inspired attractions and entertainment.

Yet Disney went even further to ensure its parks aligned with Chinese norms. In China, extended families often travel together, and because there was a one-child limit, adults often outnumber children. Disney responded by designing more entertainment options for parents and grandparents accompanying children, recognizing that the new park must appeal to adults as well as children.

When entering unfamiliar markets, companies are susceptible to unforeseen challenges. For Disney, this challenge came in the form of air pollution in Shanghai. To combat the bad publicity of smoggy skies, the Chinese government forced the closure of more than 150 factories near the park. Indeed, it appears that both Disney and Shanghai have a vested interested in the new park's public reception. However, its true success will likely hinge on how well classic Disney themes and Chinese cultural elements merge.[77]

Discussion Questions

1. What elements are part of Disney's multinational strategy of entering China?
2. Why does Disney's new park in Shanghai, China, need to appeal to adults?
3. What are some unique attractions at Shanghai Disneyland?

The highest level of international business involvement is the **multinational corporation (MNC)**, a corporation, such as IBM or ExxonMobil, that operates on a worldwide scale, without significant ties to any one nation or region. Table 3-5 lists 10 well-known multinational corporations. MNCs are more than simple corporations. They often have greater assets than some of the countries in which they do

multinational corporation (MNC)
a corporation that operates on a worldwide scale, without significant ties to any one nation or region.

TABLE 3-5
Large Multinational Companies

Company	Country	Description
Royal Dutch Shell	Netherlands	Oil and gas; largest company in the world in terms of revenue
Toyota	Japan	Largest automobile manufacturer in the world
Walmart	United States	Largest retailer in the world; largest private employer in the world
Siemens	Germany	Engineering and electronics; largest engineering company in Europe
Nestlé	Switzerland	Nutritional, snack-food, and health-related consumer goods
Samsung	South Korea	Subsidiaries specializing in electronics, electronic components, telecommunications equipment, medical equipment, and more
Unilever	United Kingdom	Consumer goods including cleaning and personal care, foods, beverages
Boeing	United States	Aerospace and defense; largest U.S. exporter
Lenovo	China	Computer technology; highest share of PC market
Subway	United States	Largest fast-food chain; fastest growing franchises in 105 countries

Airbnb is a website for people to list, find, and rent lodging from across the world. Because it did not operate as a brick-and-mortar business, Airbnb was able to get involved in international business almost immediately.

© ArthurStock/Shutterstock

business. Nestlé, with headquarters in Switzerland, operates more than 400 factories around the world and receives revenues from Europe; North, Central, and South America; Africa; and Asia.[78] The Royal Dutch/Shell Group, one of the world's major oil producers, is another MNC. Its main offices are located in The Hague and London. Other MNCs include BASF, British Petroleum, Matsushita, Mitsubishi, Siemens, Toyota, and Unilever. Many MNCs have been targeted by antiglobalization activists at global business forums, and some protests have turned violent. The activists contend that MNCs increase the gap between rich and poor nations, misuse and misallocate scarce resources, exploit the labor markets in LDCs, and harm their natural environments.[79]

International Business Strategies

Contrast two basic strategies used in international business.

Planning in a global economy requires businesspeople to understand the economic, legal, political, and sociocultural realities of the countries in which they will operate. These factors will affect the strategy a business chooses to use outside its own borders.

Developing Strategies

multinational strategy
a plan, used by international companies, that involves customizing products, promotion, and distribution according to cultural, technological, regional, and national differences.

Companies doing business internationally have traditionally used a **multinational strategy,** customizing their products, promotion, and distribution according to cultural, technological, regional, and national differences. When McDonald's opened its first restaurant in Vietnam, it offered its traditional menu items as well as McPork sandwiches specifically targeted toward Vietnam consumers.[80] Many soap and detergent manufacturers have adapted their products to local water conditions, washing equipment, and washing habits. For customers in some LDCs, Colgate-Palmolive Co. has developed an inexpensive, plastic, hand-powered washing machine for use in households that have no electricity. Even when products are standardized, advertising often has to be modified to adapt to language and cultural differences. Also, celebrities used in advertising in the United States may be unfamiliar to foreign consumers and thus would not be effective in advertising products in other countries.

global strategy (globalization)
a strategy that involves standardizing products (and, as much as possible, their promotion and distribution) for the whole world, as if it were a single entity.

More and more companies are moving from this customization strategy to a **global strategy (globalization),** which involves standardizing products (and, as much as possible, their promotion and distribution) for the whole world, as if it were a single entity. Examples of globalized products are American clothing, movies, music, and cosmetics. Social media sites are an important channel brands are using to connect with their global customers. 3M, Pampers, and Corona had the highest engagement with their global followers on Twitter.[81]

Before moving outside their own borders, companies must conduct environmental analyses to evaluate the potential of and problems associated with various markets and to determine what strategy is best for doing business in those markets. Failure to do so may result in losses and even negative publicity. Some companies rely on local managers to gain greater insights and faster response to changes within a country. Astute businesspeople today "think globally, act locally." That is, while constantly being aware of the total picture, they adjust their firms' strategies to conform to local needs and tastes.

Managing the Challenges of Global Business

As we've pointed out in this chapter, many past political barriers to trade have fallen or been minimized, expanding and opening new market opportunities. Managers who can meet the challenges of creating and implementing effective and sensitive business strategies for the global marketplace can help lead their companies to success. For example, the Commercial Service is the global business solutions unit of the U.S. Department of Commerce that offers U.S. firms wide and deep practical knowledge of international markets and industries, a unique global network, inventive use of information technology, and a focus on small and mid-sized businesses. Another example is the benchmarking of best international practices that benefits U.S. firms, which is conducted by the network of CIBERs (Centers for International Business Education and Research) at leading business schools in the United States. These CIBERs are funded by the U.S. government to help U.S. firms become more competitive globally. A major element of the assistance that these governmental organizations can provide firms (especially for small and medium-sized firms) is knowledge of the internationalization process.[82] Small businesses, too, can succeed in foreign markets when their managers have carefully studied those markets and prepared and implemented appropriate strategies. Being globally aware is therefore an important quality for today's managers and will become a critical attribute for managers of the 21st century.

⊖ So You Want a Job in Global Business

Have you always dreamt of traveling the world? Whether backpacking your way through Central America or sipping espressos at five-star European restaurants is your style, the increasing globalization of business might just give you your chance to see what the world has to offer. Most new jobs will have at least some global component, even if located within the United States, so being globally aware and keeping an open mind to different cultures is vital in today's business world. Think about the 1.3 billion consumers in China who have already purchased mobile phones. In the future, some of the largest markets will be in Asia.

Many jobs discussed in chapters throughout this book tend to have strong international components. For example, product management and distribution management are discussed as marketing careers in the chapter "Dimensions of Marketing Strategy." As more and more companies sell products around the globe, their function, design, packaging, and promotions need to be culturally relevant to many different people in many different places. Products very often cross multiple borders before reaching the final consumer, both in their distribution and through the supply chain to produce the products.

Jobs exist in export and import management, product and pricing management, distribution and transportation, and advertising. Many "born global" companies such as Google operate virtually and consider all countries their market. Many companies sell their products through eBay and other Internet sites and never leave the United States. Today, communication and transportation facilitates selling and buying products worldwide with delivery in a few days. You may have sold or purchased a product on eBay outside the United States without thinking about how easy and accessible international markets are to business. If you have, welcome to the world of global business.

To be successful, you must have an idea not only of differing regulations from country to country, but of different language, ethics, and communication styles and varying needs and wants of international markets. From a regulatory side, you may need to be aware of laws related to intellectual property, copyrights, antitrust, advertising, and pricing in every country. Translating is never only about translating the language. Perhaps even more important is ensuring that your message gets through. Whether on a product label or in advertising or promotional materials, the use of images and words varies widely across the globe.

Review Your Understanding

Explore some of the factors within the international trade environment that influence business.

International business is the buying, selling, and trading of goods and services across national boundaries. Importing is the purchase of products and raw materials from another nation; exporting is the sale of domestic goods and materials to another nation. A nation's balance of trade is the difference in value between its exports and imports; a negative balance of trade is a trade deficit. The difference between the flow of money into a country and the flow of money out of it is called the balance of payments. An absolute or comparative advantage in trade may determine what products a company from a particular nation will export.

Investigate some of the economic, legal, political, social, cultural, and technological barriers to international business.

Companies engaged in international trade must consider the effects of economic, legal, political, social, and cultural differences between nations. Economic barriers are a country's level of development (infrastructure) and exchange rates. Wide-ranging legal and political barriers include differing laws (and enforcement), tariffs, exchange controls, quotas, embargoes, political instability, and war. Ambiguous cultural and social barriers involve differences in spoken and body language, time, holidays and other observances, and customs.

Specify some of the agreements, alliances, and organizations that may encourage trade across international boundaries.

Among the most important promoters of international business are the General Agreement on Tariffs and Trade, the World Trade Organization, the North American Free Trade Agreement, the European Union, the Asia-Pacific Economic Cooperation, the Association of Southeast Asian Nations, the World Bank, and the International Monetary Fund.

Summarize the different levels of organizational involvement in international trade.

A company may be involved in international trade at several levels, each requiring a greater commitment of resources and effort, ranging from importing/exporting to multinational corporations.

Countertrade agreements occur at the import/export level and involve bartering products for other products instead of currency. At the next level, a trading company links buyers and sellers in different countries to foster trade. In licensing and franchising, one company agrees to allow a foreign company the use of its company name, products, patents, brands, trademarks, raw materials, and production processes in exchange for a flat fee or royalty. Contract manufacturing occurs when a company hires a foreign company to produce a specified volume of the firm's product to specification; the final product carries the domestic firm's name. A joint venture is a partnership in which companies from different countries agree to share the costs and operation of the business. The purchase of overseas production and marketing facilities is direct investment. Outsourcing, a form of direct investment, involves transferring manufacturing to countries where labor and supplies are cheap. Offshoring is the relocation of business processes by a company or subsidiary to another country; it differs from outsourcing because the company retains control of the offshored processes. A multinational corporation is one that operates on a worldwide scale, without significant ties to any one nation or region.

Contrast two basic strategies used in international business.

Companies typically use one of two basic strategies in international business. A multinational strategy customizes products, promotion, and distribution according to cultural, technological, regional, and national differences. A global strategy (globalization) standardizes products (and, as much as possible, their promotion and distribution) for the whole world, as if it were a single entity.

Assess the opportunities and problems facing a small business that is considering expanding into international markets.

The "Solve the Dilemma" feature at the end of this chapter presents a small business considering expansion into international markets. Based on the material provided in the chapter, analyze the business's position, evaluating specific markets, anticipating problems, and exploring methods of international involvement.

Revisit the World of Business

1. Why is it necessary for fast-food restaurants to customize their menu items when entering different countries?

2. Describe how Domino's became so popular with consumers in India.

3. Why did Pizza Hut not do well in sub-Saharan Africa initially, and how is it changing its tactics this time around?

Learn the Terms

absolute advantage 75
Asia-Pacific Economic Cooperation (APEC) 89
Association of Southeast Asian Nations (ASEAN) 90
balance of payments 77
balance of trade 76
cartel 82
comparative advantage 75
contract manufacturing 93
countertrade agreements 92
direct investment 94
dumping 82
embargo 81

European Union (EU) 87
exchange controls 81
exchange rate 78
exporting 75
franchising 92
General Agreement on Tariffs and Trade (GATT) 85
global strategy (globalization) 96
import tariff 80
importing 76
infrastructure 78
international business 74
International Monetary Fund (IMF) 90
joint venture 94

licensing 92
multinational corporation (MNC) 95
multinational strategy 96
North American Free Trade Agreement (NAFTA) 85
offshoring 94
outsourcing 75
quota 81
strategic alliance 94
trade deficit 76
trading company 92
World Bank 90
World Trade Organization (WTO) 85

Check Your Progress

1. Distinguish between an absolute advantage and a comparative advantage. Cite an example of a country that has an absolute advantage and one with a comparative advantage.

2. What effect does devaluation have on a nation's currency? Can you think of a country that has devaluated or revaluated its currency? What have been the results?

3. What effect does a country's economic development have on international business?

4. How do political issues affect international business?

5. What is an import tariff? A quota? Dumping? How might a country use import tariffs and quotas to control its balance of trade and payments? Why can dumping result in the imposition of tariffs and quotas?

6. How do social and cultural differences create barriers to international trade? Can you think of any additional social or cultural barriers (other than those mentioned in this chapter) that might inhibit international business?

7. Explain how a countertrade agreement can be considered a trade promoter. How does the World Trade Organization encourage trade?

8. At what levels might a firm get involved in international business? What level requires the least commitment of resources? What level requires the most?

9. Compare and contrast licensing, franchising, contract manufacturing, and outsourcing.

10. Compare multinational and global strategies. Which is better? Under what circumstances might each be used?

Get Involved

1. If the United States were to impose additional tariffs on cars imported from Japan, what would happen to the price of Japanese cars sold in the United States? What would happen to the price of American cars? What action might Japan take to continue to compete in the U.S. automobile market?

2. Although NAFTA has been controversial, it has been a positive factor for U.S. firms desiring to engage in international business. What industries and specific companies have the greatest potential for opening stores in Canada and Mexico? What opportunities exist for small businesses that cannot afford direct investment in Mexico and Canada?

3. Identify a local company that is active in international trade. What is its level of international business involvement and why? Analyze the threats and opportunities it faces in foreign markets, as well as its strengths and weaknesses in meeting those challenges. Based on your analysis, make some recommendations for the business's future involvement in international trade. (Your instructor may ask you to share your report with the class.)

Build Your Skills

Global Awareness

Background

As American businesspeople travel the globe, they encounter and must quickly adapt to a variety of cultural norms quite different from the United States. When encountering individuals from other parts of the world, the best attitude to adopt is, "Here is my way. Now what is yours?" The more you see that you are part of a complex world and that your culture is different from, not better than, others, the better you will communicate and the more effective you will be in a variety of situations. It takes time, energy, understanding, and tolerance to learn about and appreciate other cultures. Naturally you're more comfortable doing things the way you've always done them. Remember, however, that this fact will also be true of the people from other cultures with whom you are doing business.

Task

You will "travel the globe" by answering questions related to some of the cultural norms that are found in other countries. Form groups of four to six class members and determine the answers to the following questions. Your instructor has the answer key, which will allow you to determine your group's Global Awareness IQ, which is based on a maximum score of 100 points (10 points per question).

Match the country with the cultural descriptor provided.

A. Saudi Arabia	**F.** China
B. Japan	**G.** Greece
C. Great Britain	**H.** Korea
D. Germany	**I.** India
E. Venezuela	**J.** Mexico

_____ 1. When people in this country table a motion, they want to discuss it. In America, "to table a motion" means to put off discussion.

_____ 2. In this country, special forms of speech called *keigo* convey status among speakers. When talking with a person in this country, one should know the person's rank. People from this country will not initiate a conversation without a formal introduction.

_____ 3. People from this country pride themselves on enhancing their image by keeping others waiting.

_____ 4. When writing a business letter, people in this country like to provide a great deal of background information and detail before presenting their main points.

_____ 5. For a man to inquire about another man's wife (even a general question about how she is doing) is considered very offensive in this country.

_____ 6. When in this country, you are expected to negotiate the price on goods you wish to purchase.

_____ 7. While North Americans want to decide the main points at a business meeting and leave the details for later, people in this country need to have all details decided before the meeting ends to avoid suspicion and distrust.

_____ 8. Children in this country learn from a very early age to look down respectfully when talking to those of higher status.

_____ 9. Until recently in this country, the eldest male was legally the ruler of the household, and the custom was to keep the women hidden.

_____ 10. Many businesspeople from the United States experience frustration because yes does not always mean the same thing in other cultures. For example, the word *yes* in this country means, "OK, I want to respect you and not offend you." It does not necessarily show agreement.

Solve the Dilemma

Global Expansion or Business as Usual?

Audiotech Electronics, founded in 1959 by a father and son, currently operates a 35,000-square-foot factory with 75 employees. The company produces control consoles for television and radio stations and recording studios. It is involved in every facet of production—designing the systems, installing the circuits in its computer boards, and even manufacturing and painting the metal cases housing the consoles. The company's products are used by all the major broadcast and cable networks. The firm's newest products allow television

Assess the opportunities and problems facing a small business that is considering expanding into international markets.

correspondents to simultaneously hear and communicate with their counterparts in different geographic locations. Audiotech has been very successful meeting its customers' needs efficiently.

Audiotech sales have historically been strong in the United States, but recently, growth is stagnating. Even though Audiotech is a small, family-owned firm, it believes it should evaluate and consider global expansion.

Discussion Questions

1. What are the key issues that need to be considered in determining global expansion?
2. What are some of the unique problems that a small business might face in global expansion that larger firms would not?
3. Should Audiotech consider a joint venture? Should it hire a sales force of people native to the countries it enters?

Build Your Business Plan

Business in a Borderless World

Think about the good/service you are contemplating for your business plan. If it is an already established good or service, try to find out if the product is currently being sold internationally. If not, can you identify opportunities to do so in the future? What countries do you think would respond most favorably to your product? What problems would you encounter if you attempted to export your product to those countries?

If you are thinking of creating a new good or service for your business plan, think about the possibility of eventually

marketing that product in another country. What countries or areas of the world do you think would be most responsive to your product?

Are there countries the United States has trade agreements or alliances with that would make your entry into the market easier? What would be the economic, social, cultural, and technological barriers you would have to recognize before entering the prospective country(ies)? Think about the specific cultural differences that would have to be taken into consideration before entering the prospective country.

See for Yourself Videocase

Electra Bikes: Better, Cooler, Awesomer!

Twenty-three years ago, Swiss snowboard designer Benno Bänziger and his German business partner Jeano Erforth decided they wanted to make bike riding fun again. At the time, cruiser bikes were out of style and were in danger of disappearing. Bänziger and Erforth converted their T-shirt company in Vista, California, into a bicycle manufacturer called Electra Bikes. However, they did not want to manufacture just any type of cruiser bike. They wanted their bikes to look hip with a vintage style, based off rockabilly culture and resembling the look of muscle cars. The shop went from selling a few hundred the first year it was in business to becoming a global sensation. Electra eventually caught the attention of Trek Bicycle Corporation, which acquired the firm in 2014.

As Electra began to expand globally, it found that it had a comparative advantage its bigger competitors did not have. First of all, many bike enthusiasts worldwide appreciated the vintage look combined with the most up-to-date technology of Electra bicycles. One particular advantage Electra has is its patented Flat Foot Technology®. This technology enables better leg extension, making the ride more comfortable. Because of its patent, Electra is currently the only company that can use the technology it developed. These advantages combined with its "genuine Americana message" proved to be a hit overseas.

Global expansion offered Electra the unique opportunity to reach new market niches of bicycle enthusiasts. It started slowly, expanding first into markets that were closer to the United States, including Canada and Australia. The company currently has distributors in 26 countries that sell its bikes. In addition to offices in the United States, Electra opened a European office that supports sales for 25 countries. Like many other firms, Electra outsources production to Taiwan and China. Using freight ships, the firm ships its products to markets such as Australia, the European Union, and the domestic American market. By outsourcing production, the firm is able to save more money than if it had the bikes produced in the United States.

Like most companies that expand globally, Electra is subject to import duties that can vary depending upon where the bicycles are manufactured. It is also subject to regulations that vary from country to country. Sometimes, Electra must have additional features due to safety laws. For instance, some bikes shipped to certain countries have front brakes, while others have lighting systems or fenders. While these different features add to costs, they ensure that Electra stays on the right side of the laws within the countries in which they do business.

Regulations can vary by type of product as well. Kevin Cox, president of Electra Bicycle, describes how Electra had to take this into consideration when designing a bicycle with a motor called the Townie Go. According to Cox, "There are certain speed regulations that exist, and those regulations are different between Europe and [the] U.S." The company chose to adopt the stricter U.S. standard, although it meant a slower speed because it would give Electra "one product platform that has global reach."

Electra also faces economic and geographical challenges as well. "Currency fluctuation in Asia, that's a big one because that in and of itself can skew the cost of our bicycle," Cox says. Additionally, certain areas such as Europe and many parts of the United States have highly seasonal weather that limits bike riding to certain times of the year. These weather variations cause fluctuations in demand based upon the season. However, Cox also points out that having a global reach helps to balance out these fluctuations "because while it's winter in the U.S., I'm enjoying a nice summer in Australia." In other words, there is a constant worldwide demand for bicycles year-round.

As Electra expanded globally, the infrastructure of operating a global network became more complex. This is why, in 2014, Electra made the decision to sell the company to Trek. The decision benefits Electra because it can now utilize Trek's extensive network to reach new markets. At the same time, tapping into Trek's distribution networks frees Electra to focus less on distribution concerns and more on its core competency: developing high-quality, durable, vintage bicycles.[83]

Discussion Questions

1. Describe how Electra maintains a worldwide comparative advantage.

2. What are some global difficulties Electra had to overcome when it expanded into different countries?

3. Why did Electra—which markets itself with a "genuine Americana" message—decide to outsource production to Asia? Do you believe this is appropriate?

You can find the related video in the Video Library in Connect. Ask your instructor how you can access Connect.

Team Exercise

Visit Transparency International's Country Corruption Index website: http://www.transparency.org/cpi2015. Form groups and select two countries. Research some of the economic, ethical, legal, regulatory, and political barriers that would have an impact on international trade. Be sure to pair a fairly ethical country with a fairly unethical country (Sweden with Myanmar, Australia with Haiti). Report your findings.

Endnotes

1. Adam Janofsky, "Why Burger King Is Selling a Squid-Ink Burger," *The Wall Street Journal,* May 26, 2015, p. R4; Janice Kew and Chris Spillane, "Pizza Hut Wants to Roll Its Dough in Africa," *Bloomberg Businessweek,* February 19, 2015, pp. 24–25; Saritha Rai, "How Dominos Won India," *Fast Company,* February 2015, pp. 54–58.

2. "Subway," *Fortune,* http://www.forbes.com/companies/subway/ (accessed February 26, 2016).

3. Nick Parker, "BMWs Billion-Dollar Bet on Mexico," *CNN Money,* July 8, 2014, http://money.cnn.com/2014/07/08/news/companies/bmw-mexico/ (accessed February 29, 2016).

4. Deloitte, "2016 Global Manufacturing Competitiveness Index," 2016, http://www2.deloitte.com/global/en/pages/about-deloitte/articles/global-manufacturing-competitiveness-index.html (accessed February 29, 2016).

5. Starbucks, "Starbucks Coffee International," http://www.starbucks.com/business/international-stores (accessed February 26, 2016).

6. Elisabeth Sullivan, "Choose Your Words Wisely," *Marketing News,* February 15, 2008, p. 22.

7. Matt Rosoff, "China Has Passed Europe as Apple's No. 2 Market," *Business Insider,* April 27, 2015, http://www.businessinsider.com/china-apple-top-foreign-market-2015-4 (accessed February 29, 2016).

8. Statista, "Total Population in the United States from 2003 to 2013 (in millions)," 2013, www.statista.com/statistics/263762/total-population-of-the-united-states/ (accessed February 24, 2014).

9. Sullivan, "Choose Your Words Wisely."

10. Economist staff, "Europes Unlikely Star," *The Economist,* June 28, 2014, p. 13.

11. Paul Davidson, "We Produce More at Home with New Drilling Methods," *USA Today,* February 11, 2014, p. 1B.

12. U.S. Bureau of the Census, Foreign Trade Division, U.S. Trade in Goods and Services—Balance of Payments (BOP) Basis, February 5, 2016, www.census.gov/foreign-trade/statistics/historical/gands.pdf (accessed February 27, 2014).

13. Ibid.

14. Ibid.

15. Ian Bremmer, "Sea of Troubles," *Time* 185, no. 1 (2015), p. 18.

16. Economist staff, "Shaken, not stirred," *The Economist,* January 24, 2015, p. 48.

17. Yepoka Yeebo, "Cleaning Up Drug Lane," *Bloomberg Businessweek,* August 1, 2015, pp. 58–61; "Ghanaian SMS Start Up Tackles Fake Drug Scourge," mPedigree, http://mpedigree.net/articles/ghanaian-sms-start-tackles-fake-drug-scourge (accessed October 28, 2015); Bright Simons, "35 Innovators Under 35," *MIT Technology Review,* 2013, http://www.technologyreview.com/lists/innovators-under-35/2013/entrepreneur/bright-simons/ (accessed October 28, 2015); Tom Jackson, "mPedigree Moves into Ghanas Textile Industry," *Disrupt Africa,* March 5, 2015, http://disrupt-africa.com/2015/03/mpedigree-moves-ghanas-textile-industry/ (accessed October 28, 2015); "About Us," mPedigree, http://www.mpedigree.us/about-us (accessed October 28, 2015).

18. Anant Vijay Kala and Preetika Rana, "India Eases Retailer Requirements, Lifts Some Foreign Investment Limits," *The Wall Street Journal,* November 10, 2015, http://www.wsj.com/articles/india-eases-retailer-requirements-lifts-some-foreign-investment-limits-1447173462 (accessed February 29, 2016).

19. Joe Harpaz, "Will Irish Tax Law Change Stop Corporate Inversions?" *Forbes,* October 15, 2014, http://www.forbes.com/sites/joeharpaz/2014/10/15/will-irish-tax-law-change-stop-corporate-inversions/ (accessed February 26, 2016); Robert W. Wood, "Whopper? Microsoft Skirts Billions In Taxes, Google, HP & Apple Have It Their Way Too," *Forbes,* August 26, 2014, http://www.forbes.com/sites/robertwood/2014/08/26/whopper-microsoft-skirts-billions-in-taxes-google-hp-apple-have-it-their-way-too/#6142ec6546de (accessed February 26, 2016).

20. "The Restricted Zone in Mexico," Penner & Associates—Mexico Law Firm and Business Consulting for Mexico, www.mexicolaw.com/LawInfo17.htm (accessed February 29, 2016).

21. BSA, "Security Threats Rank as Top Reason Not to Use Unlicensed Software," http://globalstudy.bsa.org/2013/ (accessed February 29, 2016).

22. Sonja Elmquist, "U.S. Calls for 256% Tariff on Imports of Steel from China," *Bloomberg Business,* December 22, 2015, http://www.bloomberg.com/news/articles/2015-12-22/u-s-commerce-department-to-put-256-tariff-on-chinese-steel (accessed February 29, 2016).

23. Kitty Bean Yancey, "Back to Cuba: People-to-People Trips Get the Green Light," *USA Today,* August 4, 2011, p. 4A; Alan Gomez, "Feds Approve First U.S. Factory in Cuba," *USA Today,* February 16, 2016, p. 1B.

24. Kitty Bean Yancey and Laura Bly, "Door May Be Inching Open for Tourism," *USA Today,* February 20, 2008, p. A5; Sue Kirchhoff and Chris Woodyard, "Cuba Trade Gets New Opportunity," *USA Today,* February 20, 2008, p. B1.

25. European Commission, "EU Wins a WTO Dispute on Chinese Anti-Dumping Duties," February 13, 2015, http://trade.ec.europa.eu/doclib/press/index.cfm?id=1257 (accessed February 29, 2016).

26. Ibid.

27. Laurie Burkitt, "Tiffany Finds Sparkle in Overseas Markets," *The Wall Street Journal,* December 26, 2013, p. B4.

28. Julie Jargon, "Starbucks Shifts in Europe," *The Wall Street Journal,* November 30–December 1, 2013, p. B3.

29. "Slogans Gone Bad," Joe-ks, www.joe-ks.com/archives_apr2004/slogans_gone_bad.htm (accessed April 9, 2014).

30. Nina Lakhani, "Coca-Cola Apologizes for Indigenous People Ad Intended as 'Message of Unity,'" *The Guardian,* December 5, 2015, http://www.theguardian.com/world/2015/dec/05/coca-cola-mexico-ad-indigenous-people (accessed February 29, 2016).

31. J. Bonasia, "For Web, Global Reach Is Beauty—and Challenge," *Investor s Business Daily,* June 13, 2001, p. A6.

32. Gartner, "Gartner Says Worldwide PC Shipments Declined 9.5 Percent in Second Quarter of 2015," July 9, 2015, http://www.gartner.com/newsroom/id/3090817 (accessed February 29, 2016).

33. "What Is the WTO," World Trade Organization (n.d.), www.wto.org/english/thewto_e/whatis_e/whatis_e.htm (accessed April 9, 2014).

34. European Commission, "EU Wins a WTO Dispute on Chinese Anti-Dumping Duties."

35. "The North American Free Trade Agreement (NAFTA)," export.gov, http://export.gov/FTA/nafta/index.asp (accessed January 5, 2016).

36. Central Intelligence Agency, "Guide to Country Comparisons," *World Factbook,* https://www.cia.gov/library/publications/the-world-factbook/rankorder/rankorderguide.html (accessed January 8, 2016).

37. U.S. Census Bureau, "Trade in Goods with Canada," https://www.census.gov/foreign-trade/balance/c1220.html (accessed February 5, 2016).

38. Statistics Canada, "Table 1 Merchandise Trade: Canadas Top 10 Principal Trading Partners—Seasonally Adjusted, Current Dollars," December 5, 2014, http://www.statcan.gc.ca/daily-quotidien/141205/t141205b001-eng.htm (accessed January 5, 2016).

39. Central Intelligence Agency, "Guide to Country Comparisons."

40. U.S. Census Bureau, "Trade in Goods with Mexico," Foreign Trade, https://www.census.gov/foreign-trade/balance/c2010.html (accessed February 5, 2016).

41. Jen Wieczner, "Why 2014 Could Be Mexico s Year," *Fortune,* January 13, 2014, pp. 37–38.

42. "A Tale of Two Mexicos: North and South," *The Economist,* April 26, 2008, pp. 53–54.

43. U.S. Census Bureau, "Top Trading Partners—December 2013: Year-to-Date Total Trade," www.census.gov/foreign-trade/statistics/highlights/top/top1312yr.html (accessed February 29, 2016).

44. Pete Engardio and Geri Smith, "Business Is Standing Its Ground," *BusinessWeek,* April 20, 2009, pp. 34–39.

45. "Countries," European Union, http://europa.eu/about-eu/countries/index_en.htm (accessed February 29, 2016).

46. Central Intelligence Agency, "Country Comparison: GDP (Purchasing Power Parity)," *The World Factbook,* https://www.cia.gov/library/publications/resources/the-world-factbook/rankorder/2001rank.html (accessed February 29, 2016).

47. Stanley Reed, with Ariane Sains, David Fairlamb, and Carol Matlack, "The Euro: How Damaging a Hit?" *BusinessWeek,* September 29, 2003, p. 63; Irene Chapple, "How the Euro Became a Broken Dream," *CNN,* November 3, 2011, http://www.cnn.com/2011/09/23/business/europe-euro-creation-maastricht-chapple/ (accessed February 29, 2016).

48. Matthew Dalton, "EU Criticized for Effort To Overhaul GMO Rules," *The Wall Street Journal,* April 22, 2015, p. B3; "UPDATE 2—France Bolsters Ban on Genetically Modified Crops," *Reuters,* September 17, 2015, http://www.reuters.com/article/2015/09/17/france-gmo-idUSL5N11N16620150917 (accessed September 29, 2015); Monsanto, "Safety of Genetically Modified Sweet Corn," http://www.monsanto.com/products/pages/safety-of-gm-sweet-corn.aspx (accessed September 29, 2015).

49. Julia Fioretti, "EU watchdogs to apply right to be forgotten rule on Web worldwide," *Reuters,* November 26, 2014, http://www.reuters.com/article/2014/11/26/us-google-eu-privacy-idUSKCN0JA1HU20141126 (accessed January 16, 2015); The Economist staff, "Drawing the Line," *The Economist,* October 4, 2014, http://www.economist.com/news/international/21621804-google-grapples-consequences-controversial-ruling-boundary-between (accessed January 16, 2015); Samuel Gibbs, "European parliament votes yes on Google breakup motion," *The Guardian,* November 27, 2014, http://www.theguardian.com/technology/2014/nov/27/european-parliament-votes-yes-google-breakup-motion (accessed February 9, 2015).

50. Abigail Moses, "Greek Contagion Concern Spurs European Sovereign Default Risk to Record," *Bloomberg,* April 26, 2010, www.bloomberg.com/news/2010-04-26/greek-contagion-concern-spurs-european-sovereign-default-risk-to-record.html (accessed March 18, 2011).

51. James G. Neuger and Joe Brennan, "Ireland Weighs Aid as EU Spars over Debt-Crisis Remedy," *Bloomberg,* www.bloomberg.com/news/2010-11-16/ireland-discusses-financial-bailout-as-eu-struggles-to-defuse-debt-crisis.html (accessed March 18, 2011).

52. Charles Forelle and Marcus Walker, "Dithering at the Top Turned EU Crisis to Global Threat," *The Wall Street Journal,* December 29, 2011, p. A1; Jeff Cox, "US, Europe Face More Ratings Cuts in Coming Years," *CNBC,* January 20, 2012, www.cnbc.com/id/46072354?__source=google%7Ceditorspicks%7C&par=google (accessed January 20, 2012); Charles Forelle, "Greece Defaults and Tries to Move On," *The Wall Street Journal,* March 10, 2012, http://online.wsj.com/article/SB10001424052970204603004577270542625035960.html (accessed July 19, 2012).

53. Mac William Bishop and Alastair Jamieson, "'Brexit' Vote: Why Britain Could Quit E.U. and Why America Cares,"

NBC News, February 28, 2016, http://www.nbcnews.com/news/world/brexit-vote-why-britain-could-quit-e-u-why-america-n526386 (accessed February 29, 2016).

54. "Powerhouse Deutschland," *Bloomberg Businessweek,* January 3, 2011, p. 93; Alan S. Blinder, "The Euro Zone's German Crisis," *The Wall Street Journal,* http://online.wsj.com/article/SB1000142405297020343040457709431370790708.html (accessed February 29, 2016).

55. "About APEC," Asia-Pacific Economic Cooperation, http://www.apec.org/home.aspx (accessed January 5, 2016).

56. Ibid.

57. Bloomberg News, "China's Economic Growth Rate Is Seen Falling Until at Least 2018," *Bloomberg Businessweek,* December 15, 2015, http://www.bloomberg.com/news/articles/2015-12-15/china-s-economic-growth-rate-is-seen-falling-until-at-least-2018 (accessed February 29, 2016).

58. Charles Riley and Feng Ke, "China to Overtake U.S. as World's Top Trader," *CNN,* January 10, 2014, http://money.cnn.com/2014/01/10/news/economy/china-us-trade/ (accessed February 29, 2016).

59. U.S. Environmental Protection Agency, "Global Greenhouse Gas Emissions Data," www.epa.gov/climatechange/ghgemissions/global.html (accessed February 29, 2016); Joshua Keating, "China Passes U.S. as World's Largest Oil Importer," *Slate,* October 11, 2013, www.slate.com/blogs/the_world_/2013/10/11/china_now_world_s_largest_net_oil_importer_surpassing_united_states.html (accessed February 29, 2016).

60. "The Rise of Capitalism," *The Economist,* January 21, 2012, p. 11.

61. Dexter Roberts, "Corporate China's Black Hole of Debt," *Bloomberg Businessweek,* November 19–22, 2012, pp. 15–16.

62. Kathy Chu, "China Loses Edge on Labor Costs," *The Wall Street Journal,* December 3, 2015, B1, B4. b

63. "Overview," Association of Southeast Asian Nations, www.aseansec.org/64.htm (accessed April 10, 2014).

64. "ASEAN Economic Community: 12 Things to Know," *Asian Development Bank,* December 29, 2015, http://www.adb.org/features/asean-economic-community-12-things-know (accessed January 6, 2016).

65. Simon Long, "Safety in Numbers," *The Economist,* The World In 2015 Edition, p. 68.

66. R.C., "No Brussels Sprouts in Bali," *The Economist,* November 18, 2011, www.economist.com/blogs/banyan/2011/11/asean-summits (accessed February 29, 2016).

67. "Thaksin Times," *The Economist,* January 31, 2015, p. 31.

68. Eric Bellman, "Asia Seeks Integration Despite EU s Woes," *The Wall Street Journal,* July 22, 2011, p. A9.

69. David J. Lynch, "The IMF is . . . Tired Fund Struggles to Reinvent Itself," *USA Today,* April 19, 2006. p. B1.

70. WTSC Industrial Group website, http://www.wtsc.eu/ (accessed January 6, 2016).

71. Walter B. Wriston, "Ever Heard of Insourcing?" Commentary, *The Wall Street Journal,* March 24, 2004, p. A20.

72. James Hagerty and Mark Magnier, "Companies Tiptoe Back toward 'Made in U.S.A.,'" *The Wall Street Journal,* January 13, 2015, http://www.wsj.com/articles/companies-tiptoe-back-toward-made-in-the-u-s-a-1421206289 (accessed February 29, 2016).

73. Sobia Khan, "Shell to Open Largest Offshore Delivery Centre Globally in Bengaluru," *Economic Times,* June 5, 2015, http://economictimes.indiatimes.com/jobs/shell-to-open-largest-offshore-delivery-centre-globally-in-bengaluru/articleshow/47548572.cms (accessed February 29, 2016).

74. Paul Mozer, "Qualcomm in Venture with Chinese Chip Maker," *The New York Times,* June 23, 2015, http://www.nytimes.com/2015/06/24/business/international/qualcomm-in-venture-with-chinese-chip-maker.html?_r=0 (accessed January 6, 2016).

75. Calum Fuller, "EY and LinkedIn announce strategic alliance," *Accountancy Age,* October 30, 2015, http://www.accountancyage.com/aa/news/2432737/ey-and-linkedin-announce-strategic-alliance (accessed January 6, 2016).

76. Laura Stevens, "UPS Invests to Learn about Direct Online Sales," *The Wall Street Journal,* September 30, 2015, http://www.wsj.com/articles/ups-invests-to-learn-about-direct-online-sales-1443654181 (accessed February 29, 2016).

77. Christopher Palmeri, "Shanghai Disneyland Is Customized for the Chinese Family," *Bloomberg,* July 20, 2015, http://www.bloomberg.com/news/articles/2015-07-09/shanghai-disneyland-is-customized-for-the-chinese-family (accessed September 16, 2015). Shanghai Disney Resort; https://www.shanghaidisneyresort.com.cn/en/about/disney-unveils-new-magic-in-shanghai/ (accessed September 16, 2015); Steve Mollman, "China Will Close 150 Factories to Make Sure Shanghai Disneyland Has Blue Skies," *Quartz,* September 8, 2015, http://qz.com/497132/china-will-close-150-factories-to-make-sure-shanghai-disneyland-has-blue-skies/ (accessed September 16, 2015).

78. Guo Changdong and Ren Ruqin, "Nestle CEO visits Tianjin," *China Daily,* August 12, 2010, www.chinadaily.com.cn/m/tianjin/e/2010-08/12/content_11146560.htm (accessed March 1, 2016); Nestlé, "How Many Factories Do You Have," http://www.nestle.com/ask-nestle/our-company/answers/how-many-factories-do-you-have (accessed March 1, 2016).

79. O. C. Ferrell, John Fraedrich, and Linda Ferrell, *Business Ethics,* 6th ed. (Boston: Houghton Mifflin, 2005), pp. 227–30.

80. Vu Trong Khanh, "Vietnam Gets Its First McDonald s," *The Wall Street Journal,* February 11, 2014, p. B4.

81. Kimberlee Morrison, "Who Are the Most (and Least) Engaged Brands on Twitter?" *Ad Week,* March 16, 2015, http://www.adweek.com/socialtimes/the-most-and-least-engaged-brands-on-twitter/617045 (accessed March 1, 2016).

82. Export.gov, www.export.gov/about/index.asp (accessed March 1, 2016); CIBER Web, http://CIBERWEB.msu.edu (accessed March 1, 2016).

83. McGraw-Hill video, http://www.viddler.com/embed/50051953/?f=1&autoplay=0&player=full&disablebranding=0 (accessed April 11, 2016); Brain Staff, "Trek Announces Acquisition of Electra," *Bicycle Retailer,* January 6, 2014, http://www.bicycleretailer.com/north-america/2014/01/06/trek-announces-acquisition-electra#.Vwu7TjArLIV (accessed April 11, 2016); Ron Callahan, "Electra Bicycle Company Opens Global Headquarters with Slowest Bicycle Race," *Bike World News,* November 10, 2012, http://www.bikeworldnews.com/2012/11/10/electra-bicycle-company-opens-global-headquarters-slowest-bicycle-race/ (accessed April 11, 2016); Electra Bicycle Company website, http://www.electrabike.com/ (accessed April 11, 2016).

PART 2

Starting and Growing a Business

© Ken Wolter/Shutterstock

4 Options for Organizing Business

Learning Objectives

After reading this chapter, you will be able to:

LO 4-1 Define and examine the advantages and disadvantages of the sole proprietorship form of organization.

LO 4-2 Identify two types of partnership and evaluate the advantages and disadvantages of the partnership form of organization.

LO 4-3 Describe the corporate form of organization and cite the advantages and disadvantages of corporations.

LO 4-4 Define and debate the advantages and disadvantages of mergers, acquisitions, and leveraged buyouts.

LO 4-5 Propose an appropriate organizational form for a startup business.

Enter the World of Business ⊖

Ace Is the Place: Or Is It?

Big-box retailers like Home Depot, Lowes, and online retailer Amazon.com have large selections of home improvement products at competitive prices. They are able to offer customer services such as same-day delivery that many smaller companies cannot. Yet their large size has not deterred Ace Hardware from gaining a significant share of the market.

Unlike its larger competitors, Ace Hardware is a co-op of more than 4,700 stores spread across the United States. Each Ace store is owned by an independent business owner. However, unlike a franchise, each store owner is a shareholder in the Ace Hardware co-op. Ace stores are much smaller than their big-box competitors, which means they retain more of a neighborhood feel and allow employees to form stronger relationships with consumers in the area. As a result, Ace ranks the highest in customer satisfaction for home-improvement chains. The co-op structure also enables Ace to leverage collective bargaining power to receive competitive pricing from suppliers.

Marketing is a team effort at Ace, with each store contributing toward a central advertising budget that collectively benefits the entire chain. Although Ace appeals to a growing consumer niche seeking the convenience of a smaller store, the chain is also taking steps to be more competitive with its big-box rivals. The co-op is experimenting with same day delivery and continually working to improve its image as a neighborhood store, a unique quality that its larger competitors lack.[1]

Introduction

The legal form of ownership taken by a business is seldom of great concern to you as a customer. When you eat at a restaurant, you probably don't care whether the restaurant is owned by one person (a sole proprietorship), has two or more owners who share the business (a partnership), or is an entity owned by many stockholders (a corporation); all you want is good food. If you buy a foreign car, you probably don't care whether the company that made it has laws governing its form of organization that are different from those for businesses in the United States. All businesses must select a form of organization that is most appropriate for their owners and the scope of their business. A business's legal form of ownership affects how it operates, how much it pays in taxes, and how much control its owners have.

This chapter examines three primary forms of business ownership—sole proprietorship, partnership, and corporation—and weighs the advantages and disadvantages of each. These forms are the most often used whether the business is a traditional bricks-and-mortar company, an online-only one, or a combination of both. We also take a look at S corporations, limited liability companies, and cooperatives and discuss some trends in business ownership. We also touch on one of the most common forms of organizations for nonprofits. You may wish to refer to Table 4-1 to compare the various forms of business ownership mentioned in the chapter.

Need help understanding forms of business ownership? Visit your Connect ebook video tab for a brief animated explanation.

Define and examine the advantages and disadvantages of the sole proprietorship form of organization.

sole proprietorships
businesses owned and operated by one individual; the most common form of business organization in the United States.

Sole Proprietorships

Sole proprietorships, businesses owned and operated by one individual, are the most common form of business organization in the United States. Common examples include many retailers such as restaurants, hair salons, flower shops, dog kennels, and independent grocery stores. Sole proprietors also include independent contractors who complete projects or engage in entrepreneurial activities for different organizations but who are not employees. These include drivers for Uber and those engaged in direct selling for firms such as Mary Kay, Avon, or Tupperware. Many sole proprietors focus on services—small retail stores, financial counseling, automobile

TABLE 4-1   Various Forms of Business Ownership

Structure	Ownership	Taxation	Liability	Use
Sole Proprietorship	One owner	Individual income taxed	Unlimited	Owned by a single individual and is the easiest way to conduct business
Partnership	Two or more owners	Individual owners' income taxed	Somewhat limited	Easy way for two individuals to conduct business
Corporation	Any number of shareholders	Corporate and shareholder taxed	Limited	A legal entity with shareholders or stockholders
S Corporation	Up to 100 shareholders	Taxed as a partnership	Limited	A legal entity with tax advantages for restricted number of shareholders
Limited Liability Company	Unlimited number of shareholders	Taxed as a partnership	Limited	Avoid personal lawsuits

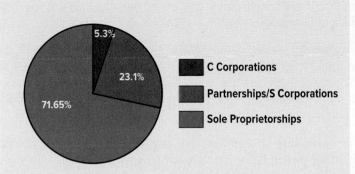

FIGURE 4-1

Comparison of Sole Proprietorships, Partnerships/S Corporations, and C Corporations

Source: Scott A. Hodge, "The U.S. Has More Individually Owned Businesses than Corporations," *Tax Foundation,* January 13, 2014, http://taxfoundation.org/blog/us-has-more-individually-owned-businesses-corporations (accessed March 2, 2016).

repair, child care, and the like—rather than on the manufacture of goods, which often requires large sums of money not available to most small businesses. As you can see in Figure 4-1, proprietorships far outnumber corporations. However, they net far fewer sales and less income. Differences between S corporations and C corporations will be discussed later in this text.

Sole proprietorships are typically small businesses employing fewer than 50 people. (We'll look at small businesses in greater detail in the chapter "Small Business, Entrepreneurship, and Franchising.") Sole proprietorships constitute approximately three-fourths of all businesses in the United States. It is interesting to note that women business owners are less likely to get access to credit than their male counterparts.[2] In many areas, small businesses make up the vast majority of the economy.

Advantages of Sole Proprietorships

Sole proprietorships are generally managed by their owners. Because of this simple management structure, the owner/manager can make decisions quickly. This is just one of many advantages of the sole proprietorship form of business.

Ease and Cost of Formation.   Forming a sole proprietorship is relatively easy and inexpensive. In some states, creating a sole proprietorship involves merely announcing the new business in the local newspaper. Other proprietorships, such as barber shops and restaurants, may require state and local licenses and permits because of the nature of the business. The cost of these permits may run from $25 to $100. Lawyers are not usually needed to create such enterprises, and the owner can usually take care of the required paperwork without much assistance.

Of course, an entrepreneur starting a new sole proprietorship must find a suitable site from which to operate the business, even if it is an online business. Some sole proprietors look no farther than their garage or a spare bedroom when seeking a workshop or office. Among the more famous businesses that sprang to life in their founders' homes are Google, Walt Disney, Dell, eBay, Hewlett-Packard, Apple, and Mattel.[3] Computers, personal copiers, scanners, and websites have been a boon for home-based businesses, permitting them to interact quickly with customers, suppliers, and others. Many independent salespersons and contractors can perform their work using a smartphone or tablet computer as they travel. E-mail and social networks have made it possible for many proprietorships to develop in the services area. Internet connections also allow small businesses to establish websites to promote their products and even to make low-cost long-distance phone calls with voice-over

Internet protocol (VoIP) technology. One of the most famous services using VoIP is Skype, which allows people to make free calls over the Internet.

Secrecy.   Sole proprietorships make possible the greatest degree of secrecy. The proprietor, unlike the owners of a partnership or corporation, does not have to discuss publicly his or her operating plans, minimizing the possibility that competitors can obtain trade secrets. Financial reports need not be disclosed, as do the financial reports of publicly owned corporations.

Distribution and Use of Profits.   All profits from a sole proprietorship belong exclusively to the owner. He or she does not have to share them with any partners or stockholders. The owner decides how to use the funds—for expansion of the business, for salary increases, for travel to purchase additional inventory, or to find new customers.

Flexibility and Control of the Business.   The sole proprietor has complete control over the business and can make decisions on the spot without anyone else's approval. This control allows the owner to respond quickly to competitive business conditions or to changes in the economy. The ability to quickly change prices or products can provide a competitive advantage for the business.

Government Regulation.   Sole proprietorships have the most freedom from government regulation. Many government regulations—federal, state, and local—apply only to businesses that have a certain number of employees, and securities laws apply only to corporations that issue stock. Nonetheless, sole proprietors must ensure that they follow all laws that do apply to their business. For example, sole proprietorships must be careful to obey employee and consumer protection regulation.

Taxation.   Profits from sole proprietorships are considered personal income and are taxed at individual tax rates. The owner, therefore, pays one income tax that includes the business and individual income. Another tax benefit is that a sole proprietor is allowed to establish a tax-exempt retirement account or a tax-exempt profit-sharing account. Such accounts are exempt from current income tax, but payments taken after retirement are taxed when they are received.

Many local restaurants are sole proprietorships.
© Image Source

Closing the Business.   A sole proprietorship can be dissolved easily. No approval of co-owners or partners is necessary. The only legal condition is that all financial obligations must be paid or resolved. If a proprietor does a going-out-of-business sale, most states require that the business actually close.

Disadvantages of Sole Proprietorships

What may be seen as an advantage by one person may turn out to be a disadvantage to another. For profitable businesses managed by capable owners, many of the following factors do not cause problems. On the other hand, proprietors starting out with little management experience and little money are likely to encounter many of the disadvantages.

Unlimited Liability.   The sole proprietor has unlimited liability in meeting the debts of the business. In other words, if the business cannot pay its creditors, the owner may be forced to use personal, nonbusiness holdings such as a car or a home to pay off the debts. There are only a few states in which houses and homesteads cannot be taken by creditors, even if the proprietor declares bankruptcy. The more wealth an individual has, the greater is the disadvantage of unlimited liability.

Limited Sources of Funds.   Among the relatively few sources of money available to the sole proprietorship are banks, friends, family, the Small Business Administration, or his or her own funds. The owner's personal financial condition determines his or her credit standing. Additionally, sole proprietorships may have to pay higher interest rates on funds borrowed from banks than do large corporations because they are considered greater risks. More proprietors are using nonbank financial institutions for transactions that charge higher interest rates than banks. Often, the only way a sole proprietor can borrow for business purposes is to pledge a car, a house, other real estate, or other personal assets to guarantee the loan. If the business fails, the owner may lose the personal assets as well as the business. Publicly owned corporations, in contrast, can not only obtain funds from commercial banks but can sell stocks and bonds to the public to raise money. If a public company goes out of business, the owners do not lose personal assets. However, they will lose the value of their stocks or bonds.

Limited Skills.   The sole proprietor must be able to perform many functions and possess skills in diverse fields such as management, marketing, finance, accounting, bookkeeping, and personnel management. Specialized professionals, such as accountants or attorneys, can be hired by businesses for help or advice. Sometimes, sole proprietors need assistance with certain business functions. For instance, Network Solutions offers web services for small and medium-sized businesses that want to grow their online presence. The company offers website hosting, or storage space and access for websites, as well as tools to help build a website and online marketing services.[4] In the end, however, it is up to the business owner to make the final decision in all areas of the business.

Lack of Continuity.   The life expectancy of a sole proprietorship is directly linked to that of the owner and his or her ability to work. The serious illness of the owner could result in failure of the business if competent help cannot be found.

It is difficult to arrange for the sale of a proprietorship and, at the same time, assure customers that the business will continue to meet their needs. For instance, how does one sell a veterinary practice? A veterinarian's major asset is

Sole proprietorships often have greater difficulty attracting talented employees because of competition from larger companies.

© Blend Images/Alamy

Millennium Products Dominates Kombucha Market

Millennium Products Inc.

Founder: GT Dave

Founded: 1995, in Beverly Hills, California

Success: GT Dave's kombucha products, manufactured by Millennium Products Inc., is estimated to hold more than half of the $600 million kombucha beverages market.

GT Dave believes kombucha helped his mom beat breast cancer. In 1995, his mother Laraine was diagnosed with a deadly form of cancer, but the cancer never metastasized. Laraine credits this to her consumption of kombucha beverages. Kombucha is a green tea that ferments for a month with a culture of bacteria and yeast. The resulting probiotic beverage is thought to have health benefits. Laraine encouraged her son to sell the beverage on a wide scale. GT Dave called his company Millennium Products Inc. Although he incorporated Millennium Products, he owns 100 percent of the company.

Consumers loved the product, especially after Whole Foods picked it up. But in 2010, a crisis hit when tests demonstrated some beverages had too much alcohol to be sold as nonalcoholic and were pulled from shelves. However, rather than turning off customers, kombucha only grew in demand. GT Dave reformulated the product and now has a line of 17 flavors of kombucha beverages suitable for all ages as well as his original kombucha product available to those 21 years and older.[5]

Discussion Questions

1. What entrepreneurial qualities does GT Dave possess that has contributed toward his success?
2. What type of organization is GT Dave? Who owns the company?
3. What are some of the challenges GT Dave has faced in popularizing kombucha?

---

patients. If the vet dies suddenly, the equipment can be sold, but the patients will not necessarily remain loyal to the office. On the other hand, a veterinarian who wants to retire could take in a younger partner and sell the practice to the partner over time. One advantage to the partnership is that some of the customers are likely to stay with the business, even if ownership changes.

Lack of Qualified Employees.   It is sometimes difficult for a small sole proprietorship to match the wages and benefits offered by a large competing corporation because the proprietorship's profits may not be as high. In addition, there may be less room for advancement within a sole proprietorship, so the owner may have difficulty attracting and retaining qualified employees. On the other hand, the trend of large corporations downsizing and outsourcing tasks has created renewed opportunities for small businesses to acquire well-trained employees.

Taxation.   Although we listed taxation as an advantage for sole proprietorships, it can also be a disadvantage, depending on the proprietor's income. Under current tax rates, sole proprietors pay a higher marginal tax rate than do small corporations on income of less than $75,000. However, sole proprietorships avoid the double taxation of corporate and personal taxes that occurs with corporations. The tax effect often determines whether a sole proprietor chooses to incorporate his or her business.

Partnerships

LO 4-2

Identify two types of partnership and evaluate the advantages and disadvantages of the partnership form of organization.

One way to minimize the disadvantages of a sole proprietorship and maximize its advantages is to have more than one owner. Most states have a model law governing partnerships based on the Uniform Partnership Act. This law defines a **partnership** as "an association of two or more persons who carry on as co-owners of a business for profit." Partnerships are the least used form of business. They are typically larger than sole proprietorships but smaller than corporations.

I. Keep profit sharing equitable based on contributions.
2. Partners should have different skill sets or resource contributions.
3. Ethics and compliance is required.
4. Must maintain effective communication skills.
5. Maintain transparency with stakeholders.
6. Must be realistic in resource and financial management.
7. Previous experience related to business is helpful.
8. Maintain life balance in time spent on business.
9. Focus on customer satisfaction and product quality.
10. Maintain resources in line with sales and growth expectations and planning.

TABLE 4-2
Keys to Success in
Business Partnerships

Partnerships can be a fruitful form of business, as long as you follow some basic keys to success, which are outlined in Table 4-2.

Types of Partnership

There are two basic types of partnership: general partnership and limited partnership. A **general partnership** involves a complete sharing in the management of a business. In a general partnership, each partner has unlimited liability for the debts of the business. For example, Webco, a military retail service provider, is a general partnership with locations in the United States. These locations are strategic business units that focus on many product categories at once. This strategy has allowed the company to become a leader in category management in the military retail market, sustaining its business for more than 50 years.[6] Professionals such as lawyers, accountants, and architects often join together in general partnerships.

A **limited partnership** has at least one general partner, who assumes unlimited liability, and at least one limited partner, whose liability is limited to his or her investment in the business. Limited partnerships exist for risky investment projects where the chance of loss is great. The general partners accept the risk of loss; the limited partners' losses are limited to their initial investment. Limited partners do not participate in the management of the business but share in the profits in accordance with the terms of a partnership agreement. Usually the general partner receives a larger share of the profits after the limited partners have received their initial investment back. A *master limited partnership* (MLP) is a limited partnership traded on securities exchanges. MLPs have the tax benefits of a limited partnership but the liquidity (ability to convert assets into cash) of a corporation. Popular examples of MLPs include oil and gas companies and pipeline operators.[7]

Articles of Partnership

Articles of partnership are legal documents that set forth the basic agreement between partners. Most states require articles of partnership, but even if they are not required, it makes good sense for partners to draw them up. Articles of partnership usually list the money or assets that each partner has contributed (called *partnership capital*), state each partner's individual management role or duty, specify how the profits and losses of the

partnership
a form of business organization defined by the Uniform Partnership Act as "an association of two or more persons who carry on as co-owners of a business for profit."

general partnership
a partnership that involves a complete sharing in both the management and the liability of the business.

limited partnership
a business organization that has at least one general partner, who assumes unlimited liability, and at least one limited partner, whose liability is limited to his or her investment in the business.

articles of partnership
legal documents that set forth the basic agreement between partners.

TABLE 4-3
Issues and Provisions in
Articles of Partnership

I. Name, purpose, location
2. Duration of the agreement
3. Authority and responsibility of each partner
4. Character of partners (i.e., general or limited, active or silent)
5. Amount of contribution from each partner
6. Division of profits or losses
7. Salaries of each partner
8. How much each partner is allowed to withdraw
9. Death of partner
10. Sale of partnership interest
II. Arbitration of disputes
12. Required and prohibited actions
13. Absence and disability
14. Restrictive covenants
15. Buying and selling agreements

partnership will be divided among the partners, and describe how a partner may leave the partnership as well as any other restrictions that might apply to the agreement. Table 4-3 lists some of the issues and provisions that should be included in articles of partnership.

Advantages of Partnerships

Law firms, accounting firms, and investment firms with several hundred partners have partnership agreements that are quite complicated in comparison with the partnership agreement among two or three people owning a computer repair shop. The advantages must be compared with those offered by other forms of business organization, and not all apply to every partnership.

Ease of Organization.   Starting a partnership requires little more than drawing up articles of partnership. No legal charters have to be granted, but the name of the business should be registered with the state.

Availability of Capital and Credit.   When a business has several partners, it has the benefit of a combination of talents and skills and pooled financial resources. Partnerships tend to be larger than sole proprietorships and, therefore, have greater earning power and better credit ratings. Because many limited partnerships have

In 1996, Stanford students Sergey Brin and Larry Page partnered to form the search engine Google, now named Alphabet, as part of a research project. The company was incorporated in 1998 and is now the world's top search engine.

© Ben Margot/AP Images

Brew Hound Brewery No Longer a Lone Wolf

Kenny Thacker always dreamed about brewing beer, so after he became unemployed, the former construction worker set out to make his dream a reality. Using a $25,000 loan from his father, Thacker opened Brew Hound Brewery in 2012. The brewery proved popular with the locals, but nonetheless, the business tanked financially in the three years it was open. There were not enough customers in the small town where the brewery was located for Thacker to turn a profit. As a sole business owner, he did not have all the skills needed to succeed financially.

Help came when Thacker partnered with Frank Becker, a restaurant franchise manager, and Rick Cash, a retired manager from Philip Morris. The three men reopened Brew Hound Brewery in 2015, this time in a more desirable location where the brewery could develop a stronger customer base. The various business responsibilities of running the brewery were split up among the three men. Thacker focused on perfecting his brewing recipes, while his two partners addressed the marketing, operations and financing aspects of the business. The brewery was a hit when it opened. Finding the right business partners helped transform the fledgling brewery into a successful business. Revenue at the brewery approached $500,000 in its first year, and Thacker, Becker, and Cash expect that number to surpass $1 million in 2017.[8]

Discussion Questions

1. What made the brewery more successful after Thacker brought on his two business partners?
2. Why was it important for Thacker, Becker, and Cash to share in the responsibility of running the brewery?
3. How did the owners of Brew Hound Brewery grow its customer base?

---

been formed for tax purposes rather than for economic profits, the combined income of all U.S. partnerships is quite low. Nevertheless, the professional partnerships of many lawyers, accountants, and banking firms make quite large profits. For instance, the more than 700 partners at the international law firm Morgan, Lewis & Bockius LLP take home large incomes as the firm earns revenues of more than $1 billion a year.[9]

Combined Knowledge and Skills. Partners in the most successful partnerships acknowledge each other's talents and avoid confusion and conflict by specializing in a particular area of expertise such as marketing, production, accounting, or service. The diversity of skills in a partnership makes it possible for the business to be run by a management team of specialists instead of by a generalist sole proprietor. Co-founders Justin Wetherill, Edward Trujillo, and David Reiff credit diversity as being a key component to the success of their company uBreakiFix, an iPhone repair service. In just seven years, the startup has grown to 58 locations, generating more than $17 million in revenue. They have also embarked upon a franchising strategy, which is sure to spur further growth.[10] Service-oriented partnerships in fields such as law, financial planning, and accounting may attract customers because clients may think that the service offered by a diverse team is of higher quality than that provided by one person. Larger law firms, for example, often have individual partners who specialize in certain areas of the law—such as family, bankruptcy, corporate, entertainment, and criminal law.

Decision Making. Small partnerships can react more quickly to changes in the business environment than can large partnerships and corporations. Such fast reactions are possible because the partners are involved in day-to-day operations and can make decisions quickly after consultation. Large partnerships with hundreds of partners in many states are not common. In those that do exist, decision making is likely to be slow. However, some partnerships have been successful despite their large size. The accounting firm Ernst & Young is the second largest accounting and advisory firm in the United States. In one year, it promoted 753 individuals to the rank of partner, 30 percent of which consisted of women. With global revenues of more than $28 billion, some have attributed Ernst & Young's success to its strong approach to diversity and the innovation of its teams.[11]

Regulatory Controls.   Like a sole proprietorship, a partnership has fewer regulatory controls affecting its activities than does a corporation. A partnership does not have to file public financial statements with government agencies or send out quarterly financial statements to several thousand owners, as do corporations such as Apple and Ford Motor Co. A partnership does, however, have to abide by all laws relevant to the industry or profession in which it operates as well as state and federal laws relating to financial reports, employees, consumer protection, and environmental regulations, just as the sole proprietorship does.

Disadvantages of Partnerships

Partnerships have many advantages compared to sole proprietorships and corporations, but they also have some disadvantages. Limited partners have no voice in the management of the partnership, and they may bear most of the risk of the business, while the general partner reaps a larger share of the benefits. There may be a change in the goals and objectives of one partner but not the other, particularly when the partners are multinational organizations. This can cause friction, giving rise to an enterprise that fails to satisfy both parties or even forcing an end to the partnership. Many partnership disputes wind up in court or require outside mediation. A partnership can be jeopardized when two business partners cannot resolve disputes. For instance, two co-founders of photo-sharing mobile application Snapchat reached a financial settlement with their former fraternity brother, who sued the co-founders because the business was based around his idea.[12] In some cases, the ultimate solution may be dissolving the partnership. Major disadvantages of partnerships include the following.

Unlimited Liability.   In general partnerships, the general partners have unlimited liability for the debts incurred by the business, just as the sole proprietor has unlimited liability for his or her business. Such unlimited liability can be a distinct disadvantage to one partner if his or her personal financial resources are greater than those of the others. A potential partner should check to make sure that all partners have comparable resources to help the business in time of trouble. This disadvantage is eliminated for limited partners, who can lose only their initial investment.

Business Responsibility.   All partners are responsible for the business actions of all others. Partners may have the ability to commit the partnership to a contract without approval of the other partners. A bad decision by one partner may put the other partners' personal resources in jeopardy. Personal problems such as a divorce can eliminate a significant portion of one partner's financial resources and weaken the financial structure of the whole partnership.

Life of the Partnership.   A partnership is terminated when a partner dies or withdraws. In a two-person partnership, if one partner withdraws, the firm's liabilities would be paid off and the assets divided between the partners. Obviously, the partner who wishes to continue in the business would be at a serious disadvantage. The business could be disrupted, financing would be reduced, and the management skills of the departing partner would be lost. The remaining partner would have to find another or reorganize the business as a sole proprietorship. In very large partnerships such as those found in law firms and investment banks, the continuation of the partnership may be provided for in the articles of partnership. The provision may simply state the terms for a new partnership agreement among the remaining partners. In such cases, the disadvantage to the other partners is minimal.

Selling a partnership interest has the same effect as the death or withdrawal of a partner. It is difficult to place a value on a partner's share of the partnership. No public value is placed on the partnership, as there is on publicly owned corporations. What is a law firm worth? What is the local hardware store worth? Coming up with a fair value that all partners can agree to is not easy. Selling a partnership interest is easier if the articles of partnership specify a method of valuation. Even if there is not a procedure for selling one partner's interest, the old partnership must still be dissolved and a new one created. In contrast, in the corporate form of business, the departure of owners has little effect on the financial resources of the business, and the loss of managers does not cause long-term changes in the structure of the organization.

Distribution of Profits.   Profits earned by the partnership are distributed to the partners in the proportions specified in the articles of partnership. This may be a disadvantage if the division of the profits does not reflect the work each partner puts into the business. You may have encountered this disadvantage while working on a student group project: You may have felt that you did most of the work and that the other students in the group received grades based on your efforts. Even the perception of an unfair profit-sharing agreement may cause tension between the partners, and unhappy partners can have a negative effect on the profitability of the business.

Limited Sources of Funds.   As with a sole proprietorship, the sources of funds available to a partnership are limited. Because no public value is placed on the business (such as the current trading price of a corporation's stock), potential partners do not always know what one partnership share is worth, although third parties can access the value. Moreover, because partnership shares cannot be bought and sold easily in public markets, potential owners may not want to tie up their money in assets that cannot be readily sold on short notice. Accumulating enough funds to operate a national business, especially a business requiring intensive investments in facilities and equipment, can be difficult. Partnerships also may have to pay higher interest rates on funds borrowed from banks than do large corporations because partnerships may be considered greater risks.

Taxation of Partnerships

Partnerships are quasi-taxable organizations. This means that partnerships do not pay taxes when submitting the partnership tax return to the Internal Revenue Service. The tax return simply provides information about the profitability of the organization and the distribution of profits among the partners. Partners must report their share of profits on their individual tax returns and pay taxes at the income tax rate for individuals. Master limited partnerships require financial reports similar to corporations, which are discussed in the next section.

Corporations

When you think of a business, you probably think of a huge corporation such as General Electric, Procter & Gamble, or Sony because a large portion of your consumer dollars go to such corporations. A **corporation** is a legal entity, created by the state, whose assets and liabilities are separate from its owners. As a legal entity, a

Describe the corporate form of organization and cite the advantages and disadvantages of corporations.

corporation
a legal entity, created by the state, whose assets and liabilities are separate from its owners.

corporation has many of the rights, duties, and powers of a person, such as the right to receive, own, and transfer property. Corporations can enter into contracts with individuals or with other legal entities, and they can sue and be sued in court.

Corporations account for the majority of all U.S. sales and income. Thus, most of the dollars you spend as a consumer probably go to incorporated businesses. Most corporations are not mega-companies like General Mills or Ford Motor Co.; even small businesses can incorporate. As we shall see later in the chapter, many smaller firms elect to incorporate as "S Corporations," which operate under slightly different rules and have greater flexibility than do traditional "C Corporations" like General Mills.

stock
shares of a corporation that may be bought or sold.

Corporations are typically owned by many individuals and organizations who own shares of the business, called **stock** (thus, corporate owners are often called *shareholders* or *stockholders*). Stockholders can buy, sell, give or receive as gifts, or inherit their shares of stock. As owners, the stockholders are entitled to all profits that are left after all the corporation's other obligations have been paid. These profits may be distributed in the form of cash payments called **dividends.** For example, if a corporation earns $100 million after expenses and taxes and decides to pay the owners $40 million in dividends, the stockholders receive 40 percent of the profits in cash dividends. However, not all after-tax profits are paid to stockholders in dividends. Some corporations may retain profits to expand the business. For example, Google retains its earnings and does not pay out dividends. The company claims it needs cash on hand to remain flexible and competitive. However, with cash reserves at $65 billion, investors have begun placing pressure on the firm to provide a return to stockholders through dividends or by repurchasing some of its shares. Corporations do have to pay taxes on all profits, just like individuals.[13]

dividends
profits of a corporation that are distributed in the form of cash payments to stockholders.

Creating a Corporation

A corporation is created, or incorporated, under the laws of the state in which it incorporates. The individuals creating the corporation are known as *incorporators.* Each state has a specific procedure, sometimes called *chartering the corporation,* for incorporating a business. Most states require a minimum of three incorporators; thus, many small businesses can be and are incorporated. Another requirement is that the new corporation's name cannot be similar to that of another business. In most states, a corporation's name must end in "company," "corporation," "incorporated," or "limited" to show that the owners have limited liability. (In this text, however, the word *company* means any organization engaged in a commercial enterprise and can refer to a sole proprietorship, a partnership, or a corporation.)

The incorporators must file legal documents generally referred to as *articles of incorporation* with the appropriate state office (often the secretary of state). The articles of incorporation contain basic information about the business. The following 10 items are found in the Model Business Corporation Act, issued by the American Bar Association, which is followed by most states:

1. Name and address of the corporation.
2. Objectives of the corporation.
3. Classes of stock (common, preferred, voting, nonvoting) and the number of shares for each class of stock to be issued.
4. Expected life of the corporation (corporations are usually created to last forever).
5. Financial capital required at the time of incorporation.
6. Provisions for transferring shares of stock between owners.

7. Provisions for the regulation of internal corporate affairs.
8. Address of the business office registered with the state of incorporation.
9. Names and addresses of the initial board of directors.
10. Names and addresses of the incorporators.

Based on the information in the articles of incorporation, the state issues a **corporate charter** to the company. After securing this charter, the owners hold an organizational meeting at which they establish the corporation's bylaws and elect a board of directors. The bylaws might set up committees of the board of directors and describe the rules and procedures for their operation.

corporate charter
a legal document that the state issues to a company based on information the company provides in the articles of incorporation.

Types of Corporations

If the corporation does business in the state in which it is chartered, it is known as a *domestic corporation*. In other states where the corporation does business, it is known as a *foreign corporation*. If a corporation does business outside the nation in which it is incorporated, it is called an *alien corporation*. A corporation may be privately or publicly owned.

A **private corporation** is owned by just one or a few people who are closely involved in managing the business. These people, often a family, own all the corporation's stock, and no stock is sold to the public. Many corporations are quite large, yet remain private, including Publix Super Markets. It is the nation's ninth largest privately held corporation with annual revenues of more than $30 billion. Founded in 1930, today the company is run by the founder's grandson, who is the fourth family member to lead the company.[14] Other well-known privately held companies include HJ Heinz, Mars, Inc., Toys 'R' Us, and Amway.[15] Privately owned corporations are not required to disclose financial information publicly, but they must, of course, pay taxes.

private corporation
a corporation owned by just one or a few people who are closely involved in managing the business.

A **public corporation** is one whose stock anyone may buy, sell, or trade. Table 4-4 lists 10 U.S. corporations with more than half of their revenue coming from outside of the United States. Despite its high revenue, Amazon did not make a profit for years. A small profit in 2015 caused its stock to spike.[16] Thousands of smaller public corporations in the United States have sales under $10 million. In large public corporations such as AT&T, the stockholders are often far removed from the management of the company. In other public corporations, the managers are often the founders and the major shareholders. Facebook CEO Mark Zuckerberg, for example, holds more than $1 billion in Facebook stock. While he announced that he would donate 99 percent of his shares to charity, he will retain his voting majority position in the firm.[17] *Forbes'* Global 2000 companies generate around $39 trillion in revenues, $3 trillion in profits, and $162 trillion in assets. They are worth $39 trillion in market value.[18] Asia-Pacific companies account for the majority of the Global 2000 companies, but other nations are catching up. The rankings of the Global 2000 span across 60 countries.[19] Publicly owned corporations must disclose financial information to the public under specific laws that regulate the trade of stocks and other securities.

public corporation
a corporation whose stock anyone may buy, sell, or trade.

A private corporation that needs more money to expand or to take advantage of opportunities may have to obtain financing by "going public" through an **initial public offering (IPO),** that is, becoming a public corporation by selling stock so that it can be traded in public markets. Digital media companies are leading a surge in initial public offerings. Chinese e-commerce company Alibaba released the largest IPO globally at $25 billion.[20]

initial public offering (IPO)
selling a corporation's stock on public markets for the first time.

Also, privately owned firms are occasionally forced to go public with stock offerings when a major owner dies and the heirs have large estate taxes to pay. The tax payment may only be possible with the proceeds of the sale of stock. This happened

TABLE 4-4
American Companies with More than Half of Their Revenues from Outside the United States

Company	Description
Caterpillar Inc.	Designs, manufactures, markets, and sells machinery, engines, and financial products
Dow Chemical	Manufactures chemicals, with products including plastics, oil, and crop technology
General Electric	Operates in the technology infrastructure, energy, capital finance, and consumer and industrial fields, with products including appliances, locomotives, weapons, lighting, and gas
General Motors	Sells automobiles with brands including Chevrolet, Buick, Cadillac, and Isuzu
IBM	Conducts technological research, develops intellectual property including software and hardware, and offers consulting services
Intel	Manufactures and develops semiconductor chips and microprocessors
McDonald's	Operates second-largest chain of fast-food restaurants worldwide after Subway
Nike	Designs, develops, markets, and sells athletic shoes and clothing
Procter & Gamble	Sells consumer goods with brands including Tide, Bounty, Crest, and Iams
Yum! Brands	Operates and licenses restaurants including Taco Bell, Kentucky Fried Chicken, and Pizza Hut

to the brewer Adolph Coors Inc. After Adolph Coors died, the business went public and his family sold shares of stock to the public in order to pay the estate taxes.

On the other hand, public corporations can be "taken private" when one or a few individuals (perhaps the management of the firm) purchase all the firm's stock so that it can no longer be sold publicly. Taking a corporation private may be desirable when owners want to exert more control over the firm or they want the flexibility to make decisions for restructuring operations. For example, Michael Dell took his company private in order to set a new direction as PC sales continue to decline. Becoming a private company again allows Dell to focus on the needs of the company more fully without having to worry about the stock price for investors.[21] Taking a corporation private is also one technique for avoiding a takeover by another corporation.

Quasi-public corporations and nonprofits are two types of public corporations. **Quasi-public corporations** are owned and operated by the federal, state, or local government. The focus of these entities is to provide a service to citizens, such as mail delivery, rather than earning a profit. Indeed, many quasi-public corporations operate at a loss. Examples of quasi-public corporations include the National Aeronautics and Space Administration (NASA) and the U.S. Postal Service.

Like quasi-public corporations, **nonprofit corporations** focus on providing a service rather than earning a profit, but they are not owned by a government entity. Organizations such as the Sesame Workshop, the Elks Clubs, the American Lung Association, the American Red Cross, museums, and private schools provide services

quasi-public corporations corporations owned and operated by the federal, state, or local government.

nonprofit corporations corporations that focus on providing a service rather than earning a profit but are not owned by a government entity.

without a profit motive. To fund their operations and services, nonprofit organizations solicit donations from individuals and companies and grants from the government and other charitable foundations. Nonprofits do not have shareholders, and most are organized as 501(c)(3) organizations. A 501(c)(3) organization receives certain tax exemptions, and donors contributing to these organizations may reduce their tax deductibility for their donations. Organizations that have 501(c)(3) status include public charities (e.g. the Leukemia & Lymphoma Society), private foundations (e.g. the Daniels Fund), and private operating foundations that sponsor and fund their own programs (e.g. day camp for underprivileged children).[22]

Elements of a Corporation

The Board of Directors.

A **board of directors,** elected by the stockholders to oversee the general operation of the corporation, sets the long-range objectives of the corporation. It is the board's responsibility to ensure that the objectives are achieved on schedule. Board members have a duty of care and loyalty to oversee the management of the firm or for any misuse of funds. An important duty of the board of directors is to hire corporate officers, such as the president and the chief executive officer (CEO), who are responsible to the directors for the management and daily operations of the firm. The role and expectations of the board of directors took on greater significance after the accounting scandals of the early 2000s and the passage of the Sarbanes-Oxley Act.[23] As a result, most corporations have restructured how they compensate board directors for their time and expertise.

board of directors
a group of individuals, elected by the stockholders to oversee the general operation of the corporation, who set the corporation's long-range objectives.

However, some experts now speculate that Sarbanes-Oxley did little to motivate directors to increase company oversight. Seven board members stepped down after American Apparel CEO Dov Charney was ousted after years of alleged misconduct.[24] At the same time, the pay rate of directors is rising. On average, corporate directors are paid around $255,000, with compensation ranging from $0 to more than $1 million. Over the past several years, the trend of increasing directors' pay continues to reach higher and higher limits. Although such pay is meant to attract top-quality directors, concerns exist over whether excessive pay will have unintended consequences. Some believe that this trend is contributing to the declining effectiveness in corporate governance.[25]

Directors can be employees of the company *(inside directors)* or people unaffiliated with the company *(outside directors).* Inside directors are usually the officers responsible for running the company. Outside directors are often top executives from other companies, lawyers, bankers, even professors. Directors today are increasingly chosen for their expertise, competence, and ability to bring diverse perspectives to strategic discussions. Outside directors are also thought to bring more independence to the monitoring function because they are not bound by past allegiances, friendships, a current role in the company, or some other issue that may create a conflict of interest. Many of the corporate scandals uncovered in recent years might have been prevented if each of the companies' boards of directors had been better qualified, more knowledgeable, and more independent.

There is a growing shortage of available and qualified board members. Boards are increasingly telling their own CEOs that they should be focused on serving their company, not serving on outside boards. Because of this, the average CEO sits on less than one outside board. This represents a decline from a decade ago when the average was two. Because many CEOs are turning down outside positions, many companies have taken steps to ensure that boards have experienced directors. They have increased the

The boards of directors are elected by stockholders to oversee the general operation of the corporation.

© Minerva Studio/Getty Images

preferred stock
a special type of stock whose owners, though not generally having a say in running the company, have a claim to profits before other stockholders do.

common stock
stock whose owners have voting rights in the corporation, yet do not receive preferential treatment regarding dividends.

mandatory retirement age to 72 or older, and some have raised it to 75 or even older. Minimizing the amount of overlap between directors sitting on different boards helps to limit conflicts of interest and provides for independence in decision making.

Stock Ownership. Corporations issue two types of stock: preferred and common. Owners of **preferred stock** are a special class of owners because, although they generally do not have any say in running the company, they have a claim to profits before any other stockholders do. Other stockholders do not receive any dividends unless the preferred stockholders have already been paid. Dividend payments on preferred stock are usually a fixed percentage of the initial issuing price (set by the board of directors). For example, if a share of preferred stock originally cost $100 and the dividend rate was stated at 7.5 percent, the dividend payment will be $7.50 per share per year. Dividends are usually paid quarterly. Most preferred stock carries a cumulative claim to dividends. This means that if the company does not pay preferred-stock dividends in one year because of losses, the dividends accumulate to the next year. Such dividends unpaid from previous years must also be paid to preferred stockholders before other stockholders can receive any dividends.

Although owners of **common stock** do not get such preferential treatment with regard to dividends, they do get some say in the operation of the corporation. Their ownership gives them the right to vote for members of the board of directors and on other important issues. Common stock dividends may vary according to the profitability of the business, and some corporations do not issue dividends at all, but instead plow their profits back into the company to fund expansion.

Common stockholders are the voting owners of a corporation. They are usually entitled to one vote per share of common stock. During an annual stockholders' meeting, common stockholders elect a board of directors. Some boards find it easier than others to attract high profile individuals. For example, the board of Procter & Gamble consists of Ernesto Zedillo, former president of Mexico; Kenneth I. Chenault, chairman and CEO of the American Express Company; Scott D. Cook, chairman of the executive committee of Intuit Inc.; Patricia A. Woertz, CEO of Archer Daniels Midland;

Owners of preferred stock have first claim to profits.

© Stockbyte/Getty Images

W. James McNerney Jr., chairman of the board of Boeing; Margaret C. Whitman, CEO of Hewlett-Packard; and others.[26] Because they can choose the board of directors, common stockholders have some say in how the company will operate. Common stockholders may vote by *proxy,* which is a written authorization by which stockholders assign their voting privilege to someone else, who then votes for his or her choice at the stockholders' meeting. It is a normal practice for management to request proxy statements from shareholders who are not planning to attend the annual meeting. Most owners do not attend annual meetings of the very large companies, such as Westinghouse or Boeing, unless they live in the city where the meeting is held.

Common stockholders have another advantage over preferred shareholders. In most states, when the corporation decides to sell new shares of common stock in the marketplace, common stockholders have the first right, called a *preemptive right,* to purchase new shares of the stock from the corporation. A preemptive right is often included in the articles of incorporation. This right is important because it allows stockholders to purchase new shares to maintain their original positions. For example, if a stockholder owns 10 percent of a corporation that decides to issue new shares, that stockholder has the right to buy enough of the new shares to retain the 10 percent ownership.

Advantages of Corporations

Because a corporation is a separate legal entity, it has some very specific advantages over other forms of ownership. The biggest advantage may be the limited liability of the owners.

Limited Liability.   Because the corporation's assets (money and resources) and liabilities (debts and other obligations) are separate from its owners', in most cases the stockholders are not held responsible for the firm's debts if it fails. Their liability or potential loss is limited to the amount of their original investment. Although a creditor can sue a corporation for not paying its debts, even forcing the corporation into bankruptcy, it cannot make the stockholders pay the corporation's debts out of their personal assets. Occasionally, the owners of a private corporation may pledge personal assets to secure a loan for the corporation; this would be most unusual for a public corporation.

Ease of Transfer of Ownership.   Stockholders can sell or trade shares of stock to other people without causing the termination of the corporation, and they can do this without the prior approval of other shareholders. The transfer of ownership (unless it is a majority position) does not affect the daily or long-term operations of the corporation.

Perpetual Life.   A corporation usually is chartered to last forever unless its articles of incorporation stipulate otherwise. The existence of the corporation is unaffected by the death or withdrawal of any of its stockholders. It survives until the owners sell it or liquidate its assets. However, in some cases, bankruptcy ends a corporation's life. Bankruptcies occur when companies are unable to operate and earn profits. Eventually, uncompetitive businesses must close or seek protection from creditors in bankruptcy court while the business tries to reorganize.

External Sources of Funds.   Of all the forms of business organization, the public corporation finds it easiest to raise money. When a large or public corporation needs to raise more money, it can sell more stock shares or issue bonds (corporate "IOUs," which pledge to repay debt), attracting funds from anywhere in the United States and

Multinational oil corporation Royal Dutch Shell is the third largest company in the world.

© Vytautas Kielaitis/Shutterstock

even overseas. The larger a corporation becomes, the more sources of financing are available to it. We take a closer look at some of these in "Money and the Financial System."

Expansion Potential.   Because large public corporations can find long-term financing readily, they can easily expand into national and international markets. And, as a legal entity, a corporation can enter into contracts without as much difficulty as a partnership.

Disadvantages of Corporations

Corporations have some distinct disadvantages resulting from tax laws and government regulation.

Double Taxation.   As a legal entity, the corporation must pay taxes on its income just like you do. The United States has one of the highest corporate tax rates in the world, with a maximum rate of 35 percent.[27] Global companies such as Apple and Caterpillar have to pay foreign taxes as well as U.S. taxes when profits are brought back into the country. When after-tax corporate profits are paid out as dividends to the stockholders, the dividends are taxed a second time as part of the individual owner's income. This process creates double taxation for the stockholders of dividend paying corporations. Double taxation does not occur with the other forms of business organization.

Forming a Corporation.   The formation of a corporation can be costly. A charter must be obtained, and this usually requires the services of an attorney and payment of legal fees. Filing fees ranging from $25 to $150 must be paid to the state that awards the corporate charter, and certain states require that an annual fee be paid to maintain the charter. Today, a number of Internet services such as LegalZoom.com and Business .com make it easier, quicker, and less costly to form a corporation. However, in making it easier for people to form businesses without expert consultation, these services have increased the risk that people will not choose the kind of organizational form that is right for them. Sometimes, one form works better than another. The business's founders may fail to take into account disadvantages, such as double taxation with corporations.

Disclosure of Information.   Corporations must make information available to their owners, usually through an annual report to shareholders. The annual report contains financial information about the firm's profits, sales, facilities and equipment, and debts, as well as descriptions of the company's operations, products, and plans for the future. Public corporations must also file reports with the Securities and Exchange Commission (SEC), the government regulatory agency that regulates securities such as stocks and bonds. The larger the firm, the more data the SEC requires. Because all reports filed with the SEC are available to the public, competitors can access them. Additionally, complying with securities laws takes time.

DID YOU KNOW? The first corporation with a net income of more than $1 billion in one year was General Motors, with a net income in 1955 of $1,189,477,082.[28]

Employee–Owner Separation.   Many employees are not stockholders of the company for which they work. This separation of owners and employees may cause employees to feel that their work benefits only the owners. Employees without an ownership stake do not always see how they fit into the corporate picture and may not understand the importance of profits to the health of the organization. If managers are part owners but other employees are not, management–labor relations take on a different, sometimes difficult, aspect from those in partnerships and sole proprietorships. However, this situation is changing as more corporations establish employee stock ownership plans (ESOPs), which give shares of the company's stock to its employees. Such plans build a partnership between employee and employer and can boost productivity because they motivate employees to work harder so that they can earn dividends from their hard work as well as from their regular wages.

Other Types of Ownership

In this section, we take a brief look at joint ventures, S corporations, limited liability companies, and cooperatives—businesses formed for special purposes.

Joint Ventures

A **joint venture** is a partnership established for a specific project or for a limited time. The partners in a joint venture may be individuals or organizations, as in the case of the international joint ventures discussed in "Business in a Borderless World." Control of a joint venture may be shared equally, or one partner may control decision making. Joint ventures are especially popular in situations that call for large investments, such as extraction of natural resources and the development of new products. Joint ventures are especially popular in situations that call for large investments and can even take place between businesses and governments. Sprint developed a joint venture with Europe's leading wireless retailer Dixons Carphone to open up to 500 Sprint-branded stores across the United States. The two companies each own a 50 percent stake in the venture.[29]

joint venture
a partnership established for a specific project or for a limited time.

S Corporations

An **S corporation** is a form of business ownership that is taxed as though it were a partnership. Net profits or losses of the corporation pass to the owners, thus eliminating double taxation. The benefit of limited liability is retained. Formally known as Subchapter S Corporations, they have become a popular form of business ownership for entrepreneurs and represent almost half of all corporate filings.[30] The owners of an S corporation get the benefits of tax advantages and limited liability. Advantages of S corporations include the simple method of taxation, the limited liability of shareholders, perpetual life, and the ability to shift income and appreciation to others. Disadvantages include restrictions on the number (100) and types (individuals, estates, and certain trusts) of shareholders and the difficulty of formation and operation.

S corporation
corporation taxed as though it were a partnership with restrictions on shareholders.

Limited Liability Companies

A **limited liability company (LLC)** is a form of business ownership that provides limited liability, as in a corporation, but is taxed like a partnership. Although relatively new in the United States, LLCs have existed for many years abroad. Professionals such as lawyers, doctors, and engineers often use the LLC form of ownership. Many consider the LLC a blend of the best characteristics of corporations, partnerships, and sole proprietorships. One of the major reasons for the LLC form of ownership is to protect the

limited liability company (LLC)
form of ownership that provides limited liability and taxation like a partnership but places fewer restrictions on members.

Crimson Midstream Embraces Green

Crimson Midstream Limited Liability Company (LLC) is a holding company specializing in petroleum pipelines, the shipping of petrochemicals, and specialty asphalt products. The LLC designation allows the company to have as many members or owners as it pleases of all different types (that is, individuals, corporations, partnerships, and so on). It also gives the company the ability to choose how much and when to pay distributions to stockholders, giving it more control over its finances.

As a holding company, it is able to generate independent business units with slightly different functions within the same industry. Denver-based Crimson Renewable Energy Limited Partnership (LP) is one such business unit that produces oil and gas with a focus on biodiesel fuels. As an LP, Crimson Renewable Energy has limited its liability to its own business, while Crimson Midstream LLC serves as the general partner that holds unlimited liability for the LP.

Crimson Renewable Energy produces 25 million gallons of biodiesel per year. It invests heavily in its ability to transform natural materials such as used cooking oil waste, vegetable oils, algae oils, animal fats, and waste corn oil derived from ethanol production into biofuels. With more than 20 years of experience, the firm oversees the quality of its operations in-house through testing and has the capacity to customize fuel for customers to meet certain price points, function requirements, or climate considerations. Crimson Renewable Energy's supply chain consists of those who are dedicated to sustainable practices. The company also sources locally when possible.[31]

Discussion Questions

1. Crimson Midstream organized as a limited liability corporation. What are some of the advantages of an LLC?
2. What protections does Crimson Renewable receive by organizing one of its divisions as a limited partnership?
3. What does it mean that Crimson Midstream holds unlimited liability for Crimson Renewable LP?

---

cooperative (co-op)
an organization composed of individuals or small businesses that have banded together to reap the benefits of belonging to a larger organization.

members' personal assets in case of lawsuits. LLCs are flexible, simple to run, and do not require the members to hold meetings, keep minutes, or make resolutions, all of which are necessary in corporations. Mrs. Fields Famous Brands LLC—known for its cookies and brownies—is an example of a limited liability company.[32]

Cooperatives

Another form of organization in business is the **cooperative** or **co-op,** an organization composed of individuals or small businesses that have banded together to reap

REI is organized as a consumer cooperative.

© Ken Wolter/123RF

the benefits of belonging to a larger organization. Berkshire Co-op Market, for example, is a grocery store cooperative based in Massachusetts;[33] Ocean Spray is a cooperative of cranberry farmers. REI operates a bit differently because it is owned by consumers rather than farmers or small businesses. A co-op is set up not to make money as an entity. It exists so that its members can become more profitable or save money. Co-ops are generally expected to operate without profit or to create only enough profit to maintain the co-op organization.

Many cooperatives exist in small farming communities. The co-op stores and markets grain; orders large quantities of fertilizer, seed, and other supplies at discounted prices; and reduces costs and increases efficiency with good management. A co-op can purchase supplies in large quantities and pass the savings on to its members. It also can help distribute the products of its members more efficiently than each could on an individual basis. A cooperative can advertise its members' products and thus generate demand. Ace Hardware, a cooperative of independent hardware store owners, allows its members to share in the savings that result from buying supplies in large quantities; it also provides advertising, which individual members might not be able to afford on their own.

Trends in Business Ownership: Mergers and Acquisitions

Define and debate the advantages and disadvantages of mergers, acquisitions, and leveraged buyouts.

Companies large and small achieve growth and improve profitability by expanding their operations, often by developing and selling new products or selling current products to new groups of customers in different geographic areas. Such growth, when carefully planned and controlled, is usually beneficial to the firm and ultimately helps it reach its goal of enhanced profitability. But companies also grow by merging with or purchasing other companies.

A **merger** occurs when two companies (usually corporations) combine to form a new company. An **acquisition** occurs when one company purchases another, generally by buying most of its stock. The acquired company may become a subsidiary of the buyer, or its operations and assets may be merged with those of the buyer. The government sometimes scrutinizes mergers and acquisitions in an attempt to protect customers from monopolistic practices. For example, the decision to authorize American Airlines' acquisition of U.S. Airways was carefully analyzed. Google paid $3.2 billion for smart home company, Nest Labs.[34] The company was just one of many that Google acquired during the year. While these acquisitions have the potential to diversify Google's service offerings and benefit it financially, some believe that Google might be investing in companies of which it has little knowledge. In these cases, acquisitions could end up harming the acquiring company. Perhaps partially for this reason, Google restructured to become a holding firm called Alphabet Inc. Divisions such as Google Nest are now operated as semi-independent businesses.[35] Acquisitions sometimes involve the purchase of a division or some other part of a company rather than the entire company. The late 1990s saw a merger and acquisition frenzy, which is slowing in the 21st century (see Table 4-5).

When firms that make and sell similar products to the same customers merge, it is known as a *horizontal merger,* as when Martin Marietta and Lockheed, both defense contractors, merged to form Lockheed Martin. Horizontal mergers, however, reduce the number of corporations competing within an industry, and for this reason they are usually reviewed carefully by federal regulators before the merger is allowed to proceed.

When companies operating at different but related levels of an industry merge, it is known as a *vertical merger.* In many instances, a vertical merger results when one corporation merges with one of its customers or suppliers. For example, if Burger King were to purchase a large Idaho potato farm—to ensure a ready supply of potatoes for its french fries—a vertical merger would result.

A *conglomerate merger* results when two firms in unrelated industries merge. For example, the purchase of Sterling Drug, a pharmaceutical firm, by Eastman Kodak, best-known for its films and cameras, represented a conglomerate merger because

merger
the combination of two companies (usually corporations) to form a new company.

acquisition
the purchase of one company by another, usually by buying its stock.

TABLE 4-5   Major Mergers and Acquisitions Worldwide 2000–2015

Rank	Year	Acquirer	Target	Transaction Value (in millions of U.S. dollars)
1	2000	America Online Inc. (AOL) (*Merger*)	Time Warner	$164,747
2	2000	Glaxo Wellcome Plc.	SmithKline Beecham Plc.	75,961
3	2004	Royal Dutch Petroleum Co.	Shell Transport & Trading Co.	74,559
4	2006	AT&T Inc.	BellSouth Corporation	72,671
5	2001	Comcast Corporation	AT&T Broadband & Internet Svcs.	72,041
6	2004	JP Morgan Chase & Co.	Bank One Corporation	58,761
7	2013	American Airlines	U.S. Airways	11,000
8	2015	Albertson's	Safeway	9,400
9	2008	Bank of America	Countrywide	4,000
10	2008	JP Morgan Chase & Co	Bear Stearns Companies Inc.	1,100

Unless noted, deal was an acquisition.

Sources: Institute of Mergers, Acquisitions and Alliances Research, Thomson Financial, www.imaa-institute.org/en/publications+mergers+acquisitions+m&a.php#Reports (accessed March 16, 2010); "JPMorgan Chase Completes Bear Stearns Acquisition," JPMorganChase News Release, May 31, 2008, www.bearstearns.com/includes/pdfs/ PressRelease_BSC_31May08.pdf(accessed March 1, 2010); "Southwest Completes Purchase of Orlando-Based AirTran," Orlando Sentinel, May 2, 2011, http://articles. orlandosentinel.com/2011-05-02/business/os-southwest-airtran-reuters-update2-20110502_1_southwest-executive-vice-president-southwest-brand-airtran-holdings(accessed January 27, 2012).

the two companies were of different industries. (Kodak later sold Sterling Drug to a pharmaceutical company.)

When a company (or an individual), sometimes called a *corporate raider,* wants to acquire or take over another company, it first offers to buy some or all of the other company's stock at a premium over its current price in a *tender offer.* Most such offers are "friendly," with both groups agreeing to the proposed deal, but some are "hostile," when the second company does not want to be taken over. Energizer Holdings put controls in place to prevent a takeover after it split into two independent companies. With the split making the companies more vulnerable to takeover, it adopted a 10 percent trigger to prevent any one stockholder from gaining majority control. This means that if a stockholder gained control of 10 percent or more of the shares, the firm would release more shares to dilute the stock. Energizer claimed it would keep this trigger until the companies had been separated for six months.[36]

To head off a hostile takeover attempt, a threatened company's managers may use one or more of several techniques. They may ask stockholders not to sell to the raider, file a lawsuit in an effort to abort the takeover, institute a *poison pill* as Energizer did (in which the firm allows stockholders to buy more shares of stock at prices lower than the current market value) or *shark repellant* (in which management requires a large majority of stockholders to approve the takeover), or seek a *white knight* (a more acceptable firm that is willing to acquire the threatened company). In some cases, management may take the company private or even take on more debt so that the heavy debt obligation will "scare off" the raider.

In a **leveraged buyout (LBO),** a group of investors borrows money from banks and other institutions to acquire a company (or a division of one), using the assets of the purchased company to guarantee repayment of the loan. In some LBOs, as much as

leveraged buyout (LBO)
a purchase in which a group of investors borrows money from banks and other institutions to acquire a company (or a division of one), using the assets of the purchased company to guarantee repayment of the loan.

95 percent of the buyout price is paid with borrowed money, which eventually must be repaid.

Because of the explosion of mergers, acquisitions, and leveraged buyouts in the 1980s and 1990s, financial journalists coined the term *merger mania*. Many companies joined the merger mania simply to enhance their own operations by consolidating them with the operations of other firms. Mergers and acquisitions enabled these companies to gain a larger market share in their industries, acquire valuable assets such as new products or plants and equipment, and lower their costs. Mergers also represent a means of making profits quickly, as was the case during the 1980s when many companies' stock was undervalued. Quite simply, such companies represent a bargain to other companies that can afford to buy them. Additionally, deregulation of some industries has permitted consolidation of firms within those industries for the first time, as is the case in the banking and airline industries.

Some people view mergers and acquisitions favorably, pointing out that they boost corporations' stock prices and market value, to the benefit of their stockholders. In many instances, mergers enhance a company's ability to meet foreign competition in an increasingly global marketplace. Additionally, companies that are victims of hostile takeovers generally streamline their operations, reduce unnecessary staff, cut costs, and otherwise become more efficient with their operations, which benefits their stockholders whether or not the takeover succeeds.

Critics, however, argue that mergers hurt companies because they force managers to focus their efforts on avoiding takeovers rather than managing effectively and profitably. Some companies have taken on a heavy debt burden to stave off a takeover, later to be forced into bankruptcy when economic downturns left them unable to handle the debt. Mergers and acquisitions also can damage employee morale and productivity, as well as the quality of the companies' products.

Many mergers have been beneficial for all involved; others have had damaging effects for the companies, their employees, and customers. No one can say whether mergers will continue to slow, but many experts say the utilities, telecommunications, financial services, natural resources, computer hardware and software, gaming, managed health care, and technology industries are likely targets.

So You'd Like to Start a Business

If you have a good idea and want to turn it into a business, you are not alone. Small businesses are popping up all over the United States, and the concept of entrepreneurship is hot. Entrepreneurs seek opportunities and creative ways to make profits. Business emerges in a number of different organizational forms, each with its own advantages and disadvantages. Sole proprietorships are the most common form of business organization in the United States. They tend to be small businesses and can take pretty much any form—anything from a hair salon to a scuba shop, from an organic produce provider to a financial advisor. Proprietorships are everywhere serving consumers' wants and needs. Proprietorships have a big advantage in that they tend to be simple to manage—decisions get made quickly when the owner and the manager are the same person and they are fairly simple and inexpensive to set up. Rules vary by state, but at most all you will need is a license from the state.

Many people have been part of a partnership at some point in their life. Group work in school is an example of a partnership. If you ever worked as a DJ on the weekend with your friend and split the profits, then you have experienced a partnership. Partnerships can be either general or limited. General partners have unlimited liability and share completely in the management, debts, and profits of the business. Limited partners, on the other hand, consist of at least one general partner and one or more limited partners who do not participate in the management of the company but share in the profits. This form of partnership is used more often in risky investments where the limited partner stands only to lose his or her initial investment. Real estate limited partnerships are an example of how investors can minimize their financial exposure, given the poor performance of the real estate market in recent years. Although it has its advantages, partnership is the least utilized form of business. Part of the reason is that all partners are responsible for the actions and decisions of all other partners, whether or not all of the partners were involved. Usually, partners will have to write up an Articles of Partnership that outlines respective responsibilities in the business. Even in states where it is not required, it is a good idea to draw up this document as a way to cement each partner's role and hopefully minimize conflict. Unlike a corporation, proprietorships and partnerships both expire upon the death of one or more of those involved.

Corporations tend to be larger businesses, but do not need to be. A corporation can consist of nothing more than a small group of family members. In order to become a corporation, you will have to file in the state under which you wish to incorporate. Each state has its own procedure for incorporation, meaning there are no general guidelines to follow. You can make your corporation private or public, meaning the company issues stocks, and shareholders are the owners. While incorporating is a popular form of organization because it gives the company an unlimited lifespan and limited liability (meaning that if your business fails, you cannot lose personal funds to make up for losses), there is a downside. You will be taxed as a corporation and as an individual, resulting in double taxation. No matter what form of organization suits your business idea best, there is a world of options out there for you if you want to be or experiment with being an entrepreneur.

Review Your Understanding

Define and examine the advantages and disadvantages of the sole proprietorship form of organization.

Sole proprietorships—businesses owned and managed by one person—are the most common form of organization. Their major advantages are the following: (1) They are easy and inexpensive to form, (2) they allow a high level of secrecy, (3) all profits belong to the owner, (4) the owner has complete control over the business, (5) government regulation is minimal, (6) taxes are paid only once, and (7) the business can be closed easily. The disadvantages include the following: (1) The owner may have to use personal assets to borrow money, (2) sources of external funds are difficult to find, (3) the owner must have many diverse skills, (4) the survival of the business is tied to the life of the owner and his or her ability to work, (5) qualified employees are hard to find, and (6) wealthy sole proprietors pay a higher tax than they would under the corporate form of business.

Identify two types of partnership and evaluate the advantages and disadvantages of the partnership form of organization.

A partnership is a business formed by several individuals; a partnership may be general or limited. Partnerships offer the following advantages: (1) They are easy to organize, (2) they may have higher credit ratings because the partners possibly have more combined wealth, (3) partners can specialize, (4) partnerships can make decisions faster than larger businesses, and (5) government regulations are few. Partnerships also have several disadvantages: (1) General partners have unlimited liability for the debts of the partnership, (2) partners are responsible for each other's decisions, (3) the death or termination of one partner requires a new partnership agreement to be drawn up, (4) it is difficult to sell a partnership interest at a fair price, (5) the distribution of profits may not correctly reflect the amount of work done by each partner, and (6) partnerships cannot find external sources of funds as easily as can large corporations.

Describe the corporate form of organization and cite the advantages and disadvantages of corporations.

A corporation is a legal entity created by the state, whose assets and liabilities are separate from those of its owners. Corporations are chartered by a state through articles of incorporation. They have a board of directors made up of corporate officers or people from outside the company. Corporations, whether private or public, are owned by stockholders. Common stockholders have the right to elect the board of directors. Preferred stockholders do not have a vote but get preferential dividend treatment over common stockholders.

Advantages of the corporate form of business include the following: (1) The owners have limited liability, (2) ownership (stock) can be easily transferred, (3) corporations usually last forever, (4) raising money is easier than for other forms of business, and (5) expansion into new businesses is simpler because of the ability of the company to enter into contracts. Corporations also have disadvantages: (1) The company is taxed on its income, and owners pay a second tax on any profits received as dividends; (2) forming a corporation can be expensive; (3) keeping trade secrets is difficult because so much information must be made available to the public and to government agencies; and (4) owners and managers are not always the same and can have different goals.

Define and debate the advantages and disadvantages of mergers, acquisitions, and leveraged buyouts.

A merger occurs when two companies (usually corporations) combine to form a new company. An acquisition occurs when one company buys most of another company's stock. In a leveraged buyout, a group of investors borrows money to acquire a company, using the assets of the purchased company to guarantee the loan. They can help merging firms to gain a larger market share in their industries, acquire valuable assets such as new products or plants and equipment, and lower their costs. Consequently, they can benefit stockholders by improving the companies' market value and stock prices. However, they also can hurt companies if they force managers to focus on avoiding takeovers at the expense of productivity and profits. They may lead a company to take on too much debt and can harm employee morale and productivity.

Propose an appropriate organizational form for a startup business.

After reading the facts in the "Solve the Dilemma" feature at the end of this chapter and considering the advantages and disadvantages of the various forms of business organization described in this chapter, you should be able to suggest an appropriate form for the startup nursery.

Revisit the World of Business

1. What qualities give Ace Hardware a competitive advantage over its rivals?

2. How does a co-op structure benefit Ace Hardware?

3. Can you think of any disadvantages of having a co-op versus a corporate structure?

Learn the Terms

acquisition 129
articles of partnership 115
board of directors 123
common stock 124
cooperative (co-op) 128
corporate charter 121
corporation 119
dividends 120

general partnership 115
initial public offering (IPO) 121
joint venture 127
leveraged buyout (LBO) 130
limited liability company (LLC) 127
limited partnership 115
merger 129
nonprofit corporations 122

partnership 114
preferred stock 124
private corporation 121
public corporation 121
quasi-public corporations 122
S corporation 127
sole proprietorships 110
stock 120

Check Your Progress

1. Name five advantages of a sole proprietorship.
2. List two different types of partnerships and describe each.
3. Differentiate among the different types of corporations. Can you supply an example of each type?
4. Would you rather own preferred stock or common stock? Why?
5. Contrast how profits are distributed in sole proprietorships, partnerships, and corporations.
6. Which form of business organization has the least government regulation? Which has the most?

7. Compare the liability of the owners of partnerships, sole proprietorships, and corporations.
8. Why would secrecy in operating a business be important to an owner? What form of organization would be most appropriate for a business requiring great secrecy?
9. Which form of business requires the most specialization of skills? Which requires the least? Why?
10. The most common example of a cooperative is a farm co-op. Explain the reasons for this and the benefits that result for members of cooperatives.

Get Involved

1. Select a publicly owned corporation and bring to class a list of its subsidiaries. These data should be available in the firm's corporate annual report, *Standard & Poor's Corporate Records,* or *Moody Corporate Manuals.* Ask your librarian for help in finding these resources.

2. Select a publicly owned corporation and make a list of its outside directors. Information of this nature can be found in several places in your library: the company's annual report, its list of corporate directors, and various financial sources. If possible, include each director's title and the name of the company that employs him or her on a full-time basis.

Build Your Skills

Selecting a Form of Business

Background

Ali Bush sees an opportunity to start her own website development business. Ali has just graduated from the University of Mississippi with a master's degree in computer science. Although she has many job opportunities outside the Oxford area, she wishes to remain there to care for her aging parents. She already has most of the computer equipment necessary to start the business, but she needs additional software. She is considering the purchase of a server to maintain websites for small businesses. Ali feels she has the ability to take this start-up firm and create a long-term career opportunity for herself and others. She knows she can hire Ole Miss students to work on a part-time basis to support her business. For now, as she starts the business, she can work out of the extra bedroom of her apartment. As the business grows, she'll hire the additional full- and/or part-time help needed and reassess the location of the business.

LO 4-5

Propose an appropriate organizational form for a startup business.

Task

1. Using what you've learned in this chapter, decide which form of business ownership is most appropriate for Ali. Use the tables provided to assist you in evaluating the advantages and disadvantages of each decision.

Sole Proprietorships	
Advantages	Disadvantages
•	•
•	•
•	•
•	•
•	•

Corporation	
Advantages	Disadvantages
•	•
•	•
•	•
•	•
•	•

Limited Liability Company	
Advantages	Disadvantages
•	•
•	•
•	•
•	•
•	•

Solve the Dilemma

To Incorporate or Not to Incorporate

Thomas O'Grady and Bryan Rossisky have decided to start a small business buying flowers, shrubs, and trees wholesale and reselling them to the general public. They plan to contribute $5,000 each in startup capital and lease a 2.5-acre tract of land with a small, portable sales office.

Thomas and Bryan are trying to decide what form of organization would be appropriate. Bryan thinks they should create a corporation because they would have limited liability and the image of a large organization. Thomas thinks a partnership would be easier to start and would allow them to rely on the combination of their talents and financial resources. In addition, there might be fewer reports and regulatory controls to cope with.

Discussion Questions

1. What are some of the advantages and disadvantages of Thomas and Bryan forming a corporation?
2. What are the advantages and disadvantages of their forming a partnership?
3. Which organizational form do you think would be best for Thomas and Bryan's company and why?

Build Your Business Plan

Options for Organizing Business

Your team needs to think about how you should organize yourselves that would be most efficient and effective for your business plan. The benefits of having partners include having others to share responsibilities with and to toss ideas off of each other. As your business evolves, you will have to decide whether one or two members will manage the business while the other members are silent partners. Or perhaps you will all decide on working in the business to keep costs down, at least initially. However you decide on team member involvement in the business, it is imperative to have a written agreement so that all team members understand what their responsibilities are and what will happen if the partnership dissolves.

It is not too soon for you and your partners to start thinking about how you might want to find additional funding for your business. Later on in the development of your business plan, you might want to show your business plan to family members. Together, you and your partners will want to develop a list of potential investors in your business.

See for Yourself Videocase

PODS Excels at Organizing a Business

What happens when homeowners need to store their belongings temporarily? Before 1998, people would choose to either rent storage space, which can be costly and inconvenient, or store their belongings in their front yards. Yet, starting in 1998, another option was introduced: PODS.

PODS, short for Portable On Demand Storage, was founded after a group of firemen noticed the difficulties that many people faced when they needed to store their belongings for a short period. PODS delivers storage containers and leaves them in front of a house or business. A specially made hydraulic lift called Podzilla is able to place the container on ground level, which makes it easier for owners to store their belongings inside the container. PODS will then pick up the containers and move them to either its warehouses for storage or to anywhere else in the country.

When PODS was first started, banks and financial institutions were uncertain about how successful the moving and storage services company would be. Another issue was the expense of the actual containers. PODS containers, made of plywood over steel frames, cost between $2,200 and $2,500 each. If the company failed, the banks could repossess the containers. However, because PODS was a first-mover and there were no other comparable companies around, the banks feared that they would not be able to resell the containers. The risk for banks and financial institutions was high. This meant that PODS initially depended on venture capitalists for funding.

Once the company got started, however, PODS proved it was well worth the investment. More than a decade later, PODS can be found on three continents and has more than 200 million customers across the United States, Canada, the United Kingdom, and Australia. More franchises are planned for France, South Africa, Europe, Asia, Latin America, and South America. In addition to its convenience, PODS has also become known for its high-quality services and social responsibility. For instance, the company provided PODS containers to help recovery efforts in Hurricane Katrina. In 2011, PODS became a finalist in the National Association of Professional Organizers award for best service provider.

As PODS has expanded, its business organization has also undergone changes. Originally, PODS was formed as a sole proprietorship. Many businesses start off as sole proprietorships because of the benefits involved, such as ease of formation and greater control over operations. PODS's initial name was PODS LLC, meaning that it was a limited liability company. Limited liability companies provide more protection to owners so that their personal belongings will not be seized to pay the company's debts. It also frees owners from some of the restrictions that exist for corporations.

However, as businesses grow nationally, they become much more difficult for one or two individuals to handle. PODS soon realized that its rapid expansion required a new form of business organization. PODS decided to become a private corporation and renamed itself PODS Enterprises Inc. Although more people became involved in the ownership of the company, a small group of individuals maintains control over much of the general corporate operations. PODS stock is not issued publicly.

Eventually, PODS also decided to adopt a franchise model. The corporation began to allow other entrepreneurs, called franchisees, to license its name and products for a fee. This provided PODS with additional funding as well as the opportunity to expand into more areas. Because PODS is already successful, franchisees have a lower failure rate than starting their own businesses from scratch. Franchisees also understand their particular markets better than a corporation can.

"Franchisees bring another advantage, though, and that is their knowledge and connections in the local market, so they can take advantage of particularities in a market," said the senior vice president of Franchise Operations. This increases PODS's adaptability when it expands into other areas.

On the other hand, because corporations are able to bring together several knowledgeable individuals, PODS corporate headquarters finds that it is better able to handle larger markets such as Los Angeles and Chicago. With this business model, PODS has figured out how to meet the needs of both local markets, through franchisees, and larger markets. Because of PODS's ability to understand the best ways of organizing its business, the company has been able to reap the benefits from all types of market sizes.[37]

Discussion Questions

1. What are some advantages of sole proprietorships for PODS? What are some disadvantages?

2. What are some advantages of private corporations for PODS? What are some disadvantages?

3. How has adopting a franchise model made PODS more adaptable?

You can find the related video in the Video Library in Connect. Ask your instructor how you can access Connect.

Team Exercise

Form groups and find examples of mergers and acquisitions. Mergers can be broken down into traditional mergers, horizontal mergers, and conglomerate mergers. When companies are found, note how long the merger or acquisition took, if there were any requirements by the government before approval of the merger or acquisition, and if any failed mergers or acquisitions were found that did not achieve government approval. Report your findings to the class, and explain what the companies hoped to gain from the merger or acquisition.

Endnotes

1. Clare O'Connor, "Safety in Numbers," *Forbes*, March 2, 2015, 39, 41; "Home Depot Plans to Offer Same-Day Delivery to Customers," *Trefis*, December 12, 2013, http://www.trefis.com/stock/hd/articles/218709/maryhome-depot-plans-to-offer-same-day-delivery-to-customers/2013-12-12 (accessed August 24, 2015); Maria Landon, "Independent Hardware Stores Thrive in Niche Markets," *grbj.com*, October 25, 2013, http://www.grbj.com/articles/78153-independent-hardware-stores-thrive-in-niche-markets (accessed August 24, 2015); J.D. Power, "Ace Hardware Ranks Highest in Customer Satisfaction among Home Improvement Retailers for an Eight Consecutive Years," June 4, 2014, http://www.jdpower.com/press-releases/2014-home-improvement-retailer-satisfaction-study (accessed August 24, 2015).

2. The Entrepreneurs Help Page, www.tannedfeet.com/sole_proprietorship.htm (accessed April 10, 2014); Kent Hoover, "Startups Down for Women Entrepreneurs, Up for Men," *San Francisco Business Times*, May 2, 2008, http://sanfrancisco.bizjournals.com/sanfrancisco/stories/2008/05/05/smallb2.html (accessed April 10, 2014).

3. Maggie Overfelt, "Start-Me-Up: How the Garage Became a Legendary Place to Rev Up Ideas," *Fortune Small Business*, September 1, 2003, http://money.cnn.com/magazines/fsb/fsb_archive/2003/09/01/350784/index.htm (accessed April 10, 2014).

4. Network Solutions LLC, "Hosting Options," 2015, http://www.networksolutions.com/web-hosting/index-v5.jsp (accessed February 23, 2015); Network Solutions LLC, Network Solutions website, http://www.networksolutions.com/web-hosting/index-v5.jsp (accessed February 23, 2015).

5. Tom Foster, "The King of Kombucha," *Inc.,* March 2015, pp. 88–96; Synergy Drinks website, http://synergydrinks.com/index.php (accessed July 24, 2015); Hannah Crum and Alex LaGory, "The Kombucha Crisis: One Year Later," *BevNet,* August 23, 2011, http://www.bevnet.com/news/2011/the-kombucha-crisis-one-year-later (accessed July 24, 2015).

6. Webco, "Webcos General Partnership," ww2.webcogp.com/webcos-approach.html (accessed March 2, 2016).

7. "Master Limited Partnership – MLP," *Investopedia,* http://www.investopedia.com/terms/m/mlp.asp (accessed March 1, 2016).

8. Kerry Hannon, "How an Unemployed Construction Worker Became a Craft Beer Entrepreneur," *Money,* June 12, 2015, http://time.com/money/3919129/beer-hound-brewery-kenny-thacker/ (accessed November 5, 2015); Alicia Adamczyk, "Advice From 7 Baby Boomers Who Reinvented Their Careers," *Money,* August 13, 2015, http://time.com/money/3992427/second-act-career-baby-boomers/ (accessed November 5, 2015); Allison Brophy Champion, "Culpeper-Crafted Olde Yella Beer Wins Gold," *Culpeper Star Exponent,* August 24, 2015, http://www.dailyprogress.com/starexponent/culpeper-crafted-olde-yella-beer-wins-gold/article_27097080-4a8f-11e5-9c64-53ea5f4e6b78.html (accessed November 5, 2015); Kenny Thacker, "Beer Hound Brewery-Grand Opening," *CvilleCalendar.com,* October 9, 2012, http://www.cvillecalendar.com/calendar/Beer_Hound_BreweryGrand_Openi_10132012 (accessed November 5, 2015).

9. Ranker, "100 Largest Law Firms in the World," 2016, http://www.ranker.com/list/100-largest-law-firms-in-the-world/business-and-company-info (accessed March 1, 2016); Chambers & Partners, "Morgan, Lewis & Bockius LLP," 2016, http://www.chambersandpartners.com/usa/firm/64563/morgan-lewis-bockius (accessed March 1, 2016).

10. Bill Orben, "uBreakiFix Launches Franchise Unit, Sets Sights on 125 Stores This Year," *Orlando Business Journal,* February 20, 2013, http://www.bizjournals.com/orlando/blog/2013/02/ubreakifix-launches-franchise-unit.html (accessed March 1, 2016); "About uBreakiFix," uBreakiFix Careers website, http://careers.ubreakifix.com/about-ubreakifix/#.VOuVr3nTBVI (accessed March 1, 2016).

11. Ernst & Young, "EY Reports 2015 Global Revenues Up by 11.6%," September 15, 2016, http://www.ey.com/GL/en/Newsroom/News-releases/news-ey-reports-2015-global-revenues-up-eleven-point-six-percent (accessed March, 1, 2016); Ernst & Young, "EY Promotes 753 New Partners Worldwide," July 1, 2015, http://www.ey.com/GL/en/Newsroom/News-releases/News-EY-promotes-753-new-partners-worldwide (accessed March 1, 2016).

12. Sarah Griffiths, "Snapchat Settles Lengthy Lawsuit with Former University Classmate—and Admit the App WAS His Idea," *Daily Mail,* September 10, 2014, http://www.dailymail.co.uk/sciencetech/article-2750807/Snapchat-founders-settle-lengthy-lawsuit-former-classmate-admit-app-WAS-idea.html (accessed March 1, 2016).

13. Charles Sizemore, "Note to Google: Stop Being a Baby and Pay a Dividend," *Forbes,* June 8, 2015, http://www.forbes.com/sites/moneybuilder/2015/06/08/note-to-google-stop-being-such-a-baby-and-pay-a-dividend/#47eb5bf96fbc (accessed March 1, 2016).

14. "Publix Super Markets: America's Largest Private Companies," *Forbes,* http://www.forbes.com/companies/publix-super-markets/ (accessed March 1, 2016).

15. "Americas Largest Private Companies," *Forbes,* http://www.forbes.com/largest-private-companies/ (accessed March 1, 2016).

16. David Streitfeld, "Amazon Reports Unexpected Profit, and Stock Soars," *The New York Times,* July 23, 2015, http://www.nytimes.com/2015/07/24/technology/amazon-earnings-q2.html?_r=0&module=ArrowsNav&contentCollection=Technology&action=keypress®ion=FixedLeft&pgtype=article (accessed March 1, 2016).

17. Vindu Goel and and Nick Wingfield, "Mark Zuckerberg Vows to Donate 99% of His Facebook Shares for Charity," *The New York Times,* December 1, 2015, http://www.nytimes.com/2015/12/02/technology/mark-zuckerberg-facebook-charity.html (accessed March 1, 2016).

18. Forbes Corporate Communications, "The World's Largest Companies 2015," *Forbes,* http://www.forbes.com/sites/liyanchen/2015/05/06/the-worlds-largest-companies/#2bd78d3f4fe5 (accessed March 1, 2016).

19. Ibid.

20. Leslie Picker and Lulu Yilun Chen, "Alibabas Banks Boost IPO Size to Record of $25 Billion," *Bloomberg,* September 22, 2014, http://www.bloomberg.com/news/articles/2014-09-22/alibaba-s-banks-said-to-increase-ipo-size-to-record-25-billion (accessed March 1, 2016).

21. Brendan Marasco, "3 Reasons Dell Went Private," *The Motley Fool,* November 1, 2013, www.fool.com/investing/general/2013/11/01/3-reasons-dell-went-private.aspx (accessed March 1, 2016); Katherine Noyes, "As a Private Company, Dell-EMC Will Enjoy a Freedom HP Can Only Dream of," *CIO,* October 12, 2015, http://www.cio.com/article/2991551/as-a-private-company-dell-emc-will-enjoy-a-freedom-hp-can-only-dream-of.html (accessed March 1, 2016).

22. Elko & Associates Limited, "Private Operating Foundations," February 23, 2011, http://blog.elkocpa.com/nonprofit-tax-exempt/private-operating-foundations (accessed February 23, 2015); Foundation Group, "What Is a 501(c)(3)?" http://www.501c3.org/what-is-a-501c3/ (accessed March 1, 2016).

23. O. C. Ferrell, John Fraedrich, and Linda Ferrell, *Business Ethics: Ethical Decision Making and Cases,* 8th ed. (Mason, OH: South-Western Cengage Learning, 2011), p. 109.

24. P. Nash Jenkins, "American Apparel Fires Controversial Founder and CEO Dov Charney," *Time,* June 19, 2014, http://time.com/2898151/

american-apparel-fires-controversial-founder-and-ceo-dov-charney/ (accessed March 1, 2016); Hayley Peterson, "American Apparel Strikes Deal," *Business Insider,* July 9, 2014, http://www.businessinsider.com/american-apparel-gets-25-million-investment-2014-7 (accessed March 1, 2016).

25. Theo Francis and Joann S. Lublin, "Corporate Directors' Pay Ratchets Higher as Risks Grow," *The Wall Street Journal,* February 24, 2015, http://www.wsj.com/articles/corporate-directors-pay-ratchets-higher-as-risks-grow-1456279452 (accessed April 22, 2016).

26. P&G, "Board Composition," http://us.pg.com/who_we_are/structure_governance/corporate_governance/board_composition (accessed March 1, 2016).

27. Richard Rubin, "Bid to Lower Corporate Tax Rate Stirs Backlash From Business," *Bloomberg,* January 13, 2015, http://www.bloomberg.com/news/articles/2015-01-13/bid-to-lower-corporate-tax-rate-stirs-backlash-from-businesses (accessed March 1, 2016).

28. Joseph Nathan Kane, *Famous First Facts,* 4th ed. (New York: The H.W. Wilson Company, 1981), p. 202.

29. Sprint, "Sprint Announces Joint Venture with Dixons Carphone—Europe's Leading Wireless Retailer," February 29, 2016, http://newsroom.sprint.com/news-releases/sprint-announces-joint-venture-with-dixons-carphone-europes-leading-wireless-retailer.htm (accessed March 2, 2016).

30. Robert D. Hisrich and Michael P. Peters, *Entrepreneurship,* 5th ed. (Boston: McGraw-Hill, 2002), pp. 315–16.

31. Crimson Renewable website, www.crimsonrenewable.com/ (accessed August 5, 2013); Stephanie Paul, "LLC or LP: What's Best for Your Business?" Legal Zoom, February 2011, www.legalzoom.com/business-management/starting-your-business/llc-or-lp-whats-best (accessed August 14, 2013); Celia Lamb, "Biodiesel Company Eyes Port of Sacramento for Manufacturing, Storage Facility," *Sacramento Business Journal,* July 13, 2008, www.bizjournals.com/sacramento/stories/2008/07/14/story10.html (accessed August 23, 2013).

32. "Company Overview of Mrs. Fields Famous Brands, LLC," *Bloomberg Business,* February 23, 2015, http://www.bloomberg.com/research/stocks/private/snapshot.asp?privcapId=3553769 (accessed February 23, 2015).

33. Coop Directory, "Coop Directory Service Listing," www.coopdirectory.org/directory.htm#Massachusetts (accessed March 2, 2016).

34. Aaron Tilley, "Google Acquires Smart Thermostat Maker Nest for $3.2 Billion," *Forbes,* January 13, 2014, www.forbes.com/sites/aarontilley/2014/01/13/google-acquires-nest-for-3-2-billion/ (accessed March 2, 2016).

35. Eric Savitz, "Did Google Buy a Lemon? Motorola Mobility Whiffs Q4," *Forbes,* January 8, 2012, www.forbes.com/sites/ericsavitz/2012/01/08/did-google-buy-a-lemon-motorola-mobility-whiffs-q4/ (accessed March 2, 2016); Richard Nieva, "Alphabet? Google? Either Way, It's Ready to Rumble," *CNET,* January 29, 2016, http://www.cnet.com/news/larry-page-sergey-brin-google-alphabet/ (accessed March 2, 2016).

36. Lisa Beilfuss, "Energizer Adopts Poison Pill Ahead of Split," *The Wall Street Journal,* May 22, 2015, http://www.wsj.com/articles/energizer-adopts-poison-pill-ahead-of-split-1432298780 (accessed March 2, 2016).

37. "PODS LLC: Company Profile," *Bloomberg,* http://www.bloomberg.com/profiles/companies/751647Z:US-pods-llc (accessed March 29, 2016); "PODS Taking a Chunk Out of Moving and Storage Market," *USA Today,* August 4, 2006, www.usatoday.com/money/smallbusiness/2006-08-04-pods_x.htm (accessed March 29, 2016); Consortium Media Services, "PODS Recognized as One of the Nation's Best Service Providers by Professional Organizing Association," *Yahoo!® Voices,* February 28, 2011, http://voices.yahoo.com/pods-recognized-as-one-nationsbest-service-7701664.html (accessed July 26, 2012); Soti, "Portable On Demand Storage (PODS) Case Study," http://www.soti.net/PDF/PODS-SOTI-Casestudy.pdf (accessed March 29, 2016); World Franchis Associates, "PODS Multi-unit Franchise," 2015, http://www.worldfranchisecentre.com/p-detail.php?bid=91 (accessed March 29, 2016).

© John Lund/Nevada Wier/Blend Images

5 Small Business, Entrepreneurship, and Franchising

Learning Objectives

After reading this chapter, you will be able to:

LO 5-1 Define *entrepreneurship* and *small business.*

LO 5-2 Investigate the importance of small business in the U.S. economy and why certain fields attract small business.

LO 5-3 Specify the advantages of small-business ownership.

LO 5-4 Summarize the disadvantages of small-business ownership and analyze why many small businesses fail.

LO 5-5 Describe how you go about starting a small business and what resources are needed.

LO 5-6 Evaluate the demographic, technological, and economic trends that are affecting the future of small business.

LO 5-7 Explain why many large businesses are trying to "think small."

LO 5-8 Assess two entrepreneurs' plans for starting a small business.

Enter the World of Business

A V.I.P. Moving Experience

For families and National Football League teams, V.I.P. Moving & Storage offers customized services to meet all your moving and storage needs. The company prides itself on its strong service orientation. Because it is not affiliated with a major van line, it can offer personalized services in moving, packing, unpacking, storing, and setting up valuables. It offers its customers guaranteed prices and no hidden costs.

Owner Marshall Powell Ledbetter III comes from a family of entrepreneurs. The company was started more than 80 years ago by his grandfather under a different name. His son purchased the company, and Powell purchased the company from his father's estate in 2000 and changed the name to V.I.P. Moving & Storage. He was only able to purchase the warehouse, requiring him to buy new trucks and trailers. By owning its own fleet, the company is able to offer the ultimate in customization.

V.I.P. Moving & Storage has also caught the attention of NFL teams. For 19 years, it has been the official mover for the Tennessee Titans and has also worked with the New York Jets, St. Louis Rams, Seattle Seahawks, and New England Patriots. The company's movers will meet the teams at the airport to transport their equipment, set up the locker rooms, and tear them down when finished. The organization is highly unique with only a small handful of moving and transportation firms in the United States that provide such a high level of customized services. V.I.P. is committed toward offering the best service experience for moving and storage—one box at a time.[1]

Introduction

Although many business students go to work for large corporations upon graduation, others may choose to start their own business or find employment opportunities in small organizations. Small businesses employ about half of all private-sector employees.[2] Each small business represents the vision of its owners to succeed through providing new or better products. Small businesses are the heart of the U.S. economic and social system because they offer opportunities and demonstrate the freedom of people to make their own destinies. Today, the entrepreneurial spirit is growing around the world, from Russia and China to India, Germany, Brazil, and Mexico. Countries with the healthiest "entrepreneurship ecosystems" include the United States, Canada, Australia, Denmark, and Sweden.[3]

This chapter surveys the world of entrepreneurship and small business. First, we define entrepreneurship and small business and examine the role of small business in the American economy. Then, we explore the advantages and disadvantages of small-business ownership and analyze why small businesses succeed or fail. Next, we discuss how an entrepreneur goes about starting a business and the challenges facing small businesses today. Finally, we look at entrepreneurship in larger organizations.

Define *entrepreneurship* and *small business*.

entrepreneurship
the process of creating and managing a business to achieve desired objectives.

The Nature of Entrepreneurship and Small Business

In "The Dynamics of Business and Economics," we defined an entrepreneur as a person who risks his or her wealth, time, and effort to develop for profit an innovative product or way of doing something. **Entrepreneurship** is the process of creating and managing a business to achieve desired objectives. Many large businesses you may recognize (Levi Strauss and Co., Procter & Gamble, McDonald's, Dell Computers, Microsoft, and Google) all began as small businesses based on the visions of their founders. Some entrepreneurs who start small businesses have the ability to see emerging trends; in response, they create a company to provide a product that serves customer needs. For example, rather than inventing a major new technology, an innovative company may take advantage of technology to create new markets, such as Amazon .com. Or they may offer a familiar product that has been improved or placed in a unique retail environment, such as Starbucks and its coffee shops. A company may innovate by focusing on a particular market segment and delivering a combination of features that consumers in that segment could not find anywhere else. The sharing economy, or gig economy, can use technology to connect service providers or homeowners. Porch.com was founded as a way to connect homeowners with contractors. Founder Matt Ehrlichman conceived of the idea after becoming frustrated with problems in building his own house. Porch.com's software provides a more transparent way to link homeowners with licensed professionals. Approximately $1.5 trillion worth of home remodeling projects have been featured through the site. The software is so effective that home improvement store Lowe's installed it in 1,700 retail locations.[4]

Of course, smaller businesses do not have to evolve into such highly visible companies to be successful, but those entrepreneurial efforts that result in rapidly growing businesses gain visibility along with success. Entrepreneurs who have achieved success—like Michael Dell (Dell Computers), Bill Gates (Microsoft), Larry Page and Sergey Brin (Google), and the late Steve Jobs (Apple)—are some of the most well known. Table 5-1 lists some of the greatest entrepreneurs of the past century.

The entrepreneurship movement is accelerating, and many new, smaller businesses are emerging. Many entrepreneurs with five or fewer employees are considered

Company	Entrepreneur
Hewlett-Packard	Bill Hewlett, David Packard
Walt Disney Productions	Walt Disney
Starbucks	Howard Schultz
Amazon.com	Jeff Bezos
Dell	Michael Dell
Microsoft	Bill Gates
Apple	Steve Jobs
Walmart	Sam Walton
Google	Larry Page, Sergey Brin
Ben & Jerry's	Ben Cohen, Jerry Greenfield
Ford	Henry Ford
General Electric	Thomas Edison

TABLE 5-1
Great Entrepreneurs of Innovative Companies

microentrepreneurs. Technology once available only to the largest firms can now be obtained by a small business. Websites, podcasts, online videos, social media, cellular phones, and even expedited delivery services enable small businesses to be more competitive with today's giant corporations. Small businesses can also form alliances with other companies to produce and sell products in domestic and global markets.

Another growing trend among small businesses is social entrepreneurship. **Social entrepreneurs** are individuals who use entrepreneurship to address social problems. They operate by the same principles as other entrepreneurs but view their organizations as vehicles to create social change. Although these entrepreneurs often start their own nonprofit organizations, they can also operate for-profit organizations committed to solving social issues. Blake Mycoskie, the founder of Toms Shoes, is an example of a social entrepreneur. He founded the firm with the purpose of donating one pair of shoes to a child in need for every pair of shoes sold to consumers. The firm has since expanded this one-for-one model with other products and has developed a fund to invest in other social entrepreneurial startups.[5] Muhammad Yunus, founder of micro-lending organization Grameen Bank, is another example of a social entrepreneur. Yunus seeks to combat poverty by providing small loans to low-income individuals to start their own businesses.

social entrepreneurs individuals who use entrepreneurship to address social problems

What Is a Small Business?

This question is difficult to answer because smallness is relative. In this book, we will define a **small business** as any independently owned and operated business that is not dominant in its competitive area and does not employ more than 500 people. Microentrepreneurs, sometimes called micropreneurs, that employ five or fewer employees are growing rapidly. A local Mexican restaurant may be the most patronized Mexican restaurant in your community, but because it does not dominate the restaurant industry as a whole, the restaurant can be considered a small business. This definition is similar to the one used by the **Small Business Administration (SBA),** an independent agency of the federal government that offers managerial and financial assistance to

small business any independently owned and operated business that is not dominant in its competitive area and does not employ more than 500 people.

Small Business Administration (SBA) an independent agency of the federal government that offers managerial and financial assistance to small businesses.

TABLE 5-2
Importance of Small
Businesses to Our
Economy

Small firms represent 99.7 percent of all employer firms.
Small firms have generated 63 percent of net new jobs.
Small firms hire approximately 37 percent of high-tech workers (such as scientists, engineers, computer programmers, and others).
Small firms produce 16 times more patents per employee than large patenting firms.
Small firms employ nearly half of all private-sector employees.
Small firms pay 42 percent of the total U.S. private payroll.

Source: Small Business Administration Department of Advocacy, "Frequently Asked Questions," March 2014, www.sba.gov/sites/default/files/FAQ_March_2014_0.pdf (accessed March 3, 2016).

small businesses. On its website, the SBA outlines the first steps in starting a small business and offers a wealth of information to current and potential small-business owners.

The Role of Small Business in the American Economy

No matter how you define a small business, one fact is clear: They are vital to the American economy. As you can see in Table 5-2, more than 99 percent of all U.S. firms are classified as small businesses, and they employ about half of private workers. Small firms are also important as exporters, representing 98 percent of U.S. exporters of goods and contributing 33 percent of the value of exported goods.[6] In addition, small businesses are largely responsible for fueling job creation and innovation. Small businesses also provide opportunities for minorities and women to succeed in business. Women own more than 9 million businesses nationwide, with great success in the professional services, retail, communication, and administrative services areas.[7] Minority-owned businesses have been growing faster than other classifiable firms as well, representing 28.6 percent of all small businesses.[8] For example, Mexican-born José de Jesús Legaspi went into the real estate business and focused his market niche on inner city areas with a high percentage of Hispanic consumers. When Legaspi decided to begin investing in struggling malls, he refashioned the malls he acquired as cultural centers appealing to Hispanic consumers of all generations. One of his malls, renamed La Gran Plaza, went from being 20 percent occupied to 80 percent.[9]

Job Creation.   The energy, creativity, and innovative abilities of small-business owners have resulted in jobs for many people. About 63 percent of net new jobs annually were created by small businesses.[10] Table 5-3 indicates that 99.7 percent of all

TABLE 5-3
Number of Firms by
Employment Size

Firm Size	Number of Firms	Percentage of All Firms
0–19 employees	5,168,122	89.5
20–99 employees	503,033	8.7
100–499 employees	85,264	1.5
500+ employees	18,636	0.3

Source: "Statistics of U.S. Businesses (SUSB)," Statistics of U.S. Businesses, www.census.gov/econ/susb/index.html (accessed March 3, 2016).

businesses employ fewer than 500 people. Businesses employing 19 or fewer people account for 89.5 percent of all businesses.[11]

Many small businesses today are being started because of encouragement from larger ones. Many new jobs are also created by big-company/small-company alliances. Whether through formal joint ventures, supplier relationships, or product or marketing cooperative projects, the rewards of collaborative relationships are creating numerous jobs for small-business owners and their employees. In India, for example, many small information technology (IT) firms provide IT services to global markets. Because of lower costs, international companies can often find Indian businesses to provide their information processing solutions.[12]

E-commerce site Etsy sells homemade and vintage items. This small firm became publicly traded in 2015 and was valued at over $3 billion.

© Matthew Chattle/Alamy Stock Photo

Innovation.   Perhaps one of the most significant strengths of small businesses is their ability to innovate and to bring significant benefits to customers. Small firms produce more than half of all innovations. Among the important 20th-century innovations by U.S. small firms are the airplane, the audio tape recorder, fiber-optic examining equipment, the heart valve, the optical scanner, the pacemaker, the personal computer, soft contact lenses, the Internet, and the zipper. For instance, the founder and CEO of the small firm UniKey, Phil Dumas, invented a new way for consumers to keep their doors locked. Dumas invented Kevo, a motorized deadbolt lock that links to users' iPhones. With just the touch of a finger, consumers can lock and unlock their doors from remote locations. Since then, UniKey has expanded into the smart home market with new partnerships. This is just one example of a small company with the ability to innovate and contribute to the benefit of customers.[13]

The innovation of successful firms take many forms. For instance, franchises make up approximately 2 percent of all small businesses. Many of today's largest businesses started off as small firms that used innovation to achieve success.[14] Small businessman Ray Kroc found a new way to sell hamburgers and turned his ideas into one of the most successful fast-food franchises in the world—McDonald's. David Galboa co-founded the successful company Warby Parker, an online retailer that sells stylish glasses at lower prices. Similar to Toms Shoes, Warby Parker is a social enterprise that gives a pair of glasses to seeing-impaired individuals in developing countries for every pair of glasses sold. The company has sold more than 1 million pairs of glasses.[15] Entrepreneurs provide fresh ideas and usually have greater flexibility to change than do large companies.

Industries That Attract Small Business

Small businesses are found in nearly every industry, but retailing and wholesaling, services, manufacturing, and high technology are especially attractive to entrepreneurs. These fields are relatively easy to enter and require low initial financing. Small-business owners in these industries also find it easier to focus on specific groups of consumers; new firms in these industries initially suffer less from heavy competition than do established firms.

Investigate the importance of small business in the U.S. economy and why certain fields attract small business.

Retailing.   Retailers acquire goods from producers or wholesalers and sell them to consumers. Main streets, shopping centers, and malls are generally lined with independent music stores, sporting-goods stores, dry cleaners, boutiques, drugstores, restaurants, caterers, service stations, and hardware stores that sell directly to consumers. Retailing attracts entrepreneurs because gaining experience and exposure in retailing is relatively easy. Additionally, an entrepreneur opening a new retail store or establishing a new website does not have to spend the large sums of money for the equipment and distribution systems that a manufacturing business requires. All that a new retailer needs is the ability to understand the market and provide a product that satisfied a need. However, it is important for entrepreneurs to anticipate the costs of opening a retail or wholesale business beforehand. Plenty Grocery & Deli in Chicago, for instance, raised $15,000 on Kickstarter, a crowdfunding site, to open its small neighborhood grocery store.[16]

Many opportunities exist for nonstore retailing as well. Nonstore retailing involves selling products outside of a retail facility. There are two types of nonstore retailing: direct marketing—which uses the telephone, catalogs, and other media to give consumers an opportunity to place orders by mail, telephone, or the Internet—and direct selling. Nonstore retailing is an area that provides great opportunity for entrepreneurs because of a lower cost of entry. JCPenney also found that it significantly affects sales. The organization decided to engage in more direct marketing by resurrecting its catalog—which it had discontinued in 2010—based on market research findings suggesting that catalog users are more inspired to purchase items online.[17] Smaller businesses can engage in a form of direct marketing by featuring their products on eBay, Amazon, or Etsy.

Direct selling involves the marketing of products to ultimate consumers through face-to-face sales presentations at home, in the workplace, and in party environments. Well-known direct selling companies include Amway, Avon, Herbalife, and Mary Kay. The cost of getting involved in direct selling is low and often involves buying enough inventory to get started. Many people view direct selling as a part-time business opportunity. Often, those who become independent contractors for direct selling companies are enthusiastic about the product and have the opportunity to recruit other distributors and receive commissions on their sales.

Wholesaling. Wholesalers provide both goods and services to producers and retailers. They can assist their customers with almost every business function. Wholesalers supply products to industrial, retail, and institutional users for resale or for use in making other products. Wholesaling activities range from planning and negotiating for supplies, promoting, and distributing (warehousing and transporting) to providing management and merchandising assistance to clients. Wholesalers are extremely important for many products, especially consumer goods,

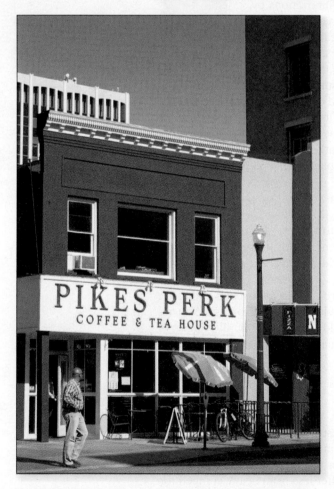

The retailing industry is particularly attractive to entrepreneurs. Pike's Perk Coffee & Tea House is a small locally owned coffee shop in Colorado Springs, Colorado.

© Richard Cummins/Getty Images

Going Green

Is 100 Percent Biodegradable Plastic Possible?

What can we do about plastic? Plastic is a component of our everyday lives, but it is causing havoc on the environment. It is estimated that plastic and other nonrecyclable materials floating in the ocean between Japan and the West Coast of North America is so vast that it is equivalent to the size of Texas.

Enter Meridian Holdings Group Inc., better known as MHG. MHG is a biopolymer firm located in Bainbridge, Georgia. Formed by a merger of two companies in 2014, MHG produces a substitute for plastic that can biodegrade in weeks. Conversely, regular plastic takes 500 to 1,000 years to biodegrade. Biopolymer technology uses plant fatty acids to turn canola oil from seeds harvested from nearby farmers into a type of plastic. This plastic can be used in anything from beverage bottles to bandages.

In 2015, the company was awarded "OK biodegradable MARINE" certification from Vinçotte, an organization that certifies compostable products using international standards. This particular certification is confirmation to stakeholders that MHG's biopolymer plastic will biodegrade in the ocean—a quality that could go far in reducing the amount of plastic waste that ends up in the sea. As a result, this small company of 100 employees has the potential to make a big difference in the quest to preserve the environment.[18]

Discussion Questions

1. How might MHG—a small business of 100 employees—have the potential to revolutionize the plastics industry?
2. MHG was formed by a merger of two companies. Why do you think this was more beneficial than starting from scratch?
3. MHG is attempting to grow on a global scale. What challenges might it face as it grows bigger?

---

because of the marketing activities they perform. Although it is true that wholesalers themselves can be eliminated, their functions must be passed on to some other organization such as the producer, or another intermediary, often a small business. Frequently, small businesses are closer to the final customers and know what it takes to keep them satisfied. Some smaller businesses start out manufacturing, but find their real niche as a supplier or distributor of larger firms' products. Sysco is a full-service wholesaler for food products that serves restaurants and other institutions.

Services. The service sector includes businesses that do not actually produce tangible goods. Services include intangible products that involve a performance, inauguration, or any effort to provide something of value that cannot be physically possessed. Services can also be part of the wholesale market and involve any product that is intangible and therefore cannot be touched. The service sector accounts for 80 percent of U.S. jobs, excluding farmworkers. Real estate, insurance and personnel agencies, barbershops, banks, television and computer repair shops, copy centers, dry cleaners, and accounting firms are all service businesses. Services also attract individuals—such as beauticians, morticians, jewelers, doctors, and veterinarians—whose skills are not usually required by large firms. Many of these service providers are retailers who provide their services to ultimate consumers. An example of a growing service sector is home sourcing, where individuals are involved in customer contact jobs such as call centers.

Manufacturing. Manufacturing goods can provide unique opportunities for small businesses. Consider the craft brewer Three Floyds Brewing in Munster, Indiana. In the first year it was founded, Three Floyds produced 300 barrels of beer. Nearly 20 years later, it is producing 50,000 barrels per year and has purchased a new building to use as a distillery. Several of its beers have been nominated as being among the best beers in the world.[19] Small businesses sometimes have an advantage over large firms because they can customize products to meet specific customer needs and wants. Such products include custom artwork, jewelry, clothing, and furniture.

Technology.   *High technology* is a broad term used to describe businesses that depend heavily on advanced scientific and engineering knowledge. People who were able to innovate or identify new markets in the fields of computers, biotechnology, genetic engineering, robotics, and other markets have become today's high-tech giants. One innovative technology was developed by a teenager interested in virtual reality. Only a few years ago, virtual reality was considered a dead technology past its prime. However, when 19-year-old Palmer Luckey developed a virtual gaming headset, it caught the attention of programmer John Carmack. Together, they brought virtual reality to a new level for gamers. The company, Oculus Rift, was sold to Facebook for $2 billion.[21] In general, high-technology businesses require greater capital and have higher initial startup costs than do other small businesses. Many of the biggest, nonetheless, started out in garages, basements, kitchens, and dorm rooms.

sharing economy
an economic model involving the sharing of underutilized resources.

Sharing Economy.   The past few years have seen a rise in the **sharing economy,** an economic model involving the sharing of underutilized resources. Under this model, entrepreneurs earn income by renting out an underutilized resource such as lodging or vehicles.[22] The ride sharing service Uber is the company most associated with the sharing economy. Rather than employing people outright, Uber acts more as a "labor broker," providing a mobile app that connects buyers (passengers) with sellers (drivers).[23] Although Uber does maintain control over variables such as rates, drivers act as independent contractors taking on jobs whenever or wherever they desire. Airbnb is another well-known company operating in the sharing economy. Its website connects those in need of lodging with sellers of those services. The sharing economy has become a $26 billion industry.[24]

The sharing economy is often referred to as the "gig economy" because independent contractors earn income going from job to job.[25] Although the work can be unstable and is not always consistent, the sharing economy offers opportunities for those who want to be their own entrepreneurs or who cannot find stable employment. It is estimated that independent contractors grew by 2.1 million between 2010 and 2014.[26] About 7 percent of Americans work as service providers in the sharing economy. Most of this growth has occurred among consumers between the ages of 25 and 44.[27] Services offered through this model often cost less than more traditional services such as hotels. This has caused sharing services to soar. It is even taking market share away from established firms. For instance, Airbnb averages 22 percent more customers per night than Hilton Worldwide.[28]

Despite the opportunities in the sharing economy, Uber and similar firms have been experiencing pressure over whether workers are independent contractors or employees. For instance, Uber faced a setback after a judge found that a driver should have been classified as an employee rather than as an independent contractor. As independent contractors, workers act as their own bosses and pay their own taxes and benefits, unlike employees of a firm. The judge ruled that Uber exerted too much control over drivers, including placing limits on some driver activities, similar to what an employer would do.[29] Uber denied the charges, but other companies are taking note of these challenges and have begun offering some employee benefits to their contractors.[30] In spite of the controversy, however, overall perception of the sharing economy appears to be high. According to one study, approximately 86 percent of respondents believe the sharing economy makes life more affordable, while 78 percent believe the sharing of underutilized resources reduces waste.[31]

Advantages of Small-Business Ownership

There are many advantages to establishing and running a small business. These can be categorized into personal advantages and business advantages. Table 5-4 lists some of the traits that can help entrepreneurs succeed.

LO 5-3

Specify the advantages of small-business ownership.

Independence

Independence is probably one of the leading reasons that entrepreneurs choose to go into business for themselves. Being a small-business owner means being your own boss. Many people start their own businesses because they believe they will do better for themselves than they could do by remaining with their current employer or by changing jobs. They may feel stuck on the corporate ladder and that no business would take them seriously enough to fund their ideas. Sometimes people who venture forth to start their own small business are those who simply cannot work for someone else. Such people may say that they just do not fit the "corporate mold."

More often, small-business owners just want the freedom to choose whom they work with, the flexibility to pick where and when to work, and the option of working in a family setting. The availability of the computer, copy machine, and Internet has permitted many people to work at home. In the past, most of them would have needed the support that an office provides.

Costs

As already mentioned, small businesses often require less money to start and maintain than do large ones. Obviously, a firm with just 25 people in a small factory spends less money on wages and salaries, rent, utilities, and other expenses than does a firm employing tens of thousands of people in several large facilities. Rather than maintain the expense of keeping separate departments for accounting, advertising, and legal counseling, small businesses often hire other firms (sometimes small businesses themselves) to supply these services as they are needed. Additionally, small-business owners can sometimes rely on friends and family members to help them save money by volunteering to work on a difficult project.

Flexibility

With small size comes the flexibility to adapt to changing market demands. Small businesses usually have only one layer of management—the owners. Decisions

TABLE 5-4   Successful Traits of Young Entrepreneurs

Trait	Definition	Trait	Definition
Intuitive	Using one's intuition to derive what's true without conscious reasoning	Innovative	Being able to come up with new and creative ideas
Productive	Being able to produce large amounts of something during a specific time period	Risk-taker	Having the ability to pursue risky endeavors despite the possibility of failure
Resourceful	Understanding how to use and spend resources wisely	Persistent	Continuing in a certain action in spite of obstacles
Charismatic	Having the ability to inspire others behind a central vision	Friendly	Being able to have mutually beneficial interactions with people

therefore can be made and executed quickly. In larger firms, decisions about even routine matters can take weeks because they must pass through multiple levels of management before action is authorized. When Taco Bell introduces a new product, for example, it must first research what consumers want, then develop the product and test it before introducing it nationwide—a process that sometimes takes years. An independent snack shop, however, can develop and introduce a new product (perhaps to meet a customer's request) in a much shorter time.

Focus

Small firms can focus their efforts on a precisely defined market niche—that is, a specific group of customers. Many large corporations must compete in the mass market or for large market segments. Smaller firms can develop products for particular groups of customers or to satisfy a need that other companies have not addressed. For example, Megan Tamte launched a chain of boutiques called Evereve targeted toward young mothers. As a young mother herself, she recognized the many problems mothers faced when they take their young children out shopping. Evereve stores were built with double-wide aisles to accommodate strollers, large dressing rooms, and play areas for children. It has since opened 59 stores and experienced a 30 percent annual growth rate.[32] By targeting small niches or product needs, businesses can sometimes avoid competition from larger firms, helping them to grow into stronger companies.

Reputation

Reputation, or how a firm is perceived by its various stakeholders, is highly significant to an organization's success. Small firms, because of their capacity to focus on narrow niches, can develop enviable reputations for quality and service. A good example of a small business with a formidable reputation is W. Atlee Burpee and Co., which has the country's premier bulb and seed catalog. Burpee has an unqualified returns policy (complete satisfaction or your money back) that demonstrates a strong commitment to customer satisfaction.

Summarize the disadvantages of small-business ownership and analyze why many small businesses fail.

Disadvantages of Small-Business Ownership

The rewards associated with running a small business are so enticing that it's no wonder many people dream of it. However, as with any undertaking, small-business ownership has its disadvantages.

High Stress Level

A small business is likely to provide a living for its owner, but not much more (although there are exceptions as some examples in this chapter have shown). There are ongoing worries about competition, employee problems, new equipment, expanding inventory, rent increases, or changing market demand. In addition to other stresses, small-business owners tend to be victims of physical and psychological stress. The small-business person is often the owner, manager, sales force, shipping and receiving clerk, bookkeeper, and custodian. Having to multitask can result in long hours for most small-business owners. Many creative persons fail, not because of their business concepts, but rather because of difficulties in managing their business.

High Failure Rate

Despite the importance of small businesses to our economy, there is no guarantee of success. Half of all new employer firms fail within the first five years.[33] Restaurants

Responding to Business Challenges

Walmart Embraces a Diversity of Suppliers

It's not easy getting into Walmart, but small-scale entrepreneurs are given the opportunity with its Made in USA "Open Call." The event was started in 2014 to increase Walmart's purchase of products that support American jobs by $250 billion within the next 10 years. During the call, suppliers are given 30 minutes to pitch their products to Walmart executives to try to get them on stores shelves. Walmart has recognized that after price, the biggest consideration for Walmart shoppers is whether the products are made in the United States.

Getting onto Walmart shelves poses many challenges. Price is a key consideration, so entrepreneurs must find ways to keep costs down. However, products that impress can soon be sold in hundreds of stores. Chef Jenn, for example, is a line of seafood products accepted in the 2014 "Open Call." Entrepreneur Jennifer McCullough, who had started developing the line in her Memphis kitchen, secured a place on Walmart shelves in 300 to 400 stores. Seven months later, her products were being sold in more than 800 Walmart locations.

Getting into Walmart, however, is no guarantee of success. Entrepreneur Karen Posada got her organic pasta sauce onto Walmart shelves but found herself competing against Walmart's own lower-priced Great Value brand. She has since developed packaged pouches of smoothies that she hopes to retail in Walmart for under $2.[34]

Discussion Questions

1. Why is getting on Walmart shelves so important to many entrepreneurs?
2. What are some of the challenges entrepreneurs face in trying to get Walmart to accept their products?
3. Although Karen Posada got her organic pasta sauce into Walmart stores, she found herself competing against lower-priced store brands. What lessons can entrepreneurs hoping to sell through Walmart learn from this?

---

are a case in point. Look around your own neighborhood, and you can probably spot the locations of several restaurants that are no longer in business.

Small businesses fail for many reasons (see Table 5-5). A poor business concept—such as insecticides for garbage cans (research found that consumers are not concerned with insects in their garbage)—will produce disaster nearly every time. Expanding a hobby into a business may work if a genuine market niche exists, but all too often people start such a business without identifying a real need for the good or service. Other notable causes of small-business failure include the burdens imposed by government regulation, insufficient funds to withstand slow sales, and vulnerability to competition from larger companies. However, three major causes of small-business failure deserve a close look: undercapitalization, managerial inexperience or incompetence, and inability to cope with growth.

Undercapitalization. The shortest path to failure in business is **undercapitalization,** the lack of funds to operate a business normally. Too many entrepreneurs think that all they need is enough money to get started, that the business can survive on cash generated from sales soon thereafter. But almost all businesses suffer from seasonal variations in sales, which make cash tight, and few businesses make money from the start. Many small rural operations cannot obtain financing within their own communities because small rural

Some entrepreneurs choose to start their businesses from scratch so they can run their businesses as they see fit. While they might start off small and struggle to attract customers, they are not limited by the restrictions of a franchise agreement.

© Atomazul/Shutterstock

TABLE 5-5
Challenges in Starting a New Business

1. Underfunded (not providing adequate startup capital)
2. Not understanding your competitive niche
3. Lack of effective utilization of websites and social media
4. Lack of a marketing and business plan
5. If operating a retail store, poor site selection
6. Pricing mistakes-too high or too low
7. Underestimating the time commitment for success
8. Not finding complementary partners to bring in additional experience
9. Not hiring the right employees and/or not training them properly
10. Not understanding legal and ethical responsibilities

banks often lack the necessary financing expertise or assets sizable enough to counter the risks involved with small-business loans. Without sufficient funds, the best small-business idea in the world will fail.

Managerial Inexperience or Incompetence.   Poor management is the cause of many business failures. Just because an entrepreneur has a brilliant vision for a small business does not mean he or she has the knowledge or experience to manage a growing business effectively. A person who is good at creating great product ideas and marketing them may lack the skills and experience to make good management decisions in hiring, negotiating, finance, and control. Moreover, entrepreneurs may neglect those areas of management they know little about or find tedious, at the expense of the business's success.

Inability to Cope with Growth. Sometimes, the very factors that are advantages for a small business turn into serious disadvantages when the time comes to grow. Growth often requires the owner to give up a certain amount of direct authority, and it is frequently hard for someone who has called all the shots to give up control. It

Chipotle has become a highly popular restaurant in a short time. However, an E. coli outbreak at some of its restaurants sickened some of its customers and caused sales to plunge. This was an extreme challenge Chipotle Grill was forced to overcome.

has often been said that the greatest impediment to the success of a business is the entrepreneur. Similarly, growth requires specialized management skills in areas such as credit analysis and promotion—skills that the founder may lack or not have time to apply. The founders of many small businesses, including Dell Computers, found that they needed to bring in more experienced managers to help manage their companies through growing pains.

Poorly managed growth probably affects a company's reputation more than anything else, at least initially. And products that do not arrive on time or goods that are poorly made can quickly reverse a success. The principal immediate threats to small and mid-sized businesses include rising inflation, energy and other supply shortages or cost escalations, and excessive household and/or corporate debt. For this reason, some small-business owners choose to stay small and are not interested in wide-scale growth. These business owners, called *micropreneurs,* operate small-scale businesses with no more than five employees. It is estimated that 95 percent of small businesses are microbusinesses.[35]

Starting a Small Business

We've told you how important small businesses are, and why they succeed and fail, but *how do you go about* starting your own business in the first place? To start any business, large or small, you must have some kind of general idea. Sam Walton, founder of Walmart stores, had a vision of a discount retailing enterprise that spawned the world's largest retailing empire and changed the way companies look at business. Next, you need to devise a strategy to guide planning and development in the business. Finally, you must make decisions about form of ownership; the financial resources needed; and whether to acquire an existing business, start a new one, or buy a franchise.

LO 5-5

Describe how you go about starting a small business and what resources are needed.

The Business Plan

A key element of business success is a **business plan**—a precise statement of the rationale for the business and a step-by-step explanation of how it will achieve its goals. The business plan should include an explanation of the business, an analysis of the competition, estimates of income and expenses, and other information. It should also establish a strategy for acquiring sufficient funds to keep the business going. Many financial institutions decide whether to loan a small business money based on its business plan. A good business plan should act as a guide and reference document—not a shackle that limits the business's flexibility and decision-making ability. The business plan must be revised periodically to ensure that the firm's goals and strategies adapt to changes in the environment. Business plans allow companies to assess market potential, determine price and manufacturing requirements, identify optimal distribution channels, and refine product selection. It is also important to evaluate and update the business plan to account for changes in the company. Salem, Oregon–based Rich Duncan Construction learned this the hard way. The company rewrote part of its business plan after 14 years to account for high growth rates and identify weaknesses that needed to be addressed.[36] The SBA website provides an overview of a plan for small businesses to use to gain financing. Online Appendix A presents a comprehensive business plan.

business plan
a precise statement of the rationale for a business and a step-by-step explanation of how it will achieve its goals.

Forms of Business Ownership

After developing a business plan, the entrepreneur has to decide on an appropriate legal form of business ownership—whether it is best to operate as a sole proprietorship, partnership, or corporation—and to examine the many factors that affect that decision, which we explored in "Options for Organizing Business."

Financial Resources

The expression "it takes money to make money" holds especially true in developing a business enterprise. To make money from a small business, the owner must first provide or obtain money (capital) to get started and to keep it running smoothly. Even a small retail store will probably need at least $50,000 in initial financing to rent space, purchase or lease necessary equipment and furnishings, buy the initial inventory, and provide working capital. Often, the small-business owner has to put up a significant percentage of the necessary capital. Few new business owners have a large amount of their own capital and must look to other sources for additional financing.

Equity Financing.   The most important source of funds for any new business is the owner. Many owners include among their personal resources ownership of a home, the accumulated value in a life-insurance policy, or a savings account. A new business owner may sell or borrow against the value of such assets to obtain funds to operate a business. Additionally, the owner may bring useful personal assets—such as a computer, desks and other furniture, a car or truck—as part of his or her ownership interest in the firm. Such financing is referred to as *equity financing* because the owner uses real personal assets rather than borrowing funds from outside sources to get started in a new business. The owner can also provide working capital by reinvesting profits into the business or simply by not drawing a full salary.

venture capitalists
persons or organizations that agree to provide some funds for a new business in exchange for an ownership interest or stock.

Small businesses can also obtain equity financing by finding investors for their operations. They may sell stock in the business to family members, friends, employees, or other investors. For example, Plated, a meal-kit service that focuses on delivering sustainable meals to customers' doors, has raised $50 million from investors.[37] **Venture capitalists** are persons or organizations that agree to provide some funds for a new business in exchange for an ownership interest or stock. Venture capitalists hope to purchase the stock of a small business at a low price and then sell the stock for a profit after the business has grown successful. Although these forms of equity financing have helped many small businesses, they require that the small-business owner share the profits of the business—and sometimes control, as well—with the investors.

Debt Financing.   New businesses sometimes borrow more than half of their financial resources. Banks are the main suppliers of external financing

Small-business owners often use debt financing from banks or the Small Business Administration to start their own organization.

© Ariel Skelley/Getty Images

to small businesses. On the federal level, the SBA offers financial assistance to qualifying businesses. Entrepreneur Megan Tamte used a $75,000 SBA loan to help start Evereve.[38] They can also look to family and friends as sources for long-term loans or other assets, such as computers or an automobile, that are exchanged for an ownership interest in a business. In such cases, the business owner can usually structure a favorable repayment schedule and sometimes negotiate an interest rate below current bank rates. If the business goes bad, however, the emotional losses for all concerned may greatly exceed the money involved. Anyone lending a friend or family member money for a venture should state the agreement clearly in writing before any money changes hands.

The amount a bank or other institution is willing to loan depends on its assessment of the venture's likelihood of success and of the entrepreneur's ability to repay the loan. The bank will often require the entrepreneur to put up *collateral*, a financial interest in the property or fixtures of the business, to guarantee payment of the debt. Additionally, the small-business owner may have to provide personal property as collateral, such as his or her home, in which case the loan is called a *mortgage.* If the small business fails to repay the loan, the lending institution may eventually claim and sell the collateral or mortgage to recover its loss.

Banks and other financial institutions can also grant a small business a *line of credit*—an agreement by which a financial institution promises to lend a business a predetermined sum on demand. A line of credit permits an entrepreneur to take quick advantage of opportunities that require external funding. Small businesses may obtain funding from their suppliers in the form of a *trade credit*—that is, suppliers allow the business to take possession of the needed goods and services and pay for them at a later date or in installments. Occasionally, small businesses engage in *bartering*— trading their own products for the goods and services offered by other businesses. For example, an accountant may offer accounting services to an office supply firm in exchange for office supplies and equipment.

Additionally, some community groups sponsor loan funds to encourage the development of particular types of businesses. State and local agencies may guarantee loans, especially to minority business people or for development in certain areas.

Approaches to Starting a Small Business

Starting from Scratch versus Buying an Existing Business.   Although entrepreneurs often start new small businesses from scratch much the way we have discussed in this section, they may elect instead to buy an existing business. This has the advantage of providing a built-in network of customers, suppliers, and distributors and reducing some of the guesswork inherent in starting a new business from the ground up. However, an entrepreneur who buys an existing business also takes on any problems the business already has.

Franchising.   Many small-business owners find entry into the business world through franchising. A license to sell another's products or to use another's name in business, or both, is a **franchise.** The company that sells a franchise is the **franchiser.** Dunkin' Donuts, Subway, and Jiffy Lube are well-known franchisers with national visibility. The purchaser of a franchise is called a **franchisee.**

The franchisee acquires the rights to a name, logo, methods of operation, national advertising, products, and other elements associated with the franchiser's business in return for a financial commitment and the agreement to conduct business in accordance

franchise
a license to sell another's products or to use another's name in business, or both.

franchiser
the company that sells a franchise.

franchisee
the purchaser of a franchise.

with the franchiser's standard of operations. The initial fee to join a franchise varies greatly. In addition, franchisees buy equipment, pay for training, and obtain a mortgage or lease. The franchisee also pays the franchiser a monthly or annual fee based on a percentage of sales or profits. In return, the franchisee often receives building specifications and designs, site recommendations, management and accounting support, and perhaps most importantly, immediate name recognition. Visit the website of the International Franchise Association to learn more on this topic.

The practice of franchising first began in the United States in the 19th century when Singer used it to sell sewing machines. This method of goods distribution soon became commonplace in the automobile, gasoline, soft drink, and hotel industries. The concept of franchising grew especially rapidly during the 1960s, when it expanded to diverse industries. Table 5-6 shows the 10 fastest growing franchises and the top 10 new franchises.

The entrepreneur will find that franchising has both advantages and disadvantages. Franchising allows a franchisee the opportunity to set up a small business relatively quickly, and because of its association with an established brand, a franchise outlet often reaches the break-even point faster than an independent business would. Franchisees commonly report the following advantages:

- Management training and support.
- Brand-name appeal.
- Standardized quality of goods and services.
- National and local advertising programs.
- Financial assistance.
- Proven products and business formats.
- Centralized buying power.
- Site selection and territorial protection.
- Greater chance for success.[39]

TABLE 5-6
Fastest Growing and Hottest New Franchises

Top 10 Fastest Growing Franchises	Top 10 Hottest New Franchises
Subway	Mac Tools
Dunkin' Donuts	Rent-A-Center
Cruise Planners	The Grounds Guys LLC
Jimmy John's Gourmet Sandwiches	FirstLight HomeCare
Vanguard Cleaning Systems	Hallmark Homecare Inc.
Great Clips	Sweet Frog Premium Frozen Yogurt
Taco Bell	Fresh Healthy Vending
Bricks 4 Kidz	HUMAN Healthy Markets
McDonald's	Green Home Solutions
Sport Clips	Engineering for Kids

Sources: "2015 Fastest-Growing Franchise Rankings," Entrepreneur, http://www.entrepreneur.com/franchises/fastestgrowing (accessed April 10, 2014); "2015 Top Newest Franchises," Entrepreneur, http://www.entrepreneur.com/franchises/topnew (accessed March 3, 2016).

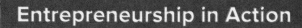

Buffalo Wild Wings Lands Rusty Taco

Rusty Taco
Founder: Steve Dunn and and Russell "Rusty" Fenton
Founded: 2010, in Dallas, Texas
Success: Rusty Taco's nine locations have attracted the attention of Buffalo Wild Wings, which bought a majority interest in the chain.

Entrepreneur Russell "Rusty" Fenton was both passionate about food and knew the perfect location for a restaurant. Teaming up with co-founder Steve Dunn in 2010, the two launched the Rusty Taco in a renovated Dallas gas station. The restaurant offers street-style breakfast and traditional tacos using fresh ingredients, with sides of melted cheese sauce, guacamole, and black beans. Consumers loved the tasty but affordable fare, and Rusty's tacos were voted as the number-one best taco in Dallas by About.com.

Not long afterward, the company began offering franchising opportunities. Startup costs include an average $350,000 and a franchise fee of $25,000. Royalties are 5 percent of gross sales. Franchisees have jumped at the opportunity, and now seven franchisees operate in the Dallas, Minneapolis, and Denver areas (the other two are company-owned). Sadly, co-founder Rusty Fenton passed away in 2014, but his idea of an affordable, fast-casual taco restaurant continues. In 2014, Buffalo Wild Wings acquired a majority stake in the promising franchise operation.[40]

Discussion Questions

1. What are some advantages of allowing other entrepreneurs to open franchises of Rusty Taco?
2. Why might entrepreneurs choose to open up a Rusty Taco franchise rather than starting their own companies from scratch?
3. Are there any disadvantages Rusty Taco may experience by operating as a franchise?

However, the franchisee must sacrifice some freedom to the franchiser. Some shortcomings experienced by franchisees include:

- Franchise fees and profit sharing with the franchiser.
- Strict adherence to standardized operations.
- Restrictions on purchasing.
- Limited product line.
- Possible market saturation.
- Less freedom in business decisions.[41]

Strict uniformity is the rule rather than the exception. Entrepreneurs who want to be their own bosses are often frustrated with the restrictions of a franchise.

Help for Small-Business Managers

Because of the crucial role that small business and entrepreneurs play in the U.S. economy, a number of organizations offer programs to improve the small-business owner's ability to compete. These include entrepreneurial training programs and programs sponsored by the SBA. Such programs provide small-business owners with invaluable assistance in managing their businesses, often at little or no cost to the owner.

Entrepreneurs can learn critical marketing, management, and finance skills in seminars and college courses. In addition, knowledge, experience, and judgment are necessary for success in a new business. While knowledge can be communicated and some experiences can be simulated in the classroom, good judgment must be developed by the entrepreneur. Local chambers of commerce and the U.S. Department of Commerce offer information and assistance helpful in operating a small business. National publications such as *Inc.* and *Entrepreneur* share statistics, advice, tips, and success/failure stories. Additionally, most urban areas have weekly business journals/newspapers that provide stories on local businesses as well as on business techniques that a manager or small business can use.

The SBA offers many types of management assistance to small businesses, including counseling for firms in difficulty, consulting on improving operations, and training for owner/managers and their employees. Among its many programs, the SBA funds Small Business Development Centers (SBDCs). These are business clinics, usually located on college campuses, that provide counseling at no charge and training at only a nominal charge. SBDCs are often the SBA's principal means of providing direct management assistance.

The Service Corps of Retired Executives (SCORE) and the Active Corps of Executives (ACE) are volunteer agencies funded by the SBA to provide advice for owners of small firms. Both are staffed by experienced managers whose talents and experience the small firms could not ordinarily afford. SCORE has more than 11,000 volunteers at 320 locations in the United States and has served more than 10 million small businesses.[42] The SBA also has organized Small Business Institutes (SBIs) on almost 500 university and college campuses in the United States. Seniors, graduate students, and faculty at each SBI provide onsite management counseling.

Finally, the small-business owner can obtain advice from other small-business owners, suppliers, and even customers. A customer may approach a small business it frequents with a request for a new product, for example, or a supplier may offer suggestions for improving a manufacturing process. Networking—building relationships and sharing information with colleagues—is vital for any businessperson, whether you work for a huge corporation or run your own small business. Incubators, or organizations created to accelerate the development and success of startup organizations, often provide network opportunities and potential capital to jumpstart a business.[43] Communicating with other business owners is a great way to find ideas for dealing with employees and government regulation, improving processes, or solving problems. New technology is making it easier to network. For example, some states are establishing social networking sites for the use of their businesses to network and share ideas.

The Future for Small Business[44]

Although small businesses are crucial to the economy, their size and limited resources can make them more vulnerable to turbulence and change in the marketplace than large businesses. Next, we take a brief look at the demographic, technological, and economic trends that will have the most impact on small business in the future.

LO 5-6

Evaluate the demographic, technological, and economic trends that are affecting the future of small business.

Demographic Trends

America's baby boom started in 1946 and ended in 1964. Many boomers are over 50, and in the next few years, millions more will pass that mark. The baby boomer generation consists of 75 million Americans.[45] This segment of the population is wealthy, but many small businesses do not actively pursue it. Some exceptions, however, include Gold Violin, which sells designer canes and other products online and through a catalog, and LifeSpring Nutrition, which delivers nutritional meals and snacks directly to the customer. Industries such as travel, financial planning, and health care will continue to grow as boomers age. Many experts believe that the boomer demographic is the market of the future.

Another market with a huge potential for small business is the echo boomers, also called millennials or Generation Y. Millennials number around 83 million and possess a number of unique characteristics.[46] Born between the early 1980s and the early 2000s, this cohort is not solely concerned about money. Those that fall into this group are also concerned with advancement, recognition, and improved capabilities. They need direct, timely feedback and frequent encouragement and recognition. Millennials do well when training sessions combine entertainment with learning. Working remotely is more acceptable to this group than previous generations, and virtual communication may become as important as face-to-face meetings.[47]

Yet another trend is the growing number of immigrants living in the United States, who now represent about 14 percent of the population. If this trend continues, by 2065 nearly one in five Americans will be classified as immigrants. The Latino population, the nation's largest minority group, is expected to grow by 86 percent between 2015 and 2050.[48]

This vast group provides still another greatly untapped market for small businesses. Retailers who specialize in ethnic products, and service providers who offer bi- or multilingual employees, will find a large amount of business potential in this market. Table 5-7 ranks top cities in the United States for small businesses and startups.

The Latino population is the biggest and fastest growing minority segment in the United States—and a lucrative market for businesses looking for ways to meet the segment's many needs.

© Karin Dreyer/Blend Images

Technological and Economic Trends

Advances in technology have opened up many new markets to small businesses. Undoubtedly, the Internet will continue to provide new opportunities for small businesses. Slack is a messaging app that allows teams to engage in efficient collaboration.

TABLE 5-7
Most Business-Friendly Cities

I. Manchester, New Hampshire
2. Dallas, Texas
3. Richmond, Virginia
4. Austin, Texas
5. Knoxville, Tennessee
6. Nashville, Tennessee
7. Houston, Texas
8. Fort Collins, Colorado

Source: "Top 10 Small Business Friendly States and Cities of 2015," Smallbusiness.com, August 18, 2015, http://smallbusiness.com/local/10-most-small-business-friendly-states-cities/ (accessed March 3, 2016).

The tool uses Internet-based computing known as the cloud to enable group collaboration. Today, Slack is valued at $2.8 billion.[49] Technology has also enabled the substantial growth of entrepreneurs working out of their houses, known as home-based businesses. Many of today's largest businesses started out from out their homes, including Mary Kay, Ford, and Apple. Approximately 52 percent of all small businesses are based out of the home. Technological advancements have increased the ability of home-based businesses to interact with customers and operate effectively.[50]

Technological advances and an increase in service exports have created new opportunities for small companies to expand their operations abroad. Changes in communications and technology can allow small companies to customize their services quickly for international customers. Also, free trade agreements and trade alliances are helping to create an environment in which small businesses have fewer regulatory and legal barriers.

In recent years, economic turbulence has provided both opportunities and threats for small businesses. As large information technology companies such as Cisco, Oracle, and Sun Microsystems had to recover from an economic slowdown and an oversupply of Internet infrastructure products, some smaller firms found new niche markets. Smaller companies can react quickly to change and can stay close to their customers. While well-funded dot-coms were failing, many small businesses were learning how to use the Internet to promote themselves and sell products online. For example, arts and crafts dealers and makers of specialty products found they could sell their wares on existing websites, such as eBay. Service providers related to tourism, real estate, and construction also found they could reach customers through their own or existing websites.

Deregulation of the energy market and interest in alternative fuels and in fuel conservation have spawned many small businesses. Southwest Windpower Inc. manufactures and markets small wind turbines for producing electric power for homes, sailboats, and telecommunications. Solar Attic Inc. has developed a process to recover heat from home attics to use in heating water or swimming pools. As entrepreneurs begin to realize that worldwide energy markets are valued in the hundreds of billions of dollars, the number of innovative companies entering this market will increase. In addition, many small businesses have the desire and employee commitment to purchase such environmentally friendly products. New Belgium Brewing Company received the U.S. Environmental Protection Agency and Department of Energy Award for leadership in conservation for making a 10-year commitment to purchase wind energy.

The future for small business remains promising. The opportunities to apply creativity and entrepreneurship to serve customers are unlimited. While large organizations such as Walmart, which has more than 2.2 million employees, typically must adapt to change slowly, a small business can adapt immediately to customer and community needs and changing trends. This flexibility provides small businesses with a definite advantage over large companies.

Making Big Businesses Act "Small"

LO 5-7

Explain why many large businesses are trying to "think small."

The continuing success and competitiveness of small businesses through rapidly changing conditions in the business world have led many large corporations to take a closer look at what makes their smaller rivals tick. More and more firms are emulating small businesses in an effort to improve their own bottom line. Beginning in the 1980s and continuing through the present, the buzzword in business has been to *downsize* or *right-size* to reduce management layers, corporate staff, and work tasks in order to make the firm more flexible, resourceful, and innovative. Many well-known U.S. companies—including IBM, Ford, Apple, General Electric, Xerox, and 3M—have downsized to improve their competitiveness, as have German, British, and Japanese firms. Other firms have sought to make their businesses "smaller" by making their operating units function more like independent small businesses, each responsible for its profits, losses, and resources. Of course, some large corporations, such as Southwest Airlines, have acted like small businesses from their inception, with great success.

Trying to capitalize on small-business success in introducing innovative new products, more and more companies are attempting to instill a spirit of entrepreneurship into even the largest firms. In major corporations, **intrapreneurs,** like entrepreneurs, take responsibility for, or "champion," the development of innovations of any kind *within* the larger organization.[51] Often, they use company resources and time to develop a new product for the company.

intrapreneurs
individuals in large firms who take responsibility for the development of innovations within the organizations.

So You Want to Be an Entrepreneur or Small-Business Owner

In times when jobs are scarce, many people turn to entrepreneurship as a way to find employment. As long as there are unfulfilled needs from consumers, there will be a demand for entrepreneurs and small businesses. Entrepreneurs and small-business owners have been, and will continue to be, a vital part of the U.S. economy, whether in retailing, wholesaling, manufacturing, technology, or services. Creating a business around your idea has a lot of advantages. For many people, independence is the biggest advantage of forming their own small business, especially for those who do not work well in a corporate setting and like to call their own shots. Smaller businesses are also cheaper to start up than large ones in terms of salaries, infrastructure, and equipment. Smallness also provides a lot of flexibility to change with the times. If consumers suddenly start demanding new and different products, a small business is more likely to deliver quickly.

Starting your own business is not easy, especially in slow economic times. Even in a good economy, taking an idea and turning it into a business has a very high failure rate. The possibility of failure can increase even more when money is tight. Reduced revenues and expensive materials can hurt a small business more than a large one because small businesses have fewer resources. When people are feeling the pinch from rising food and fuel prices, they tend to cut back on other expenditures—which could potentially harm your small business. The increased cost of materials will also affect your bottom line. However, several techniques can help your company survive:

- Set clear payment schedules for all clients. Small businesses tend to be worse about collecting payments than large ones, especially if the clients are acquaintances. However, you need to keep cash flowing into the company in order to keep business going.

- Take the time to learn about tax breaks. A lot of people do not realize all of the deductions they can claim on items such as equipment and health insurance.

- Focus on your current customers, and don't spend a lot of time looking for new ones. It is far less expensive for a company to keep its existing customers happy.

- Although entrepreneurs and small-business owners are more likely to be friends with their customers, do not let this be a temptation to give things away for free. Make it clear to your customers what the basic price is for what you are selling and charge for extra features, extra services, etc.

- Make sure the office has the conveniences employees need—like a good coffee maker and other drinks and snacks. This will not only make your employees happy, but it will also help maintain productivity by keeping employees closer to their desks.

- Use your actions to set an example. If money is tight, show your commitment to cutting costs and making the business work by doing simple things like taking the bus to work or bringing a sack lunch every day.

- Don't forget to increase productivity in addition to cutting costs. Try not to focus so much attention on cost cutting that you don't try to increase sales.

In unsure economic times, these measures should help new entrepreneurs and small-business owners sustain their businesses. Learning how to run a business on a shoestring is a great opportunity to cut the fat and to establish lean, efficient operations.[52]

Review Your Understanding

Define *entrepreneurship* and *small business.*

An entrepreneur is a person who creates a business or product and manages his or her resources and takes risks to gain a profit; entrepreneurship is the process of creating and managing a business to achieve desired objectives. A small business is one that is not dominant in its competitive area and does not employ more than 500 people.

Investigate the importance of small business in the U.S. economy and why certain fields attract small business.

Small businesses are vital to the American economy because they provide products, jobs, innovation, and opportunities. Retailing, wholesaling, services, manufacturing, high technology, and the sharing economy attract small businesses because these industries are relatively easy to enter, require relatively low initial financing, and may experience less heavy competition.

Specify the advantages of small-business ownership.

Small-business ownership offers some personal advantages, including independence, freedom of choice, and the option of working at home. Business advantages include flexibility, the ability to focus on a few key customers, and the chance to develop a reputation for quality and service.

Summarize the disadvantages of small-business ownership and analyze why many small businesses fail.

Small businesses have many disadvantages for their owners such as expense, physical and psychological stress, and a high failure rate. Small businesses fail for many reasons: undercapitalization, management inexperience or incompetence, neglect, disproportionate burdens imposed by government regulation, and vulnerability to competition from larger companies.

Describe how you go about starting a small business and what resources are needed.

First, you must have an idea for developing a small business. Next, you need to devise a business plan to guide planning and development of the business. Then, you must decide what form of business ownership to use: sole proprietorship, partnership, or corporation. Small-business owners are expected to provide some of the funds required to start their businesses, but funds also can be obtained from friends and family, financial institutions, other businesses in the form of trade credit, investors (venture capitalists), state and local organizations, and the Small Business Administration. In addition to loans, the Small Business Administration and other organizations offer counseling, consulting, and training services. Finally, you must decide whether to start a new business from scratch, buy an existing one, or buy a franchise operation.

Evaluate the demographic, technological, and economic trends that are affecting the future of small business.

Changing demographic trends that represent areas of opportunity for small businesses include more elderly people as baby boomers age, millennials, or Generation Y, and an increasing number of immigrants to the United States. Technological advances and an increase in service exports have created new opportunities for small companies to expand their operations abroad, while trade agreements and alliances have created an environment in which small business has fewer regulatory and legal barriers. Economic turbulence presents both opportunities and threats to the survival of small businesses.

Explain why many large businesses are trying to "think small."

More large companies are copying small businesses in an effort to make their firms more flexible, resourceful, and innovative and, generally, to improve their bottom line. This effort often involves downsizing (reducing management layers, laying off employees, and reducing work tasks) and intrapreneurship, when an employee takes responsibility for (champions) developing innovations of any kind within the larger organization.

Assess two entrepreneurs' plans for starting a small business.

Based on the facts given in the "Solve the Dilemma" feature at the end of this chapter and the material presented in this chapter, you should be able to assess the feasibility and potential success of Gray and McVay's idea for starting a small business.

Revisit the World of Business

1. How does V.I.P. Moving & Storage differentiate itself from other competitors?

2. As a small business, what advantages does V.I.P. Moving & Storage have that makes it appealing to customers such as the Tennessee Titans?

3. How was owner Marshall Powell Ledbetter III able to take the challenge of having to purchase an all-new fleet and turn it into an advantage?

Learn the Terms

business plan 153
entrepreneurship 142
franchise 155
franchisee 155
franchiser 155

intrapreneurs 161
sharing economy 148
small business 143
Small Business Administration
  (SBA) 143

social entrepreneurs 143
undercapitalization 151
venture capitalists 154

Check Your Progress

1. Why are small businesses so important to the U.S. economy?

2. Which fields tend to attract entrepreneurs the most? Why?

3. What are the advantages of starting a small business? The disadvantages?

4. What are the principal reasons for the high failure rate among small businesses?

5. What decisions must an entrepreneur make when starting a small business?

6. What types of financing do small entrepreneurs typically use? What are some of the pros and cons of each?

7. List the types of management and financial assistance that the Small Business Administration offers.

8. Describe the franchising relationship.

9. What demographic, technological, and economic trends are influencing the future of small business?

10. Why do large corporations want to become more like small businesses?

Get Involved

1. Interview a local small-business owner. Why did he or she start the business? What factors have led to the business's success? What problems has the owner experienced? What advice would he or she offer a potential entrepreneur?

2. Using business journals, find an example of a company that is trying to emulate the factors that make small businesses flexible and more responsive. Describe and

evaluate the company's activities. Have they been successful? Why or why not?

3. Using the business plan outline in online Appendix A, create a business plan for a business idea that you have. (A man named Fred Smith once did a similar project for a business class at Yale. His paper became the basis for the business he later founded: Federal Express!)

Build Your Skills

Creativity

Background

The entrepreneurial success stories in this chapter are about people who used their creative abilities to develop innovative products or ways of doing something that became the basis of a new business. Of course, being creative is not just for entrepreneurs or inventors; creativity is an important tool to help you find the optimal solutions to the problems you face on a daily basis. Employees rely heavily on their creativity skills to help them solve daily workplace problems.

According to brain experts, the right-brain hemisphere is the source of creative thinking; and the creative part of the brain can "atrophy" from lack of use. Let's see how much "exercise" you're giving your right-brain hemisphere.

Task

1. Take the following self-test to check your Creativity Quotient.[53]

2. Write the appropriate number in the box next to each statement according to whether the statement describes your behavior always (3), sometimes (2), once in a while (1), or never (0).

	Always 3	Sometimes 2	Once in a While 1	Never 0
1. I am a curious person who is interested in other people's opinions.				
2. I look for opportunities to solve problems.				
3. I respond to changes in my life creatively by using them to redefine my goals and revising plans to reach them.				
4. I am willing to develop and experiment with ideas of my own.				
5. I rely on my hunches and insights.				
6. I can reduce complex decisions to a few simple questions by seeing the "big picture."				
7. I am good at promoting and gathering support for my ideas.				
8. I think further ahead than most people I associate with by thinking long term and sharing my vision with others.				
9. I dig out research and information to support my ideas.				
10. I am supportive of the creative ideas from my peers and subordinates and welcome "better ideas" from others.				
11. I read books and magazine articles to stay on the "cutting edge" in my areas of interest. I am fascinated by the future.				
12. I believe I am creative and have faith in my good ideas.				
Subtotal for each column				
Grand Total				

3. **Check your score using the following scale:**

   30–36   High creativity. You are giving your right-brain hemisphere a regular workout.

   20–29   Average creativity. You could use your creativity capacity more regularly to ensure against "creativity atrophy."

   10–19   Low creativity. You could benefit by reviewing the questions you answered "never" in the above assessment and selecting one or two of the behaviors that you could start practicing.

   0–9   Undiscovered creativity. You have yet to uncover your creative potential.

Solve the Dilemma

The Small-Business Challenge

Jack Gray and his best friend, Bruce McVay, decided to start their own small business. Jack had developed recipes for fat-free and low-fat cookies and muffins in an effort to satisfy his personal health needs. Bruce had extensive experience in managing food-service establishments. They knew that a startup company needs a quality product, adequate funds, a written business plan, some outside financial support, and a good promotion program. Jack and Bruce felt they had all of this and more and were ready to embark on their new low-fat cookie/muffin store. Each had $35,000 to invest and with their homes and other resources, they had borrowing power of an additional $125,000.

However, they still have many decisions to make, including what form or organization to use, how to market their product, and how to determine exactly what products to sell—whether just cookies and muffins or additional products.

Discussion Questions

1. Evaluate the idea of a low-fat cookie and muffin retail store.

2. Are there any concerns in connection with starting a small business that Jack and Bruce have not considered?

3. What advice would you give Jack and Bruce as they start up their business?

Build Your Business Plan

Small Business, Entrepreneurship, and Franchising

Now you can get started writing your business plan! Refer to Guidelines for the Development of the Business Plan following "The Dynamics of Business and Economics," which provides you with an outline for your business plan. As you are developing your business plan, keep in mind that potential investors might be reviewing it. Or you might have plans to go to your local Small Business Development Center for an SBA loan.

At this point in the process, you should think about collecting information from a variety of (free) resources. For example, if you are developing a business plan for a local business, good, or service, you might want to check out any of the following sources for demographic information: your local Chamber of Commerce, Economic Development office, census bureau, or City Planning office.

Go on the Internet and see if there have been any recent studies done or articles on your specific type of business, especially in your area. Remember, you always want to explore any secondary data before trying to conduct your own research.

See for Yourself Videocase

Sonic—A Successful Franchise with an Old-Fashioned Drive-In Experience

For those who are nostalgic for the classic drive-in diner experience, the Sonic fast-food chain helps fill that need. Sonic offers customers a dose of nostalgia with its 1950s-style curbside speakers and carhop service. As the United States' largest drive-in fast-food chain, Sonic offers a unique and diverse menu selection that helps set it apart from a highly competitive fast-food franchise market. Founder Troy Smith launched the first Sonic Drive-In (known then as Top Hat Drive-In) in Shawnee, Oklahoma, in 1953 as a sole proprietorship. He later added a partner, Charlie Pappe, and eventually turned the business into a franchise.

Despite its traditional feel, the company has seized upon new trends and opportunities to secure more business. Customers at Sonic frequently eat in their cars or at tables outside the restaurant. However, Sonic has begun building indoor dining prototypes in colder areas to test whether this will entice more customers to eat at its locations. The prototype still makes use of the restaurant's traditional patio but encloses it to protect customers from the elements. Each of these restaurants maintains its carhop and drive-thru features in order to retain the "Sonic experience."

Today, Sonic is a publicly traded company and ranks among the top 30 restaurants among *Franchise Times'* Top 200+. Franchising is an appealing option for entrepreneurs looking to begin businesses without creating them from scratch. In the case of Sonic, when a franchisee purchases a franchise, he or she is getting a business that already has a national reputation and a national advertising campaign. The company also offers its franchisees tremendous support and training. As a pioneer, Troy Smith was required to innovate; as a Sonic franchisee, one steps into an already proven system.

That being said, successfully running a franchise is not easy. One entrepreneur who owns 22 Sonic franchises said the franchisee's job is to ensure that each customer has the best experience possible, thereby making repeat visits more likely. To accomplish this, a franchisee must build his or her locations, purchase equipment, hire excellent employees, make certain the products live up to Sonic's reputation, maintain a clean, inviting facility, and much more. In order to run 22 franchises, the entrepreneur runs his locations as limited partnerships, ensuring that a managing partner is on site at each location to keep day-to-day operations running smoothly.

Some of Sonic's success may be attributed to its stringent requirements for selecting franchisees. Although franchisees must have excellent financial credentials and prior restaurant/entrepreneurial experience, the most important factor is that each franchisee fit into the Sonic culture. Sonic offers two types of franchises. The traditional franchise, which includes the full restaurant set-up, requires an initial investment of between $1.1 million and $2 million. Franchisees are required to pay 5 percent in ongoing royalty fees and a franchise fee of $45,000. A Sonic in a travel plaza, a mall food court, or a college campus are all examples of the nontraditional model. Because these set-ups do not include the drive-in and carhop features, initial investment is less. However, royalty and advertising fees still apply.

For entrepreneurs looking for limited risk, franchises like Sonic are great options. The advantages are abundant, as discussed earlier. There is a high failure rate among small businesses. Entering into a successful franchise significantly cuts down on the risk of failure, although a franchisee does have to watch for market saturation, poor location choice, and other determining factors. However, there are also disadvantages; chiefly, franchisees are often required to follow a strict model set by the franchiser. For instance, in addition to prior restaurant experience, Sonic requires its franchisees to be financially and operationally able to open two or more drive-ins. These types of requirements may make it difficult for entrepreneurs who want to set their own terms. However, with Sonic's successful business model and brand equity, there is no shortage of individuals who would like to operate a Sonic franchise.[54]

Discussion Questions

1. What is Sonic's competitive advantage over other fast-food franchises?

2. What are the advantages of becoming a Sonic franchisee?

3. What are the disadvantages of buying into the Sonic franchise?

You can find the related video in the Video Library in Connect. Ask your instructor how you can access Connect.

Team Exercise

Explore successful global franchises. Go to the companies' websites and find the requirements for applying for three franchises. The chapter provides examples of successful franchises. What do the companies provide, and what is expected to be provided by the franchiser? Compare and contrast each group's findings for the franchises researched. For example, at Subway, the franchisee is responsible for the initial franchise fee, finding locations, leasehold improvements and equipment, hiring employees and operating restaurants, and paying an 8 percent royalty to the company and a fee into the advertising fund. The company provides access to formulas and operational systems, store design and equipment ordering guidance, a training program, an operations manual, a representative on site during opening, periodic evaluations and ongoing support, and informative publications.

Endnotes

1. Conversation with Marshall Powell Ledbetter III; V.I.P. Moving & Storage website, http://www.vipmovingandstorage.com/ (accessed July 14, 2015).

2. Small Business Administration Department of Advocacy, "Frequently Asked Questions," March 2014, www.sba.gov/sites/default/files/FAQ_March_2014_0.pdf (accessed April 10, 2014).

3. Global Entrepreneurship Development Institute, "Global Entrepreneurship Index," 2016, http://thegedi.org/global-entrepreneurship-and-development-index/ (accessed March 4, 2016).

4. Marco della Cava, "USA Today Entrepreneur of the Year," *USA Today,* December 11, 2014, pp. 1B–2B.

5. Ben Schiller, "TOMS Founder Blake Mycoskie Announces a New Fund for Social Good Startups," *Fast Company,* November 11, 2015, http://www.fastcompany.com/3053526/the-fast-company-innovation-festival/toms-founder-blake-mycoskie-announces-a-new-fund-for-so (accessed March 3, 2016).

6. Small Business Administration Department of Advocacy, "Frequently Asked Questions," March 2014, https://www.sba.gov/sites/default/files/FAQ_March_2014_0.pdf (accessed March 3, 2016).

7. National Association of Women Business Owners, "About Us," https://nawbo.org/about (accessed February 13, 2015).

8. Valentina Zarya, "Women-Owned Businesses Are Trailing in Size and Revenue," *Fortune,* September 2, 2015, http://fortune.com/2015/09/02/women-business-size-revenue/ (accessed March 3, 2016).

9. Sam Frizell, "Mercado of America," *Time,* April 28, 2015, 42-45; "About Us," The Legaspi Company website, http://www.thelegaspi.com/jos-de-jes-s-legaspi/ (accessed March 3, 2016).

10. Small Business Administration Department of Advocacy, "Frequently Asked Questions."

11. "Statistics of U.S. Businesses (SUSB)," *Statistics of U.S. Businesses,* www.census.gov/econ/susb/index.html (accessed March 3, 2016).

12. "Bittersweet Synergy: Domestic Outsourcing in India," *The Economist,* October 22, 2009, p. 74.

13. John Tozzi, "Innovation: Tap to Unlock," *Bloomberg Businessweek,* June 13, 2013, p. 42; Jennifer Hicks, "UniKey Raises Oversubscribed $10 Million Round for Smart Lock Technology," *Forbes,* April 18, 2015, http://www.forbes.com/sites/jenniferhicks/2015/04/18/unikey-raises-oversubscribed-10-million-round-for-smart-lock-technology/#6bb516c61fbe (accessed March 3, 2016).

14. SCORE Association, "Small Biz Stats & Trends," https://www.score.org/node/148155 (accessed March 3, 2016).

15. Matthew Diebel, "A Visionary Approach to Selling Eyewear," *USA Today,* December 1, 2014, p. 3B.

16. Alina Dizik, "Where Your Favorite Condiment Is Never Out of Stock," *The Wall Street Journal,* March 4, 2015, p. D3.

17. Suzanne Kapner, "J.C. Penney Resurrects Its Catalog," *The Wall Street Journal,* January 19, 2015, http://www.wsj.com/articles/j-c-penney-resurrects-its-catalog-1421695574 (accessed March 3, 2016).

18. "Fantastic Non-Plastic," *Fortune,* July 1, 2015, p. 48; MHG website, http://www.mhgbio.com/ (accessed July 14, 2015); *Reuters,* http://www.reuters.com/article/2015/04/28/ga-mhg-idUSnBw286293a=100=BSW20150428 (accessed July 14, 2015); "Biopolymer Company MHG Becomes First Company to Receive Vinçotte Certification for Marine Biodegradability," *Reuters,* April 28, 2015, http://finance.yahoo.com/news/meredian-inc-danimer-scientific-merge-171500117.html (accessed July 14, 2015).

19. Aamer Madhani, "Three Floyds: A Brewery That Really Knows Its Craft," *USA Today,* November 27, 2014, http://www.usatoday.com/story/money/business/2014/11/27/3-floyds-beer-entrepreneur-of-the-year/19273945/ (accessed March 4, 2016); Joseph S. Pete, "Three Floyds Named Fourth Best Beer in the World," *nwi.com,* February 2, 2015, http://www.nwitimes.com/business/local/three-floyds-named-fourth-best-beer-in-the-world/article_f02dd209-1999-595e-bea2-4513b549ef2d.html (accessed March 4, 2016).

20. Small Business Administration Department of Advocacy, "Frequently Asked Questions."

21. Lev Grossman, "Head Trip," *Time,* April 7, 2014, pp. 36–41.

22. Rachel Botsman presentation, "The Shared Economy Lacks a Shared Definition," *Fast Company,* November 21, 2013, http://www.fastcoexist.com/3022028/the-sharing-economy-lacks-a-shared-definition (accessed March 4, 2016); "The Rise of the Sharing Economy," *The Economist,* May 9, 2013, http://www.economist.com/news/leaders/21573104-internet-everything-hire-rise-sharing-economy (accessed March 4, 2016); Natasha Singer, "In the Sharing Economy, Workers Find Both Freedom and Uncertainty," *The New York Times,* August 16, 2014, http://www.nytimes.com/2014/08/17/technology/in-the-sharing-economy-workers-find-both-freedom-and-uncertainty.html?_r=1 (accessed March 4, 2016); "The Rise of the Sharing Economy," *The Economist,* May 9, 2013, http://www.economist.com/news/leaders/21573104-internet-everything-hire-rise-sharing-economy (accessed March 4, 2016).

23. Singer, "In the Sharing Economy, Workers Find Both Freedom and Uncertainty."

24. "The Rise of the Sharing Economy," *The Economist,* May 9, 2013, http://www.economist.com/news/leaders/21573104-internet-everything-hire-rise-sharing-economy (accessed March 4, 2016).

25. Arun Sundararajan, "The Gig Economy Is Coming. What Will It Mean for Work?" *The Guardian,* July 25, 2015, http://www.theguardian.com/commentisfree/2015/jul/26/will-we-get-by-gig-economy (accessed December 15, 2015).

26. Will Rinehart, "Independent Contractors and the Emerging Gig Economy," *American Action Forum,* July 29, 2015, http://americanactionforum.org/research/independent-contractors-and-the-emerging-gig-economy (accessed December 15, 2015).

27. PricewaterhouseCoopers, *The Sharing Economy: Consumer Intelligence Series,* 2015, https://www.pwc.com/us/en/technology/publications/assets/pwc-consumer-intelligence-series-the-sharing-economy.pdf (accessed March 4, 2016).

28. Ibid.

29. Ellen Huet, "Uber Driver Is an Employee, Not Contractor, Rules California Labor Commission," *Forbes,* June 17, 2015, http://www.forbes.com/sites/ellenhuet/2015/06/17/uber-drivers-are-employees-not-contractors-rules-california-labor-commission/#7183fe9215e4 (accessed March 4, 2016); Dan Levine, "Uber Drivers Granted Class Action Status in Lawsuit over Employment," *Reuters,* September 1, 2015, http://www.reuters.com/article/us-uber-tech-drivers-lawsuit-idUSKCN0R14O920150901 (accessed March 4, 2016).

30. Singer, "In the Sharing Economy, Workers Find Both Freedom and Uncertainty."

31. PricewaterhouseCoopers, *The Sharing Economy: Consumer Intelligence Series.*

32. David Whitford, "How a Terrible, Horrible, No Good, Very Bad Day Spawned a $70 Million Business," *Inc.,* November 2015, http://www.inc.com/magazine/201511/david-whitford/not-a-spectator-anymore.html (accessed August 9, 2016).

33. Small Business Administration Department of Advocacy, "Frequently Asked Questions."

34. Sarah Nassauer, "Inside Wal-Marts Shark Tank," *The Wall Street Journal,* July 23, 2015, p. B1; The Good Promise website, http://thegoodpromise.com/ (accessed July 24, 2015); Meagan Nichols, "Wal-Mart Wants Your Products," *Memphis Business Journal,* May 11, 2015, http://www.bizjournals.com/memphis/news/2015/05/11/wal-mart-wants-your-products.html (accessed July 24, 2015); Kim Souza, "The Supply Side: Chef Jenn Creates Gourmet Seafood for Walmart," *The City Wire,* February 23, 2015, http://www.thecitywire.com/node/36567#.VbJ2lbNViko (accessed July 24, 2015).

35. Susan Payton, "Attention, Micropreneurs: Youre Not Alone in Small Business," *Forbes,* May 12, 2014, http://www.forbes.com/sites/allbusiness/2014/05/12/attention-micropreneurs-youre-not-alone-in-small-business/ (accessed March 3, 2016).

36. Richard Duncan, "How I Blew It with My Business Plan," *The Wall Street Journal,* May 29, 2015, http://blogs.wsj.com/experts/2015/05/29/how-i-blew-it-with-my-business-plan/ (accessed March 4, 2016).

37. Elizabeth Segran, "Out of the Box," *Fast Company,* October 2015, pp. 72–76.

38. David Whitford, "Not a Spectator Anymore," *Inc.,* November 2015, pp. 26–34.

39. Thomas W. Zimmerer and Norman M. Scarborough, *Essentials of Entrepreneurship and Small Business Management,* 6th ed. (Upper Saddle River, NJ: Pearson Prentice Hall, 2005), pp. 118–24.

40. Rusty Taco, http://www.rustytaco.com/index.html (accessed July 23, 2015); Ron Ruggless, "Breakout Brands 2015: Rusty Taco," *Nations Restaurant News,* February 12, 2015, http://nrn.com/emerging-chains/breakout-brands-2015-rusty-taco (accessed July 23, 2015); Kirk Dooley, "Rusty Fenton Left Behind More than Just Tacos," *Dallas News,* September 12, 2014, http://www.dallasnews.com/news/community-news/park-cities/kirk-dooley/20140912-rusty-fenton-left-behind-more-than-just-tacos.ece (accessed July 23, 2015);

Angela Patterson, "10 Best Tacos in Dallas," About.com, http://dallas.about.com/od/restaurants/tp/BestTacosDallas.htm (accessed July 23, 2015); Rick Nelson, "Now Open: Rusty Taco," *Star Tribune,* April 13, 2011, http://www.startribune.com/now-open-rusty-taco/119297249/ (accessed July 23, 2015).

41. Thomas W. Zimmerer and Norman M. Scarborough, *Essentials of Entrepreneurship and Small Business Management,* 6th ed. (Upper Saddle River, NJ: Pearson Prentice Hall, 2005), pp. 118–24.

42. "Find a Chapter," SCORE, https://www.score.org/chapters-map (accessed March 1, 2016); SCORE Staten Island website, https://statenisland.score.org/ (accessed March 1, 2016).

43. Entrepreneur Media Inc., "Getting Started With Business Incubators," *Entrepreneur,* http://www.entrepreneur.com/article/52802 (accessed February 13, 2015).

44. Adapted from "Tomorrows Entrepreneur," *Inc. State of Small Business* 23, no. 7 (2001), pp. 80–104.

45. Cheryl Corley, "Millennials Now Out Number Baby Boomers, Census Bureau Says," *NPR,* July 7, 2015, http://www.npr.org/2015/06/25/417349199/millenials-now-out-number-baby-boomers-census-bureau-says (accessed March 4, 2016).

46. Ibid.

47. Molly Smith, "Managing Generation Y as They Change the Workforce," *Reuters,* January 8, 2008, www.reuters.com/article/2008/01/08/idUS129795=08-Jan-2008=BW20080108 (accessed March 4, 2016).

48. Jens Manuel Krogstad, "With Fewer New Arrivals, Census Lowers Hispanic Population Projections," *Pew Research Center,* December 16, 2014, http://www.pewresearch.org/fact-tank/2014/12/16/with-fewer-new-arrivals-census-lowers-hispanic-population-projections-2/ (accessed March 4, 2016); "Chapter 2: Immigration's Impact on Past and Future U.S. Population Change," *Pew Research Center,* September 28, 2015, http://www.pewhispanic.org/2015/09/28/chapter-2-immigrations-impact-on-past-and-future-u-s-population-change/ (accessed March 4, 2016).

49. Jeff Bercovici, "Gimme Some Slack: Company of the Year," *Inc.,* December 2015/January 2016, 114–119; Slack website, https://slack.com/ (accessed March 4, 2016).

50. Jason Nazar, "16 Surprising Statistics Facts about Small Businesses," *Forbes,* September 9, 2013, http://www.forbes.com/sites/jasonnazar/2013/09/09/16-surprising-statistics-about-small-businesses/ (accessed February 13, 2015); U.S. Small Business Administration, "Home-Based Businesses," https://www.sba.gov/content/home-based-businesses (accessed February 13, 2015).

51. Gifford Pinchott III, *Intrapreneuring* (New York: Harper & Row, 1985), p. 34.

52. Paul Brown, "How to Cope with Hard Times," *The New York Times,* June 10, 2008, www.nytimes.com/2008/06/10/business/smallbusiness/10toolkit.html?_r%205%20 1&ref%205%20smallbusiness&orefslogin&gwh=A256B424 94736F9E2C604851BF6451DC&gwt=regi (accessed April 22, 2014).

53. Adapted from Carol Kinsey Gorman, *Creativity in Business: A Practical Guide for Creative Thinking,* Crisp Publications Inc., 1989, pp. 5–6. © Crisp Publications Inc., 1200 Hamilton Court, Menlo Park, CA 94025.

54. Sonic Beach website, http://www.sonicbeach.com/ (accessed March 29, 2016); Sonic website, www.sonicdrivein.com (accessed March 29, 2016); "Strictly Speaking," Sonic website, www.sonicdrivein.com/business/franchise/faq.jsp (accessed July 27, 2012); Sonic, "Awards," https://www.sonicdrivein.com/corporate/awards (accessed March 29, 2016); Entrepreneur Media, Inc., "Sonic Drive-In Restaurants," *Entrepreneur,* 2016, https://www.sonicdrivein.com/corporate/awards (accessed March 29, 2016).

PART 3

Managing for Quality and Competitiveness

Introduction

For any organization—small or large, for profit or nonprofit—to achieve its objectives, it must have resources to support operations, employees to make and sell the products, and financial resources to purchase additional goods and services, pay employees, and generally operate the business. To accomplish this, it must also have one or more managers to plan, organize, staff, direct, and control the work that goes on.

This chapter introduces the field of management. It examines and surveys the various functions, levels, and areas of management in business. The skills that managers need for success and the steps that lead to effective decision making are also discussed.

The Importance of Management

Management is a process designed to achieve an organization's objectives by using its resources effectively and efficiently in a changing environment. *Effectively* means having the intended result; *efficiently* means accomplishing the objectives with a minimum of resources. **Managers** make decisions about the use of the organization's resources and are concerned with planning, organizing, directing, and controlling the organization's activities so as to reach its objectives. For instance, managers at Dow Chemical and DuPont engaged in planning, organizing, directing, and controlling the decision to merge their two firms together to form DowDuPont.[2] Management is universal. It takes place not only in business, but also in government, the military, labor unions, hospitals, schools, and religious groups—any organization requiring the coordination of resources.

Every organization must acquire resources (people, services, raw materials and equipment, financial, and information) to effectively pursue its objectives and coordinate their use to turn out a final good or service. Employees are one of the most important resources in helping a business attain its objectives. Hiring people to carry out the work of the organization is known as **staffing.** Beyond recruiting people for positions within the firm, managers must determine what skills are needed for specific jobs, how to motivate and train employees, how much to pay, what benefits to provide, and how to prepare employees for higher-level jobs in the firm at a later date. Sometimes, they must also make the difficult decision to reduce the workforce. This is known as **downsizing,** the elimination of significant numbers of employees from an organization. After a downsizing situation, an effective manager will promote optimism and positive thinking and minimize criticism and fault-finding. These elements of staffing will be explored in detail in Chapters 9 and 10.

Acquiring suppliers is another important part of managing resources and ensuring that products are made available to customers. As firms reach global markets, companies such as Walmart, Corning, and Charles Schwab enlist hundreds of diverse suppliers that provide goods and services to support operations. A good supplier maximizes efficiencies and provides creative solutions to help the company reduce expenses and reach its objectives. Finally, the manager needs adequate financial resources to pay for essential activities. Primary funding comes from owners and shareholders, as well as banks and other financial institutions. All these resources and activities must be coordinated and controlled if the company is to earn a profit.

---

management
a process designed to achieve an organization's objectives by using its resources effectively and efficiently in a changing environment.

LO 6-1

Define *management* and explain its role in the achievement of organizational objectives.

managers
those individuals in organizations who make decisions about the use of resources and who are concerned with planning, organizing, staffing, directing, and controlling the organization's activities to reach its objectives.

staffing
the hiring of people to carry out the work of the organization.

downsizing
the elimination of a significant number of employees from an organization.

Under Mary Barra's leadership, General Motors received record earnings in 2016.

© Bill Pugliano/Getty Images

Organizations must also have adequate supplies of resources of all types, and managers must carefully coordinate their use if they are to achieve the organization's objectives.

Management Functions

To harmonize the use of resources so that the business can develop, produce, and sell products, managers engage in a series of activities: planning, organizing, directing, and controlling (Figure 6-1). Although this book discusses each of the four functions separately, they are interrelated; managers may perform two or more of them at the same time.

LO 6-2

Describe the major functions of management.

Planning

Planning, the process of determining the organization's objectives and deciding how to accomplish them, is the first function of management. Planning is a crucial activity because it designs the map that lays the groundwork for the other functions. It involves forecasting events and determining the best course of action from a set of options or choices. The plan itself specifies what should be done, by whom, where, when, and how. For some managers, one major decision that requires extensive planning is selecting the right type of automation for warehouses and distribution facilities. Data gathering is a major phase of the planning process to determine what the facilities need and which automation can maximize order efficiency. Potential pitfalls in this process that managers should plan for include being swayed by advanced technology that is not needed, under-automating the facility, or over-automating the facility.[3] All businesses—from the smallest restaurant to the largest multinational corporation—need to develop plans for achieving success. But before an organization can plan a course of action, it must first determine what it wants to achieve.

planning
the process of determining the organization's objectives and deciding how to accomplish them; the first function of management.

Mission.   A **mission,** or mission statement, is a declaration of an organization's fundamental purpose and basic philosophy. It seeks to answer the question: "What business are we in?" Good mission statements are clear and concise statements that explain the organization's reason for existence. A well-developed mission statement, no matter what the industry or size of business, will answer five basic questions:

mission
the statement of an organization's fundamental purpose and basic philosophy.

1. Who are we?
2. Who are our customers?
3. What is our operating philosophy (basic beliefs, values, ethics, etc.)?
4. What are our core competencies and competitive advantages?
5. What are our responsibilities with respect to being a good steward of environmental, financial, and human resources?

FIGURE 6-1
The Functions of Management

Fiat-Chrylser is modifying its five-year strategic plan to better compete with its worldwide competitors.

© foto76/Shutterstock

A mission statement that delivers a clear answer to these questions provides the foundation for the development of a strong organizational culture, a good marketing plan, and a coherent business strategy. IKEA states that its mission is to "create a better everyday life for the many people."[4]

Goals.   A goal is the result that a firm wishes to achieve. A company almost always has multiple goals, which illustrates the complex nature of business. A goal has three key components: an attribute sought, such as profits, customer satisfaction, or product quality; a target to be achieved, such as the volume of sales or extent of management training to be achieved; and a time frame, which is the time period in which the goal is to be achieved. For instance, Starwood Hotels & Resorts made the goals to reduce energy consumption 30 percent and water consumption 20 percent by 2020.[5] To be successful at achieving goals, it is necessary to know what is to be achieved, how much, when, and how succeeding at a goal is to be determined.

Objectives   Objectives, the ends or results desired by an organization, derive from the organization's mission. A business's objectives may be elaborate or simple.

Herbalife does businesses in 90 countries, and contingency plans must often be made for fluctuating exchange rates.

© Patrick Fallon/Bloomberg via Getty Images

Entrepreneurship in Action

Former Bronco Tackles Dietary Trends

Pat's Gourmet LLC

Founder: Mike Lodish

Founded: 2011, in Birmingham, Michigan

Success: Since introducing his peanut brittle, sales volume has doubled, and it is now stocked in 30 Detroit specialty stores.

Mike Lodish, who spent 11 years as a defensive tackle in the NFL playing for the Buffalo Bills and the Denver Broncos, has traded the football field for a kitchen. In 2011, he started a company that sells vegan and gluten-free peanut brittle. Lodish knew his family's brittle recipe was good, but to be sure it would sell, he conducted market research and sampled many other varieties of brittle. In the end, he determined that his family brittle recipe was the best choice because of its unique crunchy texture.

As owner and sole full-time employee of Pat's Gourmet LLC, Lodish performs critical managerial functions like planning strategic objectives and controlling top management duties, as well as acting as a front-line supervisor for the company's contract employees. Aside from the day-to-day operational needs of the company, Lodish is also responsible for promotion. Lodish is so committed to the success of his company that he forgoes a salary and invests profits back into the business. Although Lodish has been successful, he continues to work at developing a better business, hoping one day to sell his brittle nationally.[6]

Questions for Discussion

1. As sole owner, what are some managerial roles Mike Lodish fills?
2. Mike Lodish is responsible for strategic planning of his company. What does this entail?
3. How important was it that Mike Lodish conduct market research prior to selling his family's brittle recipe?

Common objectives relate to profit, competitive advantage, efficiency, and growth. The principal difference between goals and objectives is that objectives are generally stated in such a way that they are measurable. Organizations with profit as an objective want to have money and assets left over after paying off business expenses. Objectives regarding competitive advantage are generally stated in terms of percentage of sales increase and market share, with the goal of increasing those figures. Efficiency objectives involve making the best use of the organization's resources. Growth objectives relate to an organization's ability to adapt and to get new products to the marketplace in a timely fashion. One of the most important objectives for businesses is sales. Nike, for example, has set an objective to grow sales on women-related apparel and products from $5.7 billion to $11 billion in the next five years. The company plans to focus more on selling tights and sports bras to this target market.[7] Objectives provide direction for all managerial decisions; additionally, they establish criteria by which performance can be evaluated.

Plans. There are three general types of plans for meeting objectives—strategic, tactical, and operational. A firm's highest managers develop its **strategic plans,** which establish the long-range objectives and overall strategy or course of action by which the firm fulfills its mission. Strategic plans generally cover periods ranging from one year or longer. They include plans to add products, purchase companies, sell unprofitable segments of the business, issue stock, and move into international markets. For example, after DuPont and Dow Chemical merge, the newly combined firm plans to spin off into three separate units focusing on agriculture, specialty products, and industrial materials. This strategic plan will take place over a three-year period.[8] Strategic plans must take into account the organization's capabilities and resources, the changing business environment, and organizational objectives. Plans should be market-driven, matching customers' desire for value with operational capabilities, processes, and human resources.[9]

strategic plans
those plans that establish the long-range objectives and overall strategy or course of action by which a firm fulfills its mission.

tactical plans
short-range plans designed to implement the activities and objectives specified in the strategic plan.

Tactical plans are short range and designed to implement the activities and objectives specified in the strategic plan. These plans, which usually cover a period of one year or less, help keep the organization on the course established in the strategic plan. General Motors, for instance, developed tactical plans to release redesigned versions of its vehicles that target millennials as part of its strategic plan to grow market share and reduce rental deliveries.[10] Because tactical plans allow the organization to react to changes in the environment while continuing to focus on the company's overall strategy, management must periodically review and update them. Declining performance or failure to meet objectives set out in tactical plans may be one reason for revising them. The differences between the two types of planning result in different activities in the short term versus the long term. For instance, a strategic plan might include the use of social media to reach consumers. A tactical plan could involve finding ways to increase traffic to the site or promoting premium content to those who visit the site. A fast-paced and ever-changing market requires companies to develop short-run or tactical plans to deal with the changing environment.

A retailing organization with a five-year strategic plan to invest $5 billion in 500 new retail stores may develop five tactical plans (each covering one year) specifying how much to spend to set up each new store, where to locate, and when to open each new store. Tactical plans are designed to execute the overall strategic plan. Because of their short-term nature, they are easier to adjust or abandon if changes in the environment or the company's performance so warrant.

operational plans
very short-term plans that specify what actions individuals, work groups, or departments need to accomplish in order to achieve the tactical plan and ultimately the strategic plan.

Operational plans are very short term and specify what actions specific individuals, work groups, or departments need to accomplish in order to achieve the tactical plan and ultimately the strategic plan. They apply to details in executing activities in one month, week, or even day. For example, a work group may be assigned a weekly production quota to ensure there are sufficient products available to elevate market share (tactical goal) and ultimately help the firm be number one in its product category (strategic goal). Returning to our retail store example, operational plans may specify the schedule for opening one new store, hiring and training new employees, obtaining merchandise, and opening for actual business.

crisis management (contingency planning)
an element in planning that deals with potential disasters such as product tampering, oil spills, fire, earthquake, computer virus, or airplane crash.

Another element of planning is **crisis management** or **contingency planning,** which deals with potential disasters such as product tampering, oil spills, fire, earthquake, computer viruses, or even a reputation crisis due to unethical or illegal conduct by one or more employees. Unfortunately, many businesses do not have updated contingency plans to handle the types of crises that their companies might encounter. As a result, it is estimated that approximately 25 percent of businesses fail to reopen after a serious disaster.[11] Businesses that have correct and well-thought-out contingency plans tend to respond more effectively when problems occur than do businesses who lack such planning.

Many companies, including Ashland Oil, H. J. Heinz, and Johnson & Johnson, have crisis management teams to deal specifically with problems, permitting other managers to continue to focus on their regular duties. Some companies even hold periodic disaster drills to ensure that their employees know how to respond when a crisis does occur. After the horrific earthquake in Japan, many companies in U.S. earthquake zones reevaluated their crisis management plans. Crisis management plans generally cover maintaining business operations throughout a crisis and communicating with the public, employees, and officials about the nature of and the company's response to the problem. Communication is especially important to minimize panic and damaging rumors; it also demonstrates that the company is aware of the problem and plans to respond.

Sometimes, disasters occur that no one can anticipate, but companies can still plan for how to react to the disaster. Seats Inc.—a Wisconsin-based manufacturer of quality seating for highway driving, school buses, locomotive operations, and more—is one company that displayed exemplary disaster recovery planning. When a fire destroyed the facility used to mold the foam used for its seats, the company immediately sprang into action. Partnering with another foam manufacturer, Seats Inc. retooled some of its equipment and sent its employees to the other facility to restore operations. Because of its quick action, the company was back in operation within a month after the fire.[12] Incidents such as this highlight the importance of planning for crises and the need to respond publicly and quickly when a disaster occurs.

Organizing

Rarely are individuals in an organization able to achieve common goals without some form of structure. **Organizing** is the structuring of resources and activities to accomplish objectives in an efficient and effective manner. Managers organize by reviewing plans and determining what activities are necessary to implement them; then, they divide the work into small units and assign it to specific individuals, groups, or departments. As companies reorganize for greater efficiency, more often than not, they are organizing work into teams to handle core processes such as new product development instead of organizing around traditional departments such as marketing and production. Organizing occurs continuously because change is inevitable.

organizing
the structuring of resources and activities to accomplish objectives in an efficient and effective manner.

Organizing is important for several reasons. It helps create synergy, whereby the effect of a whole system equals more than that of its parts. It also establishes lines of authority, improves communication, helps avoid duplication of resources, and can improve competitiveness by speeding up decision making. Volvo Group reorganized its heavy truck operations into four separate operations. The company claimed that this reorganization would create a simpler organization in which decisions regarding the different truck brands can be made faster.[13] Because organizing is so important, we'll take a closer look at it in Chapter 7.

Directing

During planning and organizing, staffing occurs and management must direct the employees. **Directing** is motivating and leading employees to achieve organizational objectives. Good directing involves telling employees what to do and when to do it through the implementation of deadlines and then encouraging them to do their work. For example, as a sales manager, you would need to learn how to motivate salespersons, provide leadership, teach sales teams to be responsive to customer needs, and manage organizational issues as well as evaluate sales results. Finally, directing also involves determining and administering appropriate rewards and recognition. All managers are involved in directing, but it is especially important for lower-level managers who interact daily with the employees operating the organization. For example, an assembly-line supervisor for Frito-Lay must ensure that her workers know how to use their equipment properly and have the resources needed to carry out their jobs safely and efficiently, and she must motivate her workers to achieve their expected output of packaged snacks.

directing
motivating and leading employees to achieve organizational objectives.

Managers may motivate employees by providing incentives—such as the promise of a raise or promotion—for them to do a good job. But most workers want more than money from their jobs: They need to know that their employer values their ideas and input. Managers should give younger employees some decision-making authority as soon as possible. Smart managers, therefore, ask workers to contribute ideas for reducing costs, making equipment more efficient, improving customer service, or even developing new products. This participation also serves to increase employee morale. Recognition and appreciation are often the best motivators. Employees who understand more about their effect on the financial success of the company may be induced to work harder for that success, and managers who understand the needs and desires of workers can encourage their employees to work harder and more productively. The motivation of employees is discussed in detail in Chapter 9.

Controlling

controlling
the process of evaluating and correcting activities to keep the organization on course.

Planning, organizing, staffing, and directing are all important to the success of an organization, whether its objective is earning a profit or something else. But what happens when a firm fails to reach its goals despite a strong planning effort? **Controlling** is the process of evaluating and correcting activities to keep the organization on course. Control involves five activities: (1) measuring performance, (2) comparing present performance with standards or objectives, (3) identifying deviations from the standards, (4) investigating the causes of deviations, and (5) taking corrective action when necessary.

Controlling and planning are closely linked. Planning establishes goals and standards. By monitoring performance and comparing it with standards, managers can determine whether performance is on target. When performance is substandard, management must determine why and take appropriate actions to get the firm back on course. In short, the control function helps managers assess the success of their plans. You might relate this to your performance in this class. If you did not perform as well on early projects or exams, you must take corrective action such as increasing studying or using website resources to achieve your overall objective of getting an A or B in the course. When the outcomes of plans do not meet expectations, the control process facilitates revision of the plans. Control can take many forms such as visual inspections, testing, and statistical modeling processes. The basic idea is to ensure that operations meet requirements and are satisfactory to reach objectives.

The control process also helps managers deal with problems arising outside the firm. For example, if a firm is the subject of negative publicity, management should use the control process to determine why, and to guide the firm's response.

Types of Management

LO 6-3

Distinguish among three levels of management and the concerns of managers at each level.

All managers—whether the sole proprietor of a jewelry store or the hundreds of managers of a large company such as Paramount Pictures—perform the four functions just discussed. In the case of the jewelry store, the owner handles all the functions, but in a large company with more than one manager, responsibilities must be divided and delegated. This division of responsibility is generally achieved by establishing levels of management and areas of specialization—finance, marketing, and so on.

Levels of Management

As we have hinted, many organizations have multiple levels of management—top management, middle management, and first-line, or supervisory management. These levels form a pyramid, as shown in Figure 6-2. As the pyramid shape implies, there are

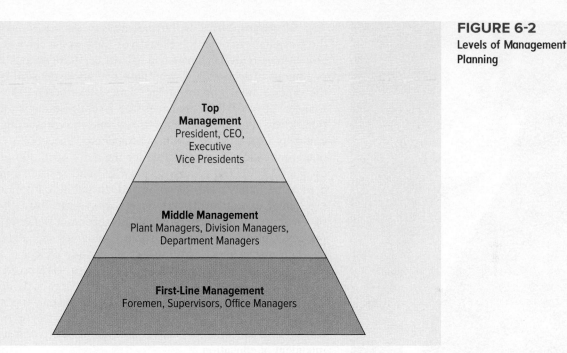

FIGURE 6-2
Levels of Management Planning

Top Management
President, CEO, Executive Vice Presidents

Middle Management
Plant Managers, Division Managers, Department Managers

First-Line Management
Foremen, Supervisors, Office Managers

generally more middle managers than top managers and still more first-line managers. Very small organizations may have only one manager (typically, the owner), who assumes the responsibilities of all three levels. Large businesses have many managers at each level to coordinate the use of the organization's resources. Managers at all three levels perform all four management functions, but the amount of time they spend on each function varies, as we shall see (Figure 6-3).

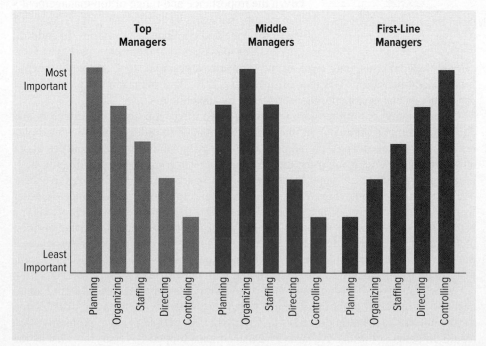

FIGURE 6-3
Importance of Management Functions to Managers in Each Level

Discovery Communication's CEO David Zaslav earned more than $150 million in compensation.

© Sam Simmonds/Polaris/Newscom

DID YOU KNOW? Only 4 percent of S&P 500 CEOs are women.[15]

top managers
the president and other top executives of a business, such as the chief executive officer (CEO), chief financial officer (CFO), and chief operations officer (COO), who have overall responsibility for the organization.

Top Management. In businesses, **top managers** include the president and other top executives, such as the chief executive officer (CEO), chief financial officer (CFO), and chief operations officer (COO), who have overall responsibility for the organization. For example, Mark Zuckerberg, CEO and founder of Facebook, manages the overall strategic direction of the company and plays a key role in representing the company to stakeholders. Sheryl Sandberg, Facebook's chief operating officer, is responsible for the daily operation of the company. The COO reports to the CEO and is often considered to be number two in command. In public corporations, even chief executive officers have a boss—the firm's board of directors. With technological advances accelerating and privacy concerns increasing, some companies are adding a new top management position—chief privacy officer (CPO). The position of privacy officer has grown so widespread that the International Association of Privacy Professionals boasts 20,000 members in 83 countries.[14] In government, top management refers to the president, a governor, or a mayor or city manager; in education, a chancellor of a university or a superintendent of education.

Top-level managers spend most of their time planning. They make the organization's strategic decisions, decisions that focus on an overall scheme or key idea for using resources to take advantage of opportunities. They decide whether to add products, acquire companies, sell unprofitable business segments, and move into foreign markets. Top managers also represent their company to the public and to government regulators.

Given the importance and range of top management's decisions, top managers generally have many years of varied experience and command top salaries. In addition to salaries, top managers' compensation packages typically include bonuses, long-term incentive awards, stock, and stock options. Table 6-1 lists the compensation packages of different CEOs. Top management may also get perks and special treatment that is criticized by stakeholders.

Compensation committees are increasingly working with boards of directors and CEOs to attempt to keep pay in line with performance in order to benefit stockholders and key stakeholders. The majority of major companies cite their concern about attracting capable leadership for the CEO and other top executive positions in their organizations. However, many firms are trying to curb criticism of excessive executive compensation by trying to align CEO compensation with performance. In other words, if the company performs poorly, the CEO will not be paid as well. This type of compensation method is making a difference.[16] For instance, the compensation of Chipotle's CEO was decreased by half due to the *E. coli* outbreaks at stores.[17] Successful management translates into happy stockholders who are willing to compensate their top executives fairly and in line with performance.

Workforce diversity is an important issue in today's corporations. Effective managers at enlightened corporations have found that diversity is good for workers and for the bottom line. Putting together different kinds of people to solve problems often results in better solutions. Novartis Pharmaceuticals topped DiversityInc's list as the

CEO	Company	Compensation*
David Zaslav	Discovery Communications	$156.1 million
Robert Iger	Walt Disney Productions	$84.3 million
Tim Cook	Apple	$65.2 million
Muhtar Kent	Coca-Cola	$25.2 million
Kenneth I. Chennault	American Express	$25.1 million
James P. Gorman	Morgan Stanley	$22.5 million
Meg Whitman	Hewlett-Packard	$19.6 million
Virginia Rometty	IBM	$19.3 million
Jeff Bezos	Amazon	$1.68 million
Warren Buffett	Berkshire Hathaway	$464,011

TABLE 6-1

Compensation Packages of CEOs

Compensation results compiled from publicly available data.

most diverse company. It was ranked two years in a row because of its emphasis on increasing opportunities for underrepresented groups to excel and earn a place among top management.[18] A diverse workforce is better at making decisions regarding issues related to consumer diversity. Reaching fast-growing demographic groups such as Hispanics, African Americans, Asian Americans, and others will be beneficial to large companies as they begin to target these markets.[19] Managers from companies devoted to workforce diversity devised five rules that make diversity recruiting work (see Table 6-2). Diversity is explored in greater detail in Chapter 10.

Rule	Action
1. Involve employees	Educate all employees on the tangible benefits of diversity recruiting to garner support and enthusiasm for those initiatives.
2. Communicate diversity	Prospective employees are not likely to become excited about joining your company just because you say that your company is diversity-friendly; they need to see it.
3. Support diversity initiatives and activities	By supporting community-based diversity organizations, your company will generate the priceless word-of-mouth publicity that will lead qualified diversity candidates to your company.
4. Delegate resources	If you are serious about diversity recruiting, you will need to spend some money getting your message out to the right places.
5. Promote your diversity initiatives	Employers need to sell their company to prospective diversity employees and present them with a convincing case as to why their company is a good fit for the diversity candidate.

TABLE 6-2

Five Rules of Successful Diversity Recruiting

Source: Adapted from Juan Rodriguez, "The Five Rules of Successful Diversity Recruiting," Diversityjobs.com, www.diversityjobs. com/Rules-of-Successful-Diversity-Recruiting (accessed February 25, 2010).

IT managers are responsible for implementing, maintaining, and controlling technology applications in business, such as computer networks.

© michaeljung/Shutterstock

middle managers
those members of an organization responsible for the tactical planning that implements the general guidelines established by top management.

first-line managers
those who supervise both workers and the daily operations of an organization.

LO 6-4

Specify the skills managers need in order to be successful.

technical expertise
the specialized knowledge and training needed to perform jobs that are related to particular areas of management.

Middle Management. Rather than making strategic decisions about the whole organization, **middle managers** are responsible for tactical and operational planning that will implement the general guidelines established by top management. Thus, their responsibility is more narrowly focused than that of top managers. Middle managers are involved in the specific operations of the organization and spend more time organizing than other managers. In business, plant managers, division managers, and department managers make up middle management. The product manager for laundry detergent at a consumer products manufacturer, the department chairperson in a university, and the head of a state public health department are all middle managers. The ranks of middle managers have been shrinking as more and more companies downsize to be more productive.

First-Line Management. Most people get their first managerial experience as **first-line managers,** those who supervise workers and the daily operations of the organization. They are responsible for implementing the plans established by middle management and directing workers' daily performance on the job. They spend most of their time directing and controlling. Common titles for first-line managers are foreman, supervisor, and office service manager.

Areas of Management

At each level, there are managers who specialize in the basic functional areas of business: finance, production and operations, human resources (personnel), marketing, IT, and administration.

Each of these management areas is important to a business's success. For instance, a firm cannot survive without someone obtaining needed financial resources (financial managers) or staff (human resources managers). While larger firms will most likely have all of these managers, and even more depending upon that particular firm's needs, in smaller firms these important tasks may fall onto the owner or a few employees. Yet whether or not companies have managers for specific areas, every company must have someone responsible for obtaining financial resources, transforming resources into finished products for the marketplace, hiring and/or dealing with staff, marketing goods and services, handling the firm's information technology resources, and managing a business segment or the overall business. These different types of managers are discussed in more detail in Table 6-3.

Skills Needed by Managers

Managers are typically evaluated using the metrics of how effective and efficient they are. Managing effectively and efficiently requires certain skills—technical expertise, conceptual skills, analytical skills, human relations skills, and leadership. Table 6-4 describes some of the roles managers may fulfill.

Technical Expertise

Managers need **technical expertise,** the specialized knowledge and training required to perform jobs related to their area of management. Accounting managers need to be able to perform accounting jobs, and production managers need to be able to perform production jobs. Although a production manager may not actually perform a job, he or she needs technical expertise to train employees, answer questions, provide

TABLE 6-3   **Areas of Management**

Manager	Function
Financial manager	Focus on obtaining the money needed for the successful operation of the organization and using that money in accordance with organizational goals.
Production and operations manager	Develop and administer the activities involved in transforming resources into goods, services, and ideas ready for the marketplace.
Human resources manager	Handle the staffing function and deals with employees in a formalized manner.
Marketing manager	Responsible for planning, pricing, and promoting products and making them available to customers through distribution.
Information technology (IT) manager	Responsible for implementing, maintaining, and controlling technology applications in business, such as computer networks.
Administrative manager	Manage an entire business or a major segment of a business; do not specialize in a particular function.

guidance, and solve problems. Technical skills are most needed by first-line managers and are least critical to top-level managers.

Conceptual Skills

Conceptual skills, the ability to think in abstract terms, and to see how parts fit together to form the whole, are needed by all managers, but particularly top-level managers. Top management must be able to evaluate continually where the company will be in the future. Conceptual skills also involve the ability to think creatively. Recent scientific research has revealed that creative thinking, which is behind the development of many innovative products and ideas, can be learned. As a result, IBM, AT&T, GE, Hewlett-Packard, Intel, and other top U.S. firms hire creative consultants to teach their managers how to think creatively.

This financial manager of a city hedge fund analyzes data from financial charts. Financial managers are responsible for obtaining the necessary funding for organizations to succeed, both in the short term and in the long term.
© NANIO4/iStockphoto

conceptual skills
the ability to think in abstract terms and to see how parts fit together to form the whole.

analytical skills
the ability to identify relevant issues, recognize their importance, understand the relationships between them, and perceive the underlying causes of a situation.

Analytical Skills

Analytical skills refer to the ability to identify relevant issues and recognize their importance, understand the relationships between them, and perceive the underlying causes of a situation. When managers have identified critical factors and causes, they can take appropriate action. All managers need to think logically, but this skill is probably most important to the success of top-level managers. To be analytical, it is necessary to think about a broad range of issues and to weigh different options before taking action. Because analytical skills are so important, questions that require analytical skills are often a part of job interviews. Questions such as "Tell me how you would resolve a problem at work if you had access to a large amount of data?" may be part of the interview process. The answer would require the interviewee to try to explain how to sort data to find relevant facts that could resolve the issue. Analytical thinking is required in complex or difficult situations where the solution is often not clear. Resolving ethical issues often requires analytical skills.

TABLE 6-4
Managerial Roles

General Role Category	Specific Role	Example Activity
Interpersonal	Figure	Attending award banquet
	Liaison	Coordinating production schedule with supply manager
	Leadership	Conducting performance appraisal for subordinates
Informational	Monitor	Contacting government regulatory agencies
	Disseminator	Conducting meetings with subordinates to pass along policy safety
	Spokesperson	Meeting with consumer group to discuss product safety
Decisional	Entrepreneur	Changing work process
	Disturbance handler	Deciding which unit moves into new facilities
	Resource allocator	Deciding who receives new computer equipment
	Negotiator	Settling union grievance

Source: Roles developed by management professor Henry Mintzberg.

financial managers
those who focus on obtaining needed funds for the successful operation of an organization and using those funds to further organizational goals.

production and operations managers
those who develop and administer the activities involved in transforming resources into goods, services, and ideas ready for the marketplace.

human resources managers
those who handle the staffing function and deal with employees in a formalized manner.

marketing manager
those who are responsible for planning, pricing, and promoting products and making them available to customers.

information technology (IT) managers
those who are responsible for implementing, maintaining, and controlling technology applications in business, such as computer networks.

administrative managers
those who manage an entire business or a major segment of a business; they are not specialists but coordinate the activities of specialized managers.

human relations skills
the ability to deal with people, both inside and outside the organization.

leadership
the ability to influence employees to work toward organizational goals.

Human Relations Skills

People skills, or **human relations skills,** are the ability to deal with people, both inside and outside the organization. Those who can relate to others, communicate well with others, understand the needs of others, and show a true appreciation for others are generally more successful than managers who lack such skills. People skills are especially important in hospitals, airline companies, banks, and other organizations that provide services. For example, Southwest Airlines places great value on its employees. New hires go through extensive training to teach employees about the airline and its reputation for impeccable customer service. All employees in management positions at Southwest take mandatory leadership classes that address skills related to listening, staying in touch with employees, and handling change without compromising values.

Leadership

Leadership is the ability to influence employees to work toward organizational goals. Strong leaders manage and pay attention to the culture of their organizations and the needs of their customers. Table 6-5 offers some requirements for successful leadership.

Managers often can be classified into three types based on their leadership style. *Autocratic leaders* make all the decisions and then tell employees what must be done and how to do it. They generally use their authority and economic rewards to get employees to comply with their directions. Martha Stewart is an example of an autocratic leader. She built up her media empire by paying close attention to every detail.[20] *Democratic leaders* involve their employees in decisions. The manager presents a situation and encourages his or her subordinates to express opinions and contribute ideas. The manager then considers the employees' points of view and makes the decision. Herb Kelleher, co-founder of Southwest Airlines, had a democratic leadership style. Under his leadership, employees were encouraged to discuss concerns and provide input.[21] *Free-rein leaders* let their employees work without much interference.

Responding to Business Challenges

Social Entrepreneurship: From South Africa to Whole Foods

Social entrepreneur Lisa Curtis founded Kuli Kuli on the principle of providing sustenance to impoverished people. While working for the Peace Corps in South Africa, Curtis was introduced to the highly nutritious leaves of the moringa tree. She learned that moringa leaves could be used as a base for various types of foods and beverages, which later inspired her to develop moringa food bars and energy drinks. She also saw moringa leaves as an opportunity to address the growing problem of malnutrition. Curtis sought to make moringa leaves more accessible while paying the farmers who grew it above-market wages. Aside from supporting local farmers, Kuli Kuli also donates a portion of its sales to a nonprofit fighting against world hunger.

Curtis is also a skilled businesswoman. She has strong human relations skills and expertly uses social media to share Kuli Kuli's story and attract top talent to work for her company. In its most recent crowdfunding campaign, Kuli Kuli raised the nearly $100,000 necessary to manufacture moringa energy shots, the company's first product to be sold in Whole Foods stores.

Curtis manages a diverse team made up of experienced engineers, entrepreneurs, and product development specialists to aid in the decision making process. She also attracted a long list of advisors passionate about Kuli Kuli's grassroots focus. Many have experience in the food and beverage industry and are eager to help Kuli Kuli succeed.[22]

Discussion Questions

1. How do you think Lisa Curtis used the decision-making process to make Kuli Kuli successful?
2. How did Lisa Curtis attract investors, employees, and advisors who believed in the mission of Kuli Kuli?
3. What personal traits enabled Lisa Curtis to grow Kuli Kuli as a grassroots movement against world hunger?

The manager sets performance standards and allows employees to find their own ways to meet them. For this style to be effective, employees must know what the standards are, and they must be motivated to attain them. The free-rein style of leadership can be a powerful motivator because it demonstrates a great deal of trust and confidence in the employee. Warren Buffett, CEO of Berkshire Hathaway, exhibits free-rein leadership among the managers who run the company's various businesses.

The effectiveness of the autocratic, democratic, and free-rein styles depends on several factors. One consideration is the type of employees. An autocratic style of leadership is generally best for stimulating unskilled, unmotivated employees; highly skilled, trained, and motivated employees may respond better to democratic or free-rein leadership styles. Employees who have been involved in decision making generally require less supervision than those not similarly involved. Other considerations are the manager's abilities and the situation itself. When a situation requires quick decisions, an autocratic style of leadership may be best because the manager does not have to consider input from a lot of people. If a special task force must be set up to solve a quality-control problem, a normally democratic manager may give free rein to the task force.

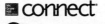

Need help understanding leaders vs. managers? Visit your Connect ebook video tab for a brief animated explanation.

• Communicate objectives and expectations.
• Gain the respect and trust of stakeholders.
• Develop shared values.
• Acquire and share knowledge.
• Empower employees to make decisions.
• Be a role model for appropriate behavior.
• Provide rewards and take corrective action to achieve goals.

TABLE 6-5
Requirements for Successful Leadership

Many managers, however, are unable to use more than one style of leadership. Some are incapable of allowing their subordinates to participate in decision making, let alone make any decisions. Thus, what leadership style is "best" depends on specific circumstances, and effective managers will strive to adapt their leadership style as circumstances warrant. Many organizations offer programs to develop goal leadership skills. When plans fail, very often leaders are held responsible for what goes wrong. For example, McDonald's former CEO Don Thompson was booted out of the position after being unable to turn around the company after years of stagnant sales.[24]

Another type of leadership style that has been gaining in popularity is *authentic leadership*. Authentic leadership is a bit different from the other three leadership styles because it is not exclusive. Both democratic and free-rein leaders could qualify as authentic leaders depending upon how they conduct themselves among stakeholders. Authentic leaders are passionate about the goals and mission of the company, display corporate values in the workplace, and form long-term relationships with stakeholders.[25] Former CEO of Ford Alan Mulally is a frequently cited example of an authentic leader. Mulally created trust with employees, developed values and a vision everyone in the firm could share, and always attempted to improve upon any shortcomings.[26]

While leaders might incorporate different leadership styles depending on the business and the situation, all leaders must be able to align employees behind a common vision to be effective.[27] Strong leaders also realize the value that employees can provide by participating in the firm's corporate culture. It is important that companies develop leadership training programs for employees. Because managers cannot oversee everything that goes on in the company, empowering employees to take more responsibility for their decisions can aid in organizational growth and productivity. Leadership training also enables a smooth transition when an executive or manager leaves the organization. Many smaller firms encounter difficulties when the founder or leader exits the firm, so it is highly important to have a succession plan in place.

Going Green

Patagonia: Lean, Mean, and Green

Since its establishment in 1970, Patagonia has produced apparel for the most extreme outdoor enthusiasts. The company also has a reputation for environmental stewardship and social responsibility. One percent of sales are donated to environmental organizations, and organic cotton has been used in its clothing since 1996. Many of Patagonia's garments are also made from recyclable materials, reducing the company's environmental impact.

When Rose Marcario became CEO in 2008, her goal was to take Patagonia's green initiatives even further. This required her to use conceptual skills to find creative new ways to increase the company's sustainability—especially since so much had already been done to make Patagonia environmentally friendly. Under her leadership, the company scrutinized its supply chain to look for ways to be more efficient while contributing toward a smaller environmental footprint. In 2014, it

began sourcing 100 percent traceable down feather from birds that were never force-fed or live plucked. Marcario focused on expanding these company green initiatives while also helping to double Patagonia's scale of operations and getting it certified as a B-Corporation—a designation given to companies committed to environmental and social responsibility.

Under Marcario's tenure, Patagonia has expanded its operations while remaining a diligent corporate citizen. If history is any indication, Patagonia will continue promoting its social and environmental initiatives while remaining an industry leader in outdoor apparel.[23]

Discussion Questions
1. What are some of Patagonia's green initiatives?
2. Why did Patagonia scrutinize its supply chain?
3. Who represents Patagonia's target market?

Howard Schultz, CEO of Starbucks, has great human relations skills and leadership abilities, as demonstrated by his ability to relate to others. Under his leadership, Starbucks decided to offer health insurance to its part-time workers and free college tuition due to its partnership with Arizona State University.

© Sakchai Lalit/AP

For example, J.M. Smucker Company implemented a transition plan that would allow the new CEO to replace the exiting CEO with minimal disruption.[28]

Employee Empowerment

Businesses are increasingly realizing the benefits of participative corporate cultures characterized by employee empowerment. **Employee empowerment** occurs when employees are provided with the ability to take on responsibilities and make decisions about their jobs. Employee empowerment does not mean that managers are not needed. Managers are important for guiding employees, setting goals, making major decisions, and other responsibilities emphasized throughout this chapter. However, companies that have a participative corporate culture have been found to be beneficial because employees feel like they are taking an active role in the firm's success.

Leaders who wish to empower employees adopt systems that support an employee's ability to provide input and feedback on company decisions. *Participative decision making,* a type of decision making that involves both manager and employee input, supports employee empowerment within the organization. One of the best ways to encourage participative decision making is through employee and managerial training. As mentioned earlier, employees should be trained in leadership skills, including

employee empowerment when employees are provided with the ability to take on responsibilities and make decisions about their jobs.

teamwork, conflict resolution, and decision making. Managers should also be trained in ways to empower employees to make decisions while also guiding employees to challenging situations in which the right decision might not be so clear.[29]

A section on leadership would not be complete without a discussion of leadership in teams. In today's business world, decisions made by teams are becoming the norm. Employees at Zappos, for instance, often work in teams and are encouraged to make decisions that they believe will reinforce the company's mission and values. Teamwork has often been an effective way for encouraging employee empowerment. Although decision making in teams is collective, the most effective teams are those in which all employees are encouraged to contribute their ideas and recommendations. Because each employee can bring in his or her own unique insights, teams often result in innovative ideas or decisions that would not have been reached by only one or two people. However, truly empowering employees in team decision making can be difficult. It is quite common for more outspoken employees to dominate the team and engage in groupthink, in which team members go with the majority rather than what they think is the right decision. Training employees how to listen to one another and provide relevant feedback can help to prevent these common challenges. Another way is to rotate the team leader so that no one person can assume dominancy.[30]

LO 5

Summarize the systematic approach to decision making used by many business managers.

Decision Making

Managers make many different kinds of decisions, such as the hours in a workday, which employees to hire, what products to introduce, and what price to charge for a product. Decision making is important in all management functions and at all levels, whether the decisions are on a strategic, tactical, or operational level. A systematic approach using the following six steps usually leads to more effective decision making: (1) recognizing and defining the decision situation, (2) developing options to resolve the situation, (3) analyzing the options, (4) selecting the best option, (5) implementing the decision, and (6) monitoring the consequences of the decision (Figure 6-4).

Recognizing and Defining the Decision Situation

The first step in decision making is recognizing and defining the situation. The situation may be negative—for example, huge losses on a particular product—or positive—for example, an opportunity to increase sales.

Situations calling for small-scale decisions often occur without warning. Situations requiring large-scale decisions, however, generally occur after some warning signs. Effective managers pay attention to such signals. Declining profits, small-scale losses in previous years, inventory buildup, and retailers' unwillingness to stock a product

FIGURE 6-4

Steps in the Decision-Making Process

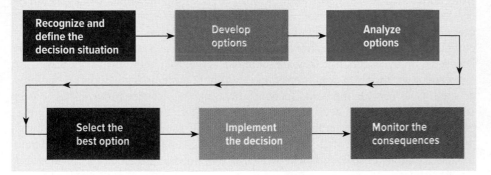

are signals that may foreshadow huge losses to come. If managers pay attention to such signals, problems can be contained.

Once a situation has been recognized, management must define it. Losses reveal a problem—for example, a failing product. One manager may define the situation as a product quality problem; another may define it as a change in consumer preference. These two viewpoints may lead to vastly different solutions. The first manager, for example, may seek new sources of raw materials of better quality. The second manager may believe that the product has reached the end of its lifespan and decide to discontinue it. This example emphasizes the importance of carefully defining the problem rather than jumping to conclusions.

Developing Options

Once the decision situation has been recognized and defined, the next step is to develop a list of possible courses of action. The best lists include both standard and creative plans. **Brainstorming,** a technique in which group members spontaneously suggest ideas to solve a problem, is an effective way to encourage creativity and explore a variety of options. As a general rule, more time and expertise are devoted to the development stage of decision making when the decision is of major importance. When the decision is of less importance, less time and expertise will be spent on this stage. Options may be developed individually, by teams, or through analysis of similar situations in comparable organizations. Creativity is a very important part of selecting the most viable option. Creativity depends on new and useful ideas, regardless of where they originate or the method used to create them. The best option can range from a required solution to an identified problem or a volunteered solution to an observed problem by an outside work group member.[31]

brainstorming
a technique in which group members spontaneously suggest ideas to solve a problem.

Analyzing Options

After developing a list of possible courses of action, management should analyze the practicality and appropriateness of each option. An option may be deemed impractical because of a lack of financial resources, legal restrictions, ethical and social responsibility considerations, authority constraints, technological constraints, economic limitations, or simply a lack of information and expertise. For example, a small computer manufacturer may recognize an opportunity to introduce a new type of computer but lack the financial resources to do so. Other options may be more practical for the computer company: It may consider selling its technology to another computer company that has adequate resources, or it may allow itself to be purchased by a larger company that can introduce the new technology.

When assessing appropriateness, the decision maker should consider whether the proposed option adequately addresses the situation. When analyzing the consequences of an option, managers should consider its impact on the situation and on the organization as a whole. For example, when considering a price cut to boost sales, management must think about the consequences of the action on the organization's cash flow and consumers' reaction to the price change.

Technology can help managers maintain an agenda, analyze options, and make decisions.

© Mutlu Kurtbas/Getty Images

Selecting the Best Option

When all courses of action have been analyzed, management must select the best one. Selection is often a subjective procedure because many situations do not lend themselves to quantitative analysis. Of course, it is not always necessary to select only one option and reject all others; it may be possible to select and use a combination of several options. William Wrigley Jr. made a decision to sell his firm to Mars for $23 billion. The firm was founded by his great-grandfather in 1891, but hard times forced Wrigley to take what was considered to be the best option. This option was to create the Mars-Wrigley firm, currently the world's largest confectionary company with a distribution network in 180 countries.[32] A different set of choices would have been available to the company had it been able to purchase Hershey for $12 billion a few years earlier.

Implementing the Decision

To deal with the situation at hand, the selected option or options must be put into action. Implementation can be fairly simple or very complex, depending on the nature of the decision. Effective implementation of a decision to abandon a product, close a plant, purchase a new business, or something similar requires planning. For example, when a product is dropped, managers must decide how to handle distributors and customers and what to do with the idle production facility. Additionally, they should anticipate resistance from people within the organization. (People tend to resist change because they fear the unknown.) Finally, management should be ready to deal with the unexpected consequences. No matter how well planned implementation is, unforeseen problems will arise. Management must be ready to address these situations when they occur.

Monitoring the Consequences

After managers have implemented the decision, they must determine whether it has accomplished the desired result. Without proper monitoring, the consequences of decisions may not be known quickly enough to make efficient changes. If the desired result is achieved, management can reasonably conclude that it made a good choice. If the desired result is not achieved, further analysis is warranted. Was the decision simply wrong, or did the situation change? Should some other option have been implemented?

If the desired result is not achieved, management may discover that the situation was incorrectly defined from the beginning. That may require starting the decision-making process all over again. Finally, management may determine that the decision was good even though the desired results have not yet shown up, or it may determine a flaw in the decision's implementation. In the latter case, management would not change the decision but would change the way in which it is implemented.

Management in Practice

Management is not exact and calculated. There is no mathematical formula for managing an organization and achieving organizational goals, although many managers passionately wish for one! Managers plan, organize, direct, and control, but management expert John P. Kotter says even these functions can be boiled down to two basic activities:

1. Figuring out what to do despite uncertainty, great diversity, and an enormous amount of potentially relevant information, and

2. Getting things done through a large and diverse set of people despite having little direct control over most of them.[33]

Managers spend as much as 75 percent of their time working with others—not only with subordinates but with bosses, people outside their hierarchy at work, and people outside the organization itself. In these interactions, they discuss anything and everything remotely connected with their business.

Managers spend a lot of time establishing and updating an agenda of goals and plans for carrying out their responsibilities. An **agenda** contains both specific and vague items, covering short-term goals and long-term objectives. Like a calendar, an agenda helps the manager figure out what must be done and how to get it done to meet the objectives set by the organization. Technology tools such as smartphones can help managers manage their agendas, contacts, communications, and time.

Managers also spend a lot of time **networking**—building relationships and sharing information with colleagues who can help them achieve the items on their agendas. Managers spend much of their time communicating with a variety of people and participating in activities that on the surface do not seem to have much to do with the goals of their organization. Nevertheless, these activities are crucial to getting the job done. Networks are not limited to immediate subordinates and bosses; they include other people in the company as well as customers, suppliers, and friends. These contacts provide managers with information and advice on diverse topics. Managers ask, persuade, and even intimidate members of their network in order to get information and to get things done. Networking helps managers carry out their responsibilities. Social media sites have increased the ability of both managers and subordinates to network. Internal social networks such as Yammer allow employees to connect with one another, while social networks such as Facebook or Twitter enable managers to connect with customers. Sales managers are even using social networks to communicate with their distributors. LinkedIn has been used for job networking and is gaining in popularity among the younger generation as an alternative to traditional job hunting. Some speculate that social networks might eventually replace traditional résumés and job boards.[34]

Finally, managers spend a great deal of time confronting the complex and difficult challenges of the business world today. Some of these challenges relate to rapidly changing technology (especially in production and information processing), increased scrutiny of individual and corporate ethics and social responsibility, the impact of social media, the changing nature of the workforce, new laws and regulations, increased global competition and more challenging foreign markets, declining educational standards (which may limit the skills and knowledge of the future labor and customer pool), and time itself—that is, making the best use of it. But such diverse issues cannot simply be plugged into a computer program that supplies correct, easy-to-apply solutions. It is only through creativity and imagination that managers can make effective decisions that benefit their organizations.

agenda
a calendar, containing both specific and vague items, that covers short-term goals and long-term objectives.

networking
the building of relationships and sharing of information with colleagues who can help managers achieve the items on their agendas.

Websites like LinkedIn are helping managers and employees network with one another to achieve their professional goals.

© Ingvar Björk/Alamy Stock Photo

So You Want to Be a Manager

What Kind of Manager Do You Want to Be?

Managers are needed in a wide variety of organizations. Experts suggest that employment will increase by millions of jobs in upcoming years. But the requirements for the jobs become more demanding with every passing year—with the speed of technology and communication increasing by the day, and the stress of global commerce increasing pressures to perform. However, if you like a challenge and if you have the right kind of personality, management remains a viable field. Even as companies are forced to restructure, management remains a vital role in business. In fact, the Bureau of Labor Statistics predicts that management positions in public relations, marketing, and advertising will increase 9 percent overall between 2014 and 2024. Demand for financial managers is estimated to increase 7 percent in the same time period. Computer and IT managers will continue to be in strong demand, with the number of jobs increasing 15 percent between 2014 and 2024.[35]

Salaries for managerial positions remain strong overall. While pay can vary significantly depending on your level of experience, the firm where you work, and the region of the country where you live, below is a list of the nationwide average incomes for a variety of different managers:

Chief executive: $180,700
Computer and IT manager: $136,280
Marketing manager: $137,400
Financial manager: $130,230
General and operations manager: $117,200
Medical/health services manager: $103,680
Administrative services manager: $92,250
Human resources manager: $114,140
Sales manager: $126,040[36]

In short, if you want to be a manager, there are opportunities in almost every field. There may be fewer middle management positions available in firms, but managers remain a vital part of most industries and will continue to be long into the future—especially as navigating global business becomes ever more complex.

Review Your Understanding

Define *management* and explain its role in the achievement of organizational objectives.

Management is a process designed to achieve an organization's objectives by using its resources effectively and efficiently in a changing environment. Managers make decisions about the use of the organization's resources and are concerned with planning, organizing, directing, and controlling the organization's activities so as to reach its objectives.

Describe the major functions of management.

Planning is the process of determining the organization's objectives and deciding how to accomplish them. Organizing is the structuring of resources and activities to accomplish those objectives efficiently and effectively. Directing is motivating and leading employees to achieve organizational objectives. Controlling is the process of evaluating and correcting activities to keep the organization on course.

Distinguish among three levels of management and the concerns of managers at each level.

Top management is responsible for the whole organization and focuses primarily on strategic planning. Middle management develops plans for specific operating areas and carries out the general guidelines set by top management. First-line, or supervisory, management supervises the workers and day-to-day operations. Managers can also be categorized as to their area of responsibility: finance, production and operations, human resources, marketing, IT, or administration.

Specify the skills managers need in order to be successful.

To be successful, managers need leadership skills (the ability to influence employees to work toward organizational goals), technical expertise (the specialized knowledge and training needed to perform a job), conceptual skills (the ability to think in abstract terms and see how parts fit together to form the whole), analytical skills (the ability to identify relevant issues and recognize their importance, understand the relationships between issues, and perceive the underlying causes of a situation), and human relations (people) skills.

Summarize the systematic approach to decision making used by many business managers.

A systematic approach to decision making follows these steps: recognizing and defining the situation, developing options, analyzing options, selecting the best option, implementing the decision, and monitoring the consequences.

Recommend a new strategy to revive a struggling business.

Using the decision-making process described in this chapter, analyze the struggling company's problems described in "Solve the Dilemma" feature at the end of this chapter and formulate a strategy to turn the company around and aim it toward future success.

Revisit the World of Business

1. What similarities do Lei and Jobs share?

2. Do you think Lei's business model that is so successful in China will have the same success in the United States? Why or why not?

3. What are the advantages and disadvantages of Xiaomi selling its phones directly to consumers?

Learn the Terms

administrative managers 183
agenda 191
analytical skills 183
brainstorming 189
conceptual skills 183
controlling 178
crisis management or contingency planning 176
directing 177
downsizing 172
employee empowerment 187

financial managers 183
first-line managers 182
human relations skills 184
human resources managers 183
information technology (IT) managers 183
leadership 184
management 172
managers 172
marketing managers 183
middle managers 182

mission 173
networking 191
operational plans 176
organizing 177
planning 173
production and operations managers 183
staffing 172
strategic plans 175
tactical plans 176
technical expertise 182
top managers 180

Check Your Progress

1. Why is management so important, and what is its purpose?

2. Explain why the American Heart Association would need management, even though its goal is not profit related.

3. Why must a company have financial resources before it can use human and physical resources?

4. Name the four functions of management, and briefly describe each function.

5. Identify the three levels of management. What is the focus of managers at each level?

6. In what areas can managers specialize? From what area do top managers typically come?

7. What skills do managers need? Give examples of how managers use these skills to do their jobs.

8. What are three styles of leadership? Describe situations in which each style would be appropriate.

9. Explain the steps in the decision-making process.

10. What is the mathematical formula for perfect management? What do managers spend most of their time doing?

Get Involved

1. Give examples of the activities that each of the following managers might be involved in if he or she worked for the Coca-Cola Company:

   Financial manager

   Production and operations manager

   Personnel manager

   Marketing manager

   Administrative manager

   Information technology manager

   Foreman

2. Interview a small sample of managers, attempting to include representatives from all three levels and all areas of management. Discuss their daily activities and relate these activities to the management functions of planning, organizing, directing, and controlling. What skills do the managers say they need to carry out their tasks?

3. You are a manager of a firm that manufactures conventional ovens. Over the past several years, sales of many of your products have declined; this year, your losses may be quite large. Using the steps of the decision-making process, briefly describe how you arrive at a strategy for correcting the situation.

Build Your Skills

Functions of Management

Background

Although the text describes each of the four management functions separately, you learned that these four functions are interrelated, and managers sometimes perform two or more of them at the same time. Here you will broaden your perspective of how these functions occur simultaneously in management activities.

Task

1. Imagine that you are the manager in each scenario described in the following table and you have to decide which management function(s) to use in each.

2. Mark your answers using the following codes:

Codes	Management Functions
P	Planning
O	Organizing
D	Directing
C	Controlling

No.	Scenario	Answer(s)
1	Your group's work is centered on a project that is due in two months. Although everyone is working on the project, you have observed your employees involved in what you believe is excessive socializing and other time-filling behaviors. You decide to meet with the group to have them help you break down the project into smaller subprojects with mini-deadlines. You believe this will help keep the group members focused on the project and that the quality of the finished project will then reflect the true capabilities of your group.	
2	Your first impression of the new group you'll be managing is not too great. You tell your friend at dinner after your first day on the job: "Looks like I got a baby sitting job instead of a management job."	
3	You call a meeting of your work group and begin it by letting them know that a major procedure used by the work group for the past two years is being significantly revamped, and your department will have to phase in the change during the next six weeks. You proceed by explaining to them the reasoning your boss gave you for this change. You then say, "Let's take the next 5 to 10 minutes to let you voice your reactions to this change." After 10 minutes elapse with the majority of comments being critical of the change, you say: "I appreciate each of you sharing your reactions; and I, too, recognize that *all* change creates problems.	

	The way I see it, however, is that we can spend the remaining 45 minutes of our meeting focusing on why we don't want the change and why we don't think it's necessary; or we can work together to come up with viable solutions to solve the problems that implementing this change will most likely create." After about five more minutes of comments being exchanged, the consensus of the group is that the remainder of the meeting needs to be focused on how to deal with the potential problems the group anticipates having to deal with as the new procedure is implemented.	
4	You are preparing for the annual budget allocation meetings to be held in the plant manager's office next week. You are determined to present a strong case to support your department getting money for some high-tech equipment that will help your employees do their jobs better. You will stand firm against any suggestions of budget cuts in your area.	
5	Early in your career, you learned an important lesson about employee selection. One of the nurses on your floor unexpectedly quit. The other nurses were putting pressure on you to fill the position quickly because they were overworked even before the nurse left, and then things were really bad. After a hasty recruitment effort, you made a decision based on insufficient information. You ended up regretting your quick decision during the three months of problems that followed until you finally had to discharge the new hire. Since then, you have never let anybody pressure you into making a quick hiring decision.	

Solve the Dilemma

Making Infinity Computers Competitive

Infinity Computers Inc. produces notebook computers, which it sells through direct mail catalog companies under the Infinity name and in some retail computer stores under their private brand names. Infinity's products are not significantly different from competitors', nor do they have extra product-enhancing features, although they are very price competitive. The strength of the company has been its CEO and president, George Anderson, and a highly motivated, loyal workforce. The firm's weakness is having too many employees and too great a reliance on one product. The firm switched to computers with the Intel Core i7 processors after it saw a decline in its netbook computer sales.

Recognizing that the strategies that initially made the firm successful are no longer working effectively, Anderson wants to reorganize the company to make it more responsive and competitive and to cut costs. The threat of new technological developments and current competitive conditions could eliminate Infinity.

Recommend a new strategy to revive a struggling business.

Discussion Questions

1. Evaluate Infinity's current situation and analyze its strengths and weaknesses.

2. Evaluate the opportunities for Infinity, including using its current strategy, and propose alternative strategies.

3. Suggest a plan for Infinity to compete successfully over the next 10 years.

Build Your Business Plan

The Nature of Management

The first thing you need to be thinking about is "What is the mission of your business? What is the shared vision your team members have for this business? How do you know if there is demand for this particular business?" Remember, you need to think about the customer's *ability and willingness* to try this particular product.

Think about the various processes or stages of your business in the creation and selling of your good or service. What functions need to be performed for these processes to be completed? These functions might include buying, receiving, selling, customer service, and/or merchandising.

Operationally, if you are opening up a retail establishment, how do you plan to provide your customers with superior customer service? What hours will your customers expect you to be open? At this point in time, how many employees are you thinking you will need to run your business? Do you (or one of your partners) need to be there all the time to supervise?

See for Yourself Videocase

Panera Bread: Strategy Leads to Success

 Panera Bread has made a lot of strategic decisions in its history to bring it where it is at today. Its CEO and founder Ron Shaich was there nearly every step of the way. Under his leadership, Panera Bread has expanded to almost 2,000 restaurants across most of the United States.

Ron started out with a mission: "change the world by changing the way America eats." He wanted to offer healthier, handmade, artisanal foods that people would enjoy. He believed that 30 to 40 percent of the market wanted something more than fast food. In 1981, he formed Au Bon Pain, the precursor to Panera Bread. Over the next several years, Shaich continued to purchase restaurants, including a company that became the sister brand to Au Bon Pain—Panera Bread. Panera went public in 1991.

As the restaurants evolved, Shaich engaged in the planning process to improve sales. Some of these changes were more tactical in nature to achieve Shaich's bigger strategic plan to modify the concept. For instance, in 1997 the restaurants added bagels to the menu. Although only a small change, it caused the restaurant's average unit volume to grow.

Two years later, Shaich would make a strategic decision that would change the course of the company's future—sell all the businesses, including Au Bon Pain, and focus on the Panera brand. Implementing this strategic plan took years and was difficult for Shaich. However, as a leader, he recognized that the business—which had expanded into four divisions— was stretching itself too thin. As manager, Shaich took these actions to control the strategic direction of the company, solidifying its current status as a nationally recognized brand.

Although Shaich had the skills to recognize opportunities and take appropriate risks, he recognizes that the restaurants are nothing without its employees. As the CEO, Shaich leads top managers directly in executing plans to make the restaurant locations a success. However, he also indirectly manages front-line managers and rank-and-file employees by helping middle management organize the steps necessary to achieve Panera's goals. Shaich recognizes the importance of loyal employees.

"People work for people; they don't work for companies," Shaich says. "So we spend a great deal of time focused on how do we execute and how do we execute well, through local franchisees, local joint venture partners, and highly skilled and committed people at the local level."

Shaich's human relations skills extend beyond employees. He also solicits feedback from customers, often walking throughout one of the restaurants and asking them about how satisfied they are with their service. Shaich uses the controlling function of management when he uses this feedback to analyze Panera's strengths, weaknesses, opportunities, and threats. The desire of Panera is to exploit its strengths, turn its weaknesses into strengths, and transform external threats into opportunities.

One potential threat that Panera Bread is turning into an opportunity is the changing technological environment. Technology changes rapidly, making it hard for businesses to keep up. For this reason, Panera embarked upon what it calls the Panera 2.0 initiative to coordinate a number of different technological tools in order to transform the guests' experience. For instance, Panera uses digital technology that enables customers at certain locations to come into the restaurant and order with their phones without having to go up to the counter. It is also experimenting with small-order delivery using digital tools. Although this has been a significant investment and took more than four years to implement, customers seem to appreciate this added convenience. Digital sales increased by 12 percent.

Despite all the major changes the company has gone through, one thing has remained the same. The company continues to hold major planning sessions to upgrade the firm's strategic plans. During these sessions, the management team asks themselves where they see the company in five years and then writes down goals for the next year. As Schaih maintains, although elements of the strategic plan change, it continues to align with a vision the company developed in 1994 that describes the essence of the firm and how it will compete in the marketplace. He sees the achievement of this vision as ensuring Panera's long-term success.

"What we're trying to do is get closer and closer to that vision that we wrote in 1994," Shaich says. "And to be frank, we're probably at 80 percent of where we wanted to get to in 1994. But it forces us to stay in the future. It forces us to look at where we're trying to get to."[37]

Discussion Questions

1. Describe how Ron Shaich uses the functions of management.

2. What skills does Ron Shaich need to be an effective manager?

3. Why is it necessary for Panera to continually engage in the strategic planning process?

You can find the related video in the Video Library in Connect. Ask your instructor how you can access Connect.

Team Exercise

Form groups and assign the responsibility of locating examples of crisis management implementation for companies dealing with natural disasters (explosions, fires, earthquakes, etc.), technology disasters (viruses, plane crashes, compromised customer data, etc.), or ethical or legal disasters. How did these companies communicate with key stakeholders? What measures did the company take to provide support to those involved in the crisis? Report your findings to the class.

Endnotes

1. Scott Austin, Chris Canape, and Sarah Slobin, "The Billion Dollar Startup Club," *The Wall Street Journal,* February 18, 2015, http://graphics.wsj.com/billion-dollar-club/?co=Xiaomi (accessed September 28, 2015); Russell Flannery, "Xiaomis Lei Jun: The Steve Jobs of China," *Forbes,* January 28, 2015, http://forbesindia.com/article/cross-border/xiaomis-lei-jun-the-steve-jobs-of-china/39455/1 (accessed September 28, 2015); Russell Flannery, "Xiaomi Breaks World Record for Online Mobile Phones Sales in a Day," *Forbes,* April 9, 2015, http://www.forbes.com/sites/russellflannery/2015/04/09/xiaomi-breaks-world-record-for-smartphone-sales-in-a-day/ (accessed September 28, 2015); "#16. Lei Jun," *Forbes,* http://www.forbes.com/profile/lei-jun/ (accessed September 28, 2015); Connie Guglielmo, "A Day in the Life of Steve Jobs," *Forbes,* May 7, 2012, http://www.forbes.com/sites/connieguglielmo/2012/05/07/a-day-in-the-life-of-steve-jobs/ (accessed September 28, 2015).

2. Jacob Bunge and Rachel Feintzeig, "Dow and DuPont Strive to Find the Right Chemistry," *The Wall Street Journal,* January 12, 2016, http://www.wsj.com/articles/dow-and-dupont-strive-to-find-the-right-chemistry-1452630298 (accessed March 7, 2016).

3. Suzanne Heyn, "Sorting through Options," *Inbound Logistics,* May 2014, pp. 48–52.

4. Tim Nudd, "Infographic: The 24 Most Inspirational Company Mission Statements," *Ad Week,* September 30, 2015, http://www.adweek.com/adfreak/infographic-24-most-inspirational-company-mission-statements-167260 (accessed March 7, 2016).

5. Starwood Hotels & Resorts, "Environmental Initiatives," http://www.starwoodhotels.com/corporate/about/citizenship/environment.html?language=en_US (accessed March 7, 2016).

6. Alexandra Fenwick, "An NFL Veteran Tackles a Sweet New Gig," *Fortune,* August 1, 2015, pp. 23, 27; Pats Gourmet, "Why It Started," Lodishs Champion Brittle, 2012, http://www.lodishschampionbrittle.com/index.php/about-us/why-it-started (accessed September 10, 2015); Kieran Darcy, "From Super Bowls to Super Sweet," *ESPN,* January 26, 2014, http://espn.go.com/new-york/nfl/story/_/id/10349205/mike-lodish-goes-six-super-bowls-peanut-brittle-maker (accessed September 10, 2015).

7. John Kell, "Nike Just Promised to Reach $50 Billion in Sales by 2020," *Fortune,* October 14, 2015, http://fortune.com/2015/10/14/nike-50-billion/ (accessed March 7, 2016).

8. Jacob Bunge and Rachel Feintzeig, "Dow and DuPont Strive to Find the Right Chemistry," *The Wall Street Journal,* January 12, 2016, http://www.wsj.com/articles/dow-and-dupont-strive-to-find-the-right-chemistry-1452630298 (accessed March 7, 2016).

9. G. Tomas, M. Hult, David W. Cravens, and Jagdish Sheth, "Competitive Advantage in the Global Marketplace: A Focus on Marketing Strategy," *Journal of Business Research* 51 (January 2001), p. 1.

10. General Motors, "Chevrolet Remains the Industry's Fastest-Growing Full-Line Brand, with 11 Consecutive Months of Growth," March 1, 2016, https://www.gm.com/investors/sales/us-sales-production.html (accessed March 7, 2016).

11. U.S. Small Business Administration, "Disaster Planning: Planning for Disasters in Advance," https://www.sba.gov/content/disaster-planning (accessed March 7, 2016).

12. Ed Legge, "Seats Rebounds after Fire," WiscNews, February 11, 2015, http://www.wiscnews.com/news/local/article_75d9e84e-7e7a-5db8-8c14-bea1dd85311d.html (accessed February 16, 2015).

13. Triad Journal, "Volvo Group to Reorganize Heavy Truck Business, Effective March 1," February 18, 2016, http://www.bizjournals.com/triad/blog/morning-edition/2016/02/volvo-group-to-reorganize-heavy-truck-business.html (accessed March 7, 2016).

14. International Association of Privacy Professionals, "Information Privacy Professionals Credentials from the IAAP Receive ANSI Accreditation," August 11, 2015, https://iapp.org/about/information-privacy-professionals-credentials-from-the-iapp-receive-ansi-accreditation (accessed March 7, 2016).

15. "Women CEOs of the S&P 500" Catalyst, February 3, 2016, http://www.catalyst.org/knowledge/women-ceos-sp-500 (accessed March 7, 2016).

16. Ross Kerber, "Growth in Compensation for U.S. CEOs May Have Slowed," *Reuters,* March 17, 2014, www.reuters.com/article/2014/03/17/us-compensation-ceos-2013-insight-idUSBREA2G05520140317 (accessed March 29, 2014).

17. Ezequiel Minaya, "Chipotle Co-CEOs' Compensation Slashed by Half in 2015," *The Wall Street Journal,* March 11, 2015, http://www.wsj.com/articles/chipotle-co-ceos-compensation-slashed-by-half-in-2015-1457736200 (accessed March 15, 2016).

18. "No. 1 Novartis Pharmaceutical Corporation DiversityInc Top 50," DiversityInc, 2015, http://www.diversityinc.com/novartis-pharmaceuticals-corporation/ (accessed March 7, 2016).

19. Laura Nichols, "Agencies Called to Step Up the Pace on Diversity Efforts," *PRWeek,* February 7, 2014, www.prweekus.com/article/agencies-called-step-pace-diversity-efforts/1283550 (accessed March 29, 2014).

20. Del Jones, "Autocratic Leadership Works—Until It Fails," *USA Today,* June 5, 2003, www.usatoday.com/news/nation/2003-06-05-raines-usat_x.htm (accessed March 7, 2016).

21. George Manning and Kent Curtis, *The Art of Leadership* (New York: McGraw-Hill, 2003), p. 125.

22. Mike Hower, "Kuli Kuli's Moringa Green Energy Shots Create Jobs, Fight Deforestation in Haiti," *Startups,* October 6, 2015, http://www.sustainablebrands.com/news_and_views/startups/mike_hower/moringa_green_energy_shot_creates_jobs_fights_deforestation_haiti (accessed October 7, 2015); Steve Nicastro, "Small Business Success Story:Kuli Kulis Collaboration with Indiegogo," *NerdWallet,* January 19, 2015, https://www.nerdwallet.com/blog/small-business/small-business-success-story-kuli-kulis-collaboration-indiegogo/ (accessed November 19, 2015); Kuli Kuli, "About Us," https://www.kulikulifoods.com/about#our-mission (accessed November 19, 2015); Lisa Curtis, "The Moringa Green Energy Shot to Revitalize Haiti," *Indiegogo,* https://www.indiegogo.com/projects/the-moringa-green-energy-shot-to-revitalize-haiti#/ (accessed November 18, 2015).

23. Ryan Bradley, "The Woman Driving Patagonia to Be (Even More) Radical," *Fortune,* September 14, 2015, http://fortune.com/2015/09/14/rose-marcario-patagonia/ (accessed November 10, 2015); Patagonia, "Environmental and Social Responsibility," http://www.patagonia.com/us/environmentalism (accessed November 17, 2015); "B Corporations Certified," https://www.bcorporation.net (accessed November 17, 2015); Patagonia, "Stories from Our Supply Chain," http://www.patagonia.com/eu/enGB/footprint (accessed November 17, 2015).

24. Craig Giammona, "McDonald's CEO Don Thompson to Step Down," *Bloomberg,* January 28, 2015, http://www.bloomberg.com/news/articles/2015-01-28/mcdonald-s-names-steve-easterbrook-ceo-as-thompson-steps-down (accessed March 7, 2016).

25. Bruce J. Avolio and William L. Gardner, "Authentic Leadership Development: Getting to the Root of Positive Forms of Leadership," *The Leadership Quarterly,* 2005, pp. 315–38.

26. Bill George, "Becoming a More Authentic Leader," *Harvard Business Review,* December 10, 2015, https://hbr.org/ideacast/2015/12/becoming-a-more-authentic-leader (accessed March 7, 2016); Bill George, "The Triumph of Authentic Leaders," *The Huffington Post,* July 13, 2015, http://www.huffingtonpost.com/bill-george/the-triumph-of-authentic_b_7784044.html (accessed March 7, 2016).

27. John P. Kotter, "What Leaders Really Do," *Harvard Business Review,* December 2001, http://fs.ncaa.org/Docs/DIII/What%20Leaders%20Really%20Do.pdf (accessed April 30, 2014).

28. Lee Schuh, "Succession Planning Critical for Business," *Pacific Coast Business Times,* February 19, 2016, http://www.pacbiztimes.com/2016/02/19/succession-planning-critical-for-business/ (accessed March 7, 2016); "The J.M. Smucker Company Announces Leadership Transition to Foster Next Chapter of Growth and Success," *PR Newswire,* March 7, 2016, http://www.prnewswire.com/news-releases/the-jm-smucker-company-announces-leadership-transition-to-foster-next-chapter-of-growth-and-success-300231865.html (accessed March 7, 2016).

29. C. L. Pearce and C. C. Manz, "The New Silver Bullets of Leadership: The Importance of Self- and Shared Leadership in Knowledge Work," *Organizational Dynamics,* 34, no. 2 (2005), pp. 130–140.

30. Deborah Harrington-Mackin, *The Team Building Tool Kit* (New York: New Directions Management, 1994); Joseph P. Folger, Marshall Scott Poole, and Randall K. Stutman, *Working through Conflict: Strategies for Relationships, Groups, and Organizations,* 6th ed. (Upper Saddle River, NJ: Pearson Education, 2009).

31. Kerrie Unsworth, "Unpacking Creativity," *Academy of Management Review,* 26 (April 2001), pp. 289–297.

32. Pallavi Gogoi, "A Bittersweet Deal or Wrigley," *BusinessWeek,* May 12, 2008, p. 34; "About Us," Wrigley, www.wrigley.com/global/about-us.aspx (accessed March 7, 2016).

33. *Harvard Business Review* 60 (November–December 1982), p. 160.

34. Dan Schwabel, "5 Reasons Why Your Online Presence Will Replace Your Resume in 10 Years," *Forbes,* February 21, 2012, www.forbes.com/sites/danschawbel/2011/02/21/5-reasons-why-your-online-presence-will-replace-your-resume-in-10-years/ (accessed April 30, 2014).

35. U.S. Bureau of Labor Statistics, "Occupational Outlook Handbook," December 17, 2015, http://www.bls.gov/ooh/ (accessed March 7, 2016).

36. Bureau of Labor Statistics, "May 2014 Occupation Profiles," http://www.bls.gov/oes/current/oes_stru.htm#00-0000 (accessed March 7, 2016).

37. Panera Bread video, http://www.viddler.com/embed/2204ea03/?f=1&autoplay=0&player=full&disablebranding=0%22%20width=%22545%22%20height=%22451%22%20frameborder=%220%22 (accessed

April 21, 2016); Ron Shaich website, http://www.ronshaich.com/meetron.php (accessed April 21, 2016); Panera Bread, "Our History," https://www.panerabread.com/en-us/company/about-panera/our-history.html (accessed April 21, 2016); Jenna Goudreau, "Here Are the Epiphanies That Made Panera a $4.5 Billion Restaurant Chain," *Business Insider,* November 11, 2014, http://www.businessinsider.com/panera-bread-founder-ron-shaich-on-growth-strategies-2014-11 (accessed April 21, 2016); Kelsey Nash, "Panera's 'Strategic Plan' Is Driving Sales but Slashing Profits," *Restaurant Business,* October 28, 2015, http://www.restaurantbusinessonline.com/news/panera-s-strategic-plan-driving-sales-slashing-profits (accessed April 21, 2016).

© Chris Ryan/age fotostock

7 Organization, Teamwork, and Communication

Learning Objectives

After reading this chapter, you will be able to:

LO 7-1   Explain the importance of organizational culture.

LO 7-2   Define *organizational structure* and relate how organizational structures develop.

LO 7-3   Describe how specialization and departmentalization help an organization achieve its goals.

LO 7-4   Determine how organizations assign responsibility for tasks and delegate authority.

LO 7-5   Compare and contrast some common forms of organizational structure.

LO 7-6   Distinguish between groups and teams and identify the types of groups that exist in organizations.

LO 7-7   Describe how communication occurs in organizations.

LO 7-8   Analyze a business's use of teams.

Enter the World of Business ⊖———————

W.L. Gore: Where Everyone Is the Boss

W.L. Gore, the chemical and manufacturing company best known for Gore-Tex fabric, is a fascinating success story. It has more than 10,000 employees at offices in more than 50 countries, ranked 22nd on *Fortune*'s 2015 "100 Best Companies to Work For" list, and—from its founding in 1958—has never posted an operating loss. During this time, it has held to a unique management structure: Almost no formalized bosses, no structured hierarchy, and no set chains of command. In doing so, it has proven that a structure antithetical to a traditional hierarchical management structure can work well if done correctly.

Gore uses what it calls a "team-based, flat lattice" organizational structure. The company is built around self-creating, multidisciplinary teams, which form in response to problems, opportunities, or shared skills and interests. Each employee can choose their own projects but in return hold themselves, and each other, strictly accountable to deliver results. As CEO Terri Kelly puts it, "There are two sides to the coin: freedom to decide and a commitment to deliver on your promises." Leaders emerge naturally from these teams and gain management power not by formalized titles or privileges but by the demonstrated willingness of others to follow them. Compensation is determined by a detailed peer-review process meant to award employees who have contributed most to the company with the highest salaries.

Gore does not pretend that it has overcome the need for company organization, strong leadership, employee accountability, and high performance needed for all organizations. Instead, it simply claims to have found alternative ways to achieve them, such as a strong focus on exemplifying company values and a powerful peer-review and accountability system. Whatever analysts might say about the company's unusual approach, It has been successful.[1]

Introduction

An organization's structure determines how well it makes decisions and responds to problems, and it influences employees' attitudes toward their work. A suitable structure can minimize a business's costs and maximize its efficiency. Even companies that operate within the same industry may utilize different organizational structures. For example, in the consumer electronics industry, Samsung is organized as a conglomerate with separate business units or divisions. Samsung is largely decentralized. Apple, under CEO Tim Cook, has moved from a hierarchical structure to a more collaborative approach among divisions.[2]

Because a business's structure can so profoundly affect its success, this chapter will examine organizational structure in detail. First, we discuss how an organization's culture affects its operations. Then we consider the development of structure, including how tasks and responsibilities are organized through specialization and departmentalization. Next, we explore some of the forms organizational structure may take. Finally, we consider communications within business.

LO 7-1

Explain the importance of organizational culture.

organizational culture
a firm's shared values, beliefs, traditions, philosophies, rules, and role models for behavior.

Organizational Culture

One of the most important aspects of organizing a business is determining its **organizational culture,** a firm's shared values, beliefs, traditions, philosophies, rules, and role models for behavior. Also called corporate culture, an organizational culture exists in every organization, regardless of size, organizational type, product, or profit objective. Sometimes behaviors, programs, and policies enhance and support the organizational culture. For instance, the sixth largest accounting firm Grant Thornton established an unlimited vacation policy to give its employees more freedom. Less than 1 percent of American firms have this policy, but it seems to be growing in companies like Netflix where employees have greater autonomy. Some speculate, however, that these policies will only work at firms with employees who are already highly motivated to work hard and are less likely to take vacations in the first place.[3] A firm's culture may be expressed formally through its mission statement, codes of ethics, memos, manuals, and ceremonies, but it is more commonly expressed informally. Examples of informal expressions of culture include dress codes (or the lack thereof), work habits, extracurricular activities, and stories. Employees often learn the accepted standards through discussions with co-workers.

The organizational culture at the Four Seasons hotel chain is service-oriented with its adoption of the universal rule: treat others the way you would like to be treated. To encourage employees to be dedicated to service, the Four Seasons offers unique perks such as the ability to request transfers among its 90 properties around the world.[4] McDonald's has organizational cultures focused on cleanliness, value, and service. Nordstrom stresses a culture of excellent customer service. As a result, employees are empowered to use their best judgment in delivering the best services.[5] When such values and philosophies are shared by all members of an organization, they will be expressed in its relationships with stakeholders. However, organizational cultures that lack such positive values may result in employees who are unproductive and indifferent and have poor attitudes, which will be reflected externally to customers. The corporate culture may have contributed to the misconduct at a number of well-known companies. A survey found that many professionals working in the financial industry continue to believe wrongdoing is common in their field, and 27 percent of respondents believe that the industry fails to put client interests first.[6]

Organizational culture helps ensure that all members of a company share values and suggests rules for how to behave and deal with problems within the organization.

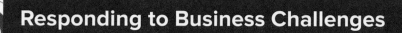

Responding to Business Challenges

Amazon: Expedited Service and Employment

Amazon revolutionized e-commerce, but the mega-company is also coming under fire for allegedly having a stressful and oppressive organizational culture, a claim Amazon's CEO Jeff Bezos denies. Aside from being one of the largest sellers of cloud-based content, such as audiobooks, music, and movies, Amazon features millions of physical items that can be quickly shipped from its large network of fulfillment centers spanning the world.

As the largest U.S. Internet retailer with a market value surpassing that of even Walmart, Amazon has demanding employee expectations. Metrics track every aspect of employee performance, and each year those ranked as underachievers are fired. Employees are expected to send comments and complaints about co-workers directly to management, and some employee disagreement is encouraged in a quest for greater efficiency and innovation. Many employees claim to work weekends, holidays, and even while on vacation to keep up with the immense workload and exhausting expectations.

For his role, Bezos disagrees with characterizations that his company employs unempathetic management policies, which push employees to their limits despite personal hardships. Indeed, while many criticize Amazon's unorthodox organizational culture as cut-throat and overcompetitive, most also see it as a major factor contributing to the company's success. Consequently, while effective communication and a certain level of teamwork will always be expected at Amazon, so will an ambitious and competitive drive toward excellence.[7]

Discussion Questions

1. Instead of always trying to foster teamwork and harmony, why does Amazon sometimes encourage employee disagreement?
2. How does Amazon's employee ranking system affect teamwork and competitiveness among co-workers?
3. Do co-worker comments and complaints sent directly to management enhance or disrupt communication and teamwork at Amazon?

Figure 7-1 confirms that business and HR leaders in this study believe that corporate culture and engagement is very important for organizational performance and employee satisfaction. The key to success in any organization is satisfying stakeholders, especially customers. Establishing a positive organizational culture sets the tone for all other decisions, including building an efficient organizational structure.

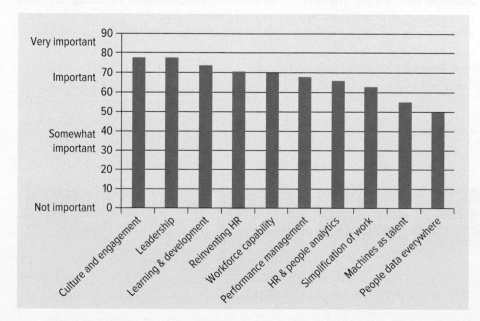

FIGURE 7-1

Desired Attitudes and Behaviors Associated with Corporate Cultures

Source: Deloitte University Press, *Global Human Capital Trends 2015,* http://d2mtr37y39tpbu. cloudfront.net/wp-content/uploads/2015/08/DUP_GlobalHumanCapitalTrends2015.pdf (accessed March 9, 2016).

N = 3,333 business and human resources professionals

Developing Organizational Structure

Structure is the arrangement or relationship of positions within an organization. Rarely is an organization, or any group of individuals working together, able to achieve common objectives without some form of structure, whether that structure is explicitly defined or only implied. A professional baseball team such as the Colorado Rockies is a business organization with an explicit formal structure that guides the team's activities so that it can increase game attendance, win games, and sell souvenirs such as T-shirts. But even an informal group playing softball for fun has an organization that specifies who will pitch, catch, bat, coach, and so on. Governments and nonprofit organizations also have formal organizational structures to facilitate the achievement of their objectives. Getting people to work together efficiently and coordinating the skills of diverse individuals require careful planning. Developing appropriate organizational structures is, therefore, a major challenge for managers in both large and small organizations.

An organization's structure develops when managers assign work tasks and activities to specific individuals or work groups and coordinate the diverse activities required to reach the firm's objectives. When Macy's, for example, has a sale, the store manager must work with the advertising department to make the public aware of the sale, with department managers to ensure that extra salespeople are scheduled to handle the increased customer traffic, and with merchandise buyers to ensure that enough sale merchandise is available to meet expected consumer demand. All the people occupying these positions must work together to achieve the store's objectives.

The best way to begin to understand how organizational structure develops is to consider the evolution of a new business such as a clothing store. At first, the business is a sole proprietorship in which the owner does everything—buys, prices, and displays the merchandise; does the accounting and tax records; and assists customers. As the business grows, the owner hires a salesperson and perhaps a merchandise buyer to help run the store. As the business continues to grow, the owner hires more salespeople. The growth and success of the business now require the owner to be away from the store frequently, meeting with suppliers, engaging in public relations, and attending trade shows. Thus, the owner must designate someone to manage the salespeople and maintain the accounting, payroll, and tax functions. If the owner decides to expand by opening more stores, still more managers will be needed. Figure 7-2

FIGURE 7-2   The Evolution of a Clothing Store, Phases I, 2, and 3

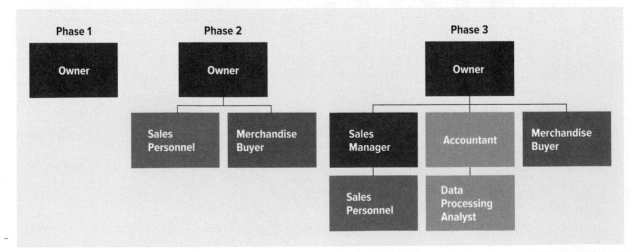

shows these stages of growth with three **organizational charts** (visual displays of organizational structure, chain of command, and other relationships).

Growth requires organizing—the structuring of human, physical, and financial resources to achieve objectives in an effective and efficient manner. Growth necessitates hiring people who have specialized skills. With more people and greater specialization, the organization needs to develop a formal structure to function efficiently. Often organizations undergo structural changes when the current structure is no longer deemed effective. For instance, Zappos adopted an organizational structure called a holacracy, a structure in which job titles are abandoned, traditional managers are eliminated, and authority is distributed to teams. Although these constitute massive changes for the firm, CEO Tony Hsieh believes this more fluid organizational structure will allow Zappos to grow in size while simultaneously increasing in productivity.[8] Zappos, as an online retailer of shoes, has a major focus on service, but its structure might not work for a manufacturing firm like Ford. As we shall see, structuring an organization requires that management assign work tasks to specific individuals and departments and assign responsibility for the achievement of specific organizational objectives.

Disney World embraces a corporate culture that focuses on the guest. It is all about putting on a show for park visitors. Employees are even referred to as cast members.
© Gino Santa Maria/123RF

Assigning Tasks

For a business to earn profits from the sale of its products, its managers must first determine what activities are required to achieve its objectives. At Celestial Seasonings, for example, employees must purchase herbs from suppliers, dry the herbs and place them in tea bags, package and label the tea, and then ship the packages to grocery stores around the country. Other necessary activities include negotiating with supermarkets and other retailers for display space, developing new products, planning advertising, managing finances, and managing employees. All these activities must be coordinated, assigned to work groups, and controlled. Two important aspects of assigning these work activities are specialization and departmentalization.

Specialization

After identifying all activities that must be accomplished, managers then break these activities down into specific tasks that can be handled by individual employees. This division of labor into small, specific tasks and the assignment of employees to do a single task is called **specialization.**

The rationale for specialization is efficiency. People can perform more efficiently if they master just one task rather than all tasks. In *The Wealth of Nations,* 18th-century economist Adam Smith discussed specialization, using the manufacture of straight

LO 7-3

Describe how specialization and departmentalization help an organization achieve its goals.

organizational chart
a visual display of the organizational structure, lines of authority (chain of command), staff relationships, permanent committee arrangements, and lines of communication.

specialization
the division of labor into small, specific tasks and the assignment of employees to do a single task.

Job specialization is common in automobile manufacturing. By dividing work into smaller specialized tasks, employees can perform their work more quickly and efficiently.

© Ulrich Baumgarten/Getty Images

pins as an example. Individually, workers could produce 20 pins a day when each employee produced complete pins. Thus, 10 employees working independently of each other could produce 200 pins a day. However, when one worker drew the wire, another straightened it, a third cut it, and a fourth ground the point, 10 workers could produce 48,000 pins per day.[9] To save money and achieve the benefits of specialization, some companies outsource and hire temporary workers to provide key skills. Many highly skilled, diverse, experienced workers are available through temp agencies.

Specialization means workers do not waste time shifting from one job to another, and training is easier. However, efficiency is not the only motivation for specialization. Specialization also occurs when the activities that must be performed within an organization are too numerous for one person to handle. Recall the example of the clothing store. When the business was young and small, the owner could do everything; but when the business grew, the owner needed help waiting on customers, keeping the books, and managing other business activities.

Overspecialization can have negative consequences. Employees may become bored and dissatisfied with their jobs, and the result of their unhappiness is likely to be poor quality work, more injuries, and high employee turnover. In extreme cases, employees in crowded specialized electronic plants are unable to form working relationships with one another. In some factories in Asia, workers are cramped together and overworked. Fourteen global vehicle manufacturers pledged to increase their oversight of the factories in their supply chain to ensure human rights and healthy working conditions. However, the task is monumental for these global companies because their supply chains encompass many different countries with different labor practices, and it can be difficult to oversee the operations of dozens of supplier and subcontractors.[10] This is why some manufacturing firms allow job rotation so that employees do not become dissatisfied and leave. Although some degree of specialization is necessary for efficiency, because of differences in skills, abilities, and interests, all people are not equally suited for all jobs. We examine some strategies to overcome these issues in Chapter 9.

Departmentalization

departmentalization
the grouping of jobs into working units usually called departments, units, groups, or divisions.

After assigning specialized tasks to individuals, managers next organize workers doing similar jobs into groups to make them easier to manage. **Departmentalization** is the grouping of jobs into working units usually called departments, units, groups, or divisions. As we shall see, departments are commonly organized by function, product, geographic region, or customer (Figure 7-3). Most companies use more than one departmentalization plan to enhance productivity. For instance, many consumer goods manufacturers have departments for specific product lines (beverages, frozen dinners, canned goods, and so on) as well as departments dealing with legal, purchasing, finance, human resources, and other business functions. For smaller companies, accounting can be set up online, almost as an automated department. Accounting software can handle electronic transfers so you never have to worry about a late bill. Many city governments also have departments for specific services (e.g., police, fire, waste disposal) as well as departments for legal, human resources, and other business functions. Figure 7-4 depicts the organizational chart for the fictional city of Pineapple Paradise, showing these departments.

Functional Departmentalization.   Functional departmentalization groups jobs that perform similar functional activities, such as finance, manufacturing, marketing,

functional departmentalization
the grouping of jobs that perform similar functional activities, such as finance, manufacturing, marketing, and human resources.

FIGURE 7-3   Departmentalization

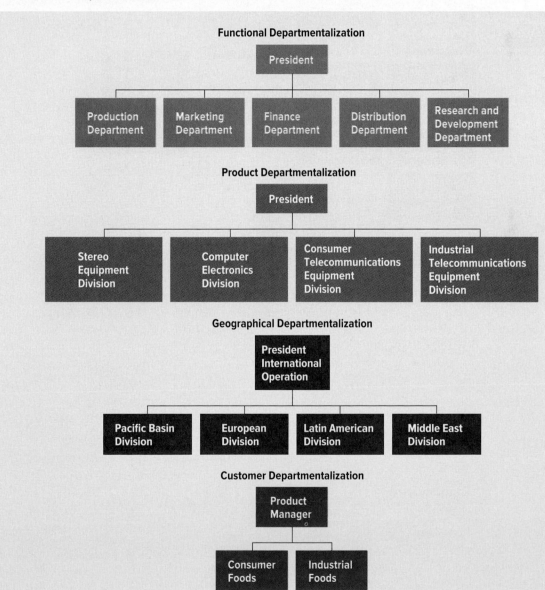

FIGURE 7-4 An Organizational Chart for Pineapple Paradise

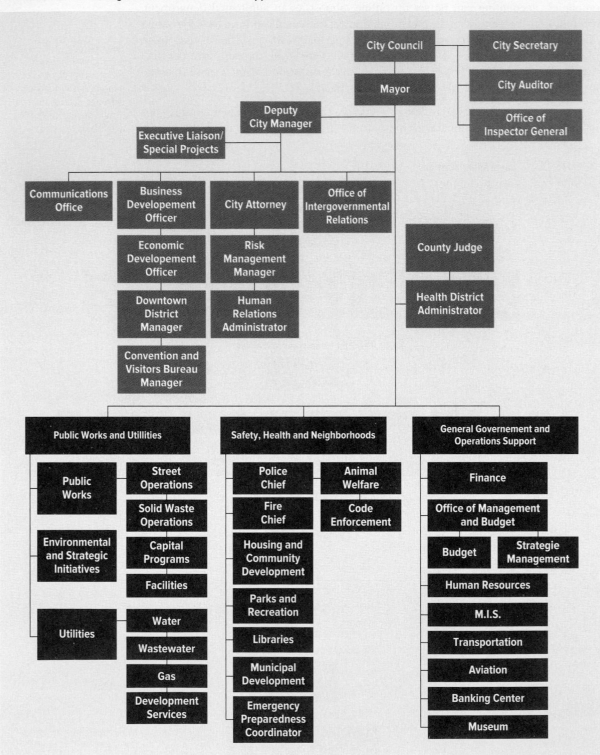

and human resources. Each of these functions is managed by an expert in the work done by the department—an engineer supervises the production department; a financial executive supervises the finance department. This approach is common in small organizations. Keurig Green Mountain Coffee is departmentalized into functions, although it has begun to adopt elements of other structures as it expands globally. A weakness of functional departmentalization is that, because it tends to emphasize departmental units rather than the organization as a whole, decision making that involves more than one department may be slow, and it requires greater coordination. Thus, as businesses grow, they tend to adopt other approaches to organizing jobs.

Product Departmentalization.   Product departmentalization, as you might guess, organizes jobs around the products of the firm. Unilever has global units, including personal care, foods, refreshment, and home care.[11] Each division develops and implements its own product plans, monitors the results, and takes corrective action as necessary. Functional activities—production, finance, marketing, and others—are located within each product division. Consequently, organizing by products duplicates functions and resources and emphasizes the product rather than achievement of the organization's overall objectives. However, it simplifies decision making and helps coordinate all activities related to a product or product group. PepsiCo Inc. is organized into six business units: (1) North America Beverages; (2) Frito-Lay North America; (3) Quaker Foods North America; (4) Latin America; (5) Europe Sub-Saharan Africa; and (6) Asia, Middle East & North Africa. PepsiCo has actually adopted a combination of two types of departmentalization. While it clearly uses product departmentalization in North America, the company also chooses to divide its segments into geographic regions—a type of geographic departmentalization.[12]

> **product departmentalization**
> the organization of jobs in relation to the products of the firm.

Geographical Departmentalization.   Geographical departmentalization groups jobs according to geographic location, such as a state, region, country, or continent. Diageo, the premium beverage company known for brands such as Johnny Walker and Tanqueray, is organized into five geographic regions, allowing the company to get closer to its customers and respond more quickly and efficiently to regional competitors.[13] Multinational corporations often use a geographical approach because of vast differences between different regions. Coca-Cola, General Motors, and Caterpillar are organized by region. However, organizing by region requires a large administrative staff and control system to coordinate operations, and tasks are duplicated among the different regions.

> **geographical departmentalization**
> the grouping of jobs according to geographic location, such as state, region, country, or continent.

Customer Departmentalization.   Customer departmentalization arranges jobs around the needs of various types of customers. This allows companies to address the unique requirements of each group. Airlines, such as British Airways and Delta, provide prices and services customized for either business/frequent travelers or infrequent/vacationing customers. Customer departmentalization, like geographical departmentalization, does not focus on the organization as a whole and therefore requires a large administrative staff to coordinate the operations of the various groups.

> **customer departmentalization**
> the arrangement of jobs around the needs of various types of customers.

Assigning Responsibility

LO 7-4

Determine how organizations assign responsibility for tasks and delegate authority.

After all workers and work groups have been assigned their tasks, they must be given the responsibility to carry them out. Management must determine to what extent it will delegate responsibility throughout the organization and how many employees will report to each manager.

Delegation of Authority

delegation of authority
giving employees not only tasks, but also the power to make commitments, use resources, and take whatever actions are necessary to carry out those tasks.

Delegation of authority means not only giving tasks to employees, but also empowering them to make commitments, use resources, and take whatever actions are necessary to carry out those tasks. Let's say a marketing manager at Nestlé has assigned an employee to design a new package that is less wasteful (more environmentally responsible) than the current package for one of the company's frozen dinner lines. To carry out the assignment, the employee needs access to information and the authority to make certain decisions on packaging materials, costs, and so on. Without the authority to carry out the assigned task, the employee would have to get the approval of others for every decision and every request for materials.

As a business grows, so do the number and complexity of decisions that must be made; no one manager can handle them all. 3M delegates authority to its employees by encouraging them to share ideas and make decisions. 3M believes employee ideas can have such an impact on the firm that it encourages them to spend 15 percent of their time working on and sharing their own projects.[14] Delegation of authority frees a manager to concentrate on larger issues, such as planning or dealing with problems and opportunities.

responsibility
the obligation, placed on employees through delegation, to perform assigned tasks satisfactorily and be held accountable for the proper execution of work.

Delegation also gives a **responsibility,** or obligation, to employees to carry out assigned tasks satisfactorily and holds them accountable for the proper execution of their assigned work. The principle of **accountability** means that employees who accept an assignment and the authority to carry it out are answerable to a superior for the outcome. Returning to the Nestlé example, if the packaging design prepared by the employee is unacceptable or late, the employee must accept the blame. If the new design is innovative, attractive, and cost-efficient, as well as environmentally responsible, or is completed ahead of schedule, the employee will accept the credit.

accountability
the principle that employees who accept an assignment and the authority to carry it out are answerable to a superior for the outcome.

The process of delegating authority establishes a pattern of relationships and accountability between a superior and his or her subordinates. The president of a firm delegates responsibility for all marketing activities to the vice president of marketing. The vice president accepts this responsibility and has the authority to obtain all relevant information, make certain decisions, and delegate any or all activities to his or her subordinates. The vice president, in turn, delegates all advertising activities to the advertising manager, all sales activities to the sales manager, and so on. These managers then delegate specific tasks to their subordinates. However, the act of delegating authority to a subordinate does not relieve the superior of accountability for the delegated job. Even though the vice president of marketing delegates work to subordinates, he or she is still ultimately accountable to the president for all marketing activities.

Degree of Centralization

The extent to which authority is delegated throughout an organization determines its degree of centralization.

centralized organization
a structure in which authority is concentrated at the top, and very little decision-making authority is delegated to lower levels.

Centralized Organizations.   In a **centralized organization,** authority is concentrated at the top, and very little decision-making authority is delegated to lower levels. Although decision-making authority in centralized organizations rests with top levels of management, a vast amount of responsibility for carrying out daily and routine procedures is delegated to even the lowest levels of the organization. Many government organizations, including the U.S. Army, the Postal Service, and the IRS, are centralized.

Going Green

Rainforest Alliance: Sustainable Workplace

When you envision nonprofit organizations, you may imagine bare-bones organizations, little money flowing through the organization, and poor working conditions for employees more dedicated to a cause than their careers. The Rainforest Alliance, a highly recognized nonprofit organization that promotes biodiversity and sustainability, defies this stereotype. In fact, the company works hard to ensure a positive workplace. With 35,000 members and supporters and an operating budget of $52.9 million, the Rainforest Alliance has been fighting globally for the environment and communities since 1987 by working to change business practices and consumer behavior. An organization such as the Rainforest Alliance requires dedicated employees; therefore, the company promotes a motivational, encouraging work environment.

The Rainforest Alliance has grown rapidly in the past five years and now employs more than 250 employees worldwide. Thanks in part to expansion, the Rainforest Alliance is a decentralized organization, delegating authority by encouraging employees at all ranks to take charge of projects. These individuals are promoted as a result of their efforts. This allows employees to follow their own interests within the organization, which builds morale. The company also offers U.S. employees opportunities to work in foreign offices, which provides the chance to travel along with the learning experience. For individuals looking to aid the environment and support small growers, the Rainforest Alliance is a great place to work.[17]

Discussion Questions

1. How does the Rainforest Alliance balance employee welfare with pursuing its mission as a nonprofit?
2. How does its decentralized structure affect the responsibilities that employees take on?
3. Do you you think it is important to believe in the mission of the organization in order to be a satisfied employee of the Rainforest Alliance?

Businesses tend to be more centralized when the decisions to be made are risky and when low-level managers are not highly skilled in decision making. In the banking industry, for example, authority to make routine car loans is given to all loan managers, while the authority to make high-risk loans, such as for a large residential development, may be restricted to upper-level loan officers.

Overcentralization can cause serious problems for a company, in part because it may take longer for the organization as a whole to implement decisions and to respond to changes and problems on a regional scale. McDonald's, for example, was one of the last chains to introduce a chicken sandwich because of the amount of research, development, test marketing, and layers of approval the product had to go through. Too much hierarchy can also prevent lower-level employees from providing their own perspectives or reporting problems.[15]

Decentralized Organizations. A **decentralized organization** is one in which decision-making authority is delegated as far down the chain of command as possible. Decentralization is characteristic of organizations that operate in complex, unpredictable environments. Businesses that face intense competition often decentralize to improve responsiveness and enhance creativity. Lower-level managers who interact with the external environment often develop a good understanding of it and thus are able to react quickly to changes. Johnson & Johnson has a very decentralized, flat organizational structure.

Delegating authority to lower levels of managers may increase the organization's productivity. Decentralization requires that lower-level managers have strong decision-making skills. In recent years, the trend has been toward more decentralized organizations, and some of the largest and most successful companies, including GE, IBM, Google, and Nike, have decentralized decision-making authority. McDonald's, Taco Bell, and Pizza Hut have established themselves in the growing Indian market

decentralized organization an organization in which decision-making authority is delegated as far down the chain of command as possible.

by decentralizing operations by varying products in specific markets to better meet customer demands. McDonald's, for example, has implemented spicy and vegetarian menu options in India to appeal to the native tastes. Becoming decentralized, however, can be difficult for a fast-food restaurant that relies on standardized processes and core products. Burger King's core offering, the Whopper, would not be well accepted in India because beef is rarely eaten. As a result, the chain began offering six vegetarian sandwich options. The response was so positive that Burger King is considering extending its vegetarian options to the United States and the United Kingdom.[16] Diversity and decentralization are the keys to being better, not just bigger. Nonprofit organizations benefit from decentralization as well.

Span of Management

How many subordinates should a manager manage? There is no simple answer. Experts generally agree, however, that top managers should not directly supervise more than four to eight people, while lower-level managers who supervise routine tasks are capable of managing a much larger number of subordinates. For example, the manager of the finance department may supervise 25 employees, whereas the vice president of finance may supervise only five managers. **Span of management** refers to the number of subordinates who report to a particular manager. A *wide span of management* exists when a manager directly supervises a very large number of employees. A *narrow span of management* exists when a manager directly supervises only a few subordinates (Figure 7-5). At Whole Foods, the best employees are recruited and placed in small teams. Employees are empowered to discount, give away, and sample products, as well as to assist in creating a respectful workplace where goals are achieved, individual employees succeed, and customers are core in business decisions. Whole Foods teams get to vote on new employee hires as well. This approach allows Whole Foods to offer unique and "local market" experiences in each of its stores. This level of customization is in contrast to more centralized national supermarket chains such as Kroger, Safeway, and Publix.[18]

Should the span of management be wide or narrow? To answer this question, several factors need to be considered. A narrow span of management is appropriate when superiors and subordinates are not in close proximity, the manager has many responsibilities in addition to the supervision, the interaction between superiors and subordinates is frequent, and problems are common. However, when superiors and subordinates are located close to one another, the manager has few responsibilities other than supervision, the level of interaction between superiors and subordinates is low, few problems arise, subordinates are highly competent, and a set of specific operating procedures governs the activities of managers and their subordinates, a wide span of management will be more appropriate. Narrow spans of management are typical in centralized organizations, while wide spans of management are more common in decentralized firms.

Organizational Layers

Complementing the concept of span of management is **organizational layers,** the levels of management in an organization. A company with many layers of managers is considered tall; in a tall organization, the span of management is narrow (see Figure 7-5). Because each manager supervises only a few subordinates, many layers of management are necessary to carry out the operations of the business. McDonald's, for example, has a tall organization with many layers, including store

span of management
the number of subordinates who report to a particular manager.

organizational layers
the levels of management in an organization.

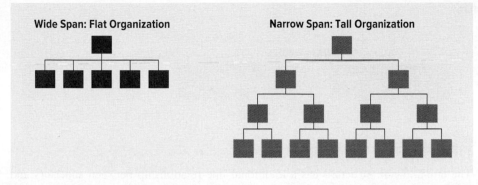

FIGURE 7-5
Span of Management:
Wide Span and
Narrow Span

managers, district managers, regional managers, and functional managers (finance, marketing, and so on), as well as a chief executive officer and many vice presidents. Because there are more managers in tall organizations than in flat organizations, administrative costs are usually higher. Communication is slower because information must pass through many layers.

Organizations with few layers are flat and have wide spans of management. When managers supervise a large number of employees, fewer management layers are needed to conduct the organization's activities. Managers in flat organizations typically perform more administrative duties than managers in tall organizations because there are fewer of them. They also spend more time supervising and working with subordinates.

Many of the companies that have decentralized also flattened their structures and widened their spans of management, often by eliminating layers of middle management. As mentioned earlier in this chapter, Johnson & Johnson has both a decentralized and flat organizational structure. Other corporations, including Avon, AT&T, and Ford Motor Company, embraced a more decentralized structure to reduce costs, speed up decision making, and boost overall productivity.

Forms of Organizational Structure

LO 7-5

Compare and contrast some common forms of organizational structure.

Along with assigning tasks and the responsibility for carrying them out, managers must consider how to structure their authority relationships—that is, what structure the organization itself will have and how it will appear on the organizational chart. Common forms of organization include line structure, line-and-staff structure, multidivisional structure, and matrix structure.

Line Structure

The simplest organizational structure, **line structure,** has direct lines of authority that extend from the top manager to employees at the lowest level of the organization. For example, a convenience store employee at 7-Eleven may report to an assistant manager, who reports to the store manager, who reports to a regional manager, or, in an independent store, directly to the owner (Figure 7-6). This structure has a clear chain of command, which enables managers to make decisions quickly. A mid-level manager facing a decision must consult only one person, his or her immediate supervisor. However, this structure requires that managers possess a wide range of knowledge and skills. They are responsible for a variety of activities and must be knowledgeable about them all. Line structures are most common in small businesses.

line structure
the simplest organizational structure, in which direct lines of authority extend from the top manager to the lowest level of the organization.

FIGURE 7-6   Line Structure

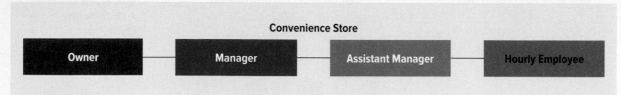

Convenience Store

| Owner | — | Manager | — | Assistant Manager | — | Hourly Employee |

Line-and-Staff Structure

line-and-staff structure
a structure having a traditional line relationship between superiors and subordinates and also specialized managers–called staff managers–who are available to assist line managers.

The **line-and-staff structure** has a traditional line relationship between superiors and subordinates, and specialized managers—called staff managers—are available to assist line managers (Figure 7-7). Line managers can focus on their area of expertise in the operation of the business, while staff managers provide advice and support to line departments on specialized matters such as finance, engineering, human resources, and the law. In the city of Pineapple Paradise (refer back for Figure 7-4), for example, assistant city managers are line managers who oversee groups of related departments. However, the city attorney, police chief, and fire chief are effectively staff managers who report directly to the city manager (the city equivalent of a business chief executive officer). Staff managers do not have direct authority over line managers or over the line manager's subordinates, but they do have direct authority over subordinates in their

FIGURE 7-7
Line-and-Staff Structure

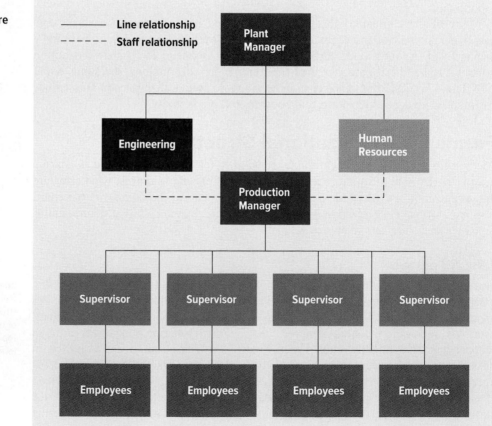

own departments. However, line-and-staff organizations may experience problems with overstaffing and ambiguous lines of communication. Additionally, employees may become frustrated because they lack the authority to carry out certain decisions.

Multidivisional Structure

As companies grow and diversify, traditional line structures become difficult to coordinate, making communication difficult and decision making slow. When the weaknesses of the structure—the "turf wars," miscommunication, and working at cross-purposes—exceed the benefits, growing firms tend to restructure, or change the basic structure of an organization. Growing firms tend to restructure into the divisionalized form. A multidivisional structure organizes departments into larger groups called divisions. Just as departments might be formed on the basis of geography, customer, product, or a combination of these, so too divisions can be formed based on any of these methods of organizing. Within each of these divisions, departments may be organized by product, geographic region, function, or some combination of all three. Indra Nooyi, CEO of PepsiCo, rearranged the company's organizational structure after taking the helm. Prior to her tenure, PepsiCo was organized geographically. She created new units that span international boundaries and make it easier for employees in different geographic regions to share business practices.[19]

Multidivisional structures permit delegation of decision-making authority, allowing divisional and department managers to specialize. They allow those closest to the action to make the decisions that will affect them. Delegation of authority and divisionalized work also mean that better decisions are made faster, and they tend to be more innovative. Most importantly, by focusing each division on a common region, product, or customer, each is more likely to provide products that meet the needs of its particular customers. However, the divisional structure inevitably creates work duplication, which makes it more difficult to realize the economies of scale that result from grouping functions together.

Matrix Structure

Another structure that attempts to address issues that arise with growth, diversification, productivity, and competitiveness, is the matrix. A matrix structure, also called a project management structure, sets up teams from different departments, thereby creating two or more intersecting lines of authority (Figure 7-8). One of the first organizations to design and implement a matrix structure was the National Aeronautics and Space Administration (NASA) for the space program because it needed to coordinate different projects at the same time. The matrix structure superimposes project-based departments on the more traditional, function-based departments. Project teams bring together specialists from a variety of areas to work together on a single project, such as developing a new fighter jet. In this arrangement, employees are responsible to two managers—functional managers and project managers. Matrix structures are usually temporary: Team members typically go back to their functional or line department after a project is finished. However, more firms are becoming permanent matrix structures, creating and dissolving project teams as needed to meet customer needs. The aerospace industry was one of the first to apply the matrix structure, but today it is used by universities and schools, accounting firms, banks, and organizations in other industries.

Matrix structures provide flexibility, enhanced cooperation, and creativity, and they enable the company to respond quickly to changes in the environment by giving

connect

▶ Need help understanding line vs. staff employees? Visit your Connect ebook video tab for a brief animated explanation.

restructure
to change the basic structure of an organization

multidivisional structure
a structure that organizes departments into larger groups called divisions.

matrix structure
a structure that sets up teams from different departments, thereby creating two or more intersecting lines of authority; also called a project-management structure.

FIGURE 7-8
Matrix Structure

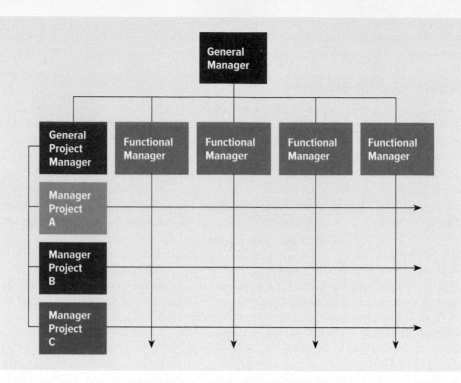

special attention to specific projects or problems. However, they are generally expensive and quite complex, and employees may be confused as to whose authority has priority—the project manager's or the immediate supervisor's.

Distinguish between groups and teams and identify the types of groups that exist in organizations.

The Role of Groups and Teams in Organizations

Regardless of how they are organized, most of the essential work of business occurs in individual work groups and teams, so we'll take a closer look at them now. There has been a gradual shift toward an emphasis on teams and managing them to enhance individual and organizational success. Some experts now believe that highest productivity results only when groups become teams.[20]

Traditionally, a **group** has been defined as two or more individuals who communicate with one another, share a common identity, and have a common goal. A **team** is a small group whose members have complementary skills; have a common purpose, goals, and approach; and hold themselves mutually accountable.[21] Think of a team like a sports team. Members of a basketball team have different skill sets and work together to score and win the game. All teams are groups, but not all groups are teams. Table 7-1 points out some important differences between them. Work groups emphasize individual work products, individual accountability, and even individual leadership. Your class is a group that can further be separated into teams of two or three classmates. Work teams share leadership roles, have both individual and mutual accountability, and create collective work products. In other words, a work group's performance depends on what its members do as individuals, while a team's performance is based on creating a knowledge center and a competency to work together to

group
two or more individuals who communicate with one another, share a common identity, and have a common goal.

team
a small group whose members have complementary skills; have a common purpose, goals, and approach; and hold themselves mutually accountable.

Working Group	Team
Has strong, clearly focused leader	Has shared leadership roles
Has individual accountability	Has individual and group accountability
Has the same purpose as the broader organizational mission	Has a specific purpose that the team itself delivers
Creates individual work products	Creates collective work products
Runs efficient meetings	Encourages open-ended discussion and active problem-solving meetings
Measures its effectiveness indirectly by its effects on others (e.g., financial performance of the business)	Measures performance directly by assessing collective work products
Discusses, decides, and delegates	Discusses, decides, and does real work together

TABLE 7-1
Differences between Groups and Teams

Source: Robert Gatewood, Robert Taylor, and O. C. Ferrell, Management: Comprehension Analysis and Application, 1995, p. 427. Copyright © 1995 Richard D. Irwin, a Times Mirror Higher Education Group, Inc., company. Reproduced with permission of the McGraw-Hill Companies.

accomplish a goal. On the other hand, it is also important for team members to retain their individuality and avoid becoming just "another face in the crowd." The purpose of teams should be toward collaboration versus collectivism. Although the team is working toward a common goal, it is important that all team members actively contribute their ideas and work together to achieve this common goal.[22]

The type of groups an organization establishes depends on the tasks it needs to accomplish and the situation it faces. Some specific kinds of groups and teams include committees, task forces, project teams, product-development teams, quality-assurance teams, and self-directed work teams. All of these can be *virtual teams*—employees in different locations who rely on e-mail, audio conferencing, fax, Internet, videoconferencing, or other technological tools to accomplish their goals. Virtual teams are becoming a part of everyday business, with the number of employees working remotely from their employer increasing more than 80 percent in the last several years.[23] Virtual teams have also opened up opportunities for different companies. For instance, inside salespeople use virtual technology such as email and social media to connect with prospects and clients.[24]

Committees

A **committee** is usually a permanent, formal group that does some specific task. For example, many firms have a compensation or finance committee to examine the effectiveness of these areas of operation as well as the need for possible changes. Ethics committees are formed to develop and revise codes of ethics, suggest methods for implementing ethical standards, and review specific issues and concerns.

commitee
a permanent, formal group that performs a specific task.

Task Forces

A **task force** is a temporary group of employees responsible for bringing about a particular change. They typically come from across all departments and levels of an organization. Task force membership is usually based on expertise rather than organizational position. Occasionally, a task force may be formed from individuals outside a company. Coca-Cola has often used task forces to address problems

task force
a temporary group of employees responsible for bringing about a particular change.

Amazon is known for its use of teams. According to CEO Jeff Bezos, the size of the teams should be no bigger than the number of people you can feed with two pizzas.

© Geoffrey Robinson/Alamy Stock Photo

and provide recommendations for improving company practices or products. While some task forces might last a few months, others last for years. When Coca-Cola faced lawsuits alleging discrimination practices in hiring and promotion, it developed a five-year task force to examine pay and promotion practices among minority employees. Its experiences helped Coca-Cola realize the advantages of having a cross-functional task force made up of employees from different departments, and it continued to use task forces to tackle major company issues. Other companies that have also recognized the benefits of task forces include IBM, Prudential, and General Electric.[25]

Teams

Teams are becoming far more common in the U.S. workplace as businesses strive to enhance productivity and global competitiveness. In general, teams have the benefit of being able to pool members' knowledge and skills and make greater use of them than can individuals working alone. Team building is becoming increasingly popular in organizations, with around half of executives indicating their companies had team-building training. Teams require harmony, cooperation, synchronized effort, and flexibility to maximize their contribution.[26] Teams can also create more solutions to problems than can individuals. Furthermore, team participation enhances employee acceptance of, understanding of, and commitment to team goals. Teams motivate workers by providing internal rewards in the form of an enhanced sense of accomplishment for employees as they achieve more, and external rewards in the form of praise and certain perks. Consequently, they can help get workers more involved. They can help companies be more innovative, and they can boost productivity and cut costs.

According to psychologist Ivan Steiner, team productivity peaks at about five team members. People become less motivated and group coordination becomes more difficult after this size. Jeff Bezos, Amazon.com CEO, says that he has a "two-pizza rule": If a team cannot be fed by two pizzas, it is too large. Keep teams small enough where everyone gets a piece of the action.[27]

project teams
groups similar to task forces that normally run their operation and have total control of a specific work project.

product-development teams
a specific type of project team formed to devise, design, and implement a new product.

Project Teams. **Project teams** are similar to task forces, but normally they run their operation and have total control of a specific work project. Like task forces, their membership is likely to cut across the firm's hierarchy and be composed of people from different functional areas. They are almost always temporary, although a large project, such as designing and building a new airplane at Boeing Corporation, may last for years.

Product-development teams are a special type of project team formed to devise, design, and implement a new product. Sometimes product-development teams exist within a functional area—research and development—but now they more frequently include people from numerous functional areas and may even include customers to help ensure that the end product meets the customers' needs. Intel informs its product development process through indirect input from customers. It has a social scientist on staff who leads a research team on how customers actually use products. This is done mainly by observation and asking questions. Once enough information is gathered, it is relayed to the product-development team and incorporated into Intel's designs.[28]

Quality-Assurance Teams. Quality-assurance teams, sometimes called **quality circles,** are fairly small groups of workers brought together from throughout the organization to solve specific quality, productivity, or service problems. Although the *quality circle* term is not as popular as it once was, the concern about quality is stronger than ever. Companies such as IBM and Xerox as well as companies in the automobile industry have used quality circles to shift the organization to a more participative culture. The use of teams to address quality issues will no doubt continue to increase throughout the business world.

quality-assurance teams (or quality circles)
small groups of workers brought together from throughout the organization to solve specific quality, productivity, or service problems.

Self-directed Work Teams. A **self-directed work team (SDWT)** is a group of employees responsible for an entire work process or segment that delivers a product to an internal or external customer.[29] SDWTs permit the flexibility to change rapidly to meet the competition or respond to customer needs. The defining characteristic of an SDWT is the extent to which it is empowered or given authority to make and implement work decisions. Thus, SDWTs are designed to give employees a feeling of "ownership" of a whole job. Employees at 3M as well as an increasing number of companies encourage employees to be active to perform a function or operational task. With shared team responsibility for work outcomes, team members often have broader job assignments and cross-train to master other jobs, thus permitting greater team flexibility.

self-directed work team (SDWT)
a group of employees responsible for an entire work process or segment that delivers a product to an internal or external customer.

Communicating in Organizations

LO 7-7

Describe how communication occurs in organizations.

Communication within an organization can flow in a variety of directions and from a number of sources, each using both oral and written forms of communication. The success of communication systems within the organization has a tremendous effect on the overall success of the firm. Communication mistakes can lower productivity and morale.

DID YOU KNOW? A survey of employees revealed that approximately 65 percent consider how their employers communicate with them to be a key factor in their job satisfaction.[30]

Alternatives to face-to-face communications—such as meetings—are growing, thanks to technology such as voice-mail, e-mail, social media, and online newsletters. Many companies use internal networks called intranets to share information with employees. Intranets increase communication across different departments and levels of management and help with the flow of everyday business activities. Another innovative approach is cloud computing. Rather than using physical products, companies using cloud computing technology can access computing resources and information over a network. Cloud computing allows companies to have more control over computing resources and can be less expensive than hardware or software. Salesforce.com uses cloud computing in its customer relationship management solutions.[31] Companies can even integrate aspects of social media into their intranets, allowing employees to post comments and pictures, participate in polls, and create group calendars. However, increased access to the Internet at work has also created many problems, including employee abuse of company e-mail and Internet access.[32] The increasing use of e-mail as a communication

New cloud-based technology is transforming internal communications at firms. It allows employees to share documents, collaborate with their teams, and even work from home.

© Vladyslav Starozhylo/Alamy

TABLE 7-2   Types of Formal Communication

Type	Definition	Examples
Upward	Flows from lower to higher levels of the organization	Progress reports, suggestions for improvement, inquiries, grievances
Downward	Traditional flow of communication from upper organizational levels to lower organizational levels	Directions, assignments of tasks and responsibilities, performance feedback, details about strategies and goals, speeches, employee handbooks, job descriptions
Horizontal	Exchange of information among colleagues and peers on the same organizational level, such as across or within departments, inform, support, and coordinate activities both within the department and between other departments	Task forces, project teams, communication from the finance department to the marketing department concerning budget requirements
Diagonal	When individuals from different levels and different departments communicate	A manager from the finance department communicates with a lower-level manager from the marketing department

tool also inundates employees and managers with e-mails, making it easier to overlook individual communications. For this reason, it is advised that employees place a specific subject in the subject line, keep e-mails brief, and avoid using e-mail if a problem would be better solved through face-to-face interaction.[33]

Formal and Informal Communication

Formal channels of communication are intentionally defined and designed by the organization. They represent the flow of communication within the formal organizational structure, as shown on organizational charts. Table 7-2 describes the different forms of formal communication. Traditionally, formal communication patterns were classified as vertical and horizontal, but with the increased use of teams and matrix structures, formal communication may occur in a number of patterns (Figure 7-9).

FIGURE 7-9
The Flow of Communication in an Organizational Hierarchy

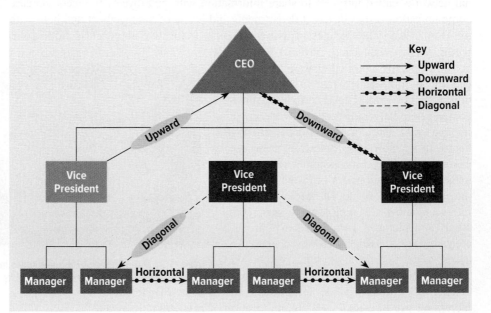

Along with the formal channels of communication shown on an organizational chart, all firms communicate informally as well. Communication between friends, for instance, cuts across department, division, and even management-subordinate boundaries. Such friendships and other nonwork social relationships comprise the *informal organization* of a firm, and their impact can be great.

The most significant informal communication occurs through the **grapevine,** an informal channel of communication, separate from management's formal, official communication channels. Grapevines exist in all organizations. Information passed along the grapevine may relate to the job or organization, or it may be gossip and rumors unrelated to either. The accuracy of grapevine information has been of great concern to managers.

grapevine
an informal channel of communication, separate from management's formal, official communication channels.

Managers can turn the grapevine to their advantage. Using it as a "sounding device" for possible new policies is one example. Managers can obtain valuable information from the grapevine that could improve decision making. Some organizations use the grapevine to their advantage by floating ideas, soliciting feedback, and reacting accordingly. People love to gossip, and managers need to be aware that grapevines exist in every organization. Managers who understand how the grapevine works also can use it to their advantage by feeding it facts to squelch rumors and incorrect information. For instance, rather than confronting employees about gossip and placing them on the defense, some employers ask employees—especially those who are the spreaders of gossip—for assistance in squelching the untrue rumors. This tactic turns employees into advocates for sharing truthful information.[34]

Monitoring Communications

Technological advances and the increased use of electronic communication in the workplace have made monitoring its use necessary for most companies. Failing to monitor employees' use of e-mail, social media, and the Internet can be costly. Many companies require that employees sign and follow a policy on appropriate Internet use. These agreements often require that employees will use corporate computers only for work-related activities. Additionally, several companies use software programs to monitor employee computer usage.[35] Instituting practices that show respect for employee privacy but do not abdicate employer responsibility are increasingly necessary in today's workplace. Merck, for instance, has a section on employee privacy in its code of conduct that reassures both current and former employees that their information will be protected and used only for legitimate business purposes.[36]

Improving Communication Effectiveness

Without effective communication, the activities and overall productivity of projects, groups, teams, and individuals will be diminished. Communication is an important area for a firm to address at all levels of management. Apple supplier Foxconn is one example of how essential communication is to a firm. Despite criticisms of unfair labor conditions, the Fair Labor Association determined that Foxconn had formal procedures in place at its factories to prevent many major accidents. However, it concluded that the firm had a communication problem. These procedures were not being communicated to the factory workers, contributing to unsafe practices and two tragic explosions.[37]

One of the major issues of effective communication is in obtaining feedback. If feedback is not provided, then communication will be ineffective and can drag down

From a Small Coffee Shop to a Big Sugar Bowl

Sugar Bowl Bakery
Founders: Tom, Binh, Andrew, Sam, and Paul Ly
Founded: 1984, in San Francisco, California
Success: The bakery has expanded to a 120,000-square-foot production facility and was prominently featured in *Costco Connection* in 2009.

In the 1980s, a family of refugees from Vietnam came to the United States to start a new life. Brothers Tom, Binh, Andrew, Sam, and Paul Ly had a deeply ingrained spirit of teamwork. Despite limited baking experience, the brothers decided to purchase a struggling coffee shop. To purchase the shop, they worked any jobs they could find and pooled together their money. After the bakery was opened, they shared operational responsibility. Andrew Ly took English language night courses so he could build business connections and promote the company.

While Sugar Bowl Bakery began as a coffee and donut shop, today its dessert products are manufactured with modern technology and can be found in nationwide retailers including Costco and Walgreens. It is still very much a team endeavor, with Andrew Ly as CEO and 8 of 12 second-generation children working at the bakery. Even now, the brothers hold monthly meetings to discuss conflicts and new ideas. This culture of shared responsibility has led to continual success for more than 30 years. Today, it is in one of America's largest family-owned national minority bakery manufacturers.[38]

Discussion Questions

1. How did teamwork contribute to the Ly brothers' successful bakery?
2. Why is it important to continue meeting regularly to discuss conflicts and ideas?
3. None of the Ly brothers spoke English when they immigrated to the United States. How was the communication barrier overcome?

overall performance. Managers should always encourage feedback, including concerns and challenges about issues. Listening is a skill that involves hearing, and most employees listen much more than they actively communicate to others. Therefore, managers should encourage employees to provide feedback—even if it is negative. It is interesting to note that employees list a failure to listen to their concerns as a top complaint in the workplace.[39] Employees often notice issues that managers overlook, and employee feedback can alert managers to these issues. This will allow the organization to identify strengths and weaknesses and make adjustments when needed. At the same time, strong feedback mechanisms help to empower employees as they feel that their voices are being heard.

Interruptions can be a serious threat to effective communication. Various activities can interrupt the message. For example, interjecting a remark can create discontinuance in the communication process or disrupt the uniformity of the message. Even small interruptions can be a problem if the messenger cannot adequately understand or interpret the communicator's message. One suggestion is to give the communicator space or time to make another statement rather than quickly responding or making your own comment.

Strong and effective communication channels are a requirement for companies to distribute information to different levels of the company. Businesses have several channels for communication, including face-to-face, e-mail, phone, and written communication (for example, memos). Each channel has advantages and disadvantages, and some are more appropriate to use than others. For instance, a small task requiring little instruction might be communicated through a short memo or e-mail. An in-depth task would most likely require a phone conversation or face-to-face contact. E-mail has become especially helpful for businesses, and both employees and managers are increasingly using e-mail rather than memos or phone conversations. However, it is important that employees use e-mail correctly. Inappropriate use of e-mail can include forwarding sexually explicit or otherwise offensive material. Additionally, many employees have used work e-mail accounts to send personal information. This may be against company policy. It is important for employees to remember that e-mail sent from corporate accounts is the property of the firm, so they should exert caution in making sure their e-mail messages contain appropriate content. It is, therefore, important for companies to communicate their e-mail policies throughout the organization. Communicators using e-mail, whether managers or employees, must exert caution before pushing that "Send" button.

Communication is necessary in helping every organizational member understand what is expected of him or her. Many business problems can be avoided if clear communication exists within the company. Even the best business strategies are of little use if those who will oversee them cannot understand what is intended. Communication might not seem to be as big of a concern to management as finances, human resources, and marketing, but in reality it can make the difference between successful implementation of business activities or failure.

So You Want a Job in Managing Organizational Culture, Teamwork, and Communication

Jobs dealing with organizational culture and structure are usually at the top of the organization. If you want to be a CEO or high-level manager, you will help shape these areas of business. On the other hand, if you are an entrepreneur or small-business person, you will need to make decisions about assigning tasks, departmentalization, and assigning responsibility. Even managers in small organizations have to make decisions about decentralization, span of management, and forms of organizational structure. Micro-entrepreneurs with five or fewer employees still have to make decisions about assigning tasks and whether to work as a group or a team. While these decisions may be part of your job, there are usually no job titles dealing with these specific areas. Specific jobs that attempt to improve organizational culture could include ethics and compliance positions as well as those who are in charge of communicating memos, manuals, and policies that help establish the culture. These positions will be in communications, human resources, and positions that assist top organizational managers.

Teams are becoming more common in the workplace, and it is possible to become a member of a product development group or quality assurance team. There are also human resource positions that encourage teamwork through training activities. The area of corporate communications provides lots of opportunities for specific jobs that facilitate communication systems. Thanks to technology, there are job positions to help disseminate information through online newsletters, intranets, or internal computer networks to share information to increase collaboration. In addition to the many advances using electronic communications, there are technology concerns that create new job opportunities. Monitoring workplace communications such as the use of e-mail and the Internet has created new industries. There have to be internal controls in the organization to make sure that the organization does not engage in any copyright infringement. If this is an area of interest, there are specific jobs that provide an opportunity to use your technological skills to assist in maintaining appropriate standards in communicating and using technology.

If you go to work for a large company with many divisions, you can expect a number of positions dealing with the tasks discussed here. If you go to work for a small company, you will probably engage in most of these tasks as a part of your position. Organizational flexibility requires individual flexibility, and those employees willing to take on new domains and challenges will be the employees who survive and prosper in the future.

Review Your Understanding

Explain the importance of organizational culture.

Organizational culture is the firm's shared values, beliefs, traditions, philosophies, and role models for behavior. It helps ensure that all members of a company share values and suggests rules for how to behave and deal with problems within the organization.

Define *organizational structure* and relate how organizational structures develop.

Structure is the arrangement or relationship of positions within an organization; it develops when managers assign work activities to work groups and specific individuals and coordinate the diverse activities required to attain organizational objectives. Organizational structure evolves to accommodate growth, which requires people with specialized skills.

Describe how specialization and departmentalization help an organization achieve its goals.

Structuring an organization requires that management assign work tasks to specific individuals and groups. Under specialization, managers break labor into small, specialized tasks and assign employees to do a single task, fostering efficiency. Departmentalization is the grouping of jobs into working units (departments, units, groups, or divisions). Businesses may departmentalize by function, product, geographic region, or customer, or they may combine two or more of these.

Distinguish between groups and teams and identify the types of groups that exist in organizations.

A group is two or more persons who communicate, share a common identity, and have a common goal. A team is a small group whose members have complementary skills, a common purpose, goals, and approach and who hold themselves mutually accountable. The major distinction is that individual performance is most important in groups, while collective work group performance counts most in teams. Special kinds of groups include task forces, committees, project teams, product-development teams, quality-assurance teams, and self-directed work teams.

Determine how organizations assign responsibility for tasks and delegate authority.

Delegation of authority means assigning tasks to employees and giving them the power to make commitments, use resources, and take whatever actions are necessary to accomplish the tasks. It lays responsibility on employees to carry out assigned tasks satisfactorily and holds them accountable to a superior for the proper execution of their assigned work. The extent to which authority is delegated throughout an organization determines its degree of centralization. Span of management refers to the number of subordinates who report to a particular manager. A wide span of management occurs in flat organizations; a narrow one exists in tall organizations.

Compare and contrast some common forms of organizational structure.

Line structures have direct lines of authority that extend from the top manager to employees at the lowest level of the organization. The line-and-staff structure has a traditional line relationship between superiors and subordinates, and specialized staff managers are available to assist line managers. A multidivisional structure gathers departments into larger groups called divisions. A matrix, or project-management, structure sets up teams from different departments, thereby creating two or more intersecting lines of authority.

Describe how communication occurs in organizations.

Communication occurs both formally and informally in organizations. Formal communication may be downward, upward, horizontal, and even diagonal. Informal communication takes place through friendships and the grapevine.

Analyze a business's use of teams.

The "Solve the Dilemma" feature at the end of this chapter introduces Quest Star's attempt to restructure to a team environment. Based on the material presented in this chapter, you should be able to evaluate the Quest Star's efforts and make recommendations for resolving the problems that have developed.

Revisit the World of Business

1. Why does W.L. Gore's unique management structure work?
2. What trade-offs does Gore make by using the flat lattice structure? In other words, are there certain disadvantages

that Gore has chosen to accept in return for other benefits?
3. Would you like to work in a flat lattice-style organization? Why or why not?

Learn the Terms

accountability 210
centralized organization 210
committee 217
customer departmentalization 209
decentralized organization 211
delegation of authority 210
departmentalization 206
functional departmentalization 207
geographical
  departmentalization 209
grapevine 221

group 216
line-and-staff structure 214
line structure 213
matrix structure 215
multidivisional structure 215
organizational chart 205
organizational culture 202
organizational layers 212
product departmentalization 209
product-development teams 218
project teams 218

quality-assurance teams
  (or quality circles) 219
responsibility 210
restructure 215
self-directed work team (SDWT) 219
span of management 212
specialization 205
structure 204
task force 217
team 216

Check Your Progress

1. Identify four types of departmentalization and give an example of each type.
2. Explain the difference between groups and teams.
3. What are self-managed work teams and what tasks might they perform that traditionally are performed by managers?
4. Explain how delegating authority, responsibility, and accountability are related.
5. Distinguish between centralization and decentralization. Under what circumstances is each appropriate?
6. Define *span of management.* Why do some organizations have narrow spans and others wide spans?

7. Discuss the different forms of organizational structure. What are the primary advantages and disadvantages of each form?
8. Discuss the role of the grapevine within organizations. How can managers use it to further the goals of the firm?
9. How have technological advances made electronic oversight a necessity in many companies?
10. Discuss how an organization's culture might influence its ability to achieve its objectives. Do you think that managers can "manage" the organization's culture?

Get Involved

1. Explain, using a specific example (perhaps your own future business), how an organizational structure might evolve. How would you handle the issues of specialization, delegation of authority, and centralization? Which structure would you use? Explain your answers.

2. Interview the department chairperson in charge of one of the academic departments in your college or university. Using Table 7-1 as a guideline, explore whether the professors function more like a group or a team. Contrast what you learned here with what you see on your school's basketball, football, or baseball team.

Build Your Skills

Teamwork

Background
Think about all the different kinds of groups and teams you have been a member of or been involved with. Here's a checklist to help you remember them—with "Other" spaces to fill in ones not listed. Check all that apply.

School Groups/Teams

- ☐ Sports teams
- ☐ Cheerleading squads
- ☐ Musical groups
- ☐ Hobby clubs
- ☐ Foreign language clubs
- ☐ Study groups
- ☐ Other_____

Community Groups/Teams

- ☐ Fund-raising groups
- ☐ Religious groups
- ☐ Sports teams
- ☐ Political groups
- ☐ Boy/Girl Scout troops
- ☐ Volunteer organizations
- ☐ Other_____

Employment Groups/Teams

- ☐ Problem-solving teams
- ☐ Work committees
- ☐ Project teams
- ☐ Labor union groups
- ☐ Work crews
- ☐ Other_____

Task

1. Of those you checked, circle those that you would categorize as a "really great team."

2. Examine the following table[40] and circle those characteristics from columns 2 and 3 that were represented in your "really great" team experiences.

Indicator	Good Team Experience	Not-So-Good Team Experience
Members arrive on time?	Members are prompt because they know others will be.	Members drift in sporadically, and some leave early.
Members prepared?	Members are prepared and know what to expect.	Members are unclear what the agenda is.
Meeting organized?	Members follow a planned agenda.	The agenda is tossed aside, and freewheeling discussion ensues.
Members contribute equally?	Members give each other a chance to speak; quiet members are encouraged.	Some members always dominate the discussion; some are reluctant to speak their minds.
Discussions help members make decisions?	Members learn from others' points of view, new facts are discussed, creative ideas evolve, and alternatives emerge.	Members reinforce their belief in their own points of view, or their decisions were made long before the meeting.
Any disagreement?	Members follow a conflict-resolution process established as part of the team's policies.	Conflict turns to argument, angry words, emotion, blaming.
More cooperation or more conflict?	Cooperation is clearly an important ingredient.	Conflict flares openly, as well as simmering below the surface.
Commitment to decisions?	Members reach consensus before leaving.	Compromise is the best outcome possible; some members don't care about the result.
Member feelings after team decision?	Members are satisfied and are valued for their ideas.	Members are glad it's over, not sure of results or outcome.
Members support decision afterward?	Members are committed to implementation.	Some members second-guess or undermine the team's decision.

3. What can you take with you from your positive team experiences and apply to a work-related group or team situation in which you might be involved?

_____
_____
_____
_____

Solve the Dilemma

Quest Star in Transition

Quest Star (QS), which manufactures quality stereo loudspeakers, wants to improve its ability to compete against Japanese Arms. Accordingly, the company has launched a comprehensive quality-improvement program for its Iowa plant. The QS Intracommunication Leadership Initiative (ILI) has flattened the layers of management. The program uses teams and peer pressure to accomplish the plant's goals instead of multiple management layers with their limited opportunities for communication. Under the initiative, employees make all decisions within the boundaries of their responsibilities, and they elect team representatives to coordinate with other teams. Teams are also assigned tasks ranging from establishing policies to evaluating on-the-job safety.

However, employees who are not self-motivated team players are having difficulty getting used to their peers' authority within this system. Upper-level managers face stress and frustration because they must train workers to supervise themselves.

LO 7-8

Analyze a business's use of teams.

Discussion Questions

1. What techniques or skills should an employee have to assume a leadership role within a work group?

2. If each work group has a team representative, what problems will be faced in supervising these representatives?

3. Evaluate the pros and cons of the system developed by QS.

Build Your Business Plan

Organization, Teamwork, and Communication

Developing a business plan as a team is a deliberate move of your instructor to encourage you to familiarize yourself with the concept of teamwork. You need to realize that you are going to spend a large part of your professional life working with others. At this point in time, you are working on the business plan for a grade, but after graduation, you will be "teaming" with co-workers, and the success of your endeavor may determine whether you get a raise or a bonus. It is important that you be comfortable as soon as possible with working with others and holding them accountable for their contributions.

Some people are natural "leaders," and leaders often feel that if team members are not doing their work, they take

it upon themselves to "do it all." This is not leadership, but rather micro-managing.

Leadership means holding members accountable for their responsibilities. Your instructor may provide ideas on how this could be implemented, possibly by utilizing peer reviews. Remember, you are not doing a team member a favor by doing their work for them.

If you are a "follower" (someone who takes directions well) rather than a leader, try to get into a team where others are hard workers and you will rise to their level. There is nothing wrong with being a follower; not everyone can be a leader!

See for Yourself Videocase

Hot Topic Tees Up an Employee Culture

Hot Topic Inc. founded Hot Topic-branded stores and Torrid, a subsidiary of Hot Topic. Hot Topic-branded stores sell edgy, cultural-related apparel, accessories, and music. Approximately

40 percent of its sales are from licensed T-shirts. Torrid sells fashionable apparel for plus-sized women. Corporate culture takes a front stage role at both types of stores. Hot Topic Inc. employees are given a unique opportunity to have fun on the

job and make meaningful contributions to the organization. With its emphasis on music, pop culture, and fashion, Hot Topic wants employees to be passionate about their products. It encourages a culture that promotes employee passion through communication, teamwork, and recognition.

Hot Topic Inc. was founded in 1988 to sell hip, music-inspired accessories. In 2001, Hot Topic opened the fashion retailer Torrid after recognizing that plus-sized women often had trouble finding fashionable clothing in their sizes. During the latest recession, Hot Topic refocused on music, with an emphasis on emerging bands. Hot Topic was able to soar through the recession by utilizing employee passion to come up with new product ideas and events. For instance, it began featuring free acoustic shows called Local Static that featured bands chosen by Hot Topic's salespeople.

This emphasis on employee involvement is a strong part of Hot Topic's culture. Hot Topic Inc. welcomes feedback from employees on concerns or product recommendations. The company stresses an open communication culture where employees can approach management on any topic. At the Hot Topic headquarters in Industry City, California, there are no cubicles to separate employees. Management believes this shared environment encourages cooperation and teamwork.

"You'll notice there are no walls and there are no doors, and all of us sit in one big room and we share space," says former Hot Topic CEO Betsy McLaughlin. "Collaboration is really important to all of us. Keeping a pulse on the culture, I believe, is directly attributable to the kind of space that we all share on a daily basis."

Employees at Hot Topic's headquarters and distribution centers meet on a regular basis to discuss updates and accomplishments. For each district, store managers meet with their assistant store managers twice annually, and district managers meet with headquarters twice a year. This keeps Hot Topic's management fully informed about how the company is doing while simultaneously giving Hot Topic employees the opportunity to participate in the operational process.

One of the incentives Hot Topic provides to its employees is the Concert Reimbursement program. Any associate who attends a concert is eligible for up to $25 in reimbursement for his or her ticket. However, this is not only a way to reward employees; it also serves as another method of soliciting employee feedback. To be eligible for reimbursement, Hot Topic concert-goers fill out a fashion report of what they saw people wearing at the concert. Hot Topic's Merchandise team then uses this feedback to generate new ideas for fashion products to sell in stores.

A core part of creating a strong and cohesive culture is the adoption of values that all members can share. For example, its subsidiary Torrid lists five core values on its website for employees to adopt: (1) customer service, (2) communication, (3) development and recognition, (4) community, and (5) fun. In terms of employee recognition, Hot Topic Inc. rewards its promoted employees by recognizing them at its quarterly meetings. These values are fundamental to the identity of Torrid.

Hot Topic Inc. has a more decentralized organizational structure. Although it is similar to other retailers in structure and design, employees are empowered to make decisions. Front-line employees are encouraged to take reasonable risks to satisfy customers or solve problems. Allowing employees to make these types of decisions gives the company the opportunity to utilize the diverse talents of their employees.

The corporate culture is so important to Hot Topic that it promotes internally. It desires to promote individuals who are well versed in the company's culture and values. Through internal promoting, Hot Topic ensures that employees carry corporate values to the highest echelons of the organization.[41]

Discussion Questions

1. How would you describe the corporate culture for employees who work at Hot Topic?

2. What are the advantages in having a decentralized organizational structure at Hot Topic?

3. Evaluate Hot Topic subsidiary Torrid's values—customer service, communication, development and recognition, community, and fun.

You can find the related video in the Video Library in Connect. Ask your instructor how you can access Connect.

Team Exercise

Assign the responsibility of providing the organizational structure for a company one of your team members has worked for. Was your organization centralized or decentralized in terms of decision making? Would you consider the span of control to be wide or narrow? Were any types of teams, committees, or task forces utilized in the organization? Report your work to the class.

Endnotes

1. "The 100 Best Companies to Work For," Fortune, 2015, http://fortune.com/best-companies/w-l-gore-associates-17/ (accessed October 21, 2015); W.L. Gore, "A Team-Based Flats Lattice Structure," http://www.gore.com/en_xx/aboutus/culture/index.html (accessed October 15, 2014); Gary Hamel, "W.L. Gore: Lessons from a Management Revolutionary," The Wall Street Journal, March 18, 2010, http://blogs.wsj.com/management/2010/03/18/wl-gore-lessons-from-a-management-revolutionary/ (accessed March 8, 2015).

2. Horace Dediu, "Understanding Apple's Organizational Structure," Asymco, July 3, 2013, www.asymco.com/2013/07/03/understanding-apples-organizational-structure/ (accessed March 10, 2016); Sam Grobart, "How Samsung Became the World's No. 1 Smartphone Maker," Bloomberg Businessweek, March 28, 2013, www.businessweek.com/articles/2013-03-28/how-samsung-became-the-worlds-no-dot-1-smartphone-maker#p1(accessed March 10, 2016); Jay Yarow, "Apple's New Organizational Structure Could Help It Move Faster," Business Insider, May 1, 2013, www.businessinsider.com/apples-new-organizational-structure-could-help-it-move-faster-2013-5 (accessed March 10, 2016).

3. Megan McArdle, "'Unlimited Vacation' Is Code for 'No Vacation,'" September 30, 2015, Bloomberg, September 30, 2015,http://www.bloombergview.com/articles/2015-09-30/-unlimited-vacation-is-code-for-no-vacation- (accessed March 9, 2015).

4. Robert Hackett, "A Globe of Opportunity," Fortune, February 1, 2015, p. 22.

5. Micah Solomon, "Take These Two to Rival Nordstrom's Customer Service Experience," Forbes, March 15, 2014, http://www.forbes.com/sites/micahsolomon/2014/03/15/the-nordstrom-two-part-customer-experience-formula-lessons-for-your-business/#2ebc60a92335 (accessed March 10, 2016).

6. Larry Alton, "Report: 'Unethical Behavior' Continues to Plague Financial Services Industry," Business Ethics, May 28, 2015, http://business-ethics.com/2015/05/28/0920-survey-unethical-behavior-continues-to-plague-financial-services-industry/ (accessed March 9, 2016).

7. Jodi Kantor and David Streitfeld, "Inside Amazon: Wrestling Big Ideas in a Bruising Workplace," The New York Times, August 15, 2015,http://www.nytimes.com/2015/08/16/technology/inside-amazon-wrestling-big-ideas-in-a-bruising-workplace.html?_r=1 (accessed November 23, 2015); Rem Rieder, "Amazon A Prime Media Target," USA Today, August 18, 2015, p. 2B; Shannon Pettypiece, "Amazon Passes Wal-Mart as Biggest Retailer by Market Value," Bloomberg Business, July 23, 2015, http://www.bloomberg.com/news/articles/2015-07-23/amazon-surpasses-wal-mart-as-biggest-retailer-by-market-value, (accessed November 23, 2015); Brett Molina and Elizabeth Weise, "Bezos Defends Working Conditions at Amazon," USA Today, August 17, 2015,http://www.usatoday.com/story/tech/2015/08/17/bezos-defends-working-conditions-amazon/31843547/ (accessed November 23, 2015).

8. CNN Money, "How Zappos Will Run with No Job Titles," YouTube, February 17, 2014, https://www.youtube.com/watch?v=-DYigfNJQlg (accessed March 10, 2016).

9. Adam Smith, Wealth of Nations (New York: Modern Library, 1937; originally published in 1776).

10. Ben Dipietro, "Automakers Face 'Herculean' Task in Implementing Supply Chain Guidelines," The Wall Street Journal, May 28, 2014,http://blogs.wsj.com/riskandcompliance/2014/05/28/automakers-face-herculean-task-in-implementing-supply-chain-guidelines/ (accessed March 5, 2015).

11. Unilever, "Brands," https://www.unilever.com/brands/ (accessed March 10, 2016).

12. PepsiCo Inc., The New York Times, March 31, 2014,http://topics.nytimes.com/top/news/business/companies/pepsico_inc/index.html (accessed March 31, 2014). PepsiCo Inc., "Global Divisions,"http://www.pepsico.com/Company/Global-Divisions (accessed March 8, 2016).

13. Diageo, "Regions," www.diageo.com/en-row/ourbusiness/ourregions/Pages/default.aspx (accessed March 10, 2016).

14. 3M, "Employee Engagement," http://www.3m.com/3M/en_US/sustainability-report/strategy/employee-engagement/ (accessed March 10, 2016).

15. "Hierarchy, High Pressure & Risk," BizEd, June 2015, p. 16.

16. Claire Groden, "Burger King Considers Rolling Out Vegetarian Options," Fortune, June 30, 2015, http://fortune.com/2015/06/30/burger-king-vegetarian/ (accessed March 10, 2016).

17. Kelly K. Spors, "Top Small Workplaces 2008," The Wall Street Journal, February 2, 2009, http://www.wsj.com/articles/SB122347733961315417?alg=y (accessed November 23, 2015); Richard Donovan, "Rainforest Alliance Launches TREES," Forest Stewardship Council, December 15, 2001,https://us.fsc.org/newsletter.239.55.htm (accessed November 23, 2015); Rainforest Alliance, http://www.rainforest-alliance.org/ (accessed November 23, 2015).

18. Why Work Here?" www.wholefoodsmarket.com/careers/workhere.php (accessed March 10, 2016).

19. "PepsiCo Unveils New Organizational Structure, Names CEOs of Three Principle Operating Units," PR Newswire, November 5, 2007, www.prnewswire.com/news-releases/pepsico-unveils-new-organizational-structure-names-ceos-of-three-principal-operating-units-58668152.html (accessed March 10, 2016); "The PepsiCo Family," PepsiCo,www.pepsico.com/Company/The-Pepsico-Family/PepsiCo-Americas-Beverages.html (accessed April 30, 2014).

20. Jon R. Katzenbach and Douglas K. Smith, "The Discipline of Teams," Harvard Business Review, 71 (March- April 1993), p. 19.

21. Ibid.

22. John Baldoni, "The Secret to Team Collaboration: Individuality," *Inc.,* January 18, 2012, www.inc.com/john-baldoni/the-secret-to-team-collaboration-is-individuality.html (accessed March 11, 2016).

23. Gregory Ciotti, "Why Remote Teams Are the Future (and How to Make Them Work)," *Help Scout,* October 23, 2013, www.helpscout.net/blog/virtual-teams/ (accessed March 11, 2016).

24. Anneke Seley, "Outside In: The Rise of the Inside Sales Team,"*Salesforce.com Blog,* February 3, 2015,http://blogs.salesforce.com/company/2015/02/outside-in-rise-inside-sales-team-gp.html (accessed March 5, 2015).

25. Patrick Kiger, "Task Force Training Develops New Leaders, Solves Real Business Issues and Helps Cut Costs," *Workforce,* September 7, 2011,www.workforce.com/article/20070521/NEWS02/305219996/task-force-training-develops-new-leaders-solves-real-business-issues-and-helps-cut-costs (accessed March 10, 2016; Duane D. Stanford, "Coca-Cola Woman Board Nominee Bucks Slowing Diversity Trend," *Bloomberg,* February 22, 2013, www.bloomberg.com/news/2013-02-22/coca-cola-s-woman-director-nominee-bucks-slowing-diversity-trend.html (accessed March 10, 2016).

26. Jerry Useem, "What's That Spell? TEAMWORK," *Fortune,* June 12, 2006, p. 66.

27. Jia Lynnyang, "The Power of Number 4.6," *Fortune,* June 12, 2006, p. 122.

28. Natasha Singer, "Intel's Sharp-Eyed Social Scientist," *The New York Times,* February 15, 2014, www.nytimes.com/2014/02/16/technology/intels-sharp-eyed-social-scientist.html?_r=0 (accessed March 10, 2016).

29. Richard S. Wellins, William C. Byham, and Jeanne M. Wilson, *Empowered Teams: Creating Self-Directed Work Groups That Improve Quality, Productivity, and Participation* (San Francisco: Jossey-Bass Publishers, 1991), p. 5.

30. TheIRapp, LLC, "theEMPLOYEEapp™ Survey: Internal Communications Affects Job Satisfaction and Employee Engagement," *APPrise Mobile,* May 20, 2014, http://www.thecommsapp.com/media-center/press-releases/theemployeeapp-survey-internal-communications-affects-job-satisfaction-and-employee-engagement (accessed March 5, 2015).

31. Peter Mell and Timothy Grance, "The NIST Definition of Cloud Computing," National Institute of Standards and Technology, Special Publication 800-145, September 2011, http://csrc.nist.gov/publications/nistpubs/800-145/SP800-145.pdf (accessed April 30, 2014).

32. Michael Christian, "Top 10 Ideas: Making the Most of Your Corporate Intranet," April 2, 2009, www.claromentis.com/blog/top-10-ideas-making-the-most-of-your-corporate-intranet/ (accessed March 11, 2016).

33. Verne Harnish, "Five Ways to Liberate Your Team From Email Overload," *Fortune,* June 16, 2014, p. 52.

34. Sue Shellenbarger, "They're Gossiping About You," *The Wall Street Journal,* October 8, 2014, pp. D1–D2.

35. Kim Komando, "Why You Need a Company Policy on Internet Use," www.microsoft.com/business/en-us/resources/management/employee-relations/why-you-need-a-company-policy-on-internet-use.aspx?fbid=HEChiHWK7CU (accessed April 30, 2014).

36. Merck, "Our Values and Standards: The Basis of Our Success," https://www.merck.com/abo0ut/code_of_conduct.pdf (accessed March 16, 2015).

37. PBSNewsHour, "Apple Supplier Foxconn Pledges Better Working Conditions, but Will It Deliver?" *YouTube,* www.youtube.com/watch?v=ZduorbCkSBQ (accessed March 10, 2016).

38. Dinah Eng, "The Sweet Taste of Success," *Fortune,* June 1, 2015, pp. 9–20; Sugar Bowl Bakery, "The Costco Connection," http://sugarbowlbakery.com/2009/02/the-costco-connection/ (accessed September 9, 2015); Sugar Bowl Bakery, "About," http://sugarbowlbakery.com/about/ (accessed September 9, 2015).

39. Susan M. Heathfield, "Top Ten Employee Complaints," About.com, http://humanresources.about.com/od/retention/a/emplo_complaint.htm (accessed March 16, 2015).

40. Michael D. Maginn, *Effective Teamwork,* 1994, p. 10. © 1994 Richard D. Irwin, a Times Mirror Higher Education Group Inc. Company.

41. Hot Topic, "Hot Topic Careers, http://hottopiccareers.com/ (accessed April 19, 2016); Torrid, "Jobs," http://jobs.jobvite.com/torrid (accessed April 19, 2016); Kate Rockwood, "How Hot Topic's Culture-Heavy Strategy Helped It Sizzle during the Downturn," *Fast Company,* September 1, 2009, http://www.fastcompany.com/1325764/how-hot-topics-culture-heavy-strategy-helped-it-sizzle-during-downturn (accessed April 19, 2016); Jayne O'Donnell, "Hot Topic CEO Betsy McLaughlin Lives in Two Worlds," *USA Today,* March 22, 2010, http://usatoday30.usatoday.com/money/industries/retail/2010-03-22-hottopicceo22_CV_N.htm (accessed April 19, 2016).

© Jonathan Weiss/Shutterstock

8

Managing Service and Manufacturing Operations

Learning Objectives

After reading this chapter, you will be able to:

LO 8-1 Define *operations management* and differentiate between operations and manufacturing.

LO 8-2 Explain how operations management differs in manufacturing and service firms.

LO 8-3 Describe the elements involved in planning and designing an operations system.

LO 8-4 Specify some techniques managers may use to manage the logistics of transforming inputs into finished products.

LO 8-5 Assess the importance of quality in operations management.

LO 8-6 Evaluate a business's dilemma and propose a solution.

Enter the World of Business ⊖

Operations Challenges Inside the Chipotle Kitchen

The Chipotle business model of serving farm-grown, ethically sourced, and oftentimes local ingredients has helped the restaurant attract health-conscious consumers, but at the cost of increasing operational complexity. To satisfy desires many have for less-processed fresh food, Chipotle has its more than 1,700 restaurants prepare guacamole from scratch; chop ingredients such as lettuce, tomatoes, and cilantro in-house; and prepare its full line of menu items in front of the customer. This means the company spends much more on resources than comparable restaurants, but it allows the company to maintain more control over processes and procedures. Because Chipotle sources costly ingredients that are often processed at each individual restaurant, employees are taught to follow strict portioning, cooking, and serving guidelines. This is intended to keep costs down while ensuring the food adheres to certain quality and taste expectations. Additionally, despite its customizable made-to-order menu, Chipotle ensures customers are served quickly.

While sales at Chipotle have increased over the past decade, the restaurant chain is not immune to danger. In 2015, an *E. coli* outbreak linked to 11 locations in Washington and Oregon forced restaurant closures and sent sales plummeting. Chipotle acted quickly by implementing more stringent food safety practices, but the company faced much criticism and government scrutiny. However, despite its recent trouble, many anticipate Chipotle will bounce back. The chain has a strong track record of increasing sales, even in times when fast-food sales have largely declined.[1]

Introduction

All organizations create products—goods, services, or ideas—for customers. Thus, organizations as diverse as Toyota, Campbell Soup, UPS, and a public hospital share a number of similarities relating to how they transform resources into the products we consume. Most hospitals use similar admission procedures, while online social media companies, like Facebook and Twitter, use their technology and operating systems to create social networking opportunities and sell advertising. Such similarities are to be expected. But even organizations in unrelated industries take similar steps in creating goods or services. The check-in procedures of hotels and commercial airlines are comparable, for example. The way Subway assembles a sandwich and the way GMC assembles a truck are similar (both use automation and an assembly line). These similarities are the result of operations management, the focus of this chapter.

Here, we discuss the role of production or operations management in acquiring and managing the resources necessary to create goods and services. Production and operations management involves planning and designing the processes that will transform those resources into finished products, managing the movement of those resources through the transformation process, and ensuring that the products are of the quality expected by customers.

The Nature of Operations Management

Define *operations management* and differentiate between operations and manufacturing.

operations management (OM)
the development and administration of the activities involved in transforming resources into goods and services.

manufacturing
the activities and processes used in making tangible products; also called production.

production
the activities and processes used in making tangible products; also called manufacturing.

operations
the activities and processes used in making both tangible and intangible products.

Operations management (OM), the development and administration of the activities involved in transforming resources into goods and services, is of critical importance. Operations managers oversee the transformation process and the planning and designing of operations systems, managing logistics, quality, and productivity. Quality and productivity have become fundamental aspects of operations management because a company that cannot make products of the quality desired by consumers, using resources efficiently and effectively, will not be able to remain in business. OM is the "core" of most organizations because it is responsible for the creation of the organization's goods and services. Some organizations like General Motors produce tangible products, but service is an important part of the total product for the customer.

Historically, operations management has been called "production" or "manufacturing" primarily because of the view that it was limited to the manufacture of physical goods. Its focus was on methods and techniques required to operate a factory efficiently. The change from "production" to "operations" recognizes the increasing importance of organizations that provide services and ideas. Additionally, the term *operations* represents an interest in viewing the operations function as a whole rather than simply as an analysis of inputs and outputs.

Today, OM includes a wide range of organizational activities and situations outside of manufacturing, such as health care, food service, banking, entertainment, education, transportation, and charity. Thus, we use the terms **manufacturing** and **production** interchangeably to represent the activities and processes used in making *tangible* products, whereas we use the broader term **operations** to describe those processes used in the making of *both tangible and intangible products*. Manufacturing provides tangible products such as the Apple Watch, and operations provides intangibles such as a stay at Wyndham Hotels and Resorts.

The Transformation Process

At the heart of operations management is the transformation process through which **inputs** (resources such as labor, money, materials, and energy) are converted into **outputs** (goods, services, and ideas). The transformation process combines inputs in predetermined ways using different equipment, administrative procedures, and technology to create a product (Figure 8-1). To ensure that this process generates quality products efficiently, operations managers control the process by taking measurements (feedback) at various points in the transformation process and comparing them to previously established standards. If there is any deviation between the actual and desired outputs, the manager may take some sort of corrective action. For example, if an airline has a standard of 90 percent of its flights departing on time but only 80 percent depart on time, a 10 percent negative deviation exists. All adjustments made to create a satisfying product are a part of the transformation process.

Transformation may take place through one or more processes. In a business that manufactures oak furniture, for example, inputs pass through several processes before being turned into the final outputs—furniture that has been designed to meet the desires of customers (Figure 8-2). The furniture maker must first strip the oak trees of their bark and saw them into appropriate sizes—one step in the transformation process. Next, the firm dries the strips of oak lumber, a second form of transformation. Third, the dried wood is routed into its appropriate shape and made smooth. Fourth, workers assemble and treat the wood pieces, then stain or varnish the piece of assembled furniture. Finally, the completed piece of furniture is stored until it can be shipped to customers at the appropriate time. Of course, many businesses choose to eliminate some of these stages by purchasing already processed materials—lumber, for example—or outsourcing some tasks to third-party firms with greater expertise.

Operations Management in Service Businesses

Different types of transformation processes take place in organizations that provide services, such as airlines, colleges, and most nonprofit organizations. An airline transforms inputs such as employees, time, money, and equipment through processes such as booking flights, flying airplanes, maintaining equipment, and training crews. The

inputs
the resources—such as labor, money, materials, and energy—that are converted into outputs.

outputs
the goods, services, and ideas that result from the conversion of inputs.

Need help understanding the transformation process for goods and services? Visit your Connect ebook video tab for a brief animated explanation.

LO 8-2

Explain how operations management differs in manufacturing and service firms.

FIGURE 8-1
The Transformation Process of Operations Management

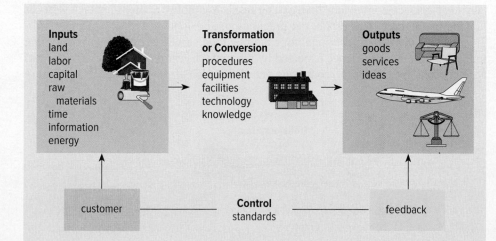

Entrepreneurship in Action

Bean-to-Bar Chocolate

Olive & Sinclair
Founder: Scott Witherow
Founded: 2009, in Nashville, Tennessee
Success: Olive & Sinclair's innovative "bean-to-bar" Southern chocolate expanded internationally within four years after it first started making chocolate.

Former pastry chef Scott Witherow decided to create artisanal chocolate with a southern flair—and the entire process would be done in-house. He founded Olive & Sinclair in 2009 with the idea to make chocolate in small batches using stone mills to ground the cocoa beans. Only a few years later, Olive & Sinclair chocolate bars could be found in select Whole Foods stores, retailers, coffee shops, and internationally at the department store Selfridges London and FRESCA, Japan's online marketplace for fine foods.

The inputs at Olive & Sinclair are single-origin cocoa beans that are organic and fair-trade certified. During the transformation process, the beans are sorted, slow-roasted, and ground.

Ingredients that typify the South—including buttermilk and pure brown sugar—are added to create southern flavors. The chocolate is molded and packaged in the company's factory. In the few years Olive & Sinclair has been in business, it has learned to excel at the operations process. Even though it makes the chocolate in small batches, it has gone from producing 250 bars a day in 2009 to 2,000 today.[2]

Discussion Questions

1. What are the inputs used in Olive & Sinclair products? What are the outputs?
2. Describe some ways Olive & Sinclair uses the operations process to create competitive advantages.
3. Why do you think Olive & Sinclair chooses to make its chocolate in small batches? Would it be a good idea to increase the size of the batches to enhance productivity? Why or why not?

---

output of these processes is flying passengers and/or packages to their destinations. In a nonprofit organization like Habitat for Humanity, inputs such as money, materials, information, and volunteer time and labor are used to transform raw materials into homes for needy families. In this setting, transformation processes include fundraising and promoting the cause in order to gain new volunteers and donations of supplies, as well as pouring concrete, raising walls, and setting roofs. Transformation processes occur in all organizations, regardless of what they produce or their objectives. For most organizations, the ultimate objective is for the produced outputs to be worth more than the combined costs of the inputs.

Unlike tangible goods, services are effectively actions or performances that must be directed toward the consumers who use them. Thus, there is a significant customer-contact component to most services. Examples of high-contact services include health care, real estate, tax preparation, and food service. At King's Arms Tavern in Williamsburg, Virginia, for example, food servers are critical to delivering the perfect dining experience expected by the most discriminating diners. Wait staff are expected not only to be courteous but also to deliver an authentic 18th-century

FIGURE 8-2

Inputs, Outputs, and Transformation Processes in the Manufacture of Oak Furniture

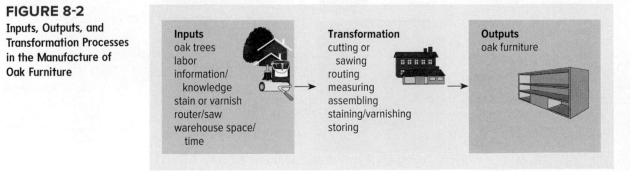

Inputs
oak trees
labor
information/
    knowledge
stain or varnish
router/saw
warehouse space/
    time

Transformation
cutting or
    sawing
routing
measuring
assembling
staining/varnishing
storing

Outputs
oak furniture

experience complete with the fashions of the day.[3] Employees at the Container Store receive 263 hours of training due to the high expectations of customer service the organization expects of them. Low-contact services, such as online auction services like eBay, often have a strong high-tech component. Table 8-1 shows common characteristics of services.

Regardless of the level of customer contact, service businesses strive to provide a standardized process, and technology offers an interface that creates an automatic and structured response. The ideal service provider will be high tech and high touch. Amazon, for instance, has one of the highest customer service ratings. It utilizes a site that is easily navigable and has fast shipping times to deliver high-quality customer service. In fact, Amazon goes above and beyond trying to satisfy its customers, with CEO Jeff Bezos encouraging customers to e-mail him directly if they have had a problem with its services.[4] Thus, service organizations must build their operations around good execution, which comes from hiring and training excellent employees, developing flexible systems, customizing services, and maintaining adjustable capacity to deal with fluctuating demand.[5]

Another challenge related to service operations is that the output is generally intangible and even perishable. Few services can be saved, stored, resold, or returned.[6] A seat on an airline or a table in a restaurant, for example, cannot be sold or used at a later date. Because of the perishability of services, it can be extremely difficult for service providers to accurately estimate the demand in order to match the right supply of a service. If an airline overestimates demand, for example, it will still have to fly each plane even with empty seats. The flight costs the same regardless of whether it is 50 percent full or 100 percent full, but the former will result in much higher costs per passenger. If the airline underestimates demand, the result can be long lines of annoyed customers or even the necessity of bumping some customers off of an overbooked flight.

Businesses that manufacture tangible goods and those that provide services or ideas are similar yet different. For example, both types of organizations must make design and operating decisions. Most goods are manufactured prior to purchase, but most services are performed after purchase. Flight attendants at Southwest Airlines, hotel service personnel, and even the New York Giants football team engage in performances that are a part of the total product. Though manufacturers and service providers often perform similar activities, they also differ in several respects. We can classify these differences in five basic ways.

Service Characteristics	Examples
Intangibility	Going to a concert or sports event such as baseball, basketball, or football
Inseparability of production and consumption	Going to a chiropractor; air travel; veterinary services
Perishability	Seats at a speaker's presentation
Customization	Haircut; legal services
Customer contact	Restaurants; direct selling such as Tupperware parties

TABLE 8-1
Characteristics of Services

Source: Adapted from Valerie A. Zeithaml, A, Parasuramanr and Leonard L. Berry, Delivering Quality Service: Balancing Customer Perceptions and Expectations (New York: Free Press, 1990); K. Douglas Hoffman and John E.G. Bateson, Essentials of Services Marketing (Mason, OH; Cengage Learning, 2001); Ian P. McCarthy, Leytand Pitt, and Pierre Berthon, "Service Customization Through Dramaturgy" Mass Customization, 2011, pp. 45–65.

Nature and Consumption of Output.   First, manufacturers and service providers differ in the nature and consumption of their output. For example, the term *manufacturer* implies a firm that makes tangible products. A service provider, on the other hand, produces more intangible outputs such as U.S. Postal Service delivery of priority mail or a business stay in a Hyatt hotel. As mentioned earlier, the very nature of the service provider's product requires a higher degree of customer contact. Moreover, the actual performance of the service typically occurs at the point of consumption. At the Hyatt, the business traveler may evaluate in-room communications and the restaurant. Automakers, on the other hand, can separate the production of a car from its actual use, but the service dimension requires closer contact with the consumer. Manufacturing, then, can occur in an isolated environment, away from the customer. However, service providers, because of their need for customer contact, are often more limited than manufacturers in selecting work methods, assigning jobs, scheduling work, and exercising control over operations. For this reason, Zappos adopted an online scheduling platform called Open Market to schedule its worker hours. Before, the process was complicated and involved workers having to write their scheduling preferences on sheets of paper. This new scheduling platform uses surge-based pricing that provides higher compensation to workers who take shifts in periods of high demand.[7] The quality of the service experience is often controlled by a service-contact employee. However, some hospitals are studying the manufacturing processes and quality control mechanisms applied in the automotive industry in an effort to improve their service quality. By analyzing work processes to find unnecessary steps to eliminate and using teams to identify and address problems as soon as they occur, these hospitals are slashing patient waiting times, decreasing inventories of wheelchairs, readying operating rooms sooner, and generally moving patients through their hospital visit more quickly, with fewer errors, and at a lower cost.[8]

Uniformity of Inputs.   A second way to classify differences between manufacturers and service providers has to do with the uniformity of inputs. Manufacturers typically have more control over the amount of variability of the resources they use than do service providers. For example, each customer calling Fidelity Investments is likely to require different services due to differing needs, whereas many of the tasks required to manufacture a Ford Focus are the same across each unit of output. Consequently, the products of service organizations tend to be more "customized" than those of their manufacturing counterparts. Consider, for example, a haircut versus a bottle of shampoo. The haircut is much more likely to incorporate your specific desires (customization) than is the bottle of shampoo.

Uniformity of Output.   Manufacturers and service providers also differ in the uniformity of their output, the final product. Because of the human element inherent in providing services, each service tends to be performed differently. Not all grocery checkers, for example, wait on customers in the same way. If a barber or stylist performs 15 haircuts in a day, it is unlikely that any two of them will be exactly the same. Consequently, human and technological elements associated with a service can result in a different day-to-day or even hour-to-hour performance of that service. The service experience can even vary at McDonald's or Burger King despite the fact that the two chains employ very similar procedures and processes. Moreover, no two customers are exactly alike in their perception of the service experience. Health care offers another excellent example of this challenge. Every diagnosis, treatment, and surgery varies because every individual is different. In manufacturing, the high degree of automation available allows manufacturers to generate uniform outputs and, thus, the operations are more effective and efficient. For example, we would expect every TAG Heuer or Rolex watch to maintain very high standards of quality and performance.

Labor Required.   A fourth point of difference is the amount of labor required to produce an output. Service providers are generally more labor-intensive (require more labor) because of the high level of customer contact, perishability of the output (must be consumed immediately), and high degree of variation of inputs and outputs (customization). For example, Adecco provides temporary support personnel. Each temporary worker's performance determines Adecco's product quality. A manufacturer, on the other hand, is likely to be more capital-intensive because of the machinery and technology used in the mass production of highly similar goods. For instance, it would take a considerable investment for Ford to make an electric car that has batteries with a longer life.

Subway's inputs are sandwich components such as bread, tomatoes, and lettuce, while its outputs are customized sandwiches.
© RosaIreneBetancourt 7/Alamy Stock Photo

Measurement of Productivity.   The final distinction between service providers and manufacturers involves the measurement of productivity for each output produced. For manufacturers, measuring productivity is fairly straightforward because of the tangibility of the output and its high degree of uniformity. For the service provider, variations in demand (for example, higher demand for air travel in some seasons than in others), variations in service requirements from job to job, and the intangibility of the product make productivity measurement more difficult. Consider, for example, how much easier it is to measure the productivity of employees involved in the production of Intel computer processors as opposed to serving the needs of Prudential Securities' clients.

It is convenient and simple to think of organizations as being either manufacturers or service providers as in the preceding discussion. In reality, however, most organizations are a combination of the two, with both tangible and intangible qualities embodied in what they produce. For example, Porsche provides customer services such as toll-free hotlines and warranty protection, while banks may sell checks and other tangible products that complement their primarily intangible product offering. Thus, we consider "products" to include both tangible physical goods and intangible service offerings. It is the level of tangibility of its principal product that tends to classify a company as either a manufacturer or a service provider. From an OM standpoint, this level of tangibility greatly influences the nature of the company's operational processes and procedures.

Planning and Designing Operations Systems

Describe the elements involved in planning and designing an operations system.

Before a company can produce any product, it must first decide what it will produce and for what group of customers. It must then determine what processes it will use to make these products as well as the facilities it needs to produce them. These decisions comprise operations planning. Although planning was once the sole realm of the production and operations department, today's successful companies involve all departments within an organization, particularly marketing and research and development, in these decisions.

Planning the Product

Before making any product, a company first must determine what consumers want and then design a product to satisfy that want. Most companies use marketing research (discussed in Chapter 11) to determine the kinds of goods and services to provide and the features they must possess. Twitter and Facebook provide new opportunities for businesses to discover what consumers want, then design the product accordingly. Approximately 39 percent of retailers use social media to facilitate planning in the product development process.[9] Marketing research can also help gauge the demand for a product and how much consumers are willing to pay for it. But when a market's environment changes, firms have to be flexible.

Developing a product can be a lengthy, expensive process. For example, Google spent $60 million in research and development for its autonomous self-driving vehicles early in the process.[10] Most companies work to reduce development time and costs. For example, Cisco and Ericsson partnered together to develop what they term "networks of the future" fueled by the rise of digitization, mobile technology, and the cloud.[11] By joining together, the companies can pool their resources together and reduce the time it takes to develop new networks. Once management has developed an idea for a product that customers will buy, it must then plan how to produce the product.

Within a company, the engineering or research and development department is charged with turning a product idea into a workable design that can be produced economically. In smaller companies, a single individual (perhaps the owner) may be solely responsible for this crucial activity. Regardless of who is responsible for product design, planning does not stop with a blueprint for a product or a description of a service; it must also work out efficient production of the product to ensure that enough is available to satisfy consumer demand. How does a lawn mower company transform steel, aluminum, and other materials into a mower design that satisfies consumer and environmental requirements? Operations managers must plan for the types and quantities of materials needed to produce the product, the skills and quantity of people needed to make the product, and the actual processes through which the inputs must pass in their transformation to outputs.

Designing the Operations Processes

Before a firm can begin production, it must first determine the appropriate method of transforming resources into the desired product. Often, consumers' specific needs and desires dictate a process. Customer needs, for example, require that all 3/4-inch bolts have the same basic thread size, function, and quality; if they did not, engineers and builders could not rely on 3/4-inch bolts in their construction projects. A bolt manufacturer, then, will likely use a standardized process so that every 3/4-inch bolt produced is like every other one. On the other hand, a bridge often must be customized so that it is appropriate for the site and expected load; furthermore, the bridge must be constructed on site rather than in a factory. Typically, products are designed to be manufactured by one of three processes: standardization, modular design, or customization.

Standardization. Most firms that manufacture products in large quantities for many customers have found that they can make them cheaper and faster by standardizing designs. **Standardization** is making identical, interchangeable components or even complete products. With standardization, a customer may not get exactly what he or she wants, but the product generally costs less than a custom-designed product. Television sets, ballpoint pens, and tortilla chips are standardized products; most are manufactured on an assembly line. Standardization speeds up production and quality control and reduces production costs. And, as in the example of the 3/4-inch bolts, standardization provides consistency so that customers who need certain products to function uniformly all the time will get a product that meets their expectations. Standardization becomes more complex on a global scale because different countries have different standards for quality. To help solve this problem, the International Organization for Standardization (ISO) has developed a list of global standards that companies can adopt to assure stakeholders that they are complying with the highest quality, environmental, and managerial guidelines.

standardization
the making of identical interchangeable components or products.

Modular Design.   Modular design involves building an item in self-contained units, or modules, that can be combined or interchanged to create different products. IKEA furniture, for example, embodies a modular design with several components. This allows for customers to mix and match components for customized design. Because many modular components are produced as integrated units, the failure of any portion of a modular component usually means replacing the entire component. Modular design allows products to be repaired quickly, thus reducing the cost of labor, but the component itself is expensive, raising the cost of repair materials. Many automobile manufacturers use modular design in the production process. Manufactured homes are built on a modular design and often cost about one-fourth the cost of a conventionally built house.

modular design
the creation of an item in self-contained units, or modules, that can be combined or interchanged to create different products.

Customization.   Customization is making products to meet a particular customer's needs or wants. Products produced in this way are generally unique. Such products include repair services, photocopy services, custom artwork, jewelry, and furniture, as well as large-scale products such as bridges, ships, and computer software. For instance, bicycles are popular products to customize. A company called Breadwinner Cycles designs eight models of bicycles in such a way that riders can customize various features and sizes to fit their specific needs.[12] Mass customization relates to making products that meet the needs or wants of a large number of individual customers. The customer can select the model, size, color, style, or design of the product. Dell can customize a computer with the exact configuration that fits a customer's needs. Services such as fitness programs and travel packages can also be custom designed for a large number of individual customers. For both goods and services, customers get to make choices and have options to determine the final product.

customization
making products to meet a particular customer's needs or wants.

Planning Capacity

Planning the operational processes for the organization involves two important areas: capacity planning and facilities planning. The term **capacity** basically refers to the maximum load that an organizational unit can carry or operate. The unit of measurement may be a worker or machine, a department, a branch, or even an entire plant. Maximum capacity can be stated in terms of the inputs or outputs provided. For example, an electric plant might state plant capacity in terms of the maximum number of kilowatt-hours that can be produced without causing a power outage, while a restaurant might state capacity in terms of the maximum number of customers who can be effectively—comfortably and courteously—served at any one particular time.

capacity
the maximum load that an organizational unit can carry or operate.

Efficiently planning the organization's capacity needs is an important process for the operations manager. Capacity levels that fall short can result in unmet demand, and consequently, lost customers. On the other hand, when there is more capacity available than needed, operating costs are driven up needlessly due to unused and often expensive resources. To avoid such situations, organizations must accurately forecast demand and then plan capacity based on these forecasts. Another reason for the importance of efficient capacity planning has to do with long-term commitment of resources. Often, once a capacity decision—such as factory size—has been implemented, it is very difficult to change the decision without incurring substantial costs. Large companies have come to realize that although change can be expensive, not adjusting to future demand and stakeholder desires will be more expensive in the long run. For this reason, Toyota and its subsidiaries have acquired ISO 14001 certification for environmental management at many of its locations worldwide.[14] These systems help firms monitor their impact on the environment.

Planning Facilities

Once a company knows what process it will use to create its products, it then can design and build an appropriate facility in which to make them. Many products are manufactured in factories, but others are produced in stores, at home, or where the product ultimately will be used. Companies must decide where to locate their operations facilities, what layout is best for producing their particular product, and even what technology to apply to the transformation process.

Many firms are developing both a traditional organization for customer contact and a virtual organization. Charles Schwab Corporation, a securities brokerage and investment company, maintains traditional offices and has developed complete telephone and Internet services for customers. Through its website, investors can obtain personal investment information and trade securities over the Internet without leaving their home or office.

Facility Location.   Where to locate a firm's facilities is a significant question because, once the decision has been made and implemented, the firm must live with it due to the high costs involved. When a company decides to relocate or open a facility at a new location, it must pay careful attention to factors such as proximity to market, availability of raw materials, availability of transportation, availability of power, climatic influences, availability of labor, community characteristics (quality of life), and taxes and inducements. Inducements and tax reductions have become an increasingly important criterion in recent years. To increase production and to provide incentives for small startups, many states are offering tax inducements for solar companies. State governments are willing to forgo some tax revenue in exchange for job growth, getting in on a burgeoning industry as well as the good publicity generated by the company. However, it is still less expensive for many firms to use overseas factories. Apple has followed the lead of other major companies by locating its manufacturing facilities in Asia to take advantage of lower labor and production costs. The facility-location decision is complex because it involves the evaluation of many factors, some of which cannot be measured with precision. Because of the long-term impact of the decision, however, it is one that cannot be taken lightly.

Facility Layout.   Arranging the physical layout of a facility is a complex, highly technical task. Some industrial architects specialize in the design and layout of

The use of robotics in manufacturing is increasing, especially in countries like the United States and Japan.
© Aaron Roeth Photography

certain types of businesses. There are three basic layouts: fixed-position, process, and product.

A company using a **fixed-position layout** brings all resources required to create the product to a central location. The product—perhaps an office building, house, hydroelectric plant, or bridge—does not move. A company using a fixed-position layout may be called a **project organization** because it is typically involved in large, complex projects such as construction or exploration. Project organizations generally make a unique product, rely on highly skilled labor, produce very few units, and have high production costs per unit.

Firms that use a **process layout** organize the transformation process into departments that group related processes. A metal fabrication plant, for example, may have a cutting department, a drilling department, and a polishing department. A hospital may have an X-ray unit, an obstetrics unit, and so on. These types of organizations are sometimes called **intermittent organizations,** which deal with products of a lesser magnitude than do project organizations, and their products are not necessarily unique but possess a significant number of differences. Doctors, makers of custom-made cabinets, commercial printers, and advertising agencies are intermittent organizations because they tend to create products to customers' specifications and produce relatively few units of each product. Because of the low level of output, the cost per unit of product is generally high.

fixed-position layout
a layout that brings all resources required to create the product to a central location.

project organization
a company using a fixed-position layout because it is typically involved in large, complex projects such as construction or exploration.

process layout
a layout that organizes the transformation process into departments that group related processes.

intermittent organizations
organizations that deal with products of a lesser magnitude than do project organizations; their products are not necessarily unique but possess a significant number of differences.

product layout
a layout requiring that production be broken down into relatively simple tasks assigned to workers, who are usually positioned along an assembly line.

continuous manufacturing organizations
companies that use continuously running assembly lines, creating products with many similar characteristics.

computer-assisted design (CAD)
the design of components, products, and processes on computers instead of on paper.

computer-assisted manufacturing (CAM)
manufacturing that employs specialized computer systems to actually guide and control the transformation processes.

flexible manufacturing
the direction of machinery by computers to adapt to different versions of similar operations.

The **product layout** requires that production be broken down into relatively simple tasks assigned to workers, who are usually positioned along an assembly line. Workers remain in one location, and the product moves from one worker to another. Each person in turn performs his or her required tasks or activities. Companies that use assembly lines are usually known as **continuous manufacturing organizations,** so named because once they are set up, they run continuously, creating products with many similar characteristics. Examples of products produced on assembly lines are automobiles, television sets, vacuum cleaners, toothpaste, and meals from a cafeteria. Continuous manufacturing organizations using a product layout are characterized by the standardized product they produce, the large number of units produced, and the relatively low unit cost of production.

Many companies actually use a combination of layout designs. For example, an automobile manufacturer may rely on an assembly line (product layout) but may also use a process layout to manufacture parts.

Technology.   Every industry has a basic, underlying technology that dictates the nature of its transformation process. The steel industry continually tries to improve steelmaking techniques. The health care industry performs research into medical technologies and pharmaceuticals to improve the quality of health care service. Two developments that have strongly influenced the operations of many businesses are computers and robotics.

Computers have been used for decades and on a relatively large scale since IBM introduced its 650 series in the late 1950s. The operations function makes great use of computers in all phases of the transformation process. **Computer-assisted design (CAD),** for example, helps engineers design components, products, and processes on the computer instead of on paper. CAD is used in 3D printing. CAD software is used to develop a 3D image. Then, the CAD file is sent to the printer. The printer is able to use layers of liquid, powder, paper, or metal to construct a 3D model.[15] **Computer-assisted manufacturing (CAM)** goes a step further, employing specialized computer systems to actually guide and control the transformation processes. Such systems can monitor the transformation process, gathering information about the equipment used to produce the products and about the product itself as it goes from one stage of the transformation process to the next. The computer provides information to an operator who may, if necessary, take corrective action. In some highly automated systems, the computer itself can take corrective action. At Dell's OptiPlex Plant, electronic instructions are sent to double-decker conveyor belts that speed computer components to assembly stations. Two-member teams are told by computers which PC or server to build, with initial assembly taking only three to four minutes. Then more electronic commands move the products to a finishing area to be customized, boxed, and sent to waiting delivery trucks.

Using **flexible manufacturing,** computers can direct machinery to adapt to different versions of similar operations. For example, with instructions from a computer, one machine can be programmed to carry out its function for several different versions of an engine without shutting down the production line for refitting.

The use of drones in business operations would vastly change the technology landscape. Drones refer to unmanned aerial vehicles and have long been used in military operations. Amazon generated excitement when CEO Jeff Bezos announced the company's future intention to used drone aircraft to deliver packages to customers in as little as 30 minutes. The new service will be called Amazon Prime Air. It is estimated that drones could save Amazon $2 per delivery. Despite its promise, use of drone technology for operations such as delivery services is uncertain due to regulatory concerns. The Federal Aviation Administration is allowing Amazon to test drones in the United States, but only with a number of restrictions. As a result, Amazon has been testing drones in the United Kingdom, Canada, and the Netherlands. While this represents an obstacle for companies in using drones for long-distance delivery, they continue to work toward more favorable legislation. Drones are estimated to generate $10 billion in new spending within the next 10 years.[16]

Robots are also becoming increasingly useful in the transformation process. These "steel-collar" workers have become particularly important in industries such as nuclear power, hazardous-waste disposal, ocean research, and space construction and maintenance, in which human lives would otherwise be at risk. Robots are used in numerous applications by companies around the world. Many assembly operations— cars, television sets, telephones, stereo equipment, and numerous other products— depend on industrial robots. The United States is one of the largest users of robotics, and it estimated that 1.2 million more advanced robots will be brought into use by 2025. China is another robotics powerhouse. The country is going through a robotics revolution, and it is estimated that one-third of industrial robots will be in China by 2018.[17] Researchers continue to make more sophisticated robots, extending their use beyond manufacturing and space programs to various industries, including laboratory research, education, medicine, and household activities. There are many advantages in using robotics, such as more successful surgeries, re-shoring manufacturing activities back to America, energy conservation, and safer work practices.

When all these technologies—CAD/CAM, flexible manufacturing, robotics, computer systems, and more—are integrated, the result is **computer-integrated manufacturing (CIM)**, a complete system that designs products, manages machines and materials, and controls the operations function. Companies adopt CIM to boost productivity and quality and reduce costs. Such technology, and computers in particular, will continue to make strong inroads into operations on two fronts—one dealing with the technology involved in manufacturing and one dealing with the administrative functions and processes used by operations managers. The operations manager must be willing to work with computers and other forms of technology and to develop a high degree of computer literacy.

computer-integrated manufacturing (CIM) a complete system that designs products, manages machines and materials, and controls the operations function.

Sustainability and Manufacturing

Manufacturing and operations systems are moving quickly to establish environmental sustainability and minimize negative impact on the natural environment. Sustainability deals with conducting activities in such a way as to provide for the long-term well-being of the natural environment, including all biological entities. Sustainability issues are becoming increasingly important to stakeholders and consumers, as they pertain to the future health of the planet. Some sustainability issues include pollution of the land, air, and water, climate change, waste management, deforestation, urban sprawl, protection of biodiversity, and genetically modified foods.

For example, Adobe was ranked as the greenest technology company due to its leadership in sustainability. The company continually monitors energy use and takes steps to reduce it. Since 2002, the firm has reduced its electricity use by 50 percent and natural gas use by 30 percent.[18] New Belgium Brewing is another company that illustrates green initiatives in operations and manufacturing. New Belgium was the first brewery to adopt 100 percent wind-powered electricity, reducing carbon emissions by 1,800 metric tons a year.

Sierra Nevada's new brewery has received LEED certification (Leadership in Energy and Environmental Design), showing that it was built using sustainable guidelines.

© Marvin McAbee/Alamy Stock Photo

Adobe and New Belgium Brewing demonstrate that reducing waste, recycling, conserving, and using renewable energy not only protect the environment, but can also gain the support of stakeholders. Green operations and manufacturing can improve a firm's reputation along with customer and employee loyalty, leading to improved profits.

Much of the movement to green manufacturing and operations is the belief that global warming and climate change must decline. It is estimated that eco-friendly buildings use 60 to 90 percent less energy than conventional buildings.[19] Companies like General Motors and Ford are adapting to stakeholder demands for greater sustainability by producing smaller and more fuel-efficient cars. Tesla has taken sustainability further by making a purely electric vehicle that also ranks at the top in safety. The company also makes sure that its manufacturing facilities operate sustainably by installing solar panels and other renewable sources of energy. Green products produced through green operations and manufacturing are our future. A report authored by the Center for American Progress cites ways that cities and local governments can play a role. For example, Chicago launched the Chicago Climate Action Plan which, among other agendas, seeks to retrofit Chicago buildings for energy efficiency and cut fees for the use of solar panels.[20] Government initiatives provide space for businesses to innovate their green operations and manufacturing.

Managing the Supply Chain

Specify some techniques managers may use to manage the logistics of transforming inputs into finished products.

supply chain management connecting and integrating all parties or members of the distribution system in order to satisfy customers.

A major function of operations is **supply chain management,** which refers to connecting and integrating all parties or members of the distribution system in order to satisfy customers.[21] Also called logistics, supply chain management includes all the activities involved in obtaining and managing raw materials and component parts, managing finished products, packaging them, and getting them to customers. The supply chain integrates firms such as raw material suppliers, manufacturers, retailers, and ultimate consumers into a seamless flow of information and products.[22] Some aspects of logistics (warehousing, packaging, distributing) are so closely linked with marketing that we will discuss them in Chapter 12. In this section, we look at purchasing, managing inventory, outsourcing, and scheduling, which are vital tasks in the transformation of raw materials into finished goods. To illustrate logistics, consider a hypothetical small business—we'll call it Rushing Water Canoes Inc.—that manufactures aluminum canoes, which it sells primarily to sporting goods stores and river-rafting expeditions. Our company also makes paddles and helmets, but the focus of the following discussion is the manufacture of the company's quality canoes as they proceed through the logistics process.

Purchasing

Purchasing, also known as procurement, is the buying of all the materials needed by the organization. The purchasing department aims to obtain items of the desired quality in the right quantities at the lowest possible cost. Rushing Water Canoes, for example, must procure not only aluminum and other raw materials, and various canoe parts and components, but also machines and equipment, manufacturing supplies (oil, electricity, and so on), and office supplies in order to make its canoes. People in the purchasing department locate and evaluate suppliers of these items. They must constantly be on the lookout for new materials or parts that will do a better job or cost less than those currently being used. The purchasing function can be quite complex and is one area made much easier and more efficient by technological advances.

Not all companies purchase all of the materials needed to create their products. Oftentimes, they can make some components more economically and efficiently than can an outside supplier. Zara, a Spanish fast fashion retailer, manufactures the majority of the clothes it sells.[23] On the other hand, firms sometimes find that it is uneconomical to make or purchase an item, and instead arrange to lease it from another organization. Some airlines, for example, lease airplanes rather than buy them. Whether to purchase, make, or lease a needed item generally depends on cost, as well as on product availability and supplier reliability.

purchasing
the buying of all the materials needed by the organization; also called procurement.

Managing Inventory

Once the items needed to create a product have been procured, some provision has to be made for storing them until they are needed. Every raw material, component, completed or partially completed product, and piece of equipment a firm uses—its inventory—must be accounted for, or controlled. There are three basic types of inventory. *Finished-goods inventory* includes those products that are ready for sale, such as a fully assembled automobile ready to ship to a dealer. *Work-in-process inventory* consists of those products that are partly completed or are in some stage of the transformation process. At McDonald's, a cooking hamburger represents work-in-process inventory because it must go through several more stages before it can be sold to a customer. *Raw materials inventory* includes all the materials that have been purchased to be used as inputs for making other products. Nuts and bolts are raw materials for an automobile manufacturer, while hamburger patties, vegetables, and buns are raw materials for the fast-food restaurant. Our fictional Rushing Water Canoes has an inventory of materials for making canoes, paddles, and helmets, as well as its inventory of finished products for sale to consumers. Inventory control is the process of determining how many supplies and goods are needed and keeping track of quantities on hand, where each item is, and who is responsible for it.

Operations management must be closely coordinated with inventory control. The production of televisions, for example, cannot be planned without some knowledge of the availability of all the necessary materials—the chassis, picture tubes, color guns, and so forth. Also, each item held in inventory—any type of inventory—carries with it a cost. For example, storing fully assembled televisions in a warehouse to sell to a dealer at a future date requires not only the use of space, but also the purchase of insurance to cover any losses that might occur due to fire or other unforeseen events.

inventory
all raw materials, components, completed or partially completed products, and pieces of equipment a firm uses.

inventory control
the process of determining how many supplies and goods are needed and keeping track of quantities on hand, where each item is, and who is responsible for it.

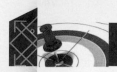

Ashley Furniture Owns Its Supply Chain

As the largest U.S. furniture maker, Ashley Furniture has good reason to ensure it has the most effective supply chain possible. Due to its size, Ashley has found it advantageous to own and operate much of its own supply chain instead of relying on external companies. For instance, Ashley operates its own fleet of delivery trucks that help the company fulfill on-time deliveries and reduce overall costs. Its trucks and warehouses utilize specially designed tilt-racks that speed up loading and unloading of furniture. Ashley also utilizes newer trucks that offer more amenities for drivers, such as a more luxurious cabin and space for a bed. Furthermore, the deep integration of Ashley's supply chain and logistics network means drivers have more predictable work schedules, freeing up time for them to spend with family. This all leads to satisfied drivers who double as ambassadors for the Ashley brand, a benefit not possible with a third-party delivery company.

La-Z-Boy, the second largest U.S. furniture maker, has taken notice of Ashley's success. It is growing its own truck fleet on the premise that it increases delivery reliability. While both of these companies are large enough to benefit from company-owned truck fleets and deeply integrated logistics and supply chain networks, smaller competitors will likely continue outsourcing parts of their supply chains. At lower volumes, outsourcing offers reduced costs and improved efficiency.[24]

Discussion Questions

1. What are some of the advantages Ashley realizes from owning its own fleet of delivery trucks?
2. How does Ashley foster high satisfaction rates among its delivery drivers? Why is this important?
3. Should all companies strive to own their own supply chains? When is outsourcing parts of the supply chain appropriate?

Inventory managers spend a great deal of time trying to determine the proper inventory level for each item. The answer to the question of how many units to hold in inventory depends on variables such as the usage rate of the item, the cost of maintaining the item in inventory, future costs of inventory and other procedures associated with ordering or making the item, and the cost of the item itself. For example, the price of copper has fluctuated greatly over the past few years. Prices have increased 243 percent in a 14-year period.[25] Firms using copper wiring for construction, copper pipes for plumbing, and other industries requiring copper have to analyze the trade-offs between inventory costs and expected changes in the price of copper. Several approaches may be used to determine how many units of a given item should be procured at one time and when that procurement should take place.

economic order quantity (EOQ) model
a model that identifies the optimum number of items to order to minimize the costs of managing (ordering, storing, and using) them.

The Economic Order Quantity Model. To control the number of items maintained in inventory, managers need to determine how much of any given item they should order. One popular approach is the **economic order quantity (EOQ) model**, which identifies the optimum number of items to order to minimize the costs of managing (ordering, storing, and using) them.

just-in-time (JIT) inventory management
a technique using smaller quantities of materials that arrive "just in time" for use in the transformation process and therefore require less storage space and other inventory management expense.

Just-in-Time Inventory Management. An increasingly popular technique is **just-in-time (JIT) inventory management,** which eliminates waste by using smaller quantities of materials that arrive "just in time" for use in the transformation process and, therefore, require less storage space and other inventory management expense. JIT minimizes inventory by providing an almost continuous flow of items from suppliers to the production facility. Many U.S. companies—including Hewlett-Packard, IBM, and Harley Davidson—have adopted JIT to reduce costs and boost efficiency.

Let's say that Rushing Water Canoes uses 20 units of aluminum from a supplier per day. Traditionally, its inventory manager might order enough for one month at a time: 440 units per order (20 units per day times 22 workdays per month). The expense of such a large inventory could be considerable because of the cost of insurance coverage, recordkeeping, rented storage space, and so on. The just-in-time approach would reduce these costs because aluminum would be purchased in smaller quantities, perhaps in lot sizes of 20, which the supplier would deliver once a day. Of course, for such an approach to be effective, the supplier must be extremely reliable and relatively close to the production facility.

On the other hand, there are some downsides to just-in-time inventory management that marketers must take into account. When an earthquake and tsunami hit Japan, resulting in a nuclear reactor crisis, several Japanese companies halted their operations. Some multinationals relied so much upon their Japanese suppliers that their supply chains were also affected. In the case of natural disasters, having only enough inventory to meet current needs could create delays in production and hurt the company's bottom line. For this reason, many economists suggest that businesses store components that are essential for production and diversify their supply chains. That way, if a natural disaster knocks out a major supplier, the company can continue to operate.[26]

Material-requirements Planning.   Another inventory management technique is **material-requirements planning (MRP)**, a planning system that schedules the precise quantity of materials needed to make the product. The basic components of MRP are a master production schedule, a bill of materials, and an inventory status file. At Rushing Water Canoes, for example, the inventory-control manager will look at the production schedule to determine how many canoes the company plans to make. He or she will then prepare a bill of materials—a list of all the materials needed to make that quantity of canoes. Next, the manager will determine the quantity of these items that RWC already holds in inventory (to avoid ordering excess materials) and then develop a schedule for ordering and accepting delivery of the right quantity of materials to satisfy the firm's needs. Because of the large number of parts and materials that go into a typical production process, MRP must be done on a computer. It can be, and often is, used in conjunction with just-in-time inventory management.

Operations managers are concerned with managing inventory to ensure that there is enough inventory in stock to meet demand.

© Andersen Ross/Digital Vision/Getty Images

material-requirements planning (MRP)
a planning system that schedules the precise quantity of materials needed to make the product.

Outsourcing

Increasingly, outsourcing has become a component of supply chain management in operations. As we mentioned in Chapter 3, outsourcing refers to the contracting of manufacturing or other tasks to independent companies, often overseas. Many companies elect to outsource some aspects of their operations to companies that can provide these products more efficiently, at a lower cost, and with greater customer satisfaction. Globalization has put pressure on supply chain managers to improve speed and balance resources against competitive pressures. Companies outsourcing to China, in particular, face heavy regulation, high transportation costs, inadequate facilities, and unpredictable supply chain execution. Therefore, suppliers need to provide useful, timely, and accurate information about every aspect of the quality requirements, schedules, and solutions to dealing with problems. Companies that hire suppliers must also make certain that their suppliers are following company standards; failure to do so could lead to criticism of the parent company.

Many high-tech firms have outsourced the production of chips, computers, and telecom equipment to Asian companies. The hourly labor costs in countries such as China, India, and Vietnam are far less than in the United States, Europe, or even Mexico. These developing countries have improved their manufacturing capabilities, infrastructure, and technical and business skills, making them more attractive regions for global sourcing. For instance, Nike outsources almost all of its production to Asian countries such as China and Vietnam. On the other hand, the cost of outsourcing halfway around the world must be considered in decisions. While information technology is often outsourced today, transportation, human resources, services, and even marketing functions can be outsourced. Our hypothetical Rushing Water Canoes might contract with a local janitorial service to clean its offices and with a local accountant to handle routine bookkeeping and tax-preparation functions.

Outsourcing, once used primarily as a cost-cutting tactic, has increasingly been linked with the development of competitive advantage through improved product quality, speeding up the time it takes products to get to the customer, and overall supply-chain efficiencies. Table 8-2 describes five of the top 100 global outsourcing providers that assist mainly in information technology. Outsourcing allows companies to free up time and resources to focus on what they do best and to create better opportunities to focus on customer satisfaction. Many executives view outsourcing as an innovative way to boost productivity and remain competitive against low-wage offshore factories. However, outsourcing may create conflict with labor and negative public opinion when it results in U.S. workers being replaced by lower-cost workers in other countries.

routing
the sequence of operations through which the product must pass.

Routing and Scheduling

After all materials have been procured and their use determined, managers must then consider the **routing,** or sequence of operations through which the product must

TABLE 8-2
Top Outsourcing Providers

Company	Services
ISS	Facility services
Accenture	Management consulting, technology, and outsourcing
Hewlett Packard Enterprises	IT, technology, and enterprise products and solutions
CBRE	Commercial real estate services
Kelly Outsourcing and Consulting Group	Talent management solutions

Source: International Association of Outsourcing, The Global Outsourcing 100, 2016, https://www.iaop.org/FORTUNE (accessed March 16, 2016).

pass. For example, before employees at Rushing Water Canoes can form aluminum sheets into a canoe, the aluminum must be cut to size. Likewise, the canoe's flotation material must be installed before workers can secure the wood seats. The sequence depends on the product specifications developed by the engineering department of the company.

Once management knows the routing, the actual work can be scheduled. **Scheduling** assigns the tasks to be done to departments or even specific machines, workers, or teams. At Rushing Water, cutting aluminum for the company's canoes might be scheduled to be done by the "cutting and finishing" department on machines designed especially for that purpose.

Many approaches to scheduling have been developed, ranging from simple trial and error to highly sophisticated computer programs. One popular method is the *Program Evaluation and Review Technique (PERT),* which identifies all the major activities or events required to complete a project, arranges them in a sequence or path, determines the critical path, and estimates the time required for each event. Producing a McDonald's Big Mac, for example, involves removing meat, cheese, sauce, and vegetables from the refrigerator; grilling the hamburger patties; assembling the ingredients; placing the completed Big Mac in its package; and serving it to the customer (Figure 8-3). The cheese, pickles, onions, and sauce cannot be put on before the hamburger patty is completely grilled and placed on the bun. The path that requires the longest time from start to finish is called the *critical path* because it determines the minimum amount of time in which the process can be completed. If any of the activities on the critical path for production of the Big Mac fall behind schedule, the sandwich will not be completed on time, causing customers to wait longer than they usually would.

scheduling
the assignment of required tasks to departments or even specific machines, workers, or teams.

FIGURE 8-3   **A Hypothetical PERT Diagram for a McDonald's Big Mac**

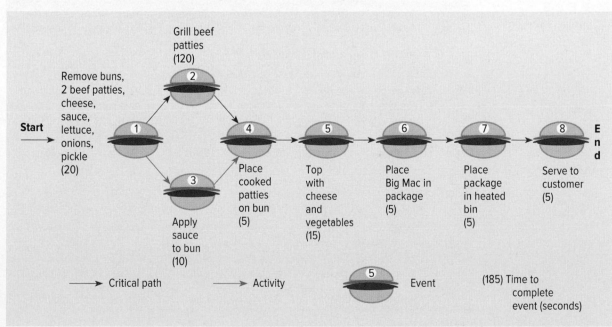

Managing Quality

Quality, like cost and efficiency, is a critical element of operations management, for defective products can quickly ruin a firm. Quality reflects the degree to which a good or service meets the demands and requirements of customers. Customers are increasingly dissatisfied with the quality of service provided by many airlines. Table 8-3 gives the rankings of U.S. airlines in certain operational areas. Determining quality can be difficult because it depends on customers' perceptions of how well the product meets or exceeds their expectations. For example, customer satisfaction on airlines can vary wildly depending on individual customers' perspectives. However, the airline industry is notorious for its dissatisfied customers. Flight delays are a common complaint from airline passengers; 30 percent of all flights arrive late. However, most passengers do not select an airline based on how often flights arrive on time.[27]

The fuel economy of an automobile or its reliability (defined in terms of frequency of repairs) can be measured with some degree of precision. Although automakers rely on their own measures of vehicle quality, they also look to independent sources such as the J.D. Power & Associates annual initial quality survey for confirmation of their quality assessment as well as consumer perceptions of quality for the industry, as indicated in Figure 8-4.

It is especially difficult to measure quality characteristics when the product is a service. A company has to decide exactly which quality characteristics it considers important and then define those characteristics in terms that can be measured. The inseparability of production and consumption and the level of customer contact influence the selection of characteristics of the service that are most important. Employees in high-contact services such as hairstyling, education, legal services, and even the barista at Starbucks are an important part of the product.

TABLE 8-3
2015 Airline Scorecard (Best to Worst)

Rank	Overall Rank	On-Time Arrival	Cancelled Flights	Baggage Handling	Bumping Passengers	Customer Complaints
1	Alaska	Alaska	Frontier	Virgin America	JetBlue	Alaska
2	Virgin America	Delta	Virgin American	JetBlue	Virgin America	Southwest
3	Delta	Southwest	Alaska	Delta	Delta	Delta
4	Southwest	Virgin American	Southwest	Spirit	Spirit	JetBlue
5	JetBlue	JetBlue	Delta	Frontier	Alaska	Virgin American
6	Frontier	United	JetBlue	United	American	United
7	United	American	Spirit	Southwest	United	American
8	Spirit	Frontier	United	Alaska	Southwest	Frontier
9	American	Spirit	American	American	Frontier	Spirit

Sources: FlightStats; U.S. Department of Transportation.

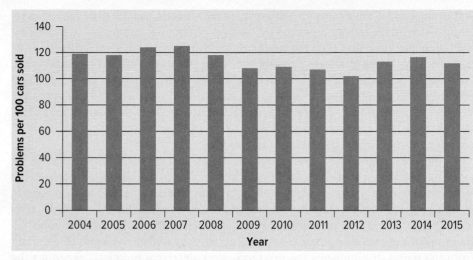

FIGURE 8-4

J.D. Power and Associates Initial Automobile Quality Study

Source: J.D. Power, "2015 U.S. Initial Quality Study (IQS)," June I7, 2015, http://www.jdpower.com/press-releases/2015-us-initial-quality-study-iqs (accessed March I6, 2016).

The Malcolm Baldrige National Quality Award is given each year to companies that meet rigorous standards of quality. The Baldrige criteria are (1) leadership, (2) information and analysis, (3) strategic planning, (4) human resource development and management, (5) process management, (6) business results, and (7) customer focus and satisfaction. The criteria have become a worldwide framework for driving business improvement. Four organizations won the award in 2015, representing four different categories: MidwayUSA (small business); Charter School of San Diego (education); Charleston Area Medical Center Health System (health care); and Mid-America Transplant Services (nonprofit).[28]

Quality is so important that we need to examine it in the context of operations management. **Quality control** refers to the processes an organization uses to maintain its established quality standards. It was a desire to create quality injection-molded parts for printers at affordable prices that prompted entrepreneur Larry Lukis to found Protomold, later renamed Proto Labs. Wanting to design a better printer, Lukis got frustrated at how expensive and long it took to receive the parts. He developed an automated process to change the industry, and the company became popular among engineers who needed quality products quickly or in small batches. Today Proto Labs has become the world's fastest provider of machined and molded parts.[29] Quality has become a major concern in many organizations, particularly in light of intense foreign competition and increasingly demanding customers. To regain a competitive edge, a number of firms have adopted a total quality management approach. **Total quality management (TQM)** is a philosophy that uniform commitment to quality in all areas of the organization will promote a culture that meets customers' perceptions of quality. It involves coordinating efforts to improve customer satisfaction, increasing employee participation, forming and strengthening supplier partnerships, and facilitating an organizational culture of continuous quality improvement. TQM requires constant improvements in all areas of the company as well as employee empowerment.

Continuous improvement of an organization's goods and services is built around the notion that quality is free; by contrast, *not* having high-quality goods and services can be very expensive, especially in terms of dissatisfied customers.[30] A primary tool of the continuous improvement process is *benchmarking*, the measuring

quality control
the processes an organization uses to maintain its established quality standards.

total quality management (TQM)
a philosophy that uniform commitment to quality in all areas of an organization will promote a culture that meets customers' perceptions of quality.

and evaluating of the quality of the organization's goods, services, or processes as compared with the quality produced by the best-performing companies in the industry.[31] Benchmarking lets the organization know where it stands competitively in its industry, thus giving it a goal to aim for over time. Now that online digital media are becoming more important in businesses, companies such as Compuware Corporation offer benchmarking tools so companies can monitor and compare the success of their websites. Such tools allow companies to track traffic to the site versus competitors' sites. Studies have shown a direct link between website performance and online sales, meaning this type of benchmarking is important.[32]

Companies employing TQM programs know that quality control should be incorporated throughout the transformation process, from the initial plans to the development of a specific product through the product and production-facility design processes to the actual manufacture of the product. In other words, they view quality control as an element of the product itself, rather than as simply a function of the operations process. When a company makes the product correctly from the outset, it eliminates the need to rework defective products, expedites the transformation process itself, and allows employees to make better use of their time and materials. One method through which many companies have tried to improve quality is **statistical process control,** a system in which management collects and analyzes information about the production process to pinpoint quality problems in the production system.

statistical process control
a system in which management collects and analyzes information about the production process to pinpoint quality problems in the production system.

ISO 9000
a series of quality assurance standards designed by the International Organization for Standardization (ISO) to ensure consistent product quality under many conditions.

International Organization for Standardization (ISO)

Regardless of whether a company has a TQM program for quality control, it must first determine what standard of quality it desires and then assess whether its products meet that standard. Product specifications and quality standards must be set so the company can create a product that will compete in the marketplace. Rushing Water Canoes, for example, may specify that each of its canoes has aluminum walls of a specified uniform thickness, that the front and back be reinforced with a specified level of steel, and that each contain a specified amount of flotation material for safety. Production facilities must be designed that can produce products with the desired specifications.

Quality standards can be incorporated into service businesses as well. A hamburger chain, for example, may establish standards relating to how long it takes to cook an order and serve it to customers, how many fries are in each order, how thick the burgers are, or how many customer complaints might be acceptable. Once the desired quality characteristics, specifications, and standards have been stated in measurable terms, the next step is inspection.

The International Organization for Standardization (ISO) has created a series of quality management standards—**ISO 9000**—designed to ensure the customer's quality standards are met. The standards provide a framework for documenting how a certified business keeps records, trains employees, tests products, and fixes defects. To obtain ISO 9000

Several of FedEx's worldwide facilities have achieved ISO 14001 certification.

© McGraw-Hill Education/Jill Braaten

A Green Apple Contributes to Supply Chain Sustainability

Electronics companies are often criticized when it comes to sustainability. Planned obsolescence, in which products are built to last for a certain amount of time before being replaced with an upgraded product, has contributed to massive amounts of electronic waste. Yet one electronics firm that seems to be making significant inroads in sustainability is Apple. For instance, 87 percent of its operations now run on renewable energy. Greenpeace has lauded Apple for taking the lead in addressing its negative impact on the environment.

Now Apple wants to extend its sustainability success to its supply chain—a much more daunting task. CEO Tim Cook admits that it will be a challenge as Apple's supply chain uses 60 times more energy than its own facilities. However, Apple is tackling this challenge head-on with new initiatives in China, where most of its manufacturing takes place. The company announced it would build two 20-megawatt solar panel farms with hopes to use this renewable energy to power more manufacturing operations. Additionally, the company has partnered with the World Wildlife Fund to preserve and responsibly manage forests in China. Although Apple has a long way to go, as one of the world's most profitable companies, it definitely seems up to the task.[34]

Discussion Questions

1. Why is planned obsolescence detrimental to the environment?
2. How does Apple plan to increase sustainability in its supply chain?
3. Why is it much more difficult to increase sustainability in Apple's supply chain than it is with its facilities?

---

certification, an independent auditor must verify that a business's factory, laboratory, or office meets the quality standards spelled out by the International Organization for Standardization. The certification process can require significant investment, but for many companies, the process is essential to being able to compete. Thousands of companies have been certified, including General Electric Analytical Instruments, which has applied ISO standards to everything from the design to the manufacturing practices of its global facilities.[33] Certification has become a virtual necessity for doing business in Europe in some high-technology businesses. ISO 9002 certification was established for service providers.

ISO 14000 is a comprehensive set of environmental standards that encourages a cleaner and safer world. ISO 14000 is a valuable standard because currently considerable variation exists between the regulations in different nations, and even regions within a nation. These variations make it difficult for organizations committed to sustainability to find acceptable global solutions to problems. The goal of the ISO 14000 standards is to promote a more uniform approach to environmental management and to help companies attain and measure improvements in their environmental performance. **ISO 19600** provides guidelines for compliance management that address risks, legal requirements, and stakeholder needs. This standard deals with both mandatory requirements such as laws and voluntary standards such as principles. Since these are guidelines rather than requirements, companies that comply with ISO 19600 cannot be certified. However, organizations that adopt this standard demonstrate they are committed toward stakeholders and continual improvement in compliance management.[35]

Inspection

Inspection reveals whether a product meets quality standards. Some product characteristics may be discerned by fairly simple inspection techniques—weighing the contents of cereal boxes or measuring the time it takes for a customer to receive his or her hamburger. As part of the ongoing quality assurance program at Hershey Foods, all wrapped Hershey Kisses are checked, and all imperfectly wrapped kisses are

ISO 14000
a comprehensive set of environmental standards that encourages a cleaner and safer world by promoting a more uniform approach to environmental management and helping companies attain and measure improvements in their environmental performance.

ISO 19600
a comprehensive set of guidelines for compliance management that address risks, legal requirements, and stakeholder needs.

rejected. Other inspection techniques are more elaborate. Automobile manufacturers use automated machines to open and close car doors to test the durability of latches and hinges. The food-processing and pharmaceutical industries use various chemical tests to determine the quality of their output. Rushing Water Canoes might use a special device that can precisely measure the thickness of each canoe wall to ensure that it meets the company's specifications.

Organizations normally inspect purchased items, work-in-process, and finished items. The inspection of purchased items and finished items takes place after the fact; the inspection of work-in-process is preventive. In other words, the purpose of inspection of purchased items and finished items is to determine what the quality level is. For items that are being worked on—an automobile moving down the assembly line or a canoe being assembled—the purpose of the inspection is to find defects before the product is completed so that necessary corrections can be made.

Sampling

An important question relating to inspection is how many items should be inspected. Should all canoes produced by Rushing Water be inspected or just some of them? Whether to inspect 100 percent of the output or only part of it is related to the cost of the inspection process, the destructiveness of the inspection process (some tests last until the product fails), and the potential cost of product flaws in terms of human lives and safety.

Some inspection procedures are quite expensive, use elaborate testing equipment, destroy products, and/or require a significant number of hours to complete. In such cases, it is usually desirable to test only a sample of the output. If the sample passes inspection, the inspector may assume that all the items in the lot from which the sample was drawn would also pass inspection. By using principles of statistical inference, management can employ sampling techniques that ensure a relatively high probability of reaching the right conclusion—that is, rejecting a lot that does not meet standards and accepting a lot that does. Nevertheless, there will always be a risk of making an incorrect conclusion—accepting a population that *does not* meet standards (because the sample was satisfactory) or rejecting a population that *does* meet standards (because the sample contained too many defective items).

Sampling is likely to be used when inspection tests are destructive. Determining the life expectancy of lightbulbs by turning them on and recording how long they last would be foolish: There is no market for burned-out lightbulbs. Instead, a generalization based on the quality of a sample would be applied to the entire population of lightbulbs from which the sample was drawn. However, human life and safety often depend on the proper functioning of specific items, such as the navigational systems installed in commercial airliners. For such items, even though the inspection process is costly, the potential cost of flawed systems—in human lives and safety—is too great not to inspect 100 percent of the output.

Integrating Operations and Supply Chain Management

Managing operations and supply chains can be complex and challenging due to the number of independent organizations that must perform their responsibilities in creating product quality. Managing supply chains requires constant vigilance and the ability to make quick tactical changes. When allegations arose that seafood sold in the United States may have come from forced labor on ships around Thailand, companies had to immediately investigate these allegations. The issue has become so serious that President Obama signed legislation to ban fish imported from Southeast Asia if slave labor was used.[36] Therefore, managing the various partners involved in supply chains and operations is important because many stakeholders hold the firm responsible for appropriate conduct related to product quality. This requires that the company exercise oversight over all suppliers involved in producing a product. Encouraging suppliers to report problems, issues, or concerns requires excellent communication systems to obtain feedback. Ideally, suppliers will report potential problems before they reach the next level of the supply chain, which reduces damage.

Despite the challenges of monitoring global operations and supply chains, there are steps businesses can take to manage these risks. All companies who work with global suppliers should adopt a Global Supplier Code of Conduct and ensure that it is effectively communicated. Additionally, companies should encourage compliance and procurement employees to work together to find ethical suppliers at reasonable costs. Those in procurement are concerned with the costs of obtaining materials for the company. As a result, supply chain and procurement managers must work together to make operational decisions to ensure the selection of the best suppliers from an ethical and cost-effective standpoint. Businesses must also work to make certain that their supply chains are diverse. Having only a few suppliers in one area can disrupt operations should a disaster strike. Finally, companies must perform regular audits on its suppliers and take action against those found to be in violation of company standards.[37]

⊖ So You Want a Job in Operations Management

While you might not have been familiar with terms such as *supply chain* or *logistics* or *total quality management* before taking this course, careers abound in the operations management field. You will find these careers in a wide variety of organizations—manufacturers, retailers, transportation companies, third-party logistics firms, government agencies, and service firms. Approximately $1.3 trillion is spent on transportation, inventory, and related logistics activities, and logistics alone accounts for more than 9.5 percent of U.S. gross domestic product.[38] Closely managing how a company's inputs and outputs flow from raw materials to the end consumer is vital to a firm's success. Successful companies also need to ensure that quality is measured and actively managed at each step.

Supply chain managers have a tremendous impact on the success of an organization. These managers are engaged in every facet of the business process, including planning, purchasing, production, transportation, storage and distribution, customer service, and more. Their performance helps organizations control expenses, boost sales, and maximize profits.

Warehouse managers are a vital part of manufacturing operations. A typical warehouse manager's duties include overseeing and recording deliveries and pickups, maintaining inventory records and the product tracking system, and adjusting inventory levels to reflect receipts and disbursements. Warehouse managers also have to keep in mind customer service and employee issues. Warehouse managers can earn up to $60,000 in some cases.

Operations management is also required in service businesses. With more than 80 percent of the U.S. economy in services, jobs exist for services operations. Many service contact operations require standardized processes that often use technology to provide an interface that provides an automatic quality performance. Consider jobs in health care, the travel industry, fast food, and entertainment. Think of any job or task that is a part of the final product in these industries. Even an online retailer such as Amazon.com has a transformation process that includes information technology and human activities that facilitate a transaction. These services have a standardized process and can be evaluated based on their level of achieved service quality.

Total quality management is becoming a key attribute for companies to ensure that quality pervades all aspects of the organization. Quality assurance managers make a median salary of $72,000. These managers monitor and advise on how a company's quality management system is performing and publish data and reports regarding company performance in both manufacturing and service industries.[39]

Review Your Understanding

Define *operations management* and differentiate between operations and manufacturing.

Operations management (OM) is the development and administration of the activities involved in transforming resources into goods and services. Operations managers oversee the transformation process and the planning and designing of operations systems, managing logistics, quality, and productivity. The terms *manufacturing* and *production* are used interchangeably to describe the activities and processes used in making tangible products, whereas *operations* is a broader term used to describe the process of making both tangible and intangible products.

Explain how operations management differs in manufacturing and service firms.

Manufacturers and service firms both transform inputs into outputs, but service providers differ from manufacturers in several ways: They have greater customer contact because the service typically occurs at the point of consumption; their inputs and outputs are more variable than manufacturers', largely because of the human element; service providers are generally more labor intensive; and their productivity measurement is more complex.

Describe the elements involved in planning and designing an operations system.

Operations planning relates to decisions about what product(s) to make, for whom, and what processes and facilities are needed to produce them. OM is often joined by marketing and research and development in these decisions. Common facility layouts include fixed-position layouts, process layouts, or product layouts. Where to locate operations facilities is a crucial decision that depends on proximity to the market, availability of raw materials, availability of transportation, availability of power, climatic influences, availability of labor, and community characteristics. Technology is also vital to operations, particularly computer-assisted design, computer-assisted manufacturing, flexible manufacturing, robotics, and computer-integrated manufacturing.

Specify some techniques managers may use to manage the logistics of transforming inputs into finished products.

Logistics, or supply chain management, includes all the activities involved in obtaining and managing raw materials and component parts, managing finished products, packaging them, and getting them to customers. The organization must first make or purchase (procure) all the materials it needs. Next, it must control its inventory by determining how many supplies and goods it needs and keeping track of every raw material, component, completed or partially completed product, and piece of equipment, how many of each are on hand, where they are, and who has responsibility for them. Common approaches to inventory control include the economic order quantity (EOQ) model, the just-in-time (JIT) inventory concept, and material-requirements planning (MRP). Logistics also includes routing and scheduling processes and activities to complete products.

Assess the importance of quality in operations management.

Quality is a critical element of OM because low-quality products can hurt people and harm the business. Quality control refers to the processes an organization uses to maintain its established quality standards. To control quality, a company must establish what standard of quality it desires and then determine whether its products meet that standard through inspection.

Evaluate a business's dilemma and propose a solution.

Based on this chapter and the facts presented in the "Solve the Dilemma" feature at the end of this chapter, you should be able to evaluate the business's problem and propose one or more solutions for resolving it.

Revisit the World of Business

1. How does Chipotle's made-to-order menu increase organizational complexity?

2. Why does Chipotle prepare menu items in front of customers?

3. Why does Chipotle employ strict cooking, preparing, and serving guidelines for its food?

Learn the Terms

capacity 241
computer-assisted design (CAD) 244
computer-assisted manufacturing (CAM) 244
computer-integrated manufacturing (CIM) 245
continuous manufacturing organizations 244
customization 241
economic order quantity (EOQ) model 248
fixed-position layout 243

Check Your Progress

1. What is operations management?

2. Differentiate among the terms *operations, production,* and *manufacturing.*

3. Compare and contrast a manufacturer versus a service provider in terms of operations management.

4. Who is involved in planning products?

5. In what industry would the fixed-position layout be most efficient? The process layout? The product layout? Use real examples.

6. What criteria do businesses use when deciding where to locate a plant?

7. What is flexible manufacturing? How can it help firms improve quality?

8. Define supply chain management and summarize the activities it involves.

9. Describe some of the methods a firm may use to control inventory.

10. When might a firm decide to inspect a sample of its products rather than test every product for quality?

Get Involved

1. Compare and contrast OM at McDonald's with that of Honda of America. Compare and contrast OM at McDonald's with that of a bank in your neighborhood.

2. Find a real company that uses JIT, either in your local community or in a business journal. Why did the company decide to use JIT? What have been the advantages and disadvantages of using JIT for that particular company? What has been the overall effect

on the quality of the company's goods or services? What has been the overall effect on the company's bottom line?

3. Interview someone from your local Chamber of Commerce and ask him or her what incentives the community offers to encourage organizations to locate there. (See if these incentives relate to the criteria firms use to make location decisions.)

Build Your Skills

Reducing Cycle Time

Background

An important goal of production and operations management is reducing cycle time—the time it takes to complete a task or process.

The goal in cycle time reduction is to reduce costs and/or increase customer service.[40] Many experts believe that the rate of change in our society is so fast that a firm must master speed and connectivity.[41] Connectivity refers to a seamless integration of customers, suppliers, employees, and organizational, production, and operations management. The use of the Internet and other telecommunications systems helps many organizations connect and reduce cycle time.

Task

Break up into pairs throughout the class. Select two businesses (local restaurants, retail stores, etc.) that both of you frequent, are employed by, and/or are fairly well acquainted with. For the first business, one of you will role-play the "manager" and the other will role-play the "customer." Reverse roles for the second business you have selected. As managers at your respective businesses, you are to prepare a list of five questions you will ask the customer during the role-play. The questions you prepare should be designed to get the customer's viewpoint on how good the cycle time is at your business. If one of the responses leads to a problem area, you may need to ask a follow-up question to determine the nature of the dissatisfaction. Prepare one main question and a follow-up, if necessary, for each of the five dimensions of cycle time:

1. **Speed**—the delivery of goods and services in the minimum time; efficient communications; the elimination of wasted time.

2. **Connectivity**—all operations and systems in the business appear connected with the customer.

3. **Interactive relationships**—a continual dialog exists among operations units, service providers, and customers that permits the exchange of feedback on concerns or needs.

4. **Customization**—each product is tailored to the needs of the customer.

5. **Responsiveness**—the willingness to make adjustments and be flexible to help customers and to provide prompt service when a problem develops.

Begin the two role-plays. When it is your turn to be the manager, listen carefully when your partner answers your prepared questions. You need to elicit information on how to improve the cycle time at your business. You will achieve this by identifying the problem areas (weaknesses) that need attention.

After completing both role-play situations, fill out the accompanying form for the role-play when you were the manager. You may not have gathered enough information to fill in all the boxes.

For example, for some categories, the customer may have had only good things to say; for others, the comments may all be negative. Be prepared to share the information you gain with the rest of the class.

I role-played the manager at (business). After listening carefully to the customer's responses to my five questions, I determined the following strengths and weaknesses as they relate to the cycle time at my business:

Dimension	Strength	Weakness
Speed		
Connectivity		
Interactive relationships		
Customization		
Responsiveness		

Solve the Dilemma

Planning for Pizza

McKing Corporation operates fast-food restaurants in 50 states, selling hamburgers, roast beef and chicken sandwiches, french fries, and salads. The company wants to diversify into the growing pizza business. Six months of tests revealed that the ideal pizza to sell was a 16-inch pie in three varieties: cheese, pepperoni, and deluxe (multiple toppings). Research found the size and toppings acceptable to families as well as to individuals (single buyers could freeze the leftovers), and the price was acceptable for a fast-food restaurant ($7.99 for cheese, $8.49 for pepperoni, and $9.99 for deluxe).

Marketing and human resources personnel prepared training manuals for employees, advertising materials, and the rationale to present to the restaurant managers (many stores are franchised). Store managers, franchisees, and employees are excited about the new plan. There is just one problem.

LO 8-6

Evaluate a business's dilemma and propose a solution.

The drive-through windows in current restaurants are too small for a 16-inch pizza to pass through. The largest size the present windows can accommodate is a 12-inch pie. The managers and franchisees are concerned that if this aspect of operations has been overlooked, perhaps the product is not ready to be launched. Maybe there are other problems yet to be uncovered.

Discussion Questions

1. What mistake did McKing make in approaching the introduction of pizza?

2. How could this product introduction have been coordinated to avoid the problems that were encountered?

3. If you were an executive at McKing, how would you proceed with the introduction of pizza into the restaurants?

Build Your Business Plan

Managing Service and Manufacturing Operations

For your business, you need to determine if you are providing raw materials that will be used in further production, or if you are a reseller of goods and services, known as a retailer. If you are the former, you need to determine what processes you go through in making your product.

The text provides ideas of breaking the process into inputs, transformation processes, and outputs. If you are a provider of a service or a link in the supply chain, you need to know exactly what your customer expectations are. Services are intangible, so it is all the more important to better understand what exactly the customer is looking for in resolving a problem or filling a need.

See for Yourself Videocase

Operations Excellence Results in a Home Run

It's not often that frozen pizza is compared favorably with fresh pizzas served in restaurants. Home Run Inn is the exception to the rule. Home Run Inn's frozen cheese pizza is considered tastier than the fresh deep dish and original pizzas from Domino's and Pizza Hut. In 2013, *Consumer Reports* named Home Run Inn as number one in the frozen pizza category. Its popularity is evident as it has become one of the fastest-growing frozen pizza companies in the nation. Today, Home Run Inn distributes pizza in more than 20 states and sells almost as much as DiGiorno and Tombstone brands combined.

Home Run Inn is a family-run business with headquarters in Chicago. The inspiration for the name happened after a baseball from a nearby sandlot crashed through Mary and Vincent Grittani's window of their new restaurant in 1923. More than 20 years later, in 1947 the Grittani's son-in-law Nick Perinno partnered with Mary Grittani to develop the recipe for the company's all-natural Home Run Inn pizza. This pizza would place the restaurant on the map.

During the 1950s, the business chose to expand into the frozen pizza business. In the 1980s, Nick's son Joe Perrino, currently the president and CEO of the business, realized that they needed to expand if they wanted to grow. He began to look at ways to improve the organization's operations through automation. "We started very basically with conveyers and ovens, and we then proceeded with different presses," he said.

Soon, demand for Home Run Inn pizzas began to eclipse supply. Home Run Inn was unable to meet this demand with its current capacity due to manufacturing limitations. Cooking the pizzas and freezing them with conventional freezing methods was complex and placed constraints on how much the company could produce. As a result, Perrino decided to purchase a cryogenic freezer that freezes using CO_2 gas. The equipment cost $250,000, which was approximately what it would cost to purchase a restaurant. However, the result was far worth the money spent. Perrino states, "We were able to produce pizzas three, four times as fast as we were currently doing with fewer people, so that really set a light bulb off in our heads."

Two years later, the company built a new facility to keep up with demand. The major reason for this high demand is the quality of the pizza. Home Run Inn guarantees that its frozen pizzas are just as good as the pizzas it serves in its restaurants (it currently has nine restaurant locations). The company does this by controlling quality in-house. Home Run Inn pizza uses all-natural ingredients and its homemade sauce, sausage, and cheese. These all-natural ingredients have enabled the company to differentiate its products, allowing it to have higher prices compared to competitors and still retain high demand.

In 2002, Home Run Inn decided to go a step further. The company partnered with former Kraft CEO Jay Williams to self-distribute its pizzas. Until then, Home Run Inn frozen pizzas were stored in warehouses and then distributed to retailers. Self-distribution required the company to have its own fleet of trucks to deliver the pizzas to the retailers. This requires Home Run Inn to keep careful track of inventory in the stores. It was a significant investment for Home Run Inn, but it also allowed the company to control its supply chain and ensure that quality was maintained from manufacturing all the way to the finished product on the shelf. According to Perrino, this move helped the firm grow from 8 percent market share to 28 percent market share.

Thanks to quality operation processes, strong supply chain control, and careful monitoring of inventory, Home Run Inn pizza has secured its place as a top-quality frozen pizza business. Despite its high price compared to rivals, customers are eager to purchase Home Run Inn frozen pizza because they know the value is worth the price.[42]

Discussion Questions

1. Describe how taking risks to increase its operational capacity turned Home Run Inn pizza into the top player in the frozen pizza industry.

2. Why is Home Run Inn able to compete at prices higher than its rivals'?

3. Why has self-distribution been so beneficial for Home Run Inn? Do you think it would be successful for every manufacturing company?

You can find the related video in the Video Library in Connect. Ask your instructor how you can access Connect.

Team Exercise

Form groups and assign the responsibility of finding companies that outsource their production to other countries. What are the key advantages of this outsourcing decision? Do you see any drawbacks or weaknesses in this approach? Why would a company not outsource when such a tactic can be undertaken to cut manufacturing costs? Report your findings to the class.

Endnotes

1. Susan Nassauer, "What's Made from Scratch?" *The Wall Street Journal,* February 25, 2015, pp. D1–D2; Candice Choi, "Chipotle Warns of Sales Slide as E. Coli Outbreak Expands," *ABC News,* December 4, 2015, http://abcnews .go.com/Health/wireStory/chipotle-tightening-food-safety-coli-cases-35577816 (accessed December 5, 2015); Chipotle Grill, "Food with Integrity," https://www.chipotle.com/ food-with-integrity (accessed December 5, 2015); Chipotle Grill, "Chipotle Mexican Grill, Inc. Announces Third Quarter 2014 Results," http://ir.chipotle.com/phoenix .zhtml?c=194775&p=irol-newsArticle&ID=1979465 (accessed December 5, 2015); Chipotle Grill, "Food Safety Update," December 10, 2015, https://www.chipotle.com/ update (accessed December 5, 2015).

2. Olive & Sinclair website, http://www.oliveandsinclair .com/ (accessed December 11, 2015); Daniel Walker, "Sensual Southern-Made Chocolate from Olive & Sinclair," *Arkansas Times,* August 22, 2013, http://www .arktimes.com/EatArkansas/archives/2013/08/22/sensual-southern-made-chocolate-from-olive-and-sinclair (accessed December 11, 2015); Christine Birkner, "Southern Sweet Spot," *Marketing News,* January 2014, https://www.ama.org/ publications/MarketingNews/Pages/southern-sweet-spot .aspx (accessed December 11, 2015); E.J. Boyer, "Olive & Sinclair Chocolate Co.'s Scott Witherow Likes Old Things and Sweets (Video)," *Nashville Business Journal,* March 13, 2014, http://www.bizjournals.com/nashville/blog/2014/03/ olive-sinclair-chocolate-co-s-scott-witherow-likes.html (accessed December 11, 2015); Steve Haruch, "Olive & Sinclair Opens East Nashville Factory with Tours and Retail Store," *Nashville Scene,* January 29, 2014, http://www .nashvillescene.com/bites/archives/2014/01/29/olive-and-sinclair-opens-east-nashville-factory-with-tours-and-retail-store (accessed December 11, 2015).

3. The Colonial Williamsburg Foundation, "King's Arms Tavern," https://www.colonialwilliamsburg.com/do/ restaurants/historic-dining-taverns/kings-arms/ (accessed March 15, 2016).

4. Michael B. Sauter, "2015's Customer Service Hall of Fame," *USA Today,* August 2, 2015,http://www.usatoday. com/story/money/business/2015/07/24/24-7-wall-st-customer-service-hall-fame/30599943/ (accessed March 15, 2016); Adam Clark Estes, "Jeff Bezos: If You Have a Problem with Amazon, Email Me,"*Gizmodo,* August 17, 2015, http://gizmodo.com/jeff-bezos-if-you-have-a-problem-with-amazon-email-me-1724561248 (accessed March 15, 2016).

5. Leonard L. Berry, *Discovering the Soul of Service* (New York: The Free Press, 1999), pp. 86–96.

6. Valerie A. Zeithaml and Mary Jo Bitner, *Services Marketing,* 3rd ed. (Boston: McGraw-Hill Irwin, 2003), pp. 3, 22.

7. Claire Zillman, "Zappos Is Bringing Uber-like Surge Pay to the Workplace," *Fortune,* January 28, 2015, http://fortune.

com/2015/01/28/zappos-employee-pay/ (accessed March 15, 2016).

8. Bernard Wysocki Jr., "To Fix Health Care, Hospitals Take Tips from the Factory Floor," *The Wall Street Journal,* April 9, 2004, viawww.chcanys.org/clientuploads/downloads/ Clinical_resources/Leadership%20Articles/LeanThinking_ ACF28EB.pdf (accessed March 16, 2016).

9. Ryan Chavis, "Survey: Retailers Looking to Expand Social Media, Tech Solutions in Product Planning," *Drug Store News,* November 4, 2014, http://www.drugstorenews.com/ article/survey-retailers-looking-expand-social-media-tech-solutions-product-planning (accessed March 11, 2015).

10. Brooke Crothers, "Google Is Leader in 'Revolutionary' Self-Driving Cars, Says IHS," *Forbes,* November 12, 2015,http:// www.forbes.com/sites/brookecrothers/2015/11/12/ google-is-leader-in-revolutionary-self-driving-cars-says-ihs/#1a371731e3e6 (accessed March 21, 2016).

11. Ericsson, "Ericsson and Cisco Partner to Create the Networks of the Future," November 9, 2015, http://www .ericsson.com/news/1965277 (accessed March 15, 2016).

12. Christina Cooke, "America's Rebel Band of Custom-Bike Builders," *The Atlantic,* April 3, 2014,www.theatlantic. com/business/archive/2014/04/americas-rebel-band-of-custom-bike-builders/360058/ (accessed April 22, 2014); Breadwinner Cycles website, http://breadwinnercycles.com/ (accessed March 15, 2016).

13. Marie Singer, "The Hershey Company—Company Information," *Market Business News,* April 14, 2014, www .marketbusinessnews.com/hershey-company-company-information/18006 (accessed March 15, 2016).

14. Toyota, "ISO 14001 Certification," http://www.toyota-industries.com/csr/environment/management/iso.html (accessed March 15, 2016).

15. Ross Toro, "How 3D Printers Work (Infographic)," *Live Science,* June 18, 2013, www.livescience.com/37513-how-3d-printers-work-infographic.html(accessed March 15, 2016).

16. Matt Schiavenza, "FAA Drone Regulations Deal Blow to Amazon," *The Atlantic,* February 15, 2015,http://www .theatlantic.com/business/archive/2015/02/faa-drone-regulations-deal-blow-to-amazon/385529/ (accessed March 15, 2016); Chris Anderson, "How I Accidentally Kickstarted the Domestic Drone Boom," June 22, 2012, http://www. wired.com/2012/06/ff_drones/all/ (accessed March 15, 2016); Jonathan Vanian, "Amazon's Drone Testing Takes Flight in Yet Another Country," *Fortune,* February 1, 2016, http://fortune.com/2016/02/01/amazon-testing-drones-netherlands/(accessed March 15, 2016).

17. Paul Davidson, "More robots coming to U.S. factories," *USA Today,* February 10, 2015, http://www.usatoday.com/story/ money/2015/02/09/bcg-report-on-factory-robots/23143259/ (accessed March 15, 2016); Ed Flanagan, " 'Workshop of the World' China Bets on a Robot Revolution," *NBC News,* December 23, 2015, http://www.nbcnews.com/news/china/ workshop-world-china-bets-robot-revolution-n482301 (accessed March 15, 2016).

18. Adobe, "Corporate Responsibility," http://www.adobe.com/ corporate-responsibility/sustainability/energy-conservation.

html (accessed March 15, 2016); Adobe, "Newsweek Ranks Adobe World's Greenest Tech Company Second Year in a Row," June 9, 2015, http://www.adobe.com/news-room/pres sreleases/201506/060915NewsweekRanksAdobeWorldsGree nestTechCompany.html (accessed March 15, 2016).

19. Ashim Paun, "Green Buildings Are Good Business," HSBC, http://www.hsbc.com/news-and-insight/2015/green-buildings-are-good-business (accessed March 16, 2016).

20. City of Chicago, "Energy Efficiency and Renewable Energy," http://www.cityofchicago.org/city/en/progs/env/ energy_efficiencyandrenewables.html (accessed March 16, 2016).

21. O. C. Ferrell and Michael D. Hartline, *Marketing Strategy* (Mason, OH: South Western, 2011), p. 215.

22. Ibid.

23. Susan Berfield and Manuel Baigorri, "Zara's Fast-Fashion Edge," *Bloomberg Businessweek,* November 14, 2013, www .businessweek.com/articles/2013-11-14/2014-outlook-zaras-fashion-supply-chain-edge (accessed March 16, 2016).

24. James R. Hagerty, "A Radical Idea: Own Your Supply Chain," *The Wall Street Journal,* April 30, 2015, p. B1; Ashley Furniture, "Operations Supply Chain Overview," http://www.ashleyfurniture.com/jobportal/pdf/ BWaldera_SupplyChain.pdf (accessed December 14, 2015); RTO Online, "Ashley Furniture's Integrated Supply Chain," http://rtoonline.com/Content/Article/aug08/rentdirect_ primetime088508.asp?ptid=9865494 (accessed December 14, 2015).

25. Teresa Matich, *Copper Investing News,* January 4, 2015, http://investingnews.com/daily/resource-investing/ base-metals-investing/copper-investing/historical-copper-prices-china-us-supply-demand-porphyry-mining/ (accessed March 16, 2016).

26. "Broken Links," *The Economist,* March 31, 2011, www .economist.com/node/18486015 (accessed May 12, 2014).

27. Susan Carey, "Airlines Play Up Improvements in On-Time Performance," *The Wall Street Journal,* February 10, 2010, p. B6; U.S. Department of Transportation, "Air Travel Consumer Report," March 2014, www.dot.gov/sites/dot. gov/files/docs/2014_March_ATCR.pdf (accessed April 23, 20014).

28. The Quality Center, "2015 Baldrige National Quality Award Winners Announced!" November 20, 2015, http://www .msqpc.com/news/2015-baldrige-national-quality-award-winners-announced/ (accessed March 16, 2016).

29. Hollie Slade, "Factory of the Future," *Forbes,* November 3, 2014, pp. 92–96; Proto Labs, "About," http://www.protolabs. com/about (accessed March 11, 2015).

30. Philip B. Crosby, *Quality Is Free: The Art of Making Quality Certain* (New York: McGraw-Hill, 1979), pp. 9–10.

31. Nigel F. Piercy, *Market-Led Strategic Change* (Newton, MA: Butterworth-Heinemann, 1992), pp. 374–385.

32. Bloomberg LLP, "Compuware Gomez Introduces Free Web Performance Benchmarking Tool," *Bloomberg,* February 16, 2010,www.bloomberg.com/apps/news?pid=newsarchive&si d=a3bTx6JLlx7I(accessed May 12, 2014).

33. "ISO 9001 Certification," GE Power & Water, www.geinstruments.com/company/iso-9001-certification.html (accessed March 16, 2016).

34. Matthew Sparkes, "Apple 'Leads the Way' on Reducing Environmental Harm," *The Telegraph,* September 3, 2014, http://www.telegraph.co.uk/technology/apple/11070662/Apple-leads-the-way-on-reducing-environmental-harm.html (accessed October 21, 2015); Apple Inc., "Apple Announces New Environmental Initiatives in China," *Apple Press Info,* May 11, 2015,https://www.apple.com/pr/library/2015/05/11Apple-Announces-New-Environmental-Initiatives-in-China.html (accessed October 21, 2015); Daisuke Wakabayashi, "Apple Expands Renewable Energy Goal," *The Wall Street Journal,* May 10, 2015, http://blogs.wsj.com/digits/2015/05/10/apple-expands-renewable-energy-goal-to-cover-supply-chain/ (accessed October 21, 2015).

35. PowerPoint presentation at 2014 ECOA conference in Atlanta, presented by Martin Tolar, GRC Institute, entitled, "The First ISO Standard in E&C: What You Need to Know," October 2, 2014; Dick Hortensius, "What Is the General Idea Behind the Proposed ISO 19600?" *Ethics Intelligence,* April 2014, http://www.ethic-intelligence.com/experts/4636-general-idea-behind-iso-19600/ (accessed October 14, 2014).

36. Ben Dipietro, "Supply Chain Slavery Comes Into Focus for Companies," *The Wall Street Journal,* March 30, 2015, http://blogs.wsj.com/riskandcompliance/2015/03/30/supply-chain-slavery-comes-into-focus-for-companies/ (accessed March 16, 2016); Ian Urbina, "U.S. Closing a Loophole on Products Tied to Slaves," *The New York Times,* February 15, 2016, http://www.nytimes.com/2016/02/16/us/politics/us-closing-a-loophole-on-products-tied-to-slaves.html?_r=0 (accessed March 16, 2016).

37. "Monitoring and Auditing Global Supply Chains Is a Must," *Ethisphere,* 2011, Q3, pp. 38–45.

38. "Employment Opportunities," Careers in Supply Chain Management, www.careersinsupplychain.org/career-outlook/empopp.asp (accessed March 16, 2016).

39. "Best Jobs in America," *CNN Money,* http://money.cnn.com/magazines/moneymag/bestjobs/2009/snapshots/48.html (accessed April 24, 2014); PayScale, "Quality Assurance Manager Salary," http://www.payscale.com/research/US/Job=Quality_Assurance_Manager/Salary (accessed March 16, 2016).

40. James Wetherbe, "Principles of Cycle Time Reduction," *Cycle Time Research*, 1995, p. iv.

41. Stan Davis and Christopher Meyer, *Blur: The Speed of Change in the Connected Economy* (Reading, MA: Addison-Wesley, 1998), p. 5.

42. "Home Run Inn," *CBS Chicago,* January 4, 2012, http://chicago.cbslocal.com/2012/01/04/home-run-inn/ (accessed August 5, 2016); Home Run Inn, "Catering," *http://*www.homeruninnpizza.com/catering (accessed August 5, 2016); "Consumer Reports Names Home Run Inn Best Frozen Pizza," *NBC,* August 20, 2013, http://www.nbcchicago.com/news/local/Home-Run-Inn-Named-Best-Frozen-Pizza-220344721.html (accessed August 5, 2016); Home Run Inn, "Best Frozen Pizza," http://www.homeruninnpizza.com/frozen-pizza (accessed August 5, 2016).

Creating the Human Resource Advantage

© Jim West/Alamy Stock Photo

9

Motivating the Workforce

Learning Objectives

After reading this chapter, you will be able to:

 LO 9-1 Define *human relations* and determine why its study is important.

 LO 9-2 Summarize early studies that laid the groundwork for understanding employee motivation.

 LO 9-3 Compare and contrast the human relations theories of Abraham Maslow and Frederick Herzberg.

 LO 9-4 Investigate various theories of motivation, including Theories X, Y, and Z; equity theory; expectancy theory; and goal-setting theory.

LO 9-5 Describe some of the strategies that managers use to motivate employees.

LO 9-6 Critique a business's program for motivating its sales force.

Enter the World of Business ⊖────────

Marriott: Take Care of Employees and That Takes Care of Your Customers

Taking care of employees means something unique for the executive staff, owners, and rank-and-file workers of Marriott. Although the Marriott family initially went into business running hot dog stands in the 1920s, when they entered the hotel business in 1957, they brought with them an entrenched desire to put employees first. Indeed, employee-centrism continues to be at the heart of the company with the philosophy that it leads to happier guests. In this regard, the company found that employee engagement leads to higher guest satisfaction and ultimately more profit.

There are many ways Marriott fosters a culture centered on its employees. Employees are motivated through job enrichment, where hard work leads to opportunities for promotion. Preshift meetings at some hotels include fun activities like music and dancing. And there is also an annual Awards of Excellence event, where around 800 hand-selected employees join the executive team for an evening of recognition. Any employee who stays with Marriott for at least 25 years is also eligible for the Quarter Century Club, which includes free weekend stays at any Marriott hotel for life.

Marriott provides an example of the benefits that can arise from a motivated and inspired workforce. Employee turnover at Marriott is lower than the industry average, and the company's stock price is well beyond the S&P 500 Index—all evidence that Marriott's employee commitment is paying off, both in guest satisfaction and financial performance.[1]

Introduction

Because employees do the actual work of the business and influence whether the firm achieves its objectives, most top managers agree that employees are an organization's most valuable resource. To achieve organizational objectives, employees must have the motivation, ability (appropriate knowledge and skills), and tools (proper training and equipment) to perform their jobs. Chapter 10 covers topics related to managing human resources, such as those listed earlier. This chapter focuses on how to motivate employees.

We examine employees' needs and motivation, managers' views of workers, and several strategies for motivating employees. Managers who understand the needs of their employees can help them reach higher levels of productivity and thus contribute to the achievement of organizational goals.

Define *human relations* and determine why its study is important.

human relations
the study of the behavior of individuals and groups in organizational settings.

motivation
an inner drive that directs a person's behavior toward goals.

Nature of Human Relations

What motivates employees to perform on the job is the focus of **human relations,** the study of the behavior of individuals and groups in organizational settings. In business, human relations involves motivating employees to achieve organizational objectives efficiently and effectively. The field of human relations has become increasingly important over the years as businesses strive to understand how to boost workplace morale, maximize employees' productivity and creativity, and motivate their ever more diverse employees to be more effective.

Motivation is an inner drive that directs a person's behavior toward goals. A goal is the satisfaction of some need, and a need is the difference between a desired state and an actual state. Both needs and goals can be motivating. Motivation explains why people behave as they do; similarly, a lack of motivation explains, at times, why people avoid doing what they should do. Motivating employees to do the wrong things or for the wrong reasons can be problematic, however. Encouraging employees to lie to customers or to create false documentation is unethical and could even have legal ramifications. A person who recognizes or feels a need is motivated to take action to satisfy the need and achieve a goal (Figure 9-1). Consider a person who takes a job as a salesperson. If his or her performance is far below other salespeople's, he or she will likely recognize a need to increase sales. To satisfy that need and achieve success, the person may try to acquire new insights from successful salespeople or obtain additional training to improve sales skills. In addition, a sales manager might try different means to motivate the salesperson to work harder and to improve his or her skills. Human relations is concerned with the needs of employees, their goals and how they try to achieve them, and the impact of those needs and goals on job performance.

Motivation is important both in business and outside of it. For instance, coaches motivate athletes before major games to increase their chances they will play their best.

© moodboard/SuperStock

Effectively motivating employees helps keep them engaged in their work. Engagement involves emotional involvement and commitment. Being engaged results in carrying out the expectations and obligations of employment. Many employees are actively engaged in their jobs, while others are not. Some employees do the minimum amount of work required to get by, and some employees are completely disengaged.

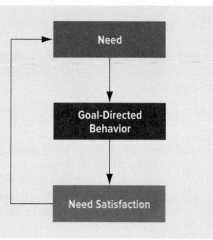

FIGURE 9-1
The Motivation Process

Motivating employees to stay engaged is a key responsibility of management. For example, to test if his onsite production managers were fully engaged in their jobs, former Van Halen frontman David Lee Roth placed a line in the band's rider asking for a bowl of M&Ms with the brown ones removed. It was a means for the band to test local stage production crews' attention to detail. Because their shows were highly technical, David Lee Roth would demand a complete recheck of everything if he found brown M&Ms in the bowl.[2]

One prominent aspect of human relations is **morale**—an employee's attitude toward his or her job, employer, and colleagues. High morale contributes to high levels of productivity, high returns to stakeholders, and employee loyalty. Conversely,

Events that engage and motivate employees can improve morale.
© a katz/Shutterstock

low morale may cause high rates of absenteeism and turnover (when employees quit or are fired and must be replaced by new employees). Wegmans Food Markets recognizes the value of happy, committed employees. It offers flexible scheduling, employee scholarship programs—nearly half of employees are 25 years or younger—and strong internal promoting. The CEO of Wegmans stresses that employee growth and satisfaction is a key goal of the organization.

Employees are motivated by their perceptions of extrinsic and intrinsic rewards. An **intrinsic reward** is the personal satisfaction and enjoyment that you feel from attaining a goal. For example, in this class you may feel personal enjoyment in learning how business works and aspire to have a career in business or to operate your own business one day. **Extrinsic rewards** are benefits and/or recognition that you receive from someone else. In this class, your grade is extrinsic recognition of your efforts and success in the class. In business, praise and recognition, pay increases, and bonuses are extrinsic rewards. If you believe that your job provides an opportunity to contribute to society or the environment, then that aspect would represent an intrinsic reward. Both intrinsic and extrinsic rewards contribute to motivation that stimulates employees to do their best in contributing to business goals.

morale
an employee's attitude toward his or her job, employer, and colleagues.

intrinsic rewards
the personal satisfaction and enjoyment felt after attaining a goal.

extrinsic rewards
benefits and/or recognition received from someone else.

TABLE 9-1
How to Retain Good Employees

1. Challenge your employees.
2. Provide adequate incentives.
3. Don't micromanage.
4. Create a work-friendly environment.
5. Provide opportunities for employee growth.

Source: Adapted from Geoff Williams, "Retaining Employees: 5 Things You Need to Know," The Huffington Post, February 2, 2012, www.huffingtonpost.com/2012/02/01/retaining-employees-5-things-you-need-to-know_n_976767.html (accessed March 24, 2016).

Respect, involvement, appreciation, adequate compensation, promotions, a pleasant work environment, and a positive organizational culture are all morale boosters. Table 9-1 lists some ways to retain good employees. Costco Wholesale, the second largest retailer in America, knows how to retain happy employees. The company pays an average annual rate of $21 per hour plus overtime, gives five weeks of vacation per year, and matches 401(k) contributions; in addition, almost 90 percent of employees are covered by company-sponsored health insurance.[4] Many companies offer a diverse array of benefits designed to improve the quality of employees' lives and increase their morale and satisfaction. Some of the "best companies to work for" offer onsite day care, concierge services (e.g., dry cleaning, shoe repair, prescription renewal), domestic partner benefits to same-sex couples, and fully paid sabbaticals. Table 9-2 offers suggestions as to how leaders can motivate employees on a daily basis.

DID YOU KNOW? Absenteeism can cost a company about 22 percent of payroll.[3]

LO 9-2

Summarize early studies that laid the groundwork for understanding employee motivation.

Historical Perspectives on Employee Motivation

Throughout the 20th century, researchers have conducted numerous studies to try to identify ways to motivate workers and increase productivity. From these studies have come theories that have been applied to workers with varying degrees of success.

TABLE 9-2
How to Motivate Employees

1. Interact with employees in a friendly and open manner.
2. Equitably dispense rewards and other incentives.
3. Create a culture of collaboration.
4. Provide both positive and negative feedback and constructive criticism.
5. Make employees feel as if they are partners rather than workers.
6. Handle conflicts in an open and professional manner.
7. Provide continuous opportunities for improvement and employee growth.
8. Encourage creativity in problem solving.
9. Recognize employees for jobs well done.
10. Allow employees to make mistakes, as these become learning opportunities.

A brief discussion of two of these theories—the classical theory of motivation and the Hawthorne studies—provides a background for understanding the present state of human relations.

Classical Theory of Motivation

The birth of the study of human relations can be traced to time and motion studies conducted at the turn of the century by Frederick W. Taylor and Frank and Lillian Gilbreth. Their studies analyzed how workers perform specific work tasks in an effort to improve the employees' productivity. These efforts led to the application of scientific principles to management.

According to the **classical theory of motivation**, money is the sole motivator for workers. Taylor suggested that workers who were paid more would produce more, an idea that would benefit both companies and workers. To improve productivity, Taylor thought that managers should break down each job into its component tasks (specialization), determine the best way to perform each task, and specify the output to be achieved by a worker performing the task. Taylor also believed that incentives would motivate employees to be more productive. Thus, he suggested that managers link workers' pay directly to their output. He developed the piece-rate system, under which employees were paid a certain amount for each unit they produced; those who exceeded their quota were paid a higher rate per unit for all the units they produced.

classical theory of motivation
theory suggesting that money is the sole motivator for workers.

We can still see Taylor's ideas in practice today in the use of financial incentives for productivity. Moreover, companies are increasingly striving to relate pay to performance at both the hourly and managerial level. Incentive planners choose an individual incentive to motivate and reward their employees. In contrast, team incentives are used to generate partnership and collaboration to accomplish organizational goals. Boeing develops sales teams for most of its products, including commercial airplanes. The team dedicated to each product shares in the sales incentive program.

More and more corporations are tying pay to performance in order to motivate—even up to the CEO level. The topic of executive pay has become controversial in recent years, and many corporate boards of directors have taken steps to link executive compensation more closely to corporate performance. Despite these changes, many top executives still receive large compensation packages. Satya Nadella, CEO of Microsoft, earns $84.3 million in annual compensation.[5]

Like most managers of the early 20th century, Taylor believed that satisfactory pay and job security would motivate employees to work hard. However, later studies showed that other factors are also important in motivating workers.

The Hawthorne Studies

Elton Mayo and a team of researchers from Harvard University wanted to determine what physical conditions in the workplace—such as light and noise levels—would stimulate employees to be most productive. From 1924 to 1932, they studied a group of workers at the Hawthorne Works Plant of the Western Electric Company and measured their productivity under various physical conditions.

What the researchers discovered was quite unexpected and very puzzling: Productivity increased regardless of the physical conditions. This phenomenon has been labeled the Hawthorne effect. When questioned about their behavior, the employees expressed satisfaction because their co-workers in the experiments were friendly

Going Green

King Arthur Flour: Employees Rule!

King Arthur Flour is far from the typical American company. In addition to being 100 percent employee owned, King Arthur prioritizes environmental and social responsibility, evidenced by its B-Corporation certification and benefit corporation status. This implies that the firm meets high criteria for social and environmental performance, as well as other factors. For instance, King Arthur Flour is continually working to reduce its energy usage and increase recycling and composting. Its sustainable activities act as a model for employees, who are empowered by the corporate culture to follow suit.

In a move away from bureaucracy, all employees at King Arthur Flour have a say in how the company is run, and taking care of employees is embedded into the company culture. Indeed, perks such as company-paid volunteer time, parental leave, free turkeys or vegetable baskets at Thanksgiving, subsidized exercise opportunities, and free baking classes all contribute to high employee satisfaction. Furthermore, King Arthur's work environment encourages employees to work hard while also having fun. In the spirit of Arthurian legend, employee recognition comes in the form of knighting ceremonies. Treating employees, the environment, and society well has been the cornerstone of King Arthur Flour for more than 200 years, and these characteristics will likely serve as a recipe for success into the future.[6]

Discussion Questions

1. Describe the ways that King Arthur addresses the needs of both employees and the environment.
2. What does B-Corporation certification indicate to stakeholders about King Arthur Flour?
3. Do you feel that employee empowerment is useful in increasing the firm's commitment to sustainability? Why or why not?

Some companies let people bring their pets to work as an added incentive to make the workplace seem more friendly.

© Image Source Plus/Alamy Stock Photo

and, more importantly, because their supervisors had asked for their help and cooperation in the study. In other words, they were responding to the attention they received, not the changing physical work conditions. The researchers concluded that social and psychological factors could significantly affect productivity and morale. The United Services Automobile Association (USAA) has a built-in psychological factor that influences employee morale. The work of the financial services company serves military and veteran families, which enlivens employees. This shows how important it is for employees to feel like their work matters.

The Hawthorne experiments marked the beginning of a concern for human relations in the workplace. They revealed that human factors do influence workers' behavior and that managers who understand the needs, beliefs, and expectations of people have the greatest success in motivating their workers.

Theories of Employee Motivation

The research of Taylor, Mayo, and many others has led to the development of a number of theories that attempt to describe what motivates employees to perform. In this section, we discuss some of the most important of these theories. The successful implementation of ideas based on these theories will vary, of course, depending on the company, its management, and its employees. It should be noted, too, that what worked in the past may no longer work today. Good managers must have the ability to adapt their ideas to an ever-changing, diverse group of employees.

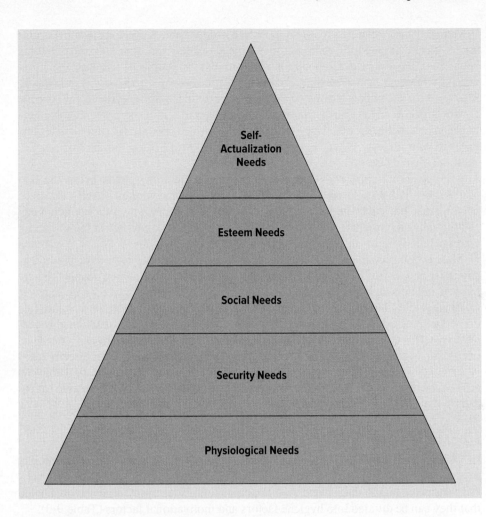

FIGURE 9-2
Maslow's Hierarchy of Needs

Source: Adapted from Abraham H. Maslow, "A Theory of Human Motivation," *Psychology Review* 50 (1943), pp. 370-396. American Psychology Association.

Maslow's hierarchy
a theory that arranges the five basic needs of people—physiological, security, social, esteem, and self-actualization—into the order in which people strive to satisfy them

Maslow's Hierarchy of Needs

Psychologist Abraham Maslow theorized that people have five basic needs: physiological, security, social, esteem, and self-actualization. **Maslow's hierarchy** arranges these needs into the order in which people strive to satisfy them (Figure 9-2).

Physiological needs, the most basic and first needs to be satisfied, are the essentials for living—water, food, shelter, and clothing. According to Maslow, humans devote all their efforts to satisfying physiological needs until they are met. Only when these needs are met can people focus their attention on satisfying the next level of needs—security.

Security needs relate to protecting yourself from physical and economic harm. Actions that may be taken to achieve security include reporting a dangerous workplace condition to management, maintaining safety equipment, and purchasing insurance with income protection in the event you become unable to work. Once security needs have been satisfied, people may strive for social goals.

Social needs are the need for love, companionship, and friendship—the desire for acceptance by others. To fulfill social needs, a person may try many things: making friends with a co-worker, joining a group, volunteering at a hospital, throwing a party, and so on. Once their social needs have been satisfied, people attempt to satisfy their need for esteem.

LO 9-3

Compare and contrast the human relations theories of Abraham Maslow and Frederick Herzberg.

physiological needs
the most basic human needs to be satisfied—water, food, shelter, and clothing.

security needs
the need to protect oneself from physical and economic harm.

social needs
the need for love, companionship, and friendship—the desire for acceptance by others.

esteem needs
the need for respect—both self-respect and respect from others.

self-actualization needs
the need to be the best one can be; at the top of Maslow's hierarchy.

Esteem needs relate to respect—both self-respect and respect from others. One aspect of esteem needs is competition—the need to feel that you can do something better than anyone else. Competition often motivates people to increase their productivity. Esteem needs are not as easily satisfied as the needs at lower levels in Maslow's hierarchy because they do not always provide tangible evidence of success. However, these needs can be realized through rewards and increased involvement in organizational activities. Until esteem needs are met, people focus their attention on achieving respect. When they feel they have achieved some measure of respect, self-actualization becomes the major goal of life.

Self-actualization needs, at the top of Maslow's hierarchy, mean being the best you can be. Self-actualization involves maximizing your potential. A self-actualized person feels that she or he is living life to its fullest in every way. For Stephen King, self-actualization might mean being praised as the best fiction writer in the world; for actress Halle Berry, it might mean winning an Oscar.

Maslow's theory maintains that the more basic needs at the bottom of the hierarchy must be satisfied before higher-level goals can be pursued. Thus, people who are hungry and homeless are not concerned with obtaining respect from their colleagues. Only when physiological, security, and social needs have been more or less satisfied do people seek esteem. Maslow's theory also suggests that if a low-level need is suddenly reactivated, the individual will try to satisfy that need rather than higher-level needs. Many laid off workers probably shift their focus from high-level esteem needs to the need for security. Managers should learn from Maslow's hierarchy that employees will be motivated to contribute to organizational goals only if they are able to first satisfy their physiological, security, and social needs through their work.

Herzberg's Two-Factor Theory

In the 1950s, psychologist Frederick Herzberg proposed a theory of motivation that focuses on the job and on the environment where work is done. Herzberg studied various factors relating to the job and their relation to employee motivation and concluded that they can be divided into hygiene factors and motivational factors (Table 9-3).

hygiene factors
aspects of Herzberg's theory of motivation that focus on the work setting and not the content of the work; these aspects include adequate wages, comfortable and safe working conditions, fair company policies, and job security.

Hygiene factors, which relate to the work setting and not to the content of the work, include adequate wages, comfortable and safe working conditions, fair company policies, and job security. These factors do not necessarily motivate employees to excel, but their absence may be a potential source of dissatisfaction and high turnover. Employee safety and comfort are clearly hygiene factors.

Many people feel that a good salary is one of the most important job factors, even more important than job security and the chance to use one's mind and abilities.

TABLE 9-3
Herzberg's Hygiene and Motivational Factors

Hygiene Factors	Motivational Factors
Company policies	Achievement
Supervision	Recognition
Working conditions	Work itself
Relationships with peers, supervisors, and subordinates	Responsibility
Salary	Advancement
Security	Personal growth

Salary and security, two of the hygiene factors identified by Herzberg, make it possible for employees to satisfy the physiological and security needs identified by Maslow. However, the presence of hygiene factors is unlikely to motivate employees to work harder. For example, many people do not feel motivated to pursue a career as a gastroenterologist (doctors who specialize in the digestive system). Although the job is important and pays nearly $300,000 on average, the tasks are routine and most patients are not looking forward to their appointments.[7]

Motivational factors, which relate to the content of the work itself, include achievement, recognition, involvement, responsibility, and advancement. The absence of motivational factors may not result in dissatisfaction, but their presence is likely to motivate employees to excel. Many companies are beginning to employ methods to give employees more responsibility and control and to involve them more in their work, which serves to motivate them to higher levels of productivity and quality. Hotels are adopting more employee-centric processes in order to better their offerings. Hilton Hotels views employees as team members. It holds an annual Team Member Appreciation Week and encourages team members to thank one another for exceptional guest services. Approximately 91 percent of employees say they are proud to work for the company.[8]

Herzberg's motivational factors and Maslow's esteem and self-actualization needs are similar. Workers' low-level needs (physiological and security) have largely been satisfied by minimum-wage laws and occupational-safety standards set by various government agencies and are therefore not motivators. Consequently, to improve productivity, management should focus on satisfying workers' higher-level needs (motivational factors) by providing opportunities for achievement, involvement, and advancement and by recognizing good performance.

> **motivational factors**
> aspects of Herzberg's theory of motivation that focus on the content of the work itself; these aspects include achievement, recognition, involvement, responsibility, and advancement.

McGregor's Theory X and Theory Y

In *The Human Side of Enterprise,* Douglas McGregor related Maslow's ideas about personal needs to management. McGregor contrasted two views of management—the traditional view, which he called Theory X, and a humanistic view, which he called Theory Y.

According to McGregor, managers adopting **Theory X** assume that workers generally dislike work and must be forced to do their jobs. They believe that the following statements are true of workers:

1. The average person naturally dislikes work and will avoid it when possible.
2. Most workers must be coerced, controlled, directed, or threatened with punishment to get them to work toward the achievement of organizational objectives.
3. The average worker prefers to be directed and to avoid responsibility, has relatively little ambition, and wants security.[9]

Managers who subscribe to the Theory X view maintain tight control over workers, provide almost constant supervision, try to motivate through fear, and make decisions in an autocratic fashion, eliciting little or no input from their subordinates. The Theory X style of management focuses on physiological and security needs and virtually ignores the higher needs discussed by Maslow. Computer Science Corporation seemed to adopt the Theory X perspective when it initiated an employee ranking system that ranked 40 percent of employees as below expectations. Employees felt that the system was unfair and the company did not have a good work-life balance. The outcry was so intense that Computer Science Corporation eventually relaxed some of its ratings criteria.[10]

LO 9-4

Investigate various theories of motivation, including Theories X, Y, and Z; equity theory; expectancy theory; and goal-setting theory.

> **Theory X**
> McGregor's traditional view of management whereby it is assumed that workers generally dislike work and must be forced to do their jobs.

Alterra: Creating Customers for Life

Alterra LLC
Founder: David Royce
Founded: 2012, in Provo, Utah
Success: Alterra is the nation's number-one, fastest-growing pest control firm according to *PCT Magazine*.

When founder David Royce founded Alterra LLC, he wanted to create a friendly work environment that would attract the best employees. Royce, who had previous experience in pest control, founded Alterra with a mission to use socially responsible practices to protect families and the natural environment. Although its eco-friendly mission statement would guide the firm, Royce wanted to find a way to motivate and attract top employees by offering Google-style incentives.

To make this a reality, Royce made the decision to invest 10 percent of firm profits into employee incentives. A basketball court, golf simulator, and free beverages are just some of the amenities found in its Utah offices. Employees

also receive larger salaries than they do at competing firms. Alterra believes improving employee happiness will translate into higher productivity. It appears this is happening, with sales managers showing 70 percent improved performance and the company experiencing a 94 percent employee retention rate. Royce's strong leadership led to his election as a finalist for the EY Entrepreneur of the Year® 2015 Award in the Utah Region.[11]

Discussion Questions

1. What perks does Alterra LLC offer its employees? Does this result in higher productivity?
2. Do employee perks primarily motivate intrinsically or extrinsically?
3. Why are companies willing to spend so much money motivating employees? How does employee investment affect the bottom line?

The Theory X view of management does not take into account people's needs for companionship, esteem, and personal growth, whereas Theory Y, the contrasting view of management, does. Managers subscribing to the **Theory Y** view assume that workers like to work and that under proper conditions employees will seek out responsibility in an attempt to satisfy their social, esteem, and self-actualization needs. McGregor describes the assumptions behind Theory Y in the following way:

Theory Y
McGregor's humanistic view of management whereby it is assumed that workers like to work and that under proper conditions employees will seek out responsibility in an attempt to satisfy their social, esteem, and self-actualization needs.

1. The expenditure of physical and mental effort in work is as natural as play or rest.
2. People will exercise self-direction and self-control to achieve objectives to which they are committed.
3. People will commit to objectives when they realize that the achievement of those goals will bring them personal reward.
4. The average person will accept and seek responsibility.
5. Imagination, ingenuity, and creativity can help solve organizational problems, but most organizations do not make adequate use of these characteristics in their employees.
6. Organizations today do not make full use of workers' intellectual potential.[12]

Obviously, managers subscribing to the Theory Y philosophy have a management style very different from managers subscribing to the Theory X philosophy. Theory Y managers maintain less control and supervision, do not use fear as the primary motivator, and are more democratic in decision making, allowing subordinates to participate in the process. Theory Y managers address the high-level needs in Maslow's hierarchy as well as physiological and security needs. For instance, the Virgin Group, which is a conglomerate of various businesses in many industries, allows CEOs and managers to run their locations as they see fit. The company has achieved success by empowering employees to make their own decisions and follow their passions.[13] Today, Theory Y enjoys widespread support and may have displaced Theory X.

Theory Z

Theory Z is a management philosophy that stresses employee participation in all aspects of company decision making. It was first described by William Ouchi in his book *Theory Z—How American Business Can Meet the Japanese Challenge.* Theory Z incorporates many elements associated with the Japanese approach to management, such as trust and intimacy, but Japanese ideas have been adapted for use in the United States. In a Theory Z organization, managers and workers share responsibilities; the management style is participative; and employment is long term and, often, lifelong. Japan has faced a significant period of slowing economic progress and competition from China and other Asian nations. This has led to experts questioning Theory Z, particularly at firms such as Sony and Toyota. On the other hand, Theory Z results in employees feeling organizational ownership. Research has found that such feelings of ownership may produce positive attitudinal and behavioral effects for employees.[14] In a Theory Y organization, managers focus on assumptions about the nature of the worker. The two theories can be seen as complementary. Table 9-4 compares Theory X, Theory Y, and Theory Z.

Theory Z
a management philosophy that stresses employee participation in all aspects of company decision making.

Equity Theory

According to **equity theory,** how much people are willing to contribute to an organization depends on their assessment of the fairness, or equity, of the rewards they will receive in exchange. In a fair situation, a person receives rewards proportional to the contribution he or she makes to the organization. However, in practice, equity is a subjective notion. Each worker regularly develops a personal input-output ratio by taking stock of his or her contribution (inputs) to the organization in time, effort, skills, and experience and assessing the rewards (outputs) offered by the organization in pay, benefits, recognition, and promotions. The worker compares his or her ratio to the input-output ratio of some other person—a "comparison other," who may be a co-worker, a friend working in another organization, or an "average" of several people working in the organization. If the two ratios are close, the individual will feel that he or she is being treated equitably.

equity theory
an assumption that how much people are willing to contribute to an organization depends on their assessment of the fairness, or equity, of the rewards they will receive in exchange.

TABLE 9-4   Comparisons of Theories X, Y, and Z

	Theory X	Theory Y	Theory Z
Countries that use this style	China	United States	Japan
Philosophy	Tight control over workers	Assume workers will seek out responsibility and satisfy social needs	Employee participation in all aspects of company decision making
Job description	Considerable specialization	Less control and supervision; address higher levels of Maslow's hierarchy	Trust and intimacy with workers sharing responsibilities
Control	Tight control	Commitment to objectives with self-direction	Relaxed but required expectations
Worker welfare	Limited concern	Democratic	Commitment to worker's total lives
Responsibility	Managerial	Collaborative	Participative

Let's say you have a high-school education and earn $25,000 a year. When you compare your input-output ratio with that of a co-worker who has a college degree and makes $35,000 a year, you will probably feel that you are being paid fairly. However, if you perceive that your personal input-output ratio is lower than that of your college-educated co-worker, you may feel that you are being treated unfairly and be motivated to seek change. Or if you learn that your co-worker who makes $35,000 has only a high-school diploma, you may feel cheated by your employer. To achieve equity, you could try to increase your outputs by asking for a raise or promotion. You could also try to have your co-worker's inputs increased or his or her outputs decreased. Failing to achieve equity, you may be motivated to look for a job at a different company.

Equity theory might explain why many consumers are upset about CEO compensation. Although the job of the CEO can be incredibly stressful, the fact that they take home millions in compensation, bonuses, and stock options has been questioned. The high unemployment rate coupled with the misconduct that occurred at some large corporations prior to the recession contributed largely to consumer frustration with executive compensation packages. To counter this perception of pay inequality, several corporations have now begun to tie CEO compensation with company performance. If the company performs poorly for the year, then firms such as Goldman Sachs will cut bonuses and other compensation.[15] While lower compensation rates might appease the general public, some companies are worried that lower pay might deter talented individuals from wanting to assume the position of CEO at their firms.

expectancy theory
the assumption that motivation depends not only on how much a person wants something but also on how likely he or she is to get it.

Because almost all the issues involved in equity theory are subjective, they can be problematic. Author David Callahan has argued that feelings of inequity may underlie some unethical or illegal behavior in business. For example, due to employee theft and shoplifting, Walmart experiences billions in inventory losses every year. Some employees may take company resources to restore what they perceive to be equity. Theft of company resources is a major ethical issue, based on a survey by the Ethics Resource Center.[16] Callahan believes that employees who do not feel they are being treated equitably may be motivated to equalize the situation by lying, cheating, or otherwise "improving" their pay, perhaps by stealing.[17] Managers should try to avoid equity problems by ensuring that rewards are distributed on the basis of performance and that all employees clearly understand the basis for their pay and benefits.

Expectancy Theory

Psychologist Victor Vroom described **expectancy theory,** which states that motivation depends not only on how much a person wants something but also on the person's perception of how likely he or she is to get it. A person who wants something and has reason to be optimistic will be strongly motivated. For example, say you really want a promotion. And let's say because

Managers should be transparent with employees about opportunities for advancement. According to expectancy theory, your motivation depends not only on how much you want something, but also on how likely you are to get it.

© Troels Graugaard/Getty Images

you have taken some night classes to improve your skills, and moreover, have just made a large, significant sale, you feel confident that you are qualified and able to handle the new position. Therefore, you are motivated to try to get the promotion. In contrast, if you do not believe you are likely to get what you want, you may not be motivated to try to get it, even though you really want it.

Goal-Setting Theory

Goal-setting theory refers to the impact that setting goals has on performance. According to this philosophy, goals act as motivators to focus employee efforts on achieving certain performance outcomes. Setting goals can positively affect performance because goals help employees direct their efforts and attention toward the outcome, mobilize their efforts, develop consistent behavior patterns, and create strategies to obtain desired outcomes.[18] For instance, if a marketer at McDonald's has the goal to increase awareness about its McCafé drinks by a specific percentage, he could investigate what types of promotion would be most effective at reaching their target market and invest his efforts in the types that would most likely obtain the company's goal.

In 1954, Peter Drucker introduced the term *management by objectives (MBO)* that has since become important to goal-setting theory. MBO refers to the need to develop goals that both managers and employees can understand and agree upon.[19] This requires managers to work with employees to set personal objectives that will be used to further organizational objectives. By linking managerial objectives with personal objectives, employees often feel a greater sense of commitment toward achieving organizational goals. Hewlett-Packard was an early adopter of MBO as a management style.[20]

goal-setting theory
refers to the impact that setting goals has on performance

Strategies for Motivating Employees

Based on the various theories that attempt to explain what motivates employees, businesses have developed several strategies for motivating their employees and boosting morale and productivity. Some of these techniques include behavior modification and job design, as well as the already described employee involvement programs and work teams.

LO 9-5

Describe some of the strategies that managers use to motivate employees.

Behavior Modification

Behavior modification involves changing behavior and encouraging appropriate actions by relating the consequences of behavior to the behavior itself. Behavior modification is the most widely discussed application of *reinforcement theory,* the theory that behavior can be strengthened or weakened through the use of rewards and punishments. The concept of behavior modification was developed by psychologist B. F. Skinner. Skinner found that behavior that is rewarded will tend to be repeated, while behavior that is punished will tend to be eliminated. For example, employees who know that they will receive a bonus such as an expensive restaurant meal for making a sale over $2,000 may be more motivated to make sales. Workers who know they will be punished for being tardy are likely to make a greater effort to get to work on time.

However, the two strategies may not be equally effective. Punishing unacceptable behavior may provide quick results but may lead to undesirable long-term side effects, such as employee dissatisfaction and increased turnover. In general, rewarding appropriate behavior is a more effective way to modify behavior.

behavior modification
changing behavior and encouraging appropriate actions by relating the consequences of behavior to the behavior itself.

Job Design

Herzberg identified the job itself as a motivational factor. Managers have several strategies that they can use to design jobs to help improve employee motivation. These include job rotation, job enlargement, job enrichment, and flexible scheduling strategies.

job rotation
movement of employees from one job to another in an effort to relieve the boredom often associated with job specialization.

Job Rotation.   Job rotation allows employees to move from one job to another in an effort to relieve the boredom that is often associated with job specialization. Businesses often turn to specialization in hopes of increasing productivity, but there is a negative side effect to this type of job design: Employees become bored and dissatisfied, and productivity declines. Job rotation reduces this boredom by allowing workers to undertake a greater variety of tasks and by giving them the opportunity to learn new skills. With job rotation, an employee spends a specified amount of time performing one job and then moves on to another, different job. The worker eventually returns to the initial job and begins the cycle again.

Job rotation is a good idea, but it has one major drawback. Because employees may eventually become bored with all the jobs in the cycle, job rotation does not totally eliminate the problem of boredom. Job rotation is extremely useful, however, in situations where a person is being trained for a position that requires an understanding of various units in an organization. Accounting firm PricewaterhouseCoopers believes in the benefits of job rotation. Sometimes this rotation involves rotating an employee to a different job across the world for a short period. This gives employees the chance to see new places as well as learn new skills.[21] Many executive training programs require trainees to spend time learning a variety of specialized jobs. Job rotation is also used to cross-train today's self-directed work teams.

job enlargement
the addition of more tasks to a job instead of treating each task as separate.

Job Enlargement.   Job enlargement adds more tasks to a job instead of treating each task as separate. Like job rotation, job enlargement was developed to overcome the boredom associated with specialization. The rationale behind this strategy is that jobs are more satisfying as the number of tasks performed by an individual increases. Employees sometimes enlarge, or craft, their jobs by noticing what needs to be done and then changing tasks and relationship boundaries to adjust. Individual orientation and motivation shape opportunities to craft new jobs and job relationships. Job enlargement strategies have been more successful in increasing job satisfaction than have job rotation strategies. IBM, AT&T, and Maytag are among the many companies that have used job enlargement to motivate employees.

job enrichment
the incorporation of motivational factors, such as opportunity for achievement, recognition, responsibility, and advancement, into a job.

Job Enrichment.   Job enrichment incorporates motivational factors such as opportunity for achievement, recognition, responsibility, and advancement into a job. It gives workers not only more tasks within the job, but more control and authority over the job. Job enrichment programs enhance a worker's feeling of responsibility and provide opportunities for growth and advancement when the worker is able to take on the more challenging tasks. Hyatt Hotels Corporation and Clif Bar use job enrichment to improve the quality of work life for their employees. The potential benefits of job enrichment are great, but it requires careful planning and execution.

flextime
a program that allows employees to choose their starting and ending times, provided that they are at work during a specified core period.

Flexible Scheduling Strategies.   Many U.S. workers work a traditional 40-hour workweek consisting of five 8-hour days with fixed starting and ending times. Facing problems of poor morale and high absenteeism as well as a diverse workforce with changing needs, many managers have turned to flexible scheduling strategies such as flextime, compressed workweeks, job sharing, part-time work, and telecommuting.

Flextime is a program that allows employees to choose their starting and ending times, as long as they are at work during a specified core period (Figure 9-3). It does

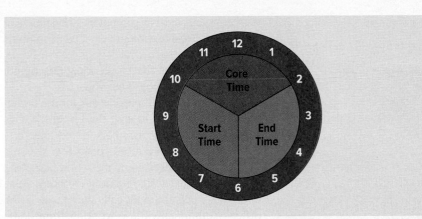

FIGURE 9-3
Flextime, Showing Core
and Flexible Hours

not reduce the total number of hours that employees work; instead, it gives employees more flexibility in choosing which hours they work. A firm may specify that employees must be present from 10:00 a.m. to 3:00 p.m. One employee may choose to come in at 7:00 a.m. and leave at the end of the core time, perhaps to attend classes at a nearby college after work. Another employee, a mother who lives in the suburbs, may come in at 9:00 a.m. in order to have time to drop off her children at a day care center and commute by public transportation to her job. Flextime provides many benefits, including improved ability to recruit and retain workers who wish to balance work and home life. Customers can be better served by allowing more coverage of customers over longer hours, workstations and facilities can be better utilized by staggering employee use, and rush hour traffic may be reduced. In addition, flexible schedules have been associated with an increase in healthy behaviors on the part of employees. More flexible schedules are associated with healthier lifestyle choices such as increased physical activity and healthier sleep habits.[22]

Related to flextime are the scheduling strategies of the compressed workweek and job sharing. The **compressed workweek** is a four-day (or shorter) period in which an employee works 40 hours. Under such a plan, employees typically work 10 hours per day for four days and have a three-day weekend. The compressed workweek reduces the company's operating expenses because its actual hours of operation are reduced. It is also sometimes used by parents who want to have more days off to spend with their families. The U.S. Bureau of Labor Statistics notes that the following career options provide greater flexibility in scheduling: medical transcriptionist, financial manager, nurse, database administrator, accountant, software developer, physical therapist assistant, paralegal, graphic designer, and private investigator.[23]

Job sharing occurs when two people do one job. One person may work from 8:00 a.m. to 12:30 p.m.; the second person comes in at 12:30 p.m. and works until 5:00 p.m. Job sharing gives both people the opportunity to work as well as time to fulfill other obligations, such as parenting or school. With job sharing, the company has the benefit of the skills of two people for one job, often at a lower total cost for salaries and benefits than one person working eight hours a day would be paid.

Two other flexible scheduling strategies attaining wider use include allowing full-time workers to work part time for a certain period and allowing workers to work at home either full- or part-time. Employees at some firms may be permitted to work part-time for several months in order to care for a new baby or an elderly parent or just to slow down for a little while to "recharge their batteries." When the employees return to full-time work, they are usually given a position comparable to their original full-time position. Other firms are allowing employees to telecommute or telework (work at home a few days of the week),

compressed workweek
a four-day (or shorter) period during which an employee works 40 hours.

job sharing
performance of one full-time job by two people on part-time hours.

Working from home is becoming increasingly common. Telecommuting, job sharing, and flextime can be beneficial for employees who cannot work normal work hours.

© Jetta Productions/Getty Images

staying connected via computers, modems, and telephones. Most telecommuters tend to combine going into the office with working from home. In fact, three out of five workers say they do not need to be in the office to be productive.[24]

Although many employees ask for the option of working at home to ease the responsibilities of caring for family members, some have discovered that they are more productive at home without the distractions of the workplace. One study found that telecommuting workers completed 13.5 percent more calls than those in the office. Additionally, those working from home worked longer hours because they did not have to spend time commuting.[25] Other employees, however, have discovered that they are not suited for working at home. For telecommuting to work, it must be a feasible alternative and must not create significant costs for the company.[26] Work-at-home programs can help reduce overhead costs for businesses. For example, some companies used to maintain a surplus of office space but have reduced the surplus through employee telecommuting, "hoteling" (being assigned to a desk through a reservation system), and "hot-desking" (several people using the same desk but at different times).

Companies are turning to flexible work schedules to provide more options to employees who are trying to juggle their work duties with other responsibilities and needs. Preliminary results indicate that flexible scheduling plans increase job satisfaction, which, in turn, leads to increases in productivity. Some recent research, however, has indicated there are potential problems with telecommuting. Some managers are reluctant to adopt the practice because the pace of change in today's workplace is faster than ever, and telecommuters may be left behind or actually cause managers more work in helping them stay abreast of changes. Some employers also worry that telecommuting workers create a security risk by creating more opportunities for computer hackers or equipment thieves. Some employees have found that working outside the office may hurt career advancement opportunities, and some report that instead of helping them balance work and family responsibilities, telecommuting increases the strain by blurring the barriers between the office and home. Co-workers call at all hours, and telecommuters are apt to continue to work when they are not supposed to (after regular business hours or during vacation time).

Importance of Motivational Strategies

Motivation is more than a tool that managers can use to foster employee loyalty and boost productivity. It is a process that affects all the

Businesses have come up with different ways to motivate employees, including rewards such as trophies and plaques to show the company's appreciation.

© ColorBlind Images/Getty Images

Acuity: Insuring Workplace Happiness

With employee turnover at just 1 percent, it is easy to see why *Fortune* magazine rated Acuity as the third best company to work for. The private insurance company Acuity offers a multitude of employee benefits that focus on the well-being and happiness of its workforce. Full-time employees are offered unlimited tuition reimbursement and outstanding 401(k) and medical plans. Additionally, employees can stay healthy by utilizing the onsite fitness center, and many appreciate the compressed work schedules that free up more time to spend with family. As an added bonus, Acuity does not limit the number of paid sick days employees can take if they become ill.

However, Acuity does more than just offer excellent employee perks. Efforts are also made to ensure employees have a say in the company. Aside from a private lunch with an executive, each employee is also encouraged to attend town hall meetings where he or she can engage with upper management. These efforts to empower and motivate employees have not gone unnoticed. For the second year in a row, Acuity has won the "We Love Our Workplace" video contest. The short videos feature passionate employees that focus on the empowerment and positive company culture Acuity fosters. This is hardly the enthusiasm one would expect from employees working for an insurance company, and it demonstrates how well an employee-centered culture can lead to a more inspired and motivated workforce.[27]

Discussion Questions

1. How does Acuity cultivate a positive work environment?
2. How do employee perks help Acuity motivate its workforce?
3. What are some advantages of an employee-centered work culture?

relationships within an organization and influences many areas such as pay, promotion, job design, training opportunities, and reporting relationships. Employees are motivated by the nature of the relationships they have with their supervisors, by the nature of their jobs, and by characteristics of the organization. Table 9-5 shows companies with

TABLE 9-5 Companies with Excellent Motivational Strategies

Company	Motivational Strategies
3M	Gives employees 15–20 percent of their time to pursue on projects
Google	Perks include a massage every other week, free gourmet lunches, tuition reimbursement, a volleyball court, and time to work on own projects
Whole Foods	Employees receive 20 percent discounts on company products, the opportunity to gain stock options, and the ability to make major decisions in small teams
Patagonia	Provides areas for yoga and aerobics, in-house child care services, organic food in its café, and opportunities to go surfing during the day
The Container Store	Provides more than 260 hours of employee training and hosts "We Love Our Employees" Day
Southwest Airlines	Gives employees permission to interact with passengers as they see fit, provides free or discounted flights, and hosts the "Adopt-a-Pilot" program to connect pilots with students across the nation
Nike	Offers tuition assistance, product discounts, onsite fitness centers, and the ability for employees to give insights on how to improve the firm
Apple	Creates a fast-paced, innovative work environment where employees are encouraged to debate ideas
Marriott	Offers discounts at hotels across the world as well as free hotel stays and travel opportunities for employees with exceptional service
Zappos	Creates a fun, zany work environment for employees and empowers them to take as much time as needed to answer customer concerns

excellent motivational strategies, along with the types of strategies they use to motivate employees. Even the economic environment can change an employee's motivation. In a slow growth or recession economy, sales can flatten or decrease and morale can drop because of the need to cut jobs. The firm may have to work harder to keep good employees and to motivate all employees to work to overcome obstacles. In good economic times, employees may be more demanding and be on the lookout for better opportunities. New rewards or incentives may help motivate workers in such economies. Motivation tools, then, must be varied as well. Managers can further nurture motivation by being honest, supportive, empathic, accessible, fair, and open. Motivating employees to increase satisfaction and productivity is an important concern for organizations seeking to remain competitive in the global marketplace.

So You Think You May Be Good at Motivating a Workforce

If you are good at mediation, smoothing conflict, and have a good understanding of motivation and human relations theories, then you might be a good leader, human resource manager, or training expert. Most organizations, especially as they grow, will need to implement human relations programs. These are necessary to teach employees about sensitivity to other cultures, religions, and beliefs, as well as for teaching the workforce about the organization so that they understand how they fit in the larger picture. Employees need to appreciate the benefits of working together to make the firm run smoothly, and they also need to understand how their contributions help the firm. To stay motivated, most employees need to feel like what they do each day contributes something of value to the firm. Disclosing information and including employees in decision-making processes will also help employees feel valuable and wanted within the firm.

There are many different ways employers can reward and encourage employees. However, employers must be careful when considering what kinds of incentives to use. Different cultures value different kinds of incentives more highly than others. For example, a Japanese worker would probably not like it if she were singled out from the group and given a large cash bonus as a reward for her work. Japanese workers tend to be more group oriented, and therefore, anything that singles out individuals would not be an effective way of rewarding and motivating. American workers, on the other hand, are very individualistic, and a raise and public praise might be more effective. However, what might motivate a younger employee (bonuses, raises, and perks) may not be the same as what motivates a more seasoned, experienced, and financially successful employee (recognition, opportunity for greater influence, and increased training). Motivation is not an easy thing to understand, especially as firms become more global and more diverse.

Another important part of motivation is enjoying where you work and your career opportunities. Here is a list of the best places to do business and start careers in the United States, according to *Forbes* magazine. Chances are, workers who live in these places have encountered fewer frustrations than those places at the bottom of the list and, therefore, would probably be more content with where they work.[28]

Best Places for Businesses and Careers

Rank	Metro Area	Job Growth Rank	Population
1.	Denver, Colorado	16	2,761,000
2.	Raleigh, North Carolina	17	1,245,800
3.	Portland, Oregon	41	2,352,700
4.	Provo, Utah	3	572,900
5.	Atlanta, Georgia	47	5,626,000
6.	Seattle, Washington	7	2,844,200
7.	Salt Lake City, Utah	23	1,155,200
8.	Indianapolis, Indiana	45	1,973,600
9.	Warren, Michigan	13	2,532,500
10.	Fort Collins, Colorado	21	325,300

Source: "Best Places for Businesses and Careers," Forbes, 2015, http://www.forbes.com/best-places-for-business/list/#tab:overall (accessed March 24, 2016).

Review Your Understanding

Define *human relations* and determine why its study is important.

Human relations is the study of the behavior of individuals and groups in organizational settings. Its focus is what motivates employees to perform on the job. Human relations is important because businesses need to understand how to motivate their increasingly diverse employees to be more effective, boost workplace morale, and maximize employees' productivity and creativity.

Summarize early studies that laid the groundwork for understanding employee motivation.

Time and motion studies by Frederick Taylor and others helped them analyze how employees perform specific work tasks in an effort to improve their productivity. Taylor and the early practitioners of the classical theory of motivation felt that money and job security were the primary motivators of employees. However, the Hawthorne studies revealed that human factors also influence workers' behavior.

Compare and contrast the human-relations theories of Abraham Maslow and Frederick Herzberg.

Abraham Maslow defined five basic needs of all people and arranged them in the order in which they must be satisfied: physiological, security, social, esteem, and self-actualization. Frederick Herzberg divided characteristics of the job into hygiene factors and motivational factors. Hygiene factors relate to the work environment and must be present for employees to remain in a job. Motivational factors—recognition, responsibility, and advancement—relate to the work itself. They encourage employees to be productive. Herzberg's hygiene factors can be compared to Maslow's physiological and security needs; motivational factors may include Maslow's social, esteem, and self-actualization needs.

Investigate various theories of motivation, including Theories X, Y, and Z; equity theory; expectancy theory; and goal-setting theory.

Douglas McGregor contrasted two views of management: Theory X (traditional) suggests workers dislike work, while Theory Y (humanistic) suggests that workers not only like work but seek out responsibility to satisfy their higher-order needs. Theory Z stresses employee participation in all aspects of company decision making, often through participative management programs and self-directed work teams. According to equity theory, how much people are willing to contribute to an organization depends on their assessment of the fairness, or equity, of the rewards they will receive in exchange. Expectancy theory states that motivation depends not only on how much a person wants something but also on the person's perception of how likely he or she is to get it. Goal-setting theory refers to the impact that setting goals has on performance.

Describe some of the strategies that managers use to motivate employees.

Strategies for motivating workers include behavior modification (changing behavior and encouraging appropriate actions by relating the consequences of behavior to the behavior itself) and job design. Among the job design strategies businesses use are job rotation (allowing employees to move from one job to another to try to relieve the boredom associated with job specialization), job enlargement (adding tasks to a job instead of treating each task as a separate job), job enrichment (incorporating motivational factors into a job situation), and flexible scheduling strategies (flextime, compressed workweeks, job sharing, part-time work, and telecommuting).

Critique a business's program for motivating its sales force.

Using the information presented in the chapter, you should be able to analyze and defend Eagle Pharmaceutical's motivation program in the "Solve the Dilemma" feature at the end of this chapter, including the motivation theories the firm is applying to boost morale and productivity.

Revisit the World of Business

I. What are some of the ways Marriott motivates its employees?

2. Why is it important to recognize and reward high-performing employees?

3. What types of extrinsic recognition does Marriot provide for its employees?

Learn the Terms

behavior modification 279	human relations 268	motivation 268
classical theory of motivation 271	hygiene factors 274	motivational factors 275
compressed workweek 281	intrinsic rewards 269	physiological needs 273
equity theory 277	job enlargement 280	security needs 273
esteem needs 274	job enrichment 280	self-actualization needs 274
expectancy theory 278	job rotation 280	social needs 273
extrinsic rewards 269	job sharing 281	Theory X 275
flextime 280	Maslow's hierarchy 273	Theory Y 276
goal-setting theory 279	morale 269	Theory Z 277

Check Your Progress

1. Why do managers need to understand the needs of their employees?

2. Describe the motivation process.

3. What was the goal of the Hawthorne studies? What was the outcome of those studies?

4. Explain Maslow's hierarchy of needs. What does it tell us about employee motivation?

5. What are Herzberg's hygiene and motivational factors? How can managers use them to motivate workers?

6. Contrast the assumptions of Theory X and Theory Y. Why has Theory Y replaced Theory X in management today?

7. What is Theory Z? How can businesses apply Theory Z to the workplace?

8. Identify and describe four job-design strategies.

9. Name and describe some flexible scheduling strategies. How can flexible schedules help motivate workers?

10. Why are motivational strategies important to both employees and employers?

Get Involved

1. Consider a person who is homeless: How would he or she be motivated and what actions would that person take? Use the motivation process to explain. Which of the needs in Maslow's hierarchy are likely to be most important? Least important?

2. View the video *Cheaper by the Dozen* (1950) and report on how the Gilbreths tried to incorporate their passion for efficiency into their family life.

3. What events and trends in society, technology, and economics do you think will shape human relations management theory in the future?

Build Your Skills

Motivating

Background

Do you think that, if employers could make work more like play, employees would be as enthusiastic about their jobs as they are about what they do in their leisure time? Let's see where this idea might take us.

Task

After reading the "Characteristics of PLAY," place a √ in column one for those characteristics you have experienced in your leisure time activities. Likewise, check column three for those "Characteristics of WORK" you have experienced in any of the jobs you've held.

All That Apply	Characteristics of PLAY	All That Apply	Characteristics of WORK
	1. New games can be played on different days.		1. Job enrichment, job enlargement, or job rotation.
	2. Flexible duration of play.		2. Job sharing.
	3. Flexible time of when to play.		3. Flextime, telecommuting.
	4. Opportunity to express oneself.		4. Encourage and implement employee suggestions.
	5. Opportunity to use one's talents.		5. Assignment of challenging projects.
	6. Skillful play brings applause, praise, and recognition from spectators.		6. Employee-of-the-month awards, press releases, employee newsletter announcements.
	7. Healthy competition, rivalry, and challenge exist.		7. Production goals with competition to see which team does best.
	8. Opportunity for social interaction.		8. Employee softball or bowling teams.
	9. Mechanisms for scoring one's performance are available (feedback).		9. Profit sharing; peer performance appraisals.
	10. Rules ensure basic fairness and justice.		10. Use tactful and consistent discipline.

Discussion Questions

1. What prevents managers from making work more like play?

2. Are these forces real or imagined?

3. What would be the likely (positive and negative) results of making work more like play?

4. Could others in the organization accept such creative behaviors?

Solve the Dilemma

Motivating to Win

Eagle Pharmaceutical has long been recognized for its innovative techniques for motivating its salesforce. It features the salesperson who has been the most successful during the previous quarter in the company newsletter, "Touchdown." The salesperson also receives a football jersey, a plaque, and $1,000 worth of Eagle stock. Eagle's "Superbowl Club" is for employees who reach or exceed their sales goal, and a "Heisman Award," which includes a trip to the Caribbean, is given annually to the top 20 salespeople in terms of goal achievement.

Eagle employs a video conference hookup between the honored salesperson and four regional sales managers to capture some of the successful tactics and strategies the winning

LO 9-6

Critique a business's program for motivating its sales force.

salesperson uses to succeed. The managers summarize these ideas and pass them along to the salespeople they manage. Sales managers feel strongly that programs such as this are important and that, by sharing strategies and tactics with one another, they can be a successful team.

Discussion Questions

I. Which motivational theories are in use at Eagle?

2. What is the value of getting employees to compete against a goal instead of against one another?

3. Put yourself in the shoes of one of the four regional sales managers and argue against potential cutbacks to the motivational program.

Build Your Business Plan

Motivating the Workforce

As you determine the size of your workforce, you are going to face the reality that you cannot provide the level of financial compensation that you would like to your employees, especially when you are starting your business.

Many employees are motivated by other things than money. Knowing that they are appreciated and doing a good job can bring great satisfaction to employees. Known as "stroking," it can provide employees with internal gratification that can be valued even more than financial incentives. Listening to

your employees' suggestions, involving them in discussions about future growth, and valuing their input can go a long way toward building loyal employees and reducing employee turnover.

Think about what you could do in your business to motivate your employees without spending much money. Maybe you will have lunch brought in once a week or offer tickets to a local sporting event to the employee with the most sales. Whatever you elect to do, you must be consistent and fair with all your employees.

See for Yourself Videocase

The Container Store's Secret to Success: Employee Satisfaction

Can you form a successful company by selling containers, boxes, and other storage products? The Container Store has shown that the answer is yes. With more than 10,000 products available, The Container Store sells items such as hanging bins, drawers, trash cans, and other items to help make a hectic life more organized. While there might have been skeptics in the beginning, particularly as the firm started out in a small 1,600 square-foot store, the idea quickly caught on with consumers.

"Word of mouth spread incredibly. It was just the oddest collection of merchandising anybody had ever seen to organize your home and to organize your life. A week into it, we knew we had something," co-founder and CEO Kip Tindell said.

Yet in addition to its unusual product mix, The Container Store is also unique for its dedication to employees. The retail

world can be difficult for employees because of high turnover, different hours every week, lower benefits, and constant interaction with people. The turnover rate in the retail industry is about 100 percent. This increases training costs, which can cause companies to decrease the amount of training offered.

This trend is reversed at The Container Store. First-year full-time employees receive 263 hours of training, much higher than the industry average of seven hours. Employees receive 50 percent more pay than at other retail establishments. Employee turnover at The Container Store is a low 10 percent. For more than a decade, The Container Store has been elected as one of the top 100 companies to work for by *Fortune* magazine.

Yet, the satisfaction that employees feel toward the company is not solely a result of higher pay. According to Frederick Herzberg's two-factor theory, good workplace conditions can prevent dissatisfaction but do not motivate the employee to go above and beyond what is required of them. As CEO of the company, Kip Tindell realizes that the amount of time and effort an employee gives to the company will determine productivity.

"The first 25 percent for any employee is mandatory. If they don't do that, they're going to get fired. But the next 75 percent of an employee's productivity for any business in the world, I believe, is more or less voluntary. You do more or less of it depending upon how you feel about your boss and your product and your company."

Therefore, to enhance productivity, the firm has made employee satisfaction a priority. Employees come first, followed by customers and then shareholders. One of the ways that The Container Store motivates its employees is by creating an open communication culture. Employees are encouraged to approach their managers on any topic. This causes employees to feel as if the organization cares about them enough to take their concerns seriously. The Container Store also holds several events to show their appreciation of employee efforts. For instance, every February 14, The Container Store holds its "We Love Our Employees" day. At one of the events, the company announced the establishment of an emergency fund for employees. The company contributed $100,000 for unexpected costs that employees may find themselves having to pay for due to natural disasters, terrorist attacks, or significant medical issues.

Employees also receive many perks for working at The Container Store, and even part-time employees are eligible for health care benefits. Because employees take precedence

at The Container Store, the company bases its decisions on what is best for employees even during hard times. During the recession, for instance, The Container Store refused to lay off employees. In addition to benefits, employees have access to all company data, including financial reports.

Does this mean that The Container Store ignores its customers for the sake of its employees? The high-quality customer service that The Container Store offers suggests just the opposite. In fact, the extensive employee training and the company's values demonstrate its high commitment to customer satisfaction. According to Tindell, the key to great customer service, however, is highly motivated employees.

"We believe that if you take better care of your employees than anybody else, they'll take better care of the customer than anybody else, and if those two guys are ecstatic, ironically enough, your shareholder's going to be ecstatic too."[29]

Discussion Questions

1. Name some of the hygiene factors at The Container Store.

2. Name some of the ways that The Container Store motivates its employees.

3. Do you believe Tindell's statement that highly satisfied employees will lead to highly satisfied customers and shareholders?

You can find the related video in the Video Library in Connect. Ask your instructor how you can access Connect.

Team Exercise

Form groups and outline a compensation package that you would consider ideal in motivating an employee, recognizing performance, and assisting the company in attaining its cost-to-performance objectives. Think about the impact of intrinsic and extrinsic motivation and recognition. How can flexible scheduling strategies be used effectively to motivate employees? Report your compensation package to the class.

Endnotes

1. Leigh Gallagher, "Why Employees Love Marriott," *Fortune*, March 5, 2015, pp. 113–118; Marriott, "Our Story," http://www.marriott.com/about/culture-and-values/history.mi (accessed September 10, 2015); Marriott, "Marriott International Again Named One of the 'Best Places to Launch a Career' by Businessweek," September 8, 2009, http://news.marriott.com/2009/09/marriott-international-again-named-one-of-the-best-places-to-launch-a-career-by-businessweek.html (accessed September 10, 2015).

2. Dan Heath and Chip Heath, "Business Advice from Van Halen," *Fast Company*, March 1, 2010, www.fastcompany.com/1550881/business-advice-van-halen (accessed March 24, 2016).

3. Society for Human Resource Management, "Total Financial Impact of Employee Absences in the U.S.," October 2014, http://www.shrm.org/Research/SurveyFindings/Documents/Kronos_US_Executive_Summary_Final.pdf (accessed March 22, 2016).

4. Brad Stone, "Costco CEO Craig Jelinek Leads the Cheapest, Happiest Company in the World," *Bloomberg Businessweek,* June 6, 2013, http://www.bloomberg.com/bw/articles/2013-06-06/costco-ceo-craig-jelinek-leads-the-cheapest-happiest-company-in-the-world (accessed March 24, 2016); Rebecca Hiscott, "7 Companies That Aren't Waiting for Congress to Raise the Minimum Wage," *The Huffington Post,* June 26, 2014, http://www.huffingtonpost.com/2014/06/26/companies-minimum-wage_n_5530835.html (accessed March 24, 2016).

5. Equilar Inc., "100 Largest Company CEOs," http://www.equilar.com/reports/17-100-largest-company-CEOs-2015.html (accessed March 22, 2016).

6. Alana Semuels, "A New Business Strategy: Treating Employees Well," *The Atlantic,* November 26, 2014, http://www.theatlantic.com/business/archive/2014/11/a-new-business-strategy-treating-employees-well/383192/ (accessed December 5, 2015); Vermont Employee Ownership Center, "Employee-Owned Company Profile: King Arthur Flour," http://www.veoc.org/kingarthurflour (accessed December 16, 2015); King Arthur Flour,. "Employees," http://www.kingarthurflour.com/about/employee-commitment.html (accessed December 16, 2015); B Lab, "Why B Corporations Matter," 2015, https://www.bcorporation.net/what-are-b-corps/why-b-corps-matter (accessed December 16, 2015); King Arthur Flour, "Our Commitment to the Environment," http://www.kingarthurflour.com/about/environmental-commitment.html (accessed December 16, 2015).

7. "25 Well-Paying Jobs That Most People Overlook (and Why)," *Business Pundit,* www.businesspundit.com/25-well-paying-jobs-that-most-people-overlook-and-why/ (accessed March 22, 2016); "Gastroenterologist Salary (United States)," PayScale, http://www.payscale.com/research/US/Job=Gastroenterologist/Salary (accessed March 22, 2016).

8. "At Hilton, a Team Commitment to Creating Exceptional Hospitality Experiences," *Fortune,* March 15, 2016, p. 38.

9. Douglas McGregor, *The Human Side of Enterprise* (New York: McGraw-Hill, 1960), pp. 33–34.

10. Thomas C. Frohlich, Michael B. Sauter, and Sam Stebbins, "The 12 Worst Companies to Work for," *MSN Money,* August 19, 2015, http://www.msn.com/en-us/money/inside-the-ticker/the-12-worst-companies-to-work-for/ar-AAcIMbT#page=3 (accessed March 24, 2016); Jill R. Aitoro, "CSC Relaxes Bell-Curve Ratings for Employee Performance,"*Washington Business Journal,* January 30, 2015, http://www.bizjournals.com/washington/blog/fedbiz_daily/2015/01/csc-relaxes-bell-curve-ratings-for-employee.html (accessed March 24, 2016).

11. "Alterra Pest Control Announces CEO David Royce EY Entrepreneur of the Year™ 2015 Award Finalist in Utah Region," *PRWeb,* April 14, 2015, http://www.prweb.com/releases/2015/04/prweb12644993.htm (accessed September 16, 2015); Rachel Feintzeig, "Google-Style Office Perks Go Mainstream," *The Wall Street Journal,* August 4, 2015,http://www.wsj.com/articles/google-style-office-perks-go-mainstream-1438680780 (accessed September 16, 2015); Michal Addady, "Why this pest control Company Spends So Much Time on Google-esque Perks," *Fortune,* August 5,

2015, http://fortune.com/tag/alterra-llc/ (accessed September 16, 2015).

12. McGregor, *The Human Side of Enterprise,* pp. 33–34.

13. Richard Branson, "Richard Branson on Giving Your Employees Freedom," *Entrepreneur,* December 31, 2012, www.entrepreneur.com/article/225272 (accessed April 24, 2014); Oscar Raymundo, "Richard Branson: Compaines Should Put Employees First," *Inc.,* October 28, 2014, http://www.inc.com/oscar-raymundo/richard-branson-companies-should-put-employees-first.html (accessed March 24, 2016).

14. Jon L. Pierce, Tatiana Kostova, and Kurt T. Kirks, "Toward a Theory of Psychological Ownership in Organizations, *Academy of Management Review,* 26, no. 2 (2001), p. 298.

15. Brad Stone, "Goldman, Morgan Stanley CEOs See 2015 Pay Cuts," *CNBC,* January 23, 2016, http://www.cnbc.com/2016/01/23/goldman-morgan-stanley-ceos-see-2015-pay-cuts.html (accessed March 24, 2016).

16. Ethics Resource Center, *2011 National Business Ethics Survey: Ethics in Transition* (Arlington, VA: Ethics Resource Center, 2012), p. 16.

17. Archie Carroll, "Carroll: Do We Live in a Cheating Culture?" *Athens Banner-Herald,* February 21, 2004, www.onlineathens.com/stories/022204/bus_20040222028.shtml (accessed March 24, 2016).

18. Edwin A. Locke, K. M. Shaw, and Gary P. Latham, "Goal Setting and Task Performance: 1969–1980," *Psychological Bulletin* 90 (1981), pp. 125–152.

19. Peter Drucker, *The Practice of Management* (New York: Harper & Row, 1954).

20. "Management by Objectives," *The Economist,* October 21, 2009, http://www.economist.com/node/14299761 (accessed March 24, 2016).

21. Lauren Weber and Leslie Kwoh, "Co-Workers Change Places," *The Wall Street Journal,* February 21, 2012, http://www.wsj.com/articles/SB10001424052970204059804577229123891255472 (accessed March 24, 2016); PricewaterhouseCoopers LLP, "Coaching and Professional Development," 2015, http://www.pwc.com/us/en/about-us/pwc-professional-development.jhtml (accessed March 24, 2016).

22. Robert Preidt, "Workplace Flexibility Can Boost Healthy Behaviors," *ABC News,* March 23, 2008, http://abcnews.go.com/Health/Healthday/story?id=4509753 (accessed March 24, 2016).

23. My Guides USA.com, "Which Jobs Offer Flexible Work Schedules?" http://jobs.myguidesusa.com/answers-to-myquestions/which-jobs-offer-flexible-workschedules?/ (accessed March 24, 2016).

24. Tara Gravel, "Empowering the Mobile Workforce," Special Advertising Section, *Bloomberg Businessweek,* 2014, http://www.businessweek.com/adsections/2014/pdf/140811_HR2.pdf (accessed March 18, 2015).

25. Intuit, "New Study Finds Telecommuting Increases Team Productivity," March 31, 2015, http://quickbase.intuit.com/

blog/new-study-finds-telecommuting-increases-team-productivity.

26. Dori Meinert, "Make Telecommuting Pay Off," Society for Human Resource Management, June 1, 2011, www.shrm.org/Publications/hrmagazine/EditorialContent/2011/0611/Pages/0611meinert.aspx (accessed March 24, 2016).

27. Claire Zillman, "Dream Job . . . Insurance Salesman?" *Fortune,* March 5, 2015, p. 123; "100 Best Companies to Work For: Acuity," *Fortune,* 2015, http://fortune.com/best-companies/acuity-3/ (accessed December 22, 2015); Great Place to Work, "ACUITY Wins the "We ♥ Our Workplace" Video Contest," 2015, http://www.greatplacetowork.com/2015-video-contest-enter (accessed December 22, 2015).

28. "Best Places for Businesses and Careers," *Forbes,* 2015, http://www.forbes.com/best-places-for-business/list/#tab:overall (accessed March 24, 2016).

29. "100 Best Companies to Work for 2009," *Fortune,* http://archive.fortune.com/magazines/fortune/bestcompanies/2009/snapshots/32.html (accessed August 5, 2016); "The Container Store: Employee Centric Retailer," UNM Daniels Fund Business Ethics Initiative, https://danielsethics.mgt.unm.edu/pdf/Container%20Store%20Case.pdf (accessed August 5, 2016); Fortune 100 Best Companies to Work For, "The Container Store," *CNN Money,* 2013, http://archive.fortune.com/magazines/fortune/best-companies/2013/snapshots/16.html (accessed August 5, 2016); The Container Store, "Employee First Culture," http://standfor.containerstore.com/putting-our-employees-first/ (accessed August 5, 2016); Bureau of Labor Statistics, "How to Become a Retail Sales Worker," January 8, 2014, http://www.bls.gov/ooh/Sales/Retail-sales-workers.htm (accessed August 5, 2016); The Container Store, "Communication IS Leadership," http://standfor.containerstore.com/our-foundation-principles/communication-is-leadership/ (accessed August 5, 2016); The Container Store, "Happy National We Love Our Employees Day," February 13, 2014, http://standfor.containerstore.com/happy-national-we-love-our-employees-day/ (accessed August 5, 2016); The Container Store, "Careers" http://www.containerstore.com/careers/index.html (accessed August 5, 2016); Maria Halkias, "The Container Store Set Up an Emergency Fund for Its Employee," *Dallas News,* February 14, 2014, http://bizbeatblog.dallasnews.com/2014/02/the-container-store-set-up-an-emergency-fund-for-its-employees.html/ (accessed August 5, 2016).

© Andrey_Popov/Shutterstock

10 Managing Human Resources

Chapter Outline

Learning Objectives

After reading this chapter, you will be able to:

LO 10-1 Define *human resources management* and explain its significance.

LO 10-2 Summarize the processes of recruiting and selecting human resources for a company.

LO 10-3 Discuss how workers are trained and their performance appraised.

LO 10-4 Identify the types of turnover companies may experience and explain why turnover is an important issue.

LO 10-5 Specify the various ways a worker may be compensated.

LO 10-6 Discuss some of the issues associated with unionized employees, including collective bargaining and dispute resolution.

LO 10-7 Describe the importance of diversity in the workforce.

LO 10-8 Assess an organization's efforts to reduce its workforce size and manage the resulting effects.

Enter the World of Business ⊖————————————

Higher Sophistication in Hiring

Face-to-face job interviews may be a thing of the past as some companies turn to a new generation of personality tests and data analytics for guidance on hiring prospective employees. The tests predict the individual beliefs and behavioral tendencies of the applicant, data which are then used to find those most likely to succeed at the company. Companies like Bridgewater Associates, a hedge fund, even use the personality tests on its current 1,400 employees to help select who should receive promotions or be fired.

Bridgewater Associates is not alone—many believe data are key to making successful hires. Yet relying too much on data also introduces a problem: possible discrimination—especially against those with disabilities. Despite laws prohibiting discrimination, hiring based on data alone—often coming from multiple choice or true-false answers—may not account for the unique challenges individuals face, including those with disabilities.

However, even with these potential limitations, companies such as Facebook, Progressive, and others are partnering with Guild, a tech recruiting company that specializes in more automated hiring processes utilizing data science and predictive analytics. Guild also uses data mining technology to find talented individuals who may not have formal qualifications but still have valuable skill sets that make them desirable. It is not clear how much reliance should be placed on the cognitive and behavioral tests that make up the majority of the data thought to optimize hiring decisions. Because of a lack of experience with the technology and the potential pitfalls of using data analytics, many companies utilize a hybrid of traditional HR hiring strategies, such as in-person interviews, with relatively new personality and behavioral tests.[1]

Introduction

If a business is to achieve success, it must have sufficient numbers of employees who are qualified and motivated to perform the required duties. Thus, managing the quantity (from hiring to firing) and quality (through training, compensating, and so on) of employees is an important business function. Meeting the challenge of managing increasingly diverse human resources effectively can give a company a competitive edge in a global marketplace.

This chapter focuses on the quantity and quality of human resources. First we look at how human resources managers plan for, recruit, and select qualified employees. Next we look at training, appraising, and compensating employees, aspects of human resources management designed to retain valued employees. Along the way, we'll also consider the challenges of managing unionized employees and workplace diversity.

human resources management (HRM) all the activities involved in determining an organization's human resources needs, as well as acquiring, training, and compensating people to fill those needs.

LO 10-1

Define *human resources management* and explain its significance.

The Nature of Human Resources Management

In "The Dynamics of Business and Economics" chapter, human resources was defined as labor, the physical and mental abilities that people use to produce goods and services. **Human resources management (HRM)** refers to all the activities involved in determining an organization's human resources needs, as well as acquiring, training, and compensating people to fill those needs. Human resources managers are concerned with maximizing the satisfaction of employees and motivating them to meet organizational objectives productively. In some companies, this function is called personnel management.

HRM has increased in importance over the past few decades, in part because managers have developed a better understanding of human relations through the work of Maslow, Herzberg, and others. How employees are treated is also important to consumers. Approximately 85 percent of consumers say that a company's corporate social responsibility (CSR) practices, including their treatment of employees, play a significant role in deciding where to take their business.[2] Moreover, the human resources themselves are changing. Employees today are concerned not only about how much a job pays; they are concerned also with job satisfaction, personal performance, recreation, benefits, the work environment, and their opportunities for advancement. Today's workforce includes significantly more women, African Americans, Hispanics, and other minorities, as well as disabled and older workers than in the past. Human resources managers must be aware of these changes and leverage them to increase the productivity of their employees. Every manager practices some of the functions of human resources management at all times.

Today's organizations are more diverse, with a greater range of women, minorities, and older workers.

© Digital Vision/Getty Images

Planning for Human Resources Needs

When planning and developing strategies for reaching the organization's overall objectives, a company must consider whether it will have the human resources necessary to carry out its plans. After determining how many employees and what skills are needed to satisfy the overall plans, the human resources department (which may range from the owner in a small business to hundreds of people in a large corporation) ascertains how many employees the company currently has and how many will be

PowerToFly: Hiring Women in Tech Worldwide

PowerToFly

Founders: Milena Berry and Katharine Zaleski

Founded: 2014, in New York City

Success: Less than a year in operation, the company has been able to raise $6.5 million in funding.

Most new mothers spend weeks on maternity leave after having a child. While parents often appreciate spending time with their new baby, some struggle with leaving work for such an extended period of time.

Recognizing that stay-at-home moms represent a valuable part of the workforce, online marketplace PowerToFly connects eager-to-work moms—the majority who live outside of the United States—with U.S. companies searching for new talent. PowerToFly hopes its platform will empower women, especially those commonly excluded from traditional job markets.

It is not just women who are benefiting—an increasing number of companies realize they can gain a competitive advantage from having remote employees. Companies can utilize remote employees located across the globe, ensuring around-the-clock continuous operation. However, while virtual work teams provide benefits, some question whether too much technology will negatively affect employee interactions and organizational culture. While opinions vary, the president of the software company Citrix claims that remote employees actually simplify human resource management and lead to a more flexible and productive workforce.[3]

Discussion Questions

1. How does PowerToFly address the issue of mothers who want to stay at home with their children but who also desire to work?
2. What are some benefits of virtual work teams? What are some disadvantages?
3. Citrix claims that remote employees simplify human resources management. Explain what you think it means by that.

---

retiring or otherwise leaving the organization during the planning period. With this information, the human resources manager can then forecast how many more employees the company will need to hire and what qualifications they must have or determine if layoffs are required to meet demand more efficiently. HRM planning also requires forecasting the availability of people in the workforce who will have the necessary qualifications to meet the organization's future needs. The human resources manager then develops a strategy for satisfying the organization's human resources needs. As organizations strive to increase efficiency through outsourcing, automation, or learning to effectively use temporary workers, hiring needs can change dramatically.

Next, managers analyze the jobs within the organization so that they can match the human resources to the available assignments. **Job analysis** determines, through observation and study, pertinent information about a job—the specific tasks that comprise it; the knowledge, skills, and abilities necessary to perform it; and the environment in which it will be performed. Managers use the information obtained through a job analysis to develop job descriptions and job specifications.

A **job description** is a formal, written explanation of a specific job that usually includes job title, tasks to be performed (for instance, waiting on customers), relationship with other jobs, physical and mental skills required (such as lifting heavy boxes or calculating data), duties, responsibilities, and working conditions. Job seekers might turn to online websites or databases to help find job descriptions for specific occupations. For instance, the Occupational Information Network has an online database with hundreds of occupational descriptors. These descriptors describe the skills, knowledge, and education needed to fulfill a particular occupation (e.g., human resources).[4] A **job specification** describes the qualifications necessary for a specific job, in terms of education (some jobs require a college degree), experience, personal characteristics (ads frequently request outgoing, hardworking persons), and physical characteristics.

job analysis
the determination, through observation and study, of pertinent information about a job—including specific tasks and necessary abilities, knowledge, and skills.

job description
a formal, written explanation of a specific job, usually including job title, tasks, relationship with other jobs, physical and mental skills required, duties, responsibilities, and working conditions.

job specification
a description of the qualifications necessary for a specific job, in terms of education, experience, and personal and physical characteristics.

Both the job description and job specification are used to develop recruiting materials such as newspapers, trade publications, and online advertisements.

Recruiting and Selecting New Employees

LO 10-2

Summarize the processes of recruiting and selecting human resources for a company.

After forecasting the firm's human resources needs and comparing them to existing human resources, the human resources manager should have a general idea of how many new employees the firm needs to hire. With the aid of job analyses, management can then recruit and select employees who are qualified to fill specific job openings.

Recruiting

recruiting
forming a pool of qualified applicants from which management can select employees.

Recruiting means forming a pool of qualified applicants from which management can select employees. There are two sources from which to develop this pool of applicants—internal and external.

Internal sources of applicants include the organization's current employees. Many firms have a policy of giving first consideration to their own employees—or promoting from within. The cost of hiring current employees to fill job openings is inexpensive when compared with the cost of hiring from external sources, and it is good for employee morale. However, hiring from within creates another job vacancy to be filled.

External sources of applicants consist of advertisements in newspapers and professional journals, employment agencies, colleges, vocational schools, recommendations from current employees, competing firms, unsolicited applications, online websites, and social networking sites such as LinkedIn. Internships are also a good way to solicit for potential employees. Many companies hire college students or recent graduates to low-paying internships that give them the opportunity to get hands-on experience on the job. If the intern proves to be a good fit, an organization may then hire the intern as a full-time worker. There are also hundreds of websites where employers can post job openings and job seekers can post their résumés, including Monster.com, USAJobs, Simply Hired, and CareerBuilder.com. TheLadders.com is a website that focuses on career-driven professionals who make salaries of $40,000 or more. Employers looking for employees for specialized jobs can use more focused sites such as computerwork.com. Increasingly, companies can turn to their own websites for potential candidates: Nearly all of the Fortune 500 firms provide career websites where they recruit, provide employment information, and take applications. Using these sources of applicants is generally more expensive than hiring from within, but it may be necessary if there are no current employees who meet the job specifications or there are better-qualified people outside of the organization. Recruiting for entry-level managerial and professional positions is often carried out on college and university campuses. For managerial or professional positions above the entry level, companies sometimes depend on employment agencies or executive search firms, sometimes called *headhunters*, that specialize in luring qualified people away from other companies. Employers are also increasingly using professional social networking sites such as LinkedIn and Viadeo as recruitment tools. Figure 10-1 shows some

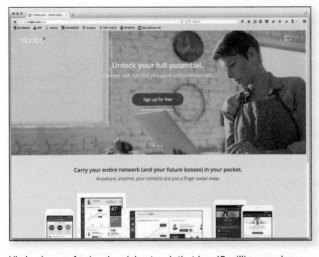

Viadeo is a professional social network that has 65 million members.

Source: Viadeo.com

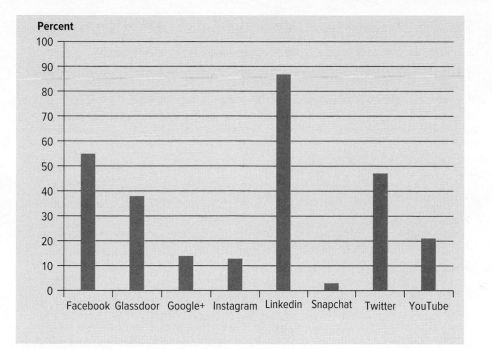

Percent

FIGURE 10-1
Recruiters' Use of
Social Networks in the
Recruitment Process

Source: Jobvite, "Recruiter Nation
Survey 2015."

social media networks that recruiters use to research job candidates during the recruitment process.

Selection

Selection is the process of collecting information about applicants and using that information to decide which ones to hire. It includes the application itself, as well as interviewing, testing, and reference checking. This process can be quite lengthy and expensive. Procter & Gamble, for example, offers online applications for jobs in approximately 100 countries. The first round of evaluation involves assessment, and if this stage goes well, the candidate interviews in the region or country to which the applicant applied.[5] Such rigorous scrutiny is necessary to find those applicants who can do the work expected and fit into the firm's structure and culture. If an organization finds the "right" employees through its recruiting and selection process, it will not have to spend as much money later in recruiting, selecting, and training replacement employees.

selection
the process of collecting information about applicants and using that information to make hiring decisions.

The Application.   In the first stage of the selection process, the individual fills out an application form and perhaps has a brief interview. The application form asks for the applicant's name, address, telephone number, education, and previous work experience. The goal of this stage of the selection process is to get acquainted with the applicants and to weed out those who are obviously not qualified for the job. For employees with work experience, most companies ask for the following information before contacting a potential candidate: current salary, reason for seeking a new job, years of experience, availability, and level of interest in the position. In addition to identifying obvious qualifications, the application can provide subtle clues about whether a person is appropriate for a particular job. For instance, an applicant who gives unusually creative answers may be perfect for a position at an advertising

TABLE 10-1
Interviewing Tips

I. Evaluate the work environment. Do employees seem to get along and work well in teams?
2. Evaluate the attitude of employees. Are employees happy, tense, or overworked?
3. Are employees enthusiastic and excited about their work?
4. What is the organizational culture, and would you feel comfortable working there?

Source: Adapted from "What to Look for During Office Visits," https://careercenter.tamu.edu/guides/interviews/lookforinoffice. cfm?sn=faculty (accessed March 31, 2016).

TABLE 10-2
Most Common Questions Asked During the Interview

I. Tell me about yourself.
2. Why should I hire you?
3. Please tell me about your future objectives.
4. Has your education prepared you for your career?
5. Have you been a team player?
6. Did you encounter any conflict with your previous professors or employer? What are the steps that you have taken to resolve this issue?
7. What is your biggest weakness?
8. How would your professors describe you?
9. What are the qualities that a manager should possess?
I0. If you could turn back time, what would you change?

Source: "Job Interview Skills Training: Top Ten Interview Questions for College Graduates," February 17, 2010, www.articlesbase .com/business-articles/job-interview-skills-training-top-ten-interview-questions-for-college-graduates-1871741.html (accessed March 31, 2016).

agency; a person who turns in a sloppy, hurriedly scrawled application probably would not be appropriate for a technical job requiring precise adjustments. Most companies now accept online applications. The online application for Target is designed not only to collect biographical data on the applicant, but also to create a picture of the applicant and how that person might contribute to the company. The completion of the survey takes about 15–45 minutes, depending on the position. To get a better view of the fit between the applicant and the company, the online application contains a questionnaire that asks applicants more specific questions, from how they might react in a certain situation to personality attributes like self-esteem or ability to interact with people.

The Interview.   The next phase of the selection process involves interviewing applicants. Table 10-1 provides some insights on finding the right work environment. Interviews allow management to obtain detailed information about the applicant's experience and skills, reasons for changing jobs, attitudes toward the job, and an idea of whether the person would fit in with the company. Table 10-2 lists some of the most common questions asked by interviewers, while Table 10-3 reveals some common mistakes candidates make in interviewing. Furthermore, the interviewer can answer the applicant's questions about the requirements for the job, compensation, working

1. Not taking the interview seriously.
2. Not dressing appropriately (dressing down).
3. Not appropriately discussing experience, abilities, and education.
4. Being too modest about your accomplishments.
5. Talking too much.
6. Too much concern about compensation.
7. Speaking negatively of a former employer.
8. Not asking enough or appropriate questions.
9. Not showing the proper enthusiasm level.
10. Not engaging in appropriate follow-up to the interview.

TABLE 10-3
Mistakes Made in Interviewing

Source: "Avoid the Top 10 Job Interview Mistakes," All Business, http://www.allbusiness.com/slideshow/avoid-the-top-10-job-interview-mistakes-16568835-1.html (accessed March 31, 2016).

conditions, company policies, organizational culture, and so on. A potential employee's questions may be just as revealing as his or her answers. Today's students might be surprised to have an interviewer ask them, "What's on your Facebook account?" or have them show the interviewer their Facebook accounts. Currently, these are legal questions for an interviewer to ask. Approximately 52 percent of employers review job candidates through social media sites.[6] It is also legal and common for companies to monitor employee work habits and e-mails. While this can be important for monitoring outside threats such as hacking or information leaks, employees might view this as the company's way of saying it does not trust them.[7]

Testing.   Another step in the selection process is testing. Ability and performance tests are used to determine whether an applicant has the skills necessary for the job. Aptitude, IQ, or personality tests may be used to assess an applicant's potential for a certain kind of work and his or her ability to fit into the organization's culture. One of the most commonly used tests is the Myers-Briggs Type Indicator. The Myers-Briggs Type Indicator Test is used worldwide by millions of people each year. Although polygraph ("lie detector") tests were once a common technique for evaluating the honesty of applicants, in 1988 their use was restricted to specific government jobs and those involving security or access to drugs. Applicants may also undergo physical examinations to determine their suitability for some jobs, and many companies require applicants to be screened for illegal drug use. Illegal drug use and alcoholism can be particularly damaging to businesses. It has been estimated that nearly 10 percent of full-time employees have had a recent substance abuse problem, while 9 percent engaged in heavy drinking within the past month.[8] Small

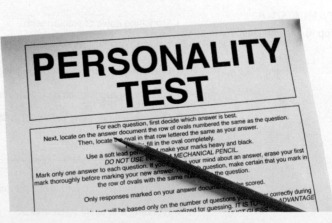

Personality tests such as Myers-Briggs are used to assess an applicant's potential for a certain kind of job. For instance, extroversion and a love of people would be good qualities for a retail job.

© Kirby Hamilton/iStock

businesses may have a higher percentage of these employees because they do not engage in systematic drug testing. Loss in productivity from substance abuse amounts to $120 million.[9] E-cigarettes are another growing concern. Many organizations have restrictions on cigarette use, but these policies do not necessarily apply to e-cigarettes. As e-cigarette use grows among employees, many of them do not know where they stand regarding their corporate policies.[10]

Reference Checking.   Before making a job offer, the company should always check an applicant's references. Reference checking usually involves verifying educational background and previous work experience. An Internet search is often done to determine social media activities or other public activities. While public Internet searches are usually deemed acceptable, asking for private information—while legal—is deemed to be intrusive by many job seekers.[11] Many states are already taking legislative action to ban this practice.[12] Public companies are likely to do more extensive background searches to make sure applicants are not misrepresenting themselves.

Background checking is important because applicants may misrepresent themselves on their applications or résumés. Research has shown that those who are willing to exaggerate or lie on their résumés are more likely to engage in unethical behaviors.[13] As Table 10-4 illustrates, some of the most common types of résumé lies include the faking of credentials, overstatements of skills or accomplishments, lies concerning education/degrees, omissions of past employment, and the falsification of references.[14]

Reference checking is a vital, albeit often overlooked, stage in the selection process. Managers charged with hiring should be aware, however, that many organizations will confirm only that an applicant is a former employee, perhaps with beginning and ending work dates, and will not release details about the quality of the employee's work.

Legal Issues in Recruiting and Selecting

Legal constraints and regulations are present in almost every phase of the recruitment and selection process, and a violation of these regulations can result in lawsuits and fines. Therefore, managers should be aware of these restrictions to avoid legal problems. Some of the laws affecting human resources management are discussed here.

TABLE 10-4
Top 10 Résumé Lies

1. Stretching dates of employment
2. Inflating past accomplishments and skills
3. Enhancing job titles and responsibilities
4. Education exaggeration and fabricating degrees
5. Unexplained gaps and periods of "self-employment"
6. Omitting past employment
7. Faking credentials
8. Fabricating reasons for leaving previous job
9. Providing fraudulent references
10. Misrepresenting military record

Source: Christopher T. Marquet and Lisa J. B. Peterson, "Résumé Fraud: The Top 10 Lies," www.marquetinternational.com/pdf/Resume%20Fraud-Top%20Ten%20Lies.pdf (accessed March 31, 2016).

Because one law pervades all areas of human resources management, we'll take a quick look at it now. **Title VII of the Civil Rights Act** of 1964 prohibits discrimination in employment. It also created the Equal Employment Opportunity Commission (EEOC), a federal agency dedicated to increasing job opportunities for women and minorities and eliminating job discrimination based on race, religion, color, sex, national origin, or handicap. As a result of Title VII, employers must not impose sex distinctions in job specifications, job descriptions, or newspaper advertisements. In 2015, workplace discrimination charges filed with the EEOC were 89,385. The EEOC received more than 6,800 charges of sexual harassment and/or sexual discrimination.[15] The Civil Rights Act of 1964 also outlaws the use of discriminatory tests for applicants. Aptitude tests and other indirect tests must be validated; in other words, employers must be able to demonstrate that scores on such tests are related to job performance, so that no one race has an advantage in taking the tests or is alternatively discriminated against. Although many hope for improvements in organizational diversity, only five Fortune 500 CEOs are African American, and only 10 CEOs are Hispanic.[16]

The Department of Labor has oversight over workplace safety, wages and work hours, unemployment benefits, and more. It often files lawsuits against firms that it believes are treating workers unfairly and violating labor laws.

© B Christopher/Alamy Stock Photo

Title VII of the Civil Rights Act
prohibits discrimination in employment and created the Equal Employment Opportunity Commission.

Other laws affecting HRM include the Americans with Disabilities Act (ADA), which prevents discrimination against disabled persons. It also classifies people with AIDS as handicapped and, consequently, prohibits using a positive AIDS test as reason to deny an applicant employment. The Age Discrimination in Employment Act specifically outlaws discrimination based on age. Its focus is banning hiring practices that discriminate against people 40 years and older. Generally, when companies need employees, recruiters head to college campuses, and when downsizing is necessary, many older workers are offered early retirement. Forced retirement based on age, however, is generally considered to be illegal in the United States, although claims of forced retirement still abound. Indeed, there are many benefits that companies are realizing in hiring older workers. Some of these benefits include the fact that they are more dedicated, punctual, honest, and detail-oriented; are good listeners; take pride in their work; exhibit good organizational skills; are efficient and confident; are mature; can be seen as role models; have good communication skills; and offer an opportunity for a reduced labor cost because of already having insurance plans.[17] Figure 10-2 shows the age ranges of employed workers in the United States.

The Equal Pay Act mandates that men and women who do equal work must receive the same wage. Wage differences are acceptable only if they are attributed to seniority, performance, or qualifications. In the United States, female employees, on average, make 79 cents for every dollar male employees make.[18] The largest pay gap exists in the computer programming industry, in which female employees are paid, on average, 72 cents per dollar earned by their male colleagues.[19] Performance quality in these jobs is relatively subjective. Jobs like engineers, actuaries, or electricians, where the performance evaluation is more objective, result in greater salary parity

FIGURE 10-2

U.S. Population Employed by Age Group (in thousands)

Source: Bureau of Labor Statistics, Labor Force Statistics from the *Current Population Survey,* http://www.bls .gov/cps/cpsaat03.pdf (accessed April 6, 2016).

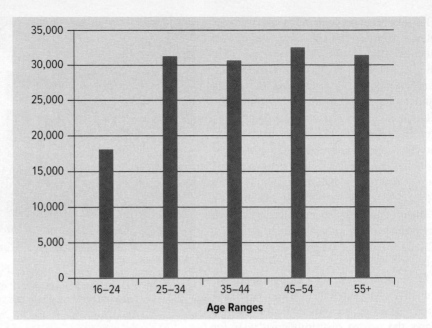

between men and women.[20] However, despite the wage inequalities that still exist, women in the workplace are becoming increasingly accepted among both genders. The working mother is no longer a novelty; in fact, many working mothers seek the same amount of achievement as working men and women who are not mothers.

Developing the Workforce

Once the most qualified applicants have been selected, have been offered positions, and have accepted their offers, they must be formally introduced to the organization and trained so they can begin to be productive members of the workforce. **Orientation** familiarizes the newly hired employees with fellow workers, company procedures, and the physical properties of the company. It generally includes a tour of the building; introductions to supervisors, co-workers, and subordinates; and the distribution of organizational manuals describing the organization's policy on vacations, absenteeism, lunch breaks, company benefits, and so on. Orientation also involves socializing the new employee into the ethics and culture of the new company. Many larger companies now show videos of procedures, facilities, and key personnel in the organization to help speed the adjustment process.

orientation
familiarizing newly hired employees with fellow workers, company procedures, and the physical properties of the company.

Training and Development

Although recruiting and selection are designed to find employees who have the knowledge, skills, and abilities the company needs, new employees still must undergo **training** to learn how to do their specific job tasks. *On-the-job training* allows workers to learn by actually performing the tasks of the job, while *classroom training* teaches employees with lectures, conferences, videos, case studies, and web-based training. For instance, McDonald's trains those interested in company operations and leadership development at the Fred L. Turner Training Center, otherwise known as Hamburger University.[21]

LO 10-3

Discuss how workers are trained and their performance appraised.

training
teaching employees to do specific job tasks through either classroom development or on-the-job experience.

Some companies will go even further and ask a more experienced individual in the organization to mentor a new employee. **Mentoring** involves supporting, training, and guiding an employee in his or her professional development. Mentoring provides employees with more of a one-on-one interaction with somebody in the organization that not only teaches them but also acts as their supporter as they progress in their jobs. It is estimated that 71 percent of *Fortune* 500 firms offer mentoring programs, including Deloitte and Sun Microsystems.[22] Even small and medium-sized firms agree on the importance of mentoring—93 percent of these organizations claim that mentoring is important to helping them succeed.[23] Another benefit of mentoring is that companies can use this process to attract talent from underrepresented areas. For instance, mentoring has been suggested as a way to attract more women into the gas and oil industry.[24]

McDonald's has expanded its famous Hamburger University into China. This branch of Hamburger University will train a new generation of Chinese students in such areas as restaurant management, leadership development, and other skills.

© Tannen Maury/Bloomberg via Getty Images

Development is training that augments the skills and knowledge of managers and professionals. Training and development are also used to improve the skills of employees in their present positions and to prepare them for increased responsibility and job promotions. Training is, therefore, a vital function of human resources management. At the Container Store, for example, first-year sales personnel receive 263 hours of training about the company's products.[25] Companies are engaging in more experiential and involvement-oriented training exercises for employees. Use of role-plays, simulations, and online training methods are becoming increasingly popular in employee training.

mentoring
involves supporting, training, and guiding an employee in his or her professional development.

Assessing Performance

Assessing an employee's performance—his or her strengths and weaknesses on the job—is one of the most difficult tasks for managers. However, performance appraisal is crucial because it gives employees feedback on how they are doing and what they need to do to improve. It also provides a basis for determining how to compensate and reward employees, and it generates information about the quality of the firm's selection, training, and development activities. Table 10-5 identifies 16 characteristics that may be assessed in a performance review.

Performance appraisals may be objective or subjective. An objective assessment is quantifiable. For example, a Westinghouse employee might be judged by how many circuit boards he typically produces in one day or by how many of his boards have defects. A Century 21 real estate agent might be judged by the number of houses she has shown or the number of sales she has closed. A company can also use tests as an objective method of assessment.

Performance appraisals are important because they provide employees with feedback on how well they are doing as well as areas for improvement.

© Eric Audras/Getty Images

TABLE 10-5
Performance
Characteristics

- **Productivity**—rate at which work is regularly produced

- **Quality**—accuracy, professionalism, and deliverability of produced work

- **Job knowledge**—understanding of the objectives, practices, and standards of work

- **Problem solving**—ability to identify and correct problems effectively

- **Communication**—effectiveness in written and verbal exchanges

- **Initiative**—willingness to identify and address opportunities for improvement

- **Adaptability**—ability to become comfortable with change

- **Planning and organization skills**—reflected through the ability to schedule projects, set goals, and maintain organizational systems

- **Teamwork and cooperation**—effectiveness of collaborations with co-workers

- **Judgment**—ability to determine appropriate actions in a timely manner

- **Dependability**—responsiveness, reliability, and conscientiousness demonstrated on the job

- **Creativity**—extent to which resourceful ideas, solutions, and methods for task completion are proposed

- **Sales**—demonstrated through success in selling products, services, yourself, and your company

- **Customer service**—ability to communicate effectively with customers, address problems, and offer solutions that meet or exceed their expectations

- **Leadership**—tendency and ability to serve as a doer, guide, decision maker, and role model

- **Financial management**—appropriateness of cost controls and financial planning within the scope defined by the position

development
training that augments the
skills and knowledge of
managers and professionals.

Whatever method they use, managers must take into account the work environment when they appraise performance objectively.

When jobs do not lend themselves to objective appraisal, the manager must relate the employee's performance to some other standard. One popular tool used in subjective assessment is the ranking system, which lists various performance factors on which the manager ranks employees against each other. Although used by many large companies, ranking systems are unpopular with many employees. Qualitative criteria, such as teamwork and communication skills, used to evaluate employees are generally hard to gauge. Such grading systems have triggered employee lawsuits that allege discrimination in grade/ranking assignments. For example, one manager may grade a company's employees one way, while another manager grades a group more harshly depending on the managers' grading style. If layoffs occur, then employees graded by the second manager may be more likely to lose their jobs. Other criticisms of grading systems include unclear wording or inappropriate words that a manager may unintentionally write in a performance evaluation, like *young* or *pretty* to describe an employee's appearance. These liabilities can all be fodder for lawsuits should employees allege that they were treated unfairly. Therefore, it is crucial that managers use clear language in performance evaluations and be consistent with all employees. Several employee grading computer packages have been developed to make performance evaluations easier for managers and clearer for employees.[26]

Figure 10-3 demonstrates that HR managers are more likely to view performance reviews as more effective than employees are.

Another performance appraisal method used by many companies is the 360-degree feedback system, which provides feedback from a panel that typically includes superiors, peers, and subordinates. Because of the tensions it may cause, peer appraisal appears to be difficult for many. However, companies that have success with 360-degree feedback tend to be open to learning, willing to experiment and are led by executives who are direct about the expected benefits as well as the challenges.[27] Managers and leaders with a high emotional intelligence (sensitivity to their own as well as others' emotions) assess and reflect upon their interactions with colleagues on a daily basis. In addition, they conduct follow-up analysis on their projects, asking the right questions and listening carefully to responses without getting defensive of their actions.[28]

Another trend occurring at some companies is the decrease of negative employee feedback. Executives have begun to recognize that hard tactics can harm employee confidence. Negative feedback tends to overshadow positive feedback, so employees may get discouraged if performance reviews are phrased too negatively. At the same time, it is important for managers to provide constructive criticism on employee weaknesses in addition to their strengths so workers know what to expect and how they are viewed.[29]

Whether the assessment is objective or subjective, it is vital that the manager discuss the results with the employee, so that the employee knows how well he or she is doing the job. The results of a performance appraisal become useful only when they are communicated, tactfully, to the employee and presented as a tool to allow the employee to grow and improve in his or her position and beyond. Performance appraisals are also used to determine whether an employee should be promoted, transferred, or terminated from the organization.

FIGURE 10-3 Beliefs that Reviews Are Effective

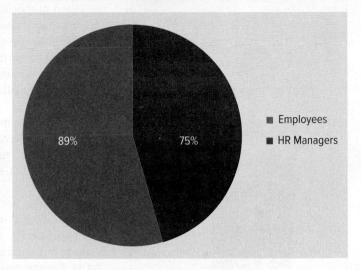

Survey developed by OfficeTeam, a Robert Half Company.

Source: PRNewswire, "Are Performance Reviews Worth It?," *OfficeTeam*, November 23, 2015, http://officeteam.rhi.mediaroom.com/2015-11-23-Are-Performance-Reviews-Worth-It (accessed March 31, 2016).

Turnover

Turnover, which occurs when employees quit or are fired and must be replaced by new employees, results in lost productivity from the vacancy, costs to recruit replacement employees, management time devoted to interviewing, training, and socialization expenses for new employees. However, some companies have created innovative solutions for reducing turnover. Diebold, a financial self-service, security and services corporation, decided that the best way to attract and retain top talent was to offer jobs in which they could work remotely. About 40 percent of its top 100 executives work far from its central office in Ohio.[30] Part of the reason for turnover may be overworked employees as a result of downsizing and a lack of training and advancement opportunities.[31] Of course, turnover is not always an unhappy occasion when it takes the form of a promotion or transfer.

Identify the types of turnover companies may experience and explain why turnover is an important issue.

turnover
occurs when employees quit or are fired and must be replaced by new employees.

Many companies in recent years are choosing to downsize by eliminating jobs. Reasons for downsizing might be due to financial constraints or the need to become more productive and competitive.

promotion
a persuasive form of communication that attempts to expedite a marketing exchange by influencing individuals, groups, and organizations to accept goods, services, and ideas

transfer
a move to another job within the company at essentially the same level and wage.

separations
employment changes involving resignation, retirement, termination, or layoff.

A **promotion** is an advancement to a higher-level job with increased authority, responsibility, and pay. In some companies and most labor unions, seniority—the length of time a person has been with the company or at a particular job classification—is the key issue in determining who should be promoted. Most managers base promotions on seniority only when they have candidates with equal qualifications. Managers prefer to base promotions on merit.

A **transfer** is a move to another job within the company at essentially the same level and wage. Transfers allow workers to obtain new skills or to find a new position within an organization when their old position has been eliminated because of automation or downsizing.

Separations occur when employees resign, retire, are terminated, or are laid off. Employees may be terminated, or fired, for poor performance, violation of work rules, absenteeism, and so on. Businesses have traditionally been able to fire employees *at will*—that is, for any reason other than for race, religion, sex, or age, or because an employee is a union organizer. However, recent legislation and court decisions now require that companies fire employees fairly, for just cause only. Managers must take care, then, to warn employees when their performance is unacceptable and may lead to dismissal, elevating the importance of performance evaluations. They should also document all problems and warnings in employees' work records. To avoid the possibility of lawsuits from individuals who may feel they have been fired unfairly, employers should provide clear, business-related reasons for any firing, supported by written documentation if possible. Employee disciplinary procedures should be carefully explained to all employees and should be set forth in employee handbooks. Table 10-6 illustrates what to do and what *not* to do when you are terminated.

Many companies have downsized in recent years, laying off tens of thousands of employees in their effort to become more productive and competitive. Layoffs are sometimes temporary; employees may be brought back when business conditions improve. When layoffs are to be permanent, employers often help employees find other jobs and may extend benefits while the employees search for new employment. Such actions help lessen the trauma of the layoffs. Fortunately, there are several business areas that are choosing not to downsize.

A well-organized human resources department strives to minimize losses due to separations and transfers because recruiting and training new employees is very expensive. Note that a high turnover rate in a company may signal problems with the selection and training process, the compensation program, or even the type of company. To help reduce turnover, companies have tried a number of strategies, including giving employees more interesting job responsibilities (job enrichment), allowing for increased job flexibility, and providing more employee benefits. When employees do choose to leave the organization, the company will often ask them to conduct an *exit interview*. An exit interview is a survey used to determine why the employee is leaving the organization. The company hopes that this feedback will alert them to processes they can improve upon to dissuade valuable employees from leaving in the future.

I. Do not criticize your boss who terminated you.
2. Do not take files or property that is not yours.
3. Do try to get a reference letter.
4. Do not criticize your former employer during job interviews.
5. Do look to the future and be positive about new job opportunities.

TABLE 10-6
Actions You Should and Shouldn't Take When You Are Terminated

Compensating the Workforce

People generally don't work for free, and how much they are paid for their work is a complicated issue. Also, designing a fair compensation plan is an important task because pay and benefits represent a substantial portion of an organization's expenses. Wages that are too high may result in the company's products being priced too high, making them uncompetitive in the market. Wages that are too low may damage employee morale and result in costly turnover. Remember that compensation is one of the hygiene factors identified by Herzberg.

Specify the various ways a worker may be compensated.

Designing a fair compensation plan is a difficult task because it involves evaluating the relative worth of all jobs within the business while allowing for individual efforts. Compensation for a specific job is typically determined through a **wage/salary survey,** which tells the company how much compensation comparable firms are paying for specific jobs that the firms have in common. Compensation for individuals within a specific job category depends on both the compensation for that job and the individual's productivity. Therefore, two employees with identical jobs may not receive exactly the same pay because of individual differences in performance.

wage/salary survey
a study that tells a company how much compensation comparable firms are paying for specific jobs that the firms have in common.

Financial Compensation

Financial compensation falls into two general categories—wages and salaries. **Wages** are financial rewards based on the number of hours the employee works or the level of output achieved. Wages based on the number of hours worked are called time wages. The federal minimum wage increased to $7.25 per hour in 2009 for covered nonexempt workers.[32] However, Congress is expected to vote on whether to increase the minimum wage to $10.10. If passed, the minimum wage would increase over the next few years. Many members of Congress want to increase the minimum wage to $15 per hour.[33] Tipped wages may be $2.13 per hour as long as tips plus the wage of $2.13 per hour equal the minimum wage of $7.25 per hour.[34] Many states also mandate minimum wages; in the case where the two wages are in conflict, the higher of the two wages prevails. There may even be differences between city and state minimum wages. In New Mexico, the minimum wage is $7.50, whereas in the state capitol of Santa Fe, the minimum wage is $10.91, due to a higher cost of living.[35] Table 10-7 compares wages and other information for Costco and Walmart, two well-known discount chains. Time wages are appropriate when employees are continually interrupted and when quality is more important than quantity. Assembly-line workers, clerks, and maintenance personnel are commonly paid on a time-wage basis. The advantage of time wages is the ease of computation. The disadvantage is that time wages provide no incentive to increase productivity. In fact, time wages may encourage employees to be less productive.

wages
financial rewards based on the number of hours the employee works or the level of output achieved.

Google IT: Employee Bonuses for Being Green

For employees at Google, it pays to be green. Google employees can save money and earn bonuses by taking advantage of the company's green incentives. For instance, employees can save fuel costs by riding to work on Google's biodiesel shuttles. This is estimated to save 29,000 metric tons of carbon dioxide annually. Employees can also use Google's GFleet car-sharing program that includes electric vehicles such as the Nissan Leaf and Chevrolet Volt. To support its GFleet program, Google has partnered with a technology firm to build the largest electric vehicle charging infrastructure in the nation. Employees are also encouraged to bike to work.

Google has also begun to tie bonuses to meeting sustainability goals—including energy reduction. This encourages employees to take an active role in increasing their sustainable behaviors. Additionally, the company itself acts as a model

for employees to follow. Google contributed toward the largest fund ever for residential solar power in the form of a $750 million investment in Solar City. The total investments it has made in renewable energy amount to more than $1.8 billion. Google makes sure to stress the importance of sustainability in every facet of its operations. The company is committed to making a difference in the field of sustainability—starting with its employees.[36]

Discussion Questions

1. Describe some of Google's green initiatives.
2. How is Google rewarding employees for adopting greener behaviors?
3. Why do you think it is important for Google to model green behaviors for employees?

To overcome these disadvantages, many companies pay on an incentive system, using piece wages or commissions. Piece wages are based on the level of output achieved. A major advantage of piece wages is that they motivate employees to supervise their own activities and to increase output. Skilled craftworkers are often paid on a piece-wage basis.

commission
an incentive system that pays a fixed amount or a percentage of the employee's sales.

The other incentive system, **commission,** pays a fixed amount or a percentage of the employee's sales. Skincare direct selling firm Rodan + Fields uses independent consultants to sell its products. Consultants earn commissions of 10 percent on whatever they sell. As consultants move up in the business, the opportunities to earn additional commissions through sponsoring other consultants or reaching certain sales levels increases.[37] This method motivates employees to sell as much as they can. Some companies also combine payment based on commission with time wages or salaries.

TABLE 10-7
Costco versus Walmart

	Costco	Walmart
Number of employees	205,000+	2,200,000+
Revenues	$114 billion	$485.7 billion
Wages at entry-level	$13/hour	$10/hour
World's most admired ranking	12	42
Strengths	Management quality; financial soundness; people management	Management quality; financial soundness; global competitiveness

Sources: Fortune, "Fortune World's Most Admired Rankings," 2016, http://fortune.com/worlds-most-admired-companies/(accessed May 5, 2014); John Kell, "Dancing in the Aisles," Fortune, December 15, 2015, p. 26; Sarah Nassauer, "Costco to Raise Minimum Wage," The Wall Street Journal, March 4, 2016, p. B3; "Wal-Mart," NY JobSource, January 16, 2016, http://nyjobsource.com/walmart.html (accessed March 31, 2016); Clare O'Connor, "Walmart Hikes Hourly Pay to $10 Minimum for Most Workers," Forbes, January 20, 2016, http://www.forbes.com/sites/clareoconnor/2016/01/20/walmart-hikes-hourly-pay-to-10-minimum-for-most-workers/#33250bac26af (accessed March 31, 2016).

A **salary** is a financial reward calculated on a weekly, monthly, or annual basis. Salaries are associated with white-collar workers such as office personnel, executives, and professional employees. Although a salary provides a stable stream of income, salaried workers may be required to work beyond usual hours without additional financial compensation.

In addition to the basic wages or salaries paid to employees, a company may offer **bonuses** for exceptional performance as an incentive to increase productivity further. Many workers receive a bonus as a "thank you" for good work and an incentive to continue working hard. Many owners and managers are recognizing that simple bonuses and perks foster happier employees and reduce turnover. Bonuses are especially popular among Wall Street firms. In 2015, bonuses among Wall Street executives dropped for the first time in four years due to uncertainty in global economic markets.[38]

Another form of compensation is **profit sharing,** which distributes a percentage of company profits to the employees whose work helped to generate those profits. Some profit-sharing plans involve distributing shares of company stock to employees. Usually referred to as *ESOPs*—employee stock ownership plans—they have been gaining popularity in recent years. One reason for the popularity of ESOPs is the sense of partnership that they create between the organization and employees. Profit sharing can also motivate employees to work hard, because increased productivity and sales mean that the profits or the stock dividends will increase. Many organizations offer employees a stake in the company through stock purchase plans, ESOPs, or stock investments through 401(k) plans. Companies are adopting broad-based stock option plans to build a stronger link between employees' interests and the organization's interests. Businesses have found employee stock options a great way to boost productivity and increase morale. Publix, consistently ranked among the best companies to work for, implemented an ESOP program in 1974. Any employee that accrues more than a thousand hours and stays over a year gets shares of company stock. Since its inception, it has averaged an annual return of 16.9 percent, resulting in significant value for long-term employees who own its stock.[39]

Benefits

Benefits are nonfinancial forms of compensation provided to employees, such as pension plans for retirement; health, disability, and life insurance; holidays and paid days off for vacation or illness; credit union membership; health programs; child care; elder care; assistance with adoption; and more. According to the Bureau of Labor Statistics, employer costs for employee compensation for civilian workers in the United States average $33.58 per hour worked. Wages and salaries account for approximately 68.7 percent of those costs, while benefits account for 31.3 percent of the cost. Legally required benefits (Social Security, Medicare, federal and state employment insurance, and workers' compensation) account for 8 percent of total compensation.[40] Such benefits increase employee security and, to a certain extent, their morale and motivation.

Although health insurance is a common benefit for full-time employees, rising health care costs have forced a growing number of employers to trim this benefit. Even government workers, whose wages and benefits used to be virtually guaranteed safe, have seen reductions in health care and other benefits. On the other hand, employee loyalty tends to increase when employees feel that the firm cares about them. Starbucks recognizes the importance of how benefits can significantly affect an employee's health and well-being. As a result, it is the only fast-food company

salary
a financial reward calculated on a weekly, monthly, or annual basis.

bonuses
monetary rewards offered by companies for exceptional performance as incentives to further increase productivity.

profit sharing
a form of compensation whereby a percentage of company profits is distributed to the employees whose work helped to generate them.

benefits
nonfinancial forms of compensation provided to employees, such as pension plans, health insurance, paid vacation and holidays, and the like.

On-site child care is just one of the benefits large companies have begun to offer employees. On-site child care can be particularly important in attracting talented individuals with children.

© Michael Hall Photography Pty Ltd/Corbis

to offer its part-time employees health insurance. Additionally, Starbucks began offering employees a benefit called College Achievement Plan in which it will pay full tuition for employees to finish a bachelor's degree at Arizona State University.[41]

A benefit increasingly offered is the employee assistance program (EAP). Each company's EAP is different, but most offer counseling for and assistance with those employees' personal problems that might hurt their job performance if not addressed. The most common counseling services offered include drug- and alcohol-abuse treatment programs, fitness programs, smoking cessation clinics, stress-management clinics, financial counseling, family counseling, and career counseling. Lowe's, for example, offers family assistance programs, smoking cessation clinics, health screenings, and other assistance programs for its employees.[42] EAPs help reduce costs associated with poor productivity, absenteeism, and other workplace issues by helping employees deal with personal problems that contribute to these issues. For example, exercise and fitness programs reduce health insurance costs by helping employees stay healthy. Family counseling may help workers trying to cope with a divorce or other personal problems to better focus on their jobs.

Companies try to provide the benefits they believe their employees want, but diverse people may want different things. In recent years, some single workers have felt that co-workers with spouses and children seem to get "special breaks" and extra time off to deal with family issues. Some companies use flexible benefit programs to allow employees to choose the benefits they would like, up to a specified amount.

Fringe benefits include sick leave, vacation pay, pension plans, health plans, and any other extra compensation. Many states and cities are adopting new policies on sick leave that mandate a certain number of paid sick days a worker can take. It is often lower-wage employees who do not receive paid sick leave, yet they are the ones who usually cannot afford to take a day off if it is unpaid.[43] Soft benefits include perks that help balance life and work. They include on-site child care, spas, food service, and even laundry services and hair salons. These soft benefits motivate employees and give them more time to focus on their job. Insurance firm Acuity provides unlimited sick leave, unlimited education reimbursement, and a 10 percent company contribution to 401(k) plans, in addition to an on-site fitness facility and massage therapists.[44]

Cafeteria benefit plans provide a financial amount to employees so that they can select the specific benefits that fit their needs. The key is making benefits flexible, rather than giving employees identical benefits. As firms go global, the need for cafeteria or flexible benefit plans becomes even more important. For some employees, benefits are a greater motivator and differentiator in jobs than wages. For many Starbucks employees who receive health insurance when working part-time, this benefit could be the most important compensation.

Over the past two decades, the list of fringe benefits has grown dramatically, and new benefits are being added every year.

Managing Unionized Employees

Employees who are dissatisfied with their working conditions or compensation have to negotiate with management to bring about change. Dealing with management on an individual basis is not always effective, however, so employees may organize themselves into **labor unions** to deal with employers and to achieve better pay, hours, and working conditions. Organized employees are backed by the power of a large group that can hire specialists to represent the entire union in its dealings with management. Union workers make significantly more than nonunion employees. The United States has a roughly 11.1 percent unionization rate. Figure 10-4 displays unionization rates by state. On average, the median usual weekly earnings of unionized full-time and salary workers are about $200 more than their nonunion counterparts.[45]

However, union growth has slowed in recent years, and prospects for growth do not look good. One reason is that most blue-collar workers, the traditional members of unions, have already been organized. Factories have become more automated and

LO 10-6

Discuss some of the issues associated with unionized employees, including collective bargaining and dispute resolution.

labor unions
employee organizations formed to deal with employers for achieving better pay, hours, and working conditions.

FIGURE 10-4 **Union Membership Rates by State**

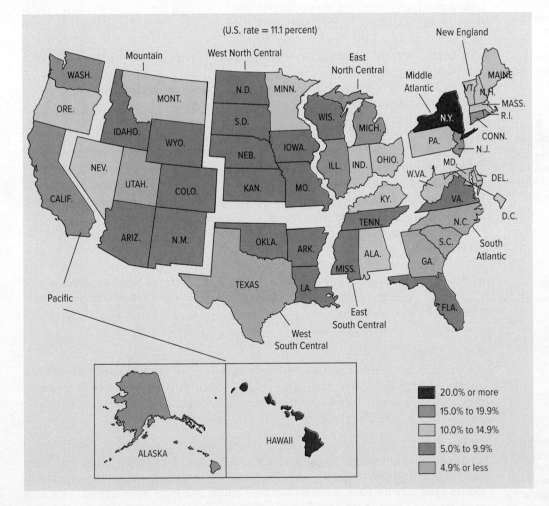

Source: Bureau of Labor Statistics, http://www.bls.gov/news.release/pdf/union2.pdf (accessed April 1, 2016).

need fewer blue-collar workers. The United States has shifted from a manufacturing to a service economy, further reducing the demand for blue-collar workers. Moreover, in response to foreign competition, U.S. companies are scrambling to find ways to become more productive and cost efficient. Job enrichment programs and participative management have blurred the line between management and workers. Because workers' say in the way plants are run is increasing, their need for union protection is decreasing. Many workers do not see the benefits of union membership if they do not have complaints or grievances against their employers.[46]

Nonetheless, labor unions have been successful in organizing blue-collar manufacturing, government, and health care workers, as well as smaller percentages of employees in other industries. Consequently, significant aspects of HRM, particularly compensation, are dictated to a large degree by union contracts at many companies. Therefore, we'll take a brief look at collective bargaining and dispute resolution in this section.

Collective Bargaining

collective bargaining
the negotiation process through which management and unions reach an agreement about compensation, working hours, and working conditions for the bargaining unit.

Collective bargaining is the negotiation process through which management and unions reach an agreement about compensation, working hours, and working conditions for the bargaining unit (Figure 10-5). The objective of negotiations is to reach agreement about a **labor contract,** the formal, written document that spells out the relationship between the union and management for a specified period of time, usually two or three years.

labor contract
the formal, written document that spells out the relationship between the union and management for a specified period of time— usually two or three years.

In collective bargaining, each side tries to negotiate an agreement that meets its demands; compromise is frequently necessary. Management tries to negotiate a labor contract that permits the company to retain control over things like work schedules; the hiring and firing of workers; production standards; promotions, transfers, and separations; the span of management in each department; and discipline. Unions tend to focus on contract issues such as magnitude of wages; better pay rates for overtime, holidays, and undesirable shifts; scheduling of pay increases; and benefits. These issues will be spelled out in the labor contract, which union members will vote to either accept (and abide by) or reject.

Many labor contracts contain a *cost-of-living escalator* (or *adjustment*) *(COLA) clause,* which calls for automatic wage increases during periods of inflation to protect the "real" income of the employees. During tough economic times, unions may be forced to accept *givebacks*—wage and benefit concessions made to employers to allow them to remain competitive or, in some cases, to survive and continue to provide jobs for union workers.

Resolving Disputes

Sometimes, management and labor simply cannot agree on a contract. Most labor disputes are handled through collective bargaining or through grievance procedures. When these processes break down, however, either side may resort to more drastic measures to achieve its objectives.

picketing
a public protest against management practices that involves union members marching and carrying antimanagement signs at the employer's plant.

Labor Tactics.   Picketing is a public protest against management practices and involves union members marching (often waving antimanagement signs and placards) at the employer's plant or work site. Picketing workers hope that their signs will arouse sympathy for their demands from the public and from other unions. Picketing may occur as a protest or in conjunction with a strike.

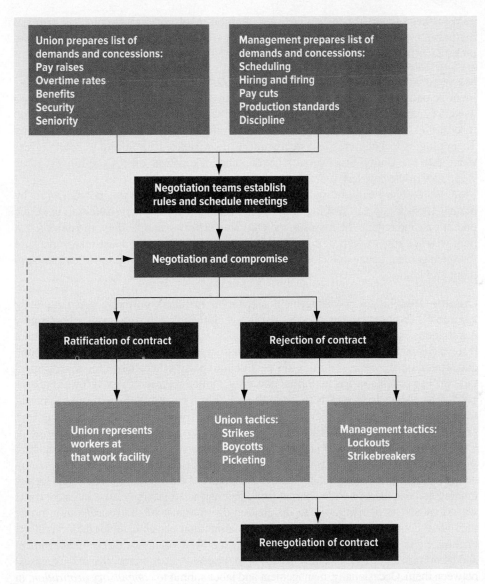

FIGURE 10-5
The Collective Bargaining
Process

Strikes (employee walkouts) are one of the most effective weapons labor has. By striking, a union makes carrying out the normal operations of a business difficult at best and impossible at worst. Strikes receive widespread publicity, but they remain a weapon of last resort. However, in extreme cases, workers may organize a strike with the help of unions and coalitions. Coca-Cola employees at two of its bottling plants in Chicago went on strike due to rising health care premiums.[47] While it is mostly the case that the mere threat of a strike is enough to make management back down, there are times when the issues are heatedly debated and regulatory agencies become involved.[48]

A **boycott** is an attempt to keep people from purchasing the products of a company. In a boycott, union members are asked not to do business with the boycotted organization. Some unions may even impose fines on members who ignore the boycott. To

strikes
employee walkouts; one of the most effective weapons labor has.

boycott
an attempt to keep people from purchasing the products of a company.

gain further support for their objectives, a union involved in a boycott may also ask the public—through picketing and advertising—not to purchase the products of the picketed firm.

lockout
management's version of a strike, wherein a work site is closed so that employees cannot go to work.

strikebreakers
people hired by management to replace striking employees; called "scabs" by striking union members.

conciliation
a method of outside resolution of labor and management differences in which a third party is brought in to keep the two sides talking.

mediation
a method of outside resolution of labor and management differences in which the third party's role is to suggest or propose a solution to the problem.

arbitration
settlement of a labor/management dispute by a third party whose solution is legally binding and enforceable.

Need help understanding mediation vs. arbitration? Visit your Connect ebook video tab for a brief animated explanation.

LO 10-7

Describe the importance of diversity in the workforce.

diversity
the participation of different ages, genders, races, ethnicities, nationalities, and abilities in the workplace.

Management Tactics.   Management's version of a strike is the **lockout**; management actually closes a work site so that employees cannot go to work. Lockouts are used, as a general rule, only when a union strike has partially shut down a plant and it seems less expensive for the plant to close completely. Pittsburgh-based Allegheny Technologies locked out 2,200 steelworkers in six states after failing to reach agreement with the United Steelworkers Union. The lockout was one of the longest work stoppages in the past few years.[49]

Strikebreakers, called "scabs" by striking union members, are people hired by management to replace striking employees. Managers hire strikebreakers to continue operations and reduce the losses associated with strikes—and to show the unions that they will not bow to their demands. Strikebreaking is generally a last-resort measure for management because it does great damage to the relationship between management and labor.

Outside Resolution.   Management and union members normally reach mutually agreeable decisions without outside assistance. Sometimes though, even after lengthy negotiations, strikes, lockouts, and other tactics, management and labor still cannot resolve a contract dispute. In such cases, they have three choices: conciliation, mediation, and arbitration. **Conciliation** brings in a neutral third party to keep labor and management talking. The conciliator has no formal power over union representatives or over management. The conciliator's goal is to get both parties to focus on the issues and to prevent negotiations from breaking down. Like conciliation, **mediation** involves bringing in a neutral third party, but the mediator's role is to suggest or propose a solution to the problem. The strike at the Coca-Cola plants ended after the firm agreed to federal mediation.[50] Mediators have no formal power over either labor or management. With **arbitration,** a neutral third party is brought in to settle the dispute, but the arbitrator's solution is legally binding and enforceable. Ride-sharing firm Uber has an arbitration clause in its contracts with drivers. The firm argues that dissatisfied drivers must submit to arbitration rather than go to court. One judge ruled that Uber's arbitration clause is unfair and, therefore, unenforceable.[51] Generally, arbitration takes place on a voluntary basis—management and labor must agree to it, and they usually split the cost (the arbitrator's fee and expenses) between them. Occasionally, management and labor submit to *compulsory arbitration,* in which an outside party (usually the federal government) requests arbitration as a means of eliminating a prolonged strike that threatens to disrupt the economy.

The Importance of Workforce Diversity

Customers, employees, suppliers—all the participants in the world of business—come in different ages, genders, races, ethnicities, nationalities, and abilities, a truth that business has come to label **diversity.** Understanding this diversity means recognizing and accepting differences as well as valuing the unique perspectives such differences can bring to the workplace.

The Characteristics of Diversity

When managers speak of diverse workforces, they typically mean differences in gender and race. While gender and race are important characteristics of diversity, others are

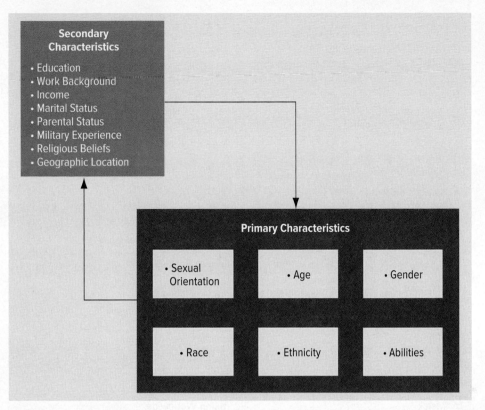

FIGURE 10-6
Characteristics of Diversity

Source: Marilyn Loden and Judy B. Rosener, *Workforce America! Managing Employee Diversity as a Vital Resource*, 1991, p. 20. Used with permission. Copyright © 1991 The McGraw-Hill Companies.

also important. We can divide these differences into primary and secondary characteristics of diversity. In the lower segment of Figure 10-6, age, gender, race, ethnicity, abilities, and sexual orientation represent *primary characteristics* of diversity that are inborn and cannot be changed. In the upper section of Figure 10-6 are eight *secondary characteristics* of diversity—work background, income, marital status, military experience, religious beliefs, geographic location, parental status, and education—which *can* be changed. We acquire, change, and discard them as we progress through our lives.

Defining characteristics of diversity as either primary or secondary enhances our understanding, but we must remember that each person is defined by the interrelation of all characteristics. In dealing with diversity in the workforce, managers must consider the complete person—not one or a few of a person's differences.

Why Is Diversity Important?

The U.S. workforce is becoming increasingly diverse. Once dominated by white men, today's workforce includes significantly more women, African Americans, Hispanics, and other minorities, as well as disabled and older workers. The Census Bureau has predicted that by 2043, minorities will make up more than 50 percent of the U.S. population.[52] These groups have traditionally faced discrimination and higher unemployment rates and have been denied opportunities to assume leadership roles in corporate America. Consequently, more and more companies are trying to improve HRM programs to recruit, develop, and retain more diverse employees to better serve their diverse customers. Some firms are providing special programs such as sponsored affinity groups, mentoring programs, and special career development

TABLE 10-8
Top 50 Companies for
Diversity

1. Kaiser Permanente	26. Eli Lilly and Company
2. Novartis Pharmaceuticals	27. Wyndham Worldwide
3. Ernst & Young	28. Dell
4. AT&T	29. Comcast NBCUniversal
5. PricewaterhouseCoopers	30. Kellogg Company
6. Sodexo	31. Northrop Grumman
7. MasterCard	32. Aetna
8. Johnson & Johnson	33. TIAA
9. Marriott International	34. Toyota Motor North America
10. Prudential Financial	35. Allstate Insurance Company
11. Deloitte	36. Colgate-Palmolive
12. Wells Fargo	37. Time Warner
13. Procter & Gamble	38. The Walt Disney Company
14. Abbott	39. TD Bank
15. Accenture	40. General Mills
16. KPMG	41. Nielsen
17. Merck	42. Hilton Worldwide
18. Cox Communications	43. Monsanto
19. Cummins	44. KeyCorp
20. IBM	45. AbbVie
21. ADP	46. Southern Company
22. Target	47. MassMutual Financial Group
23. New York Life	48. General Motors
24. BASF	49. Genentech
25. Anthem	50. Medtronic

Source: "The 2016 DiversityInc Top 50 Companies for Diversity," DiversityInc, 2016, http://www.diversityinc.com/the-diversityinc-top-50-companies-for-diversity-2016/ (accessed May 20, 2016).

opportunities. Kaiser Permanente has incorporated diversity into its goals and corporate strategies. The company has been voted as one of the top 10 companies for people with disabilities. Diversity and equal rights are so important to Kaiser Permanente that it has established the Institute for Culturally Competent Care and the Centers of Excellence to pave the way for equal health care for all, including minorities, immigrants, and those with disabilities.[53] Silicon Valley, however, has been cited for its lack of diversity. Despite attempts to increase diversity, the Silicon Valley workforce is 23 percent Asian, 8 percent Latino, 7 percent African American, and 29 percent women.[54] Table 10-8 shows the top companies for minorities according to a study by DiversityInc. Effectively managing diversity in the workforce involves cultivating and valuing its benefits and minimizing its problems.

The Benefits of Workforce Diversity

There are a number of benefits to fostering and valuing workforce diversity, including the following:

1. More productive use of a company's human resources.
2. Reduced conflict among employees of different ethnicities, races, religions, and sexual orientations as they learn to respect each other's differences.
3. More productive working relationships among diverse employees as they learn more about and accept each other.
4. Increased commitment to and sharing of organizational goals among diverse employees at all organizational levels.
5. Increased innovation and creativity as diverse employees bring new, unique perspectives to decision-making and problem-solving tasks.
6. Increased ability to serve the needs of an increasingly diverse customer base.[55]

Companies that do not value their diverse employees are likely to experience greater conflict, as well as prejudice and discrimination. Among individual employees, for example, racial slurs and gestures, sexist comments, and other behaviors by co-workers harm the individuals at whom such behavior is directed. The victims of such behavior may feel hurt, depressed, or even threatened and suffer from lowered self-esteem, all of which harm their productivity and morale. In such cases, women and minority employees may simply leave the firm, wasting the time, money, and other resources spent on hiring and training them. When discrimination comes from a supervisor, employees may also fear for their jobs. A discriminatory atmosphere not only can harm productivity and increase turnover, but it may also subject a firm to costly lawsuits and negative publicity.

affirmative action programs legally mandated plans that try to increase job opportunities for minority groups by analyzing the current pool of workers, identifying areas where women and minorities are underrepresented, and establishing specific hiring and promotion goals, with target dates, for addressing the discrepancy.

Astute businesses recognize that they need to modify their human resources management programs to target the needs of *all* their diverse employees as well as the needs of the firm itself. They realize that the benefits of diversity are long term in nature and come only to those organizations willing to make the commitment. Most importantly, as workforce diversity becomes a valued organizational asset, companies spend less time managing conflict and more time accomplishing tasks and satisfying customers, which is, after all, the purpose of business.

Affirmative Action

Many companies strive to improve their working environment through **affirmative action programs,** legally mandated plans that try to increase job opportunities for minority groups by analyzing the current pool of workers; identifying areas where women and minorities are underrepresented; and establishing specific hiring and promotion goals, along with target dates, for meeting those goals to resolve the

Some of the major benefits of diversity include a wider range of employee perspectives, greater innovation and creativity, and the ability to target a diverse customer base more effectively.

© Beathan/Corbis

Tech Industry Short-Circuits the Diversity Gap

Women and minority groups are largely underrepresented in the tech industry. However, companies like Apple and Intel are working to change this, with Apple allocating $50 million and Intel $300 million to help train and recruit more diverse employees. In the United States, fewer African American and Latino students have access to sufficient math and science courses in their early education compared to white and Asian American students. Furthermore, only half of African American and Latino students with computer science degrees end up working in the tech industry after graduation.

Intel plans to provide mentorship programs targeting freshly graduated minorities who may lack the resources, and technological background, of their nonminority counterparts. Intel also hopes that creating more diverse management teams will lead to the hiring of more diverse employees. While these efforts are noteworthy, strong social biases still make it difficult for women and other minority groups to break away from cultural stereotypes and enter underrepresented industries.

For Dropbox, a technology company headquartered in San Francisco, the solution is working to build a more inclusive culture, where women and other minorities feel welcome and appreciated. While women comprised nearly one-third of Dropbox's workforce in late 2014, fewer than 13 percent worked in technical positions, with most fulfilling nontechnical and managerial roles. Dropbox has joined Apple and Intel in striving to increase employment opportunities for minorities and women—a difficult yet important goal.[56]

Discussion Questions

1. Why does Intel want to create more diverse management teams?
2. What are some of the ways tech companies intend to create more diverse workforces?
3. What are the benefits of having more diverse employees?

---

discrepancy. Affirmative action began in 1965 as Lyndon B. Johnson issued the first of a series of presidential directives. It was designed to make up for past hiring and promotion prejudices, to overcome workplace discrimination, and to provide equal employment opportunities for blacks and whites. Since then, minorities have made solid gains.

Legislation passed in 1991 reinforces affirmative action but prohibits organizations from setting hiring quotas that might result in reverse discrimination. Reverse discrimination occurs when a company's policies force it to consider only minorities or women instead of concentrating on hiring the person who is best qualified. More companies are arguing that affirmative action stifles their ability to hire the best employees, regardless of their minority status. Because of these problems, affirmative action became politically questionable.

Trends in Management of the Workforce

Advances in information technology as well as the last recession and financial crisis have had a major impact on employment. Employee benefits, especially health care, remains a significant and controversial issue. Even with the Affordable Care Act, health care costs continue to increase, with some of these costs passed on to employees. The labor market and employment is improving as the economy continues to improve.[57]

The nature of the workplace is changing as well. Microentrepreneurs, small-scale businesses with no more than five employees, are growing rapidly. The gig economy where individuals move from one project to another is growing quickly as well. The sharing economy (online gig economy) is providing opportunities for independent contractors to own their businesses and contract their time and resources as they see fit. The rise of Uber, Airbnb, and Lyft illustrates this new form of employment. This new job market has been supported by smartphones, tablet computers, and other technologies. However, a major challenge with the increasing use of smartphones and tablet computers is the blurring between leisure and work time, with some employers calling employees after hours.[58] Employees themselves are mixing work and personal time by using social media in the office. This is requiring companies to come up with new policies that limit how employees can use social media in the workplace. On the other hand, it is estimated that 40 percent of full-time workers log more than 50 hours a week. Some CEOs have begun encouraging employees to take more vacation time to avoid burn-out.[59] Clearly, technology is changing the dynamics of the workplace in both positive and negative ways.

It is important for human resources managers to be aware of legal issues regarding worker rights. Strict criteria—such as having management responsibilities, having advanced degrees, or making more than $455 a week—determine whether an employee is exempt from overtime pay.[61] Interestingly, although it might currently be legal for employers to request an applicant's Facebook password, employees who "rant" about their employers on Facebook can receive some form of legal protection. Under the National Labor Relations Act of 1935, certain private-sector employees are allowed to complain about working conditions and pay—which seems to apply to social media sites as well. Threats, on the other hand, are not protected.[62] Additionally, the Affordable Care Act has extended coverage to millions of Americans. The new law has placed certain health care responsibilities on employers that employ full-time employees.[63] Hence, human resources managers should understand these issues to ensure that the company adheres to all applicable employment laws.

Despite the grim outlook of the past few years, hiring trends are on the rise. Companies are finding that as consumer demands rise, their current employees are hitting the limits of productivity, requiring firms to hire more workers.[64] This will require firms not only to know about relevant employee laws, but also to understand how benefits and employee morale can contribute to overall productivity. Many of the most successful firms have discovered ways to balance costs with the well-being of their employees.

DID YOU KNOW? The largest employer in the world is the U.S. Department of Defense with more than 3 million employees. The largest private employer is Walmart with more than 2 million employees.[60]

Managing human resources is a challenging and creative facet of a business. It is the department that handles the recruiting, hiring, training, and firing of employees. Because of the diligence and detail required in hiring and the sensitivity required in firing, human resources managers have a broad skill set. Human resources, therefore, is vital to the overall functioning of the business because, without the right staff, a firm will not be able to effectively carry out its plans. Like in basketball, a team is only as strong as its individual players, and those players must be able to work together to enhance strengths and downplay weaknesses. In addition, a good human resources manager can anticipate upcoming needs and changes in the business, hiring in line with the dynamics of the market and organization.

Once a good workforce is in place, human resources managers must ensure that employees are properly trained and oriented and that they clearly understand some elements of what the organization expects. Hiring new people is expensive, time consuming, and turbulent; thus, it is imperative that all employees are carefully selected, trained, and motivated so that they will remain committed and loyal to the company. This is not an easy task, but it is one of the responsibilities of the human resources manager. Because even with references, a résumé, background checks, and an interview, it can be hard to tell how a person will fit in the organization—the HR manager needs to have skills to be able to anticipate how every individual will "fit in." Human resources jobs include compensation, labor relations, benefits, training, ethics, and compliance managers. All of the tasks associated with the interface with hiring, developing, and maintaining employee motivation come into play in human resources management. Jobs are diverse and salaries will depend on responsibilities, education, and experience.

One of the major considerations for an HR manager is workforce diversity. A multicultural, multiethnic workforce consisting of men and women will help to bring in a variety of viewpoints and improve the quality and creativity of organizational decision making. Diversity is an asset and can help a company from having blind spots or harmony in thought, background, and perspective, which stifles good team decisions. However, a diverse workforce can present some management challenges. Human resources management is often responsible for managing diversity training and compliance to make sure employees do not violate the ethical culture of the organization or break the law. Different people have different goals, motivations, and ways of thinking about issues that are informed by their culture, religion, and the people closest to them. No one way of thinking is more right or more wrong than others, and they are all valuable. A human resources manager's job can become very complicated, however, because of diversity. To be good at human resources, you should be aware of the value of differences, strive to be culturally sensitive, and ideally should have a strong understanding and appreciation of different cultures and religions. Human resources managers' ability to manage diversity and those differences will affect their overall career success.

Review Your Understanding

Define *human resources management* and explain its significance.

Human resources, or personnel, management refers to all the activities involved in determining an organization's human resources needs and acquiring, training, and compensating people to fill those needs. It is concerned with maximizing the satisfaction of employees and improving their efficiency to meet organizational objectives.

Summarize the processes of recruiting and selecting human resources for a company.

First, the human resources manager must determine the firm's future human resources needs and develop a strategy to meet them. Recruiting is the formation of a pool of qualified applicants from which management will select employees; it takes place both internally and externally. Selection is the process of collecting information about applicants and using that information to decide which ones to hire; it includes the application, interviewing, testing, and reference checking.

Discuss how workers are trained and their performance appraised.

Training teaches employees how to do their specific job tasks; development is training that augments the skills and knowledge of managers and professionals, as well as current employees. Appraising performance involves identifying an employee's strengths and weaknesses on the job. Performance appraisals may be subjective or objective.

Identify the types of turnover companies may experience and explain why turnover is an important issue.

A promotion is an advancement to a higher-level job with increased authority, responsibility, and pay. A transfer is a move to another job within the company at essentially the same level and wage. Separations occur when employees resign, retire, are terminated, or are laid off. Turnovers due to separation are expensive because of the time, money, and effort required to select, train, and manage new employees.

Specify the various ways a worker may be compensated.

Wages are financial compensation based on the number of hours worked (time wages) or the number of units produced (piece wages). Commissions are a fixed amount or a percentage of a sale paid as compensation. Salaries are compensation calculated on a weekly, monthly, or annual basis, regardless of the number of hours worked or the number of items produced. Bonuses and profit sharing are types of financial incentives. Benefits are nonfinancial forms of compensation, such as vacation, insurance, and sick leave.

Discuss some of the issues associated with unionized employees, including collective bargaining and dispute resolution.

Collective bargaining is the negotiation process through which management and unions reach an agreement on a labor contract—the formal, written document that spells out

the relationship written between the union and management. If labor and management cannot agree on a contract, labor union members may picket, strike, or boycott the firm, while management may lock out striking employees, hire strikebreakers, or form employers' associations. In a deadlock, labor disputes may be resolved by a third party—a conciliator, mediator, or arbitrator.

Describe the importance of diversity in the workforce.

When companies value and effectively manage their diverse workforces, they experience more productive use of human resources, reduced conflict, better work relationships among workers, increased commitment to and sharing of organizational goals, increased innovation and creativity, and enhanced ability to serve diverse customers.

Assess an organization's efforts to reduce its workforce size and manage the resulting effects.

Based on the material in this chapter, you should be able to answer the questions posed in the "Solve the Dilemma" feature at the end of the chapter and evaluate the company's efforts to manage the human consequences of its downsizing.

Revisit the World of Business

1. What are some advantages of using data to optimize hiring?

2. What are some of the potential problems of relying too much on data to analyze potential employees?

3. Why do you think most companies still utilize traditional HR strategies in addition to personality and behavioral tests?

Learn the Terms

affirmative action programs 317
arbitration 314
benefits 309
bonuses 309
boycott 313
collective bargaining 312
commission 308
conciliation 314
development 303
diversity 314
human resources management (HRM) 294

job analysis 295
job description 295
job specification 295
labor contract 312
labor unions 311
lockout 314
mediation 314
mentoring 303
orientation 302
picketing 312
profit sharing 309
promotion 306

recruiting 296
salary 309
selection 297
separations 306
strikebreakers 314
strikes 313
Title VII of the Civil Rights Act 301
training 302
transfer 306
turnover 305
wage/salary survey 307
wages 307

Check Your Progress

1. Distinguish among job analysis, job descriptions, and job specifications. How do they relate to planning in human resources management?

2. What activities are involved in acquiring and maintaining the appropriate level of qualified human resources? Name the stages of the selection process.

3. What are the two types of training programs? Relate training to kinds of jobs.

4. What is the significance of a performance appraisal? How do managers appraise employees?

5. Why does turnover occur? List the types of turnover. Why do businesses want to reduce turnover due to separations?

6. Relate wages, salaries, bonuses, and benefits to Herzberg's distinction between hygiene and motivation factors. How does the form of compensation relate to the type of job?

7. What is the role of benefits? Name some examples of benefits.

8. Describe the negotiation process through which management and unions reach an agreement on a contract.

9. Besides collective bargaining and the grievance procedures, what other alternatives are available to labor and management to handle labor disputes?

10. What are the benefits associated with a diverse workforce?

Get Involved

1. Although many companies screen applicants and test employees for illegal drug use, such testing is somewhat controversial. Find some companies in your community that test applicants and/or employees for drugs. Why do they have such a policy? How do the employees feel about it? Using this information, debate the pros and cons of drug testing in the workplace.

2. If collective bargaining and the grievance procedures have not been able to settle a current labor dispute,

what tactics would you and other employees adopt? Which tactics would be best for which situations? Give examples.

3. Find some examples of companies that value their diverse workforces, perhaps some of the companies mentioned in the chapter. In what ways have these firms derived benefits from promoting cultural diversity? How have they dealt with the problems associated with cultural diversity?

Build Your Skills

Appreciating and Valuing Diversity

Background

Here's a quick self-assessment to get you to think about diversity issues and evaluate the behaviors you exhibit that reflect your level of appreciation of other cultures:

Do you . . .	Regularly	Sometimes	Never
1. Make a conscious effort not to think stereotypically?			
2. Listen with interest to the ideas of people who don't think like you do?			
3. Respect other people's opinions, even when you disagree?			
4. Spend time with friends who are not your age, race, gender, or the same economic status and education?			
5. Believe your way is not the only way?			
6. Adapt well to change and new situations?			

Do you . . .	Regularly	Sometimes	Never
7. Enjoy traveling, seeing new places, eating different foods, and experiencing other cultures?			
8. Try not to offend or hurt others?			
9. Allow extra time to communicate with someone whose first language is not yours?			
10. Consider the effect of cultural differences on the messages you send and adjust them accordingly?			

Scoring

Number of **Regularly** checks _____ multiplied by 5 = _____

Number of **Sometimes** checks _____ multiplied by 3 = _____

Number of **Never** checks _____ multiplied by 0 = _____

TOTAL _____

Indications from score

40–50   You appear to understand the importance of valuing diversity and exhibit behaviors that support your appreciation of diversity.

6–39   You appear to have a basic understanding of the importance of valuing diversity and exhibit some behaviors that support that understanding.

13–5   You appear to lack a thorough understanding of the importance of valuing diversity and exhibit only some behaviors related to valuing diversity.

0–1   You appear to lack an understanding of valuing diversity and exhibit few, if any, behaviors of an individual who appreciates and values diversity.

Task

In a small group or class discussion, share the results of your assessment. After reading the following list of ways you can increase your knowledge and understanding of other cultures, select one of the items that you have done and share how it helped you learn more about another culture. Finish your discussion by generating your own ideas on other ways you can learn about and understand other cultures and fill in those ideas on the blank lines at the end.

- Be alert to and take advantage of opportunities to talk to and get to know people from other races and ethnic groups. You can find them in your neighborhood, in your classes, at your fitness center, at a concert or sporting event—just about anywhere you go. Take the initiative to strike up a conversation and show a genuine interest in getting to know the other person.

- Select a culture you're interested in and immerse yourself in that culture. Read novels, look at art, take courses, see plays.

- College students often have unique opportunities to travel inexpensively to other countries—for example, as a member of a performing arts group, with a humanitarian mission group, or as part of a college course studying abroad. Actively seek out travel opportunities that will expose you to as many cultures as possible during your college education.

- Study a foreign language.

- Expand your taste buds. The next time you're going to go to a restaurant, instead of choosing that old familiar favorite, find a restaurant that serves ethnic food you've never tried before.

- Many large metropolitan cities sponsor ethnic festivals, particularly in the summertime, where you can go and take in the sights and sounds of other cultures. Take advantage of these opportunities to have a fun time learning about cultures that are different from yours.

- _____

- _____

Solve the Dilemma

Morale among the Survivors

Medallion Corporation manufactures quality carpeting and linoleum for homes throughout the United States. A recession and subsequent downturn in home sales has sharply cut the company's sales. Medallion found itself in the unenviable position of having to lay off hundreds of employees in the home office (the manufacturing facilities) as well as many salespeople. Employees were called in on Friday afternoon and told about their status in individual meetings with their supervisors. The laid-off employees were given one additional month of work and a month of severance pay, along with the opportunity to sign up for classes to help with the transition, including job search tactics and résumé writing.

Several months after the cutbacks, morale was at an all-time low for the company, although productivity had improved. Medallion brought in consultants, who suggested that the leaner, flatter organizational structure would be suitable for more team activities. Medallion, therefore, set up task forces and teams to deal with employee concerns, but the diversity of the workforce led to conflict and misunderstandings among team members. Medallion is evaluating how to proceed with this new team approach.

LO 10-8

Assess an organization's efforts to reduce its workforce size and manage the resulting effects

Discussion Questions

1. What did Medallion's HRM department do right in dealing with the employees who were laid off?

2. What are some of the potential problems that must be dealt with after an organization experiences a major trauma such as massive layoffs?

3. What can Medallion do to make the team approach work more smoothly? What role do you think diversity training should play?

Build Your Business Plan

Managing Human Resources

Now is the time to start thinking about the employees you will need to hire to implement your business plan. What kinds of background/skills are you going to look for in potential employees? Are you going to require a certain amount of work experience?

When you are starting a business, you are often only able to hire part-time employees because you cannot afford to pay the benefits for a full-time employee. Remember at the end of the last chapter we discussed how important it is to think of ways to motivate your employees when you cannot afford to pay them what you would like.

You need to consider how you are going to recruit your employees. When you are first starting your business, it is often a good idea to ask people you respect (and not necessarily members of your family) for any recommendations of potential employees they might have. You probably won't be able to afford to advertise in the classifieds, so announcements in sources such as church bulletins or community bulletin boards should be considered as an excellent way to attract potential candidates with little, if any, investment.

Finally, you need to think about hiring employees from diverse backgrounds, especially if you are considering targeting diverse segments. The more diverse your employees, the greater the chance you will be able to draw in diverse customers.

See for Yourself Videocase

The Importance of Hollywood Labor Unions

You might be familiar with unions for teachers or autoworkers. But what about unions for actors, radio artists, and screenwriters? Because we tend to view Hollywood as a glamorous place, we are tempted to view unions as unnecessary for these types of professions. Yet Hollywood unions were, and continue to be, important players in the careers of Hollywood artists.

When actors first became mainstream in the early 20th century, working conditions for the industry included long work weeks and low pay. Studios essentially "owned" their artists, which meant that rival studios would not hire actors or actresses once their contracts ended. Actors were forced to work for the same studio to advance their careers. Negotiations with studios often proved fruitless.

Because strikes can be so disruptive and risky, they are often used as a last resort. Yet, in 1919 the Actors' Equity Association, a union for theatrical performers, and the American Federation of Labor staged a Broadway strike to protest harsh working conditions. The strike resulted in a five-year contract and promises to improve labor conditions. Although the event happened off Broadway and not in Hollywood, it would inspire other artists to begin forming their own unions.

Working conditions might have improved somewhat for theatrical actors, but radio artists, film actors, and screenwriters still had to bear with hard conditions. For instance, radio artists might do an entire show and then receive only a dollar. Film actors would work around the clock with few (if any) breaks. Screenwriters experienced salary cuts. As individuals, these artists did not have much bargaining power with studios. Realizing that banding together could improve conditions, the Masquers Club (later the Screen Actors Guild of America) was created in 1925. It was followed by the Screenwriters Guild (later renamed the Writers Guild of America) in 1933 and the American Federation of Radio Artists in 1937.

It would take lawsuits, strikes, and hardline negotiations for Hollywood artists to receive more rights. This often required artists to take risks such as suspensions or firings in the hope of better treatment. In 1988, the Writers Guild of America organized the longest strike in Hollywood history after disagreements with producers over payments and creative rights. The strike, which lasted five months, was estimated to cost the industry $500 million.

Now that working conditions seem to have improved, it might be tempting to discard Hollywood unions as no longer useful. Yet, even today, conflicts often occur between artists and studios. For instance, the Screen Actors Guild of America (SAG) watches to make sure that low-budget actors know their rights and are not exploited by producers. Unequal treatment still happens in the entertainment industry. For instance, minorities and female actors/actresses still tend to be paid less than Caucasian and male actors. The introduction of new media venues, particularly the Internet, may also warrant additional negotiations.

To address these challenges, many unions are banding together to address mutual concerns in the industry. In 2012, SAG united with the American Federation of Television and Radio Artists (AFTRA). This increases the bargaining power of the combined union. Additionally, Hollywood unions work closely with the American Federation of Labor and Congress of Industrial Organizations (AFL-CIO), which represents a federation of labor unions. The merger between SAG and AFTRA creates solidarity in the industry's unions through the formation of an Industry Coordinating Committee. This allows for coordination of activity among 10 or 12 major unions within the industry.

Although these unions are for movie stars and other artists, the goal is much the same as for other unions across the nation. As the industry expands, Hollywood unions feel that they must work together to secure benefits for their members while striving to arrive at mutually beneficial agreements with studios, producers, and other stakeholders in the entertainment industry.

Discussion Questions

1. Why are Hollywood labor unions considered necessary?

2. Why is striking often avoided if possible?

3. Why do you think unions in the entertainment industry are banding together?

You can find the related video in the Video Library in Connect. Ask your instructor how you can access Connect.

Team Exercise

Form groups and go to monster.com and look up job descriptions for positions in business (account executive in advertising, marketing manager, human resource director, production supervisor, financial analyst, bank teller, etc.). What are the key requirements for the position that you have been assigned (education, work experience, language/computer skills, etc.)? Does the position announcement provide a thorough understanding of the job? Was any key information that you would have expected omitted? Report your findings to the class.

Endnotes

1. Emma Byrne, "Hiring with Science: Big Data Brings Better Recruits," *Forbes,* July 24, 2014, http://www .forbes.com/sites/netapp/2014/07/24/hire-big-data-science/ (accessed December 18); Eliza Gray, "Questions to Answer in the Age of Optimized Hiring," *Time,* June 11, 2015, pp. 40-46 (accessed December 18, 2015); Guild website, https://www.gild.com (accessed December 27, 2015).

2. Christine Birkner, "Taking Care of Their Own," *Marketing News,* February 2015, pp. 44–49.

3. Marco della Cava, "Site Helps Moms Stay at Home, Work," *USA Today,* July 1, 2015, p. 3B; Joe McKendrick, "'100 Percent Distributed': 12 Companies That Only Hire Virtual Workers," *ZDNet.com,* March 23, 2014, http://www.zdnet.com/article/25-companies-that-hire-virtual-workers/ (accessed December 18, 2015); Brett Caine, "Rethink Workplace Flexibility," *The Huffington Post,* February 14, 2011, http://www.huffingtonpost.com/brett-caine/rethink-workplace-flexibi_b_822827.html (accessed December 22, 2015); Deborah Gage, "PowerToFly Raises $6.5 Million to Match Women with Jobs," *The Wall Street Journal,* June 30, 2015, http://blogs.wsj.com/venturecapital/2015/06/30/powertofly-raises-6-5-million-to-match-women-with-jobs/ (accessed December 22, 2015).

4. "About O*NET," O*NET Resource Center, www.onetcenter.org/overview.html (accessed March 31, 2016).

5. "P&G Careers," www.pg.com/en_US/careers/career_main.shtml (accessed March 31, 2016).

6. Olivera Perkins, "More than Half of Employers Now Use Social Media to Screen Job Candidates, Poll Says; Even Send Friend Requests," Cleveland.com, May 14, 2015, http://www.cleveland.com/business/index.ssf/2015/05/more_than_half_of_employers_no_1.html (accessed March 31, 2016).

7. Dune Lawrence, "Tracking the Enemy Within," *Bloomberg Businessweek,* March 16–22, 2015, pp. 39–41.

8. Join Together Staff, "Almost 10 Percent of Full-Time Workers Have Had Recent Substance Abuse Problem," Partnership for Drug-Free Kids, April 22, 2015, http://www.drugfree.org/join-together/almost-10-percent-full-time-workers-recent-substance-abuse-problem/ (accessed March 31, 2016).

9. Office of National Drug Control Policy, "How Illicit Drug Affects Business and the Economy," https://www.whitehouse.gov/ondcp/ondcp-fact-sheets/how-illicit-drug-use-affects-business-and-the-economy (accessed March 31, 2016).

10. Lauren Weber and Mike Esterl, "E-Cigarette Rise Poses Quandary For Employers," *The Wall Street Journal,* January 16, 2014, p. A2.

11. Shannon McFarland, "Job Seekers Getting Asked for Facebook Passwords," *USA Today,* March 20, 2012, http://usatoday30.usatoday.com/tech/news/story/2012-03-20/job-applicants-facebook/53665606/1 (accessed March 31, 2016).

12. Jonathan Dame, "Will Employers Still Ask for Facebook Passwords in 2014?" *USA Today,* January 10, 2014, http://www.usatoday.com/story/money/business/2014/01/10/facebook-passwords-employers/4327739/ (accessed March 31, 2016).

13. Allison Linn, "Desperate Measures: Why Some People Fake Their Resumes," *CNBC,* February 7, 2014, www.cnbc.com/id/101397212 (accessed March 31, 2016).

14. Christopher T. Marquet and Lisa J. B. Peterson, "Résumé Fraud: The Top Ten Lies," Marquet International, Ltd., www.marquetinternational.com/pdf/Resume%20Fraud-Top%20Ten%20Lies.pdf (accessed March 31, 2016).

15. U.S. Equal Employment Opportunity Commission, "Charge Statistics: FY 1997 through FY 2015," http://www.eeoc.gov/eeoc/statistics/enforcement/charges.cfm (accessed March 31, 2016); Equal Employment Opportunity Commission, "Charges Alleging Sexual Harassment FY 2010–FY 2015," http://www.eeoc.gov/eeoc/statistics/enforcement/sexual_harassment_new.cfm (accessed March 31, 2016).

16. Ellen McGirt, "An Inside Look at What's Keeping Black Men Out of the C-Suite," *Fortune,* February 1, 2016, http://fortune.com/black-executives-men-c-suite/ (accessed March 31, 2016); KJ Mariño, "Top 10 Latino CEOs at Fortune 500 Companies You Should Know About," *Latin Post,* January 8, 2016, http://www.latinpost.com/articles/107285/20160108/top-10-latino-ceos-at-fortune-500-companies-you-should-know-about.htm (accessed March 31, 2016).

17. Stephen Bastien, "12 Benefits of Hiring Older Workers," *Entrepreneur.com,* September 20, 2006, www.entrepreneur.com/article/167500 (accessed May 29, 2014).

18. Catherine Hill, "The Simple Truth about the Gender Pay Gap (Spring 2016)," *AAUW,* http://www.aauw.org/research/the-simple-truth-about-the-gender-pay-gap/ (accessed March 31, 2016).

19. Georgia Wells, "Mind the Gender Pay Gap: Female Computer Programmers Earn 72 Cents on the Dollar, Study Says," *The Wall Street Journal,* March 24, 2016, http://blogs.wsj.com/digits/2016/03/24/mind-the-gender-pay-gap-female-computer-programmers-earn-72-cents-on-the-dollar-study-says/ (accessed March 31, 2016).

20. Catherine Rampell, "The Gender Wage Gap, Around the World," March 9, 2010, http://economix.blogs.nytimes.com/2010/03/09/the-gender-wage-gap-around-the-world/?_php=true&_type=blogs&_r=0 (accessed March 31, 2016).

21. "Our Curriculum," Hamburger University, www.aboutmcdonalds.com/mcd/careers/hamburger_university/our_curriculum.html (accessed March 31, 2016).

22. Chronus Corporation, "How to Use Mentoring in Your Workplace," http://chronus.com/how-to-use-mentoring-in-your-workplace (accessed March 31, 2016).

23. The Sage Group PLC, "Mentoring Statistics," 2015, http://www.sage.com/businessnavigators/research (accessed March 31, 2016).

24. Sue Lam, "Why Mentoring Is More Important for Women in Workplace than You Think," *APQC,* March 10, 2015, http://www.apqc.org/blog/why-mentoring-more-important-women-workplace-you-think (accessed March 24, 2015).

25. "Our Employee First Culture," The Container Store, http://standfor.containerstore.com/putting-our-employees-first (accessed March 31, 2016).

26. Doug Stewart, "Employee-Appraisal Software," *Inc.,* www.inc.com/magazine/19940615/3288_pagen_2.html (accessed March 31, 2016).

27. Maury A. Peiperl, "Getting 360-Degree Feedback Right," *Harvard Business Review,* January 2001, pp. 142–148.

28. Chris Musselwhite, "Self Awareness and the Effective Leader," Inc.com, www.inc.com/resources/leadership/articles/20071001/musselwhite.html (accessed March 31, 2016).

29. Rachel Feintzeig, "You're Awesome! Firms Scrap Negative Feedback," *The Wall Street Journal,* February 11, 2015, pp. B1, B5.

30. Leslie Patton, "Diebold's New Executive Suite," *Bloomberg Businessweek,* August 10–23, 2015, pp. 21–23.

31. Marcia Zidle, "Employee Turnover: Seven Reasons Why People Quit Their Jobs," Alrakoba, http://ezinearticles.com/?Employee-Turnover:-Seven-Reasons-Why-People-Quit-Their-Jobs&id=42531 (accessed March 31, 2016).

32. Peter Coy, "Is a $15 Minimum Wage Too High?" *Bloomberg Businessweek,* August 10–23, 2015, pp. 14–16.

33. Ibid.

34. "Fair Labor Standards Act Advisor," U.S. Department of Labor, www.dol.gov/elaws/faq/esa/flsa/002.htm (accessed March 31, 2016).

35. City of Santa Fe, "Living Wage," https://www.santafenm.gov/living_wage_1 (accessed March 31, 2016); National Conferences of State Legislatures, "2016 Minimum Wage by State," March 30, 2016, http://www.ncsl.org/research/labor-and-employment/state-minimum-wage-chart.aspx (accessed March 31, 2016).

36. Christopher Martin, "Google Is Making Its Biggest Ever Bet on Renewable Energy," *Bloomberg Business,* February 26, 2015, http://www.bloomberg.com/news/articles/2015-02-26/google-makes-biggest-bet-on-renewables-to-fund-solarcity (accessed December 11, 2015); Google, "Campus Operations," Google Green, https://www.google.com/green/efficiency/oncampus/ (accessed December 11, 2015); Lauren Hepler, "Apple, Google and Bribing Employees to Hit Corporate Climate Goals," *GreenBiz,* November 5, 2015, http://www.greenbiz.com/article/apple-google-and-bribing-employees-hit-corporate-climate-goals (accessed December 11, 2015).

37. Rodan + Fields, Compensation Plan at a Glance, https://www.rodanandfields.com/images/Archives/CompPlan_update.pdf (accessed March 31, 2016).

38. Justin Baer, "Wall Street Bracing for Lower Bonuses for First Time in Years," *The Wall Street Journal,* November 8, 2015, http://www.wsj.com/articles/wall-street-bracing-for-lower-bonuses-for-first-time-in-years-1447030800 (accessed March 31, 2016).

39. Christopher Tkaczyk, "My Five Days of 'Bleeding Green,'" *Fortune,* March 15, 2016, pp. 166–176.

40. Bureau of Labor Statistics, "Employer Costs for Employee Compensation," December 2015, http://www.bls.gov/news.release/ecec.nr0.htm (accessed April 29, 2014).

41. Christine Birkner, "Taking Care of Their Own," *Marketing News,* February 2015, pp. 44–49.

42. "Wellness Benefits," Lowe's, http://mylowesbenefits.com/part-time/wellness-benefits/ (accessed April 1, 2016).

43. Angus Loten and Sarah E. Needleman, "Laws on Paid Sick Leave Divide Businesses," *The Wall Street Journal,* February 6, 2014, p. B5.

44. "Job Requirement: Have Fun at Work," *Fortune,* March 15, 2016, p. 30.

45. Bureau of Labor Statistics, http://www.bls.gov/news.release/pdf/union2.pdf (accessed April 1, 2016).

46. Tom Walsh, "UAW Needs Stronger Message," *USA Today,* February 17, 2014, p. 1B.

47. Mike Esterl, "Walkout Affects Coca-Cola Plants," *The Wall Street Journal,* December 19–20, 2015, p. B4.

48. Josh Eidelson, "Walmart Fires Eleven Strikers in Alleged Retaliation," *The Nation,* June 22, 2013, www.thenation.com/blog/174937/walmart-fires-eleven-strikers-alleged-retaliation# (accessed April 29, 2014); Carlyn Kolker, "U.S. Labor Board May Issue Complaint Against Wal-Mart on Strikes," *Reuters,* November 18, 2013, www.reuters.com/article/2013/11/19/us-usa-employment-walmart-idUSBRE9AI00S20131119 (accessed April 29, 2014); Dave Jamieson, "Feds Charge Walmart with Breaking Labor Law in Black Friday Strikes," *Huffington Post,* January 25, 2014, www.huffingtonpost.com/2014/01/15/walmart-complaint_n_4604069.html (accessed April 29, 2014).

49. Steven Greenhouse, "In Pennsylvania, a Steel Mill and Its Workers at a Crossroads," *The New York Times,* December 3, 2015, http://www.nytimes.com/2015/12/04/business/in-pennsylvania-a-steel-mill-and-its-workers-at-a-crossroads.html?_r=0 (accessed April 1, 2016).

50. Alexia Elejalde-Ruiz, "Coca-Cola, Union Agree to Federal Mediation as Strike Continues," *Chicago Tribune,* December 9, 2015, http://www.chicagotribune.com/business/ct-coke-strike-letter-1209-biz-20151207-story.html (accessed March 31, 2016).

51. Joel Rosenblatt, "Uber Tells Judges to Read the Fine Print," *Bloomberg Businessweek,* September 24, 2015, pp. 33–34.

52. Carolina Moreno, "10 Reasons You'll Love Living in a Majority-Minority America," *The Huffington Post,* May 7, 2015, http://www.huffingtonpost.com/2015/05/07/majority-minority-america_n_7205688.html (accessed April 1, 2016).

53. Melanie Tervalon, "At a Decade: Centers of Excellence in Culturally Competent Care," *The Permanente Journal,* 13, no. 1 (2009), pp. 87–91; Kaiser Permanente, "Kaiser Permanente Named No. 2 on DiversityInc's Top 50 Companies for Diversity® List for 2015," April 24, 2015, http://share.kaiserpermanente.org/article/kaiser-permanente-named-no-2-on-diversityincs-top-50-companies-for-diversity-list-for-2015/ (accessed April 1, 2016).

54. Judy Woodruff, "How Silicon Valley Is Trying to Fix Its Diversity Problem," *PBS,* March 17, 2016, http://www.pbs.org/newshour/bb/how-silicon-valley-is-trying-to-fix-its-diversity-problem/ (accessed March 28, 2016).

55. Taylor H. Cox Jr., "The Multicultural Organization," *Academy of Management Executives* 5 (May 1991), pp. 34–47; Marilyn Loden and Judy B. Rosener,

Workforce America! Managing Employee Diversity as a Vital Resource (Homewood, IL: Business One Irwin, 1991).

56. Jessica Guynn, "Dropbox Thinks Outside the Box on Diversity," *USA Today,* November 6, 2014, http://www.usatoday.com/story/tech/2014/11/05/dropbox-diversity/18473517/ (accessed December 18, 2015); J. J. McCorvey, "Can Intel Solve Tech's Diversity Problem?" *Fast Company,* April 23, 2015, http://www.fastcompany.com/3044260/can-intel-solve-techs-diversity-problem (accessed December 18, 2015); Rani Molla and Renee Lightner, "Diversity in Tech," *The Wall Street Journal,* December 30, 2014, http://graphics.wsj.com/diversity-in-tech-companies/ (accessed December 27, 2015).

57. Susannah Snider, "7 Workplace and Employment Trends to Anticipate in 2016," *US News,* January 4, 2016, http://money.usnews.com/money/careers/articles/2016-01-04/7-workplace-and-employment-trends-to-anticipate-in-2016 (accessed March 28, 2016).

58. Paul Davidson, "Overworked and Underpaid?" *USA Today,* April 16, 2012, pp. 1A–2A.

59. Jennifer Alsever, "Take It Easy. That's An Order!" *Fortune,* December 15, 2015, p. 46.

60. Niall McCarthy, "The World's Biggest Employers [Infographic]," *Forbes,* June 23, 2015m http://www.forbes.com/sites/niallmccarthy/2015/06/23/the-worlds-biggest-employers-infographic/#5305848251d0 (accessed April 4, 2016).

61. Ibid.

62. Melanie Trottman, "For Angry Employees, Legal Cover for Rants," *The Wall Street Journal,* December 2, 2011, http://online.wsj.com/article/SB10001424052970203710704577049822809710332.html (accessed May 29, 2014).

63. IRS, "Affordable Care Act Tax Provisions for Large Employers," https://www.irs.gov/Affordable-Care-Act/Employers/Affordable-Care-Act-Tax-Provisions-for-Large-Employers (accessed April 4, 2016).

64. Martin Crutsinger, "Hiring Grows as Companies Hit Limits with Workers,"*MPR News,* March 7, 2012, http://minnesota.publicradio.org/display/web/2012/03/07/hiring-grows-as-companies-hit-limit/ (accessed May 29, 2014).

PART 5

Marketing: Developing Relationships

SERVINGS OF FRUIT*
PER BOTTLE

Bolthouse FARMS

Berry Boost™

with the juice of
42
BERRIES
per bottle

© dave willman/123RF

11 Customer-Driven Marketing

Learning Objectives

After reading this chapter, you will be able to:

LO 11-1 Define *marketing* and describe the exchange process.

LO 11-2 Specify the functions of marketing.

LO 11-3 Explain the marketing concept and its implications for developing marketing strategies.

LO 11-4 Examine the development of a marketing strategy, including market segmentation and marketing mix.

LO 11-5 Investigate how marketers conduct marketing research and study buying behavior.

LO 11-6 Summarize the environmental forces that influence marketing decisions.

LO 11-7 Assess a company's marketing plans and propose a solution for resolving its problem.

Enter the World of Business ⊖───────────

Campbell's Soup: You Can't Always Get What You Want

Campbell Soup Company, famous for established staples like condensed soup and Goldfish crackers, hopes to target consumers interested in purchasing healthier food. A major challenge, however, is offering convenient and tasty food that consumers perceive as healthy. For instance, a few years ago Campbell's abandoned its lower-sodium reformulation of its soups after flagging sales suggested that lower salt levels led to less tasty food products. The trick is to create healthier, tasty products that consumers can easily differentiate from the competition.

In general, processing foods to make them more convenient makes them less healthy. Many consumers are avoiding foods containing preservatives and additives due to health concerns, leading to a call for fresher foods. At the same time, fewer Americans are cooking meals at home, increasing the demand for quick and easy food choices.

To meet consumer demands, Campbell's introduced its new Campbell's Fresh Division, which offers snack-sized carrots, hummus, and cold pressed juices. To differentiate its fresh products, Campbell's offers its seemingly common products with innovative twists. For instance, after acquiring Bolthouse Farms, Campbell's began offering Bolthouse's baby carrots product with a dry seasoning that tastes like ranch dressing. Campbell's also acquired Plum Organics, a company specializing in organic baby foods, because it wished to develop more fresh foods in convenient, squeezable pouches instead of traditional jars and cans. For adults, it offers microwavable soup containers that are easy to use. Responding to these fluctuating consumer preferences has helped Campbell's retain its lead in the processed and packaged food industry.[1]

Introduction

Marketing involves planning and executing the development, pricing, promotion, and distribution of ideas, goods, and services to create exchanges that satisfy individual and organizational goals. These activities ensure that the products consumers want to buy are available at a price they are willing to pay and that consumers are provided with information about product features and availability. Organizations of all sizes and objectives engage in these activities.

In this chapter, we focus on the basic principles of marketing. First we define and examine the nature of marketing. Then we look at how marketers develop marketing strategies to satisfy the needs and wants of their customers. Next we discuss buying behavior and how marketers use research to determine what consumers want to buy and why. Finally, we explore the impact of the environment on marketing activities.

Nature of Marketing

LO 11-1

Define *marketing* and describe the exchange process.

marketing
a group of activities designed to expedite transactions by creating, distributing, pricing, and promoting goods, services, and ideas.

A vital part of any business undertaking, **marketing** is a group of activities designed to expedite transactions by creating, distributing, pricing, and promoting goods, services, and ideas. These activities create value by allowing individuals and organizations to obtain what they need and want. A business cannot achieve its objectives unless it provides something that customers value. But just creating an innovative product that meets many users' needs isn't sufficient in today's volatile global marketplace. Products must be conveniently available, competitively priced, and uniquely promoted.

Marketing is an important part of a firm's overall strategy. Other functional areas of the business—such as operations, finance, and all areas of management—must be coordinated with marketing decisions. Marketing has the important function of providing revenue to sustain a firm. Only by creating trust and effective relationships with customers can a firm succeed in the long run. Businesses try to respond to consumer wants and needs and to anticipate changes in the environment. Unfortunately, it is difficult to understand and predict what consumers want: Motives are often unclear; few principles can be applied consistently; and markets tend to fragment, each desiring customized products, new value, or better service.

It is important to note what marketing is not: It is not manipulating consumers to get them to buy products they do not want. It is not just selling and advertising; it is a systematic approach to satisfying consumers. Marketing focuses on the many activities—planning, pricing, promoting, and distributing products—that foster exchanges. Unfortunately, the mass media and movies sometimes portray marketing as unethical or as not adding value to business. In this chapter, we point out that marketing is essential and provides important benefits in making products available to consumers.

The Exchange Relationship

exchange
the act of giving up one thing (money, credit, labor, goods) in return for something else (goods, services, or ideas).

At the heart of all business is the **exchange,** the act of giving up one thing (money, credit, labor, goods) in return for something else (goods, services, or ideas). Businesses exchange their goods, services, or ideas for money or credit supplied by customers in a voluntary *exchange relationship,* illustrated in Figure 11-1. The buyer must feel good about the purchase, or the exchange will not continue. If your cell phone service works everywhere, you will probably feel good about using its services. But if you have a lot of dropped calls, you will probably use another phone service next time.

For an exchange to occur, certain conditions are required. As indicated by the arrows in Figure 11-1, buyers and sellers must be able to communicate about the

Companies find that communicating with customers through digital media sites can enhance customer relationships and create value for their brands.

© kenary820/Shutterstock

"something of value" available to each. An exchange does not necessarily take place just because buyers and sellers have something of value to exchange. Each participant must be willing to give up his or her respective "something of value" to receive the "something" held by the other. You are willing to exchange your "something of value"—your money or credit—for soft drinks, football tickets, or new shoes because you consider those products more valuable or more important than holding on to your cash or credit potential.

When you think of marketing products, you may think of tangible things—cars, smartphones, or books, for example. What most consumers want, however, is a way to get a job done, solve a problem, or gain some enjoyment. You may purchase a Hoover vacuum cleaner not because you want a vacuum cleaner but because you want clean carpets. Starbucks serves coffee drinks at a premium price, providing convenience, quality, and an inviting environment. It claims that it is not in the "coffee business serving people" but is in the "people business serving coffee." Therefore, the tangible product itself may not be as important as the image or the benefits associated with the product. This intangible "something of value" may be capability gained from using a product or the image evoked by it, or even the brand name. Good examples of brand names that are easy to remember include Avon's Skin So Soft, Tide detergent, and the Ford Mustang. The label or brand name may also offer the added bonus of being a conversation piece in a social environment, such as Dancing Bull or Smoking Loon wine.

FIGURE 11-1
The Exchange Process:
Giving Up One Thing in
Return for Another

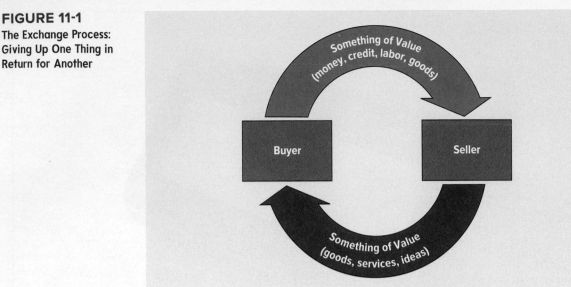

Functions of Marketing

Specify the functions of
marketing.

Marketing focuses on a complex set of activities that must be performed to accomplish objectives and generate exchanges. These activities include buying, selling, transporting, storing, grading, financing, marketing research, and risk taking.

Buying.   Everyone who shops for products (consumers, stores, businesses, governments) decides whether and what to buy. A marketer must understand buyers' needs and desires to determine what products to make available.

Selling.   The exchange process is expedited through selling. Marketers usually view selling as a persuasive activity that is accomplished through promotion (advertising, personal selling, sales promotion, publicity, and packaging).

Transporting.   Transporting is the process of moving products from the seller to the buyer. Marketers focus on transportation costs and services.

Storing.   Like transporting, storing is part of the physical distribution of products and includes warehousing goods. Warehouses hold some products for lengthy periods in order to create time utility. Time utility has to do with being able to satisfy demand in a timely manner. This especially pertains to a seasonal good such as orange juice. Fresh oranges are only available for a few months annually, but consumers demand juice throughout the entire year. Sellers must arrange for cold storage of orange juice concentrate so that they can maintain a steady supply all of the time.

Grading.   Grading refers to standardizing products by dividing them into subgroups and displaying and labeling them so that consumers clearly understand their nature and quality. Many products, such as meat, steel, and fruit, are graded according to a set of standards that often are established by the state or federal government.

Financing.   For many products, especially large items such as automobiles, refrigerators, and new homes, the marketer arranges credit to expedite the purchase.

Marketing Research.   Through research, marketers ascertain the need for new goods and services. By gathering information regularly, marketers can detect new trends and changes in consumer tastes.

Risk Taking.   Risk is the chance of loss associated with marketing decisions. Developing a new product creates a chance of loss if consumers do not like it enough to buy it. Spending money to hire a sales force or to conduct marketing research also involves risk. The implication of risk is that most marketing decisions result in either success or failure.

Creating Value with Marketing[2]

Value is an important element of managing long-term customer relationships and implementing the marking concept. We view **value** as a customer's subjective assessment of benefits relative to costs in determining the worth of a product (customer value = customer benefits – customer costs).

> **value**
> a customer's subjective assessment of benefits relative to costs in determining the worth of a product.

Customer benefits include anything a buyer receives in an exchange. Hotels and motels, for example, basically provide a room with a bed and bathroom, but each firm provides a different level of service, amenities, and atmosphere to satisfy its guests. Motel 6 offers the minimum services necessary to maintain a quality, efficient, low-price overnight accommodation. In contrast, the Ritz-Carlton provides every imaginable service a guest might desire and strives to ensure that all service is of the highest quality. Customers judge which type of accommodation offers them the best value according to the benefits they desire and their willingness and ability to pay for the costs associated with the benefits.

Customer costs include anything a buyer must give up to obtain the benefits the product provides. The most obvious cost is the monetary price of the product, but nonmonetary costs can be equally important in a customer's determination of value. Two nonmonetary costs are the time and effort customers expend to find and purchase desired products. To reduce time and effort, a company can increase product availability, thereby making it more convenient for buyers to purchase the firm's products. Another nonmonetary cost is risk, which can be reduced by offering good basic warranties for an additional charge. Another risk-reduction strategy is increasingly popular in today's catalog/telephone/Internet shopping environment. L.L. Bean, for example, uses a guarantee to reduce the risk involved in ordering merchandise from its catalogs.

In developing marketing activities, it is important to recognize that customers receive benefits based on their experiences. For example, many computer buyers consider services such as fast delivery, ease of installation, technical advice, and training assistance to be important elements of the product. Customers also derive benefits from the act of shopping and selecting products. These benefits can be affected by the atmosphere or environment of a store, such as Red Lobster's nautical/seafood theme.

LO 11-3

Explain the marketing concept and its implications for developing marketing strategies.

The Marketing Concept

A basic philosophy that guides all marketing activities is the **marketing concept,** the idea that an organization should try to satisfy customers' needs through coordinated activities that also allow it to achieve its own goals. According to the marketing concept, a business must find out what consumers desire and then develop the good, service, or idea that fulfills their needs or wants. The business must then get the product to the customer. In addition, the business must continually alter, adapt, and develop

> **marketing concept**
> the idea that an organization should try to satisfy customers' needs through coordinated activities that also allow it to achieve its own goals.

Mattel has begun to release Barbie dolls that come in different sizes. This comes after years of criticism that Barbie's figure was unrealistic and could be damaging to young girls who want to emulate the dolls. Mattel is embracing the marketing concept by providing features that consumers want into their products.

© Mattel/Splash News/Newscom

products to keep pace with changing consumer needs and wants. For instance, after years of criticism regarding her unrealistic body shape, Mattel released its iconic Barbie doll in three different shape sizes. Barbie will also have different skin tones and hairstyles. These new dolls are meant to reflect the multicultural diversity around the world.[3] To remain competitive, companies must be prepared to add to or adapt their product lines to satisfy customers' desires for new fads or changes in eating habits. Each business must determine how best to implement the marketing concept, given its own goals and resources.

Trying to determine customers' true needs is increasingly difficult because no one fully understands what motivates people to buy things. However, Estée Lauder, founder of her namesake cosmetics company, had a pretty good idea. When a prestigious store in Paris rejected her perfume in the 1960s, she "accidentally" dropped a bottle on the floor where nearby customers could get a whiff of it. So many asked about the scent that Galeries Lafayette was obliged to place an order. Lauder ultimately built an empire using then-unheard-of tactics like free samples and gifts with purchases to market her "jars of hope."[4]

Although customer satisfaction is the goal of the marketing concept, a business must also achieve its own objectives, such as boosting productivity, reducing costs, or achieving a percentage of a specific market. If it does not, it will not survive. For example, Lenovo could sell computers for $50 and give customers a lifetime guarantee, which would be great for customers but not so great for Lenovo. Obviously, the company must strike a balance between achieving organizational objectives and satisfying customers.

To implement the marketing concept, a firm must have good information about what consumers want, adopt a consumer orientation, and coordinate its efforts throughout the entire organization; otherwise, it may be awash with goods, services, and ideas that consumers do not want or need. Successfully implementing the marketing concept requires that a business view the customer's perception of value as the ultimate measure of work performance and improving value, and the rate at which this is done, as the measure of success.[5] Everyone in the organization who interacts with customers—*all* customer-contact employees—must know what customers want. They are selling ideas, benefits, philosophies, and experiences—not just goods and services.

Someone once said that if you build a better mousetrap, the world will beat a path to your door. Suppose you do build a better mousetrap. What will happen? Actually, consumers are not likely to beat a path to your door because the market is so competitive. A coordinated effort by everyone involved with the mousetrap is needed to sell the product. Your company must reach out to customers and tell them about your mousetrap, especially how your mousetrap works better than those offered by competitors. If you do not make the benefits of your product widely known, in most cases, it will not be successful. One reason that Apple is so successful is because of its stores. Apple's more than 400 national and international retail stores market computers and electronics in a way unlike any other computer manufacturer or retail establishment. The upscale stores, located in high-rent shopping districts, show off Apple's products in modern, spacious settings to encourage consumers to try new things—like making a movie on a computer.[6] So for some companies, like Apple Inc., you need to create stores to sell your product to consumers. You could also find stores that are willing to sell your product to consumers for you. In either situation, you must implement the marketing concept by making a product with satisfying benefits and making it available and visible.

Orville Wright said that an airplane is "a group of separate parts flying in close formation." This is what most companies are trying to accomplish: They are striving for a team effort to deliver the right good or service to customers. A breakdown at any point in the organization—whether it be in production, purchasing, sales, distribution, or advertising—can result in lost sales, lost revenue, and dissatisfied customers.

Evolution of the Marketing Concept

The marketing concept may seem like the obvious approach to running a business and building relationships with customers. However, businesspeople are not always focused on customers when they create and operate businesses. Many companies fail to grasp the importance of customer relationships and fail to implement customer strategies. A firm's marketing department needs to share information about customers and their desires with the entire organization. Our society and economic system have changed over time, and marketing has become more important as markets have become more competitive. Although this is an oversimplification, these time periods help us to understand how marketing has evolved. There have always been some firms that have practiced the marketing concept.

The Production Orientation. During the second half of the 19th century, the Industrial Revolution was well under way in the United States. New technologies, such as electricity, railroads, internal combustion engines, and mass-production techniques, made it possible to manufacture goods with ever increasing efficiency. Together with new management ideas and ways of using labor, products poured into the marketplace, where demand for manufactured goods was strong.

The Sales Orientation. By the early part of the 20th century, supply caught up with and then exceeded demand, and businesspeople began to realize they would have to "sell" products to buyers. During the first half of the 20th century, businesspeople viewed sales as the primary means of increasing profits in what has become known as a sales orientation. Those who adopted the sales orientation perspective believed the most important marketing activities were personal selling and advertising. Today, some people still inaccurately equate marketing with a sales orientation.

The Market Orientation. By the 1950s, some businesspeople began to recognize that even efficient production and extensive promotion did not guarantee sales. These businesses, and many others since, found that they must first determine what customers want and then produce it, rather than making the products first and then trying to persuade customers that they need them. Managers at General Electric first suggested that the marketing concept was a companywide philosophy of doing business. As more organizations realized the importance of satisfying customers' needs, U.S. businesses entered the marketing era, one of market orientation.

market orientation
an approach requiring organizations to gather information about customer needs, share that information throughout the firm, and use that information to help build long-term relationships with customers.

A **market orientation** requires organizations to gather information about customer needs, share that information throughout the entire firm, and use it to help build long-term relationships with customers. Top executives, marketing managers, non-marketing managers (those in production, finance, human resources, and so on), and customers all become mutually dependent and cooperate in developing and carrying out a market orientation. Nonmarketing managers must communicate with marketing managers to share information important to understanding the customer. Consider the 125-year history of Wrigley's gum. In 1891, the gum was given away to promote sales of baking powder (the company's original product). The gum was launched as its own product in 1893, and after four generations of Wrigley family CEOs, the company continues to reinvent itself and focus on consumers. Eventually, the family made the decision to sell the company to Mars. Wrigley now functions as a stand-alone subsidiary of Mars. The deal combined such popular brands as Wrigley's gums and Life Savers with Mars' M&M's, Snickers, and Skittles to form the world's largest confectionary company.

Trying to assess what customers want, which is difficult to begin with, is further complicated by the rate at which trends, fashions, and tastes can change. Businesses today want to satisfy customers and build meaningful long-term relationships with them. It is more efficient and less expensive for the company to retain existing customers and even increase the amount of business each customer provides the organization than to find new customers. Most companies' success depends on increasing the amount of repeat business; therefore, relationship building between company and customer is key. Many companies are turning to technologies associated with customer relationship management to help build relationships and boost business with existing customers.

Although it might be easy to dismiss customer relationship management as time-consuming and expensive, this mistake could destroy a company. Customer relationship management (CRM) is important in a market orientation because it can result in loyal and profitable customers. Without loyal customers, businesses would not survive; therefore, achieving the full profit potential of each customer relationship should be the goal of every marketing strategy. At the most basic level, profits can be obtained through relationships by acquiring new customers, enhancing the profitability of existing customers, and extending the duration of customer relationships. The profitability of loyal customers throughout their relationship with the company (their lifetime customer value) should not be underestimated. For instance, Pizza Hut has a lifetime customer value of approximately $8,000, whereas Cadillac's lifetime customer value is approximately $332,000.[7]

Communication remains a major element of any strategy to develop and manage long-term customer relationships. By providing multiple points of interactions with customers—that is, websites, telephone, fax, e-mail, and personal contact—companies can personalize customer relationships.[8] Like many online retailers, Amazon.com stores and analyzes purchase data in an attempt to understand

Tesla meets the needs of consumers who care about the environment and wish to improve their environmental footprint by driving an electric vehicle.

each customer's interests. This information helps the online retailer improve its ability to satisfy individual customers and thereby increase sales of books, music, movies, and other products to each customer. The ability to identify individual customers allows marketers to shift their focus from targeting groups of similar customers to increasing their share of an individual customer's purchases. Regardless of the medium through which communication occurs, customers should ultimately be the drivers of marketing strategy because they understand what they want. Customer relationship management systems should ensure that marketers listen to customers in order to respond to their needs and concerns and build long-term relationships.

Developing a Marketing Strategy

LO 11-4

Examine the development of a marketing strategy, including market segmentation and marketing mix.

To implement the marketing concept and customer relationship management, a business needs to develop and maintain a **marketing strategy,** a plan of action for developing, pricing, distributing, and promoting products that meet the needs of specific customers. This definition has two major components: selecting a target market and developing an appropriate marketing mix to satisfy that target market.

Selecting a Target Market

A **market** is a group of people who have a need, purchasing power, and the desire and authority to spend money on goods, services, and ideas. A **target market** is a more specific group of consumers on whose needs and wants a company focuses its marketing efforts. Target markets can be further segmented into business markets and consumer markets.

Business-to-business (B2B) marketing involves marketing products to customers who will use the product for resale, direct use in daily operations, or direct use in making other products. John Deere, for instance, sells earth-moving equipment to construction firms and tractors to farmers. Most people, however, tend to think of *business-to-consumer marketing (B2C),* or marketing directly to the end consumer. Sometimes products are used by both types of markets. Cleaning supplies such as Windex are consumer products when sold to households but business products when sold for janitorial purposes. Consumer products are purchased to satisfy personal and family needs.

Marketing managers may define a target market as a relatively small number of people within a larger market, or they may define it as the total market (Figure 11-2). Rolls Royce, for example, targets its products at a very exclusive, high-income market—people who want the ultimate in prestige in an automobile. On the other hand, Ford Motor Company manufactures a variety of vehicles including Lincolns, Mercurys, and Ford Trucks in order to appeal to varied tastes, needs, and desires.

Some firms use a **total-market approach,** in which they try to appeal to everyone and assume that all buyers have similar needs and wants. Sellers of salt, sugar, and many agricultural products use a total-market approach because everyone is a potential consumer of these products. This approach is also referred to as *mass marketing*. Most firms, though, use **market segmentation** and divide the total market into groups of people. A **market segment** is a collection of individuals, groups, or organizations who share one or more characteristics and thus have relatively similar product needs and desires. Women are the largest market segment, with 51 percent of the U.S. population. At the household level, segmentation can identify each woman's social attributes, culture, and stages in life to determine preferences and needs.

marketing strategy
a plan of action for developing, pricing, distributing, and promoting products that meet the needs of specific customers.

market
a group of people who have a need, purchasing power, and the desire and authority to spend money on goods, services, and ideas.

target market
a specific group of consumers on whose needs and wants a company focuses its marketing efforts.

total-market approach
an approach whereby a firm tries to appeal to everyone and assumes that all buyers have similar needs.

market segmentation
a strategy whereby a firm divides the total market into groups of people who have relatively similar product needs.

market segment
a collection of individuals, groups, or organizations who share one or more characteristics and thus have relatively similar product needs and desires.

FIGURE 11-2
Target Market Strategies

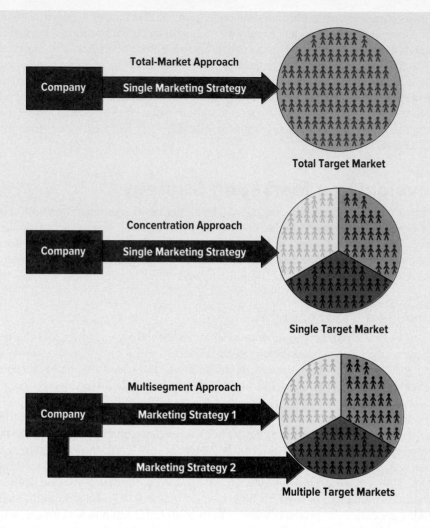

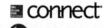
Another market segment on which many marketers are focusing is the growing Hispanic population. Target launched advertisements showing three generations of a family at a dinner table after the food had been removed to demonstrate the Latin American practice of *sombremesa,* or spending time chatting after the meal. This is part of a campaign Target has launched using cultural concepts that resonate with the Hispanic culture, rather than simply translating marketing campaigns into the Spanish language.[9] The companies hope to create relationships with Hispanic consumers in order to gain their loyalty. One of the challenges for marketers in the future will be to effectively address an increasingly racially diverse United States. In future decades, the purchasing power of minority market segments is set to grow by leaps and bounds. Table 11-1 shows the buying power of minority groups in the United States. Today, multicultural buying power exceeds $3.4 trillion.[10] Companies will have to learn how to most effectively reach these growing segments. Companies use market segmentation to focus their efforts and resources on specific target markets so that they can

	1990	2000	2010	2012	2015
Total	$4,200	$7,300	$11,200	$12,200	$15,100
Black	316	600	947	1,000	1,300
Native American	20	40	87	103	148
Asian	115	272	609	718	1,000
Hispanic*	210	488	1,000	1,200	1,700

TABLE 11-1
Buying Power of U.S. Minorities by Race (billions)

* Earnings per share are for the latest 12-month period and do not necessarily match year-end numbers.

Source: Jeffrey M. Humphreys, The Multicultural Economy 2012 (Athens, GA: The University of Georgia Terry College of Business Selig Center for Economic Growth, 2013).

develop a productive marketing strategy. Two common approaches to segmenting markets are the concentration approach and the multisegment approach.

Market Segmentation Approaches. In the **concentration approach,** a company develops one marketing strategy for a single market segment. The concentration approach allows a firm to specialize, focusing all its efforts on the one market segment. Porsche, for example, directs all its marketing efforts toward high-income individuals who want to own high-performance vehicles. A firm can generate a large sales volume by penetrating a single market segment deeply. The concentration approach may be especially effective when a firm can identify and develop products for a segment ignored by other companies in the industry.

concentration approach a market segmentation approach whereby a company develops one marketing strategy for a single market segment.

In the **multisegment approach,** the marketer aims its marketing efforts at two or more segments, developing a marketing strategy for each. Many firms use a multisegment approach that includes different advertising messages for different segments. Companies also develop product variations to appeal to different market segments. The U.S. Post Office, for example, offers personalized stamps, while Mars Inc. sells personalized M&M's through mymms.com. Many other firms also attempt to use a multisegment approach to market segmentation, such as the manufacturer of Raleigh bicycles, which has designed separate marketing strategies for racers, tourers, commuters, and children.

multisegment approach a market segmentation approach whereby the marketer aims its efforts at two or more segments, developing a marketing strategy for each.

Niche marketing is a narrow market segment focus when efforts are on one small, well-defined group that has a unique, specific set of needs. Niche segments are usually very small compared to the total market for the products. Many airlines cater to first-class flyers, who comprise only 10 percent of international air travelers. To meet the needs of these elite customers, airlines include special perks along with the spacious seats. Freshpet makes all-natural gourmet pet food that mimics the type of food humans like. This company is targeting a growing niche of pet owners who want the best food for their pets.[11]

For a firm to successfully use a concentration or multisegment approach to market segmentation, several requirements must be met:

1. Consumers' needs for the product must be heterogeneous.
2. The segments must be identifiable and divisible.
3. The total market must be divided in a way that allows estimated sales potential, cost, and profits of the segments to be compared.

4. At least one segment must have enough profit potential to justify developing and maintaining a special marketing strategy.

5. The firm must be able to reach the chosen market segment with a particular market strategy.

Bases for Segmenting Markets.   Companies segment markets on the basis of several variables:

1. *Demographic*—age, sex, race, ethnicity, income, education, occupation, family size, religion, social class. These characteristics are often closely related to customers, product needs and purchasing behavior, and they can be readily measured. For example, deodorants are often segmented by sex: Secret and Soft n' Dri for women; Old Spice and Mennen for men.

2. *Geographic*—climate, terrain, natural resources, population density, subcultural values. These influence consumer needs and product usage. Climate, for example, influences consumer purchases of clothing, automobiles, heating and air conditioning equipment, and leisure activity equipment.

3. *Psychographic*—personality characteristics, motives, lifestyles. Soft-drink marketers provide their products in several types of packaging, including two-liter bottles and cases of cans, to satisfy different lifestyles and motives.

4. *Behavioristic*—some characteristic of the consumer's behavior toward the product. These characteristics commonly involve some aspect of product use. Benefit segmentation is also a type of behavioristic segmentation. For instance, low-fat, low-carb food products would target those who desire the benefits of a healthier diet.

Developing a Marketing Mix

The second step in developing a marketing strategy is to create and maintain a satisfying marketing mix. The **marketing mix** refers to four marketing activities—product, price, distribution, and promotion—that the firm can control to achieve specific goals within a dynamic marketing environment (Figure 11-3). The buyer or the target market is the central focus of all marketing activities.

marketing mix
the four marketing activites—product, price, promotion, and distribution—that the firm can control to achieve specific goals within a dynamic marketing environment.

Product.   A product—whether a good, a service, an idea, or some combination—is a complex mix of tangible and intangible attributes that provide satisfaction and benefits. A *good* is a physical entity you can touch. A Porsche Cayenne, a Hewlett-Packard printer, and a kitten available for adoption at an animal shelter are examples of goods. A *service* is the application of human and mechanical efforts to people or objects to provide intangible benefits to customers. Air travel, dry cleaning, haircuts, banking, insurance, medical care, and day care are examples of services. *Ideas* include concepts, philosophies, images, and issues. For instance, an attorney, for a fee, may advise you about what rights you have in the event that the IRS decides to audit your tax return. Other marketers of ideas include political parties, churches, and schools.

A product has emotional and psychological, as well as physical, characteristics that include everything that the buyer receives from an exchange. This definition includes supporting services such as installation, guarantees, product information, and promises of repair. Products usually have both favorable and unfavorable attributes; therefore, almost every purchase or exchange involves trade-offs as consumers try to maximize their benefits and satisfaction and minimize unfavorable attributes.

FIGURE 11-3

The Marketing Mix:
Product, Price, Promotion,
and Distribution

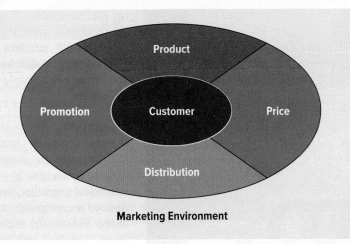

Product

Promotion   Customer   Price

Distribution

Marketing Environment

Products are among a firm's most visible contacts with consumers. If they do not meet consumer needs and expectations, sales will be difficult, and product life spans will be brief. The product is an important variable—often the central focus—of the marketing mix; the other variables (price, promotion, and distribution) must be coordinated with product decisions.

Price.   Almost anything can be assessed by a price, a value placed on an object exchanged between a buyer and a seller. Although the seller usually establishes the price, it may be negotiated between the buyer and the seller. The buyer usually exchanges purchasing power—income, credit, wealth—for the satisfaction or utility associated with a product. Because financial price is the measure of value commonly used in an exchange, it quantifies value and is the basis of most market exchanges.

price
a value placed on an object exchanged between a buyer and a seller.

DID YOU KNOW? During its first year of operation, sales of Coca-Cola averaged just nine drinks per day for total first-year sales of $50. Today, Coca-Cola products are consumed at the rate of 1.9 billion drinks per day.[12]

Marketers view price as much more than a way of assessing value, however. It is a key element of the marketing mix because it relates directly to the generation of revenue and profits. Prices can also be changed quickly to stimulate demand or respond to competitors' actions. The sudden increase in the cost of commodities such as oil can create price increases or a drop in consumer demand for a product. When gas prices rise, consumers purchase more fuel-efficient cars; when prices fall, consumers return to larger vehicles.[13]

Distribution.   Distribution (sometimes referred to as "place" because it helps to remember the marketing mix as the "4 Ps") is making products available to customers in the quantities desired. For example, consumers can rent movies and videogames from a physical store, a vending machine, or an online service. Intermediaries, usually wholesalers and retailers, perform many of the activities required to move products efficiently from producers to consumers or industrial buyers. These activities involve transporting, warehousing, materials handling, and inventory control, as well as packaging and communication.

distribution
making products available to customers in the quantities desired.

Critics who suggest that eliminating wholesalers and other middlemen would result in lower prices for consumers do not recognize that eliminating intermediaries would not do away with the need for their services. Other institutions would have to perform those services, and consumers would still have to pay for them. In addition,

TABLE 11-2
Companies with the Best
Customer Service

Rank	Companies	Excellence Rating (%)
1	Amazon.com	59.4
2	Chick-fil-A	47.0
3	Apple	40.0
4	Marriott	39.2
5	Kroger	38.6
6	FedEx	37.7
7	Trader Joe's	37.7
8	Sony	37.0
9	Samsung Electronics	36.9
10	UPS	36.7

Source: Michael B. Sauter, Thomas C. Frohlich, and Samuel Stebbins, "Customer Service Hall of Fame," 24/7 Wall St., July 23, 2015, http://247wallst.com/special-report/2015/07/23/customer-service-hall-of-fame-2/ (accessed April 1, 2016).

research, the approach can help marketers determine what consumers really think about their products and how different ethnic or demographic groups react to them.

secondary data
information that is compiled inside or outside an organization for some purpose other than changing the current situation.

Secondary data are compiled inside or outside the organization for some purpose other than changing the current situation. Marketers typically use information compiled by the U.S. census bureau and other government agencies, databases created by marketing research firms, as well as sales and other internal reports, to gain information about customers.

Online Marketing Research

The marketing of products and collecting of data about buying behavior—information on what people actually buy and how they buy it—represents marketing research of the future. New information technologies are changing the way businesses learn about their customers and market their products. Interactive multimedia research, or *virtual testing,* combines sight, sound, and animation to facilitate the testing of concepts as well as packaging and design features for consumer products. The evolving development of telecommunications and computer technologies is allowing marketing researchers quick and easy access to a growing number of online services and a vast database of potential respondents.

Marketing research can use digital media and social networking sites to gather useful information for marketing decisions. Sites such as Twitter, Facebook, and LinkedIn can be good substitutes for focus groups. Online surveys can serve as an alternative to mail, telephone, or personal interviews.

Social networks are a great way to obtain information from consumers who are willing to share their experiences about products and companies. In a way, this process identifies those consumers who develop an identity or passion for certain products, as well as those consumers who have concerns about quality or performance. It is possible for firms to tap into existing online social networks and simply "listen" to what consumers have on their mind. Firms can also encourage consumers to join a community or group so that they can share their opinions with the business.

A good outcome from using social networks is the opportunity to reach new voices and gain varied perspectives on the creative process of developing new products and promotions. For instance, Kickstarter gives aspiring entrepreneurs the ability to market their ideas online. Funders can then choose whether to fund those ideas in return for a finished product or a steep discount.[20] To some extent, social networking is democratizing design by welcoming consumers to join in the development process for new products.[21]

Online surveys are becoming an important part of marketing research. Traditionally, the process of conducting surveys online involved sending questionnaires to respondents either through email or through a website. However, digital communication has increased the ability of marketers to conduct polls on blogs and social networking sites. The benefits of online market research include lower costs and quicker feedback. For instance, Lego encourages fans to submit their own ideas for Lego sets on their Lego Ideas crowdsourcing platform. Other fans can vote on the ideas, and enough votes make the idea eligible for review and possible commercialization. This allows Lego to solicit creative ideas from passionate fans at low cost.[22] By monitoring consumers' feedback, companies can understand customer needs and adapt their goods or services.

Coffee shops attempt to influence consumers' buying behavior by offering free Wi-Fi and a comfortable retail environment.

© Ken Seet/Corbis Images/SuperStock

Finally, *marketing analytics* uses data that has been collected to measure, interpret, and evaluate marketing decisions. This emerging area uses advanced software that can track, store, and analyze data. Marketing analytics is becoming an increasingly important part of a company's marketing activities that are integrated into daily decision making. Nearly all marketers use analytical tools to measure their website, traffic, and performance.

Buying Behavior

Carrying out the marketing concept is impossible unless marketers know what, where, when, and how consumers buy; conducting marketing research into the factors that influence buying behavior helps marketers develop effective marketing strategies. **Buying behavior** refers to the decision processes and actions of people who purchase and use products. It includes the behavior of both consumers purchasing products for personal or household use and organizations buying products for business use. Marketers analyze buying behavior because a firm's marketing strategy should be guided by an understanding of buyers. For instance, men's shopping habits are changing. Men's shopping habits used to be more targeted and fast. Today, they tend to buy more clothes on impulse, search websites or mobile phones for style ideas, and try out new brands. As a result, retailers such as Saks and Barney's have begun expanding the men's areas in their stores.[23] Both psychological and social variables are important to an understanding of buying behavior.

buying behavior
the decision processes and actions of people who purchase and use products.

Psychological Variables of Buying Behavior

Psychological factors include the following:

perception
the process by which a person selects, organizes, and interprets information received from his or her senses.

motivation
an inner drive that directs a person's behavior toward goals.

learning
changes in a person's behavior based on information and experience.

attitude
knowledge and positive or negative feelings about something.

personality
the organization of an individual's distinguishing character traits, attitudes, or habits.

- **Perception** is the process by which a person selects, organizes, and interprets information received from his or her senses, as when experiencing an advertisement or touching a product to better understand it.
- **Motivation,** as we said in Chapter 9, is an inner drive that directs a person's behavior toward goals. A customer's behavior is influenced by a set of motives rather than by a single motive. A buyer of a tablet computer, for example, may be motivated by ease of use, ability to communicate with the office, and price.
- **Learning** brings about changes in a person's behavior based on information and experience. For instance, a smartphone app that provides digital news or magazine content could eliminate the need for print copies. If a person's actions result in a reward, he or she is likely to behave the same way in similar situations. If a person's actions bring about a negative result, however—such as feeling ill after eating at a certain restaurant—he or she will probably not repeat that action.
- **Attitude** is knowledge and positive or negative feelings about something. For example, a person who feels strongly about protecting the environment may refuse to buy products that harm the earth and its inhabitants.
- **Personality** refers to the organization of an individual's distinguishing character traits, attitudes, or habits. Although market research on the relationship between personality and buying behavior has been inconclusive, some marketers believe that the type of car or clothing a person buys reflects his or her personality.

Social Variables of Buying Behavior

social roles
a set of expectations for individuals based on some position they occupy.

Social factors include **social roles,** which are a set of expectations for individuals based on some position they occupy. A person may have many roles: mother, wife, student, executive. Each of these roles can influence buying behavior. Consider a woman choosing an automobile. As a mother, she might prefer to purchase a safe, gasoline-efficient car such as a Volvo. Her environmentally supportive colleagues at work might urge her to forgo buying a car and instead use public transportation and Uber. Because millennials (those between the ages of 18 and 34) tend to prefer vehicles that represent how they see themselves,[24] the woman's outdoorsy 18-year-old son may want her to purchase a Ford Explorer to take on camping trips, while her 20-year-old daughter thinks she should buy a cool, classy car such as a Ford Mustang. Thus, in choosing which car to buy, the woman's buying behavior may be affected by the opinions and experiences of her family and friends and by her roles as mother, daughter, and employee.

Other social factors include reference groups, social classes, and culture.

reference groups
groups with whom buyers identify and whose values or attitudes they adopt.

social classes
a ranking of people into higher or lower positions of respect.

- **Reference groups** include families, professional groups, civic organizations, and other groups with whom buyers identify and whose values or attitudes they adopt. A person may use a reference group as a point of comparison or a source of information. A person new to a community may ask other group members to recommend a family doctor, for example.
- **Social classes** are determined by ranking people into higher or lower positions of respect. Criteria vary from one society to another. People within a particular social class may develop common patterns of behavior. People in the upper-middle class, for example, might buy a Lexus or a BMW as a symbol of their social class.

IOLLA Sees Eyewear Differently

IOLLA
Founders: Stefan Hunter and Brian McGuire
Founded: 2015, in Glasgow, United Kingdom
Success: IOLLA's showroom has gained positive reviews from customers and bloggers in its quest to change the eyewear industry.

When Brian McGuire and Stefan Hunter began IOLLA, their objective was to bring fashionable, high-quality, affordable eyeglasses to Scotland. Knowing that nearly an infinite variety of glasses could be purchased online, the two men implemented a unique marketing strategy to gain the attention of potential customers. First, in an effort to resonate with consumers, they named their variety of glass frames after influential individuals in Scottish culture. Second, they designed an unusual, yet inviting, showroom—one equipped with a coffee bar—to enable potential customers to try on glasses before purchasing.

All of IOLLA's glasses are designed in house by Stefan Hunter, a strategy the company claims cuts down on costs. The company sources materials from around Europe and assembles the glasses in Scotland, reducing shipping costs. Although IOLLA is a young company, its popularity is increasing thanks to exposure on social media—IOLLA recently invited bloggers to a launch party to celebrate the opening of its new showroom. Looking toward the future, its founders intend to take IOLLA global.[25]

Discussion Questions
1. Describe how the entrepreneurs used customer-driven marketing to develop IOLLA.
2. How does IOLLA target a market niche?
3. How have the entrepreneurs used social media for promotional purposes?

- **Culture** is the integrated, accepted pattern of human behavior, including thought, speech, beliefs, actions, and artifacts. Culture determines what people wear and eat and where they live and travel. Many Hispanic Texans and New Mexicans, for example, buy *masa trigo*, the dough used to prepare flour tortillas, which are basic to Southwestern and Mexican cuisine.

culture
the integrated, accepted pattern of human behavior, including thought, speech, beliefs, actions, and artifacts.

Understanding Buying Behavior

Although marketers try to understand buying behavior, it is extremely difficult to explain exactly why a buyer purchases a particular product. The tools and techniques for analyzing consumers are not exact. Marketers may not be able to determine accurately what is highly satisfying to buyers, but they know that trying to understand consumer wants and needs is the best way to satisfy them. Marriott International's Innovation Lab, for instance, tests out new hotel designs for its brands to target millennials and other desirable demographics. Wi-Fi, lighting, and more soundproof rooms are among the top desirable traits travelers desire. Another trend is that travelers are not unpacking their suitcases as much. As a result, Marriott has begun reducing the size of closets and the number of hangers to save room.[26]

The Marketing Environment

A number of external forces directly or indirectly influence the development of marketing strategies; the following political, legal, regulatory, social, competitive, economic, and technological forces comprise the marketing environment.

- *Political, legal, and regulatory forces*—laws and regulators' interpretation of laws, law enforcement and regulatory activities, regulatory bodies, legislators and legislation, and political actions of interest groups. Specific laws, for example, require that advertisements be truthful and that all health claims be documented.

LO 11-6

Summarize the environmental forces that influence marketing decisions.

Going Green

Volkswagen Hits a Bump in the Road: The Quest to Rebuild Trust

Volkswagen had marketed its diesel vehicles for their low carbon emissions, only to have the Environmental Protection Agency discover it used a "defeat device" in its software to change performance during emissions testing. During testing, the software made the cars run below performance, causing them to release fewer emissions. Once on the road, however, the cars ran at maximum performance—and gave off emissions that were 40 times past the allowable limit in the United States. Volkswagen estimates that 11 million cars worldwide have been affected. A class-action lawsuit was subsequently filed against the firm. Now, many global regulatory agencies are investigating Volkswagen for charges ranging from deceptive advertising to fraud.

Perhaps the most damaging aspect of the scandal, however, is the impact on consumer trust. The scandal has dealt a blow to diesel's reputation as consumers now wonder how sustainable it really is over traditional engines. Additionally, other carmakers are being scrutinized to make sure they did not commit similar misconduct. When a major company betrays customer trust in such a way, it not only affects the firm, but every organization in the industry.

Volkswagen has begun to take steps to restore consumer trust. For instance, it is recalling vehicles and offering a $1,000 goodwill package to its American car owners. Yet even with incentives, Volkswagen will have to face this loss of goodwill for years to come. Consumer trust is easily lost and is not restored overnight.[27]

Discussion Questions

1. How will this scandal affect the trustworthiness of VW's future marketing claims?
2. Describe the impact you believe the scandal will have on vehicles sold by competitors.
3. Do you think Volkswagen will ultimately be able to recover? Why or why not?

- *Social forces*—the public's opinions and attitudes toward issues such as living standards, ethics, the environment, lifestyles, and quality of life. For example, social concerns have led marketers to design and market safer toys for children.
- *Competitive and economic forces*—competitive relationships such as those in the technology industry, unemployment, purchasing power, and general economic conditions (prosperity, recession, depression, recovery, product shortages, and inflation).
- *Technological forces*—computers and other technological advances that improve distribution, promotion, and new-product development.

Marketing requires creativity and consumer focus because environmental forces can change quickly and dramatically. Changes can arise from social concerns and economic forces such as price increases, product shortages, and altering levels of demand for commodities. Recently, climate change, global warming, and the impact of carbon emissions on our environment have become social concerns and are causing businesses to rethink marketing strategies. These environmental issues have persuaded governments to institute stricter limits on greenhouse gas emissions. For instance, in the United States, the government has mandated that by 2025, vehicles must be able to reach 54.5 miles per gallon on average.[28] This is causing automobile companies like General Motors to investigate ways to make their cars more fuel-efficient without significantly raising the price. At the same time, these laws are also introducing opportunities for new products. Concerns over the environment are encouraging automobile companies to begin releasing electric vehicles, such as the Chevrolet Bolt and the Nissan Leaf.

Because such environmental forces are interconnected, changes in one may cause changes in others. Consider that because of evidence linking children's consumption of soft drinks and fast foods to health issues such as obesity, diabetes, and osteoporosis, marketers of such products have experienced negative publicity and calls for legislation regulating the sale of soft drinks in public schools.

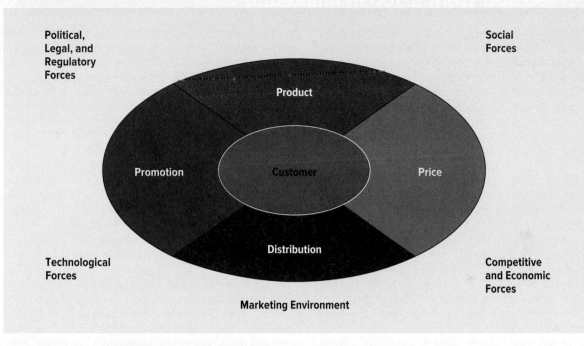

FIGURE 11-4   The Marketing Mix and the Marketing Environment

Although the forces in the marketing environment are sometimes called uncontrollables, they are not totally so. A marketing manager can influence some environmental variables. For example, businesses can lobby legislators to dissuade them from passing unfavorable legislation. Figure 11-4 shows the variables in the marketing environment that affect the marketing mix and the buyer.

Importance of Marketing to Business and Society

As this chapter has shown, marketing is a necessary function to reaching consumers, establishing relationships, and creating revenue. While some critics might view marketing as a way to change what consumers want, marketing is essential in communicating the value of goods and services. For consumers, marketing is necessary to ensure that they get the products they desire at the right places in the right quantities at a reasonable price. From the perspective of businesses, marketing is necessary in order to form valuable relationships with customers to increase profitability and customer support.

It is not just for-profit businesses that engage in marketing activities. Nonprofit organizations, government institutions, and even people must market themselves to spread awareness and achieve desired outcomes. All organizations must reach their target markets, communicate their offerings, and establish high-quality services. For instance, nonprofit organization The Leukemia and Lymphoma Society uses print, radio, web, and other forms of media to market its Team in Training racing events to recruit participants and solicit support. Without marketing, it would be nearly impossible for organizations to connect with their target audiences. Marketing is, therefore, an important contributor to business and societal well-being.

So You Want a Job in Marketing

You probably did not think as a child how great it would be to grow up and become a marketer. That's because, often, marketing is associated with sales jobs, but opportunities in marketing, public relations, product management, advertising, e-marketing, and customer relationship management and beyond represent almost one-third of all jobs in today's business world. To enter any job in the marketing field, you must balance an awareness of customer needs with business knowledge while mixing in creativity and the ability to obtain useful information to make smart business decisions.

Marketing starts with understanding the customer. Marketing research is a vital aspect in marketing decision making and presents many job opportunities. Market researchers survey customers to determine their habits, preferences, and aspirations. Activities include concept testing, product testing, package testing, test-market research, and new-product research. Salaries vary, depending on the nature and level of the position as well as the type, size, and location of the firm. A market analyst may make between $36,000 to $76,000, while a market research director earns a median salary of more than $107,000.

One of the most dynamic areas in marketing is direct marketing, where a seller solicits a response from a consumer using direct communications methods such as telephone, online communication, direct mail, or catalogs. Jobs in direct marketing include buyers, catalog managers, research/mail-list managers, or order fulfillment managers. Most positions in direct marketing involve planning and market analysis. Some require the use of databases to sort and analyze customer information and sales history.

Use of the Internet for retail sales is growing, and the Internet continues to be very useful for business-to-business sales. E-marketing offers many career opportunities, including customer relationship management (CRM). CRM helps companies market to customers through relationships, maintaining customer loyalty. Information technology plays a huge role in such marketing jobs because you need to combine technical skills and marketing knowledge to effectively communicate with customers. Job titles include e-marketing manager, customer relationship manager, and e-services manager. A CRM manager earns a median salary of approximately $67,000, and experienced individuals may earn as much as $116,000.

A job in any of these marketing fields will require a strong sense of the current trends in business and marketing. Customer service is vital to many aspects of marketing, so the ability to work with customers and to communicate their needs and wants is important. Marketing is everywhere, from the corner grocery or local nonprofit organization to the largest multinational corporations, making it a shrewd choice for an ambitious and creative person. We will provide additional job opportunities in marketing in Chapter 12.[29]

Review Your Understanding

Define *marketing* and describe the exchange process.

Marketing is a group of activities designed to expedite transactions by creating, distributing, pricing, and promoting goods, services, and ideas. Marketing facilitates the exchange, the act of giving up one thing in return for something else. The central focus of marketing is to satisfy needs.

Specify the functions of marketing.

Marketing includes many varied and interrelated activities: buying, selling, transporting, storing, grading, financing, marketing research, and risk taking.

Explain the marketing concept and its implications for developing marketing strategies.

The marketing concept is the idea that an organization should try to satisfy customers' needs through coordinated activities that also allow it to achieve its goals. If a company does not implement the marketing concept by providing products that consumers need and want while achieving its own objectives, it will not survive.

Examine the development of a marketing strategy, including market segmentation and marketing mix.

A marketing strategy is a plan of action for creating a marketing mix (product, price, distribution, promotion) for a specific target market (a specific group of consumers on whose needs and wants a company focuses its marketing efforts). Some firms use a total-market approach, designating everyone as the target market. Most firms divide the total market into segments of people who have relatively similar product needs. A company using a concentration approach develops one marketing strategy for a single market segment, whereas a multisegment approach aims marketing efforts at two or more segments, developing a different marketing strategy for each.

Investigate how marketers conduct marketing research and study buying behavior.

Carrying out the marketing concept is impossible unless marketers know what, where, when, and how consumers buy; marketing research into the factors that influence buying behavior helps marketers develop effective marketing strategies. Marketing research is a systematic, objective process of getting information about potential customers to guide marketing decisions. Buying behavior is the decision processes and actions of people who purchase and use products.

Summarize the environmental forces that influence marketing decisions.

There are several forces that influence marketing activities: political, legal, regulatory, social, competitive, economic, and technological.

Assess a company's marketing plans and propose a solution for resolving its problem.

Based on the material in this chapter, you should be able to answer the questions posed in the "Solve the Dilemma" feature at the end of the chapter and help the business understand what went wrong and how to correct it.

Revisit the World of Business

1. How important is unique packaging and novel food design in attracting health-minded consumers?

2. Should Campbell's ignore fresh foods altogether and focus on its core competencies—processed and prepared foods? Why?

3. Should Campbell's sell its fresh foods under the traditional Campbell's brand or create a new separate brand for its fresh foods division?

Learn the Terms

attitude 348	market segmentation 339	price 343
buying behavior 347	marketing 332	primary data 345
concentration approach 341	marketing concept 335	promotion 344
culture 349	marketing mix 342	reference groups 348
distribution 343	marketing research 344	secondary data 346
exchange 332	marketing strategy 339	social classes 348
learning 348	motivation 348	social roles 348
market 339	multisegment approach 341	target market 339
market orientation 338	perception 348	total-market approach 339
market segment 339	personality 348	value 335

Check Your Progress

1. What is marketing? How does it facilitate exchanges?

2. Name the functions of marketing. How does an organization use marketing activities to achieve its objectives?

3. What is the marketing concept? Why is it so important?

4. What is a marketing strategy?

5. What is market segmentation? Describe three target market strategies.

6. List the variables in the marketing mix. How is each used in a marketing strategy?

7. Why are marketing research and information systems important to an organization's planning and development of strategy?

8. Briefly describe the factors that influence buying behavior. How does understanding buying behavior help marketers?

9. Discuss the impact of technological forces and political and legal forces on the market.

Get Involved

1. With some or all of your classmates, watch several hours of television, paying close attention to the commercials. Pick three commercials for products with which you are somewhat familiar. Based on the commercials, determine who the target market is. Can you surmise the marketing strategy for each of the three?

2. Discuss the decision process and influences involved in purchasing a personal computer.

Build Your Skills

The Marketing Mix

Background

You've learned the four variables—product, promotion, price, and distribution—that the marketer can select to achieve specific goals within a dynamic marketing environment. This exercise will give you an opportunity to analyze the marketing strategies of some well-known companies to determine which of the variables received the most emphasis to help the company achieve its goals.

Task

In groups of three to five students, discuss the examples below and decide which variable received the most emphasis.

A. Product

B. Distribution

C. Promotion

D. Price

_____ 1. Starbucks Coffee began selling bagged premium specialty coffee through an agreement with Kraft Foods to gain access to more than 30,000 supermarkets.

_____ 2. Skype is a software application that allows consumers to make telephone calls over the web. Calls to Skype subscribers are free, while calls to land line and mobile phones cost around 2 cents per minute.

_____ 3. Amid great anticipation, Apple released its iPad, selling more than 3 million within three months. The slim tablet computer is a major step forward in reading e-books, watching movies, and playing games.

_____ 4. After decades on the market, WD-40 is in about 80 percent of U.S. households—more than any other branded product. Although WD-40 is promoted as a product that can stop squeaks, protect metal, loosen rusted parts, and free sticky mechanisms, the WD-40 Company has received letters from customers who have sprayed the product on bait to attract fish, on pets to cure mange, and even on people to cure arthritis. Despite more than 200 proposals to expand the WD-40 product line and ideas to change the packaging and labeling, the company stands firmly behind its one highly successful and respected original product.

_____ 5. Southwest Airlines makes flying fun. Flight attendants try to entertain passengers, and the airline has an impeccable customer service record. Employees play a key role and take classes that emphasize that having fun translates into great customer service.

_____ 6. Hewlett-Packard offered a $100 rebate on a $799 HP LaserJet printer when purchased with an HP LaserJet toner cartridge. To receive the rebate, the buyer had to return a mail-in certificate to certify the purchase. A one-page ad with a coupon was used in *USA Today* stating, "We're taking $100 off the top."

_____ 7. Denny's, the largest full-service family restaurant chain in the United States, serves more than 1 million customers a day. The restaurants offer the Build Your Own Grand Slam Breakfast for about $7.15, lunch basket specials for $4–$6, and a value menu with prices ranging from $2 to $8.

Solve the Dilemma

Will It Go?

Ventura Motors makes midsized and luxury automobiles in the United States. Best selling models include its basic four-door sedans (priced from $20,000 to $25,000) and two-door and four-door luxury automobiles (priced from $40,000 to $55,000). The success of two-seat sports cars like the Mazda RX-8 started the company evaluating the market for a two-seat sports car priced midway between the moderate and luxury market. Research found that there was indeed significant demand and that Ventura needed to act quickly to take advantage of this market opportunity.

Ventura took the platform of the car from a popular model in its moderate line, borrowing the internal design from its luxury line. The car was designed, engineered, and produced in just over two years, but the coordination needed to bring the design together resulted in higher than anticipated costs. The price for this two-seat car, the Olympus, was set at $32,000. Dealers were anxious to take delivery on the car, and salespeople were well trained on techniques to sell this new model.

However, initial sales have been slow, and company executives are surprised and concerned. The Olympus was introduced relatively quickly, made available at all Ventura dealers, priced midway between luxury and moderate models, and advertised heavily since its introduction.

Assess a company's marketing plans and propose a solution for resolving its problem.

Discussion Questions

1. What do you think were the main concerns with the Olympus two-door sports coupe? Is there a market for a two-seat, $32,000 sports car when the RX-8 sells for significantly less?

2. Evaluate the role of the marketing mix in the Olympus introduction.

3. What are some of the marketing strategies auto manufacturers use to stimulate sales of certain makes of automobiles?

Build Your Business Plan

Customer-Driven Marketing

The first step is to develop a marketing strategy for your good or service. Who will be the target market you will specifically try to reach? What group(s) of people has the need, ability, and willingness to purchase this product? How will you segment customers within your target market? Segmenting by demographic and geographic variables are often the easiest segmentation strategies to attempt. Remember that you would like to have the customers in your segment be as homogeneous and accessible as possible. You might target several segments if you feel your good or service has broad appeal.

The second step in your marketing strategy is to develop the marketing mix for your good or service. Whether you are dealing with an established product or you are creating your own good or service, you need to think about what is the differential advantage your product offers. What makes it unique? How should it be priced? Should the product be priced below, above, or at the market? How will you distribute the product? And last but certainly not least, you need to think about the promotional strategy for your product.

What about the uncontrollable variables you need to be aware of? Is your product something that can constantly be technologically advanced? Is your product a luxury that will not be considered by consumers when the economy is in a downturn?

See for Yourself Videocase

Marriott: Your Home Away from Home

With 4,400 hotel properties in 87 countries, Marriott knows how to target different types of travelers. Its 19 brands use careful segmentation strategies based on demographic and psychographic variables to determine what their guests want and how best to meet their needs. Its extensive customer research allows the firm to identify its customers, understand cultural or generational changes, and adapt its hotels to target these different travelers more effectively. It also helps Marriott develop strategies to stay ahead of the competition and the emerging rental sharing sites such as Airbnb and VRBO (vacation rental by owner).

"Segmentation is really important because it really helps us to design the guest experience for a particular brand," says Tina Edmundson, Global Brand Officer, Luxury & Lifestyle Brands for Marriott International.

Marriott uses price and service as a major form of differentiation among its hotels. For instance, it separates its brands using terms like Upper Upscale and Select Service. Upper Upscale has all the amenities a traveler is looking for in a luxury hotel, including room service, a bar, doormen, and more. Marriott's Ritz-Carlton brand, known for offering the highest in guest amenities, fits this category. Select Service still offers guests a great experience but lacks some features such as room service and bellhops. Marriott's Moxy hotels is more of a do-it-yourself hotel without doormen or room service. It is positioned as being a stylish, but affordable, hotel. Each one targets a specific type of customer: Upper Upscale is for those who are willing to pay high prices for a luxurious experience, while Select Service targets customers who are looking for quality experiences at lower prices.

Marriott also segments its customers based on lifestyle characteristics. The Discoverer category is interested in exploration and experiencing local culture. Marriott's luxurious Renaissance Hotels targets this market with "local" themes. Renaissance Hotels come equipped with a focused concierge service called Navigator to provide suggestions for local experiences.

Although marketers at Marriott have become experts at customer segmentation, they constantly face new challenges. Millennials, for instance, differ significantly from baby boomers in their hotel preferences. Baby boomers enjoy familiarity and comfort, something Marriott's high-quality hotels have been able to achieve. For many consumers, consistency of the service and atmosphere is important—they want the J.W. Marriott they stay at in Milan, Italy, to be similar in service and design as the one in New York City.

Millennials go in the opposite direction. They desire an unpredictable adventure and are less likely to want to stay at large hotel chains. They are also more likely to travel globally;

millennials are 23 percent more interested in traveling abroad than non-millennials. These wide-scale differences among two large demographic groups represents a challenge for Marriott—one it is tackling head-on.

For this reason, Marriott partnered with consulting firm Fahrenheit 212, which specializes in marketing to millennials. Preliminary research shows that millennials need to be convinced of the value of a hotel, requiring the Marriott to "tell a story" about its hotels. Marriott also tapped into the insights of local entrepreneurs and hotel employees. They were challenged to come up with creative ideas that would attract both travelers and locals to the hotel. Teams whose ideas were adopted were awarded $50,000. In this way, Marriott is able to utilize local talent who are familiar with the city and know the culture.

One hotel that has been developed to target millennials is Moxy Hotels. Marriott partnered with IKEA to develop a hotel that is *specifically targeted* to the millennial traveler. Moxy Hotels combine a stylish atmosphere, functional guest rooms, affordable prices, and the types of amenities that tech-savvy millennials care about the most (e.g. Wi-Fi, televisions, and public areas with computers). Unlike some of the other generations, millennials tend to be more self-sufficient, so Moxy does not have room service or bellhops. This keeps prices down for millennials, who tend to have higher unemployment or lower-paying jobs than other age groups.

No matter who the target market is, they all have one thing in common: They seek a pleasurable experience. As Tina Edmundson explains, "It's no longer about filling rooms anymore. It is really about providing experiences that resonate with guests personally."[30]

Discussion Questions

1. How does Marriott use psychographic and demographic variables to segment the market?

2. Why is the millennial traveler market posing challenges for Marriott and other hotels?

3. Describe some ways that Marriott uses market research to discover what their customers want.

You can find the related video in the Video Library in Connect. Ask your instructor how you can access Connect.

Team Exercise

Form groups and assign the responsibility of finding examples of companies that excel in one dimension of the marketing mix (price, product, promotion, and distribution). Provide several company and product examples, and defend why this would be an exemplary case. Present your research to the class.

Endnotes

1. Eliza Gray, "Thinking Outside the Can," *Time,* February 2, 2015, pp. 44–47; Katie Koerner, "Are Preservatives in Food Bad for My Health?" *Greatist,* August 27, 2012, http://greatist.com/health/are-preservatives-food-bad-my-health (accessed August 24, 2015); Claire Groden, "Here's How Campbell's Is Moving beyond Soup," *Fortune,* June 9, 2015, http://fortune.com/2015/06/09/campbells-garden-fresh-gourmet/(accessed August 24, 2015); Bolthouse Farms, "Baby Carrot Shakedowns® Ranch," http://www.bolthouse.com/product/babycarrotshakedownsranch (accessed August 24, 2015); Nadia Arumugam, "Campbell Soup Increases Sodium as New Studies Vindicate Salt," *Forbes,* July 18, 2011, http://www.forbes.com/sites/nadiaarumugam/2011/07/18/campbell-soup-increases-sodium-as-new-studies-vindicate-salt/ (accessed August 24, 2015).

2. Adapted from Wiliam M. Pride and O. C. Ferrell, "Value-Driven Marketing," *Foundations of Marketing,* 4th ed. (Mason, OH: South-Western Cengage Learning), pp. 13–14.

3. Mary Bowerman and Hadley Malcolm, "New Barbies Are Tall, Petite, Curvy," *USA Today,* January 29, 2016, p. 3B.

4. "Beauty Queen," *People,* May 10, 2004, p. 187.

5. Michael Treacy and Fred Wiersema, *The Discipline of Market Leaders* (Reading, MA: Addison Wesley, 1995), p. 176.

6. Jefferson Graham, "At Apple Stores, iPads at Your Service," *USA Today,* May 23, 2011, p. 1B; Ana Swanson, "How the Apple Store Took Over the World," *The Washington Post,* July 21, 2015,https://www.washingtonpost.com/news/wonk/wp/2015/07/21/the-unlikely-success-story-of-the-apple-retail-store/ (accessed April 4, 2016).

7. Customer Insight Group Inc., "Program Design: Loyalty and Retention," www.customerinsightgroup.com/loyalty_retention.php (accessed January 4, 2011).

8. Venky Shankar, "Multiple Touch Point Marketing," American Marketing Association, Faculty Consortium on Electronic Commerce, Texas A&M University, July 14–17, 2001.

9. Samantha Masunaga, "Target Takes Aim at Latinos with New Marketing Campaign," *Los Angeles Times,* April 18, 2015, http://www.latimes.com/business/la-fi-target-latino-marketing-20150418-story.html (accessed April 4, 2016).

10. Nielsen, "The Making of a Multicultural Super Consumer," March 18, 2015, http://www.nielsen.com/us/en/insights/news/2015/the-making-of-a-multicultural-super-consumer-.html (accessed April 4, 2016).

11. Craig Giammona, "Hey Mom, Set Another Place at Dinner for Fido," *Bloomberg Businessweek,* November 12, 2105, pp. 26–27.

12. "The Coca-Cola Company Fact Sheet," http://assets.coca-colacompany.com/90/11/5f21b88444bab46d430b4c578e80/Company_Fact_Sheet.pdf (accessed April 4, 2016); Coca-Cola, "Coca-Cola Can Sales Per Day," http://www.coca-cola.co.uk/faq/products/how-many-cans-of-coca-cola-are-sold-worldwide-in-a-day/ (accessed April 4, 2016).

13. William Fierman, "This Is Why the SUV Is Here to Stay," *Business Insider,*March 9, 2016, http://www.businessinsider.com/suv-sales-continue-to-grow (accessed April 4, 2016).

14. "Google AdWords," Google, https://www.google.com/adwords/ (accessed April 4, 2016).

15. Twitter, "What Are Promoted Tweets?" Twitter Help Center, https://support.twitter.com/articles/142101-what-are-promoted-tweets# (accessed April 4, 2016).

16. Christine Birkner, "10 Minutes with . . . Raul Murguia Villegas," *Marketing News,* July 30, 2011, pp. 26–27.

17. Parmy Olson, "A Massive Social Experiment on You Is Under Way, and You Will Love It," *Forbes,* January 21, 2015, http://www.forbes.com/sites/parmyolson/2015/01/21/jawbone-guinea-pig-economy/ (accessed September 28, 2015); John McCann and Lily Prasuethsut, "Best Smartwatch 2015: What's the Best Wearable Tech for You?" *Tech Radar,* 2015,http://www.techradar.com/us/news/wearables/best-smart-watches-what-s-the-best-wearable-tech-for-you--1154074 (accessed September 28, 2015); Fitbit Inc., "Charge HR," 2015, https://www.fitbit.com/chargehr (accessed September 28, 2015); Lisa Eadicicco, "A New Wave of Gadgets Can Collect Your Personal Information Like Never Before," *Business Insider,* October 9, 2014, http://www.businessinsider.com/privacy-fitness-trackers-smartwatches-2014-10 (accessed September 28, 2015).

18. "MSPA North America," Mystery Shopping Providers Association, http://mysteryshop.org/ (accessed April 4, 2016).

19. Piet Levy, "10 Minutes with . . . Robert J. Morais," *Marketing News,* May 30, 2011, pp. 22–23.

20. Steven Kurutz, "On Kickstarter, Designers' Dream Materialize," *The New York Times,* September 21, 2011, www.nytimes.com/2011/09/22/garden/on-kickstarter-designers-dreams-materialize.html (accessed April 4, 2016).

21. Mya Frazier, "CrowdSourcing," *Delta Sky Mag,* February 2010, p. 73.

22. Lego, "LEGO Ideas—How It Works," https://ideas.lego.com/howitworks (accessed April 4, 2016).

23. Ray A. Smith, "Men Shop More Like Women," *The Wall Street Journal,* February 17, 2016, pp. D1–D2.

24. Mike Floyd, "Editor's Letter: What Drives Millennials?" *Automobile Magazine,* May 2015, p. 12.

25. Jill Castle, "Sight to Behold: Glasgow Entrepreneurs Hope Scots Made Glasses Business Will Have Specs Appeal," *Evening Times,* September 24, 2015,http://www.eveningtimes.co.uk/news/13783857.Sight_toehold__Glasgow_entrepreneurs_hope_Scots_made_glassesusiness_will_have_specs_appeal/ (accessed January

4, 2016); "IOLLA Prescription Eyewear," *Transatlantic Blonde,* September 12, 2015, http://transatlanticblonde .blogspot.com/2015/09/iolla-prescription-eyewear .html (accessed January 4, 2016); IOLLA website, http:// iolla.com/pages/about#design (accessed January 4, 2016); "Last Year's Looks: See with IOLLA," *Last Year's Girl,* August 30, 2015, http://lastyearsgirl.pixlet.net/last-years-looks-see-with-iolla/ (accessed January 4, 2016).

26. Andrea Petersen, "Secrets of a Hotel Test Lab," *The Wall Street Journal,* October 1, 2015, pp. D1–D2.

27. Sarah Sloat, "Volkswagen to Offer $1,000 Package to U.S. Customers Hit by Emissions Scandal," *The Wall Street Journal,* November 9, 2015, http://www.wsj.com/articles/ volkswagen-to-offer-1-000-package-to-u-s-customers-hit-by-emissions-scandal-1447088254?alg=y (accessed November 9, 2015); Russell Hotten, "Volkswagen: The Scandal Explained," *BBC News,* November 4, 2015, http://www.bbc .com/news/business-34324772 (accessed November 9, 2015); Associated Press, "VW Scandal Widens: Vehicles Don't Meet Standard for Second Pollutant," *NBC News,* November 3, 2015, http://www.nbcnews.com/business/autos/ vw-scandal-widens-vehicles-dont-meet-standard-second-pollutant-n456726 (accessed November 9, 2015); Chris Woodyard, "Volkswagen Faces Lawsuits over Emissions Deception," *USA Today,* September 22, 2015, http://www .usatoday.com/story/money/cars/2015/09/22/volkswagen-vw-emissions-lawsuits/72604396/ (accessed November 9, 2015); Sam Abuelsamid, "Does VW Diesel Cheating Threaten Consumer Trust of Automotive Software?" *Forbes,* October 21, 2015, http://www.forbes .com/sites/pikeresearch/2015/10/21/vw-diesel/(accessed November 9, 2015).

28. Environmental Protection Agency, "EPA and NHTSA Set Standards to Reduce Greenhouse Gases and Improve Fuel Economy for Model Years 2017-2025 Cars and Light Trucks," https://www3.epa.gov/otaq/climate/ documents/420f12051.pdf (accessed May 20, 2016).

29. PayScale, Inc., "Customer Relationship Manager," http://www.payscale.com/research/US/Job=Customer_ Relationship_Management_(CRM)_Manager/ Salary (accessed April 5, 2016); PayScale, Inc., "Marketing Analyst Salary," http://www.payscale.com/research/US/ Job=Marketing_Analyst/Salary (accessed April 5, 2016); PayScale, Inc., "Marketing Research Director," http://www .payscale.com/research/US/Job=Marketing_Research_ Director/Salary (accessed April 5, 2016).

30. McGraw-Hill video, http://www.viddler.com/embed/16 eb2415/?f=1&autoplay=0&player=full&disablebrand ing=0 (accessed April 11, 2016); Elizabeth Segran, "Inside Marriot's Attempt to Win Over Millennials," *Fast Company,* June 26, 2015, http://www.fastcompany.com/3047872/ innovation-agents/inside-marriotts-attempt-to-win-over-millennials (accessed April 8, 2016); Brad Tuttle, "Marriott & IKEA Launch a Hotel Brand for Millennials: What Does That Even Mean?" *Time,* March 8, 2013, http://business. time.com/2013/03/08/marriott-ikea-launch-a-hotel-brand-for-millennials-what-does-that-even-mean/ (accessed April 8, 2016); Larry Olmstead, "Luxury Hotels: Marriott Bets Big with 8 Brands, Explosive Growth," *Forbes,* June 6, 2014, http://www.forbes.com/sites/larryolmsted/2014/06/06/ luxury-hotels-marriott-bets-big-with-8-brands-explosive-growth/#3414c894886d (accessed April 8, 2016); Marriott website, https://www.marriott.com/marriott/aboutmarriott .mi (accessed April 8, 2016).

Introduction

The key to developing a marketing strategy is selecting a target market and maintaining a marketing mix that creates long-term relationships with customers. Getting just the right mix of product, price, promotion, and distribution is critical if a business is to satisfy its target customers and achieve its own objectives (implement the marketing concept).

In Chapter 11, we introduced the marketing concept and the various activities important in developing a marketing strategy. In this chapter, we'll take a closer look at the four dimensions of the marketing mix—product, price, distribution, and promotion—used to develop the marketing strategy. The focus of these marketing mix elements is a marketing strategy that builds customer relationships and satisfaction.

The Marketing Mix

The marketing mix is the part of marketing strategy that involves decisions regarding controllable variables. After selecting a target market, marketers have to develop and manage the dimensions of the marketing mix to give their firm an advantage over competitors. Successful companies offer at least one dimension of value usually associated with a marketing mix element that surpasses all competitors in the marketplace in meeting customer expectations. However, this does not mean that a company can ignore the other dimensions of the marketing mix; it must maintain acceptable, and if possible distinguishable, differences in the other dimensions as well.

DID YOU KNOW? Less than 10 percent of new products succeed in the marketplace, and 90 percent of successes come from a handful of companies.[2]

Walmart, for example, emphasizes price ("Save money, live better"). Procter & Gamble is well known for its promotion of top consumer brands such as Tide, Cheer, Crest, Ivory, and Head & Shoulders. Xiaomi, a Chinese consumer electronics company established in 2010, has achieved impressive scale by utilizing a low-cost, feature-rich strategy. Today, it is the fifth largest smartphone maker in the world.[3]

Product Strategy

Describe the role of product in the marketing mix, including how products are developed, classified, and identified.

As mentioned previously, the term *product* refers to goods, services, and ideas. Because the product is often the most visible of the marketing mix dimensions, managing product decisions is crucial. In this section, we'll consider product development, classification, mix, life cycle, and identification.

Developing New Products

Each year, thousands of products are introduced, but few of them succeed. Even established firms launch unsuccessful products. For example, Mini Cooper discontinued its Coupe and Roadster models after overexpanding its product lines.[4] Figure 12-1 shows the different steps in the product development process. Before introducing a new product, a business must follow a multistep process: idea development, the screening of new ideas, business analysis, product development, test marketing, and commercialization. A firm can take considerable time to get a product ready for the market: It took more than 20 years for the first photocopier, for example. Additionally, sometimes an idea or product prototype might be shelved only to be returned to later. Former Apple CEO Steve Jobs admitted that the iPad actually came before the iPhone in the product development process. Once it was realized that the scrolling mechanism he was thinking of using could be used to develop a phone, the iPad idea was placed on a shelf for the time

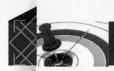

Responding to Business Challenges

IKEA "Sees" Each Store as Unique

IKEA is going to great lengths to collect consumer information it hopes will help the company boost sales. In a bid to better understand its customers and create products that are in demand, IKEA is ramping up its relatively unorthodox marketing research strategy by showing up at the homes of hundreds of customers to observe their behavior—including food habits and daily routines—and determine what furniture would best meet their future needs. The findings, combined with survey data from thousands of people around the world, is published in IKEA's quarterly "Life at Home" report. Ultimately, IKEA intends to use the consumer research data to customize its store offerings to meet the unique customer demands in the geographic regions where its stores are located.

Despite opening up new stores in recent years, the company has seen a decline in overall sales. In an era where nearly any type of customizable furniture can be purchased online, fewer are drawn to IKEA's streamlined, mass-marketed products that sometimes cost more to ship than rival products. This is why IKEA is aggressively searching for new, more functional designs to attract customers. More recently, the company is focusing its efforts on introducing new products for the kitchen—a high-growth area for IKEA. Ultimately, IKEA hopes that better understanding its customers will lead to the development of more successful products and greater sales volume.[5]

Discussion Questions

1. How does IKEA collect its consumer research data?
2. Why does IKEA intend to customize its store offerings?
3. What are the advantages of surveys inside the homes of potential customers?

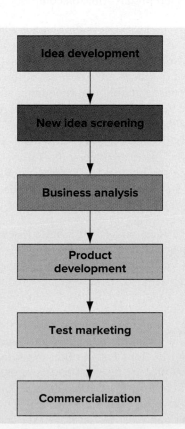

FIGURE 12-1
Product Development Process

Idea development

↓

New idea screening

↓

Business analysis

↓

Product development

↓

Test marketing

↓

Commercialization

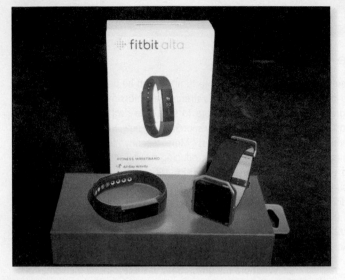

Entrepeneurs James Park and Eric Friedman came up with the idea of activity trackers that could be used to record a variety of activities related to health, from number of steps walked during the day to the quality of sleep. The product was highly successful, and an IPO for the company was filed in 2015.

© lev radin/Shutterstock

being. Apple later returned to develop the product and released the iPad in 2010.[6]

Idea Development. New ideas can come from marketing research, engineers, and outside sources such as advertising agencies and management consultants. Nike has a separate division—Nike Sport Research Lab—where scientists, athletes, engineers, and designers work together to develop technology of the future. The teams research ideas in biomechanics, perception, athletic performance, and physiology to create unique, relevant, and innovative products. These final products are tested in environmental chambers with real athletes to ensure functionality and quality before being introduced into the market.[7] As we said in Chapter 11, ideas sometimes come from customers, too. Other sources are brainstorming and intracompany incentives or rewards for good ideas. New ideas can even create a company. When Jeff Bezos came up with the idea to sell books over the Internet in 1992, he had no idea it would evolve into a billion-dollar firm. After failing to convince his boss of the idea, Bezos left to start Amazon.com.[8]

New Idea Screening. The next step in developing a new product is idea screening. In this phase, a marketing manager should look at the organization's resources and objectives and assess the firm's ability to produce and market the product. Important aspects to be considered at this stage are consumer desires; the competition; technological changes; social trends; and political, economic, and environmental considerations. Basically, there are two reasons new products succeed: They are able to meet a need or solve a problem better than products already available, or they add variety to the product selection currently on the market. Bringing together a team of knowledgeable people—including designers, engineers, marketers, and customers—is a great way to screen ideas. Using the Internet to encourage collaboration represents a rich opportunity for marketers to screen ideas. Most new product ideas are rejected during screening because they seem inappropriate or impractical for the organization.

Business Analysis. Business analysis is a basic assessment of a product's compatibility in the marketplace and its potential profitability. Both the size of the market and competing products are often studied at this point. The most important question relates to market demand: How will the product affect the firm's sales, costs, and profits?

Product Development. If a product survives the first three steps, it is developed into a prototype that should reveal the intangible attributes it possesses as perceived by the consumer. Product development is often expensive, and few product ideas make it to this stage. New product research and development costs vary. Adding a new color to an existing item may cost $100,000 to $200,000, but launching a completely new product can cost millions of dollars. During product development, various elements of the marketing mix must be developed for testing. Copyrights, tentative

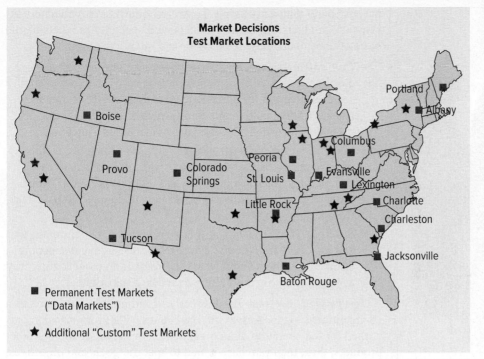

**Market Decisions
Test Market Locations**

Portland
Albany
Boise
Columbus
Peoria
Colorado
Springs
Evansville
Provo
St. Louis
Lexington
Little Rock
Charlotte
Charleston
Tucson
Jacksonville
Baton Rouge

■ Permanent Test Markets
("Data Markets")

★ Additional "Custom" Test Markets

FIGURE 12-2
Common Test Market Cities
Source: The Nielsen Company

advertising copy, packaging, labeling, and descriptions of a target market are integrated to develop an overall marketing strategy.

Test Marketing.   **Test marketing** is a trial minilaunch of a product in limited areas that represent the potential market. It allows a complete test of the marketing strategy in a natural environment, giving the organization an opportunity to discover weaknesses and eliminate them before the product is fully launched. Mamma Chia test marketed one of its products in Portland through a company known as SamplingLab. SamplingLab provides free samples for consumers in a retail environment, acting as a type of focus group. In exchange for free samples, consumers fill out surveys about their perceptions of the products.[9] Because test marketing requires significant resources and expertise, market research companies like ACNielsen can assist firms in test marketing their products. Figure 12-2 shows a sample of test markets marketing research firms often use to test products to predict how successful they might be on a nationwide scale.

test marketing
a trial minilaunch of a product in limited areas that represent the potential market.

Commercialization.   **Commercialization** is the full introduction of a complete marketing strategy and the launch of the product for commercial success. During commercialization, the firm gears up for full-scale production, distribution, and promotion. Firms such as AquAdvantage Salmon are getting ready to release genetically modified salmon into the market. The Food and Drug Administration has approved the salmon as fit for consumption. Federal approval is one major step for AquAdvantage in its plans for large-scale commercialization. However, even with federal regulatory approval, AquAdvantage may face hurdles from consumer and environmental groups.[10]

commercialization
the full introduction of a complete marketing strategy and the launch of the product for commercial success.

Classifying Products

Products are usually classified as either consumer products or industrial products. **Consumer products** are for household or family use; they are not intended for any

consumer products
products intended for household or family use.

Coca-Cola BläK is a coffee-flavored soft drink that Coca-Cola introduced in 2006. It is an example of product that did not survive. Many consumers did not like the taste, and Coca-Cola discontinued the drink in 2008.

© McGraw-Hill Education/John Flournoy, photographer

business products
products that are used directly or indirectly in the operation or manufacturing processes of businesses.

product line
a group of closely related products that are treated as a unit because of similar marketing strategy, production, or end-use considerations.

purpose other than daily living. They can be further classified as convenience products, shopping products, and specialty products on the basis of consumers' buying behavior and intentions.

- *Convenience products,* such as beverages, granola bars, gasoline, and batteries, are bought frequently, without a lengthy search, and often for immediate consumption. Consumers spend virtually no time planning where to purchase these products and usually accept whatever brand is available.
- *Shopping products,* such as computers, smartphones, clothing, and sporting goods, are purchased after the consumer has compared competitive products and "shopped around." Price, product features, quality, style, service, and image all influence the decision to buy.
- *Specialty products,* such as motorcycles, designer clothing, art, and rock concerts, require even greater research and shopping effort. Consumers know what they want and go out of their way to find it; they are not willing to accept a substitute.

Business products are used directly or indirectly in the operation or manufacturing processes of businesses. They are usually purchased for the operation of an organization or the production of other products; thus, their purchase is tied to specific goals and objectives. They too can be further classified:

- *Raw materials* are natural products taken from the earth, oceans, and recycled solid waste. Iron ore, bauxite, lumber, cotton, and fruits and vegetables are examples.
- *Major equipment* covers large, expensive items used in production. Examples include earth-moving equipment, stamping machines, and robotic equipment used on auto assembly lines.
- *Accessory equipment* includes items used for production, office, or management purposes, which usually do not become part of the final product. Computers, calculators, and hand tools are examples.
- *Component parts* are finished items, ready to be assembled into the company's final products. Tires, window glass, batteries, and spark plugs are component parts of automobiles.
- *Processed materials* are things used directly in production or management operations but are not readily identifiable as component parts. Varnish, for example, is a processed material for a furniture manufacturer.
- *Supplies* include materials that make production, management, and other operations possible, such as paper, pencils, paint, cleaning supplies, and so on.
- *Industrial services* include financial, legal, marketing research, security, janitorial, and exterminating services. Purchasers decide whether to provide these services internally or to acquire them from an outside supplier.

Product Line and Product Mix

Product relationships within an organization are of key importance. A **product line** is a group of closely related products that are treated as a unit because of a similar

FIGURE 12-3   Colgate-Palmolive's Product Mix and Product Lines

←—————————————————— **Product Mix** ——————————————————→

Oral Care	**Personal Care**	**Home Care**	**Pet Nutrition**
Toothpaste	*Deodorant*	*Dishwashing*	Hill's Prescription Diet
Colgate Total	Speed Stick	Palmolive	Hill's Science Diet
Colgate Optic White	Lady Speed Stick	AJAX	Hill's Ideal Balance
Colgate Enamel Health		Dermassage	
Colgate Sensitive	*Body Wash*		
MaxFresh	Softsoap	*Fabric Conditioner*	
	Irish Spring	Suavitel	
Colgate Kids			
Dora the Explorer	*Bar Soap*	*Household cleaner*	
SpongeBob SquarePants	Irish Spring	Murphy Oil Soap	
Teenage Mutant Ninja Turtles	Softsoap	Fabuloso	
Monster High		AJAX	
Transformers	*Liquid Soap*		
Minion	Softsoap		
Toothbrushes	*Toiletries for Men*		
Colgate 360°	Afta		
Colgate MaxFresh	Skin Bracer		
Colgate Total			
Colgate Optic White			

Source: Colgate Palmolive, "Colgate World of Care," www.colgatepalmolive.com/app/Colgate/US/CompanyHomePage.cvsp (accessed April 5, 2016).

marketing strategy. At Colgate-Palmolive, for example, the personal-care product line includes deodorant, body wash, bar soap, liquid soap, and toiletries for men. A **product mix** is all the products offered by an organization. Figure 12-3 displays a sampling of the product mix and product lines of the Colgate-Palmolive Company.

Product Life Cycle

Like people, products are born, grow, mature, and eventually die. Some products have very long lives. Ivory Soap was introduced in 1879 and still exists (although competition leading to decreased sales may soon put the future of Ivory Soap in question). In contrast, a new computer chip is usually outdated within a year because of technological breakthroughs and rapid changes in the computer industry. There are four stages in the life cycle of a product: introduction, growth, maturity, and decline (Figure 12-4). The stage a product is in helps determine marketing strategy. In the personal computer industry, desktop computers are in the decline stage, laptop computers have reached the maturity stage, and tablet computers are currently in the growth stage of the product life cycle (although growth has slowed in recent years). Manufacturers of these products are adopting different advertising and pricing strategies to maintain or increase demand for these types of computers.

In the *introductory stage,* consumer awareness and acceptance of the product are limited, sales are zero, and profits are negative. Profits are negative because the firm has spent money on research, development, and marketing to launch the product. During the introductory stage, marketers focus on making consumers aware of the product and its benefits. Smartwatches are still in the early stages of the product development cycle. However, it may quickly jump into the growth stage, with analysts

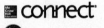

▶ Need help understanding product life cycle? Visit your Connect ebook video tab for a brief animated explanation.

product mix
all the products offered by an organization.

FIGURE 12-4
The Life Cycle of a Product

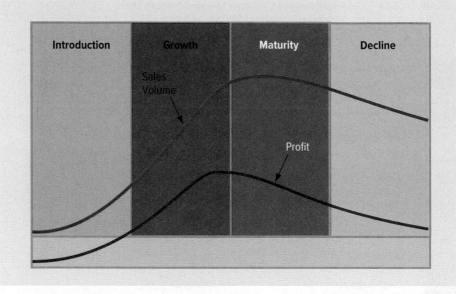

predicting it achieving 12 percent global market growth by 2020.[11] It is not unusual for technology products to go quickly through the life cycle as the rate of new technology innovations continues to increase. Table 12-1 shows some familiar products at different stages of the product life cycle. Sales accelerate as the product enters the growth stage of the life cycle.

In the *growth stage,* sales increase rapidly and profits peak, then start to decline. One reason profits start to decline during the growth stage is that new companies enter the market, driving prices down and increasing marketing expenses. Drones for both recreational and business uses are growing rapidly and are a good example of a product in the growth stage. During the growth stage, the firm tries to strengthen its position in the market by emphasizing the product's benefits and identifying market segments that want these benefits.

Sales continue to increase at the beginning of the *maturity stage,* but then the sales curve peaks and starts to decline while profits continue to decline. This stage is characterized by severe competition and heavy expenditures. In the United States, soft drinks have hit the maturity stage. Firms such as PepsiCo and Coca-Cola have taken many steps to try and revitalize sales. Pepsi made the decision to replace aspartame, a controversial sweetener, in its Diet Pepsi product with sucralose in an attempt to allay customer concerns over aspartame. However, the initial reaction to the change were negative, with many consumers reportedly disliking the taste.[12]

TABLE 12-1
Products at Different Stages of the Product Life Cycle

Introduction	Growth	Maturity	Decline
Ultra HD 4K television	3D printers	Laptop computer	Desktop computer
Smartwatch	Airbnb lodging sharing	Disney theme parks	Landline phones
Hydrogen fuel automobiles	Gluten-free products	Soft drinks	Print newspaper

During the *decline stage,* sales continue to fall rapidly. Profits also decline and may even become losses as prices are cut and necessary marketing expenditures are made. As profits drop, firms may eliminate certain models or items. To reduce expenses and squeeze out any remaining profits, marketing expenditures may be cut back, even though such cutbacks accelerate the sales decline. Finally, plans must be made for phasing out the product and introducing new ones to take its place. Apple iPods have been in decline in recent years as tablets and phones are being designed to serve as music listening devices. The iPod Touch, however, is not yet being prepared for exit from the marketplace, and a new version was released to take advantage of consumers still loyal to the iPod.[13]

At the same time, it should be noted that product stages do not always go one way. Some products that have moved to the maturity stage or to the decline stage can still rebound through redesign or new uses for the product. One prime example is baking soda. Originally, baking soda was only used for cooking, which meant it reached the maturity stage very quickly. However, once it was discovered that baking soda could be used as a deodorizer, sales shot up and bumped baking soda back into the growth stage.[14]

Identifying Products

Branding, packaging, and labeling can be used to identify or distinguish one product from others. As a result, they are key marketing activities that help position a product appropriately for its target market.

Branding. Branding is the process of naming and identifying products. A *brand* is a name, term, symbol, design, or combination that identifies a product and distinguishes it from other products. Consider that Google, iTunes, and TiVo are brand names that are used to identify entire product categories, much like Xerox has become synonymous with photocopying and Kleenex with tissues. Protecting a brand name is important in maintaining a brand identity. The world's 10 most valuable brands are shown in Table 12-2. The brand name is the part of the brand that can be spoken and consists of letters, words, and numbers—such as WD-40 lubricant. A *brand mark* is the part of the brand that is a distinctive design, such as the silver star on the hood of a Mercedes or McDonald's golden arches logo. A trademark is a brand that is registered with the U.S. Patent and Trademark Office and is thus legally protected from use by any other firm.

Two major categories of brands are manufacturer brands and private distributor brands. Manufacturer brands are brands initiated and owned by the manufacturer to identify products from the point of production to the point of purchase. Kellogg's, Sony, and Chevron are examples. Private distributor brands, which may be less expensive than manufacturer brands, are owned and controlled by a wholesaler or retailer, such as Pantry Essentials (Safeway), 355 Everyday Value (Whole Foods), Great Value (Walmart), and Member's Mark (Sam's Wholesale Club). The names of private brands do not usually identify their manufacturer. While private-label brands were once considered cheaper and of poor quality, such as Walmart's Ol'Roy dog food, many private-label brands are increasing in quality and image and are competing with national brands. Even Amazon.com has noticed the lucrative opportunities of private-label brands. The firm has begun hiring employees with fashion experience to help develop its own private-label clothing brand.[15] Today there are private label brands in nearly every food and beverage category, and the private-label food and beverage market is expected to grow at a compound annual growth rate of 4.65 percent between 2015 and 2019.[16] Manufacturer brands are fighting hard against private distributor brands to retain their market share.

branding
the process of naming and identifying products.

trademark
a brand that is registered with the U.S. Patent and Trademark Office and is thus legally protected from use by any other firm.

manufacturer brands
brands initiated and owned by the manufacturer to identify products from the point of production to the point of purchase.

private distributor brands
brands, which may cost less than manufacturer brands, that are owned and controlled by a wholesaler or retailer.

TABLE 12-2
The 10 Most Valuable
Brands in the World

Rank	Brand	Brand Value ($ Millions)	Brand Value % Change
1	Apple	246,992	67
2	Google	173,652	9
3	Microsoft	115,500	28
4	IBM	93,987	−13
5	Visa	91,962	16
6	AT&T	89,492	15
7	Verizon	86,009	36
8	Coca-Cola	83,841	4
9	McDonald's	81,162	−5
10	Marlboro	80,352	19

Source: Millward Brown Optimer, "Brandz™ Top 100 Most Valuable Global Brands 2014," http://www.millwardbrown.com/ BrandZ/2015/Global/2015_BrandZ_Top100_Chart.pdf (accessed April 5, 2016).

generic products
products with no brand name that often come in simple packages and carry only their generic name.

Another type of brand that has developed is **generic products**—products with no brand name at all. They often come in plain simple packages that carry only the generic name of the product—peanut butter, tomato juice, aspirin, dog food, and so on. They appeal to consumers who may be willing to sacrifice quality or product consistency to get a lower price. Sales of generic brands have significantly decreased in recent years, although generic pharmaceuticals are commonly purchased due to their lower prices.

Companies use two basic approaches to branding multiple products. In one, a company gives each product within its complete product mix its own brand name. Warner-Lambert, which was acquired by Pfizer in 2000, sells many well-known consumer products—Dentyne, Chiclets, Listerine, Halls, Rolaids, and Trident—each individually branded. This branding policy ensures that the name of one product does not affect the names of others, and different brands can be targeted at different segments of the same market, increasing the company's market share (its percentage of the sales for the total market for a product). Another approach to branding is to develop a family of brands with each of the firm's products carrying the same name or at least part of the name. Gillette, Sara Lee, and IBM use this approach. Finally, consumers may react differently to domestic versus foreign brands. Table 12-3 provides a snapshot of the most popular car brands.

packaging
the external container that holds and describes the product.

Packaging. The **packaging,** or external container that holds and describes the product, influences consumers' attitudes and their buying decisions. Surveys have shown that consumers are willing to pay more for certain packaging attributes. One of the attributes includes clearly stated nutrition and ingredient labeling, especially those characteristics indicating whether a product is organic, gluten free, or environmentally friendly. Recyclable and biodegradable packaging is also popular.[17] It is estimated that consumers' eyes linger only 2.5 seconds on each product on an average shopping trip; therefore, product packaging should be designed to attract and hold consumers' attention.

Ranking	Vehicle Model	Country of Origin
1	Toyota Corolla	Japan
2	Hyundai Elantra	South Korea
3	Wuling Sunshine	China
4	Ford Focus	United States
5	Kia Rio	South Korea
6	Ford Fiesta	United States
7	Volkswagen Jetta	Germany
8	Toyota Camry	Japan
9	Chevrolet Cruze	United States
10	Volkswagen Golf	Germany

TABLE 12-3
Best-Selling Car Brands in the World

Source: "The Best-Selling Cars in the World," Forbes, 2015, http://www.forbes.com/pictures/mkk45ekfi/ford-fiesta-in-shanghai-by-night/ (accessed April 5, 2016).

A package can perform several functions, including protection, economy, convenience, and promotion. IKEA is constantly trying to investigate new ways for more efficient packaging to save on shipping costs.[18] Packaging can also be used to appeal to emotions. For example, pet food packaging appeals to the emotions of pet owners with illustrations of animals happily running, eating, or looking serene.[19] On the other hand, organizations must also exert caution before changing the designs of highly popular products. There was plenty of online criticism levied against Google when it changed its logo design by using a "friendlier" sans serif font.[20]

labeling
the presentation of important information on a package.

quality
the degree to which a good, service, or idea meets the demands and requirements of customers.

Labeling.   **Labeling,** the presentation of important information on the package, is closely associated with packaging. The content of labeling, often required by law, may include ingredients or content, nutrition facts (calories, fat, etc.), care instructions, suggestions for use (such as recipes), the manufacturer's address and toll-free number, website, and other useful information. This information can have a strong impact on sales. The labels of many products, particularly food and drugs, must carry warnings, instructions, certifications, or manufacturers' identifications.

Product Quality.   **Quality** reflects the degree to which a good, service, or idea meets the demands and requirements of customers. Quality products are often referred to as reliable, durable, easily maintained, easily used, a good value, or a trusted brand name. The level of quality is the amount of quality that a product possesses, and the consistency of quality depends on the product maintaining the same level of quality over time.

Gillette uses a family branding strategy so that consumers will recognize when a product is affiliated with the brand.

© Kristoffer Tripplaar/Alamy Stock Photo

Apple is the most valuable brand in the world. Its iPhones, iPods, and iPads have revolutionized the electronics and computing industry.

© Stockbroker/age fotostock

Quality of service is difficult to gauge because it depends on customers' perceptions of how well the service meets or exceeds their expectations. In other words, service quality is judged by consumers, not the service providers. For this reason, it is quite common for perceptions of quality to fluctuate from year to year. For instance, General Motors recalled millions of vehicles due to quality control issues. Problems included faulty ignition switches that prompted General Motors to issue a recall on the Chevy Cobalt. These recalls had a negative impact on GM's reputation for quality vehicles. A bank may define service quality as employing friendly and knowledgeable employees, but the bank's customers may be more concerned with waiting time, ATM access, security, and statement accuracy. Similarly, an airline traveler considers on-time arrival, on-board Internet or TV connections, and satisfaction with the ticketing and boarding process. The American Customer Satisfaction Index produces customer satisfaction scores for 10 economic sectors, 43 industries, and more than 300 companies. The latest results show that overall customer satisfaction was 73.4 (out of a possible 100), with increases in some industries balancing out drops in others.[21] Table 12-4 shows the customer satisfaction rankings of some of the most popular personal care and cleaning product companies.

The quality of services provided by businesses on the Internet can be gauged by consumers on such sites as ConsumerReports.org and BBBOnline. The subscription service offered by ConsumerReports.org provides consumers with a view of digital marketing sites' business, security, and privacy policies, while BBBOnline is dedicated to promoting responsibility online. As consumers join in by posting business and product reviews on the Internet on sites such as Yelp, the public can often get a much better idea of the quality of certain goods and services. Quality can also be associated with where the product is made. For example, "Made in U.S.A." labeling can be perceived as having a different value and quality. This includes strict laws on how much of a product can be made outside of the United States to still qualify for the "Made in USA" label. There are differences in the perception of quality and

TABLE 12-4
Personal Care and Cleaning Products Customer Satisfaction Ratings

Company	Score
Clorox	82
Unilever	80
Colgate-Palmolive	79
Dial	79
Procter & Gamble	75

Source: American Customer Satisfaction Index, "Benchmarks by Industry: Personal Care and Cleaning Products," 2016, http://www.theacsi.org/index.php?option=com_content&view=article&id=147&catid=&Itemid=212&i=Personal+Care+and+Cleaning+Products (accessed April 5, 2016).

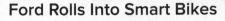

Going Green

Ford Rolls Into Smart Bikes

When Henry Ford started the Ford Motor Company in 1903, it is unlikely he ever imagined that one day his firm would be designing electronic bikes, nearly 115 years after the first Ford Model A rolled off the production line.

Yet from today's perspective it is not entirely surprising Ford chose to invest in the new e-bike prototypes, which seem to fit well with the auto maker's move into more environmentally-friendly vehicles. The prototype bikes are compact, highly customizable, and remarkably practical. Ford's third and newest e-bike prototype, the MoDe:Flex, syncs with a smartphone and smartwatch app to provide riders with useful information before and during the trip, including weather conditions, traffic congestion, parking costs, and turn-by-turn directions.

Along with traditional peddling power from the rider, the e-bike also includes a battery assist system to help get up steep hills and provide additional power based on heart rate input from the rider. An ultrasonic sensor on the back of the bike serves as a safety feature and alerts riders of approaching vehicles by inducing a vibration in the handlebars.

Ford believes the technology in its e-bikes will make multimodal travel more efficient. And instead of serving solely as an alternative transportation method, Ford e-bikes are designed to closely integrate with vehicles. For instance, the e-bike smartphone app can be used to locate and unlock the cyclist's vehicle, which can then be used to charge the e-bike's battery.[22]

Discussion Questions

1. At what stage in the product development process are Ford's e-bikes?
2. If Ford's e-bikes are released to the public, what type of product would they be? Convenience, shopping, or specialty products?
3. If Ford's e-bikes are released, how do you think the market would react? Do you believe the e-bikes would quickly jump to the growth stage of the product life cycle, or would they stay in the introductory stage for an extended period of time?

---

value between U.S. consumers and Europeans when comparing products made in the United States, Japan, Korea, and China.[23] Chinese brands are usually perceived as lower quality, while Japanese and Korean products are perceived as being of higher quality. However, China is trying to change consumer perceptions of its low brand quality. The increase in middle and upper classes in China has seen a rise in Chinese-branded luxury goods.[24]

Pricing Strategy

LO 12-2

Define *price* and discuss its importance in the marketing mix, including various pricing strategies a firm might employ.

Previously, we defined price as the value placed on an object exchanged between a buyer and a seller. Buyers' interest in price stems from their expectations about the usefulness of a product or the satisfaction they may derive from it. Because buyers have limited resources, they must allocate those resources to obtain the products they most desire. They must decide whether the benefits gained in an exchange are worth the buying power sacrificed. Almost anything of value can be assessed by a price. Many factors may influence the evaluation of value, including time constraints, price levels, perceived quality, and motivations to use available information about prices.[25] Figure 12-5 illustrates a method for calculating the value of a product. Indeed, consumers vary in their response to price: Some focus solely on the lowest price, while others consider quality or the prestige associated with a product and its price. Some types of consumers are increasingly "trading up" to more status-conscious products, such as automobiles, home appliances, restaurants, and even pet food, yet remain price-conscious for other products such as cleaning and grocery goods. In setting prices, marketers must consider not just a company's cost to produce a good or service, but the perceived value of that item in the marketplace. Products' perceived

FIGURE 12-5 Calculating the Value of a Product

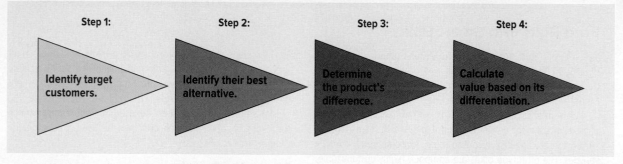

Source: Rafi Mohammed, "Use Price to Profit and Grow," Forbes.com, March 25, 2010, http://www.forbes.com/2010/03/25/profit-gain-value-mckinsey-sears-whirlpool-cmo-network-rafi-mohammed.html (accessed April 11, 2016).

value has benefited marketers at Starbucks, Sub-Zero, BMW, and Petco—which can charge premium prices for high-quality, prestige products—as well as Sam's Clubs and Costco—which offer basic household products at everyday low prices.

Price is a key element in the marketing mix because it relates directly to the generation of revenue and profits. In large part, the ability to set a price depends on the supply of and demand for a product. For most products, the quantity demanded goes up as the price goes down, and as the price goes up, the quantity demanded goes down. Changes in buyers' needs, variations in the effectiveness of other marketing mix variables, the presence of substitutes, and dynamic environmental factors can influence demand. The demand and price for coal has decreased as the price for natural gas has decreased due to an increase in supply.

Price is probably the most flexible variable in the marketing mix. Although it may take years to develop a product, establish channels of distribution, and design and implement promotion, a product's price may be set and changed in a few minutes. Under certain circumstances, of course, the price may not be so flexible, especially if government regulations prevent dealers from controlling prices. Of course, price also depends on the cost to manufacture a good or provide a service or idea. A firm may temporarily sell products below cost to match competition, to generate cash flow, or even to increase market share, but in the long run, it cannot survive by selling its products below cost.

Pricing Objectives

Pricing objectives specify the role of price in an organization's marketing mix and strategy. They usually are influenced not only by marketing mix decisions but also by finance, accounting, and production factors. Maximizing profits and sales, boosting market share, maintaining the status quo, and survival are four common pricing objectives.

Specific Pricing Strategies

Pricing strategies provide guidelines for achieving the company's pricing objectives and overall marketing strategy. They specify how price will be used as a variable in the marketing mix. Significant pricing strategies relate to the pricing of new products, psychological pricing, and price discounting.

Pricing New Products.   Setting the price for a new product is critical: The right price leads to profitability; the wrong price may kill the product. In general, there are two basic strategies to setting the base price for a new product. **Price skimming** is charging the highest possible price that buyers who want the product will pay. Price skimming is used with luxury goods items. Ultra-D (3D television without the use of glasses) often run into the thousands of dollars. Price skimming is often used to allow the company to generate much-needed revenue to help offset the costs of research and development. Conversely, a **penetration price** is a low price designed to help a product enter the market and gain market share rapidly. When Netflix entered the market, it offered its rentals at prices much lower than the average rental stores and did not charge late fees. Netflix quickly gained market share and eventually drove many rental stores out of business. Penetration pricing is less flexible than price skimming; it is more difficult to raise a penetration price than to lower a skimming price. Penetration pricing is used most often when marketers suspect that competitors will enter the market shortly after the product has been introduced.

Psychological Pricing. **Psychological pricing** encourages purchases based on emotional rather than rational responses to the price. For example, the assumption behind *even/odd pricing* is that people will buy more of a product for $9.99 than $10 because it seems to be a bargain at the odd price. The assumption behind *symbolic/prestige pricing* is that high prices connote high quality. Thus the prices of certain fragrances and cosmetics are set artificially high to give the impression of superior quality. Some over-the-counter drugs are priced high because consumers associate a drug's price with potency.

Reference Pricing. **Reference pricing** is a type of psychological pricing in which a lower-priced item is compared to a more expensive brand in hopes that the consumer will use the higher price as a comparison price. The main idea is to make the item appear less expensive compared with other alternatives. For example, Walmart might place its Great Value brand next to a manufacturer's brand such as Bayer or Johnson & Johnson so that the Great Value brand will look like a better deal.

Price Discounting. Temporary price reductions, or **discounts,** are often employed to boost sales. Although there are many types, quantity, seasonal, and promotional discounts are among the most widely used. Quantity discounts reflect the economies of purchasing in large volumes. Seasonal discounts to buyers who purchase goods or services out of season help even out production capacity. Promotional discounts attempt to improve sales by advertising price reductions on selected products to increase customer interest. Often, promotional pricing is geared toward increased profits. For instance, bare-bones German grocery chain Aldi is attempting to compete against Trader Joe's as it expands into the United States through the offering of higher-end food and price discounts.[26]

Distribution Strategy

The best products in the world will not be successful unless companies make them available where and when customers want to buy them. In this section, we will explore dimensions of distribution strategy, including the channels through which products are distributed, the intensity of market coverage, and the physical handling of products during distribution.

Marketing Channels

A **marketing channel,** or channel of distribution, is a group of organizations that moves products from their producer to customers. Marketing channels make products

price skimming
charging the highest possible price that buyers who want the product will pay.

penetration price
a low price designed to help a product enter the market and gain market share rapidly.

psychological pricing
encouraging purchases based on emotional rather than rational responses to the price.

reference pricing
a type of psychological pricing in which a lower-priced item is compared to a more expensive brand in hopes that the consumer will use the higher price as a comparison price.

discounts
temporary price reductions, often employed to boost sales.

LO 12-3

Identify factors affecting distribution decisions, such as marketing channels and intensity of market coverage.

marketing channel
a group of organizations that moves products from their producer to customers; also called a channel of distribution.

TABLE 12-5 General Merchandise Retailers

Type of Retailer	Description	Examples
Department store	Large, full-service stores organized by departments	Nordstrom, Macy's, Neiman Marcus
Discount store	Offers less services than department stores; store atmosphere reflects value pricing	Walmart, Stein Mart, Target
Convenience store	Small, self-service stores carrying many items for immediate consumption	Circle K, 7-Eleven, Allsups
Supermarket	Large stores carrying most food items as well as nonfood items for daily family use	Trader Joe's, Albertsons, Wegman's
Superstore	Very large stores that carry most food and nonfood products that are routinely purchased	Super Walmart, Meijer
Hypermarket	The largest retail store that takes the foundation of the discount store and provides even more food and nonfood products	Carrefour, Tesco Extra
Warehouse club	Large membership establishments with food and nonfood products and deep discounts	Costco, BJ's Wholesale Club, Sam's Club
Warehouse showroom	Large facilities with products displayed that are often retrieved from a less expensive adjacent warehouse	IKEA, Cost Plus

available to buyers when and where they desire to purchase them. Organizations that bridge the gap between a product's manufacturer and the ultimate consumer are called *middlemen,* or intermediaries. They create time, place, and ownership utility. Two intermediary organizations are retailers and wholesalers.

retailers
intermediaries who buy products from manufacturers (or other intermediaries) and sell them to consumers for home and household use rather than for resale or for use in producing other products.

Retailers buy products from manufacturers (or other intermediaries) and sell them to consumers for home and household use rather than for resale or for use in producing other products. Toys 'R' Us, for example, buys products from Mattel and other manufacturers and resells them to consumers. By bringing together an assortment of products from competing producers, retailers create utility. Retailers arrange for products to be moved from producers to a convenient retail establishment (place utility). They maintain hours of operation for their retail stores to make merchandise available when consumers want it (time utility). They also assume the risk of ownership of inventories (ownership utility). Table 12-5 describes various types of general merchandise retailers.

Today, there are too many stores competing for too few customers, and, as a result, competition among similar retailers has never been more intense. In addition, retailers face challenges such as shoplifting. Further, competition among different types of stores is changing the nature of retailing. Supermarkets compete with specialty food stores, wholesale clubs, and discount stores. Department stores compete with nearly every other type of store, including specialty stores, off-price chains, category killers, discount stores, and online retailers. As a result, department store sales are decreasing.[27] For this reason, many businesses have turned to nonstore retailing to sell their products. Some nonstore retailing is performed by traditional retailers to complement their in-store offerings. For instance, Walmart and Macy's have created online shopping sites to retain customers and compete against other businesses. Other companies retail outside of physical stores entirely.

direct marketing
the use of nonpersonal media to communicate products, information, and the opportunity to purchase via media such as mail, telephone, or the Internet.

Some companies rely on **direct marketing,** which is the use of nonpersonal media to communicate products, information, and the opportunity to purchase via media

TABLE 12-6   Major Wholesaling Functions

Physical distribution	• Inventory management
	• Transportation
	• Warehousing
	• Materials handling
Promotion	• Personal selling
	• Publicity
	• Sales promotion
	• Advertising
Inventory control and data processing	• Management information systems
	• Inventory control
	• Transaction monitoring
	• Financial and accounting data analysis
Risk-taking	• Inventory decisions
	• Product deterioration
	• Theft control
Financing and budgeting	• Investment capital
	• Credit management
	• Managing cash flow and receivables
Marketing research and information systems	• Conducting primary market research
	• Analyzing big data
	• Utilizing marketing analytics

such as mail, telephone, or the Internet. For example, Duluth Trading has stores but specializes in catalog marketing, especially with products such as jeans, work boots, and hats. Another form of nonstore retailing is **direct selling**, which involves the marketing of products to ultimate consumers through face-to-face sales presentations at home or in the workplace. The top three global direct selling companies are Amway, Avon, and Herbalife. Most individuals who engage in direct selling work on a part-time basis because they like the product and often sell to their own social networks.

Wholesalers are intermediaries who buy from producers or from other wholesalers and sell to retailers. They usually do not sell in significant quantities to ultimate consumers. Wholesalers perform the functions listed in Table 12-6.

Wholesalers are extremely important because of the marketing activities they perform, particularly for consumer products. Although it is true that wholesalers can be eliminated, their functions must be passed on to some other entity, such as the producer, another intermediary, or even the customer. Wholesalers help consumers and retailers by buying in large quantities, then selling to retailers in smaller quantities. By stocking an assortment of products, wholesalers match products to demand. Sysco is a food wholesaler for the food services industry. The company provides food, preparation, and serving products to restaurants, hospitals, and other institutions that provide meals outside of the home.[28] *Merchant wholesalers* like Sysco take title to the goods, assume risks, and

direct selling
the marketing of products to ultimate consumers through face-to-face sales presentations at home or in the workplace.

wholesalers
intermediaries who buy from producers or from other wholesalers and sell to retailers.

sell to other wholesalers, business customers, or retailers. *Agents* negotiate sales, do not own products, and perform a limited number of functions in exchange for a commission.

Supply Chain Management.   In an effort to improve distribution channel relationships among manufacturers and other channel intermediaries, supply chain management creates alliances between channel members. In Chapter 8, we defined supply chain management as connecting and integrating all parties or members of the distribution system in order to satisfy customers. It involves long-term partnerships among marketing channel members working together to reduce costs, waste, and unnecessary movement in the entire marketing channel in order to satisfy customers. It goes beyond traditional channel members (producers, wholesalers, retailers, customers) to include *all* organizations involved in moving products from the producer to the ultimate customer. In a survey of business managers, a disruption in the supply chain was viewed as the number-one crisis that could decrease revenue.[29]

The focus shifts from one of selling to the next level in the channel to one of selling products *through* the channel to a satisfied ultimate customer. Information, once provided on a guarded, "as needed" basis, is now open, honest, and ongoing. Perhaps most importantly, the points of contact in the relationship expand from one-on-one at the salesperson–buyer level to multiple interfaces at all levels and in all functional areas of the various organizations.

Channels for Consumer Products.   Typical marketing channels for consumer products are shown in Figure 12-6. In channel A, the product moves from the producer directly to the consumer. Farmers who sell their fruit and vegetables to consumers at

FIGURE 12-6
Marketing Channels for Consumer Products

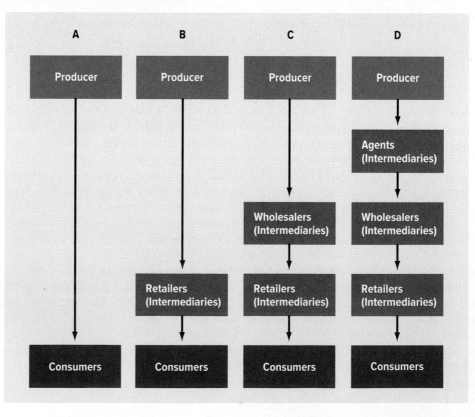

Entrepreneurship in Action

Heidi Ho Organics: Cheese Fit for a Shark

Heidi Ho
Founders: Heidi Lovig and Lyssa Story
Founded: 2011, in Portland, Oregon
Success: After deciding to develop their own vegan cheese substitutes, the founders of Heidi Ho went on to generate funding from the hit reality show *Shark Tank* and gained entry into Whole Foods Markets.

After becoming a vegan, entrepreneur Heidi Lovig was disappointed in the lack of vegan cheese alternatives available. Together with partner Lyssa Story, the two devised a dairy and gluten-free vegan cheese substitute they hoped would gain acceptance among vegan consumers. They decided to specialize in plant-based cheeses made from organic ingredients.

Five months after it was created, Heidi Ho was offered shelf space in Whole Foods Market, a leading national retailer of organic and natural health food. The Whole Foods deal put Heidi Ho on the radar of consumers across the country, drastically increasing the popularity and securing the success of the fledgling startup. The company soon had the resources to expand its product offerings and obtain certified organic status from the U.S. Department of Agriculture (USDA). Perhaps most importantly, the company gained recognition as a suitable cheese alternative deserving of a presence in the grocery aisle. Indeed, the company's appeal was confirmed in 2014 when Heidi Lovig represented her company on the reality show *Shark Tank* and successfully raised $125,000 for 30 percent equity in the company.[30]

Discussion Questions

1. Describe the different elements of the marketing strategy that Heidi Ho adopted in developing and popularizing its products.
2. What is the target market of Heidi Ho's vegan cheese substitutes?
3. What variables of buying behavior would be most likely to influence a consumer's purchase of vegan cheese substitutes?

---

roadside stands or farmers' markets use a direct-from-producer-to-consumer marketing channel.

In channel B, the product goes from producer to retailer to consumer. This type of channel is used for products such as college textbooks, automobiles, and appliances. In channel C, the product is handled by a wholesaler and a retailer before it reaches the consumer. Producer-to-wholesaler-to-retailer-to-consumer marketing channels distribute a wide range of products including refrigerators, televisions, soft drinks, cigarettes, clocks, watches, and office products. In channel D, the product goes to an agent, a wholesaler, and a retailer before going to the consumer. This long channel of distribution is especially useful for convenience products. Candy and some produce are often sold by agents who bring buyers and sellers together.

Services are usually distributed through direct marketing channels because they are generally produced *and* consumed simultaneously. For example, you cannot take a haircut home for later use. Many services require the customer's presence and participation: The sick patient must visit the physician to receive treatment; the child must be at the day care center to receive care; the tourist must be present to sight-see and consume tourism services.

Channels for Business Products.   In contrast to consumer goods, more than half of all business products, especially expensive equipment or technically complex products, are sold through direct marketing channels. Business customers like to communicate directly with producers of such products to gain the technical assistance and personal assurances that only the producer can offer. For this reason, business buyers prefer to purchase expensive and highly complex mainframe computers directly from IBM, Unisys, and other mainframe producers. Other business products may be distributed through channels employing wholesaling intermediaries such as industrial distributors and/or manufacturer's agents.

The Jessica Simpson Collection is a line of fashion products for women. The collection is distributed through retailers including Macy's, Dillard's, Nordstrom, and Lord & Taylor.

© Jamie McCarthy/Getty Images for Jessica Simpson Collection

intensive distribution
a form of market coverage whereby a product is made available in as many outlets as possible.

selective distribution
a form of market coverage whereby only a small number of all available outlets are used to expose products.

exclusive distribution
the awarding by a manufacturer to an intermediary of the sole right to sell a product in a defined geographic territory.

Intensity of Market Coverage

A major distribution decision is how widely to distribute a product—that is, how many and what type of outlets should carry it. The intensity of market coverage depends on buyer behavior, as well as the nature of the target market and the competition. Wholesalers and retailers provide various intensities of market coverage and must be selected carefully to ensure success. Market coverage may be intensive, selective, or exclusive.

Intensive distribution makes a product available in as many outlets as possible. Because availability is important to purchasers of convenience products such as toothpaste, yogurt, candy, beverages, and chewing gum, a nearby location with a minimum of time spent searching and waiting in line is most important to the consumer. To saturate markets intensively, wholesalers and many varied retailers try to make the product available at every location where a consumer might desire to purchase it. Zoom Systems provides robotic vending machines for products beyond candy and drinks. Zoom has 1,500 machines in airports and hotels across the United States. Through partnering with different companies, today's ZoomShops sell a variety of brands, including products from The Honest Company, Best Buy, Macy's, and Nespresso.[31]

Selective distribution uses only a small number of all available outlets to expose products. It is used most often for products that consumers buy only after shopping and comparing price, quality, and style. Many products sold on a selective basis require salesperson assistance, technical advice, warranties, or repair service to maintain consumer satisfaction. Typical products include automobiles, major appliances, clothes, and furniture. Ralph Lauren is a brand that uses selective distribution.

Exclusive distribution exists when a manufacturer gives an intermediary the sole right to sell a product in a defined geographic territory. Such exclusivity provides an incentive for a dealer to handle a product that has a limited market. Exclusive distribution is the opposite of intensive distribution in that products are purchased and consumed over a long period of time, and service or information is required to develop a satisfactory sales relationship. Products distributed on an exclusive basis include high-quality musical instruments, yachts, airplanes, and high-fashion leather goods. Aircraft manufacturer Piper Aircraft uses exclusive distribution by choosing only a few dealers in each region. The company has more than 30 locations in several countries, including the Americas and China.[32]

Physical Distribution

Physical distribution includes all the activities necessary to move products from producers to customers—inventory control, transportation, warehousing, and materials handling. Physical distribution creates time and place utility by making products available when they are wanted, with adequate service and at minimum cost. Both goods and services require physical distribution. Many physical distribution activities are part of supply chain management, which we discussed in Chapter 8; we'll take a brief look at a few more now.

Transportation.   Transportation, the shipment of products to buyers, creates time and place utility for products, and thus is a key element in the flow of goods and services from producer to consumer. The five major modes of transportation used to move products between cities in the United States are railways, motor vehicles, inland waterways, pipelines, and airways.

Although air freight is the most expensive mode of transportation, it is also the fastest. Its speed is particularly important for perishable products such as foods.

© stockphoto mania/Shutterstock

Railroads are a cost-effective method of transportation for many products. Heavy commodities, foodstuffs, raw materials, and coal are examples of products carried by railroads. Trucks have greater flexibility than railroads because they can reach more locations. Trucks handle freight quickly and economically, offer door-to-door service, and are more flexible in their packaging requirements than are ships or airplanes. Air transport offers speed and a high degree of dependability but is the most expensive means of transportation; shipping is less expensive and is the slowest form. Pipelines are used to transport petroleum, natural gas, semi-liquid coal, wood chips, and certain chemicals. Pipelines have the lowest costs for products that can be transported via this method. Many products can be moved most efficiently by using more than one mode of transportation.

Factors affecting the selection of a mode of transportation include cost, capability to handle the product, reliability, and availability, and, as suggested, selecting transportation modes requires trade-offs. Unique characteristics of the product and consumer desires often determine the mode selected.

Warehousing.   Warehousing is the design and operation of facilities to receive, store, and ship products. A warehouse facility receives, identifies, sorts, and dispatches goods to storage; stores them; recalls, selects, or picks goods; assembles the shipment; and finally, dispatches the shipment.

Companies often own and operate their own private warehouses that store, handle, and move their own products. Firms might want to own or lease a private warehouse when their goods require special handling and storage or when it has large warehousing needs in a specific geographic area. Private warehouses are beneficial because they provide customers with more control over their goods. However, fixed costs for maintaining these warehouses can be quite high.[33] They can also rent storage and related physical distribution services from public warehouses. While public warehouses store goods for more than one company, providing firms with less control over distribution, they are often less expensive than private warehouses and are useful for seasonal production or low-volume storage.[34] Regardless of whether a private or a public warehouse is used, warehousing is important because it makes products available for shipment to match demand at different geographic locations.

physical distribution
all the activities necessary to move products from producers to customers— inventory control, transportation, warehousing, and materials handling.

transportation
the shipment of products to buyers.

warehousing
the design and operation of facilities to receive, store, and ship products.

materials handling
the physical handling and
movement of products
in warehousing and
transportation.

Materials Handling.   Materials handling is the physical handling and movement of products in warehousing and transportation. Handling processes may vary
significantly due to product characteristics. Efficient materials-handling procedures increase a warehouse's useful capacity and improve customer service. Well-
coordinated loading and movement systems increase efficiency and reduce costs.

Importance of Distribution in a Marketing Strategy

Distribution decisions are among the least flexible marketing mix decisions. Products
can be changed over time; prices can be changed quickly; and promotion is usually
changed regularly. But distribution decisions often commit resources and establish
contractual relationships that are difficult if not impossible to change. As a company
attempts to expand into new markets, it may require a complete change in distribution. Moreover, if a firm does not manage its marketing channel in the most efficient
manner and provide the best service, then a new competitor will evolve to create a
more effective distribution system.

LO 12-4

Specify the activities involved
in promotion, as well as promotional strategies and promotional positioning.

**integrated marketing
communications**
coordinating the promotion
mix elements and
synchronizing promotion as a
unified effort.

advertising
a paid form of nonpersonal
communication transmitted
through a mass medium, such
as television commercials or
magazine advertisements.

advertising campaign
designing a series of
advertisements and placing
them in various media to
reach a particular target
market.

Need help under-
standing integrated
marketing com-
munications? Visit
your Connect
ebook video tab
for a brief animated
explanation.

Promotion Strategy

The role of promotion is to communicate with individuals, groups, and organizations
to facilitate an exchange directly or indirectly. It encourages marketing exchanges
by attempting to persuade individuals, groups, and organizations to accept goods,
services, and ideas. Promotion is used not only to sell products but also to influence opinions and attitudes toward an organization, person, or cause. The state of
Michigan, for example, has successfully used its "Pure Michigan" campaign to influence tourists to visit Michigan. The economic impact of the campaign was estimated
at $1.2 billion.[35] Most people probably equate promotion with advertising, but it also
includes personal selling, publicity, and sales promotion. The role that these elements
play in a marketing strategy is extremely important.

The Promotion Mix

Advertising, personal selling, publicity, and sales promotion are collectively known
as the promotion mix because a strong promotion program results from the careful
selection and blending of these elements. The process of coordinating the promotion
mix elements and synchronizing promotion as a unified effort is called integrated
marketing communications. When planning promotional activities, an integrated
marketing communications approach results in the desired message for customers.
Different elements of the promotion mix are coordinated to play their appropriate
roles in delivery of the message on a consistent basis.

Advertising.   Perhaps the best-known form of promotion, advertising is a paid
form of nonpersonal communication transmitted through a mass medium, such as
television commercials, magazine advertisements, or online ads. Pharmaceutical
firms have long used advertisements to promote medications for lifestyle conditions.
However, more recently it has begun releasing advertisements promoting life-saving,
often expensive medications that specialist doctors prescribe.[36] Commercials featuring celebrities, customers, or unique creations serve to grab viewers' attention and
pique their interest in a product.

An advertising campaign involves designing a series of advertisements and placing
them in various media to reach a particular target audience. The basic content and form
of an advertising campaign are a function of several factors. A product's features, uses,

and benefits affect the content of the campaign message and individual ads. Characteristics of the people in the target audience—gender, age, education, race, income, occupation, lifestyle, and other attributes—influence both content and form. When Procter & Gamble promotes Crest toothpaste to children, the company emphasizes daily brushing and cavity control, whereas it promotes tartar control and whiter teeth when marketing to adults. To communicate effectively, advertisers use words, symbols, and illustrations that are meaningful, familiar, and attractive to people in the target audience.

An advertising campaign's objectives and platform also affect the content and form of its messages. If a firm's advertising objectives involve large sales increases, the message may include hard-hitting, high-impact language and symbols. When campaign objectives aim at increasing brand awareness, the message may use much repetition of the brand name and words and illustrations associated with it. Thus, the advertising platform is the foundation on which campaign messages are built.

Hot Wheels uses celebrities like Danica Patrick, colorful packaging, and fun advertisements to appeal to children.

© Tony Ding/AP Images for Mattel, Inc

Advertising media are the vehicles or forms of communication used to reach a desired audience. Print media include newspapers, magazines, direct mail, and billboards, while electronic media include television, radio, and Internet advertising. Choice of media obviously influences the content and form of the message. Effective outdoor displays and short broadcast spot announcements require concise, simple messages. Magazine and newspaper advertisements can include considerable detail and long explanations. Because several kinds of media offer geographic selectivity, a precise message can be tailored to a particular geographic section of the target audience. For example, a company advertising in *Time* might decide to use one message in the New England region and another in the rest of the nation. A company may also choose to advertise in only one region. Such geographic selectivity lets a firm use the same message in different regions at different times. On the other hand, some companies are willing to pay extensive amounts of money to reach national audiences. Marketers spent approximately $5 million for one 30-second advertising slot during the 2016 Super Bowl due to its national reach and popularity.[37]

The use of online advertising is increasing. However, advertisers are demanding more for their ad dollars and proof that they are working, which is why Google AdWords only charges companies when users click on the ad. Certain types of ads are more popular than pop-up ads and banner ads that consumers find annoying. One technique is to blur the lines between television and online advertising. TV commercials may point viewers to a website for more information, where short "advertainment" films continue the marketing message. Marketers might also use the Internet to show advertisements or videos that were not accepted by mainstream television. People for the Ethical Treatment of Animals (PETA) often develop racy commercials that are denied Super Bowl spots. However, these ads can be viewed online through YouTube and other sites.[38]

Infomercials—typically 30-minute blocks of radio or television air time featuring a celebrity or upbeat host talking about and demonstrating a product—have evolved

Personal selling is important with high-risk items. In-store representatives can assist customers in discussing the benefits of a product, financing arrangements, and any warranties or guarantees.

© Juice Images/Alamy

personal selling
direct, two-way communication with buyers and potential buyers.

publicity
nonpersonal communication transmitted through the mass media but not paid for directly by the firm.

as an advertising method. Toll-free numbers and website addresses are usually provided so consumers can conveniently purchase the product or obtain additional information. Although many consumers and companies have negative feelings about infomercials, apparently they get results.

Personal Selling. **Personal selling** is direct, two-way communication with buyers and potential buyers. For many products—especially large, expensive ones with specialized uses, such as cars, appliances, and houses—interaction between a salesperson and the customer is probably the most important promotional tool.

Personal selling is the most flexible of the promotional methods because it gives marketers the greatest opportunity to communicate specific information that might trigger a purchase. Only personal selling can zero in on a prospect and attempt to persuade that person to make a purchase. Although personal selling has a lot of advantages, it is one of the most costly forms of promotion. A sales call on an industrial customer can cost more than $400.

There are three distinct categories of salespersons: order takers (for example, retail sales clerks and route salespeople), creative salespersons (for example, automobile, furniture, and insurance salespeople), and support salespersons (for example, customer educators and goodwill builders who usually do not take orders). For most of these salespeople, personal selling is a six-step process:

1. *Prospecting:* Identifying potential buyers of the product.
2. *Approaching:* Using a referral or calling on a customer without prior notice to determine interest in the product.
3. *Presenting:* Getting the prospect's attention with a product demonstration.
4. *Handling objections:* Countering reasons for not buying the product.
5. *Closing:* Asking the prospect to buy the product.
6. *Following up:* Checking customer satisfaction with the purchased product.

Publicity. **Publicity** is nonpersonal communication transmitted through the mass media but not paid for directly by the firm. A firm does not pay the media cost for publicity and is not identified as the originator of the message; instead, the message is presented in news story form. Obviously, a company can benefit from publicity by releasing to news sources newsworthy messages about the firm and its involvement with the public. Many companies have *public relations* departments to try to gain favorable publicity and minimize negative publicity for the firm.

Although advertising and publicity are both carried by the mass media, they differ in several major ways. Advertising messages tend to be informative, persuasive, or both; publicity is mainly informative. Advertising is often designed to have an immediate impact or to provide specific information to persuade a person to act; publicity describes what a firm is doing, what products it is launching, or other newsworthy information, but seldom calls for action. When advertising is used, the organization must pay for media time and select the media that will best reach target audiences. The mass media willingly carry publicity because they believe it has general public interest. Advertising can be repeated a number of times; most publicity appears in the mass media once and is not repeated.

Advertising, personal selling, and sales promotion are especially useful for influencing an exchange directly. Publicity is extremely important when communication focuses on a company's activities and products and is directed at interest groups, current and potential investors, regulatory agencies, and society in general.

A variation of traditional advertising is buzz marketing, in which marketers attempt to create a trend or acceptance of a product. Companies seek out trendsetters in communities and get them to "talk up" a brand to their friends, family, co-workers, and others. One unusual method that Nagoya, Japan used to attract more job applicants to the city was adopting a spokes-ape. The city used an ape at the local zoo that not only became a recruitment tool with his face on posters and T-shirts but also a national celebrity.[39] Other marketers using the buzz technique include Hebrew National ("mom squads" grilled the company's hot dogs), and Red Bull (its sponsorship of the stratosphere space diving project). The idea behind buzz marketing is that an accepted member of a particular social group will be more credible than any form of paid communication.[40] The concept works best as part of an integrated marketing communication program that also includes traditional advertising, personal selling, sales promotion, and publicity.

A related concept is viral marketing, which describes the concept of getting Internet users to pass on ads and promotions to others. The jewelry brand Pandora released "The Unique Connection" campaign that blindfolded children and then asked them to identify their mothers based on their jewelry, facial structure, clothing, and hair. Each child did so successfully. The advertisement went viral, with more than 17 million viewings on YouTube.[41]

Sales Promotion. Sales promotion involves direct inducements offering added value or some other incentive for buyers to enter into an exchange. Sales promotions are generally easier to measure and less expensive than advertising. The major tools of sales promotion are store displays, premiums, samples and demonstrations, coupons, contests and sweepstakes, refunds, and trade shows. Coupon-clipping in particular became common due to the recent recession. While coupons in the past decade traditionally had a fairly low redemption rate, with about 2 percent being redeemed, the recent recession caused an upsurge in coupon usage. There has also been a major upsurge in the use of mobile coupons, or coupons sent to consumers over mobile devices. The redemption rate for mobile coupons is 8 times higher than that of traditional coupons.[42] While coupons can be a valuable tool in sales promotion, they cannot be relied upon to stand by themselves, but should be part of an overall promotion mix. Sales promotion stimulates customer purchasing and increases dealer effectiveness in selling products. It is used to enhance and supplement other forms of promotion.

sales promotion
direct inducements offering added value or some other incentive for buyers to enter into an exchange.

Companies use a pull strategy by offering coupons in the hopes of convincing customers to visit their stores.

© Casper1774 Studio/Shutterstock

FIGURE 12-7   Push and Pull Strategies

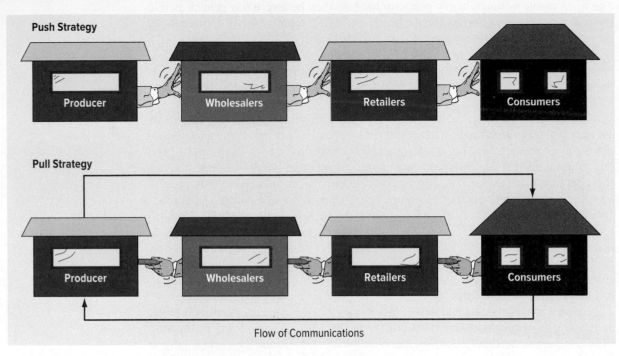

Flow of Communications

Sampling a product may also encourage consumers to buy. This is why many grocery stores provide free samples in the hopes of influencing consumers' purchasing decisions. In a given year, almost three-fourths of consumer product companies may use sampling.

Promotion Strategies: To Push or to Pull

push strategy
an attempt to motivate intermediaries to push the product down to their customers.

In developing a promotion mix, organizations must decide whether to fashion a mix that pushes or pulls the product (Figure 12-7). A **push strategy** attempts to motivate intermediaries to push the product down to their customers. When a push strategy is used, the company attempts to motivate wholesalers and retailers to make the product available to their customers. Sales personnel may be used to persuade intermediaries to offer the product, distribute promotional materials, and offer special promotional incentives for those who agree to carry the product. For example, salespeople from pharmaceutical companies will often market new products to doctors in the hope that the doctors will recommend their products to their clients. A **pull strategy** uses promotion to create consumer demand for a product so that consumers exert pressure on marketing channel members to make it available. For a while, T-Mobile was the only major carrier that did not have the iPhone. The iPhone was not compatible with T-Mobile's 3G frequencies, so Apple largely sidestepped T-Mobile. However, the popularity of the iPhone and decreasing market share caused T-Mobile to revamp its spectrum to run on the iPhone better. This is an example of how consumer pull caused a company to change its practices.[43] Additionally, offering free samples prior to a product rollout encourages consumers to request the product from their favorite retailer.

pull strategy
the use of promotion to create consumer demand for a product so that consumers exert pressure on marketing channel members to make it available.

A company can use either strategy, or it can use a variation or combination of the two. The exclusive use of advertising indicates a pull strategy. Personal selling to marketing channel members indicates a push strategy. The allocation of promotional resources to various marketing mix elements probably determines which strategy a marketer uses.

Objectives of Promotion

The marketing mix a company uses depends on its objectives. It is important to recognize that promotion is only one element of the marketing strategy and must be tied carefully to the goals of the firm, its overall marketing objectives, and the other elements of the marketing strategy. Firms use promotion for many reasons, but typical objectives are to stimulate demand, to stabilize sales, and to inform, remind, and reinforce customers.

Increasing demand for a product is probably the most typical promotional objective. Stimulating demand, often through advertising and sales promotion, is particularly important when a firm is using a pull strategy.

Another goal of promotion is to stabilize sales by maintaining the status quo—that is, the current sales level of the product. During periods of slack or decreasing sales, contests, prizes, vacations, and other sales promotions are sometimes offered to customers to maintain sales goals. Advertising is often used to stabilize sales by making customers aware of slack use periods. For example, auto manufacturers often provide rebates, free options, or lower-than-market interest rates to stabilize sales and thereby keep production lines moving during temporary slowdowns. A stable sales pattern allows the firm to run efficiently by maintaining a consistent level of production and storage and utilizing all its functions so that it is ready when sales increase.

An important role of any promotional program is to inform potential buyers about the organization and its products. A major portion of advertising in the United States, particularly in daily newspapers, is informational. Providing information about the availability, price, technology, and features of a product is very important in encouraging a buyer to move toward a purchase decision. Nearly all forms of promotion involve an attempt to help consumers learn more about a product and a company.

Promotion is also used to remind consumers that an established organization is still around and sells certain products that have uses and benefits. Often advertising reminds customers that they may need to use a product more frequently or in certain situations. Pennzoil, for example, has run television commercials reminding car owners that they need to change their oil every 3,000 miles to ensure proper performance of their cars.

Reinforcement promotion attempts to assure current users of the product that they have made the right choice and tells them how to get the most satisfaction from the product. Also, a company could release publicity statements through the news media about a new use for a product. Additionally, firms can have salespeople communicate with current and potential customers about the proper use and maintenance of a product—all in the hope of developing a repeat customer.

Promotional Positioning

Promotional positioning uses promotion to create and maintain an image of a product in buyers' minds. It is a natural result of market segmentation. In both

promotional positioning the use of promotion to create and maintain an image of a product in buyers' minds.

promotional positioning and market segmentation, the firm targets a given product or brand at a portion of the total market. A promotional strategy helps differentiate the product and makes it appeal to a particular market segment. For example, to appeal to safety-conscious consumers, Volvo heavily promotes the safety and crashworthiness of Volvo automobiles in its advertising. Promotion can be used to change or reinforce an image. Effective promotion influences customers and persuades them to buy.

Importance of Marketing Strategy

Marketing creates value through the marketing mix. For customers, value means receiving a product in which the benefit of the product outweighs the cost, or price paid for it. For marketers, value means that the benefits (usually monetary) received from selling the product outweigh the costs it takes to develop and sell it. This requires carefully integrating the marketing mix into an effective marketing strategy. One misstep could mean a loss in profits, whether it be from a failed product idea, shortages or oversupply of a product, a failure to effectively promote the product, or prices that are too high or too low. And while some of these marketing mix elements can be easily fixed, other marketing mix elements such as distribution can be harder to adapt.

On the other hand, firms that develop an effective marketing mix to meet customer needs will gain competitive advantages over those that do not. Often, these advantages occur when the firm excels at one or more elements of the marketing mix. Walmart has a reputation for its everyday low prices, while Tiffany's is known for its high-quality jewelry. However, excelling at one element of the marketing mix does not mean that a company can neglect the others. The best product cannot succeed if consumers do not know about it or if they cannot find it in stores. Additionally, firms must constantly monitor the market environment to understand how demand is changing and whether adaptations in the marketing mix are needed. It is therefore essential that every element of the marketing mix be carefully evaluated and synchronized with the marketing strategy. Only then will firms be able to achieve the marketing concept of providing products that satisfy customers' needs while allowing the organization to achieve its goals.

So You Want to Be a Marketing Manager

Many jobs in marketing are closely tied to the marketing mix functions: distribution, product, promotion, and price. Often the job titles could be sales manager, distribution or supply chain manager, advertising account executive, or store manager.

A distribution manager arranges for transportation of goods within firms and through marketing channels. Transportation can be costly, and time is always an important factor, so minimizing their effects is vital to the success of a firm. Distribution managers must choose one or a combination of transportation modes from a vast array of options, taking into account local, federal, and international regulations for different freight classifications; the weight, size, and fragility of products to be shipped; time schedules; and loss and damage ratios. Manufacturing firms are the largest employers of distribution managers.

A product manager is responsible for the success or failure of a product line. This requires a general knowledge of advertising, transportation modes, inventory control, selling and sales management, promotion, marketing research, packaging, and pricing. Frequently, several years of selling and sales management experience are prerequisites for such a position as well as college training in business administration. Being a product manager can be rewarding both financially and psychologically.

Some of the most creative roles in the business world are in the area of advertising. Advertising pervades our daily lives, as businesses and other organizations try to grab our attention and tell us about what they have to offer. Copywriters, artists, and account executives in advertising must have creativity, imagination, artistic talent, and expertise in expression and persuasion. Advertising is an area of business in which a wide variety of educational backgrounds may be useful, from degrees in advertising itself, to journalism or liberal arts degrees. Common entry-level positions in an advertising agency are found in the traffic department, account service (account coordinator), or the media department (media assistant). Advertising jobs are also available in many manufacturing or retail firms, nonprofit organizations, banks, professional associations, utility companies, and other arenas outside of an advertising agency.

Although a career in retailing may begin in sales, there is much more to retailing than simply selling. Many retail personnel occupy management positions, focusing on selecting and ordering merchandise, promotional activities, inventory control, customer credit operations, accounting, personnel, and store security. Many specific examples of retailing jobs can be found in large department stores. A section manager coordinates inventory and promotions and interacts with buyers, salespeople, and consumers. The buyer's job is fast-paced, often involving much travel and pressure. Buyers must be open-minded and foresighted in their hunt for new, potentially successful items. Regional managers coordinate the activities of several retail stores within a specific geographic area, usually monitoring and supporting sales, promotions, and general procedures. Retail management can be exciting and challenging. Growth in retailing is expected to accompany the growth in population and is likely to create substantial opportunities in the coming years.

While a career in marketing can be very rewarding, marketers today agree that the job is getting tougher. Many advertising and marketing executives say the job has gotten much more demanding in the past 10 years, viewing their number one challenge as balancing work and personal obligations. Other challenges include staying current on industry trends or technologies, keeping motivated/inspired on the job, and measuring success. If you are up to the challenge, you may find that a career in marketing is just right for you to utilize your business knowledge while exercising your creative side as well.

Review Your Understanding

Describe the role of product in the marketing mix, including how products are developed, classified, and identified.

Products (goods, services, ideas) are among a firm's most visible contacts with consumers and must meet consumers' needs and expectations to ensure success. New-product development is a multistep process: idea development, the screening of new ideas, business analysis, product development, test marketing, and commercialization. Products are usually classified as either consumer or business products. Consumer products can be further classified as convenience, shopping, or specialty products. The business product classifications are raw materials, major equipment, accessory equipment, component parts, processed materials, supplies, and industrial services. Products also can be classified by the stage of the product life cycle (introduction, growth, maturity, and decline). Identifying products includes branding (the process of naming and identifying products), packaging (the product's container), and labeling (of information, such as content and warnings, on the package).

Define *price* and discuss its importance in the marketing mix, including various pricing strategies a firm might employ.

Price is the value placed on an object exchanged between a buyer and a seller. It is probably the most flexible variable of the marketing mix. Pricing objectives include survival, maximization of profits and sales volume, and maintaining the status quo. When a firm introduces a new product, it may use price skimming or penetration pricing. Psychological pricing and price discounting are other strategies.

Identify factors affecting distribution decisions, such as marketing channels and intensity of market coverage.

Making products available to customers is facilitated by middlemen, or intermediaries, who bridge the gap between the producer of the product and its ultimate user. A marketing channel is a group of marketing organizations that directs the flow of products from producers to consumers. Market coverage relates to the number and variety of outlets that make products available to customers; it may be intensive, selective, or exclusive. Physical distribution is all the activities necessary to move products from producers to consumers, including inventory planning and control, transportation, warehousing, and materials handling.

Specify the activities involved in promotion, as well as promotional strategies and promotional positioning.

Promotion encourages marketing exchanges by persuading individuals, groups, and organizations to accept goods, services, and ideas. The promotion mix includes advertising (a paid form of nonpersonal communication transmitted through a mass medium), personal selling (direct, two-way communication with buyers and potential buyers), publicity (nonpersonal communication transmitted through the mass media but not paid for directly by the firm), and sales promotion (direct inducements offering added value or some other incentive for buyers to enter into an exchange). A push strategy attempts to motivate intermediaries to push the product down to their customers, whereas a pull strategy tries to create consumer demand for a product so that consumers exert pressure on marketing channel members to make the product available. Typical promotion objectives are to stimulate demand; stabilize sales; and inform, remind, and reinforce customers. Promotional positioning is the use of promotion to create and maintain in the buyer's mind an image of a product.

Evaluate an organization's marketing strategy plans.

Based on the material in this chapter, you should be able to answer the questions posed in the "Solve the Dilemma" feature at the end of the chapter and evaluate the company's marketing strategy plans, including its target market and marketing mix.

Revisit the World of Business

1. What is the product that Disney is selling through its theme parks?

2. What are some of the problems Disney may experience from incorporating too much technology into its parks?

Is it necessary to improve technology in the parks if the company is already successful?

3. Besides technological improvement, what are other ways Disney can improve consumer experience?

Learn the Terms

advertising 382 ✓
advertising campaign 382
branding 369 ✓
business products 366
commercialization 365 ✓
consumer products 365 ✓
direct marketing 376
direct selling 377
discounts 375
exclusive distribution 380
generic products 370
integrated marketing
  communications 382
intensive distribution 380

labeling 371
manufacturer brands 369
marketing channel 375
materials handling 382
packaging 370
penetration price 375 ✓
personal selling 384
physical distribution 380
price skimming 375 ✓
private distributor brands 369
product line 366
product mix 367
promotional positioning 387
psychological pricing 375

publicity 384
pull strategy 386
push strategy 386
quality 371
reference pricing 375
retailers 376
sales promotion 385
selective distribution 380
test marketing 365 ✓
trademark 369
transportation 381
warehousing 381
wholesalers 377

Check Your Progress

1. What steps do companies generally take to develop and introduce a new product?

2. What is the product life cycle? How does a product's life cycle stage affect its marketing strategy?

3. Which marketing mix variable is probably the most flexible? Why?

4. Distinguish between the two ways to set the base price for a new product.

5. What is probably the least flexible marketing mix variable? Why?

6. Describe the typical marketing channels for consumer products.

7. What activities are involved in physical distribution? What functions does a warehouse perform?

8. How do publicity and advertising differ? How are they related?

9. What does the personal selling process involve? Briefly discuss the process.

10. List the circumstances in which the push and pull promotional strategies are used.

Get Involved

1. Pick three products you use every day (in school, at work, or for pleasure—perhaps one of each). Determine what phase of the product life cycle each is in. Evaluate the marketer's strategy (product, price, promotion, and distribution) for the product and whether it is appropriate for the life-cycle stage.

2. Design a distribution channel for a manufacturer of stuffed toys.

3. Pick a nearby store, and briefly describe the kinds of sales promotion used and their effectiveness.

Build Your Skills

Analyzing Motel 6's Marketing Strategy

Background

Made famous through the well-known radio and TV commercials spoken in the distinctive "down-home" voice of Tom Bodett, the Dallas-based Motel 6 chain of budget motels is probably familiar to you. Based on the information provided here and any personal knowledge you may have about the company, you will analyze the marketing strategy of Motel 6.

Task

Read the following paragraphs; then complete the questions that follow.

Motel 6 was established in 1962 with the original name emphasizing its low-cost, no-frills approach. Rooms at that time were $6 per night. Today, Motel 6 has more than 760 units, and the average nightly cost is $49.99. Motel 6 is the largest company-owned and operated lodging chain in the United States. Customers receive HBO, ESPN, free morning coffee, and free local phone calls, and most units have pools and some business services. Motel 6 has made a name for itself by offering clean, comfortable rooms at the lowest prices of any national motel chain and by standardizing both its product offering and its operating policies and procedures. The company's national spokesperson, Tom Bodett, is featured in radio and television commercials that use humorous stories to show why it makes sense to stay at Motel 6 rather than a pricey hotel.

In appealing to pleasure travelers on a budget as well as business travelers looking to get the most for their dollar, one commercial makes the point that all hotel and motel rooms look the same at night when the lights are out—when customers are getting what they came for, a good night's sleep. Motel 6 location sites are selected based on whether they provide convenient access to the highway system and whether they are close to areas such as shopping centers, tourist attractions, or business districts.

1. In SELECTING A TARGET MARKET, which approach is Motel 6 using to segment markets?

   a. concentration approach

   b. multisegment approach

2. In DEVELOPING A MARKETING MIX, identify in the second column of the table what the current strategy is and then identify any changes you think Motel 6 should consider for carrying it successfully through the next five years.

Marketing Mix Variable	Current Strategy	5-Year Strategy
a. Product		
b. Price		
c. Distribution		
d. Promotion		

Solve the Dilemma

Better Health with Snacks

Deluxe Chips is one of the leading companies in the salty-snack industry, with almost one-fourth of the $10 billion market. Its Deluxos tortilla chips are the number-one selling brand in North America, and its Ridgerunner potato chip is also a market share leader. Deluxe Chips wants to stay on top of the market by changing marketing strategies to match changing consumer needs and preferences. Promoting specific brands to market segments with the appropriate price and distribution channel is helping Deluxe Chips succeed.

As many middle-aged consumers modify their snacking habits, Deluxe Chips is considering a new product line of light snack foods with less fat and cholesterol and targeted at the 35- to 50-year-old consumer who enjoys snacking but wants to be more health conscious. Marketing research suggests

that the product will succeed as long as it tastes good and that consumers may be willing to pay more for it. Large expenditures on advertising may be necessary to overcome the competition. However, it may be possible to analyze customer profiles and retail store characteristics and then match the right product with the right neighborhood. Store-specific micromarketing would allow Deluxe Chips to spend its promotional dollars more efficiently.

LO 12-5

Evaluate an organization's marketing strategy plans.

Discussion Questions

1. Design a marketing strategy for the new product line.
2. Critique your marketing strategy in terms of its strengths and weaknesses.
3. What are your suggestions for implementation of the marketing strategy?

Build Your Business Plan

Dimensions of Marketing Strategy

If you think your product/business is truly new to or unique to the market, you need to substantiate your claim. After a thorough exploration on the web, you want to make sure there has not been a similar business/product recently launched in your community. Check with your Chamber of Commerce or Economic Development Office that might be able to provide you with a history of recent business failures. If you are not confident about the ability or willingness of customers to try your new good or service, collecting your own primary data to ascertain demand is highly advisable.

The decision of where to initially set your prices is a critical one. If there are currently similar products in the market, you

need to be aware of the competitors' prices before you determine yours. If your product is new to the market, you can price it high (market skimming strategy) as long as you realize that the high price will probably attract competitors to the market more quickly (they will think they can make the same product for less), which will force you to drop your prices sooner than you would like. Another strategy to consider is market penetration pricing, a strategy that sets price lower and discourages competition from entering the market as quickly. Whatever strategy you decide to use, don't forget to examine your product elasticity.

At this time, you need to start thinking about how to promote your product. Why do you feel your product is different or new to the market? How do you want to position your product so customers view it favorably? Remember this is all occurring *within the consumer's mind.*

See for Yourself Videocase

Spirit Airlines: Flying below Customer Expectations

Flyers seem to hate Florida-based Spirit Airlines. In a survey examining tweets from passengers, Spirit topped the list of airline complaints, followed by Frontier and American Airlines. The American Customer Satisfaction Index ranked it 54 out of 100, placing it last among American airline firms. Yet Spirit has been experiencing a whopping 30

percent annual growth in capacity. How does Spirit achieve such impressive growth with complaints so high?

The answer—ultra low prices. Spirit Airlines acts as an ultra low cost carrier (ULCC) that offers flights at 40 to 50 percent lower than comparable airlines! This represents significant cost savings for the consumer. Spirit Airlines is able to keep prices so low by offering unbundled pricing. In other words, the ticket the customer purchases is enough to pay for the gas to get them to their destination. Everything else—including food, beverages, and overhead bags—costs passengers extra. Spirit is targeting the price-conscious consumer who is willing to sacrifice comfort for a less expensive flight.

"We survey customers all the time, and by far it's not even close, the number one thing that people say they look for in an airline is price. And so at Spirit, that's where we compete. We're not going to compete on legroom. We're not going to compete on having Wi-Fi. But we will compete on price," says Paul Berry, Director of public relations, advertising, and brand at Spirit Airlines.

Spirit operates on the basis of transparent pricing. Marketing itself as "the bare fare," Spirit does not want to charge passengers for items they do not need or desire. Each item is priced on its own, allowing customers to pick and choose what they want. Customers are attracted to Spirit's low prices, and demand has been so high that Spirit Airlines has expanded.

However, although Spirit believes its pricing strategy is transparent, not all customers agree. It is not uncommon for passengers to arrive at the airport and be surprised when they find they have to pay for their carry-on bags. This is especially true when passengers purchase tickets on third-party sites such as Expedia rather than on Spirit's website. Information about Spirit's bare fare pricing is not always seen or read on third-party sites.

Another criticism levied against Spirit is that it has a poor on-time record. Its 30 percent annual growth rate in capacity strained the company's resources. It increased its services between key hubs and began offering nonstop service between Baltimore and Boston and Detroit. These changes resulted in more flight delays and canceled flights. In turn, it led to dissatisfied customers.

Bob Fornaro, the new CEO of Spirit Airlines, seeks to change this. Under his leadership, he wants to create a more satisfying relationship with passengers while remaining transparent about its pricing model. Changes include reducing annual growth so resources are not strained, reducing the daily hours that Spirit's flights fly during peak periods, and adding additional staff.

Spirit's challenges demonstrate that although it has a competitive pricing model, it must maintain satisfying customer relationships to compete. In fact, because pricing is the most flexible variable of the marketing mix, airlines such as American are aggressively matching Spirit's pricing. While this might result in lower prices for consumers, it eats into Spirit's profitability.

Although there are obstacles Spirit must overcome, there is no denying the major impact it has had on the airline industry. It led to other ULCC competitors such as Frontier Airlines and has greatly affected how the big airlines view their pricing strategies. Perhaps best of all, Spirit allows those who could not normally afford it, to fly—albeit with a little less comfort.[44]

Discussion Questions

1. What is Spirit Airlines' target market?

2. Describe the marketing mix used by Spirit in its strategy.

3. What are the challenges Spirit faces in keeping prices low and improving service?

You can find the related video in the Video Library in Connect. Ask your instructor how you can access Connect.

Team Exercise

Form groups and search for examples of convenience products, shopping products, specialty products, and business products. How are these products marketed? Provide examples of any ads that you can find to show examples of the promotional strategies for these products. Report your findings to the class.

Endnotes

1. Austin Carr, "The Messy Business of Reinventing Happiness," *Fast Company*, May 2015, pp. 100–116; "10 Most Popular Theme Parks in the World," http://www.uscitytraveler.com/10-most-popular-theme-parks-in-the-world/ (accessed August 24, 2015); Walt Disney World, "Unlock the Magic with Your MagicBand or Card," https://disneyworld.disney.go.com/plan/my-disney-experience/bands-cards/ (accessed August 24, 2015).

2. Narendra Rao, "The Keys to New Product Success (Part1)—Collecting Unarticulated & Invisible Customer Needs," *Product Management & Strategy*, June 19, 2007, http://productstrategy.wordpress.com/2007/06/19/the-keys-to-new-product-succeess-part-1-collecting-unarticulated-invisible-customer-needs/ (accessed April 11, 2016).

3. Christina Larson, "Xiaomi," *Fast Company*, 2014, www.fastcompany.com/most-innovative-companies/2014/xiaomi (accessed April 11, 2016); Parmy Olson, "China's Xiaomi Becomes World's 5th Largest Smartphone Maker," July 31, 2014, http://www.forbes.com/sites/parmyolson/2014/07/31/chinas-xiaomi-becomes-worlds-5th-largest-smartphone-maker/#6487f9f23d7d (accessed April 11, 2016).

4. Robert Duffer, "Discontinued Car Models for 2016," *Chicago Tribune,* December 10, 2015, http://www.chicagotribune.com/classified/automotive/sc-2016-discontinued-cars-1022-20151016-story.html (accessed April 11, 2016).

5. Hadley Malcolm, "Ikea Wants to Get Personal," *USA Today,* June 15, 2015, p. 6B, (accessed December 11, 2015); Denise Lee Yohn, "How IKEA Designs Its Brand Success," *Forbes,* June 10, 2015, http://www.forbes.com/sites/deniselyohn/2015/06/10/how-ikea-designs-its-brand-success/ (accessed December 27, 2015); IKEA, Life at Home Report website, http://lifeathome.ikea.com (accessed December 27, 2015).

6. Associated Press, "Jobs Says iPad Idea Came Before iPhone," June 2, 2010, www.foxnews.com/tech/2010/06/02/jobs-says-ipad-idea-came-iphone/ (accessed April 11, 2016).

7. Nike, "A Look Inside Nike's Sport Research Lab," September 8, 2014, http://news.nike.com/news/a-look-inside-nike-s-sport-research-lab (accessed April 11, 2016).

8. John A. Byrne, "Greatest Entrepreneurs of Our Time," *Fortune,* April 9, 2012, pp. 68–86; Google Finance, "Amazon.com, Inc.," April 30, 2014, www.google.com/finance?cid=660463 (accessed April 11, 2016).

9. Katy Muldoon, "Marketers Wonder: How Will It Play in Portland?" *The Wall Street Journal,* July 15, 2015, http://www.wsj.com/articles/marketers-wonder-how-will-it-play-in-portland-1436983102 (accessed April 11, 2016).

10. Andrew Pollack, "Genetically Engineered Salmon Approved for Consumption," *The New York Times,* November 19, 2015, http://www.nytimes.com/2015/11/20/business/genetically-engineered-salmon-approved-for-consumption.html (accessed April 11, 2016).

11. Business Wire, "Global Smartwatch Market Growth of 12% by 2020—Analysis, Technologies & Forecast Report 2016–2020: Key Vendors: Apple, Fitbit, Pebble—Research and Markets," March 8, 2016, http://www.businesswire.com/news/home/20160308005941/en/Global-Smartwatch-Market-Growth-12-2020— (accessed April 11, 2016).

12. Susanna Kim, "Diet Pepsi's New Sweetener Fallout Follows History of Soda Bets that Fell Flat," *ABC News,* October 9, 2015, http://abcnews.go.com/Business/diet-pepsis-sweetener-fallout-history-soda-bets-fell/story?id=34368062 (accessed April 11, 2016).

13. Gene Marks, "Why Is Apple Launching a New Version of the iPod," *Forbes,* July 20, 2015, http://www.forbes.com/sites/quickerbettertech/2015/07/20/why-is-apple-launching-a-new-version-of-the-ipod/#5268adf22e56 (accessed April 11, 2016).

14. "Product Life Cycle," Answers.com, www.answers.com/topic/product-lifecycle (accessed May 29, 2014).

15. Laura Lorenzetti, "Get Ready for Amazon's New Fashion Line," *Fortune,* February 17, 2016, http://fortune.com/2016/02/17/amazon-fashion-brand/ (accessed April 11, 2016).

16. Christopher Durham, "Private Label Market in the US 2015–2019," *My Private Brand,* March 20, 2016, http://mypbrand.com/2016/03/20/private-label-market-in-the-us-2015-2019/ (accessed April 11, 2016).

17. Mintel, "Beverage Packaging Trends—US—February 2014," February 2014, http://oxygen.mintel.com/sinatra/oxygen/list/id=680559&type=RCItem#0_1___page_RCItem=0 (accessed May 5, 2014).

18. Saabira Chaudhuri, "IKEA Can't Stop Obsessing About Its Packaging," *The Wall Street Journal,* June 17, 2015, http://www.wsj.com/articles/ikea-cant-stop-obsessing-about-its-packaging-1434533401 (accessed April 11, 2016).

19. Lindsey Beaton, "Packaging as Branding in Pet Food Marketing," Petfoodindustry.com, May 21, 2015, http://www.petfoodindustry.com/articles/5193-packaging-as-branding-in-pet-food-marketing (accessed May 1, 2015).

20. Caroline Winter, "When Did Logos Get So Friendly?" *Bloomberg,* September 17, 2015, http://www.bloomberg.com/news/articles/2015-09-17/google-s-new-logo-marks-a-trend-of-friendlier-fonts (accessed April 11, 2016).

21. American Customer Satisfaction Index, "National, Sector, and Industry Results," March 2016, http://www.theacsi.org/national-economic-indicator/national-sector-and-industry-results (accessed April 11, 2016).

22. Becca Smouse, "Ford peddles e-bike for commuters on the move," *USA Today,* June 30, 2015, 4B; Steve Dent, "Ford's latest eBike breaks down to fit in your trunk," *Endgadget,* June 24, 2015, http://www.engadget.com/2015/06/24/ford-mode-flex-ebike/ (accessed December 22, 2015); Ford, "Ford Announces MoDe:Flex eBike Prototype," https://media.ford.com/content/dam/fordmedia/North%20America/US/2015/06/fwf/MoDeFlexEbike_FactSht.pdf (accessed December 22, 2015).

23. "American Demographics 2006 Consumer Perception Survey," *Advertising Age,* January 2, 2006, p. 9. Data by Synovate.

24. "The Top 10 Most Innovative Companies in China," *Fast Company,* 2014, http://www.fastcompany.com/most-innovative-companies/2014/industry/china (accessed April 5, 2016).

25. Rajneesh Suri and Kent B. Monroe, "The Effects of Time Constraints on Consumers' Judgments of Prices and Products," *Journal of Consumer Research,* 30 (June 2003), p. 92.

26. Leslie Patton, "Aldi Tries High-End Food and Discounts, Too," *Bloomberg,* August 6, 2015, http://www.bloomberg.com/news/articles/2015-08-06/aldi-grocery-chain-tries-high-end-food-and-discounts-too (accessed April 11, 2016).

27. Matt Krantz, "Here's What's Killing Department Stores," *USA Today,* November 19, 2015, p. 1B.

28. Sysco, "The Sysco Story," www.sysco.com/about-sysco.html# (accessed April 11, 2016).

29. "Top Threats to Revenue," *USA Today,* February 1, 2006, p. A1.

30. Annie Gasparro and Leslie Josephs, "The Gatekeeper to Organic Heaven," *The Wall Street Journal,* May 7, 2015, p. B1; "Heidi Ho! Organics," Whole Foods Market, https://www.wholefoodsmarket.com/local-vendor/

heidi-ho-organics (accessed August 25, 2015); Dan K., "Heidi Ho Veganics Brings Its 'Cheese' to 'Shark Tank,'" *Empty Lighthouse Magazine,* http://emptylighthouse.com/heidi-ho-veganics-brings-its-cheese-shark-tank-349612875 (accessed August 25, 2015); "Heidi Ho Makes a Quick Deal," ABC, http://abc.go.com/shows/shark-tank/video/VDKA0_m5aydvn3 (accessed August 25, 2015).

31. ZoomSystems website, http://www.zoomsystems.com/ (accessed April 11, 2016).

32. Piper, "Piper Expands Its Global Sales Network," March 19, 2013, www.piper.com/piper-expands-global-sales-network-2/ (accessed April 11, 2016); Rick Durden, "Piper Names Dealer for China," *AV Web,* January 10, 2014, www.avweb.com/avwebflash/news/Piper-Names-Dealer-for-China221250-1.html (accessed April 11, 2016).

33. William Pride and O. C. Ferrell, *Marketing Foundations,* 5th ed. (Mason, OH: Cengage South-Western Learning, 2013), pp. 415–416.

34. Ibid.

35. Michelle Grinnell, "Pure Michigan Campaign Drives $1.2 Billion in Customer Spending," March 11, 2014, http://www.michigan.org/pressreleases/pure-michigan-campaign-drives-$1-2-billion-in-visitor-spending/ (accessed April 11, 2016).

36. Peter Loftus, "Ads for Costly Drugs Get Airtime," *The Wall Street Journal,* February 17, 2016, p. B1.

37. Claire Groden, "This Is How Much a 2016 Super Bowl Ad Costs," *Fortune,* August 6, 2015, http://fortune.com/2015/08/06/super-bowl-ad-cost/ (accessed April 11, 2016).

38. Natalie Evans, "See PETA 'Vegan Sex' Advert That's So Steamy It's Been Banned from the Super Bowl," *The Mirror,* January 26, 2016, http://www.mirror.co.uk/tv/tv-news/see-peta-vegan-sex-advert-7246273 (accessed April 11, 2016).

39. Jun Hongo and Miho Inada, "To Lure Recruits, Japanese City Tries Gorilla Marketing," *The Wall Street Journal,* February 23, 2016, pp. A1, A14.

40. Gerry Khermouch and Jeff Green, "Buzz Marketing," *BusinessWeek,* July 30, 2001, pp. 50–56.

41. Tim Nudd, "The 20 Most Viral Ads of 2015," *AdWeek,* November 19, 2015, http://www.adweek.com/news-gallery/advertising-branding/20-most-viral-ads-2015-168213 (accessed February 8, 2016); Pandora, "The Unique Connection," *YouTube,* https://www.youtube.com/watch?v=DRoqk_z2Lgg (accessed February 8, 2016).

42. PR Newswire, "70% of Consumers Still Look to Traditional Paper-Based Coupons for Savings," April 16, 2015, http://www.prnewswire.com/news-releases/70-of-consumers-still-look-to-traditional-paper-based-coupons-for-savings-300067097.html (accessed April 11, 2016).

43. Evan Niu, "At Long Last, T-Mobile Is Getting the iPhone," *Daily Finance,* December 7, 2012, www.dailyfinance.com/2012/12/07/at-long-last-t-mobile-is-getting-the-iphone/ (accessed April 11, 2016).

44. Spirit Airlines video, http://www.viddler.com/embed/7ec3ff66/?f=1&autoplay=0&player=full&disablebranding=0 (accessed April 14, 2016); Susan Carey, "Spirit Airlines New Boss Vows to Repair Image," *The Wall Street Journal,* February 12, 2016, http://www.wsj.com/articles/spirit-airlines-new-boss-vows-to-repair-image-1455319883 (accessed April 14, 2016); Charisse Jones, "Spirit Switches CEOs but Extreme Low-Cost Philosophy Stays Same," *USA Today,* January 6, 2016, http://www.usatoday.com/story/money/2016/01/05/spirit-airlines-names-new-ceo/78303058/ (accessed April 14, 2016); Christopher Elliot, "These 3 Airlines Get the Most Hate on Social Media," *Fortune,* February 18, 2016, http://fortune.com/2016/02/18/airlines-hate-social-media/ (accessed April 14, 2016); Brad Cohen, "10 Completely Serious (and Not at All Sarcastic) Reasons to Love Spirit Airlines," *Road Warrior Voices,* May 22, 2015, https://usatravel.wordpress.com/2015/05/22/10-completely-serious-and-not-at-all-sarcastic-reasons-to-love-spirit-airlines/ (accessed April 14, 2016); Martin Rivers, "Spirit Airlines Nears Its 'Ryanair Moment' under New Boss Bob Fornaro," *Forbes,* February 27, 2016, http://www.forbes.com/sites/martinrivers/2016/02/27/spirit-airlines-nears-its-ryanair-moment-under-new-boss-bob-fornaro/#53e5b898386d (accessed April 14, 2016).

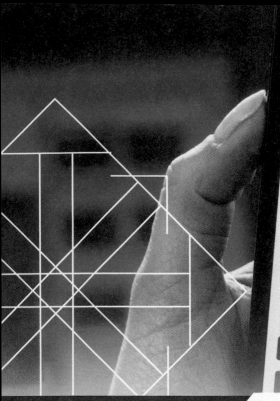

© Happy Zoe/Shutterstock.com

13 Digital Marketing and Social Networking

Learning Objectives

After reading this chapter, you will be able to:

 LO 13-1 Define *digital media* and *digital marketing* and recognize their increasing value in strategic planning.

 LO 13-2 Demonstrate the role of digital marketing and define social networking in today's business environment.

LO 13-3 Show how digital media affect the marketing mix.

LO 13-4 Illustrate how businesses can use different types of social networking media.

 LO 13-5 Identify legal and ethical considerations in digital media.

 LO 13-6 Evaluate a marketer's dilemma and propose recommendations.

Enter the World of Business ⊖————————

Pinning Your Hopes on Emerging Social Media

Social networking, something that originated as a platform to help friends, family, and acquaintances communicate, is now being used as a strategic marketing tool by many companies. Eager to reach more consumers, companies are using mobile marketing strategies to take advantage of the increased use of mobile devices. Pinterest, an online bulletin board made up of uploaded photo and video content, is one of many social media platforms trying to appeal to marketers. Pinterest users can pin pictures and videos they like to their online board, which eventually turns into a large collection of ideas representing the individual's tastes and preferences. In an effort to market through Pinterest, companies can add links to their website in photos that are uploaded to the site.

Pinterest also serves as a customer relationship management tool because the images people pin to their boards reflect interests and aspirations, thus allowing marketers to interact with users on a more personal level. Going a step further, Pinterest has now created a way for marketers to go beyond relationship management and sell products directly through the site. The company also offers a developer's program aimed at helping marketers deploy and track the success of their Pinterest ads. Advertised items are made available as buyable Pins, which users can purchase after payment information has been uploaded to their Pinterest account. Initially, Pinterest imposed no transaction fees to encourage more companies to sell on the site. Today, a long list of marketing companies already advertise and sell on Pinterest, and the company expects this list to grow in the future.[1]

Introduction[2]

The Internet and information technology have dramatically changed the environment for business. Marketers' new ability to convert all types of communications into digital media has created efficient, inexpensive ways of connecting businesses and consumers and has improved the flow and the usefulness of information. Businesses have the information they need to make more informed decisions, and consumers have access to a greater variety of products and more information about choices and quality. This has resulted in a shift in the balance of power between consumer and marketer.[3]

e-business
carrying out the goals of business through utilization of the Internet.

digital media
electronic media that function using digital codes via computers, cellular phones, smartphones, and other digital devices that have been released in recent years.

digital marketing
uses all digital media, including the Internet and mobile and interactive channels, to develop communication and exchanges with customers.

LO 13-1

Define *digital media* and *digital marketing* and recognize their increasing value in strategic planning.

The defining characteristic of information technology in the 21st century is accelerating change. New systems and applications advance so rapidly that it is almost impossible to keep up with the latest developments. Startup companies emerge that quickly overtake existing approaches to digital media. When Google first arrived on the scene, a number of search engines were fighting for dominance. With its fast, easy-to-use search engine, Google became number one and is now challenging many industries, including advertising, newspapers, mobile phones, and book publishing. Google has up to 90 percent of the market share in the European Union, raising questions about whether it might have too much power. EU antitrust regulators have charged Google with abusing its dominance in the web search market. Yet even Google faces competition in certain parts of the world, most notably Baidu in China.[4] Social networking continues to advance as the channel most observers believe will dominate digital communication in the near future. Today, people spend more time on social networking sites, such as Facebook, than they spend on e-mail.

In this chapter, we first provide some key definitions related to digital marketing and social networking. Next, we discuss using digital media in business and digital marketing. We look at marketing mix considerations when using digital media and pay special attention to social networking. Then we focus on digital marketing strategies—particularly new communication channels like social networks—and consider how consumers are changing their information searches and consumption behavior to fit emerging technologies and trends. Finally, we examine the legal and social issues associated with information technology, digital media, and e-business.

Consumers are increasingly turning to mobile apps to access company information and purchase products.

© Jeffrey Blackler/Alamy

Growth and Benefits of Digital Communication

Let's start with a clear understanding of our focus in this chapter. First, we can distinguish **e-business** from traditional business by noting that conducting e-business means carrying out the goals of business through the use of the Internet. **Digital media** are electronic media that function using digital codes—when we refer to digital media, we mean media available via computers and other digital devices, including mobile and wireless ones like smartphones.

Digital marketing uses all digital media, including the Internet and mobile and interactive channels, to develop communication and exchanges

TABLE 13-1 Characteristics of Digital Marketing

Characteristic	Definition	Example
Addressability	The ability of the marketer to identify customers before they make a purchase	Amazon installs cookies on a user's computer that allows it to identify the owner when he or she returns to the website.
Interactivity	The ability of customers to express their needs and wants directly to the firm in response to its marketing communications	Texas Instruments interacts with its customers on its Facebook page by answering concerns and posting updates.
Accessibility	The ability for marketers to obtain digital information	Google can use web searches done through its search engine to learn about customer interests.
Connectivity	The ability for consumers to be connected with marketers along with other consumers	The Avon Voices website encouraged singers to upload their singing videos, which can then be voted on by other users for the chance to be discovered.
Control	The customer's ability to regulate the information they view as well as the rate and exposure to that information	Consumers use Kayak to discover the best travel deals.

with customers. Digital marketing is a term we will use often because we are interested in all types of digital communications, regardless of the electronic channel that transmits the data. Digital marketing goes beyond the Internet and includes mobile phones, banner ads, digital outdoor marketing, and social networks.

The Internet has created tremendous opportunities for businesses to forge relationships with consumers and business customers, target markets more precisely, and even reach previously inaccessible markets at home and around the world. The Internet also facilitates business transactions, allowing companies to network with manufacturers, wholesalers, retailers, suppliers, and outsource firms to serve customers more quickly and more efficiently. The telecommunication opportunities created by the Internet have set the stage for digital marketing's development and growth.

Digital communication offers a completely new dimension in connecting with others. Some of the characteristics that distinguish digital from traditional communication are addressability, interactivity, accessibility, connectivity, and control. These terms are discussed in Table 13-1.

Using Digital Media in Business

The phenomenal growth of digital media has provided new ways of conducting business. Given almost instant communication with precisely defined consumer groups, firms can use real-time exchanges to create and stimulate interactive communication, forge closer relationships, and learn more accurately about consumer and supplier needs. Consider that Amazon.com, one of the most successful electronic businesses, ranked number 29 on the *Fortune* 500 list of America's largest corporations.[5] Many of you may not remember a world before Amazon because it has completely transformed how many people shop.

Because it is fast and inexpensive, digital communication is making it easier for businesses to conduct marketing research, provide and obtain price and product

LO 13-2

Demonstrate the role of digital marketing and define social networking in today's business environment.

information, and advertise, as well as to fulfill their business goals by selling goods and services online. Even the U.S. government engages in digital marketing activities—marketing everything from Treasury bonds and other financial instruments to oil-drilling leases and wild horses. Procter & Gamble uses the Internet as a fast, cost-effective means for marketing research, judging consumer demand for potential new products by inviting online consumers to sample new-product prototypes and provide feedback. If a product gets rave reviews from the samplers, the company might decide to introduce it.

New businesses and even industries are evolving that would not exist without digital media. Vimeo is a video website founded by filmmakers to share creative videos. The site lets users post or view videos from around the world. It has become the third most popular video website after YouTube and Netflix.[6]

The reality, however, is that Internet markets are more similar to traditional markets than they are different. Thus, successful digital marketing strategies, like traditional business strategies, focus on creating products that customers need or want, not merely developing a brand name or reducing the costs associated with online transactions. Instead of changing all industries, digital technology has had much more impact in certain industries where the cost of business and customer transactions has been very high. For example, investment trading is less expensive online because customers can buy and sell investments, such as stocks and mutual funds, on their own. Firms such as Charles Schwab Corp., the biggest online brokerage firm, have been innovators in promoting online trading. Traditional brokers such as Merrill Lynch have had to follow with online trading for their customers.

Digital media can also improve communication within and between businesses. In the future, most significant gains will come from productivity improvements within businesses. Communication is a key business function, and improving the speed and clarity of communication can help businesses save time and improve employee problem-solving abilities. Digital media can be a communications backbone that helps to store knowledge, information, and records in management information systems so co-workers can access it when faced with a problem to solve. A well-designed management information system that utilizes digital technology can, therefore, help reduce confusion, improve organization and efficiency, and facilitate clear communications. Given the crucial role of communication and information in business, the long-term impact of digital media on economic growth is substantial, and it will inevitably grow over time.

Firms also need to control access to their digital communication systems to ensure worker productivity. This can be a challenge. For example, in companies across the United States, employees are surfing the Internet for as much as an hour during each workday. Many firms are trying to curb this practice by limiting employees' access to instant messaging services, streaming music, and websites with adult content.[7]

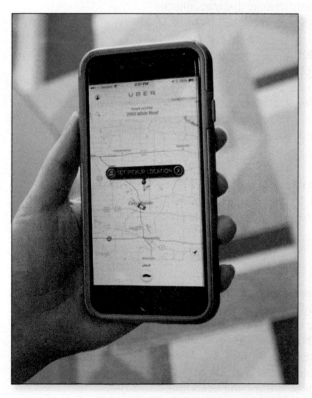

Consumers use Uber's app to locate nearby drivers to take them to their destinations.

© McGraw-Hill Education. Mark Dierker, photographer

Digital Media and the Marketing Mix

LO 13-3

Show how digital media affect the marketing mix.

While digital marketing shares some similarities with conventional marketing techniques, a few valuable differences stand out. First, digital media make customer communications faster and interactive. Second, digital media help companies reach new target markets more easily, affordably, and quickly than ever before. Finally, digital media help marketers utilize new resources in seeking out and communicating with customers. One of the most important benefits of digital marketing is the ability of marketers and customers to easily share information. Through websites, social networks, and other digital media, consumers can learn about everything they consume and use in their lives, ask questions, voice complaints, indicate preferences, and otherwise communicate about their needs and desires. Many marketers use e-mail, mobile phones, social networking, wikis, media sharing, blogs, videoconferencing, and other technologies to coordinate activities and communicate with employees, customers, and suppliers. Twitter, considered both a social network and a micro-blog, illustrates how these digital technologies can combine to create new communication opportunities.

Nielsen Marketing Research revealed that consumers now spend more time on social networking sites than they do on e-mail, and social network use is still growing. Figure 13-1 shows that while the majority of social network users are between the ages of 18 and 29, other age groups are not that far behind. With digital media, even small businesses can reach new markets through these inexpensive communication channels. Brick-and-mortar companies like Walmart utilize online catalogs and company websites and blogs to supplement their retail stores. Internet companies like Amazon and Zappos that lack physical stores let customers post reviews of their purchases on their websites, creating company-sponsored communities.

One aspect of marketing that has not changed with digital media is the importance of achieving the right marketing mix. Product, distribution, promotion, and

FIGURE 13-1   Social Networking Use by Age and Year

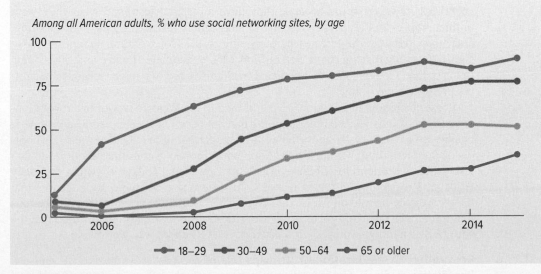

Among all American adults, % who use social networking sites, by age

18–29   30–49   50–64   65 or older

Note: No data available for 2007.

Source: Pew Research Center surveys, 2005-2006, 2008-2015.

pricing are as important as ever for successful online marketing strategies. More than 40 percent of the world's population now uses the Internet.[8] That means it is essential for businesses large and small to use digital media effectively, not only to grab or maintain market share but also to streamline their organizations and offer customers entirely new benefits and convenience. Let's look at how businesses are using digital media to create effective marketing strategies on the web.

Product Considerations.   Like traditional marketers, digital marketers must anticipate consumer needs and preferences, tailor their goods and services to meet these needs, and continually upgrade them to remain competitive. The connectivity created by digital media provides the opportunity for adding services and can enhance product benefits. Some products, such as online games, applications, and virtual worlds, are only available via digital media. The more than 1.5 million applications available on the iPad, for instance, provide examples of products that are only available in the digital world.[9] Businesses can often offer more items online than they could in a retail store.

The ability to access information for any product can have a major impact on buyer decision making. However, with larger companies now launching their own extensive marketing campaigns, and with the constant sophistication of digital technology, many businesses are finding it necessary to upgrade their product offerings to meet consumer needs. As we mentioned in a previous chapter, companies such as Julep Beauty use feedback from social media to test new products.[10] The Internet provides a major resource for learning more about consumer wants and needs.

Distribution Considerations.   The Internet is a new distribution channel for making products available at the right time, at the right place, and in the right quantities. Marketers' ability to process orders electronically and increase the speed of communications via the Internet reduces inefficiencies, costs, and redundancies while increasing speed throughout the marketing channel. Shipping times and costs have become an important consideration in attracting customers, prompting many companies to offer consumers low shipping costs or next-day delivery. Although consumers still flock to brick-and-mortar stores to purchase items, they tend to spend less time shopping because they have already determined what they want online. Approximately 73 percent of U.S. consumers research shoes, toys, clothing, and other items on the Internet before going to the store. Online shopping is also significantly increasing, with 201 million U.S. consumers finding and purchasing items online. Convenience and constant availability are two major reasons consumers prefer to shop online.[11]

These changes in distribution are not limited to the Western world. In a revolutionary shift in China, where online shopping had not been widely adopted by consumers, businesses are now realizing the benefits of marketing online. One of the first adopters of Internet selling was the Chinese company Taobao, a consumer auction site that also features sections for Chinese brands and retailers. Today, its parent company Alibaba is expanding into new markets. At the same time, there are concerns that many of the items sold on Taobao are counterfeit, and Alibaba is challenging the idea that it tolerates knockoff goods on its website. Consumer trends demonstrate that the shift of distributing through digital networks is well under way worldwide.

Promotion Considerations.   Perhaps one of the best ways businesses can utilize digital media is for promotion purposes—whether they are increasing brand awareness, connecting with consumers, or taking advantage of social networks or

Jet.com Soaring to New Heights in E-Commerce

Jet.com

Founders: Marc Lore, Nathan Faust, and Mike Hanrahan

Founded: 2015, in Hoboken, New Jersey

Success: Jet.com was able to raise $220 million in venture capital before it even launched.

New e-commerce company Jet.com hopes to stand out from rivals by providing a better shopping experience. The startup is competing head-to-head with Amazon.com by offering a similar, yet less expensive and more restrictive, subscription service that entitles customers to free shipping on orders over $35. By comparison, Amazon's subscription service is nearly twice as expensive at $99 annually, but requires no minimum order for free shipping.

Jet.com offers some unique benefits that make larger orders more appealing. Customers are rewarded with discounts as they add more items to their shopping cart, which Jet.com claims is the result of cost reductions when certain items are shipped together. Like many e-commerce sites, Jet.com uses sophisticated algorithms to help pass on cost reductions to customers. Because returns can be costly for retailers, Jet.com even offers customers a discount when they waive the right to return an item from their order. Although Jet.com is still in its infancy, the company has already raised more than $700 million from investors—an indication that many are confident in its ability to compete in the e-commerce market. In fact, it experienced such rapid growth that Walmart acquired Jet.com in 2016 for $3 billion.[12]

Discussion Questions

1. How is Jet.com attempting to differentiate itself from competitors?
2. Describe how Jet.com uses the distribution component to pass on more cost savings to the customer.
3. How does Jet.com use the pricing component of the marketing mix to attract consumers?

---

virtual worlds (discussed later) to form relationships and generate positive publicity or "buzz" about their products. Thanks to online promotion, consumers can be more informed than ever, including reading customer-generated content before making purchasing decisions. Consumer consumption patterns are radically changing, and marketers must adapt their promotional efforts to meet them.

If marketers find it difficult to adapt their promotional strategies to online marketing, many social networks offer tools to help. For instance, Facebook has its "Facebook Exchange" and "Facebook Canvas" to help businesses target their promotions to the right audiences. "Facebook Exchange" is a tool that provides marketers with the ability to target their advertisements to people based upon other activities they have done on the Internet. "Facebook Canvas" helps businesses tell their story through a combination of videos, still images, and call-to-action buttons. Lowe's used "Facebook Canvas" to share renovation stories in an attempt to inspire viewers to begin their own do-it-yourself projects. The campaign yielded a 6.7 times return on ad spend.[13] Marketers that choose to capitalize on these opportunities have the chance to significantly boost their firms' brand exposure.

Pricing Considerations. Price is the most flexible element of the marketing mix. Digital marketing can enhance the value of products by providing extra benefits such as service, information, and convenience. Through digital media, discounts and other promotions can be quickly communicated. As consumers have become better informed about their options, the demand for low-priced products has grown, leading to the creation of deal sites where consumers can directly compare prices. Expedia.com, for instance, provides consumers with a wealth of travel information about everything from flights to hotels that lets them compare benefits and prices. Many marketers offer buying incentives like online coupons or free samples to generate consumer demand for their products. For the business that wants to compete on price, digital marketing provides unlimited opportunities.

Internet users utilize social networking sites to connect with other users.

© Andriy Popov/123RF

Illustrate how businesses can use different types of social networking media.

social network
a web-based meeting place for friends, family, co-workers, and peers that lets users create a profile and connect with other users for a wide range of purposes.

Social Networking

A **social network** is a website where users can create a profile and interact with other users, post information, and engage in other forms of web-based communication. Social networks are a valued part of marketing because they are changing the way consumers communicate with each other and with firms. Sites such as Facebook and Twitter have emerged as opportunities for marketers to build communities, provide product information, and learn about consumer needs. By the time you read this, it is possible there will be new social network sites that continue to advance digital communication and opportunities for marketers.

You might be surprised to know that social networks have existed in some form or other for 40 years. The precursors of today's social networks began in the 1970s as online bulletin boards that allowed users with common interests to interact with one another. The first modern social network was SixDegrees .com, launched in 1997. This system permitted users to create a profile and connect with friends—the core attributes of today's networks.[14] Although Six Degrees eventually shut down for lack of interest, the seed of networking had been planted.[15] Other social networks followed, with each new generation becoming increasingly sophisticated. Today's sites offer a multitude of consumer benefits, including the ability to download music, games, and applications; upload photos and videos; join groups; find and chat with friends; comment on friends' posts; and post and update status messages.

As the number of social network users increases, interactive marketers are finding opportunities to reach out to consumers in new target markets. Snapchat is a mobile photo messaging application popular among teenagers. Users can send photos, messages, or videos to their friends for a certain amount of time. Afterward, the post is deleted from the recipient's phone and Snapchat servers. When Snapchat featured a live broadcast of the MTV Video Music Awards, firms such as Cover Girl, Taco Bell, and Verizon paid $200,000 per sponsor to advertise on the site.[16] We'll have more to say about how marketers utilize social networks later in this chapter.

An important question relates to how social media sites are adding value to the economy. Marketers at companies like Ford and Zappos, for instance, are using social media to promote products and build consumer relationships. Many companies are adopting the digital forum Memo, an internal social network where employees can vent anonymously and managers can respond. The forum is intended to inform managers of employee concerns without placing pressure on the employee to confront his or her supervisors.[17] While it may be too early to assess the exact economic contribution of social media to the entire economy, Facebook estimates that it has had a $227 billion global economic impact through job growth, product sales, event planning, and more.[18]

Types of Consumer-Generated Marketing and Digital Media

While digital marketing has generated exciting opportunities for companies to interact with their customers, digital media are also more consumer-driven than traditional

Facebook Smiles on Sustainability

When using Facebook, few stop to think about the environmental impact of operating such a massive online social media infrastructure. Uploading every photo and video is only made possible by utilizing huge data centers that serve as the backbone of Facebook, the most popular social media site in the world. With data centers consuming around 2 percent of all U.S. electricity, consumers are calling for the use of more renewable energy sources in the technology industry. In 2012, Facebook partnered with other large online companies—such as LinkedIn, eBay, and HP—and set the lofty goal of powering the Internet with 100 percent renewable energy sources. Its newest data center in Fort Worth, Texas, runs solely on renewable energy.

Conscious of its environmental footprint, Facebook's entire campus is also designed to reduce environmental harm. For instance, recycling and composting are offered thanks to waste diversion. In addition, special etched glass is used to protect birds that may otherwise fly into normal glass. Furthermore, the buildings are made with sustainable materials, such as energy-efficient lights and toilets. While there is still work that needs to be done to make the technology industry more energy efficient, Facebook serves as an example of a large tech company that successfully embraces sustainability efforts while also remaining profitable.[19]

Discussion Questions

1. How might Facebook's sustainability efforts affect its relationships with Internet users?
2. Do you believe Facebook's sustainability efforts will give it a competitive advantage over competitors?
3. What are some ways Facebook can communicate its sustainability efforts with stakeholders?

---

media. Internet users are creating and reading consumer-generated content as never before and are having a profound effect on marketing in the process.

Two factors have sparked the rise of consumer-generated information:

1. The increased tendency of consumers to publish their own thoughts, opinions, reviews, and product discussions through blogs or digital media.
2. Consumers' tendencies to trust other consumers over corporations. Consumers often rely on the recommendations of friends, family, and fellow consumers when making purchasing decisions.

Marketers who know where online users are likely to express their thoughts and opinions can use these forums to interact with them, address problems, and promote their companies. Types of digital media in which Internet users are likely to participate include social networks, blogs, wikis, video sharing sites, podcasts, virtual reality sites, and mobile applications. Let's look a little more closely at each.

Social Networks

The increase in social networking across the world is exponential. It is estimated that today's adults spend approximately 42.1 minutes per day on Facebook alone.[20] As social networks evolve, both marketers and the owners of social networking sites are realizing the opportunities such networks offer—an influx of advertising dollars for site owners and a large reach for the advertiser. As a result, marketers have begun investigating and experimenting with promotion on social networks. Two popular sites are Facebook and Twitter.

Facebook.   Facebook is the most popular social networking site in the world. Facebook users create profiles, which they can make public or private, and then search the network for people with whom to connect. The social networking giant has surpassed 1.5 billion users and is still growing. It has also acquired a number of companies as it expands into other services, including Instagram, WhatsApp, and Oculus.[21] Facebook also has a video feature that enables the sharing and tagging of videos.[22]

For this reason, many marketers are turning to Facebook to market products, interact with consumers, and gain free publicity. It is possible for a consumer to become a "fan" of a major company like Starbucks by clicking on the "Like" icon on the coffee retailer's Facebook page. Boosted posts, one of the features Facebook has to offer businesses, allows companies to develop an advertisement quickly from a post on their timelines, select the people who they would like the advertisement to target, and select the budget they want to spend. Boosted posts appear higher up in the News Feeds of the advertisement's target market.[23]

Additionally, social networking sites are useful for relationship marketing, or the creation of relationships that mutually benefit the business and customer. Approximately 30 percent of consumers claim social media has some influence on their purchasing decisions. As a result, firms are spending more time on the quality of their Facebook interactions. Ritz-Carlton, for instance, spends a significant amount of time analyzing its social-media conversations and reaching out to noncustomers. Businesses are shifting their emphasis from selling a product or promoting a brand to developing beneficial relationships in which brands are used to generate a positive outcome for the consumer.[24]

Twitter.   Twitter is a hybrid of a social networking site and a micro-blogging site that asks users one simple question: "What's happening?" Members can post answers of up to 140 characters, which are then available for their registered "followers" to read. It sounds simple enough, but Twitter's effect on digital media has been immense. The site quickly progressed from a novelty to a social networking staple, attracting millions of viewers each month.[25] Nearly 80 percent access the site from their mobile devices.[26]

Although 140 characters may not seem like enough for companies to send an effective message, shorter social media messages appear to be more effective. Tweets with words shorter than 100 characters are found to have a 17 percent higher engagement rate with users, and Facebook has shown similar data.[27] These efforts are having an impact; more than half of Twitter's active and monthly users follow companies or brands.[28]

Like other social networking tools, Twitter is also being used to build, or in some cases rebuild, customer relationships. For example, Taco Bell uses Twitter to interact with consumers. In addition to posting announcements and featuring polls on its Twitter site, Taco Bell has also been recognized for its humorous tweets and one-liners.[29] On the other hand, approximately 70 percent of companies ignore complaints on Twitter. This failure acts as a missed opportunity to address customer concerns and maintain strong relationships.[30]

Twitter is also expanding into video with its acquisition of the mobile application Vine. In keeping with Twitter's reputation for short, concise postings, Vine allows users to display up to 6 seconds of video and share them with other users. Vine has become highly popular among celebrities and teenagers, with 100 million users. Although most company-sponsored videos are posted on Facebook or YouTube, approximately 4 percent of branded social video content is posted on Vine.[31]

Many firms are posting photos and descriptions of their product offerings on digital media sites such as Instagram.

© Ian G Dagnall/Alamy Stock Photo

Blogs and Wikis

Today's marketers must recognize that the impact of consumer-generated material like blogs and wikis and their significance to online consumers have increased a great deal. **Blogs** (short for web logs) are web-based journals in which writers can editorialize and interact with other Internet users. More than three-fourths of Internet users read blogs.[32] In fact, the blogging site Tumblr, which allows anyone to post text, hyperlinks, pictures, and other media for free, has been called "ground zero of the viral Internet." The site Buzzfeed, well-known for its shareable and viral content, cites Tumblr as the top source from where it finds its stories. The site has 269.7 million blogs, and more than 63 million posts are posted on the site daily. In 2013, Yahoo! purchased Tumblr for $1.1 billion.[33]

blogs
web-based journals in which writers can editorialize and interact with other Internet users.

Blogs give consumers power, sometimes more than companies would like. Bloggers can post whatever they like about a company or its products, whether their opinions are positive or negative, true or false.

DID YOU KNOW? Twitter is a more popular business tool than Facebook.[34]

For instance, although companies sometimes force bloggers to remove blogs, readers often create copies of the blog post and spread it across the Internet after the original's removal. In other cases, a positive review of a good or service posted on a popular blog can result in large increases in sales. Thus, blogs can represent a potent threat or opportunity to marketers.

Rather than trying to eliminate blogs that cast their companies in a negative light, some firms are using their own blogs, or employee blogs, to answer consumer concerns or defend their corporate reputations. Bill Marriott, son of the founder of Marriott International, maintains a blog called "Marriott on the Move" where he not only discusses the hotel business but posts on a number of insightful business and inspirational topics to engage his readers.[35] As blogging changes the face of media, smart companies are using it to build enthusiasm for their products and create relationships with consumers.

Wikis are websites where users can add to or edit the content of posted articles. One of the best known is Wikipedia, an online encyclopedia with more than 38 million entries in more than 290 languages on nearly every subject imaginable. (Encyclopedia Britannica only has 120,000 entries.)[36] Wikipedia is one of the 10 most popular sites on the web, and because much of its content can be edited by anyone, it is easy for online consumers to add detail and supporting evidence and to correct inaccuracies in content. Wikipedia used to be completely open to editing, but in order to stop vandalism, the site had to make some topics off-limits that are now editable only by a small group of experts.

wiki
software that creates an interface that enables users to add or edit the content of some types of websites.

Like all digital media, wikis have advantages and disadvantages for companies. Wikis about controversial companies like Walmart and Nike often contain negative publicity, such as about workers' rights violations. However, monitoring relevant wikis can provide companies with a better idea of how consumers feel about the company or brand. Some companies also use wikis as internal tools for teams working on projects that require a great deal of documentation.[37]

There is too much at stake financially for marketers to ignore wikis and blogs. Despite this fact, statistics show that only about 21 percent of Fortune 500 companies have a corporate blog.[38] Marketers who want to form better customer relationships and promote their company's products must not underestimate the power of these two media outlets.

Media Sharing

Businesses can also share their corporate messages in more visual ways through media sharing sites. Media sharing sites allow marketers to share photos, videos, and podcasts. Media sharing sites are more limited in scope in how companies interact with consumers. They tend to be more promotional than reactive. This means that while firms can promote their products through videos or photos, they usually do not interact with consumers through personal messages or responses. At the same time, the popularity of these sites provides the potential to reach a global audience of consumers.

Video sharing sites allow virtually anybody to upload videos, from professional marketers at Fortune 500 corporations to the average Internet user. Some of the most popular video sharing sites include YouTube, Vimeo, and Dailymotion. Video sharing sites give companies the opportunity to upload ads and informational videos about their products. A few videos become viral at any given time, and although many of these gain popularity because they embarrass the subject in some way, others reach viral status because people find them entertaining. **Viral marketing** occurs when a message gets sent from person to person to person. It can be an extremely effective tool for marketers—particularly on the Internet, where one click can send a message to dozens or hundreds of people simultaneously. Marketers are taking advantage of the viral nature of video sharing sites like YouTube, either by creating their own unique videos or advertising on videos that have already reached viral status. Android released a "Friends Furever" video on YouTube showing unlikely pairs of animal friends. The videos only mentioned Android at the end and were more to generate interest and social buzz than to talk about specific products. It became the most shared video of the year with more than 6 million video shares.[39]

Posting videos on digital media sites also allows amateur entrepreneurs to showcase their talents for the chance to become successful. Ipsy founder Michelle Phan started off posting makeup tutorials to YouTube in 2007. Her videos took off, catching the interest of women across the country who valued Phan's beauty advice.[40] Her company, Ipsy, now provides a beauty subscription service to help women through Phan's beauty tutorials. She has more than 8 million subscribers. Approximately 10,000 amateur beauty bloggers help create videos in the subscription service. The company is not as involved in selling products or advertising but has been valued at $800 million for driving subscriptions.[41]

Photo-sharing sites allow users to upload and share their photos and short videos with the world. Well-known photo-sharing sites include Instagram, Imgur, Shutterfly, Photobucket, and Flickr. Owned by Yahoo!, Flickr is one of the most popular photo-sharing sites on the Internet. A Flickr user can upload images, edit them, classify the images, create photo albums, and share photos with friends without having to e-mail bulky image files or send photos through the mail. Instagram is the most popular

viral marketing
a marketing tool that uses a networking effect to spread a message and create brand awareness. The purpose of this marketing technique is to encourage the consumer to share the message with friends, family, co-workers, and peers.

Flickr is a popular photo sharing site. Marketers can use Flickr to post photos of products or company activities.

© TomBham/Alamy

mobile photo-sharing application. Instagram, owned by Facebook, allows users to be creative with their photos by using filters and tints and then sharing them with their friends. Chobani uses Instagram to build communities and suggest new uses for its yogurt products.[42] To compete against Twitter's short-form video service Vine, Facebook's Instagram app allows for 15-second videos. Instagram is one of the fastest growing social networks.[43] With more and more people using mobile apps or accessing the Internet through their smartphones, the use of photo sharing through mobile devices is likely to increase.

Other sites are emerging that take photo sharing to a new level. Pinterest is a photo sharing bulletin board site that combines photo sharing with elements of bookmarking and social networking. Users can share photos and images among other Internet users, communicating mostly through images that they "pin" to their boards. Other users can "repin" these images to their boards, follow each other, "like" images, and make comments. Marketers have found that an effective way of marketing through Pinterest is to post images conveying a certain emotion that represents their brand.[44] Because Pinterest users create boards that deal with their interests, marketers also have a chance to develop marketing messages encouraging users to purchase the product or brand that interests them. Pinterest hopes to learn how to influence a customer to proceed from showing interest in a product to having an intent to purchase. This knowledge will be helpful to advertisers marketing through Pinterest's website.[45]

Photo sharing represents an opportunity for companies to market themselves visually by displaying snapshots of company events, company staff, and/or company products. Nike, Audi, and MTV have all used Instagram in digital marketing campaigns. Zales Jewelers has topic boards on Pinterest featuring rings as well as other themes of love, including songs, wedding cake, and wedding dresses.[46] Digital marketing companies are also scanning photos and images on photo sharing sites to gather insights about how brands are being displayed or used. They hope to offer these insights to big-name companies such as Kraft. The opportunities for marketers to use photo-sharing sites to gather information and promote brands appear limitless.[47]

Podcasts are audio or video files that can be downloaded from the Internet via a subscription that automatically delivers new content to listening devices or personal computers. Podcasting offers the benefit of convenience, giving users the ability to listen to or view content when and where they choose. The markets podcasts reach are ideal for marketers, especially the 18–34 demographic, which includes the young and the affluent.[48] They also impact consumer buying habits. For instance, listening to nutrition podcasts while in the grocery store increases the likelihood that shoppers will purchase healthier items.[49]

podcast audio or video file that can be downloaded from the Internet with a subscription that automatically delivers new content to listening devices or personal computers.

As podcasting continues to catch on, radio stations and television networks like CBC Radio, NPR, MSNBC, and PBS are creating podcasts of their shows to profit from this growing trend. Many companies hope to use podcasts to create brand awareness, promote their products, and encourage customer loyalty.

Virtual Gaming

Games and programs allowing viewers to develop avatars that exist in an online virtual world have exploded in popularity in the 21st century. Virtual games include Second Life, Everquest, Sim City, and the role-playing game World of Warcraft. These sites can be described as social networks with a twist. Virtual realities are three-dimensional, user-created worlds that have their own currencies, lands, and residents that come in every shape and size. Internet users who participate in virtual realities such as Second Life choose a fictional persona, called an *avatar*. ActiveWorlds is another site that uses avatars, but in this 3D universe, Internet users can explore more than 600 worlds and environments.[50]

Real-world marketers and organizations have been eager to capitalize on the popularity of virtual reality and virtual gaming sites. For instance, *The New York Times* has provided news reports in virtual reality on topics such as Europe's refugee crisis.[51] It is estimated that consumers spend 32 percent of their time with mobile apps on gaming activities. Lexus has taken advantage of this opportunity by placing a virtual Lexus in the game *Real Racing 3*. McDonald's, Ford, and Wheat Thins plan on having in-game campaigns for their brands.[52] Even Facebook is looking into opportunities associated with virtual reality. Its purchase of Oculus Rift—a virtual reality startup—signals its interest in exploring live chatting and social virtual tours.[53] By interacting with the public virtually, businesses hope to connect with younger generations of consumers in entirely new ways.

Mobile Marketing

As digital marketing becomes increasingly sophisticated, consumers are beginning to utilize mobile devices like smartphones as a highly functional communication method. The iPhone and iPad have changed the way consumers communicate, and a growing number of travelers are using their smartphones to find online maps, travel guides, and taxis. In industries such as hotels, airlines, and car rental agencies, mobile phones have become a primary method for booking reservations and communicating about services. Other marketing uses of mobile phones include sending shoppers timely messages related to discounts and shopping opportunities.[54] Figure 13-2 breaks down smartphone users by age and activity. For these reasons, mobile marketing has exploded in recent years—mobile phones have become an important part of our everyday lives and can even affect how we shop. For instance, it is estimated that shoppers who are distracted by their phones in-store increased their unplanned purchases by 12 percent over those who are not.[55] To avoid being left behind, brands must recognize the importance of mobile marketing.

E-commerce sales on smartphones are also rapidly growing. Sales are estimated to reach $638 billion by 2018.[56] This makes it essential for companies to understand how to use mobile tools to create effective campaigns. Some of the more common mobile marketing tools include the following:

- *SMS messages:* SMS messages are text messages of 160 words or less. SMS messages have been an effective way to send coupons to prospective customers.[57]
- *Multimedia messages:* Multimedia messaging takes SMS messaging a step further by allowing companies to send video, audio, photos, and other types of media over mobile devices. The MMS market is estimated to be a $20 billion market. Approximately 98 percent of all U.S. cell phones can receive MMS.[58]
- *Mobile advertisements:* Mobile advertisements are visual advertisements that appear on mobile devices. Companies might choose to advertise through search engines, websites, or even games accessed on mobile devices. Mobile accounts for more than half of digital ad spending.[59]
- *Mobile websites:* Mobile websites are websites designed for mobile devices. More than 50 percent of e-commerce website traffic now comes through mobile devices.[60]

FIGURE 13-2
Smartphone Users by Age and Activity

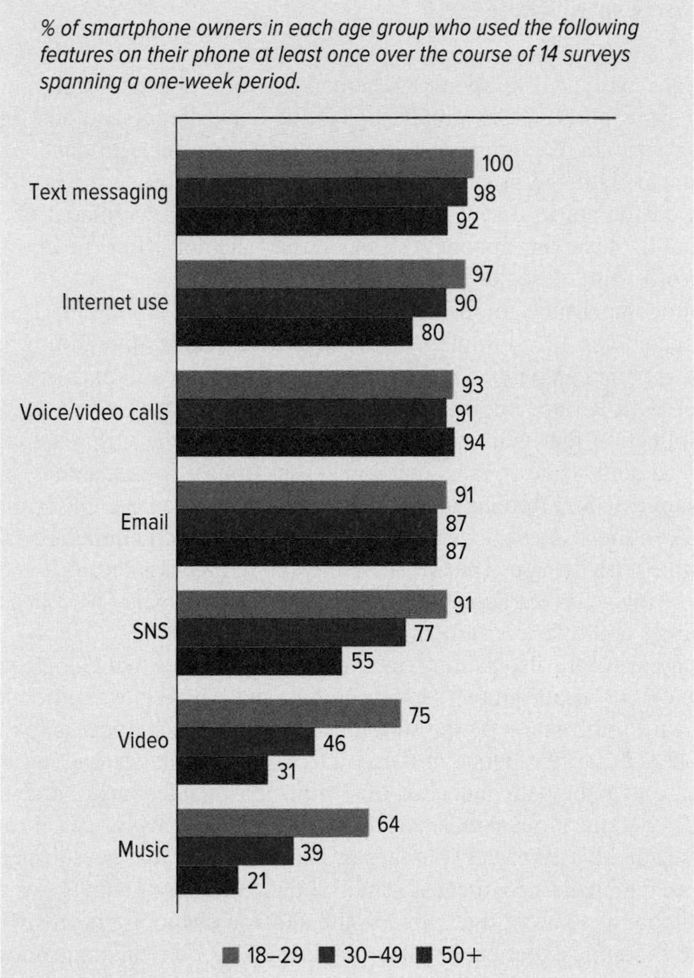

% of smartphone owners in each age group who used the following features on their phone at least once over the course of 14 surveys spanning a one-week period.

Activity	18–29	30–49	50+
Text messaging	100	98	92
Internet use	97	90	80
Voice/video calls	93	91	94
Email	91	87	87
SNS	91	77	55
Video	75	46	31
Music	64	39	21

■ 18–29 ■ 30–49 ■ 50+

Source: Pew Research Center American Trends Panel experience sampling survey, November 10–16 2014

Respondents were contacted twice a day over the course of one week (14 total surveys) and asked how they had used their phone in the preceding hour (besides completing the survey). Only those respondents who completed 10 or more surveys over the course of the study period are included in this analysis.

- *Location-based networks:* Location-based networks are built for mobile devices. Some popular location-based networks include Google Waze and Foursquare, which lets users check in and share their location with others. Foursquare introduced a new advertising network called Pinpoint for marketers. Samsung Galaxy, Olive Garden, and Jaguar Land Rover are examples of companies that have used its new service.[61]
- *Mobile applications:* Mobile applications (known as *apps*) are software programs that run on mobile devices and give users access to certain content.[62] Businesses release apps to help consumers access more information about their company or to provide incentives. Apps are discussed in further detail in the next section.

Applications and Widgets

Applications are adding an entirely new layer to the marketing environment, as Americans are estimated to spend 85 percent of their time on smartphones using apps.[63] The most important feature of apps is the convenience and cost savings they offer to the consumer. Certain apps allow consumers to scan a product's barcode and then compare it with the prices of identical products in other stores. Mobile apps also enable customers to download in-store discounts. An estimated 68 percent of American adults have smartphones, so businesses cannot afford to miss out on the chance to profit from these new trends.[64]

To remain competitive, companies are beginning to use mobile marketing to offer additional incentives to consumers. As Unilever expands into Southeast Asia, it developed a mobile campaign that gives consumers rewards in exchange for providing Unilever with certain information about themselves, such as shopping habits.[65] Another application that marketers are finding useful is the QR scanning app. QR codes are black-and-white squares that sometimes appear in magazines, posters, and storefront displays. Smartphone users who have downloaded the QR scanning application can open their smartphones and scan the code, which contains a hidden message accessible with the app. The QR scanning app recognizes the code and opens the link, video, or image on the phone's screen. Marketers are using QR codes to promote their companies and offer consumer discounts.[66]

Mobile payments are also gaining traction, and companies like Google are working to capitalize on this opportunity.[67] Google Wallet and Apple Pay are mobile apps that store credit card information on the smartphone. When the shopper is ready to check out, he or she can tap the phone at the point of sale for the transaction to be registered.[68] Square is a company launched by Twitter co-founder Jack Dorsey. The company provides organizations with smartphone swiping devices for credit cards as well as tablets that can be used to tally purchases. Bitcoin is a virtual peer-to-peer currency that can be used to make a payment via smartphone. Smaller organizations have begun to accept Bitcoin at some of their stores. The success of mobile payments in revolutionizing the shopping experience will largely depend upon retailers to adopt this payment system, but companies such as Starbucks are already jumping at the opportunity.

Widgets are small bits of software on a website, desktop, or mobile device that perform a simple purpose, such as providing stock quotes or blog updates. Marketers might use widgets to display news headlines, clocks, or games on their web pages.[69] For example, CNBC uses widgets to send alerts and financial news to subscribers. Widgets have been used by companies as a form of viral marketing—users can download the widget and send it to their friends with a click of a button.[70] Widgets downloaded to a user's desktop can update the user on the latest company or product information, enhancing relationship marketing between companies and their fans. Hotels, restaurants, and other tourist locations can download TripAdvisor widgets to their websites. These widgets display the latest company reviews, rewards, and other TripAdvisor content directly to the company's website.[71] Widgets are an innovative digital marketing tool to personalize web pages, alert users to the latest company information, and spread awareness of the company's products.

Using Digital Media to Reach Consumers

We've seen that customer-generated communications and digital media connect consumers as never before. These connections let consumers share information and experiences without company interference so they get more of the "real story" on a product or company feature. In many ways, these media take some of the professional marketer's power to control and dispense information and place it in the hands of the consumer.

However, this shift does not have to spell doom for marketers, who can choose to utilize the power of the consumer and Internet technology to their advantage. While consumers use digital media to access more product information, marketers can use the same sites to get better and more targeted information about the consumer—often more than they could gather through traditional marketing venues. Marketers increasingly use consumer-generated content to aid their own marketing efforts, even going so far as to incorporate Internet bloggers

The use of mobile coupons is increasing. Consumers appreciate these types of coupons for their convenience. Retailers like mobile coupons because they save money from having to print and distribute them.

© vectorfusionart/Shutterstock.com

in their publicity campaigns. Finally, marketers are also beginning to use the Internet to track the success of their online marketing campaigns, creating an entirely new way of gathering marketing research.

The challenge for digital media marketers is to constantly adapt to new technologies and changing consumer patterns. Unfortunately, the attrition rate for digital media channels is very high, with some dying off each year as new ones emerge. As time passes, digital media are becoming more sophisticated so as to reach consumers in more effective ways. Those that are not able to adapt and change eventually fail.

Charlene Li and Josh Bernoff of Forrester Research, a technology and market research company, emphasize the need for marketers to understand these changing relationships in the online media world. By grouping consumers into different segments based on how they utilize digital media, marketers can gain a better understanding of the online market and how best to proceed.[72]

Table 13-2 shows seven ways that Forrester Research groups consumers based on their Internet activity (or lack thereof). The categories are not mutually exclusive; online consumers can participate in more than one at a time.

Creators are consumers who create their own media outlets, such as blogs, podcasts, consumer-generated videos, and wikis.[73] Consumer-generated media are increasingly important to online marketers as a conduit for addressing consumers directly. The second group of Internet users is *conversationalists*. Conversationalists regularly update their Twitter feeds or status updates on social networking sites. Although they are less involved than creators, conversationalists spend time at least once a week (and often more) on digital media sites posting updates.[74] The third category, *critics,* consists of people who comment on blogs or post ratings and reviews on review websites such as Yelp. Because many online shoppers read ratings and reviews to aid their purchasing decisions, critics should be a primary component in a company's digital marketing strategy. The next category is *collectors*. They collect information and organize content generated by critics and creators.[75] Reddit and Delicious are some popular sites for collectors. Because collectors are active members of the online community, a company story or site that catches the eye of a collector is likely to be posted, discussed on collector sites, and made available to other online users looking for information.

Joiners include all who become users of Twitter, Facebook, or other social networking sites. It is not unusual for consumers to be members of several social networking sites at once. Joiners use these sites to connect and network with other users, but as

TABLE 13-2
Social Technographics

Creators	Publish a blog
	Publish personal web pages
	Upload original video
	Upload original audio/music
	Write articles or stories and post them
Conversationalists	Update status on social networking sites
	Post updates on Twitter
Critics	Post ratings/reviews of products or services
	Comment on someone else's blog
	Contribute to online forums
	Contribute to/edit articles in a wiki
Collectors	Use RSS feeds
	Add tags to web pages or photos
	"Vote" for websites online
Joiners	Maintain profile on a social networking site
	Visit social networking sites
Spectators	Read blogs
	Watch video from other users
	Listen to podcasts
	Read online forums
	Read customer ratings/reviews
Inactives	None of the activities

Source: Charlene Li and Josh Bernoff, Groundswell (Boston: Harvard Business Press, 2008), p. 43; Christine Hsu, "Forrester Unveils New Segment of Social Technographics—The Conversationalists," 360i Digital Agency Blog, January 21, 2010, http://blog.360i.com/social-marketing/forrester-new-segment-social-technographics-conversationalists (accessed April 15, 2016).

we've seen, marketers too can take significant advantage of these sites to connect with consumers and form customer relationships.[76] The last two segments are Spectators and Inactives. *Spectators,* who read online information but do not join groups or post anywhere, are the largest group in most countries. *Inactives* are online users who do not participate in any digital online media, but their numbers are dwindling.

Marketers need to consider what proportion of online consumers are creating, conversing, rating, collecting, joining, or simply reading online materials. As in traditional marketing efforts, they need to know their target market. For instance, where spectators make up the majority of the online population, companies should post their own corporate messages through blogs and websites promoting their organizations.

Using Digital Media to Learn about Consumers

Marketing research and information systems can use digital media and social networking sites to gather useful information about consumers and their preferences. Sites such as Twitter and Facebook can be good substitutes for focus groups. Online surveys can serve as an alternative to mail, telephone, or personal interviews.

Crowdsourcing describes how marketers use digital media to find out the opinions or needs of the crowd (or potential markets). Communities of interested consumers join sites like threadless.com, which designs T-shirts, or crowdspring.com, which creates logos and print and web designs. These companies give interested consumers opportunities to contribute and give feedback on product ideas. Crowdsourcing lets companies gather and utilize consumers' ideas in an interactive way when creating new products.

Consumer feedback is an important part of the digital media equation. Ratings and reviews have become exceptionally popular. Online reviews are estimated to influence the buying decisions of approximately 90 percent of U.S. consumers.[77] Retailers such as Amazon,

About three-quarters of online shoppers read ratings and reviews before making a decision.

© Tetra Images/Getty Images

Netflix, and Priceline allow consumers to post comments on their sites about the books, movies, and travel arrangements they sell. Today, most online shoppers search the Internet for ratings and reviews before making major purchase decisions.

While consumer-generated content about a firm can be either positive or negative, digital media forums do allow businesses to closely monitor what their customers are saying. In the case of negative feedback, businesses can communicate with consumers to address problems or complaints much more easily than through traditional communication channels. Yet despite the ease and obvious importance of online feedback, many companies do not yet take full advantage of the digital tools at their disposal.

Legal and Social Issues in Internet Marketing

Identify legal and ethical considerations in digital media.

The extraordinary growth of information technology, the Internet, and social networks has generated many legal and social issues for consumers and businesses. These issues include privacy concerns, the risk of identity theft and online fraud, and the need to protect intellectual property. The U.S. Federal Trade Commission (FTC) compiles an annual list of consumer complaints related to the Internet and digital media. We discuss these in this section, as well as steps that individuals, companies, and the government have taken to address them.

Privacy

Businesses have long tracked consumers' shopping habits with little controversy. However, observing the contents of a consumer's shopping cart or the process a consumer goes through when choosing a box of cereal generally does not result in the collection of specific, personally identifying data. Although using credit cards, shopping cards, and coupons forces consumers to give up a certain degree of anonymity in the traditional shopping process, they can still choose to remain anonymous by paying cash. Shopping on the Internet, however, allows businesses to track them on a far more personal level, from the contents of their online purchases to the websites they favor. Current technology has made it possible for marketers to amass vast quantities of personal information, often without consumers' knowledge, and to share and sell this information to interested third parties.

How is personal information collected on the web? Many sites follow users online by storing a "cookie," or an identifying string of text, on users' computers. Cookies permit website operators to track how often a user visits the site, what he or she looks at while there, and in what sequence. They also allow website visitors to customize services, such as virtual shopping carts, as well as the particular content they see when they log onto a web page. Users have the option of turning off cookies on their machines, but nevertheless, the potential for misuse has left many consumers uncomfortable with this technology.

Due to consumer concerns over privacy, the FTC is considering developing regulations that would better protect consumer privacy by limiting the amount of consumer information that businesses can gather online. Other countries are pursuing similar actions. The European Union passed a law requiring companies to get users' consent before using cookies to track their information. In the United States, one proposed solution for consumer Internet privacy is a "do not track" bill, similar to the "do not call" bill for telephones, to allow users to opt out of having their information tracked.[78] While consumers may welcome such added protections, web advertisers, who use consumer information to better target advertisements to online consumers, see it as a threat. In response to impending legislation, many web advertisers are attempting self-regulation in order to stay ahead of the game. For instance, the Digital Advertising Alliance (DAA) adopted privacy guidelines for online advertisers and created a "trusted mark" icon that websites adhering to their guidelines can display. However, because it is self-regulatory, not all digital advertisers will choose to participate in its programs.[79]

Identity Theft and Online Fraud

identity theft
when criminals obtain personal information that allows them to impersonate someone else in order to use their credit to obtain financial accounts and make purchases.

Identity theft occurs when criminals obtain personal information that allows them to impersonate someone else in order to use the person's credit to access financial accounts and make purchases. This requires organizations to implement increased security measures to prevent database theft. As you can see in Figure 13-3, the most common complaints relate to government documents/benefits fraud, followed by

FIGURE 13-3
Main Sources of Identity Theft

Source: Federal Trade Commission, "Consumer Sentinel Network Data Book: January–December 2015," February 2016, https://www.ftc.gov/system/files/documents/reports/consumer-sentinel-network-data-book-january-december-2015/160229csn-2015databook.pdf (accessed April 19, 2016).

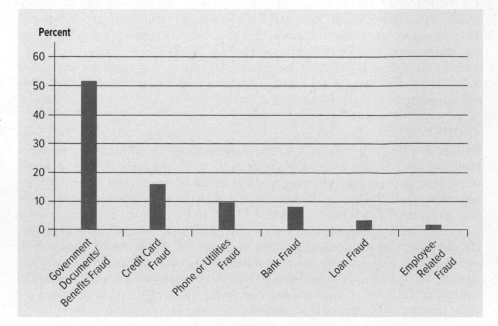

Advertising Effectiveness: Real or a Mirage?

There is a hidden type of fraud plaguing digital marketers: websites that appear to have large numbers of unique visitors but, in reality, are paying for their increase in web traffic. Much of this traffic comes from automated computers. It can be confusing for advertisers to differentiate between websites that have actual visitors versus those that artificially inflate those numbers. Websites uses their web traffic to attract digital marketers looking for popular websites to place ads. Digital marketers are charged a fee for every ad impression, or time that the ad is viewed. When computers are programmed to visit websites, they are also shown the ads, which constitutes an ad impression and drives up costs for marketers. Increasingly, marketers are turning to outside companies to determine which sites are legitimate.

While using these verification companies is helpful, they do not completely shield marketers from ad fraud. For instance, organizations possessing highly valuable online audiences, such as universities and Fortune 500 companies, had their websites targeted by large numbers of hijacked computers, called a botnet, designed to trigger fraudulent ad impressions. The botnet infected and ran undetected on private, government, and corporate computer networks. The estimated total cost of ad fraud, pirating, and ad blocking annually: more than $8 billion—more than half of which is attributed to fake, nonhuman ad impressions.[80]

Discussion Questions

1. How does this type of online ad fraud work?
2. Why do you think ad fraud is so costly?
3. How might ad fraudsters damage opportunities for legitimate websites?

---

credit card fraud, utility fraud, bank fraud, employment fraud, and loan fraud. Sadly, cyberthieves have started targeting children's identities as they offer criminals "a clean slate" for them to commit fraud, such as applying for loans or credit cards.[81]

The Internet's relative anonymity and speed make possible both legal and illegal access to databases storing Social Security numbers, drivers' license numbers, dates of birth, mothers' maiden names, and other information that can be used to establish a credit card or bank account in another person's name in order to make fraudulent transactions. One growing scam used to initiate identity theft fraud is the practice of *phishing,* whereby con artists counterfeit a well-known website and send out e-mails directing victims to it. There visitors find instructions to reveal sensitive information such as their credit card numbers. Phishing scams have faked websites for PayPal, AOL, and the Federal Deposit Insurance Corporation.

Some identity theft problems are resolved quickly, while other cases take weeks and hundreds of dollars before a victim's bank balances and credit standings are restored. To deter identity theft, the National Fraud Center wants financial institutions to implement new technologies such as digital certificates, digital signatures, and biometrics—the use of fingerprinting or retina scanning.

Online fraud includes any attempt to purposely deceive online. Many cybercriminals use hacking to commit online fraud. Hackers break into websites and steal users' personal information. Home Depot, Target, and JPMorgan are some notable cases where cybercriminals hacked into these companies' systems and stole information. Sony experienced a devastating attack that shut down its entire computer network and resulted in the theft of 27 gigabytes of files.[82]

online fraud
any attempt to conduct fraudulent activities online.

Using a different password for each website users visit is another important way to avoid becoming the victim of online fraud. Passwords should be complex enough that a cybercriminal cannot easily guess it. However, many consumers do not do this because of the hassle it takes in remembering complex passwords for multiple sites.[83]

Credit card fraud is a major type of fraud that occurs online. One way to tackle online fraud for credit cards is to use a pin number when doing online transactions.

Banks are releasing credit cards with embedded chips rather than magnetic tape to make it harder for fraud to occur. In Europe this type of credit card combined with the use of a pin number has deterred credit card fraud. This is because the consumers use their pin numbers as well as the embedded chip in their credit cards to make purchases. However, U.S. banks are not requiring Americans to input their pin numbers, which might limit their effectiveness in preventing online fraud within the United States.[84] Privacy advocates advise that the best way to stay out of trouble is to avoid giving out personal information, such as Social Security numbers or credit card information, unless the site is definitely legitimate.

Intellectual Property Theft and Other Illegal Activities

In addition to protecting personal privacy, Internet users and others want to protect their rights to property they may create, including songs, movies, books, and software. Such intellectual property consists of the ideas and creative materials developed to solve problems, carry out applications, and educate and entertain others.

Although intellectual property is generally protected by patents and copyrights, each year, losses from the illegal copying of computer programs, music, movies, compact discs, and books reach billions of dollars in the United States alone. This has become a particular problem with digital media sites. YouTube has often faced lawsuits on intellectual property infringement. With millions of users uploading content to YouTube, it can be hard for Google to monitor and remove all the videos that may contain copyrighted materials.

Illegal sharing of content is another major intellectual property problem. Consumers rationalize the pirating of software, videogames, movies, and music for a number of reasons. First, many feel they just don't have the money to pay for what they want. Second, because their friends engage in piracy and swap digital content, some users feel influenced to engage in this activity. Others enjoy the thrill of getting away with something with a low risk of consequences. And finally, some people feel being tech-savvy allows them to take advantage of the opportunity to pirate content.[85]

Illicit online marketing is also becoming a serious issue for law enforcement across the globe. The ease of the Internet and the difficulty in pinpointing perpetrators are leading drug buyers to deal in illegal drugs over the Internet. Websites that deal in illegal drugs are looking increasingly legitimate, even employing marketing strategies and customer service.[86] Sales of counterfeit goods are another problem. Knockoffs of popular products seized by federal officials annually are valued at over $1 billion. Counterfeit products, particularly from overseas, are thriving on the Internet because they can be shipped directly to customers without having to be examined by customs officials when shipped through ports. Some firms, including UGG Boots, are creating online services allowing users to type in the address to verify whether the electronic retailer is a legitimate seller.[87]

The website Pirate Bay allows users to search and download files. It was actually started by a Swedish anti-copyright organization and soon became known for copyright theft. The founders of Pirate Bay were later found guilty of copyright infringement.

© Evan Lorne/Shutterstock

Digital Media's Impact on Marketing

To be successful in business, you need to know much more than how to use a social networking site to communicate with friends. Developing a strategic understanding of how digital marketing can make business more efficient and productive is increasingly necessary. If you are thinking of becoming an entrepreneur, then the digital world can open doors to new resources and customers. Smartphones, mobile broadband, and webcams are among the tools that can make the most of an online business world, creating greater efficiency at less cost. For example, rather than using traditional phone lines, Skype helps people make and receive calls via the Internet and provides free video calling and text messaging for about 10 percent of the cost of a landline.[88] It is up to businesses and entrepreneurs to develop strategies that achieve business success using existing and future technology, software, and networking opportunities.

Traditional businesses accustomed to using print media can find the transition to digital challenging. New media may require employees with new skills or additional training for current employees. There is often a gap between technical knowledge of how to develop sites and how to develop effective digital marketing strategies to enhance business success. Determining the correct blend of traditional and new media requires careful consideration; the mix will vary depending on the business, its size, and its target market. Future career opportunities will require skills in both traditional and digital media areas so that marketers properly understand and implement marketing strategies that help businesses achieve a competitive advantage.

⊖ So You Want to be a Digital Marketer

The business world has grown increasingly dependent on digital marketing to maintain communication with stakeholders. Reaching customers is often a major concern, but digital marketing can also be used to communicate with suppliers, concerned community members, and special interest groups about issues related to sustainability, safety practices, and philanthropic activities. Many types of jobs exist: account executive directors of social media and director of marketing for digital products, as well as digital advertisers, online marketers, global digital marketers, and brand managers are prominently listed on career opportunity websites.

Entrepreneurs are taking advantage of the low cost of digital marketing, building social networking sites to help market their products. In fact, some small businesses such as specialty publishing, personal health and beauty, and other specialty products can use digital marketing as the primary channel for reaching consumers. Many small businesses are posting signs outside their stores with statements such as "Follow us on Twitter" or "Check out our Facebook page."

To utilize digital marketing, especially social networking, requires more than information technology skills related to constructing websites, graphics, videos, podcasts, etc. Most importantly, one must be able to determine how digital media can be used in implementing a marketing strategy. All

marketing starts with identifying a target market and developing a marketing mix to satisfy customers. Digital marketing is just another way to reach customers, provide information, and develop relationships. Therefore, your opportunity for a career in this field is greatly based on understanding the messages, desired level of interactivity, and connectivity that helps achieve marketing objectives.

As social media use skyrockets, digital marketing professionals will be in demand. The experience of many businesses and research indicate digital marketing is a powerful way to increase brand exposure and generate traffic. In fact, a study conducted on Social Media Examiner found that 85 percent of marketers surveyed believe generating exposure for their business is their number-one advantage in Internet marketing. As consumers use social networking for their personal communication, they will be more open to obtaining information about products through this channel. Digital marketing could be the fastest-growing opportunity in business.

To prepare yourself for a digital marketing career, learn not only the technical aspects, but also how social media can be used to maximize marketing performance. A glance at careerbuilder.com indicates that management positions such as account manager, digital marketing manager, and digital product manager can pay from $60,000 to $170,000 or more per year.

Review Your Understanding

Define *digital media* and *digital marketing* and recognize their increasing value in strategic planning.

Digital media are electronic media that function using digital codes and are available via computers, cellular phones, smartphones, and other digital devices. Digital marketing refers to the strategic process of distributing, promoting, pricing products, and discovering the desires of customers in the virtual environment of the Internet. Because they can enhance the exchange of information between the marketer and the customer, digital media have become an important component of firms' marketing strategies.

Demonstrate the role of digital marketing and define social networking in today's business environment.

Digital communication facilitates marketing research and lowers the cost of communication and consumer service and support. Through websites, social networks, and other digital media, consumers can learn about everything they purchase and use in life and businesses can reach new markets through inexpensive and interactive communication channels. Social networking is expanding so fast that no business can ignore its impact on customer relationships.

Show how digital media affect the marketing mix.

The ability to process orders electronically and increase the speed of communications via the Internet has reduced many distribution inefficiencies, costs, and redundancies while increasing speed throughout the marketing channel. Digital media help firms increase brand awareness, connect with consumers, form relationships, and spread positive publicity about their products. Because consumers are more informed than ever and consumer consumption patterns are changing, marketers must adapt their promotional efforts. The Internet gives consumers access to more information about costs and prices.

Define *social networking* and illustrate how businesses can use different types of social networking media.

Social networking occurs when online consumers interact with other users on a web-based platform to discuss or view topics of interest. Types of social networking media include social networking sites, blogs, wikis, media sharing sites, virtual reality sites, mobile marketing, mobile applications, and widgets.

Blogs not only give consumers power but also allow companies to answer consumer concerns and obtain free publicity.

Wikis give marketers a better understanding of how consumers feel about their companies. Photo-sharing sites enable companies to share images of their businesses or products with consumers and often have links that connect users to company-sponsored blogs. Video sharing is allowing many businesses to engage in viral marketing. Amateur filmmakers are also becoming a potential low-cost, effective marketing venue for companies. Podcasts are audio or video files that can be downloaded from the Internet with a subscription that automatically delivers new content to listening devices or personal computers.

Marketers have begun joining and advertising on social networking sites like Facebook and Twitter due to their global reach. Virtual realities can be fun and creative ways to reach consumers, create brand loyalty, and use consumer knowledge to benefit companies. Mobile marketing includes advertising, text messages, and other types of digital marketing through mobile devices. Mobile apps can be anything from games, to news updates, to shopping assistance. They provide a way for marketers to reach consumers via their cell phones. Apps can help consumers to perform services and make purchases more easily, such as checking in at a hotel or comparing and contrasting the price of appliances or a new dress. Widgets are small bits of software on a website, desktop, or mobile device. They can be used to inform consumers about company updates and can easily go viral.

Identify legal and ethical considerations in digital media.

Increasing consumer concerns about privacy are prompting the FTC to look into regulating the types of information marketers can gather from Internet users, while many web advertisers and trade groups try to engage in self-regulation to prevent the passage of new Internet privacy laws. Online fraud includes any attempt to conduct fraudulent activities online. Intellectual property losses cost the United States billions of dollars and have become a particular problem for sites such as YouTube, which often finds it hard to monitor the millions of videos uploaded to its site for copyright infringement.

Evaluate a marketer's dilemma and propose recommendations.

Based on the material in this chapter, you should be able to answer the questions posed in the "Solve the Dilemma" feature at the end of this chapter and evaluate where the company's marketing strategy has failed. How could Paul utilize new digital media to help promote his product and gather data on how to improve it?

Revisit the World of Business

1. Describe how marketers are using Pinterest as a customer relationship management tool.

2. According to the social technographic profile, what type of Internet users do you think use Pinterest the most? Why is this segment appealing to marketers?

3. Do you think the use of promotion in the form of advertised pins may turn off Pinterest fans? Why or why not?

Learn the Terms

blogs 407
digital marketing 398
digital media 398
e-business 398

identity theft 416
online fraud 417
podcast 409
social network 404

viral marketing 408
wiki 407

Check Your Progress

1. What is digital marketing?

2. How can marketers utilize digital media to improve business?

3. Define *accessibility, addressability, connectivity, interactivity,* and *control.* What do these terms have to do with digital marketing?

4. What is e-business?

5. How is the Internet changing the practice of marketing?

6. What impact do digital media have on the marketing mix?

7. How can businesses utilize new digital and social networking channels in their marketing campaigns?

8. What are some of the privacy concerns associated with the Internet and e-business? How are these concerns being addressed in the United States?

9. What is identity theft? How can consumers protect themselves from this crime?

10. Why do creators want to protect their intellectual property? Provide an example on the Internet where intellectual property may not be protected or where a copyright has been infringed.

Get Involved

1. Amazon.com is one of the most recognized e-businesses. Visit the site (www.amazon.com) and identify the types of products the company sells. Explain its privacy policy.

2. Visit some of the social networking sites identified in this chapter. How do they differ in design, audience, and features? Why do you think some social networking sites like Facebook are more popular than others?

3. It has been stated that digital technology and the Internet are to business today what manufacturing

was to business during the Industrial Revolution. The technology revolution requires a strategic understanding greater than learning the latest software and programs or determining which computer is the fastest. Leaders in business can no longer delegate digital media to specialists and must be the connectors and the strategists of how digital media will be used in the company. Outline a plan for how you will prepare yourself to function in a business world where digital marketing knowledge will be important to your success.

Build Your Skills

Planning a Digital Marketing and Social Networking Site

Background

Many companies today utilize digital media in a way that reflects their images and goals. They can also help to improve customer service, loyalty, and satisfaction while reaching out to new target markets. Companies use these sites in a variety of ways, sometimes setting up Facebook pages or Twitter accounts to gather customer feedback, to promote new products, or even to hold competitions.

The U.S. economy has experienced many ups and downs in recent decades, but e-commerce has been an area that has continued to grow throughout economic ups and downs. Many dot-com companies and social networking sites have risen and collapsed. Others such as Amazon.com, eBay, Facebook, and Twitter have not only survived, but thrived. Many that succeed are "niche players"; that is, they cater to a very specific market that a brick-and-mortar business (existing only in a physical marketplace) would find hard to reach. Others are able to compete with brick-and-mortar stores because they offer a wider variety of products, lower prices, or better customer service. Many new digital media outlets help companies compete on these fronts.

As a manager of Biodegradable Packaging Products Inc., a small business that produces packaging foam from recycled agricultural waste (mostly corn), you want to expand into e-business by using digital media to help market your product. Your major customers are other businesses and could include environmentally friendly companies like Tom's of Maine (natural toothpaste) and Celestial Seasonings (herbal tea). Your first need is to develop a social networking site or blog that will help you reach your potential customers. You must decide who your target market is and which medium will attract it the best.

Task

Plan a digital media marketing campaign using online social networking sites, blogs, or another digital media outlet using the following template.

Social networking/blog/other site: _____

Overall image and design of your site: _____

Strategy for attracting followers to your site: _____

Potential advertising partners to draw in more customers: _____

Solve the Dilemma

Developing Successful Freeware

Paul Easterwood, a recent graduate of Colorado State University with a degree in computer science, entered the job market during a slow point in the economy. Tech sector positions were hard to come by, and Paul felt he wouldn't be making anywhere near what he was worth. The only offer he received was from an entrepreneurial firm, Pentaverate Inc., that produced freeware. Freeware, or public domain software, is offered to consumers free of charge in exchange for revenues generated later. Makers of freeware (such as Adobe and Netscape) can earn high profits through advertisements their sites carry, from purchases made on the freeware site, or, for more specialized software, through fee-based tutorials and workshops offered to help end users. Paul did some research and found an article in *Worth* magazine documenting the enormous success of freeware.

Pentaverate Inc. offered compensation mainly in the form of stock options, which had the potential to be highly profitable if the company did well. Paul's job would be to develop freeware that people could download from the Internet and that would generate significant income for Pentaverate. With this in mind, he decided to accept the position, but he quickly realized he knew very little about business. With no real experience in marketing, Paul was at a loss to know what software he should produce that would make the company money. His first project, IOWatch, was designed to take users on virtual tours of outer space, especially the moons of Jupiter (Paul's favorite subject), by continually searching the Internet for images and video clips associated with the cosmos and downloading them directly to a PC. The images would then appear as soon as the person logged on. Advertisements would accompany each download, generating income for Pentaverate.

However, IOWatch experienced low end-user interest and drew little advertising income as a result. Historically at

LO 13-6

Evaluate a marketer's dilemma and propose recommendations.

Pentaverate, employees were fired after two failed projects. Desperate to save his job, Paul decided to hire a consultant. He needed to figure out what customers might want so he could design some useful freeware for his second project. He also needed to know what went wrong with IOWatch because he loved the software and couldn't figure out why it had failed to find an audience. The job market has not improved, so Paul realizes how important it is for his second project to succeed.

Discussion Questions

1. As a consultant, what would you do to help Paul figure out what went wrong with IOWatch?

2. What ideas for new freeware can you give Paul? What potential uses will the new software have?

3. How will it make money?

Build Your Business Plan

Digital Marketing and Social Networking

If you are considering developing a business plan for an established good or service, find out whether it is currently marketed digitally. If it is not, think about why that is the case. Can you think of how you might overcome any obstacles and engage in digital marketing on the Internet?

If you are thinking about introducing a new good or service, now is the time to think about whether you might want to market this product on the Internet. Remember, you do not have to have a brick-and-mortar store to open your own business anymore. Perhaps you might want to consider click instead of brick!

See for Yourself Videocase

Should Employees Use Social Media Sites at Work?

As Facebook and other social media sites have gained popularity and expanded, managing their use at work has become an increasingly hot topic. Studies on the use of social media in the workplace conflict over how much it inhibits productivity. Should employees be allowed to access social media at work? Approximately 38 percent of time wasters say they waste work time on social media sites. Many offices have banned access to Facebook. The results are as mixed as the research. A National Business Ethics Survey (NBES) revealed that II percent of employees who engage in social networking are "active" social networkers who spend 30 percent or more of the workday on social networking sites. Many managers are conflicted as to whether this constitutes enough of a problem to be banned outright.

Another study conducted by Nucleus Research (an IT research company) found that 77 percent of Facebook users used the site during work for as much as two hours a day; 87 percent of those surveyed admitted they were using social media sites to waste time. NBES also found that active social networkers were more likely to find certain questionable behaviors to be acceptable, such as criticizing the company or its managers on social networking sites. Procter & Gamble realized that many of its employees were using social networking sites for nonwork purposes. Its investigations revealed that employees across the company were watching an average of 50,000 five-minute YouTube videos and listening to 4,000 hours of music on Pandora daily.

However, an outright ban could cause problems. Some younger employees have expressed that they do not want to work for companies without social media access; they view restricting or eliminating access like removing a benefit. Employees at companies with an outright ban often resent the lack of trust associated with such a move and feel that management is censuring their activities. Other employees who use Facebook during their lunch hours or break times may feel that they are being punished because of others' actions. Additionally, Procter & Gamble uses YouTube and Facebook extensively for marketing purposes. Banning these sites would disrupt the firm's marketing efforts.

An Australian study indicates that employees taking time out to pursue Facebook and other social media were actually 9 percent more productive than those who did not. Brent Coker, the study's author and University of Melbourne faculty member, says people are more productive when they take time to "zone out" throughout the workday. Doing so can improve concentration. In the sales industry, a study of 100,000 employees revealed that social media "mavens" had 1.6 percent higher sales conversions.

Some companies actually encourage employees to use social networking as part of their integrated marketing strategy. In fact, not having a social media page such as Facebook or LinkedIn might be seen as a missed opportunity for marketing the firm. Even the law industry is starting to use social media on a more daily basis. One study of the top 50 highest ranked law firms in the country determined that 64 percent use Facebook and 90 percent are on Twitter. Approximately 80 percent post something every day or once a week. Although larger law firms tend not to use social media as effectively as smaller law firms, the use of social media to interact with clients is clearly gaining throughout the industry.

Despite the benefits that companies have received from allowing their employees to use social media, many companies have gone ahead with social media bans. Procter & Gamble has restricted the use of Netflix and Pandora, but not Facebook or YouTube. Companies all need to ask, "Can management use social media to benefit the company?" If so, it may be more advantageous to take the risks of employees using social media for personal use if they can also be encouraged to use social networks to publicize their organizations, connect with customers, and view consumer comments or complaints. By restricting social media use, companies may be forfeiting an effective marketing tool.[89]

Discussion Questions

1. Why do you think results are so mixed on the use of social networking in the workplace?

2. What are some possible upsides to utilizing social media as part of an integrated marketing strategy, especially in digital marketing?

3. What are the downsides to restricting employee access to social networking sites?

You can find the related video in the Video Library in Connect. Ask your instructor how you can access Connect.

Team Exercise

Develop a digital marketing promotion for a local sports team. Use Twitter, Facebook, and other social networking media to promote ticket sales for next season's schedule. In your plan, provide specific details and ideas for the content you would use on the sites. Also, describe how you would encourage fans and potential fans to go to your site. How would you use digital media to motivate sports fans to purchase tickets and merchandise and attend games?

Endnotes

1. Natalie Gagliordi, "Pinterest Launches Buyable Pins on iOS, Taps Braintree and Stripe for Processing," *ZDNet,* June 30, 2015, http://www.zdnet.com/article/pinterest-launches-buyable-pins-taps-braintree-for-processing/ (accessed December 22, 2015); Jack Marshall, "Pinterest Beefs Up Marketer Tools," *The Wall Street Journal,* April 29, 2015, p. B7; Andrew Nusca, "Pinterest CEO Ben Silbermann: We're Not a Social Network," *Fortune,* July 13, 2015, http://fortune.com/2015/07/13/pinterest-ceo-ben-silbermann/ (accessed December 22, 2015).

2. This material in this chapter is reserved for use in the authors' other textbooks and teaching materials.

3. Lauren I. Labrecque, Jonas vor dem Esche, Charla Mathwick, Thomas P. Novak, and Charles F. Hofacker, "Consumer Power: Evolution in the Digital Age," *Journal of Interactive Marketing* 27, 4 (November 2013), pp. 257–269.

4. James Kanter and Mark Scott, "Europe Challenges Google, Seeing Violations of Its Antitrust Law," *The New York Times,* April 15, 2015, http://www.nytimes.com/2015/04/16/business/international/european-union-google-antitrust-case.html?_r=0 (accessed April 17, 2015).

5. Time Inc., "Amazon.com," *Fortune,* 2016, http://fortune.com/fortune500/amazon-com-29/ (accessed April 18, 2016).

6. "Top 15 Most Popular Video Websites," eBiz MBA, April 2016, www.ebizmba.com/articles/video-websites (accessed April 18, 2016); Vimeo, "About Vimeo," http://vimeo.com/about (accessed April 18, 2016).

7. Bobby White, "The New Workplace Rules: No Video-Watching," *The Wall Street Journal,* March 4, 2008, p. B1; Ben Bryant, "Workers Waste an Hour a Day on Facebook, Shopping and Browsing Holidays, Study Finds," *The Telegraph,* July 22, 2013, www.telegraph.co.uk/news/uknews/10194322/Workers-waste-an-hour-a-day-on-Facebook-shopping-and-browsing-holidays-study-finds.html (accessed May 19, 2014).

8. InternetLiveStats, "Internet Stats," http://www.internetlivestats.com/internet-users/ (accessed April 18, 2016).

9. Daniel Nations, "How Many iApps Are in the App Store?" About.com, September 22, 2015, http://ipad.about.com/od/iPad-FAQ/f/How-Many-iPad-Apps-Are-In-The-App-Store.htm (accessed April 18, 2016).

10. Julep, "Beauty Lab," 2016, http://www.julep.com/beautylab (accessed April 15, 2016).

11. Christine Birkner, "Retail's White Elephants," *Marketing News,* April 2015, pp. 49–59.

12. Marco della Cava, "E-Commerce Turbulence Likely Ahead," *USA Today,* July 21, 2015, p. 5B; Simon Crompton, "Would-be Amazon Competitor Jet.com Raises $80 Million," *Digital Journal,* September 17, 2014, http://

www.digitaljournal.com/business/business/
would-be-amazon-competitor-jet-com-raises-80-million/
article/403885 (accessed December 22, 2015); Ben Fox
Rubin, "Why Jet.com Says It's Got a 'Smarter Way'
for You to Shop Online," *CNET*, December 21, 2015,
http://www.cnet.com/news/why-jet-com-says-its-got-a-
smarter-way-for-you-to-shop-online/ (accessed December 22,
2015); Spencer Soper, "Jet.com Opens Rivalry with
Amazon after a Ragged Trial Period," *Bloomberg*,
July 21, 2015, http://www.bloomberg.com/news/
articles/2015-07-21/jet-com-opens-rivalry-with-amazon-
after-a-ragged-trial-period (accessed December 22, 2015).

13. "Lowe's Home Improvement," Facebook for Business,
https://www.facebook.com/business/success/
lowes-home-improvement (accessed April 18, 2016);
Facebook, "Canvas," https://canvas.facebook.com/ (accessed
April 18, 2016).

14. Cameron Chapman, "The History and Evolution of Social
Media,"*WebDesigner Depot*, October 7, 2009,
www.webdesignerdepot.com/2009/10/the-history-and-
evolution-of-social-media/ (accessed April 18, 2016).

15. "Then and Now: A History of Social Networking Sites,"
CBS News, http://www.cbsnews.com/pictures/then-and-now-
a-history-of-social-networking-sites/2/ (accessed April 18,
2016).

16. Adam Kleinberg, "Thinking about Snapchat Advertising?
Snap Out of It," *Advertising Age*, August 22, 2014, http://
adage.com/article/agency-viewpoint/thinking-snapchat-
snap/294667/ (accessed January 8, 2016); Austin Carr,
"I Ain't Afraid of No Ghost," *Fast Company*, November
2015, pp. 100–122.

17. Erin Griffith, "Snitches' Brew," *Fortune*, April 1, 2015,
pp. 46–48.

18. Reed Albergotti, "Facebook Touts Economic Impact," *The
Wall Street Journal*, January 21, 2015, p. B5.

19. Ben Kepes, "It's Not So Complicated—Facebook
and Sustainability," *Forbes*, October 10, 2014, http://
www.forbes.com/sites/benkepes/2014/10/10/its-not-
so-complicated-facebook-and-sustainability/ (accessed
December 22, 2015); Ehren Goossens, "Facebook Doubles
Renewable-Energy Target to 50% by End of 2016,"
Bloomberg, July 7, 2015, http://www.bloomberg.com/news/
articles/2015-07-07/facebook-doubles-renewable-energy-
target-to-50-by-end-of-2018 (accessed December 22,
2015); Maeve Duggan, Nicole B. Ellison, Cliff Lampe,
Amanda Lenhart, and Mary Madden, "Social Media Update
2014," *Pew Research Center*, January 9, 2015, http://www.
pewinternet.org/2015/01/09/social-media-update-2014/
(accessed December 22, 2015); "Working with Tech Leaders
to Power the Internet with 100 Percent Renewable Energy,"
BSR, December 3, 2015, http://www.bsr.org/en/our-insights/
case-study-view/working-with-tech-leaders-to-power-the-
internet-with-100-percent-renewable (accessed December
22, 2015).

20. Shea Bennett, "This is How Much Time we Spend on Social
Networks Every Day," *Ad Week*, November 18, 2014,

http://www.adweek.com/socialtimes/social-media-minutes-
day/503160 (accessed April 18, 2016).

21. Harry McCracken, "Inside Mark Zuckerberg's Bold Plan for
the Future of Facebook," *Fast Company*, December 2015/
January 2016, pp. 86–100, 136.

22. Wendy Boswell, "Video Websites: The Top Ten," *About
Tech*, 2015, http://websearch.about.com/od/imagesearch/tp/
popularvideosites.htm (accessed April 18, 2016).

23. Facebook for Business, "Boost a Post," https://www
.facebook.com/business/a/boost-a-post (accessed April 18,
2016); Olsy Sorokina, "What Are Facebook Boost Posts and
How Can They Help Your Business," *Hootsuite*, October 24,
2014, https://blog.hootsuite.com/how-does-facebook-boost-
posts-work/ (accessed April 18, 2016).

24. Jeff Elder, "Facing Reality, Companies Alter Social-Media
Strategies," *The Wall Street Journal*, June 23, 2014,
pp. B1–B2.

25. Jefferson Graham, "Cake Decorator Finds Twitter a Tweet
Recipe for Success," *USA Today*, April 1, 2009, p. 5B.

26. Twitter, "About Twitter," https://about.twitter.com/company
(accessed April 18, 2016).

27. Christine Birkner, "The Goldfish Conundrum," *Marketing
News*, April 2015, pp. 18–19.

28. Stephanie Frasco, "100 Facts and Figures about Twitter,
and Why They Matter for Your Business," *Social Media
Today*, September 26, 2013, http://socialmediatoday.com/
stephaniefrasco/1770161/100-facts-figures-about-twitter-
business (accessed May 6, 2014).

29. Samantha Grossman, "The 13 Sassiest Brands on Twitter,"
Time, February 7, 2014, http://time.com/5151/sassiest-
brands-on-twitter-ranked/ (accessed January 14, 2016);
"Taco Bell," Twitter, https://twitter.com/tacobell (accessed
January 14, 2016).

30. Belinda Parmar, "50 Companies That Get Twitter—and
50 That Don't," *Harvard Business Review*, April 27, 2015,
https://hbr.org/2015/04/the-best-and-worst-corporate-
tweeters (accessed January 6, 2016).

31. Lauren Johnson, "Why Brands Are Ditching Twitter's
6-Second Vine App,"*AdWeek*, December 6, 2015, http://
www.adweek.com/news/technology/why-brands-are-
ditching-twitter-s-6-second-vine-app-168433 (accessed
January 14, 2016); "Hey Twitter Inc., It's Time to Monetize
Vine!" *Motley Fool*, August 2015, http://www.fool.com/
investing/general/2015/08/18/hey-twitter-inc-its-time-to-
monetize-vine.aspx (accessed January 14, 2016).

32. Marcelina Hardy, "Statistics on Blogging," ContentWriters.
com, August 19, 2014, https://contentwriters.com/blog/
statistics-blogging/ (accessed April 18, 2016).

33. Caitlin Dewey, "2015 Is the Year That Tumblr Became
the Front Page of the Internet," *The Washington Post*,
December 23, 2015, https://www.washingtonpost.com/
news/the-intersect/wp/2015/03/11/move-over-reddit-
tumblr-is-the-new-front-page-of-the-internet/ (accessed
April 18, 2015).

34. Hailey Gerhard, "Fortune 500 Companies Prefer Instagram over Blogs, Study Says," *Institute for Public Relations,* March 21, 2016, http://www.instituteforpr.org/fortune-500-companies-prefer-instagram-over-blogs-study-says/ (accessed April 18, 2016).

35. Niall Harbison and Lauren Fisher, "40 of the Best Corporate Blogs to Inspire You," *Ragan's PR Daily,* September 13, 2012, http://www.prdaily.com/Main/Articles/40_of_the_best_corporate_blogs_to_inspire_you_12645.aspx (accessed January 20, 2016).

36. Drake Bennett, "Ten Years of Inaccuracy and Remarkable Detail: Wikipedia," *Bloomberg Businessweek,* January 10–16, 2011, pp. 57–61; "Wikipedia: About," *Wikipedia,* http://en.wikipedia.org/wiki/Wikipedia:About (accessed April 18, 2016).

37. Charlene Li and Josh Bernoff, *Groundswell* (Boston: Harvard Business Press, 2008), pp. 25–26.

38. Chris Thilk, "Social Media and the Fortune 500," Porter Novelli, 2015, https://www.porternovelli.com/intelligence/2016/03/25/social-media-and-the-fortune-500/ (accessed April 18, 2016).

39. Lauren Johnson, "Here Are the 10 Brands with the Most-Shared Videos of 2015," *AdWeek,* December 15, 2015, http://www.adweek.com/news/technology/here-are-10-brands-most-shared-videos-2015-168637 (accessed January 20, 2016).

40. Stephanie Hayes, "Michelle Phan, a YouTube Sensation for Her Makeup Tutorials, Has Transformed Her Life," *Tampa Bay Times,* August 22, 2009, http://www.tampabay.com/features/humaninterest/michelle-phan-a-youtube-sensation-for-her-makeup-tutorials-has-transformed/1029747 (accessed April 18, 2016).

41. Nicole LaPorte, "Serious Beauty," *Fast Company,* February 2016, pp. 27–28.

42. "Photoset," Instagram, http://blog.business.instagram.com/post/78694901404/how-yogurt-maker-chobani-uses-instagram-to-open (accessed January 15, 2016).

43. "4 Key Advantages for Video Marketing on Instagram vs. Vine," *Ad Week,* March 4, 2015, http://www.adweek.com/socialtimes/sumall-dane-atkinson-video-marketing-instagram-vs-vine/616331 (accessed April 18, 2016).

44. PR Newswire, "Marketers' Interest in Pinterest," *Marketing News,* April 30, 2012, pp. 8–9; "PINTEREST INTEREST: Survey: 17 Percent of Marketers Currently Using or Planning to Join Pinterest," The Creative Group, August 22, 2012, http://creativegroup.mediaroom.com/pinterest-for-business (accessed April 18, 2016); Jason Falls, "How Pinterest Is Becoming the Next Big Thing in Social Media for Business," February 7, 2012, www.entrepreneur.com/article/222740 (accessed April 18, 2016); Pinterest website, http://pinterest.com/ (accessed April 18, 2016).

45. Jeff Bercovici, "Social Media's New Mad Men," *Forbes,* November 2014, pp. 71–82.

46. Zale Jewelers Pinterest page, www.pinterest.com/zalesjewelers (accessed April 18, 2016).

47. Douglas MacMillan and Elizabeth Dwoskin, "Smile! Marketers Are Mining Selfies," *The Wall Street Journal,* October 10, 2014, pp. B1–B2.

48. Natalie Wires, "The Rising Popularity of Podcasts: Why Listeners Are Rediscovering Podcasts," *Tunheim,* March 26, 2014, http://blog.tunheim.com/2014/03/26/rising-popularity-podcasts-listeners-rediscovering-podcasts/1438#.U2pMWYFdVc8 (accessed April 18, 2016).

49. Ann Lukits, "Podcasts Send Shoppers to Omega-3s," *The Wall Street Journal,* December 9, 2014, p. D2.

50. ActiveWorlds Inc., "About ActiveWorlds Inc.," https://www.activeworlds.com/web/cabout.php (accessed April 19, 2016).

51. Marco della Cava, "Virtual Reality Comes to Life in Swimsuit Issue," *USA Today,* February 16, 2016, p. 1B.

52. Mike Shields, "Are Mobile Games The Next Great Ad Medium?" *The Wall Street Journal,* August 18, 2014, http://blogs.wsj.com/cmo/2014/08/18/are-mobile-games-the-next-great-ad-medium/ (accessed April 18, 2016).

53. Austin Carr, "Facebook Everywhere," *Fast Company,* July/August 2014, pp. 56–98.

54. Roger Yu, "Smartphones Help Make Bon Voyages," *USA Today,* March 5, 2010, p. B1.

55. Sean Silverthorpe, "Should Retailers Worry about In-Store Mobile Use?" *Insights from Marketing Science Institute* 1 (2015), pp. 1–2.

56. Cooper Smith, "US E-Commerce Growth Is Now Far Outpacing Overall Retail Sales," *Business Insider,* April 2, 2014, www.businessinsider.com/us-e-commerce-growth-is-now-far-outpacing-overall-retail-sales-2014-4#!Kk54l (accessed April 18, 2016).

57. Mark Milian, "Why Text Messages Are Limited to 160 Characters," *Los Angeles Times,* May 3, 2009, http://latimesblogs.latimes.com/technology/2009/05/invented-text-messaging.html (accessed April 18, 2016); "Eight Reasons Why Your Business Should Use SMS Marketing," *Mobile Marketing Ratings,* www.mobilemarketingratings.com/eight-reasons-sms-marketing.html (accessed April 18, 2016).

58. James Citron, "2014: The Year the MMS Upswing Arrives and How to Take Advantage of It," *Wired,* January 21, 2014, http://insights.wired.com/profiles/blogs/2014-the-year-the-mms-upswing-arrives-and-how-to-take-advantage#axzz3xLvg3dvO (accessed January 15, 2016).

59. "Mobile to Account for More than Half of Digital Ad Spending in 2015," *eMarketer,* September 1, 2015, http://www.emarketer.com/Article/Mobile-Account-More-than-Half-of-Digital-Ad-Spending-2015/1012930 (accessed January 15, 2016).

60. Jake Jeffries, "10 Incredible Mobile Marketing Stats 2015 [INFOGRAPHIC]," *Social Media Today,* January 13, 2015, http://www.socialmediatoday.com/content/10-incredible-mobile-marketing-stats-2015-infographic (accessed January 15, 2016).

61. Christopher Heine, "Foursquare Unleashes Location Data for Cross-Mobile Ad Targeting," *AdWeek,* April 14, 2015, http://

www.adweek.com/news/technology/foursquare-finally-unleashes-location-data-cross-mobile-ad-targeting-164069 (accessed January 19, 2016).

62. Anita Campbell, "What the Heck Is an App?" *Small Business Trends,* March 7, 2011, http://smallbiztrends.com/2011/03/what-is-an-app.html (accessed April 18, 2016).

63. Sarah Perez, "Consumers Spend 85% of Time on Smartphones in Apps, But Only 5 Apps See Heavy Use," *TechCrunch,* June 22, 2015, http://techcrunch.com/2015/06/22/consumers-spend-85-of-time-on-smartphones-in-apps-but-only-5-apps-see-heavy-use/ (accessed April 18, 2016).

64. Monica Anderson, "Technology Device Ownership: 2015," October 29, 2015, http://www.pewinternet.org/2015/10/29/technology-device-ownership-2015/ (accessed April 18, 2016).

65. Michelle Yeomans, "Unilever Opts for 'Mobile Marketing Platform' to Each South-East Asia," *Cosmetics Design,* September 15, 2015, http://www.cosmeticsdesign-asia.com/Business-Financial/Unilever-opts-for-mobile-marketing-platform-to-reach-south-east-Asia (accessed January 19, 2016).

66. Umika Pidaparthy, "Marketers Embracing QR Codes, for Better or Worse,"*CNN Tech,* March 28, 2011, http://www.cnn.com/2011/TECH/mobile/03/28/qr.codes.marketing/ (accessed April 18, 2016).

67. Brad Stone and Olga Kharif, "Pay as You Go," *Bloomberg Businessweek,* July 18–24, 2011, pp. 66–71.

68. "Google Wallet," www.google.com/wallet/what-is-google-wallet.html (accessed April 18, 2016).

69. "All About Widgets," *Webopedia,* September 14, 2007, www.webopedia.com/DidYouKnow/Hardware_Software/widgets.asp (accessed April 18, 2016).

70. Rachael King, "Building a Brand with Widgets," *Bloomberg Businessweek,* March 3, 2008, www.businessweek.com/technology/content/feb2008/tc20080303_000743.htm (accessed December 12, 2014).

71. TripAdvisor, "Welcome to TripAdvisor's Widget Center," www.tripadvisor.com/Widgets (accessed April 18, 2016).

72. Li and Bernoff, *Groundswell,* p. 41.

73. Li and Bernoff, *Groundswell,* pp. 41–42.

74. "Forrester Unveils New Segment of Social Technographics—The Conversationalists," *360 Digital Connections,* January 21, 2010, http://blog.360i.com/social-marketing/forrester-new-segment-social-technographics-conversationalists (accessed April 18, 2016).

75. Li and Bernoff, *Groundswell,* p. 44.

76. Li and Bernoff, *Groundswell,* pp. 44–45.

77. Stacey Rudolph, "The Impact of Online Reviews on Customers' Buying Decisions," *Business 2 Community,* July 25, 2015, http://www.business2community.com/infographics/impact-online-reviews-customers-buying-decisions-infographic-01280945#daKeGUeQMyvjGcT6.97 (accessed April 18, 2016).

78. Jon Swartz, "Facebook Changes Its Status in Washington," *USA Today,* January 13, 2011, pp. 1B–2B; John W. Miller, "Yahoo Cookie Plan in Place," *The Wall Street Journal,* March 19, 2011, http://online.wsj.com/news/articles/SB10001424052748703512404576208700813815570 (accessed April 18, 2016).

79. Jesse Brody, "Terms and Conditions," *Marketing News,* November 2014, pp. 34–41.

80. Ben Elgin, Michael Riley, David Kocieniewski, and Joshua Brustein, "How Much of Your Audience Is Fake?" *Bloomberg Businessweek,* September 28, 2015,pp. 64–71; George Slefo, "Ad Fraud Pirated Content, Malvertising and Ad Blocking Are Costing $8.2 Billion a Year, IAB Says," *Advertising Age,* December 1, 2015, http://adage.com/article/digital/iab-puts-8-2-billion-price-tag-ad-fraud-report/301545/ (accessed December 22, 2015).

81. Priya Anand, "Cyberthieves Have a New Target: Children," *The Wall Street Journal,* February 1, 2016, p. R8.

82. Elizabeth Weise, "Sony Hack Leaves Intriguing Clues," *USA Today,* December 4, 2014, p. 1B.

83. Elizabeth Weise, "Consumers Have to Protect Themselves Online," *USA Today,* May 22, 2014, p. 1B.

84. Jim Zarroli, "U.S. Credit Cards Tackle Fraud with Embedded Chips, But No Pins," *NPR,* January 5, 2015, http://www.npr.org/blogs/alltechconsidered/2015/01/05/375164839/u-s-credit-cards-tackle-fraud-with-embedded-chips-but-no-pins (accessed April 22, 2015).

85. Kevin Shanahan and Mike Hyman "Motivators and Enablers of SCOURing," *Journal of Business Research* 63 (September–October 2010), pp. 1095–1102.

86. "The Amazons of the Dark Net," *The Economist,* November 1, 2014, pp. 57–58.

87. Erica E. Phillips, "U.S. Officials Chase Counterfeit Goods Online," *The Wall Street Journal,* November 28, 2014, http://www.wsj.com/articles/u-s-officials-chase-counterfeit-goods-online-1417217763 (accessed April 18, 2016).

88. Max Chafkin, "The Case, and the Plan, for the Virtual Company," *Inc.,* April 2010, p. 68.

89. Anthony Balderrama, "Social Media at Work—Bane or Boon?" *CNN,* March 8, 2010, www.cnn.com/2010/LIVING/worklife/03/08/cb.social.media.banned/index.html (accessed April 25, 2016); Emily Glazer, "P&G Curbs Employees Internet Use," *The Wall Street Journal,* April 4, 2012, http://online.wsj.com/article/SB10001424052702304072004577324142847006340.html (accessed April 25, 2016); Ethics Resource Center, *2011 National Business Ethics Survey®: Ethics in Transition* (Arlington, VA: Ethics Resource Center, 2012); Miral Fahmy, "Facebook, YouTube at Work Make Better Employees: Study," *San Francisco Chronicle,* April 2, 2009, www.sanfranciscosentinel.com/?p=21639 (accessed April 25, 2016); Sharon Gaudin, "Study: Facebook Use Cuts Productivity at Work," *Computer World,* July 22, 2009, www.computerworld.com/s/article/9135795/

Study_Facebook_use_cuts_productivity_at_work (accessed April 25, 2016); Sharon Gaudin, "Study: 54% of Companies Ban Facebook, Twitter at Work," *Computer World,* October 6, 2009, www.computerworld.com/s/article/9139020/Study_54_of_companies_ban_Facebook_Twitter_at_work (accessed April 25, 2016); Guy Alvarez, Brian Dalton, Joe Lamport, and Kristina Tsamis, "The Social Law Firm," *Above the Law,* http://good2bsocial.com/wp-content/uploads/2013/12/THE-SOCIAL-LAW-FIRM.pdf (accessed June 18, 2014); Cheryl Conner, "Wasting Time at Work: The Epidemic Continues," *Forbes,* July 31, 2015, http://www.forbes.com/sites/cherylsnappconner/2015/07/31/wasting-time-at-work-the-epidemic-continues/#72369bf83ac1 (accessed April 25, 2016); Barbara Siegel, "Social Media in the Workplace: Does It Impact Productivity?" *Lake Forest Graduate School of Management,* March 28, 2014, http://www.lakeforestmba.edu/blog/social-media-workplace-impact-productivity/ (accessed April 25, 2016).

PART 6

Financing the Enterprise

14 Accounting and Financial Statements

Learning Objectives

After reading this chapter, you will be able to:

LO 14-1 Define *accounting* and describe the different uses of accounting information.

LO 14-2 Demonstrate the accounting process.

LO 14-3 Examine the various components of an income statement in order to evaluate a firm's "bottom line."

LO 14-4 Interpret a company's balance sheet to determine its current financial position.

LO 14-5 Analyze financial statements, using ratio analysis, to evaluate a company's performance.

LO 14-6 Assess a company's financial position using its accounting statements and ratio analysis.

Enter the World of Business ⊖————

Accounting for Fraud

Expense fraud is a common type of fraud in organizations. According to the Association of Certified Fraud Examiners, 13.8 percent of fraud schemes involve expenses. About 27 percent of expense reimbursement fraud comes from employees who hold upper management positions. This lavish spending by top officials sets a tone at the top in which excessive spending and expense account padding is an acceptable practice.

Expense fraud reduces cash flow for an organization and is a misuse of company funds. It usually involves bogus expenses via company accounts and reimbursements for transactions that were not company-related business. For instance, employees might charge items they intend to use for personal use onto a company account. It is often easier for employees to rationalize expense accounting, especially if management is too free with spending. This can have a ripple effect on how the rest of employees treat expenses. For instance, in one organization, a manager who exaggerated his expense reports set the tone that such conduct was acceptable. Employees, therefore, assumed it was accepted practice to cheat on their expenses. The firm ended up suffering a $150,000 fraud scandal.

However, there are also many ways organizations can guard against expense fraud. Having clear policies regarding expense fraud and the consequences for violating these policies are important to show the company takes proper expense reporting seriously. Random auditing is another option, especially because it is difficult for large firms to examine every expense report for accuracy. Perhaps the biggest deterrent is for the company to remain vigilant. Much expense fraud occurs when supervisors do not adequately examine expense documents to ensure they have been filled out accurately.[1]

Introduction

Accounting, the financial "language" that organizations use to record, measure, and interpret all of their financial transactions and records, is very important in business. All businesses—from a small family farm to a giant corporation—use the language of accounting to make sure they use their money wisely and to plan for the future. Nonbusiness organizations such as charities and governments also use accounting to demonstrate to donors and taxpayers how well they are using their funds and meeting their stated objectives.

This chapter explores the role of accounting in business and its importance in making business decisions. First, we discuss the uses of accounting information and the accounting process. Then, we briefly look at some simple financial statements and accounting tools that are useful in analyzing organizations worldwide.

The Nature of Accounting

LO 14-1

Define *accounting* and describe the different uses of accounting information.

accounting
the recording, measurement, and interpretation of financial information.

Simply stated, **accounting** is the recording, measurement, and interpretation of financial information. Large numbers of people and institutions, both within and outside businesses, use accounting tools to evaluate organizational operations. The Financial Accounting Standards Board has been setting the principles and standards of financial accounting and reporting in the private sector since 1973. Its mission is to establish and improve standards of financial accounting and reporting for the guidance and education of the public, including issuers, auditors, and users of financial information. However, accounting scandals at the turn of the last century resulted when many accounting firms and businesses failed to abide by generally accepted accounting principles, or GAAP. Consequently, the federal government has taken a greater role in making rules, requirements, and policies for accounting firms and businesses through the Securities and Exchange Commission's (SEC) Public Company Accounting Oversight Board (PCAOB). For example, the PCAOB filed a disciplinary order against David A. Aronson, CPA, and his firm for repeatedly violating auditor independence, including releasing auditing reports for a company in which his son was in an accounting role. The firm also failed to get engagement quality reviews for several of its audits. This behavior violated independence requirements and was so serious that the PCAOB has forbidden Aronson from associating with registered public accounting firms in the future.[2]

To better understand the importance of accounting, we must first understand who prepares accounting information and how it is used.

Accountants

Many of the functions of accounting are carried out by public or private accountants.

certified public accountant (CPA)
an individual who has been state certified to provide accounting services ranging from the preparation of financial records and the filing of tax returns to complex audits of corporate financial records.

Public Accountants. Individuals and businesses can hire a **certified public accountant (CPA),** an individual who has been certified by the state in which he or she practices to provide accounting services ranging from the preparation of financial records and the filing of tax returns to complex audits of corporate financial records. Certification gives a public accountant the right to express, officially, an unbiased opinion regarding the accuracy of the client's financial statements. Most public accountants are either self-employed or members of large public accounting firms such as Ernst & Young, KPMG, Deloitte, and PricewaterhouseCoopers, together referred to as "the Big Four." In addition, many CPAs work for one of the second-tier accounting firms that are much smaller than the Big Four. Table 14-1 shows the revenues of the top 10 firms. VAULT.com uses a weighted ranking system based on survey results to create a score that represents work-life quality issues to reflect the prestige of the firm.

TABLE 14-1
Prestige Rankings of
Accounting Firms

Rank	Company	Revenues* (in millions)	Score	Location
1	PricewaterhouseCoopers LLP	$ 12,200.00	8.562	New York, NY
2	Deloitte LLP	$ 16,147.00	8.251	New York, NY
3	Ernst & Young	$ 11,190.00	8.250	New York, NY
4	Grant Thornton LLP	$ 1,555.56	7.939	Chicago, IL
5	KPMG LLP	$ 7,889.00	7.935	New York, NY
6	BDO USA LLP	$ 1,050.00	7.129	Chicago, IL
7	Plante Moran	$ 465.86	7.027	Southfield, MI
8	RSM US LLP	$ 1,636.87	6.751	Chicago, IL
9	Baker Tilly Virchow Krause LLP	$ 478.00	6.744	Chicago, IL
10	Dixon Hughes Goodman LLP	$ 371.00	6.712	Charlotte, NC

*Revenues taken from Accounting Today, "The 2014 Accounting Today Top 100 Firms," March 2014, Supplement P, 15-18.

Source: Accounting Today, "The 2016 Top 100 Firms and Regional Leaders," http://editiondigital.net/
publication/?i=292407#{"issue_id":292407,"page":18} (accessed April 19, 2016); Vault.com, "Vault Accounting 50," http://www.
vault.com/company-rankings/accounting/vault-accounting-50/ (accessed April 20, 2016).

While there will always be companies and individual money managers who can successfully hide illegal or misleading accounting practices for a while, eventually they are exposed. After the accounting scandals of Enron and Worldcom in the early 2000s, Congress passed the Sarbanes-Oxley Act, which required firms to be more rigorous in their accounting and reporting practices. Sarbanes-Oxley made accounting firms separate their consulting and auditing businesses and punished corporate executives with potential jail sentences for inaccurate, misleading, or illegal accounting statements. This seemed to reduce the accounting errors among nonfinancial companies, but declining housing prices exposed some of the questionable practices by banks and mortgage companies. Only five years after the passage of the Sarbanes-Oxley Act, the world experienced a financial crisis starting in 2008—part of which was due to excessive risk taking and inappropriate accounting practices. Many banks failed to understand the true state of their financial health. Banks also developed questionable lending practices and investments based on subprime mortgages made to individuals who had poor credit. When housing prices declined and people suddenly found that they owed more on their mortgages than their homes were worth, they began to default. To prevent a depression, the government intervened and bailed out some of the United States' largest banks. Congress passed the Dodd-Frank Act in 2010 to strengthen the oversight of financial institutions. This act gave the Federal Reserve Board the task of implementing the legislation. This legislation limits the types of assets commercial banks can buy; the amount of capital they must maintain; and the use of derivative instruments such as options, futures, and structured investment products.

A growing area for public accountants is *forensic accounting*, which is accounting that is fit for legal review. It involves analyzing financial documents in search of fraudulent entries or financial misconduct. Functioning

DID YOU KNOW? Corporate fraud costs are estimated at $3.7 trillion annually.[3]

KPMG is a part of the "Big Four," or the four largest international accounting firms. The other three are PricewaterhouseCoopers, Ernst & Young, and Deloitte Touche Tohmatsu.

© JPstock/Shutterstock

private accountants accountants employed by large corporations, government agencies, and other organizations to prepare and analyze their financial statements.

certified management accountants (CMAs) private accountants who, after rigorous examination, are certified by the National Association of Accountants and who have some managerial responsibility.

as much like detectives as accountants, forensic accountants have been used since the 1930s. In the wake of the accounting scandals of the early 2000s, many auditing firms are rapidly adding or expanding forensic or fraud-detection services. Additionally, many forensic accountants root out evidence of "cooked books" for federal agencies like the Federal Bureau of Investigation or the Internal Revenue Service. The Association of Certified Fraud Examiners, which certifies accounting professionals as *certified fraud examiners (CFEs),* has grown to more than 75,000 members.[4]

Private Accountants.   Large corporations, government agencies, and other organizations may employ their own **private accountants** to prepare and analyze their financial statements. With titles such as controller, tax accountant, or internal auditor, private accountants are deeply involved in many of the most important financial decisions of the organizations for which they work. Private accountants can be CPAs and may become **certified management accountants (CMAs)** by passing a rigorous examination by the Institute of Management Accountants.

Accounting or Bookkeeping?

The terms *accounting* and *bookkeeping* are often mistakenly used interchangeably. Much narrower and far more mechanical than accounting, bookkeeping is typically limited to the routine, day-to-day recording of business transactions. Bookkeepers are responsible for obtaining and recording the information that accountants require to analyze a firm's financial position. They generally require less training than accountants. Accountants, on the other hand, usually complete course work beyond their basic four- or five-year college accounting degrees. This additional training allows accountants not only to record financial information, but to understand, interpret, and even develop the sophisticated accounting systems necessary to classify and analyze complex financial information.

The Uses of Accounting Information

Accountants summarize the information from a firm's business transactions in various financial statements (which we'll look at in a later section of this chapter) for a variety of stakeholders, including managers, investors, creditors, and government agencies. Many business failures may be directly linked to ignorance of the information "hidden" inside these financial statements. Likewise, most business successes can be traced to informed managers who understand the consequences of their decisions. While maintaining and even increasing short-run profits is desirable, the failure to plan sufficiently for the future can easily lead an otherwise successful company to insolvency and bankruptcy court.

Basically, managers and owners use financial statements (1) to aid in internal planning and control and (2) for external purposes such as reporting to the Internal Revenue Service, stockholders, creditors, customers, employees, and other interested parties. Figure 14-1 shows some of the users of the accounting information generated by organizations and other stakeholders.

Internal Uses.   Managerial accounting refers to the internal use of accounting statements by managers in planning and directing the organization's activities. Perhaps management's greatest single concern is cash flow, the movement of money through an organization over a daily, weekly, monthly, or yearly basis. Obviously, for any business to succeed, it needs to generate enough cash to pay its bills as they fall due. However, it is not at all unusual for highly successful and rapidly growing companies to struggle to make payments to employees, suppliers, and lenders because of an inadequate cash flow. One common reason for a so-called cash crunch, or shortfall, is poor managerial planning.

Managerial accountants also help prepare an organization's budget, an internal financial plan that forecasts expenses and income over a set period of time. It is not unusual for an organization to prepare separate daily, weekly, monthly, and yearly budgets. Think of a budget as a financial map, showing how the company expects to move from Point A to Point B over a specific period of time. While most companies prepare *master budgets* for the entire firm, many also prepare budgets for smaller segments of the organization such as divisions, departments, product lines, or projects. "Top-down" master budgets begin at the upper management level and filter down to the individual department level, while "bottom-up" budgets start at the department or project level and are combined at the chief executive's office. Generally, the larger and more rapidly growing an organization, the greater will be the likelihood that it will build its master budget from the ground up.

Regardless of focus, the principal value of a budget lies in its breakdown of cash inflows and outflows. Expected operating expenses (cash outflows such as wages, materials costs, and taxes) and operating revenues (cash inflows in the form of payments from customers) over a set period of time are carefully forecast and subsequently compared with actual results. Deviations between the two serve as a "trip wire" or "feedback loop" to launch more detailed financial analyses in an effort to pinpoint trouble spots and opportunities.

External Uses.   Managers also use accounting statements to report the business's financial performance to outsiders. Such statements are used for filing income taxes, obtaining credit from lenders, and reporting results to the firm's stockholders. They become the basis for the information provided in the official corporate annual report,

managerial accounting
the internal use of accounting statements by managers in planning and directing the organization's activities.

cash flow
the movement of money through an organization over a daily, weekly, monthly, or yearly basis.

budget
an internal financial plan that forecasts expenses and income over a set period of time.

annual report
summary of a firm's financial information, products, and growth plans for owners and potential investors.

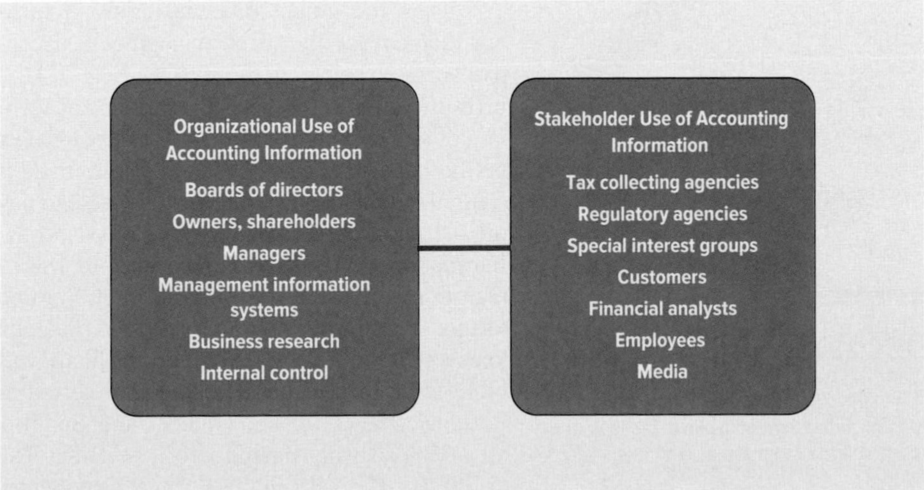

FIGURE 14-1
The Users of Accounting Information

Source: Adapted from *Principles of Accounting*, 4th edition. Houghton Mifflin Company, 1990. Authors: Belverd E. Needles, Henry R. Anderson, and James C. Caldwell.

Organizational Use of Accounting Information

Boards of directors
Owners, shareholders
Managers
Management information systems
Business research
Internal control

Stakeholder Use of Accounting Information

Tax collecting agencies
Regulatory agencies
Special interest groups
Customers
Financial analysts
Employees
Media

Environmental Costs Hit the Balance Sheet

ExxonMobil seems like an unlikely corporation to take a large step toward increasing environmental reporting. However, the energy giant has announced that it will start disclosing the value of its "stranded assets." These assets, including some oil and gas fields, come with a high environmental price and have the potential to be left unused if tougher environmental regulations are passed. While the release of this information may seem contradictory to the company's mission, this is one of the most recent examples in a growing trend toward more open green reporting. According to the CDP—a group that gathers environmental data for shareholders—of all the firms listed on the 31 largest stock exchanges, more than half report environmental data.

Attracting (or appeasing) investors is one of the largest drivers of this trend. However, companies are also seeing the benefits of promoting sustainability. Thanks in part to more extreme weather in recent years, some companies are integrating sustainability into their business strategies. Companies like UPS are also looking for sustainability initiatives that are tied closely to their business objectives to capitalize on core competencies. A research study showed that firms that focused on environmental and sustainability issues typically had higher share prices and earnings. This shift toward more green accountability has implications for the possible development of generally accepted accounting principles for sustainability concerns.[5]

Discussion Questions

1. Should companies include environmental costs, or "stranded assets," into its accounting statements?
2. Why do you think more than half of the firms listed on the 31 largest stock exchanges report environmental data?
3. What might be some advantages to reporting and monitoring environmental costs?

---

a summary of the firm's financial information, products, and growth plans for owners and potential investors. While frequently presented between slick, glossy covers prepared by major advertising firms, the single most important component of an annual report is the signature of a certified public accountant attesting that the required financial statements are an accurate reflection of the underlying financial condition of the firm. Financial statements meeting these conditions are termed *audited*. The primary external users of audited accounting information are government agencies, stockholders and potential investors, and lenders, suppliers, and employees.

During the global financial crisis, it turns out that Greece had been engaging in deceptive accounting practices, with the help of U.S. investment banks. Greece used financial techniques to hide massive amounts of debt from its public balance sheets. Eventually, the markets figured out the country might not be able to pay off its creditors. The European Union and the International Monetary Fund came up with a plan to give Greece some credit relief, but tied to this was the message to "get your financial house in order." The European problem was often referred to as the PIGS. This referred to Portugal, Italy, Ireland, Greece, and Spain— all of which were having debt problems. The PIGS caused cracks in the European Monetary

The annual report is a summary of the firm's financial information, products, and growth plans for owners and potential investors. Many investors look at a firm's annual report to determine how well the company is doing financially.

© King Wu/iStockphoto

Union. While Germany demanded austerity, others wanted more growth-oriented strategies.

To top this off, *The New York Times* reported that many states, such as Illinois and California, have the same problems as the PIGS—debt overload. These states have "budgets that will not balance, accounting that masks debt, the use of derivatives to plug holes, and armies of retired public workers who are counting on pension benefits that are proving harder and harder to pay." Fortunately for California, it was making better progress than Illinois. Clearly, the financial crisis will have some lasting effects that need clear accounting solutions.[6]

Financial statements evaluate the return on stockholders' investments and the overall quality of the firm's management team. As a result, poor performance, as documented in the financial statements, often results in changes in

As one of the biggest banks in the United States, Wells Fargo specializes in banking, mortgage, and financial services. The data it provides can be used in financial statements.

© Rob Wilson/Shutterstock

top management. Potential investors study the financial statements in a firm's annual report to determine whether the company meets their investment requirements and whether the returns from a given firm are likely to compare favorably with other similar companies.

Banks and other lenders look at financial statements to determine a company's ability to meet current and future debt obligations if a loan or credit is granted. To determine this ability, a short-term lender examines a firm's cash flow to assess its ability to repay a loan quickly with cash generated from sales. A long-term lender is more interested in the company's profitability and indebtedness to other lenders.

Labor unions and employees use financial statements to establish reasonable expectations for salary and other benefit requests. Just as firms experiencing record profits are likely to face added pressure to increase employee wages, so too are employees unlikely to grant employers wage and benefit concessions without considerable evidence of financial distress.

The Accounting Process

Many view accounting as a primary business language. It is of little use, however, unless you know how to "speak" it. Fortunately, the fundamentals—the accounting equation and the double-entry bookkeeping system—are not difficult to learn. These two concepts serve as the starting point for all currently accepted accounting principles.

Demonstrate the accounting process.

The Accounting Equation

Accountants are concerned with reporting an organization's assets, liabilities, and owners' equity. To help illustrate these concepts, consider a hypothetical floral shop called Anna's Flowers, owned by Anna Rodriguez. A firm's economic resources, or items of value that it owns, represent its **assets**—cash, inventory, land, equipment, buildings, and other tangible and intangible things. The assets of Anna's Flowers include counters, refrigerated display cases, flowers, decorations, vases, cards, and other gifts, as well as something known as "goodwill," which in this case is Anna's reputation for preparing

assets
a firm's economic resources, or items of value that it owns, such as cash, inventory, land, equipment, buildings, and other tangible and intangible things.

The owners' equity portion of this florist's balance sheet includes the money she has put into the firm.

© Ariel Skelley/Getty Images

liabilities
debts that a firm owes to others.

owners' equity
equals assets minus liabilities and reflects historical values.

accounting equation
assets equal liabilities plus owners' equity.

double-entry bookkeeping
a system of recording and classifying business transactions that maintains the balance of the accounting equation.

and delivering beautiful floral arrangements on a timely basis. **Liabilities,** on the other hand, are debts the firm owes to others. Among the liabilities of Anna's Flowers are a loan from the Small Business Administration and money owed to flower suppliers and other creditors for items purchased. The **owners' equity** category contains all of the money that has ever been contributed to the company that never has to be paid back. The funds can come from investors who have given money or assets to the company, or it can come from past profitable operations. In the case of Anna's Flowers, if Anna were to sell off, or liquidate, her business, any money left over after selling all the shop's assets and paying off its liabilities would comprise her owners' equity. The relationship among assets, liabilities, and owners' equity is a fundamental concept in accounting and is known as the **accounting equation:**

$$\text{Assets} = \text{Liabilities} + \text{Owners' equity}$$

Double-Entry Bookkeeping

Double-entry bookkeeping is a system of recording and classifying business transactions in separate accounts in order to maintain the balance of the accounting equation. Returning to Anna's Flowers, suppose Anna buys $325 worth of roses on credit from the Antique Rose Emporium to fill a wedding order. When she records this transaction, she will list the $325 as a liability or a debt to a supplier. At the same time, however, she will also record $325 worth of roses as an asset in an account known as "inventory." Because the assets and liabilities are on different sides of the accounting equation, Anna's accounts increase in total size (by $325) but remain in balance:

$$\text{Assets} = \text{Liabilities} + \text{Owners' equity}$$
$$\$325 = \$325$$

Thus, to keep the accounting equation in balance, each business transaction must be recorded in two separate accounts.

In the final analysis, all business transactions are classified as assets, liabilities, or owners' equity. However, most organizations further break down these three accounts to provide more specific information about a transaction. For example, assets may be broken down into specific categories such as cash, inventory, and equipment, while liabilities may include bank loans, supplier credit, and other debts.

Figure 14-2 shows how Anna used the double-entry bookkeeping system to account for all of the transactions that took place in her first month of business. These transactions include her initial investment of $2,500, the loan from the Small Business Administration, purchases of equipment and inventory, and the purchase of roses on credit. In her first month of business, Anna generated revenues of $2,000 by selling $1,500 worth of inventory. Thus, she deducts, or (in accounting notation that is appropriate for assets) *credits,* $1,500 from inventory and adds, or *debits,* $2,000 to the cash account. The difference between Anna's $2,000 cash inflow and her $1,500 outflow is represented by a credit to owners' equity, because it is money that belongs to her as the owner of the flower shop.

FIGURE 14-2   The Accounting Equation and Double-Entry Bookkeeping for Anna's Flowers

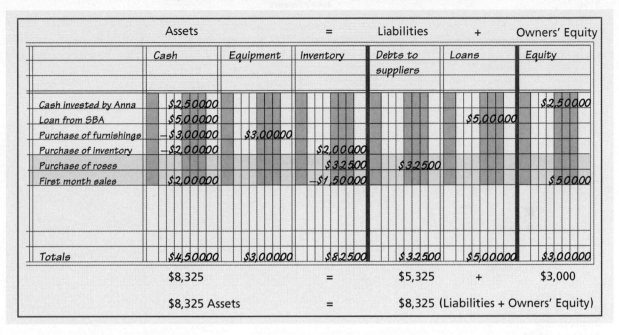

	Assets			=	Liabilities	+	Owners' Equity
	Cash	Equipment	Inventory	Debts to suppliers	Loans		Equity
Cash invested by Anna	$2,500.00						$2,500.00
Loan from SBA	$5,000.00				$5,000.00		
Purchase of furnishings	−$3,000.00	$3,000.00					
Purchase of inventory	−$2,000.00		$2,000.00				
Purchase of roses			$325.00	$325.00			
First month sales	$2,000.00		−$1,500.00				$500.00
Totals	$4,500.00	$3,000.00	$825.00	$325.00	$5,000.00		$3,000.00

$8,325   = $5,325   + $3,000

$8,325 Assets   = $8,325 (Liabilities + Owners' Equity)

The Accounting Cycle

In any accounting system, financial data typically pass through a four-step procedure sometimes called the **accounting cycle.** The steps include examining source documents, recording transactions in an accounting journal, posting recorded transactions, and preparing financial statements. Figure 14-3 shows how Anna works through them. Traditionally, all of these steps were performed using paper, pencils, and erasers (lots of erasers!), but today, the process is often fully computerized.

Step One: Examine Source Documents.   Like all good managers, Anna Rodriguez begins the accounting cycle by gathering and examining source documents—checks, credit card receipts, sales slips, and other related evidence concerning specific transactions.

Step Two: Record Transactions.   Next, Anna records each financial transaction in a **journal,** which is basically just a time-ordered list of account transactions. While most businesses keep a general journal in which all transactions are recorded, some classify transactions into specialized journals for specific types of transaction accounts.

Step Three: Post Transactions.   Anna next transfers the information from her journal into a **ledger,** a book or computer program with separate files for each account. This process is known as *posting.* At the end of the accounting period (usually yearly, but occasionally quarterly or monthly), Anna prepares a *trial balance,* a summary of the balances of all the accounts in the general ledger. If, upon totaling, the trial balance doesn't balance (that is, the accounting equation is not in balance), Anna or her accountant must look for mistakes (typically an error in one or more of the ledger entries) and correct them. If the trial balance is correct, the accountant can then begin to prepare the financial statements.

Step Four: Prepare Financial Statements.   The information from the trial balance is also used to prepare the company's financial statements. In the case of public corporations and certain other organizations, a CPA must *attest,* or certify, that the organization followed generally accepted accounting principles in preparing the financial

accounting cycle
the four-step procedure of an accounting system: examining source documents, recording transactions in an accounting journal, posting recorded transactions, and preparing financial statements.

journal
a time-ordered list of account transactions.

ledger
a book or computer file with separate sections for each account.

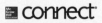

▶ Need help understanding the accounting cycle? Visit your Connect ebook video tab for a brief animated explanation.

FIGURE 14-3   The Accounting Process for Anna's Flowers

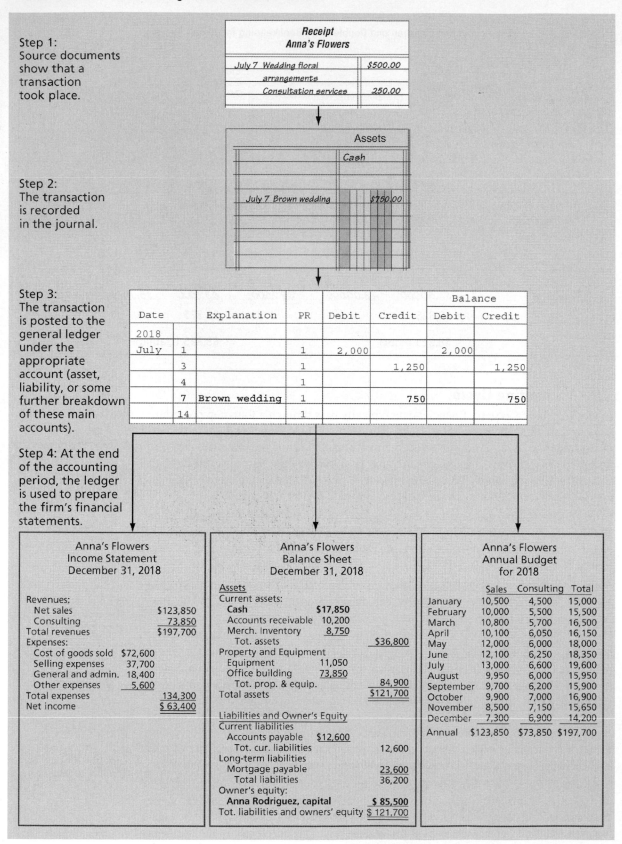

Step 1:
Source documents show that a transaction took place.

Receipt
Anna's Flowers

July 7 Wedding floral	$500.00
arrangements	
Consultation services	250.00

Step 2:
The transaction is recorded in the journal.

Assets

Cash

July 7 Brown wedding $750.00

Step 3:
The transaction is posted to the general ledger under the appropriate account (asset, liability, or some further breakdown of these main accounts).

| | | | | | Balance | |
Date	Explanation	PR	Debit	Credit	Debit	Credit
2018						
July 1		1	2,000		2,000	
3		1		1,250		1,250
4		1				
7	Brown wedding	1		750		750
14		1				

Step 4: At the end of the accounting period, the ledger is used to prepare the firm's financial statements.

Anna's Flowers
Income Statement
December 31, 2018

Revenues:
Net sales		$123,850
Consulting		73,850
Total revenues		$197,700
Expenses:
Cost of goods sold	$72,600	
Selling expenses	37,700	
General and admin.	18,400	
Other expenses	5,600	
Total expenses		134,300
Net income		$ 63,400

Anna's Flowers
Balance Sheet
December 31, 2018

Assets
Current assets:
Cash	**$17,850**	
Accounts receivable	10,200	
Merch. Inventory	8,750	
Tot. assets		$36,800
Property and Equipment
Equipment	11,050	
Office building	73,850	
Tot. prop. & equip.		84,900
Total assets		$121,700

Liabilities and Owner's Equity
Current liabilities
| Accounts payable | $12,600 | |
| Tot. cur. liabilities | | 12,600 |
Long-term liabilities
| Mortgage payable | | 23,600 |
| Total liabilities | | 36,200 |
Owner's equity:
| **Anna Rodriguez, capital** | | **$ 85,500** |
| Tot. liabilities and owners' equity | | $ 121,700 |

Anna's Flowers
Annual Budget
for 2018

	Sales	Consulting	Total
January	10,500	4,500	15,000
February	10,000	5,500	15,500
March	10,800	5,700	16,500
April	10,100	6,050	16,150
May	12,000	6,000	18,000
June	12,100	6,250	18,350
July	13,000	6,600	19,600
August	9,950	6,000	15,950
September	9,700	6,200	15,900
October	9,900	7,000	16,900
November	8,500	7,150	15,650
December	7,300	6,900	14,200
Annual	$123,850	$73,850	$197,700

statements. When these statements have been completed, the organization's books are "closed," and the accounting cycle begins anew for the next accounting period.

Financial Statements

The end result of the accounting process is a series of financial statements. The income statement, the balance sheet, and the statement of cash flows are the best-known examples of financial statements. They are provided to stockholders and potential investors in a firm's annual report as well as to other relevant outsiders such as creditors, government agencies, and the Internal Revenue Service.

It is important to recognize that not all financial statements follow precisely the same format. The fact that different organizations generate income in different ways suggests that when it comes to financial statements, one size definitely does not fit all. Manufacturing firms, service providers, and nonprofit organizations each use a different set of accounting principles or rules upon which the public accounting profession has agreed. As we have already mentioned, these are sometimes referred to as *generally accepted accounting principles (GAAP)*. Each country has a different set of rules that the businesses within that country are required to use for their accounting process and financial statements. However, a number of countries have adopted a standard set of accounting principles known as International Financial Reporting Standards. The United States has discussed adopting these standards to create a more standardized system of reporting for global investors. Moreover, as is the case in many other disciplines, certain concepts have more than one name. For example, *sales* and *revenues* are often interchanged, as are *profits, income,* and *earnings.* Table 14-2 lists a few common equivalent terms that should help you decipher their meaning in accounting statements.

The Income Statement

The question, "What's the bottom line?" derives from the income statement, where the bottom line shows the overall profit or loss of the company after taxes. Thus,

LO 14-3

Examine the various components of an income statement in order to evaluate a firm's "bottom line."

TABLE 14-2
Equivalent Terms in Accounting

Term	Equivalent Term
Revenues	Sales
	Goods or services sold
Gross profit	Gross income
	Gross earnings
Operating income	Operating profit
	Earnings before interest and taxes (EBIT)
	Income before interest and taxes (IBIT)
Income before taxes (IBT)	Earnings before taxes (EBT)
	Profit before taxes (PBT)
Net income (NI)	Earnings after taxes (EAT)
	Profit after taxes (PAT)
Income available to common stockholders	Earnings available to common stockholders

TABLE 14-3   Sample Income Statement

The following exhibit presents a sample income statement with all the terms defined and explained.

Company Name for the Year Ended December 31	
Revenues (sales)	Total dollar amount of products sold (includes income from other business services such as rental-lease income and interest income).
Less: Cost of goods sold	The cost of producing the goods and services, including the cost of labor and raw materials as well as other expenses associated with production.
Gross profit	The income available after paying all expenses of production.
Less: Selling and administrative expense	The cost of promoting, advertising, and selling products as well as the overhead costs of managing the company. This includes the cost of management and corporate staff. One noncash expense included in this category is depreciation, which approximates the decline in the value of plant and equipment assets due to use over time. In most accounting statements, depreciation is not separated from selling and administrative expenses. However, financial analysts usually create statements that include this expense.
Income before interest and taxes (operating income or EBIT)	This line represents all income left over after operating expenses have been deducted. This is sometimes referred to as operating income since it represents all income after the expenses of operations have been accounted for. Occasionally, this is referred to as EBIT, or earnings before interest and taxes.
Less: Interest expense	Interest expense arises as a cost of borrowing money. This is a financial expense rather than an operating expense and is listed separately. As the amount of debt and the cost of debt increase, so will the interest expense. This covers the cost of both short-term and long-term borrowing.
Income before taxes (earnings before taxes—EBT)	The firm will pay a tax on this amount. This is what is left of revenues after subtracting all operating costs, depreciation costs, and interest costs.
Less: Taxes	The tax rate is specified in the federal tax code.
Net income	This is the amount of income left after taxes. The firm may decide to retain all or a portion of the income for reinvestment in new assets. Whatever it decides not to keep it will usually pay out in dividends to its stockholders.
Less: Preferred dividends	If the company has preferred stockholders, they are first in line for dividends. That is one reason why their stock is called "preferred."
Income to common stockholders	This is the income left for the common stockholders. If the company has a good year, there may be a lot of income available for dividends. If the company has a bad year, income could be negative. The common stockholders are the ultimate owners and risk takers. They have the potential for very high or very poor returns since they get whatever is left after all other expenses.
Earnings per share	Earnings per share is found by taking the income available to the common stockholders and dividing by the number of shares of common stock outstanding. This is income generated by the company for each share of common stock.

income statement
a financial report that shows an organization's profitability over a period of time—month, quarter, or year.

the **income statement** is a financial report that shows an organization's profitability over a period of time, be that a month, quarter, or year. By its very design, the income statement offers one of the clearest possible pictures of the company's overall revenues and the costs incurred in generating those revenues. Other names for the income statement include profit and loss (P&L) statement or operating statement. A sample income statement with line-by-line explanations is presented in Table 14-3,

Year Ended June 30	2015	2014	2013
Revenue	$93,580	$86,833	$77,849
Cost of revenue	33,038	27,078	20,385
Gross margin	60,542	59,755	57,464
Operating expenses:			
Research and development	12,046	11,381	10,411
Sales and marketing	15,713	15,811	15,276
General and administrative	4,611	4,677	5,013
Impairment, integration, restructuring	10,011	127	0
Operating income	18,161	27,759	26,764
Other income, net	346	61	288
Income before income taxes	18,507	27,820	27,052
Provision for income taxes	6,314	5,746	5,189
Net income	$ 12,193	$22,074	$ 21,863
Earnings per share:			
Basic	$ 1.49	$ 2.66	$ 2.61
Diluted	$ 1.48	$ 2.63	$ 2.58
Weighted average shares outstanding:			
Basic	8,177	8,299	8,375
Diluted	8,254	8,399	8,470
Cash dividends declared per common share	$ 1.24	$ 1.12	$ 0.92

TABLE 14-4
Microsoft Corporation Consolidated Statement of Earnings (in millions, except share per data)

Source: Microsoft Corporation 2015 Annual Report.

while Table 14-4 presents the income statement of Microsoft. The income statement indicates the firm's profitability or income (the bottom line), which is derived by subtracting the firm's expenses from its revenues.

Revenue.   Revenue is the total amount of money received (or promised) from the sale of goods or services, as well as from other business activities such as the rental of property and investments. Nonbusiness entities typically obtain revenues through donations from individuals and/or grants from governments and private foundations. One of the controversies in accounting has been when a business should recognize revenue. For instance, should an organization book revenue during a project or after the project is completed? Differences in revenue recognition have caused similar organizations to book different accounting results. A proposed rule states that firms should book revenue when "it satisfie[s] a performance obligation by transferring a promised good or service to a customer."[7]

For most manufacturing and retail concerns, the next major item included in the income statement is the **cost of goods sold,** the amount of money the firm spent (or

revenue
the total amount of money received from the sale of goods or services, as well as from related business activities.

cost of goods sold
the amount of money a firm spent to buy or produce the products it sold during the period to which the income statement applies.

promised to spend) to buy and/or produce the products it sold during the accounting period. This figure may be calculated as follows:

Cost of goods sold = Beginning inventory + Interim purchases − Ending inventory

Let's say that Anna's Flowers began an accounting period with an inventory of goods for which it paid $5,000. During the period, Anna bought another $4,000 worth of goods, giving the shop a total inventory available for sale of $9,000. If, at the end of the accounting period, Anna's inventory was worth $5,500, the cost of goods sold during the period would have been $3,500 ($5,000 + $4,000 − $5,500 = $3,500). If Anna had total revenues of $10,000 over the same period of time, subtracting the cost of goods sold ($3,500) from the total revenues of $10,000 yields the store's **gross income** or **profit** (revenues minus the cost of goods sold required to generate the revenues): $6,500. The same process occurs at Microsoft. As indicated in Table 14-4, the cost of goods sold was more than $33 billion in 2015. Notice that Microsoft calls it cost of revenues, rather than cost of goods sold.

Expenses.   Expenses are the costs incurred in the day-to-day operations of an organization. Three common expense accounts shown on income statements are (1) selling, general, and administrative expenses; (2) research, development, and engineering expenses; and (3) interest expenses (remember that the costs directly attributable to selling goods or services are included in the cost of goods sold). Selling expenses include advertising and sales salaries. General and administrative expenses include salaries of executives and their staff and the costs of owning and maintaining the general office. Research and development costs include scientific, engineering, and marketing personnel and the equipment and information used to design and build prototypes and samples. Interest expenses include the direct costs of borrowing money.

The number and type of expense accounts vary from organization to organization. Included in the general and administrative category is a special type of expense known as **depreciation,** the process of spreading the costs of long-lived assets such as buildings and equipment over the total number of accounting periods in which they are expected to be used. Consider a manufacturer that purchases a $100,000 machine expected to last about 10 years. Rather than showing an expense of $100,000 in the first year and no expense for that equipment over the next nine years, the manufacturer is allowed to report depreciation expenses of $10,000 per year in each of the next 10 years because that better matches the cost of the machine to the years the machine is used. Each time this depreciation is "written off" as an expense, the book value of the machine is also reduced by $10,000. The fact that the equipment has a zero value on the firm's balance sheet when it is fully depreciated (in this case, after 10 years) does not necessarily mean that it can no longer be used or is economically worthless. Indeed, in some industries, machines used every day have been reported as having no book value whatsoever for more than 30 years.

Net Income.   Net income (or net earnings) is the total profit (or loss) after all expenses including taxes have been deducted from revenue. Generally, accountants divide profits into individual sections such as operating income and earnings before interest and taxes. Microsoft, for example, lists earnings before income taxes, net earnings, and earnings per share of outstanding stock (see Table 14-4). Like most companies, Microsoft presents not only the current year's results but also the previous two years' income statements to permit comparison of performance from one period to another.

Temporary Nature of the Income Statement Accounts.   Companies record their operational activities in the revenue and expense accounts during an accounting period.

---

gross income (or profit)
revenues minus the cost of goods sold required to generate the revenues.

profit
the difference between what it costs to make and sell a product and what a customer pays for it.

expenses
the costs incurred in the day-to-day operations of an organization.

depreciation
the process of spreading the costs of long-lived assets such as buildings and equipment over the total number of accounting periods in which they are expected to be used.

net income
the total profit (or loss) after all expenses, including taxes, have been deducted from revenue; also called net earnings.

Entrepreneurship in Action

Dauby O'Connor & Zaleski Make Being a CPA Less Taxing

Dauby O'Connor & Zaleski
Founders: Steve Dauby, Sean O'Connor, and Ted Zaleski
Founded: 1987, in Carmel, Indiana
Success: Dauby O'Connor & Zaleski has become well known for promoting employee health, earning it a 2015 Gold Award from the American Heart Association as a Fit-Friendly Workplace.

During tax season, certified public accountants (CPAs) work 12- to 13-hour days. This leaves little time for exercise. However, Indiana-based CPA firm Dauby O'Connor & Zaleski (DOZ) has joined a wellness program to ensure its busy CPAs get the movement they need to stay healthy. The improvement in health and mental alertness can also pay dividends in productivity and accounting.

DOZ has adopted the MOVband wristband so employees can track their physical activity. Employees are also encouraged to adopt the MOVABLE challenge of trying to move five miles each day. Rather than measuring just steps, the wristband

clocks all of the wearer's movements to provide a holistic picture of how much activity the wearer is exerting. The purpose is to keep moving and inspire the CPAs to engage in activities collectively, even during the busiest of times—such as taking group walks during lunch. Those who are able to meet goals are rewarded with prizes. Employees at CPA firm Dauby O'Connor & Zalewski LLC are so motivated that the company has been listed on the Indianapolis Star Top Work Places.[8]

Discussion Questions

1. Why is it important for DOZ to encourage its employees to take steps to stay healthy, especially during tax season?
2. What are some ways DOZ is encouraging employees to improve their fitness while maintaining productivity at their jobs?
3. How might DOZ's program improve its reputation? How might this help in gaining more clients?

Gross profit, earnings before interest and taxes, and net income are the results of calculations made from the revenues and expenses accounts; they are not actual accounts. At the end of each accounting period, the dollar amounts in all the revenue and expense accounts are moved into an account called "Retained Earnings," one of the owners' equity accounts. Revenues increase owners' equity, while expenses decrease it. The resulting change in the owners' equity account is exactly equal to the net income. This shifting of dollar values from the revenue and expense accounts allows the firm to begin the next accounting period with zero balances in those accounts. Zeroing out the balances enables a company to count how much it has sold and how many expenses have been incurred during a period of time. The basic accounting equation (Assets = Liabilities + Owners' equity) will not balance until the revenue and expense account balances have been moved or "closed out" to the owners' equity account.

One final note about income statements: You may remember that corporations may choose to make cash payments called dividends to shareholders out of their net earnings. When a corporation elects to pay dividends, it decreases the cash account (in the assets category of the balance sheet) as well as a capital account (in the owners' equity category of the balance sheet). During any period of time, the owners' equity account may change because of the sale of stock (or contributions/withdrawals by owners), the net income or loss, or the dividends paid.

Walmart is the world's second largest company with revenues of over $481 billion.

© Niloo/Shutterstock

The Balance Sheet

The second basic financial statement is the **balance sheet,** which presents a "snap-shot" of an organization's financial position at a given moment. As such, the balance sheet indicates what the organization owns or controls and the various sources of the funds used to pay for these assets, such as bank debt or owners' equity.

The balance sheet takes its name from its reliance on the accounting equation: Assets *must* equal liabilities plus owners' equity. Table 14-5 provides a sample balance sheet with line-by-line explanations. Unlike the income statement, the balance sheet does not represent the result of transactions completed over a specified accounting period. Instead, the balance sheet is, by definition, an accumulation of all financial transactions conducted by an organization since its founding. Following long-established traditions, items on the balance sheet are listed on the basis of their original cost less accumulated depreciation, rather than their present values.

Balance sheets are often presented in two different formats. The traditional balance sheet format placed the organization's assets on the left side and its liabilities and owners' equity on the right. More recently, a vertical format, with assets on top followed by liabilities and owners' equity, has gained wide acceptance. Microsoft's balance sheet for 2014 and 2015 is presented in Table 14-6. In the sections that follow, we'll briefly describe the basic items found on the balance sheet; we'll take a closer look at a number of these in Chapter 16.

Assets.   All asset accounts are listed in descending order of *liquidity*—that is, how quickly each could be turned into cash. **Current assets,** also called short-term assets, are those that are used or converted into cash within the course of a calendar year. Cash is followed by temporary investments, accounts receivable, and inventory, in that order. **Accounts receivable** refers to money owed the company by its clients or customers who have promised to pay for the products at a later date. Accounts receivable usually includes an allowance for bad debts that management does not expect to collect. The bad-debts adjustment is normally based on historical collections experience and is deducted from the accounts receivable balance to present a more realistic view of the payments likely to be received in the future, called net receivables. Inventory may be held in the form of raw materials, work-in-progress, or finished goods ready for delivery.

Long-term or fixed assets represent a commitment of organizational funds of at least one year. Items classified as fixed include long-term investments, such as plants and equipment, and intangible assets, such as corporate "goodwill," or reputation, as well as patents and trademarks.

Liabilities.   As seen in the accounting equation, total assets must be financed either through borrowing (liabilities) or through owner investments (owners' equity). **Current liabilities** include a firm's financial obligations to short-term creditors, which must be repaid within one year, while long-term liabilities have longer repayment terms. **Accounts payable** represents amounts owed to suppliers for goods and services purchased with credit. For example, if you buy gas with a BP credit card, the purchase represents an account payable for you (and an account receivable for BP). Other liabilities include wages earned by employees but not yet paid and taxes owed to the government. Occasionally, these accounts are consolidated into an **accrued expenses** account, representing all unpaid financial obligations incurred by the organization.

Owners' Equity.   Owners' equity includes the owners' contributions to the organization along with income earned by the organization and retained to finance continued

LO 14-4

Interpret a company's balance sheet to determine its current financial position.

balance sheet
a "snapshot" of an organization's financial position at a given moment.

current assets
assets that are used or converted into cash within the course of a calendar year.

accounts receivable
money owed a company by its clients or customers who have promised to pay for the products at a later date.

current liabilities
a firm's financial obligations to short-term creditors, which must be repaid within one year.

accounts payable
the amount a company owes to suppliers for goods and services purchased with credit.

accrued expenses
all unpaid financial obligations incurred by an organization.

TABLE 14-5   Sample Balance Sheet

The following exhibit presents a balance sheet in word form with each item defined or explained.

Typical Company	December 31
Assets	This is the major category for all physical, monetary, or intangible goods that have some dollar value.
Current assets	Assets that are either cash or are expected to be turned into cash within the next 12 months.
Cash	Cash or checking accounts.
Marketable securities	Short-term investments in securities that can be converted to cash quickly (liquid assets).
Accounts receivable	Cash due from customers in payment for goods received. These arise from sales made on credit.
Inventory	Finished goods ready for sale, goods in the process of being finished, or raw materials used in the production of goods.
Prepaid expense	A future expense item that has already been paid, such as insurance premiums or rent.
Total current assets	The sum of the above accounts.
Fixed assets	Assets that are long term in nature and have a minimum life expectancy that exceeds one year.
Investments	Assets held as investments rather than assets owned for the production process. Most often, the assets include small ownership interests in other companies.
Gross property, plant, and equipment	Land, buildings, and other fixed assets listed at original cost.
Less: Accumulated depreciation	The accumulated expense deductions applied to all plant and equipment over their life. Land may not be depreciated. The total amount represents, in general, the decline in value as equipment gets older and wears out. The maximum amount that can be deducted is set by the U.S. Federal Tax Code and varies by type of asset.
Net property, plant, and equipment	Gross property, plant, and equipment minus the accumulated depreciation. This amount reflects the book value of the fixed assets and not their value if sold.
Other assets	Any other asset that is long term and does not fit into the preceding categories. It could be patents or trademarks.
Total assets	The sum of all the asset values.
Liabilities and stockholders' equity	This is the major category. Liabilities refer to all indebtedness and loans of both a long-term and short-term nature. Stockholders' equity refers to all money that has been contributed to the company over the life of the firm by the owners.
Current liabilities	Short-term debt expected to be paid off within the next 12 months.
Accounts payable	Money owed to suppliers for goods ordered. Firms usually have between 30 and 90 days to pay this account, depending on industry norms.
Wages payable	Money owed to employees for hours worked or salary. If workers receive checks every two weeks, the amount owed should be no more than two weeks' pay.
Taxes payable	Firms are required to pay corporate taxes quarterly. This refers to taxes owed based on earnings estimates for the quarter.

(continued)

TABLE 14-5   Sample Balance Sheet *(continued)*

Typical Company	December 31
Notes payable	Short-term loans from banks or other lenders.
Other current liabilities	The other short-term debts that do not fit into the preceding categories.
Total current liabilities	The sum of the preceding accounts.
Long-term liabilities	All long-term debt that will not be paid off in the next 12 months.
Long-term debt	Loans of more than one year from banks, pension funds, insurance companies, or other lenders. These loans often take the form of bonds, which are securities that may be bought and sold in bond markets.
Deferred income taxes	This is a liability owed to the government but not due within one year.
Other liabilities	Any other long-term debt that does not fit the preceding two categories.
Stockholders' equity	The following three categories are the owners' investment in the company.
Common stock	The tangible evidence of ownership is a security called common stock. The par value is stated value and does not indicate the company's worth.
Capital in excess of par (a.k.a. contributed capital)	When shares of stock were sold to the owners, they were recorded at the price at the time of the original sale. If the price paid was $10 per share, the extra $9 per share would show up in this account at 100,000 shares times $9 per share, or $900,000.
Retained earnings	The total amount of earnings the company has made during its life and not paid out to its stockholders as dividends. This account represents the owners' reinvestment of earnings into company assets rather than payments of cash dividends. This account does not represent cash.
Total stockholders' equity	This is the sum of the preceding equity accounts representing the owner's total investment in the company.
Total liabilities and stockholders' equity	The total short-term and long-term debt of the company plus the owner's total investment. This combined amount *must* equal total assets.

growth and development. If the organization were to sell off all of its assets and pay off all of its liabilities, any remaining funds would belong to the owners. Not surprisingly, the accounts listed as owners' equity on a balance sheet may differ dramatically from company to company. Corporations sell stock to investors, who then become the owners of the firm. Many corporations issue two, three, or even more different classes of common and preferred stock, each with different dividend payments and/or voting rights. Google has three classes of stock, with the class B stock having more voting rights than class A shares. These are sometimes called founder's shares and allow the founders to maintain control over the company even though they do not own the majority of the shares. Ford Motor has the same type of voting structure. Because each type of stock issued represents a different claim on the organization, each must be represented by a separate owners' equity account, called contributed capital.

statement of cash flows
explains how the company's cash changed from the beginning of the accounting period to the end.

The Statement of Cash Flows

The third primary financial statement is called the **statement of cash flows,** which explains how the company's cash changed from the beginning of the accounting

TABLE 14-6   Microsoft Corporation Consolidated Balance Sheets (in millions, except per share data)

June 30	2015	2014
Assets		
Current assets:		
Cash and cash equivalents	$ 5,595	$ 8,669
Short-term investments (including securities loaned of $75 and $541)	90,931	77,040
Total cash, cash equivalents, and short-term investments	96,526	85,709
Accounts receivable, net of allowance for doubtful accounts of $335 and $301	17,908	19,544
Inventories	2,902	2,660
Deferred income taxes	1,915	1,941
Other	5,461	4,392
Total current assets	124,712	114,246
Property and equipment, net of accumulated depreciation of $17,606 and $14,793	14,731	13,011
Equity and other investments	12,053	14,597
Goodwill	16,939	20,127
Intangible assets, net	4,835	6,981
Other long-term assets	2,953	3,422
Total assets	$176,223	$ 172,384
Liabilities and Stockholders' Equity		
Current liabilities:		
Accounts payable	$ 6,591	$ 7,432
Short-term debt	4,985	2,000
Current portion of long-term debt	2,499	0
Accrued compensation	5,096	4,797
Income taxes	606	782
Short-term unearned revenue	23,223	23,150
Securities lending payable	92	558
Other	6,766	6,906
Total current liabilities	49,858	45,625
Long-term debt	27,808	20,645
Long-term unearned revenue	2,095	2,008
Deferred income taxes	2,835	2,728
Other long-term liabilities	13,544	11,594
Total liabilities	96,140	82,600

(continued)

TABLE 14-6 Microsoft Corporation Consolidated Balance Sheets (in millions, except per share data) *(continued)*

June 30	2015	2014
Commitments and contingencies		
Stockholders' equity:		
Common stock and paid-in capital-shares authorized 24,000; outstanding 8,027 and 8,239	68,465	68,366
Retained earnings	9,096	17,710
Accumulated other comprehensive Income	2,522	3,708
Total stockholders' equity	80,083	89,784
Total liabilities and stockholders' equity	$ 176,223	$ 172,384

period to the end. Cash, of course, is an asset shown on the balance sheet, which provides a snapshot of the firm's financial position at one point in time. However, many investors and other users of financial statements want more information about the cash flowing into and out of the firm than is provided on the balance sheet in order to better understand the company's financial health. The statement of cash flows takes the cash balance from one year's balance sheet and compares it with the next while providing detail about how the firm used the cash. Table 14-7 presents Microsoft's statement of cash flows.

The change in cash is explained through details in three categories: cash from (used for) operating activities, cash from (used for) investing activities, and cash from (used for) financing activities. *Cash from operating activities* is calculated by combining the changes in the revenue accounts, expense accounts, current asset accounts, and current liability accounts. This category of cash flows includes all the accounts on the balance sheet that relate to computing revenues and expenses for the accounting period. If this amount is a positive number, as it is for Microsoft, then the business is making extra cash that it can use to invest in increased long-term capacity or to pay off debts such as loans or bonds. A negative number may indicate a business that is in a declining position with regards to operations. Negative cash flow is not always a bad thing, however. Negative cash flow might indicate a company is in the rapid growth phase but not yet making a profit. This is often true of small growth companies in technology and biotech.

Cash from investing activities is calculated from changes in the long-term or fixed asset accounts. If this amount is negative, as is the case with Microsoft, we can see that the company bought $5.9 billion of property and equipment. It also purchased $98.7 billion of investments and sold $70.8 billion of investments for a total negative cash flow of $23 billion. A positive figure usually indicates a business that is selling off existing long-term assets and reducing its capacity for the future.

Finally, *cash from financing activities* is calculated from changes in the long-term liability accounts and the contributed capital accounts in owners' equity. If this amount is negative, the company is likely paying off long-term debt or returning contributed capital to investors. In the case of Microsoft, it sold some debt for an increase in cash of $10.68 billion, but repurchased stock and paid a dividend, which resulted in negative cash flow from financing.

TABLE 14-7   Microsoft Consolidated Statements of Cash Flows (in millions)

Year Ended June 30	2015	2014	2013
Operations			
Net income	$ 12,193	$ 22,074	$ 21,863
Adjustments to reconcile net income to net cash from operations:			
Goodwill impairment	7,498	0	0
Depreciation, amortization, and other	5,957	5,212	3,755
Stock-based compensation expense	2,574	2,446	2,406
Net recognized losses (gains) on investments and derivatives	(443)	(109)	80
Excess tax benefits from stock-based compensation	(588)	(271)	(209)
Deferred income taxes	224	(331`)	(19)
Deferral of unearned revenue	45,072	44,325	44,253
Recognition of unearned revenue	(44,920)	(41,739)	(41,921)
Changes in operating assets and liabilities:			
Accounts receivable	1,456	(1,120)	(1,807)
Inventories	(272)	(161)	(802)
Other current assets	62	(29)	(129)
Other long-term assets	346	(628)	(478)
Accounts payable	(1,054)	473	537
Other current liabilities	(624)	1,075	146
Other long-term liabilities	1,599	1,014	1,158
Net cash from operations	29,080	32,231	28,833
Financing			
Proceeds from issuance of short-term debt repayments, maturities of 90 days or less, net	4,481	500	0
Proceeds from issuance of debt	10,680	10,350	4,883
Repayments of debt	(1,500)	(3,888)	(1,346)
Common stock issued	634	607	931
Common stock repurchased	(14,443)	(7,316)	(5,360)
Common stock cash dividends paid	(9,882)	(8,879)	(7,455)
Excess tax benefits from stock-based compensation	588	271	209
Other	362	(39)	(10)
Net cash used in financing	(9,080)	(8,394)	(8,148)

(continued)

TABLE 14-7   Microsoft Consolidated Statements of Cash Flows (in millions)

Year Ended June 30	2015	2014	2013
Investing			
Additions to property and equipment	(5,944)	(5,485)	(4,257)
Acquisition of companies, net of cash acquired, and purchases of intangible and other assets	(3,723)	(5,937)	(1,584)
Purchases of investments	(98,729)	(72,690)	(75,396)
Maturities of investments	15,013	5,272	5,130
Sales of investments	70,848	60,094	52,464
Securities lending payable	(466)	(87)	(168)
Net cash used in investing	(23,001)	(18,833)	(23,811)
Effect of exchange rates on cash and cash equivalents	(73)	(139)	(8)
Net change in cash and cash equivalents	(3,074)	4,865	(3,134)
Cash and cash equivalents, beginning of period	8,669	3,804	6,938
Cash and cash equivalents, end of period	$ 5,595	$ 8,669	$ 3,804

LO 14-5

Analyze financial statements, using ratio analysis, to evaluate a company's performance.

ratio analysis
calculations that measure an organization's financial health.

Ratio Analysis: Analyzing Financial Statements

The income statement shows a company's profit or loss, while the balance sheet itemizes the value of its assets, liabilities, and owners' equity. Together, the two statements provide the means to answer two critical questions: (1) How much did the firm make or lose? and (2) How much is the firm presently worth based on historical values found on the balance sheet? **Ratio analysis,** calculations that measure an organization's financial health, brings the complex information from the income statement and balance sheet into sharper focus so that managers, lenders, owners, and other interested parties can measure and compare the organization's productivity, profitability, and financing mix with other similar entities.

As you know, a ratio is simply one number divided by another, with the result showing the relationship between the two numbers. For example, we measure fuel efficiency with miles per gallon. This is how we know that 55 mpg in a Toyota Prius is much better than the average car. Financial ratios are used to weigh and evaluate a firm's performance. An absolute value such as earnings of $70,000 or accounts receivable of $200,000 almost never provides as much useful information as a well-constructed ratio. Whether those numbers are good or bad depends on their relation to other numbers. If a company earned $70,000 on $700,000 in sales (a 10 percent return), such an earnings level might be quite satisfactory. The president of a company earning this same $70,000 on sales of $7 million (a 1 percent return), however, should probably start looking for another job!

Ratios by themselves are not very useful. It is the relationship of the calculated ratios to both prior organizational performance and the performance of the organization's "peers," as well as its stated goals, that really matters. Remember, while the profitability, asset utilization, liquidity, debt ratios, and per share data we'll look at here can be very useful, you will never see the forest by looking only at the trees.

Profitability Ratios

Profitability ratios measure how much operating income or net income an organization is able to generate relative to its assets, owners' equity, and sales. The numerator (top number) used in these examples is always the net income after taxes. Common profitability ratios include profit margin, return on assets, and return on equity. The following examples are based on the 2015 income statement and balance sheet for Microsoft, as shown in Table 14-4 and Table 14-6. Except where specified, all data are expressed in millions of dollars.

profitability ratios ratios that measure the amount of operating income or net income an organization is able to generate relative to its assets, owners' equity, and sales.

Microsoft's 2015 profit was decreased by $10 billion in accounting charges. A $7.5 billion charge was taken to write down goodwill related to phone hardware, and a $2.5 billion charge was taken for organizational restructuring. These changes decreased earnings per share by $1.15 and significantly reduced the profitability ratios from 2014. Profitability is expected to increase in 2016.

The **profit margin,** computed by dividing net income by sales, shows the overall percentage of profits earned by the company. It is based solely upon data obtained from the income statement. The higher the profit margin, the better the cost controls within the company and the higher the return on every dollar of revenue. Microsoft's profit margin is calculated as follows:

profit margin net income divided by sales.

$$\text{Profit margin} = \frac{\text{Net income (Net earnings)}}{\text{Sales (Total net revenues)}} = \frac{\$12,193}{\$93,580} = 13.03\%$$

Thus, for every $1 in sales, Microsoft generated profits after taxes of 13 cents.

Return on assets, net income divided by assets, shows how much income the firm produces for every dollar invested in assets. A company with a low return on assets is probably not using its assets very productively—a key managerial failing. For its construction, the return on assets calculation requires data from both the income statement and the balance sheet.

return on assets net income divided by assets.

$$
\begin{aligned}
\text{Return on assets} &= \frac{\text{Net income (Net earnings)}}{\text{Total assets}} \\
&= \frac{\$12,193}{\$176,223} \\
&= 6.92\%
\end{aligned}
$$

In the case of Microsoft, every $1 of assets generated a return of close to 7 percent, or profits of 6.92 cents per dollar.

Stockholders are always concerned with how much money they will make on their investment, and they frequently use the return on equity ratio as one of their key performance yardsticks. **Return on equity** (also called return on investment [ROI]), calculated by dividing net income by owners' equity, shows how much income is generated by each $1 the owners have invested in the firm. Obviously, a low return on equity means low stockholder returns and may indicate a need for immediate managerial attention. Because some assets may have been financed with debt not contributed by the owners, the value of the owners' equity is usually considerably lower than the total value of the firm's assets. Microsoft's return on equity is calculated as follows:

return on equity net income divided by owners' equity; also called return on investment (ROI).

$$\text{Return on equity} = \frac{\text{Net income}}{\text{Stockholders' equity}} = \frac{\$12,193}{\$80,083} = 15.23\%$$

For every dollar invested by Microsoft stockholders, the company earned a 15.23 percent return, or 15.23 cents per dollar invested.

Consider Ethics and Social Responsibility

Preserving Auditor Independence

Conflict of interest is a major risk area for auditors of accounting statements because they must remain unbiased to ensure the accuracy of reports. To preserve the independence of auditors, the Sarbanes-Oxley Act mandates that it is illegal for a registered public accounting firm to perform auditing services if a high-ranking executive if the client was employed by that accounting firm and was involved in the company's audit within the past year. In other words, if an auditor takes a high-level position with a client and has worked on auditing the company within the past year, the accounting firm must resign as auditor of that client.

This rule has not stopped companies from hiring their former auditors into executive positions. Lumber Liquidators Inc. hired a former auditor who worked on its books in the past as its interim finance chief. Previously, the auditor had worked for Lumber Liquidator's accounting firm Ernst & Young (E&Y). However, it had been 18 months since he worked on

the audit report—enough time to comply with the I-year rule. E&Y does not legally have to resign from offering audit services to Lumber Liquidators. However, is one year enough time to ensure complete objectivity? Might auditors be biased toward client companies if they believe they will get hired by these companies in the future?[9]

Discussion Questions

1. Why do you think companies like Lumber Liquidators would be interested in hiring former auditors into high-level financial positions in their firms?
2. How might an auditor's audit services be compromised if he or she predicts future employment opportunities at client firms?
3. Should Ernst & Young resign from offering auditing services to Lumber Liquidators?

Asset Utilization Ratios

asset utilization ratios
ratios that measure how well a firm uses its assets to generate each $1 of sales.

Asset utilization ratios measure how well a firm uses its assets to generate each $1 of sales. Obviously, companies using their assets more productively will have higher returns on assets than their less efficient competitors. Similarly, managers can use asset utilization ratios to pinpoint areas of inefficiency in their operations. These ratios (receivables turnover, inventory turnover, and total asset turnover) relate balance sheet assets to sales, which are found on the income statement.

receivables turnover
sales divided by accounts receivable.

The **receivables turnover,** sales divided by accounts receivable, indicates how many times a firm collects its accounts receivable in one year. It also demonstrates how quickly a firm is able to collect payments on its credit sales. Obviously, no payments means no profits. Microsoft collected its receivables 5.23 times per year, which translates to about 69 days that receivables are outstanding. This is most likely due to the trade terms it gives its corporate customers.

$$\text{Receivables turnover} = \frac{\text{Sales (Total net revenues)}}{\text{Receivables}}$$
$$= \frac{\$93,580}{\$17,908}$$
$$= 5.23 \times$$

inventory turnover
sales divided by total inventory.

Inventory turnover, sales divided by total inventory, indicates how many times a firm sells and replaces its inventory over the course of a year. A high inventory turnover ratio may indicate great efficiency but may also suggest the possibility of lost sales due to insufficient stock levels. Microsoft's inventory turnover indicates that it replaced its inventory 32.25 times last year, or about every 11 days. This high inventory turnover is a reflection that Microsoft has very little physical inventory and instead downloads its Windows programs over the Internet.

$$\text{Inventory turnover} = \frac{\text{Sales (Total net revenues)}}{\text{Inventory}}$$

$$= \frac{\$93,580}{\$2,902}$$

$$= 32.25 \times$$

Total asset turnover, sales divided by total assets, measures how well an organization uses all of its assets in creating sales. It indicates whether a company is using its assets productively. Microsoft generated $0.53 in sales for every $1 in total corporate assets. The cause of this low total asset turnover is the $96.5 billion of cash that Microsoft has on its balance sheet. Cash does not produce sales dollars.

total asset turnover
sales divided by total assets.

$$\text{Total asset turnover} = \frac{\text{Sales (Total net revenues)}}{\text{Total assets}}$$

$$= \frac{\$93,580}{\$176,223}$$

$$= 0.53 \times$$

Liquidity Ratios

Liquidity ratios compare current (short-term) assets to current liabilities to indicate the speed with which a company can turn its assets into cash to meet debts as they fall due. High liquidity ratios may satisfy a creditor's need for safety, but ratios that are too high may indicate that the organization is not using its current assets efficiently. Liquidity ratios are generally best examined in conjunction with asset utilization ratios because high turnover ratios imply that cash is flowing through an organization very quickly—a situation that dramatically reduces the need for the type of reserves measured by liquidity ratios.

liquidity ratios
ratios that measure the speed with which a company can turn its assets into cash to meet short-term debt.

The **current ratio** is calculated by dividing current assets by current liabilities. Microsoft's current ratio indicates that for every $1 of current liabilities, the firm had $2.5 of current assets on hand. The relatively high current ratio is also due to the $96.5 billion of cash, cash equivalents, and short-term investments on hand, which is part of the current asset total. If we take cash out of current assets, the numerator drops to $28,212, and the current ratio drops to 0.57.

current ratio
current assets divided by current liabilities.

$$\text{Current ratio} = \frac{\text{Current assets}}{\text{Current liabilities}}$$

$$= \frac{\$124,712}{\$49,858}$$

$$= 2.5 \times$$

The **quick ratio** (also known as the **acid test**) is a far more stringent measure of liquidity because it eliminates inventory, the least liquid current asset. It measures how well an organization can meet its current obligations without resorting to the sale of its inventory. Because Microsoft has so little inventory ($2.9 billion out of $124.7 billion of current assets), the quick ratio is almost exactly the same as the current ratio.

quick ratio (acid test)
a stringent measure of liquidity that eliminates inventory.

$$\text{Quick ratio} = \frac{\text{Current assets} - \text{Inventory}}{\text{Current liabilities}}$$

$$= \frac{\$121,810}{\$49,858}$$

$$= 2.44 \times$$

Debt Utilization Ratios

debt utilization ratios
ratios that measure how much debt an organization is using relative to other sources of capital, such as owners' equity.

Debt utilization ratios provide information about how much debt an organization is using relative to other sources of capital, such as owners' equity. Because the use of debt carries an interest charge that must be paid regularly regardless of profitability, debt financing is much riskier than equity. Unforeseen negative events such as recessions affect heavily indebted firms to a far greater extent than those financed exclusively with owners' equity. Because of this and other factors, the managers of most firms tend to keep debt-to-asset levels below 50 percent. However, firms in very stable and/or regulated industries, such as electric utilities, often are able to carry debt ratios well in excess of 50 percent with no ill effects.

debt to total assets ratio
a ratio indicating how much of the firm is financed by debt and how much by owners' equity.

The **debt to total assets ratio** indicates how much of the firm is financed by debt and how much by owners' equity. To find the value of Microsoft's total debt, you must add current liabilities to long-term debt and other liabilities.

$$\text{Debt to total assets} = \frac{\text{Debt (Total liabilities)}}{\text{Total assets}}$$
$$= \frac{\$96,140}{\$176,223}$$
$$= 55\%$$

Thus, for every \$1 of Microsoft's total assets, 55 percent is financed with debt. The remaining 45 percent is provided by owners' equity. Debt to total assets increased from 45 percent to 55 percent from 2013 to 2015 as Microsoft took advantage of low interest rates to sell debt and repurchase common stock.

times interest earned ratio
operating income divided by interest expense.

The **times interest earned ratio,** operating income divided by interest expense, is a measure of the safety margin a company has with respect to the interest payments it must make to its creditors. A low times interest earned ratio indicates that even a small decrease in earnings may lead the company into financial straits. Microsoft had so little interest expense that it did not list it as a separate item on the income statement. In this case, the analyst has to go searching through the footnotes to the financial statements. We find that interest expense was \$781 million. Putting this into the calculation, we find that interest expense is covered 23.25 times by operating income. A lender would have no worries about receiving interest payments from Microsoft.

$$\text{Times interest earned} = \frac{\text{EBIT}}{\text{Interest}}$$
$$= \frac{\$18,161}{\$781}$$
$$= 23.25 \times$$

Per Share Data

per share data
data used by investors to compare the performance of one company with another on an equal, per share basis.

Investors may use **per share data** to compare the performance of one company with another on an equal, or per share, basis. Generally, the more shares of stock a company issues, the less income is available for each share.

earnings per share
net income or profit divided by the number of stock shares outstanding.

Earnings per share is calculated by dividing net income or profit by the number of shares of stock outstanding. This ratio is important because yearly changes in earnings per share, in combination with other economywide factors, determine a company's overall stock price. When earnings go up, so does a company's stock price—and so does the wealth of its stockholders.

$$\text{Diluted earnings per share} = \frac{\text{Net income}}{\text{Number of shares outstanding (diluted)}}$$

$$= \frac{\$12,193}{8,254} = \$1.48$$

We can see from the income statement that Microsoft's basic earnings per share declined from $2.66 per share to $1.49, and this decline also shows up in diluted earnings per share. This drop in earnings can be attributed to Microsoft's write-off of $10 billion mentioned in the profitability ratios. Without the write off, diluted earnings per share would have been $2.67. You can see from the income statement that diluted earnings per share include more shares than the basic calculation; this is because diluted shares include potential shares that could be issued due to the exercise of stock options or the conversion of certain types of debt into common stock. Investors generally pay more attention to diluted earnings per share than basic earnings per share.

Dividends per share are paid by the corporation to the stockholders for each share owned. The payment is made from earnings after taxes by the corporation but is taxable income to the stockholder. Thus, dividends result in double taxation: The corporation pays tax once on its earnings, and the stockholder pays tax a second time on his or her dividend income. Since 2004, Microsoft has raised its dividend every year, from $0.16 per share to $1.24 per share. A note of clarification on the number of shares outstanding of 8,177 million versus the 7,964 million listed in the denominator. Share count for earnings per share are weighted average shares over the year. The shares on the balance sheet are those outstanding at the year's end and do not necessarily represent the shares on which dividends were actually paid.

dividends per share
the actual cash received for each share owned.

$$\text{Dividends per share} = \frac{\text{Dividends paid}}{\text{Number of shares outstanding}}$$

$$= \frac{\$9,882}{7,964}$$

$$= \$1.24$$

Industry Analysis

We have used Microsoft as a comparison to Alphabet (formerly Google) because they are competitive in many technology areas, including software and the Internet. They both have a lot of intellectual property and cash balances, and they do not produce hardware like Apple does. Alphabet has revenues of $74.9 billion. Many investors view Microsoft as an old technology company and Alphabet as a new technology company with more growth opportunities. In fact, between 2013 and 2015, Microsoft's revenues grew only 20 percent, while Alphabet's revenues grew almost 35 percent. Reflecting this growth is that investors are willing to pay more for one dollar of Alphabet's earnings per share than one dollar of Microsoft's EPS. In fact, as of April 2016, Alphabet had a price to earnings per share ratio

It was only recently that Amazon posted a profit, and the profit margin was not high. However, its efficient operations in distribution has made it a success among customers. It earned $107 billion in revenues.
© SWNS/Alamy

TABLE 14-8
Industry Analysis Year
Ending 2015

	Alphabet	Microsoft
Profit margin	21.10%	13.03%
Return on assets	10.73%	6.92%
Return on equity	13.15%	15.23%
Receivables turnover	6.49×	5.23×
Inventory turnover	n.a.	32.25×
Total asset turnover	0.51×	0.53×
Current ratio	6.46×	2.50×
Quick ratio	6.46×	2.44×
Debt to total assets	18.40%	54.56%
Times interest earned	25.16×	23.25×
Diluted earnings per share	$22.84	$1.48
Dividends per share	$0.00	$1.24

Source: Data calculated from 2015 annual reports.

(PE) of 31.5 times and Microsoft had a PE of 20 times based on adjusted earnings per share of $2.67.

Alphabet dominates Microsoft on two profitability ratios, generating a higher profit margin and return on assets. Both companies have very little accounts receivable or inventory, so they show very high receivables and inventory turnover ratios. However, because they each have large cash balances, their total asset turnover ratios are very low, which is not what you would expect with low receivables and inventory investment. At the end of 2015, Microsoft had $96.5 billion and Alphabet had $73 billion of cash, cash equivalents, and short-term investments on their balance sheets. Because of their high cash balances, both companies show high current and quick ratios and, because of very little inventory, their quick ratios are almost equal to their current ratios.

Microsoft has more debt than Alphabet, which is indicated by the debt to total assets ratio. While Microsoft has more debt than Alphabet, the times interest earned ratio indicates that Microsoft's earnings before interest and taxes cover its interest expense at a slightly lower level than does Alphabet.

Table 14-8 doesn't show earnings per share growth, but it is important in forecasting dividend growth. As you can see from the table, Alphabet does not pay a dividend even though it has cash and its earnings per share grew 21.6 percent between 2013 and 2015. Microsoft pays $1.24 per share even though its earnings per share had negative growth. Despite the negative earnings per share growth, Microsoft raised its dividends 34.8 percent over the same time period. That is easy to do when you have $96.5 billion of cash on hand and dividends only cost $9.8 billion. The moral of the story is that the faster a company grows, the more funds the company retains for future growth or, in the case of both companies, acquisitions of new technology created by smaller companies.

Importance of Integrity in Accounting

The financial crisis and the recession that followed provided another example of a failure in accounting reporting. Many firms attempted to exploit loopholes and manipulate accounting processes and statements. Banks and other financial institutions often held assets off their books by manipulating their accounts. In 2010, the examiner for the Lehman Brothers' bankruptcy found that the most common example of removing assets or liabilities from the books was entering into what is called a "repurchase agreement." In a repurchase agreement, assets are transferred to another entity with the contractual promise of buying them back at a set price. In the case of Lehman Brothers and other companies, repurchase agreements were used as a method of "cooking the books" that

As another member of the "Big Four" accounting firms, Deloitte must maintain high standards of accounting ethics to secure its reputation for integrity.

© Alex Segre/Alamy

allowed them to manipulate accounting statements so that their ratios looked better than they actually were. If the accountants, the SEC, and the bank regulators had been more careful, these types of transactions would have been discovered and corrected.

On the other hand, strong compliance to accounting principles creates trust among stakeholders. Accounting and financial planning is important for all organizational entities, even cities. The City of Maricopa in Arizona received the Government Finance Officers Association of the United States and Canada (GFOA) Distinguished Budget Presentation Award for its governmental budgeting. The city scored proficient in its policy, financial plan, operations guide, and communications device. Integrity in accounting is crucial to creating trust, understanding the financial position of an organization or entity, and making financial decisions that will benefit the organization.[10]

It is most important to remember that integrity in accounting processes requires ethical principles and compliance with both the spirit of the law and professional standards in the accounting profession. Most states require accountants preparing to take the CPA exam to take accounting ethics courses. Transparency and accuracy in reporting revenue, income, and assets develops trust from investors and other stakeholders.

So You Want to Be an Accountant

Do you like numbers and finances? Are you detail oriented, a perfectionist, and highly accountable for your decisions? If so, accounting may be a good field for you. If you are interested in accounting, there are always job opportunities available no matter the state of the economy. Accounting is one of the most secure job options in business. Of course, becoming an accountant is not easy. You will need at least a bachelor's degree in accounting to get a job, and many positions require additional training. Many states demand coursework beyond the 120 to 150 credit hours collegiate programs require for an accounting degree. If you are really serious about getting into the accounting field, you will probably want to consider getting your master's in accounting and taking the CPA exam. The field of accounting can be complicated, and the extra training provided through a master's in accounting program will prove invaluable when you go out looking for a good job. Accounting is a volatile discipline affected by changes in legislative initiatives.

With corporate accounting policies changing constantly and becoming more complex, accountants are needed to help keep a business running smoothly and within the bounds of the law. In fact, the number of jobs in the accounting and auditing field are expected to increase 16 percent between 2010 and 2020, with more than 1.4 million jobs in the United States alone by 2020. Jobs in accounting tend to pay quite well, with the median salary standing at $67,190. If you go on to get your master's degree in accounting, expect to see an even higher starting wage. Of course, your earnings could be higher or lower than these averages, depending on where you work, your level of experience, the firm, and your particular position.

Accountants are needed in the public and the private sectors, in large and small firms, in for-profit and not-for-profit organizations. Accountants in firms are generally in charge of preparing and filing tax forms and financial reports. Public-sector accountants are responsible for checking the veracity of corporate and personal records in order to prepare tax filings. Basically, any organization that has to deal with money and/or taxes in some way or another will be in need of an accountant, either for in-house service or occasional contract work. Requirements for audits under the Sarbanes-Oxley Act and rules from the Public Company Accounting Oversight Board are creating more jobs and increased responsibility to maintain internal controls and accounting ethics. The fact that accounting rules and tax filings tend to be complex virtually ensures that the demand for accountants will never decrease.[11]

Review Your Understanding

Define *accounting* and describe the different uses of accounting information.

Accounting is the language businesses and other organizations use to record, measure, and interpret financial transactions. Financial statements are used internally to judge and control an organization's performance and to plan and direct its future activities and measure goal attainment. External organizations such as lenders, governments, customers, suppliers, and the Internal Revenue Service are major consumers of the information generated by the accounting process.

Demonstrate the accounting process.

Assets are an organization's economic resources; liabilities, debts the organization owes to others; and owners' equity, the difference between the value of an organization's assets and liabilities. This principle can be expressed as the accounting equation: Assets = Liabilities + Owners' equity. The double-entry bookkeeping system is a system of recording and classifying business transactions in accounts that maintain the balance of the accounting equation. The accounting cycle involves examining source documents, recording transactions in a journal, posting transactions, and preparing financial statements on a continuous basis throughout the life of the organization.

Examine the various components of an income statement in order to evaluate a firm's "bottom line."

The income statement indicates a company's profitability over a specific period of time. It shows the "bottom line," the total profit (or loss) after all expenses (the costs incurred in the day-to-day operations of the organization) have been deducted from revenue (the total amount of money received from the sale of goods or services and other business activities). The cash flow statement details how much cash is moving through the firm and thus adds insight to a firm's "bottom line."

Interpret a company's balance sheet to determine its current financial position.

The balance sheet, which summarizes the firm's assets, liabilities, and owners' equity since its inception, portrays its financial position as of a particular point in time. Major classifications included in the balance sheet are current assets (assets that can be converted to cash within one calendar year), fixed assets (assets of greater than one year's duration), current liabilities (bills owed by the organization within one calendar year), long-term liabilities (bills due more than one year hence), and owners' equity (the net value of the owners' investment).

Analyze financial statements, using ratio analysis, to evaluate a company's performance.

Ratio analysis is a series of calculations that brings the complex information from the income statement and balance sheet into sharper focus so that managers, lenders, owners, and other interested parties can measure and compare the organization's productivity, profitability, and financing mix with similar entities. Ratios may be classified in terms of profitability (measure dollars of return for each dollar of employed assets), asset utilization (measure how well the organization uses its assets to generate $1 in sales), liquidity (assess organizational risk by comparing current assets to current liabilities), debt utilization (measure how much debt the organization is using relative to other sources of capital), and per share data (compare the performance of one company with another on an equal basis).

Assess a company's financial position using its accounting statements and ratio analysis.

Based on the information presented in the chapter, you should be able to answer the questions posed in the "Solve the Dilemma" feature at the end of the chapter. Formulate a plan for determining BrainDrain's bottom line, current worth, and productivity.

Revisit the World of Business

1. Why do you think expense fraud is common in businesses?
2. Why might expense accounting fraud be easier to rationalize than other forms of organizational fraud?
3. What are some ways that expense fraud can be controlled or deterred?

Learn the Terms

accounting 432 ✓
accounting cycle 439
accounting equation 438
accounts payable 446
accounts receivable 446
accrued expenses 446
annual report 435 ✓
asset utilization ratios 454
assets 437
balance sheet 446
budget 435
cash flow 435
certified management accountants (CMAs) 434
certified public accountant (CPA) 432 ✓
cost of goods sold 443
current assets 446

current liabilities 446
current ratio 455
debt to total assets ratio 456
debt utilization ratios 456
depreciation 444
dividends per share 457
double-entry bookkeeping 438
earnings per share 456
expenses 444
gross income (or profit) 444
income statement 442 ✓
inventory turnover 454
journal 439
ledger 439
liabilities 438
liquidity ratios 455
managerial accounting 435

net income 444
owners' equity 438
per share data 456
private accountants 434
profit 444 ✓
profit margin 453
profitability ratios 453
quick ratio (acid test) 455
ratio analysis 452
receivables turnover 454
return on assets 453
return on equity 453
revenue 443
statement of cash flows 448
times interest earned ratio 456
total asset turnover 455

Check Your Progress

1. Why are accountants so important to a corporation? What function do they perform?
2. Discuss the internal uses of accounting statements.
3. What is a budget?
4. Discuss the external uses of financial statements.
5. Describe the accounting process and cycle.
6. The income statements of all corporations are in the same format. True or false? Discuss.
7. Which accounts appear under "current liabilities"?
8. Together, the income statement and the balance sheet answer two basic questions. What are they?
9. What are the five basic ratio classifications? What ratios are found in each category?
10. Why are debt ratios important in assessing the risk of a firm?

Get Involved

1. Go to the library or the Internet and get the annual report of a company with which you are familiar. Read through the financial statements, then write up an analysis of the firm's performance using ratio analysis. Look at data over several years and analyze whether the firm's performance is changing through time.

2. Form a group of three or four students to perform an industry analysis. Each student should analyze a company in the same industry, and then all of you should compare your results. The following companies would make good group projects:

Automobiles: Fiat Chrysler, Ford, General Motors

Computers: Apple, Hewlett-Packard

Brewing: MillerCoors, Molson Coors, The Boston Beer Company

Chemicals: DuPont, Dow Chemical, Monsanto

Petroleum: Chevron, ExxonMobil, BP

Pharmaceuticals: Merck, Lilly, Amgen

Retail: Sears, JCPenney, Macy's, The Limited

Build Your Skills

Financial Analysis

Background

The income statement for Western Grain Company, a producer of agricultural products for industrial as well as consumer markets, is shown here. Western Grain's total assets are $4,237.1 million, and its equity is $1,713.4 million.

Consolidated Earnings and Retained Earnings Year Ended December 31

(Millions)	2017
Net sales	$6,295.4
Cost of goods sold	2,989.0
Selling and administrative expense	2,237.5
Operating profit	1,068.9
Interest expense	33.3
Other income (expense), net	(1.5)

Earnings before income taxes	1,034.1
Income taxes	353.4
Net earnings	680.7
(Net earnings per share)	$2.94
Retained earnings, beginning of year	3,033.9
Dividends paid	(305.2)
Retained earnings, end of year	$3,409.4

Task

Calculate the following profitability ratios: profit margin, return on assets, and return on equity. Assume that the industry averages for these ratios are as follows: profit margin, 12 percent; return on assets, 18 percent; and return on equity, 25 percent. Evaluate Western Grain's profitability relative to the industry averages. Why is this information useful?

Solve the Dilemma

Exploring the Secrets of Accounting

You have just been promoted from vice president of marketing of BrainDrain Corporation to president and CEO! That's the good news. Unfortunately, while you know marketing like the back of your hand, you know next to nothing about finance. Worse still, the "word on the street" is that BrainDrain is in danger of failure if steps to correct large and

continuing financial losses are not taken immediately. Accordingly, you have asked the vice president of finance and accounting for a complete set of accounting statements detailing the financial operations of the company over the past several years.

Recovering from the dual shocks of your promotion and feeling the weight of the firm's complete accounting report

LO 14-6

Assess a company's financial position using its accounting statements and ratio analysis.

for the very first time, you decide to attack the problem systematically and learn the "hidden secrets" of the company, statement by statement. With Mary Pruitt, the firm's trusted senior financial analyst, by your side, you delve into the accounting statements as never before. You resolve to "get to the bottom" of the firm's financial problems and set a new course for the future—a course that will take the firm from insolvency and failure to financial recovery and perpetual prosperity.

Discussion Questions

1. Describe the three basic accounting statements. What types of information does each provide that can help you evaluate the situation?
2. Which of the financial ratios are likely to prove to be of greatest value in identifying problem areas in the company? Why? Which of your company's financial ratios might you expect to be especially poor?
3. Discuss the limitations of ratio analysis.

Build Your Business Plan

Accounting and Financial Statements

After you determine your initial *reasonable selling price,* you need to estimate your sales forecasts (in terms of units and dollars of sales) for the first year of operation. Remember to be conservative and set forecasts that are more modest.

While customers may initially try your business, many businesses have seasonal patterns. A good budgeting/planning system allows managers to anticipate problems, coordinate activities of the business (so that subunits within the organization are all working toward the common goal of the organization), and control operations (how we know whether spending is "in line").

The first financial statement you need to prepare is the income statement. Beginning with your estimated sales revenue, determine what expenses will be necessary to generate that level of sales revenue.

The second financial statement you need to create is your balance sheet. Your balance sheet is a snapshot of your financial position in a moment in time. Refer to Table 14-6 to assist you in listing your assets, liabilities, and owner's equity.

The last financial statement, the cash flow statement, is the most important one to a bank. It is a measure of your ability to get and repay the loan from the bank. Referring to Table 14.7, be as realistic as possible as you are completing it. Allow yourself enough cash on hand until the point in which the business starts to support itself.

See for Yourself Videocase

Goodwill Industries: Accounting in a Nonprofit

Goodwill Industries International Inc. consists of a network of 164 independent, community-based organizations located throughout the United States and Canada. The mission of this nonprofit is to enhance the lives of individuals, families, and communities "through learning and the power of work." Local Goodwill stores sell donated goods and then donate the proceeds to fund job training programs, placement services, education, and more. Despite its nonprofit status, Goodwill establishments are in many ways run similar to for-profit businesses. One of these similarities involves the accounting function.

Like for-profit firms, nonprofit organizations like Goodwill must provide detailed information about how they are using the donations that are provided to them. Indeed, fraud can occur just as easily at a nonprofit organization as for a for-profit company, making it necessary for nonprofits to reassure stakeholders that they are using their funds legitimately. Additionally, donors want to know how much of their

donations are going toward activities such as job creation and how much is going toward operational and administrative expenses. It sometimes surprises people that nonprofits use part of the funds they receive for operational costs. Yet such a perspective fails to see that nonprofits must also pay for electricity, rent, wages, and other services.

"We have revenue and support for the revenue pieces, and then we have direct and indirect expenses for our program services, and then we have G and A, general administrative services. And we have what's called the bottom line, or other people call net profit. We have what's called net change in assets. The concept is pretty much the same as far as accounting," says Jeff McCaw, CFO of Goodwill.

Goodwill creates the equivalent of a balance sheet and income statement. Yet because Goodwill is a nonprofit entity, its financials are known by the names *statement of financial position* and *statement of activities.* These financials have some differences compared to financial statements of for-profit companies. For instance, Goodwill's statement of financial position does not have shareholder's equity but instead has net assets. The organization's financials are audited, and stakeholders can find the firm's information in form 990 through Goodwill's public website (form 990 is the IRS form for nonprofits).

Because Goodwill sells goods at its stores, the company must also figure in costs of goods sold. In fact, most of the organization's revenue comes from its store activities. In one year, the retail division or sale of donated goods and contributed goods generated $3.94 billion. The contracts division generated $666 million, which provides custodial, janitorial, and lawn maintenance service contracts to government agencies. Grants from foundations, corporations, individuals, and government account for $185 million. The fact that Goodwill is able to generate much of its own funding through store activities and contracts is important. Many nonprofits that rely solely on donated funds find it hard to be sustainable in the long run, particularly during economic downturns.

Remember that even though nonprofits are different from for-profit companies, they must still make certain that their financial information is accurate. This requires nonprofit accountants to be meticulous and thorough in gathering and analyzing information. Like all accountants, accountants at Goodwill record transactions in journals and then carefully review the information before it is recorded in the general ledger. The organization uses trial balances to ensure that everything balances out, as well as advanced software to record

transactions, reconcile any discrepancies, and provide an idea of how much cash the organization has on hand.

Finally, Goodwill uses ratio analysis to determine the financial health of the company. For instance, the common ratio allows Goodwill to determine how much revenue it brings in for every dollar it spends on costs. The organization also uses ratio analysis to compare its results to similar organizations. It is important for Goodwill to identify the best performers in its field so that it can generate ideas and even form partnerships with other organizations. By using accounting to identify how best to use its resources, Goodwill is advancing its mission of helping others.[12]

Discussion Questions

1. What are some similarities between the type of accounting performed at Goodwill compared to accounting at for-profit companies?

2. What are some differences between the type of accounting performed at Goodwill compared to accounting at for-profit companies?

3. How can Goodwill use ratio analysis to improve its operations?

You can find the related video in the Video Library in Connect. Ask your instructor how you can access Connect.

Team Exercise

You can look at websites such as Yahoo! Finance (http://finance.yahoo.com/), under the company's "key statistics" link, to find many of its financial ratios, such as return on assets and return on equity. Have each member of your team

look up a different company, and explain why you think there are differences in the ratio analysis for these two ratios among the selected companies.

Endnotes

1. Association of Certified Fraud Examiners, "Schemes Based on Perpetrator's Department," *Report to the Nations on Occupational Fraud and Abuse 2014 Global Fraud Survey,* http://www.acfe.com/rttn-perpetrator-schemes. aspx (accessed June 29, 2015); Certify, Inc., "Study Shows $13.7 Million Lost in Expense Report Fraud," October 3, 2014, https://www.certify.com/2014-10-03-Study-Shows-137-Million-Lost-in-Expense-Report-Fraud (accessed June 29, 2015); Chris Farrell, "5 Simple Steps to Prevent Expense Fraud,"*Entrepreneur,* October 21, 2014,http://www.entrepreneur.com/article/238748 (accessed June 29, 2015); Liz Galst, "A Little Extra on the Road," *The New York Times,* November 15, 2010, http://www.nytimes .com/2010/11/16/business/16expenses.html (accessed June 29, 2015); Craig L. Greene, "Expense Account and

Travel Fraud,"*McGovern & Greene LLP,* 2013,http://www.mcgoverngreene.com/archives/archive_articles/Craig_Greene_Archives/expense_acct_fraud.html (accessed June 29, 2015); Abigail Grenfell, "Employee Expense Reimbursements: Legitimate or Fraudulent?" *Minnesota Society of Certified Public Accountants,* February/March 2015,http://www.mncpa.org/publications/footnote/2015-02/employee-expense-reimbursements-legitimate-or-fraudulent .aspx (accessed June 29, 2015); Misty Norris-Carter, "Are Your Travel Expenses Monitored?" *ACFE,*September 2013, http://www.acfe.com/fraud-examiner.aspx?id=4294979665 (accessed June 29, 2015); Dan Ramey, "Detecting Fraud: The Tone at the Top," *Intuit Accountants,* May 22, 2012,http://blog.accountants.intuit.com/from-the-experts/the-tone-at-the-top/(accessed June 29, 2015);

Ashley Strickland, "Check 'Em Twice: Expense Accounts Get Some Travelers in Trouble," *CNN,* December 8, 2011, http://www.cnn.com/2011/12/05/travel/expense-account-business-travel/(accessed June 29, 2015); Yasmin Vazquez, "The Fraud Curve: White-Collar Crime in Higher Education," *ACFE,* http://www.acfe.com/fraud-examiner.aspx?id=4294972114 (accessed June 29, 2015); Candice Wierzbowski, "More Than 50% of Employees Own Up to Committing T&E Fraud," *CFO Daily News,* November 5, 2013, ">*http://*www.cfodailynews.com/more-than-50-of-employees-own-up-to-committing-te-fraud/" (accessed June 29, 2015).

2. Public Company Accounting Oversight Board, "PCAOB Imposes Sanctions Against Auditor Who Admitted Violating Independence Requirements and PCAOB Standards," October 2, 2015, http://pcaobus.org/News/Releases/Pages/2015-PCAOB-disciplinary-order-auditor-admitted-violations.aspx (accessed April 21, 2016).

3. Walter Pavlo, "Association of Certified Fraud Examiners Release 2014 Report on Fraud," *Forbes,* May 21, 2014, www.forbes.com/sites/walterpavlo/2014/05/21/association-of-certified-fraud-examiners-release-2014-report-on-fraud/ (accessed April 21, 2016).

4. Association of Certified Fraud Examiners, "About the ACFE," www.acfe.com/about-the-acfe.aspx (accessed April 20, 2016).

5. "Schumpeter: A Green Light," *The Economist,* March 29, 2014, p. 74; Heesun Wee, "Big Companies Getting Serious about Environmental Risk," *CNBC,* April 14, 2015, http://www.cnbc.com/2015/04/14/big-companies-getting-serious-about-environmental-risks.html (accessed December 11, 2015); Kurt Kuehn and Lynnette McIntire, "Sustainability a CFO Can Love," *Harvard Business Review,* April 2014, https://hbr.org/2014/04/sustainability-a-cfo-can-love (accessed December 11, 2015).

6. Mary Williams Walsh, "State Woes Grow Too Big to Camouflage," *CNBC,* March 30, 2010, www.cnbc.com/id/36096491/ (accessed March 31, 2010).

7. Sarah Johnson, "Averting Revenue-Recognition Angst," *CFO,* April 2012, p. 21.

8. Deanna White, "Wristbands Get Indiana CPA Firm Moving at Tax Time," *Accounting Web,* February 18, 2014, http://www.accountingweb.com/article/wristbands-get-indiana-cpa-firm-moving-tax-time/223103 (accessed July 21, 2015);

MOVABLE website, http://www.movable.com/platform/ (accessed July 21, 2015); Dauby O'Connor & Zalewski LLC website, http://www.doz.net/ (accessed September 19, 2014); "Central Indiana Companies Lauded in Top Workplaces 2014 List," *Indianapolis Star,* April 20, 2014, http://www.indystar.com/story/money/2014/04/20/central-indiana-companies-lauded-top-workplaces-list-indianapolis-workplacedynamics/7934931/ (accessed July 21, 2015); "Company Overview of Dauby O'Connor & Zalewski, LLC," *Bloomberg Businessweek,* September 19, 2014, http://investing.businessweek.com/research/stocks/private/snapshot.asp?privcapId=46333433 (accessed July 21, 2015); American Heart Association, "Indiana Fit-Friendly Worksites," http://www.heart.org/HEARTORG/Affiliate/Indiana-Fit-Friendly-Worksites_UCM_451379_Article.jsp (accessed July 21, 2015).

9. Emily Chasan and John Kester, "Outside Auditors Get Asked In," *The Wall Street Journal,* May 12, 2015, p. B6; John Kester and Emily Chasan, "SEC Receives at Least One Independence Query Daily," *The Wall Street Journal,* May 12, 2015, http://blogs.wsj.com/cfo/2015/05/12/sec-receives-at-least-one-audit-independence-query-daily/ (accessed June 24, 2015); "SOX 206 Forces Auditor to Resign from Firm," *Compliance Week,* August 3, 2004, https://www.complianceweek.com/news/news-article/sox-206-forces-auditor-to-resign-from-firm#.VXymuPlViko (accessed June 13, 2015); U.S. Securities and Exchange Commission, "Improper Influence on Conduct of Audits," June 26, 2003, https://www.sec.gov/rules/final/34-47890.htm (accessed June 24, 2015).

10. City of Maricopa, "City Finance Department Receives Distinguished Presentation Award for Its Budget," March 25, 2014, www.maricopa-az.gov/web/finance-administrativeservice-home/1029-citys-finance-department-recieves-distinguished-budget-presentation-award-for-its-budget (accessed June 11, 2014).

11. "Accountants and Auditors: Occupational Outlook Handbook," *Bureau of Labor Statistics,* April 6, 2012, www.bls.gov/ooh/Business-and-Financial/Accountants-and-auditors.htm (accessed April 21, 2016).

12. Goodwill website, www.goodwill.org/ (accessed April 21, 2016); Goodwill Industries International Inc., "About Us—Revenue Sources," www.goodwill.org/about-us/ (accessed April 21, 2016).

© Courtney Keating/Getty Images

15

Money and the Financial System

Learning Objectives

After reading this chapter, you will be able to:

 LO 15-1 Define *money,* its functions, and its characteristics.

 LO 15-2 Describe various types of money.

LO 15-3 Specify how the Federal Reserve Board manages the money supply and regulates the American banking system.

 LO 15-4 Compare and contrast commercial banks, savings and loan associations, credit unions, and mutual savings banks.

LO 15-5 Distinguish among nonbanking institutions such as insurance companies, pension funds, mutual funds, and finance companies.

LO 15-6 Investigate the challenges ahead for the banking industry.

LO 15-7 Recommend the most appropriate financial institution for a hypothetical small business.

Enter the World of Business ⊖———————

Brok'n: The Downside of an Increasingly Cashless Society

Credit card debt is a major problem in the United States, amounting to approximately $60 billion. Yet this pales in comparison with student loan debt. The federal loan balance for student debt is approximately $1.2 trillion. Another $150 billion is owed to lenders such as banks.

There is no denying that student loan debt is a much greater issue today. In one survey, about 30 percent of younger people cite student loan debt as their biggest financial challenge. Only one in nine older people claimed that student loan debt was a major financial issue when first starting out.

Most student loans are lent by the federal government, commercial banks, and credit unions. However, it is not uncommon to have third parties manage or even purchase these loans. Investors often purchase bundled packages of student loans, similar to the bundled mortgages investors would purchase prior to the 2007–2008 financial crisis. Borrowers may be informed that they owe penalties to a firm they do not know. Unethical debt-collection practices have also arisen. Many lenders are taking borrowers to court, even when they do not have the proper documentation to prove they own the loan.

President Obama signed a memorandum to make it easier for federal student loan borrowers to repay their student debt. One change will be that borrowers must be notified if the loans are sent to another firm. The government is also setting up systems to allow borrowers to report unethical debt-collection practices. However, this will only apply to federal student loans. Most borrowers—both old and young—agree that having financial literacy classes in high school or college would be beneficial to guard against overwhelming student debt.[1]

Introduction

From Wall Street to Main Street, both overseas and at home, money is the one tool used to measure personal and business income and wealth. **Finance** is the study of how money is managed by individuals, companies, and governments. This chapter introduces you to the role of money and the financial system in the economy. Of course, if you have a checking account, automobile insurance, a college loan, or a credit card, you already have personal experience with some key players in the financial world.

We begin our discussion with a definition of money and then explore some of the many forms money may take. Next, we examine the roles of the Federal Reserve Board and other major institutions in the financial system. Finally, we explore the future of the finance industry and some of the changes likely to occur over the course of the next several years.

Money in the Financial System

Define *money*, its functions,
and its characteristics.

money
anything generally accepted
in exchange for goods and
services.

Strictly defined, **money,** or *currency,* is anything generally accepted in exchange for goods and services. Materials as diverse as salt, cattle, fish, rocks, shells, and cloth, as well as precious metals such as gold, silver, and copper, have long been used by various cultures as money. Most of these materials were limited-supply commodities that had their own value to society (for example, salt can be used as a preservative and shells and metals as jewelry). The supply of these commodities therefore determined the supply of "money" in that society. The next step was the development of "IOUs," or slips of paper that could be exchanged for a specified supply of the underlying commodity. "Gold" notes, for instance, could be exchanged for gold, and the money supply was tied to the amount of gold available. While paper money was first used in North America in 1685 (and even earlier in Europe), the concept of *fiat money*—a paper money not readily convertible to a precious metal such as gold—did not gain full acceptance until the Great Depression in the 1930s. The United States abandoned its gold-backed currency standard largely in response to the Great Depression and converted to a fiduciary, or fiat, monetary system. In the United States, paper money is really a government "note" or promise, worth the value specified on the note.

Functions of Money

No matter what a particular society uses for money, its primary purpose is to enable a person or organization to transform a desire into an action. These desires may be for entertainment actions, such as party expenses; operating actions, such as paying for rent, utilities, or employees; investing actions, such as buying property or equipment; or financing actions, such as for starting or growing a business. Money serves three important functions: as a medium of exchange, a measure of value, and a store of value.

Medium of Exchange.   Before fiat money, the trade of goods and services was accomplished through *bartering*—trading one good or service for another of similar value. As any school-age child knows, bartering can become quite inefficient—particularly in the case of complex, three-party transactions involving peanut butter sandwiches, baseball cards, and hair ties. There had to be a simpler way, and that was to decide on a single item—money—that can be freely converted to any other good upon agreement between parties.

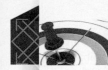

Should Firms Forgo the CFO?

It isn't too difficult to imagine a young startup company without a chief financial officer, or CFO. Recently, however, at least seven companies in the United States with revenues of more than $5 billion—including CBS and Jacobs Engineering Group—have been operating without someone in this top management role.

Another one of these corporations, Oracle, promoted its CFO, Safra Catz, to co-chief executive officer. Catz started as a classic CFO, but over time, her role changed into something more strategic, and although the official title is gone, Catz still oversees the company's financial functions in addition to the manufacturing and legal divisions. Catz's promotion reveals a new trend in today's companies: the strategic-minded CFO. CFOs today are expected to lead initiatives, develop goals, and

guide operations rooted in sound financial decision making and planning. Thanks to more complex accounting and regulations, controllers or chief accounting officers have begun to take on more of these tasks traditionally associated with the CFO. With or without a CFO, investors want to be left assured that the company's finances are in good hands.[2]

Discussion Questions

1. How are companies managing the finance function without an official CFO?
2. Describe how the role of the CFO is changing.
3. Do you think it is possible to totally eliminate the CFO function? Why or why not? How would this impact the firm?

Measure of Value.   As a measure of value, money serves as a common standard or yardstick of the value of goods and services. For example, $2 will buy a dozen large eggs and $25,000 will buy a nice car in the United States. In Japan, where the currency is known as the yen, these same transactions would cost about 210 yen and 2.75 million yen, respectively. Money, then, is a common denominator that allows people to compare the different goods and services that can be consumed on a particular income level. While a star athlete and a "burger-flipper" are paid vastly different wages, each uses money as a measure of the value of their yearly earnings and purchases.

Store of Value.   As a store of value, money serves as a way to accumulate wealth (buying power) until it is needed. For example, a person making $1,000 per week who wants to buy a $500 computer could save $50 per week for each of the next 10 weeks. Unfortunately, the value of stored money is directly dependent on the health of the economy. If, due to rapid inflation, all prices double in one year, then the purchasing power value of the money "stuffed in the mattress" would fall by half. On the other hand, deflation occurs when prices of goods fall. Deflation might seem like a good thing for consumers, but in many ways it can be just as problematic as inflation. Periods of major deflation often lead to decreases in wages and increases in debt burdens.[3] Deflation also tends to be an indicator of problems in the economy. Deflation usually indicates slow economic growth and falling prices. Over the past 25 years, we have seen deflation in Japan, and Europe has continued to struggle with deflation off and on since the financial crisis. Given a choice, central banks like the Federal Reserve would rather have a small amount of inflation than deflation.

Characteristics of Money

To be used as a medium of exchange, money must be acceptable, divisible, portable, stable in value, durable, and difficult to counterfeit.

For centuries, people on the Micronesian island of Yap have used giant round stones, like the ones shown here, for money. The stones aren't moved, but their ownership can change.

© Robert Harding World Imagery/ Alamy

Acceptability.   To be effective, money must be readily acceptable for the purchase of goods and services and for the settlement of debts. Acceptability is probably the most important characteristic of money: If people do not trust the value of money, businesses will not accept it as a payment for goods and services, and consumers will have to find some other means of paying for their purchases.

Divisibility.   Given the widespread use of quarters, dimes, nickels, and pennies in the United States, it is no surprise that the principle of divisibility is an important one. With barter, the lack of divisibility often makes otherwise preferable trades impossible, as would be an attempt to trade a steer for a loaf of bread. For money to serve effectively as a measure of value, all items must be valued in terms of comparable units—dimes for a piece of bubble gum, quarters for laundry machines, and dollars (or dollars and coins) for everything else.

Portability.   Clearly, for money to function as a medium of exchange, it must be easily moved from one location to the next. Large colored rocks could be used as money, but you couldn't carry them around in your wallet. Paper currency and metal coins, on the other hand, are capable of transferring vast purchasing power into small, easily carried (and hidden!) bundles. Few Americans realize it, but more U.S. currency is in circulation outside the United States than within. As of 2014, about $1.280 trillion of U.S. currency was in circulation, and the majority was held outside the United States.[4] Some countries, such as Panama, even use the U.S. dollar as their currency. Retailers in other countries often state prices in dollars and in their local currency.

Stability.   Money must be stable and maintain its declared face value. A $10 bill should purchase the same amount of goods or services from one day to the next. The principle of stability allows people who wish to postpone purchases and save their money to do so without fear that it will decline in value. As mentioned earlier, money declines in value during periods of inflation, when economic conditions cause prices to rise. Thus, the same amount of money buys fewer and fewer goods and services. In some countries, people spend their money as fast as they can in order to keep it from losing any more of its value. Instability destroys confidence in a nation's money and its ability to store value and serve as an effective medium of exchange. It also has an impact on other countries. When Switzerland decided to no longer hold its Swiss franc at a fixed exchange rate with the euro, other countries were concerned because they tended to view the Swiss franc as relatively "safe" for investments. This change will make Swiss exports more expensive and imports less expensive. The investment community is wary of changes in the stability of a currency, and the change caused massive losses for investors and the plunging of the Swiss stock market.[5] Ultimately, people faced with spiraling price increases avoid the increasingly worthless paper money at all costs, storing all of their savings in the form of real assets such as gold and land.

Durability.   Money must be durable. The crisp new dollar bills you trade for products at the mall will make their way all around town for about six years before being replaced (see Table 15-1). Were the value of an old, faded bill to fall in line with the deterioration of its appearance, the principles of stability and universal acceptability would fail (but, no doubt, fewer bills would pass through the washer!). Although metal coins, due to their much longer useful life, would appear to be an ideal form of money, paper currency is far more portable than metal because of its light weight. Today, coins are used primarily to provide divisibility.

TABLE 15-1   Life Expectancy of Money
How long is the life span of U.S. paper money?

When currency is deposited with a Federal Reserve Bank, the quality of each note is evaluated by sophisticated processing equipment. Notes that meet our strict quality criteria—that is, they are still in good condition—continue to circulate, while those that do not are taken out of circulation and destroyed. This process determines the life span of a Federal Reserve note.

Life span varies by denomination. One factor that influences the life span of each denomination is how the denomination is used by the public. For example, $100 notes are often used as a store of value. This means that they pass between users less frequently than lower denominations that are more often used for transactions, such as $5 notes. Thus, $100 notes typically last longer than $5 notes.

Denomination	Estimated Life Span*
$ 1	5.9 years
$ 5	4.9 years
$ 10	4.2 years
$ 20	7.7 years
$ 50	3.7 years
$ 100	15.0 years

*Estimated life spans as of December 2013. Because the $2 note does not widely circulate, we do not publish its estimated life span. The $100 dollar bill estimate is from December 2012.

Source: Board of Governors of the Federal Reserve System, "How Long Is the Life Span of U.S. Paper Money?" www.federalreserve.gov/faqs/how-long-is-the-life-span-of-us-paper-money.htm (accessed April 19, 2016).

Difficulty to Counterfeit.   Finally, to remain stable and enjoy universal acceptance, it almost goes without saying that money must be very difficult to counterfeit—that is, to duplicate illegally. Every country takes steps to make counterfeiting difficult. Most use multicolored

DID YOU KNOW? Around 75 percent of counterfeit currency is found and destroyed before it ever reaches the public.[6]

money, and many use specially watermarked papers that are virtually impossible to duplicate. Counterfeit bills represent less than 0.03 percent of the currency in circulation in the United States,[7] but it is becoming increasingly easy for counterfeiters

The U.S. government redesigns currency to stay ahead of counterfeiters and protect the public.

Source: Treasury Department

to print money. This illegal printing of money is fueled by hundreds of people who often circulate only small amounts of counterfeit bills. However, even rogue governments such as North Korea are known to make counterfeit U.S. currency. To thwart the problem of counterfeiting, the U.S. Treasury Department redesigned the U.S. currency, starting with the $20 bill in 2003, the $50 bill in 2004, the $10 bill in 2006, the $5 bill in 2008, and the $100 bill in 2010. For the first time, U.S. money includes subtle colors in addition to the traditional green, as well as enhanced security features, such as a watermark, security thread, and color-shifting ink.[8] Many countries are discontinuing large denominated bills that are used in illegal trade such as drugs or terrorism. The idea is that it is more difficult to transport or hide 100€ notes than 500€ notes. Although counterfeiting is not as much of an issue with coins, U.S. metal coins are usually worth more for the metal than their face value. It has begun to cost more to manufacture coins than what they are worth monetarily.

As Table 15-2 indicates, it costs more to produce pennies and nickels (highlighted in red numbers) than their face value. For example, we can see that in 2015 it cost $0.0143 to produce a one-cent piece, or 43 percent more than it was worth. However, what the U.S. Mint loses on pennies and nickels it makes up for with profits on dimes, quarters, and dollars. The U.S. $1 coin proved to be so unpopular that the U.S. Mint discontinued producing it after 2013. Profits fluctuate over time because of the rising and falling costs of copper, zinc, and nickel.

LO 15- 2

Describe various types of money.

Types of Money

While paper money and coins are the most visible types of money, the combined value of all of the printed bills and all of the minted coins is actually rather insignificant when compared with the value of money kept in checking accounts, savings accounts, and other monetary forms.

checking account
money stored in an account at a bank or other financial institution that can be withdrawn without advance notice; also called a demand deposit.

You probably have a **checking account** (also called a *demand deposit*), money stored in an account at a bank or other financial institution that can be withdrawn without advance notice. One way to withdraw funds from your account is by writing a *check*, a written order to a bank to pay the indicated individual or business the amount specified on the check from money already on deposit. Figure 15-1 explains the significance of the numbers found on a typical U.S. check. As legal instruments, checks serve as a substitute for currency and coins and are preferred for many transactions due to their lower risk of loss. If you lose a $100 bill, anyone who finds or steals it can spend it. If you lose a blank check, however, the risk of catastrophic loss is quite

TABLE 15-2
Costs to Produce U.S. Coins

Fiscal Year	One-Cent	Five-Cent	Dime	Quarter	$1 Coin	Total Profit From Coins (Millions)
2015	$ 0.0143	$0.0744	$0.0354	$0.0844	$ 0.0	$540.9
2014	$ 0.0166	$0.0809	$ 0.0391	$0.0895	$ 0.0	$ 289.1
2013	$ 0.0183	$ 0.0941	$0.0456	$ 0.0105	$ 0.0	$ 137.4
2012	$0.0200	$ 0.1009	$0.0499	$ 0.1130	$ 0.2111	$ 105.9
2011	$ 0.0241	$ 0.1118	$0.0565	$ 0.1114	$ 0.1803	$348.8
2010	$ 0.0179	$0.0922	$0.0569	$ 0.1278	$0.3257	$300.8

Source: Various annual reports of the U.S. Mint.

FIGURE 15-1   A Check

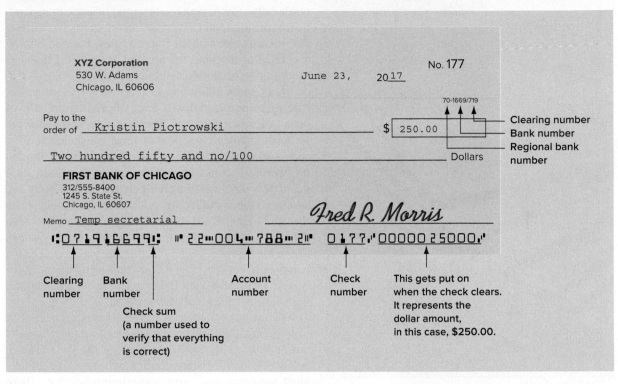

low. Not only does your bank have a sample of your signature on file to compare with a suspected forged signature, but you can render the check immediately worthless by means of a stop-payment order at your bank.

There are several types of checking accounts, with different features available for different monthly fee levels or specific minimum account balances. Some checking accounts earn interest (a small percentage of the amount deposited in the account that the bank pays to the depositor). One such interest-bearing checking account is the *NOW (Negotiable Order of Withdrawal) account* offered by most financial institutions. The interest rate paid on such accounts varies with the interest rates available in the economy but is typically quite low (more recently less than 1 percent but in the past between 2 and 5 percent).

Savings accounts (also known as *time deposits*) are accounts with funds that usually cannot be withdrawn without advance notice and/or have limits on the number of withdrawals per period. While seldom enforced, the "fine print" governing most savings accounts prohibits withdrawals without two or three days' notice. Savings accounts are not generally used for transactions or as a medium of exchange, but their funds can be moved to a checking account or turned into cash.

Money market accounts are similar to interest-bearing checking accounts, but with more restrictions. Generally, in exchange for slightly higher interest rates, the owner of a money market account can write only a limited number of checks each month, and there may be a restriction on the minimum amount of each check.

Certificates of deposit (CDs) are savings accounts that guarantee a depositor a set interest rate over a specified interval of time as long as the funds are not withdrawn before the end of the interval—six months, one year, or seven years, for example.

savings accounts
accounts with funds that usually cannot be withdrawn without advance notice; also known as time deposits.

money market accounts
accounts that offer higher interest rates than standard bank rates but with greater restrictions.

certificates of deposit (CDs)
savings accounts that guarantee a depositor a set interest rate over a specified interval as long as the funds are not withdrawn before the end of the period—six months or one year, for example.

Credit cards have many advantages, including being able to buy expensive items and pay them off a little at a time. However, this can easily lead an individual to incur spiraling credt card debt that is hard to pay off.

© Corbis Premium RF/Alamy

credit cards
means of access to preapproved lines of credit granted by a bank or finance company.

reward cards
credit cards made available by stores that carry a benefit to the user.

Money may be withdrawn from these accounts prematurely only after paying a substantial penalty. In general, the longer the term of the CD, the higher is the interest rate it earns. As with all interest rates, the rate offered and fixed at the time the account is opened fluctuates according to economic conditions.

Credit cards allow you to promise to pay at a later date by using preapproved lines of credit granted by a bank or finance company. They are a popular substitute for cash payments because of their convenience, easy access to credit, and acceptance by merchants around the world. The institution that issues the credit card guarantees payment of a credit charge to merchants and assumes responsibility for collecting the money from the cardholders. Card issuers charge a transaction fee to the merchants for performing the credit check, guaranteeing the payment, and collecting the payment. The fee is typically between 2 and 5 percent, depending on the type of card. American Express fees are usually higher than those for Visa and MasterCard.

The original American Express cards required full payment at the end of each month, but American Express now offers credit cards similar to Visa, MasterCard, and Discover that allow cardholders to make installment payments and carry a maximum balance. There is a minimum monthly payment with interest charged on the remaining balance. Some people pay off their credit cards monthly, while other make monthly payments. Charges for unpaid balances can run 18 percent or higher at an annual rate, making credit card debt one of the most expensive ways to borrow money.

Besides the major credit card companies, many stores—Target, Saks Fifth Avenue, Macy's, Bloomingdales, Sears, and others—have their own branded credit cards. They use credit rating agencies to check the credit of the cardholders and they generally make money on the finance charges. **Reward cards** are credit cards made available by stores that carry a benefit to the user. For example, gas stations such as Mobil and Shell have branded credit cards so that when you use the card you save five or six cents per gallon. Others—such as airline cards for American, Delta, and United—reward you with miles that you can use for flights. And there are cash-back credit cards that give you 1 percent or more cash back on everything you spend.

The Credit CARD (Card Accountability Responsibility and Disclosure) Act of 2009 was passed to regulate the practices of credit card companies. The law limited the ability of card issuers to raise interest rates, limited credit to young adults, gave people more time to pay bills, and made clearer due dates on billing cycles, along with several other provisions. For college students, the most important part of the law is that young adults under the age of 21 will have to have an adult co-signer or show proof that they have enough income to handle the debt limit on the card.

This act is important to all companies and cardholders. Research indicates that approximately 40 percent of lower- and middle-income households use credit cards to pay for basic necessities. Yet there is also good news. The average credit card debt for lower- and middle-income households has decreased in recent years. On the other hand, studies also show that college students tend to lack the financial literacy needed to understand credit cards and their requirements. Therefore, vulnerable segments of the population such as college students should be careful about which credit cards to choose and how often they use them.[9]

A **debit card** looks like a credit card but works like a check. The use of a debit card results in a direct, immediate, electronic payment from the cardholder's checking account to a merchant or other party. While they are convenient to carry and profitable for banks, they lack credit features, offer no purchase "grace period," and provide no hard "paper trail." Debit cards are gaining more acceptance with merchants, and consumers like debit cards because of the ease of getting cash from an increasing number of ATM machines. Financial institutions also want consumers to use debit cards because they reduce the number of teller transactions and check processing costs. Some cash management accounts at retail brokers like Merrill Lynch offer deferred debit cards. These act like a credit card but debit to the cash management account once a month. During that time, the cash earns a money market return.

debit card
a card that looks like a credit card but works like a check; using it results in a direct, immediate, electronic payment from the cardholder's checking account to a merchant or third party.

Traveler's checks, money orders, and cashier's checks are other forms of "near money." Although each is slightly different from the others, they all share a common characteristic: A financial institution, bank, credit company, or neighborhood currency exchange issues them in exchange for cash and guarantees that the purchased note will be honored and exchanged for cash when it is presented to the institution making the guarantee.

Credit Card Fraud.   More and more computer hackers have managed to steal credit card information and either use the information for Internet purchases or actually make a card exactly the same as the stolen card. Losses on credit card theft run into the billions, but consumers are usually not liable for the losses. However, consumers should be careful with debit cards because once the money is out of the account, the bank and credit card companies cannot get it back. Debit cards do not have the same level of protection as credit cards.

The American Financial System

The U.S. financial system fuels our economy by storing money, fostering investment opportunities, and making loans for new businesses and business expansion as well as for homes, cars, and college educations. This amazingly complex system includes banking institutions, nonbanking financial institutions such as finance companies, and systems that provide for the electronic transfer of funds throughout the world. Over the past 20 years, the rate at which money turns over, or changes hands, has increased exponentially. Different cultures place unique values on saving, spending, borrowing, and investing. The combination of this increased turnover rate and increasing interactions with people and organizations from other countries has created a complex money system. First, we need to meet the guardian of this complex system.

Federal Reserve Board
an independent agency of the federal government established in 1913 to regulate the nation's banking and financial industry.

The Federal Reserve System

The guardian of the American financial system is the **Federal Reserve Board,** or "the Fed," as it is commonly called, an independent agency of the federal government established in 1913 to regulate the nation's banking and financial industry. The Federal Reserve System is organized into 12 regions, each with a Federal Reserve Bank that serves its defined area (Figure 15-2). All the Federal Reserve banks except those

LO 15-3

Specify how the Federal Reserve Board manages the money supply and regulates the American banking system.

FIGURE 15-2 Federal Reserve System

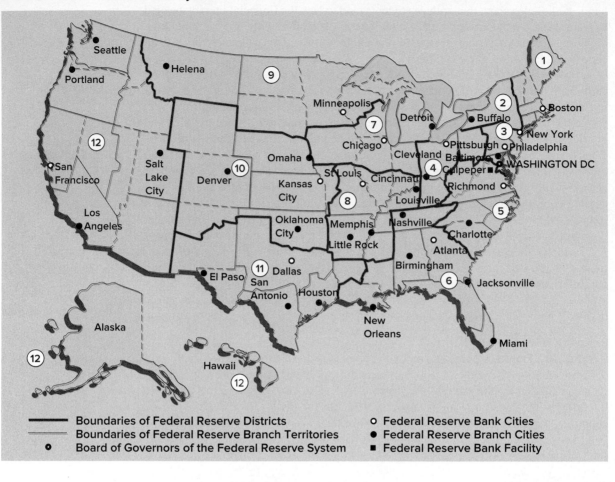

▬▬▬ Boundaries of Federal Reserve Districts	○ Federal Reserve Bank Cities
▬▬▬ Boundaries of Federal Reserve Branch Territories	● Federal Reserve Branch Cities
⊙ Board of Governors of the Federal Reserve System	■ Federal Reserve Bank Facility

in Boston and Philadelphia have regional branches. The Cleveland Federal Reserve Bank, for example, is responsible for branch offices in Pittsburgh and Cincinnati.

The Federal Reserve Board is the chief economic policy arm of the United States. Working with Congress and the president, the Fed tries to create a positive economic environment capable of sustaining low inflation, high levels of employment, a balance in international payments, and long-term economic growth. To this end, the Federal Reserve Board has four major responsibilities: (1) to control the supply of money, or monetary policy; (2) to regulate banks and other financial institutions; (3) to manage regional and national checking account procedures, or check clearing; and (4) to supervise the federal deposit insurance programs of banks belonging to the Federal Reserve System.

Monetary Policy.   The Fed controls the amount of money available in the economy through monetary policy. Without this intervention, the supply of and demand for money might not balance. This could result in either rapid price increases (inflation) because of too little money or economic recession and a slowdown of price increases (disinflation) because of too little growth in the money supply. In very rare cases (the depression of the 1930s), the United States has suffered from deflation,

monetary policy
means by which the Fed controls the amount of money available in the economy.

Activity	Effect on the Money Supply and the Economy
Buy government securities	The money supply increases; economic activity increases.
Sell government securities	The money supply decreases; economic activity slows down.
Raise discount rate	Interest rates increase; the money supply decreases; economic activity slows down.
Lower discount rate	Interest rates decrease; the money supply increases; economic activity increases.
Increase reserve requirements	Banks make fewer loans; the money supply declines; economic activity slows down.
Decrease reserve requirements	Banks make more loans; the money supply increases; economic activity increases.
Relax credit controls	More people are encouraged to make major purchases, increasing economic activity.
Restrict credit controls	People are discouraged from making major purchases, decreasing economic activity.

TABLE 15-3
Fed Tools for Regulating the Money Supply

when the actual purchasing power of the dollar has increased as prices declined. To effectively control the supply of money in the economy, the Fed must have a good idea of how much money is in circulation at any given time. This has become increasingly challenging because the global nature of our economy means that more and more U.S. dollars are circulating overseas. Using several different measures of the money supply, the Fed establishes specific growth targets that, presumably, ensure a close balance between money supply and money demand. The Fed fine-tunes money growth by using four basic tools: open market operations, reserve requirements, the discount rate, and credit controls (see Table 15-3). There is generally a lag of 6 to 18 months before the effect of these charges shows up in economic activity.

Open market operations refer to decisions to buy or sell U.S. Treasury bills (short-term debt issued by the U.S. government; also called T-bills) and other investments in the open market. The actual purchase or sale of the investments is performed by the New York Federal Reserve Bank. This monetary tool, the most commonly employed of all Fed operations, is performed almost daily in an effort to control the money supply.

When the Fed buys securities, it writes a check on its own account to the seller of the investments. When the seller of the investments (usually a large bank) deposits the check, the Fed transfers the balance from the Federal Reserve account into the seller's account, thus increasing the supply of money in the economy and, hopefully, fueling economic growth. The opposite occurs when the Fed sells investments. The buyer writes a check to the Federal Reserve, and when the funds are transferred out of the purchaser's account, the amount of money in circulation falls, slowing economic growth to a desired level.

The second major monetary policy tool is the **reserve requirement,** the percentage of deposits that banking institutions must hold in reserve ("in the vault," as it were). Funds so held are not available for lending to businesses and consumers. For example, a bank holding $10 million in deposits, with a 10 percent reserve requirement, must have reserves of $1 million. If the Fed were to reduce the reserve requirement to, say,

open market operations
decisions to buy or sell U.S. Treasury bills (short-term debt issued by the U.S. government) and other investments in the open market.

reserve requirement
the percentage of deposits that banking institutions must hold in reserve.

Need help understanding how the Federal Reserve tries to stabilize the economy? Visit your Connect ebook video tab for a brief animated explanation.

5 percent, the bank would need to keep only $500,000 in reserves. The bank could then lend to customers the $500,000 difference between the old reserve level and the new lower reserve level, thus increasing the supply of money. Because the reserve requirement has such a powerful effect on the money supply, the Fed does not change it very often, relying instead on open market operations most of the time.

discount rate
the rate of interest the Fed charges to loan money to any banking institution to meet reserve requirements.

The third monetary policy tool, the **discount rate,** is the rate of interest the Fed charges to loan money to any banking institution to meet reserve requirements. The Fed is the lender of last resort for these banks. When a bank borrows from the Fed, it is said to have borrowed at the "discount window," and the interest rates charged there are often higher than those charged on loans of comparable risk elsewhere in the economy. This added interest expense, when it exists, serves to discourage banks from borrowing from the Fed.

When the Fed wants to expand the money supply, it lowers the discount rate to encourage borrowing. Conversely, when the Fed wants to decrease the money supply, it raises the discount rate. The increases in interest rates that occurred in the United States from 2003 through 2006 were the result of more than 16 quarter-point (0.25 percent) increases in the Fed discount rate. The purpose was to keep inflation under control and to raise rates to a more normal level as the economy recovered from the recession of 2001. The Fed lowered interest rates to combat the 2007 recession, and they have remained historically low for the last 10 years as the Fed tried to stimulate a slow growing economy. In an environment where credit markets were nearly frozen, the Fed utilized monetary policy to stimulate spending. Not surprisingly, economists watch changes in this sensitive interest rate as an indicator of the Fed's monetary policy.

credit controls
the authority to establish and enforce credit rules for financial institutions and some private investors.

The final tool in the Fed's arsenal of weapons is **credit controls**—the authority to establish and enforce credit rules for financial institutions and some private investors. For example, the Fed can determine how large a down payment individuals and businesses must make on credit purchases of expensive items such as automobiles, and how much time they have to finish paying for the purchases. By raising and lowering minimum down payment amounts and payment periods, the Fed can stimulate or discourage credit purchases of "big ticket" items. The Fed also has the authority to set the minimum down payment investors must use for the credit purchases of stock. Buying stock with credit—"buying on margin"—is a popular investment strategy among individual speculators. By altering the margin requirement (currently set at 50 percent of the price of the purchased stocks), the Fed can effectively control the total amount of credit borrowing in the stock market.

Regulatory Functions.   The second major responsibility of the Fed is to regulate banking institutions that are members of the Federal Reserve System. Accordingly, the Fed establishes and enforces banking rules that affect monetary policy and the overall level of the competition between different banks. It determines which nonbanking activities, such as brokerage services, leasing, and insurance, are appropriate for banks and which should be prohibited. The Fed also has the authority to approve or disapprove mergers between banks and the formation of bank holding companies. In an effort to ensure that all rules are enforced and that correct accounting procedures are being followed at member banks, surprise bank examinations are conducted by bank examiners each year.

Check Clearing.   The Federal Reserve provides national check processing on a huge scale. Divisions of the Fed known as check clearinghouses handle almost all the checks written against a bank in one city and presented for deposit to a bank in a second city. Any banking institution can present the checks it has received from others around the country to its regional Federal Reserve Bank. The Fed passes the checks to the appropriate regional Federal Reserve Bank, which then sends the checks to the issuing bank for payment. With the advance of electronic payment systems and the passage of the Check Clearing for the 21st Century Act (Check 21 Act), checks can now be processed in a day. The Check 21 Act allows banks to clear checks electronically by presenting an electronic image of the check. This eliminates mail delays and time-consuming paper processing.

Depository Insurance.   The Fed is also responsible for supervising the federal insurance funds that protect the deposits of member institutions. These insurance funds will be discussed in greater detail in the following section.

Banking Institutions

Banking institutions accept money deposits from and make loans to individual consumers and businesses. Some of the most important banking institutions include commercial banks, savings and loan associations, credit unions, and mutual savings banks. Historically, these have all been separate institutions. However, new hybrid forms of banking institutions that perform two or more of these functions have emerged over the past two decades. The following all have one thing in common: They are businesses whose objective is to earn money by managing, safeguarding, and lending money to others. Their sales revenues come from the fees and interest that they charge for providing these financial services.

Since the financial crisis, and during the 2016 political campaign, Wall Street and banks have been the target of politicians as they continue to take out their anger at the banking world for all the economic problems that exist in the United States. You will see as you go through this section that the financial network is very complex. Because of new regulations, liquidity in the bond markets has evaporated, bank profits are down, and loans are more difficult to obtain for the average borrower. The unintended consequences of many of these regulations will show up in coming years.

Commercial Banks.   The largest and oldest of all financial institutions are **commercial banks,** which perform a variety of financial services. They rely mainly on checking and savings accounts as their major source of funds and use only a portion of these deposits to make loans to businesses and individuals. Because it is unlikely that all the depositors of any one bank will want to withdraw all of their funds at the same time, a bank can safely loan out a large percentage of its deposits.

Today, banks are quite diversified and offer a number of services. Commercial banks make loans for virtually any conceivable legal purpose, from vacations to cars, from homes to college educations. Banks in many states offer *home equity loans,* by which home owners can borrow against the appraised value of their already purchased homes. Banks also issue Visa and MasterCard credit cards and offer CDs and trusts (legal entities set up to hold and manage assets for a beneficiary). Many banks rent safe deposit boxes in bank vaults to customers who want to store jewelry, legal documents, artwork, and other valuables. In 1999, Congress passed the Financial Services Modernization Act, also

LO 15-4

Compare and contrast commercial banks, savings and loan associations, credit unions, and mutual savings banks.

commercial banks the largest and oldest of all financial institutions, relying mainly on checking and savings accounts as sources of funds for loans to businesses and individuals.

Citibank is the consumer division of Citigroup, the fourth largest bank in the United States.

© TungCheung/Shutterstock

Want Greenbacks? Then Go Green

U.S. Bancorp puts its corporate muscle behind a strong sustainability program. U.S. Bank—the leading bank of U.S. Bancorp—has been recognized by *Newsweek* in its list of greenest American companies. The bank is an Energy Star partner and a member of the U.S. Green Building Council. It has a strong environmental policy it updates periodically and an environmental affairs team that oversees sustainability activities. However, U.S. Bank not only seeks to improve the environmental footprint of its own operations, but also provides resources for stakeholders to do the same.

For instance, U.S. Bank became the first large bank to offer consumers rate reductions on auto loans for consumers who purchase "Smart Way" automobiles, a certification provided by the Environmental Protection Agency signifying environmental friendliness. It is a founding member of PayItGreen.org, a website with tools consumers can use to measure their environmental footprint.

U.S. Bank also encourages its employees to get involved. It has 37 Green Teams that participate in increasing corporate environmental stewardship in the communities in which they do business. In order for employees to improve their own environmental footprint, the bank developed sustainability kits to educate employees and show them how they can conserve resources both inside and outside of the office. It is clear that for U.S. Bank, sustainability is an investment it feels will pay off.[10]

Discussion Questions

1. How does U.S. Bank attempt to improve the sustainability of its own operations?
2. How does U.S. Bank help consumers and employees to consider their own environmental impact?
3. What are some ways that U.S. Bank can work with other stakeholders—such as suppliers, regulators, and stockholders—to increase sustainability in the banking industry?

---

known as the Gramm-Leach-Bliley Bill. This act repealed the Glass Steagall Act, which was enacted in 1929 after the stock market crash and prohibited commercial banks from being in the insurance and investment banking business. This puts U.S. commercial banks on the same competitive footing as European banks and provides a more level playing field for global banking competition. As commercial banks and investment banks have merged, the financial landscape has changed. Consolidation remains the norm in the U.S. banking industry. The financial crisis and the economic recession that began in 2007 and lasted into 2012 only accelerated the consolidation as large, healthy banks ended up buying weak banks that were in trouble. JPMorgan Chase bought Wachovia and the investment bank Bear Stearns; Wells Fargo bought Washington Mutual; and Bank of America bought Countrywide Credit and Merrill Lynch. Most of these purchases were made with financial help from the U.S. Treasury and Federal Reserve. By 2012, the banks had paid back their loans, but the financial meltdown exposed some high-risk activities in the banking industry Congress wanted to curtail. The result was the passage of the Dodd-Frank Act. This act added many new regulations, but the two most important changes raised the required capital banks had to hold on their balance sheet and limited certain types of high-risk trading activities.

Savings and Loan Associations.   Savings and loan associations (S&Ls), often called "thrifts," are financial institutions that primarily offer savings accounts and make long-term loans for residential mortgages. A mortgage is a loan made so that a business or individual can purchase real estate, typically a home; the real estate itself is pledged as a guarantee (called *collateral*) that the buyer will repay the loan. If the loan is not repaid, the savings and loan has the right to repossess the property. Prior to the 1970s, S&Ls focused almost exclusively on real estate lending and accepted only savings accounts. Today, following years of regulatory changes, S&Ls compete directly with commercial banks by offering many types of services.

savings and loan associations (S&Ls) financial institutions that primarily offer savings accounts and make long-term loans for residential mortgages; also called "thrifts."

Savings and loans have gone through a metamorphosis since the early 1990s, after having almost collapsed in the 1980s. Today, many of the largest savings and loans have merged with commercial banks. This segment of the financial services industry plays a diminished role in the mortgage lending market.

Credit Unions.   A **credit union** is a financial institution owned and controlled by its depositors, who usually have a common employer, profession, trade group, or religion. The Aggieland Credit Union in College Station, Texas, for example, provides banking services for faculty, employees, and current and former students of Texas A&M University. A savings account at a credit union is commonly referred to as a share account, while a checking account is termed a share draft account. Because the credit union is tied to a common organization, the members (depositors) are allowed to vote for directors and share in the credit union's profits in the form of higher interest rates on accounts and/or lower loan rates.

credit union
a financial institution owned and controlled by its depositors, who usually have a common employer, profession, trade group, or religion.

While credit unions were originally created to provide depositors with a short-term source of funds for low-interest consumer loans for items such as cars, home appliances, vacations, and college, today they offer a wide range of financial services. Generally, the larger the credit union, the more sophisticated its financial service offerings will be.

Mutual Savings Banks.   **Mutual savings banks** are similar to savings and loan associations, but, like credit unions, they are owned by their depositors. Among the oldest financial institutions in the United States, they were originally established to provide a safe place for savings of particular groups of people, such as fishermen. Found mostly in New England, they are becoming more popular in the rest of the country as some S&Ls have converted to mutual savings banks to escape the stigma created by the widespread S&L failures in the 1980s.

mutual savings banks
financial institutions that are similar to savings and loan associations but, like credit unions, are owned by their depositors.

Insurance for Banking Institutions.   The **Federal Deposit Insurance Corporation (FDIC),** which insures individual bank accounts, was established in 1933 to help stop bank failures throughout the country during the Great Depression. Today, the FDIC insures personal accounts up to a maximum of $250,000 at nearly 8,000 FDIC member institutions.[11] While most major banks are insured by the FDIC, small institutions in some states may be insured by state insurance funds or private insurance companies. Should a member bank fail, its depositors can recover all of their funds, up to $250,000. Amounts over $250,000, while not legally covered by the insurance, are, in fact, usually covered because the Fed understands very well the

Federal Deposit Insurance Corporation (FDIC)
an insurance fund established in 1933 that insures individual bank accounts.

enormous damage that would result to the financial system should these large depositors withdraw their money. When the financial crisis occurred, the FDIC increased the deposit insurance amount from $100,000 to $250,000 on a temporary basis to increase consumer confidence in the banking system. The Dodd-Frank Act passed on July 21, 2010, made the $250,000 insurance per account permanent. The *Federal Savings and Loan Insurance Corporation (FSLIC)* insured thrift deposits prior to its insolvency and failure during the S&L crisis of the 1980s. Now, the insurance functions once overseen by the FSLIC are handled directly by the FDIC through its

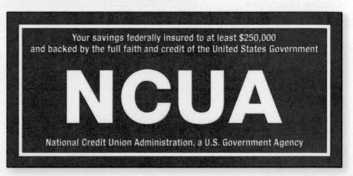

The National Credit Union Administration has the important job of regulating and chartering credit unions and insuring their deposits through its National Credit Union Insurance Fund.

Source: National Credit Union Administration

Savings Association Insurance Fund. The **National Credit Union Administration (NCUA)** regulates and charters credit unions and insures their deposits through its National Credit Union Insurance Fund.

When they were originally established, Congress hoped that these insurance funds would make people feel secure about their savings so they would not panic and withdraw their money when news of a bank failure was announced. The "bank run" scene in the perennial Christmas movie *It's a Wonderful Life,* when dozens of Bailey Building and Loan depositors attempted to withdraw their money (only to have the reassuring figure of Jimmy Stewart calm their fears), was not based on mere fiction. During the Great Depression, hundreds of banks failed and their depositors lost everything. The fact that large numbers of major financial institutions failed in the 1980s and 1990s—without a single major banking panic—underscores the effectiveness of the current insurance system. Large bank failures occurred once again during the most recent recession. According to the FDIC, 474 banks failed between January 2009 and May 31, 2014. Compare this to 52 failures between January 2000 and December 31, 2008, and you can grasp the impact of the financial crisis and long-lasting recession. For the March 2014 ending quarter, the FDIC reported that the number of problem banks had declined for 12 quarters in a row. This reflects an improving economy and a healthier financial system. It is safe to say that most depositors go to sleep every night without worrying about the safety of their savings.

Nonbanking Institutions

Distinguish among nonbanking institutions such as insurance companies, pension funds, mutual funds, and finance companies.

Nonbank financial institutions offer some financial services, such as short-term loans or investment products, but do not accept deposits. These include insurance companies, pension funds, mutual funds, brokerage firms, nonfinancial firms, and finance companies. Table 15-4 lists the assets of some diversified financial services firms.

Diversified Firms.   There are many nonfinancial firms that help finance their customers' purchases of expensive equipment. For example, Caterpillar (construction equipment), Boeing (airplanes), and General Electric (jet engines and locomotives) help their customers finance these large-scale expensive purchases through

TABLE 15-4
Leading Diversified Financial Services Firms

	2013 Assets (in millions)	2015 Assets (in millions)
JPMorgan Chase	$2,415,666	$2,351,698
Citigroup Inc.	1,880,382	1,731,210
American Express	159,103	161,184
Ameriprise	144,576	145,342
Visa	35,956	40,236
AON	30,251	27,164
Invesco	19,271	25,073
Marsh & McLennan	16,980	18,216
Apollo Investment Corp.	2,944	3,561

Source: S&P Capital IQ reports.

their finance subsidiaries. At one time, General Electric's credit subsidiary accounted for 40 percent of the company's revenues, but this is slowly falling as the company divests itself of consumer credit operations. Automobile companies such as Ford have also traditionally had credit subsidiaries to help customers finance their cars.

Insurance Companies. Insurance companies are businesses that protect their clients against financial losses from certain specified risks (death, injury, disability, accident, fire, theft, and natural disasters, for example) in exchange for a fee, called a premium. Because insurance premiums flow into the companies regularly, but major insurance losses cannot be timed with great accuracy (though expected risks can be assessed with considerable precision), insurance companies generally have large amounts of excess funds. They typically invest these or make long-term loans, particularly to businesses in the form of commercial real estate loans.

insurance companies
businesses that protect their clients against financial losses from certain specified risks (death, accident, and theft, for example).

Pension Funds. Pension funds are managed investment pools set aside by individuals, corporations, unions, and some nonprofit organizations to provide retirement income for members. One type of pension fund is the *individual retirement account (IRA),* which is established by individuals to provide for their personal retirement needs. IRAs can be invested in a variety of financial assets, from risky commodities such as oil or cocoa to low-risk financial "staples" such as U.S. Treasury securities. The choice is up to each person and is dictated solely by individual objectives and tolerance for risk. The interest earned by all of these investments may be deferred tax-free until retirement.

pension funds
managed investment pools set aside by individuals, corporations, unions, and some nonprofit organizations to provide retirement income for members.

In 1997, Congress revised the IRA laws and created a Roth IRA. Although similar to a traditional IRA in that investors may contribute $5,500 per year, the money in a Roth IRA is considered an after-tax contribution. Workers over 50 can add an extra $1,000, but in all cases, if you make too much money, you cannot fund a Roth. When the money is withdrawn at retirement, no tax is paid on the distribution. The Roth IRA is beneficial to young people who can allow a long time for their money to compound and who may be able to have their parents or grandparents fund the Roth IRA with gift money.

Most major corporations provide some kind of pension plan for their employees. Many of these are established with bank trust departments or life insurance companies. Money is deposited in a separate account in the name of each individual employee, and when the employee retires, the total amount in the account can be either withdrawn in one lump sum or taken as monthly cash payments over some defined time period (usually for the remaining life of the retiree).

Social Security, the largest pension fund, is publicly financed. The federal government collects Social Security funds from payroll taxes paid by both employers and employees. The Social Security Administration then takes these monies and makes payments to those eligible to receive Social Security benefits—the retired, the disabled, and the young children of deceased parents.

State Farm is the largest auto and home insurer. Its website allows users to input their information and receive an auto insurance quote quickly and conveniently.

© RKTPHOTO:Rachel K. Turner/Alamy Stock Photo

Pay Direct: The Big Play for Pay

Paydiant
Founders: Chris Gardner, Kevin Laracey, and Joe Paratore
Founded: 2010, in Boston, Massachusetts
Success: Paydiant provides mobile payment technology for major companies and was purchased by PayPal for about $280 million.

The war is heating up between mobile payment systems Apple Pay and CurrentC. CurrentC is a mobile payments system banks and store merchants can use to control their own branded mobile wallet applications. The startup firm behind the development of CurrentC is Paydiant, a mobile payments firm that works directly with retailers and banks to "reinvent the wallet."

Paydiant was founded to take advantage of the emerging market of mobile payments. Merchants desire Paydiant's services because it allows them to have more control. With Paydiant's technology, merchants can offer their customers their own tailored marketing incentives and customer loyalty programs through mobile devices. A consortium of companies including Verizon, Subway, Capital One, Walmart, and Sears are Paydiant clients. Rite Aid and CVS have also chosen CurrentC over Apple Pay.

This has caught the attention of top players in the digital payments industry. Because PayPal wants to increase its share of the mobile payments market, it agreed to purchase Paydiant. By acquiring Paydiant, PayPal gets instant access to Paydiant's mobile technology and its lucrative client base.[12]

Discussion Questions

1. How does Paydiant differentiate its mobile payments system from competitors?
2. Do you believe PayPal's acquisition of Paydiant is a good strategy toward gaining access to the mobile payments market?
3. As the mobile payments industry becomes more popular, how do you think this might affect the banking industry?

---

mutual fund
an investment company that pools individual investor dollars and invests them in large numbers of well-diversified securities.

Mutual Funds.   A **mutual fund** pools individual investor dollars and invests them in large numbers of well-diversified securities. Individual investors buy shares in a mutual fund in the hope of earning a high rate of return and in much the same way as people buy shares of stock. Because of the large numbers of people investing in any one mutual fund, the funds can afford to invest in hundreds (if not thousands) of securities at any one time, minimizing the risks of any single security that does not do well. Mutual funds provide professional financial management for people who lack the time and/or expertise to invest in particular securities, such as government bonds. While there are no hard-and-fast rules, investments in one or more mutual funds are one way for people to plan for financial independence at the time of retirement.

A special type of mutual fund called a *money market fund* invests specifically in short-term debt securities issued by governments and large corporations. Although they offer services such as check-writing privileges and reinvestment of interest income, money market funds differ from the money market accounts offered by banks primarily in that the former represent a pool of funds, while the latter are basically specialized, individual checking accounts. Money market funds usually offer slightly higher rates of interest than bank money market accounts.

brokerage firms
firms that buy and sell stocks, bonds, and other securities for their customers and provide other financial services.

Brokerage Firms and Investment Banks.   **Brokerage firms** buy and sell stocks, bonds, and other securities for their customers and provide other financial services. Larger brokerage firms like Merrill Lynch, Charles Schwab, and Edward Jones offer financial services unavailable at their smaller competitors. Merrill Lynch, for example, offers the Merrill Lynch Cash Management Account (CMA), which pays interest on deposits and allows clients to write checks, borrow money, and withdraw cash much like a commercial bank. The largest of the brokerage firms (including Merrill Lynch) have developed so many specialized services that they may be considered financial networks—organizations capable of offering virtually all of the services traditionally associated with commercial banks. The rise of online brokerage firms has helped investors who want to do it themselves at low costs. Firms like E-Trade, TDAmeritrade, and Scottrade offer investors the ability to buy and sell securities for $7 to $10 per trade, while the same trade at Morgan Stanley might cost $125. E-Trade offers banking services, debit cards, wire transfers, and many of the same services that the traditional brokerage firms offer.

Most brokerage firms are really part financial conglomerates that provide many different kinds of services besides buying and selling securities for clients. For example, Merrill Lynch also is an investment banker, as are Morgan Stanley and Goldman Sachs. The **investment banker** underwrites new issues of securities for corporations, states, and municipalities needed to raise money in the capital markets. The new issue market is called a *primary market* because the sale of the securities is for the first time. After the first sale, the securities trade in the *secondary markets* by brokers. The investment banker advises on the price of the new securities and generally guarantees the sale while overseeing the distribution of the securities through the selling brokerage houses. Investment bankers also act as dealers who make markets in securities. They do this by offering to sell the securities at an asked price (which is a higher rate) and buy the securities at a bid price (which is a lower rate)—the difference in the two prices represents the profit for the dealer.

investment banker underwrites new issues of securities for corporations, states, and municipalities.

Finance Companies.   **Finance companies** are businesses that offer short-term loans at substantially higher rates of interest than banks. Commercial finance companies make loans to businesses, requiring their borrowers to pledge assets such as equipment, inventories, or unpaid accounts as collateral for the loans. Consumer finance companies make loans to individuals. Like commercial finance companies, these firms require some sort of personal collateral as security against the borrower's possible inability to repay their loans. Because of the high interest rates they charge and other factors, finance companies typically are the lender of last resort for individuals and businesses whose credit limits have been exhausted and/or those with poor credit ratings.

finance companies businesses that offer short-term loans at substantially higher rates of interest than banks.

Electronic Banking

Since the advent of the computer age, a wide range of technological innovations has made it possible to move money all across the world electronically. Such "paperless" transactions have allowed financial institutions to reduce costs in what has been, and continues to be, a virtual competitive battlefield. **Electronic funds transfer (EFT)** is any movement of funds by means of an electronic terminal, telephone, computer, or magnetic tape. Such transactions order a particular financial institution to subtract money from one account and add it to another. The most commonly used forms of EFT are automated teller machines, automated clearinghouses, and home banking systems.

electronic funds transfer (EFT) any movement of funds by means of an electronic terminal, telephone, computer, or magnetic tape.

Automated Teller Machines.   Probably the most familiar form of electronic banking is the **automated teller machine (ATM),** which dispenses cash, accepts deposits, and allows balance inquiries and cash transfers from one account to another. ATMs provide 24-hour banking services—both at home (through a local bank) and far away (via worldwide ATM networks such as Cirrus and Plus). Rapid growth, driven by both strong consumer acceptance and lower transaction costs for banks (about half the cost of teller transactions), has led to the installation of hundreds of thousands of ATMs worldwide. Table 15-5 presents some interesting statistics about ATMs.

automated teller machine (ATM) the most familiar form of electronic banking, which dispenses cash, accepts deposits, and allows balance inquiries and cash transfers from one account to another.

Automated Clearinghouses.   **Automated clearinghouses (ACHs)** permit payments such as deposits or withdrawals to be made to and from a bank account by magnetic computer tape. Most large U.S. employers, and many others worldwide, use

automated clearinghouses (ACHs) a system that permits payments such as deposits or withdrawals to be made to and from a bank account by magnetic computer tape.

TABLE 15-5
Facts about ATM Use

| There are 425,000 ATM machines in use in the United States. |
| The average cash withdrawal from ATMs is $60. |
| The typical ATM consumer will visit an ATM 7.4 times per month. |
| The total ratio of people per ATM machine is 144:1. |
| Stores that install an ATM machine see a 20% average increase in sales. |
| The top ATM owners are Cardtronics, Payment Alliance, Bank of America, JPMorgan Chase, and Wells Fargo. |

Source: "ATM Machines Statistics," September 29, 2015, www.statisticbrain.com/atm-machine-statistics/ (accessed April 22, 2016).

ACHs to deposit their employees' paychecks directly to the employees' bank accounts. While direct deposit is used by only 50 percent of U.S. workers, nearly 100 percent of Japanese workers and more than 90 percent of European workers utilize it. The largest user of automated clearinghouses in the United States is the federal government, with 99 percent of federal government employees and 65 percent of the private workforce receiving their pay via direct deposit. More than 82 percent of all Social Security payments are made through an ACH system. The Social Security Administration is trying to reduce costs and reduce theft and fraud, so if you apply for Social Security benefits on or after May 1, 2011, you must receive your payments electronically.

The advantages of direct deposits to consumers include convenience, safety, and potential interest earnings. It is estimated that more than 4 million paychecks are lost or stolen annually, and FBI studies show that 2,000 fraudulent checks are cashed every day in the United States. Checks can never be lost or stolen with direct deposit. The benefits to businesses include decreased check-processing expenses and increased employee productivity. Research shows that businesses that use direct deposit can save more than $1.25 on each payroll check processed. Productivity could increase by $3 to $5 billion annually if all employees were to use direct deposit rather than taking time away from work to deposit their payroll checks.

Some companies also use ACHs for dividend and interest payments. Consumers can also use ACHs to make periodic (usually monthly) fixed payments to specific creditors without ever having to write a check or buy stamps. The estimated number of bills paid annually by consumers is 20 billion, and the total number paid through ACHs is estimated at only 8.5 billion. The average consumer who writes 10 to 15 checks each month would save $41 to $62 annually in postage alone.[13]

Computers and handheld devices have made online banking extremely convenient. However, hackers have stolen millions from banking customers by tricking them into visiting websites and downloading malicious software that gives hackers access to their passwords.

© Robin Lund/Alamy Stock Photo

Online Banking. Many banking activities are now conducted on a computer at home or at work or through wireless devices such as cell phones and tablets anywhere there is a wireless "hot spot." Consumers and small businesses can now make a bewildering array of financial transactions at home or on the go 24 hours a day. Functioning much like a vast network of personal ATMs, companies like Google and Apple provide online banking services through mobile phones, allowing sub-scribers to make sophisticated banking transactions, buy and sell stocks and bonds, and purchase products and airline tickets without ever leaving home or speaking to another human being. Many banks allow customers to log directly into their accounts to check balances, transfer money between accounts, view their account statements, and pay bills via home computer or other Internet-enabled devices. Computer and advanced telecommunications technology have revolutionized world commerce; 62 percent of adults list Internet banking as their preferred banking method, making it the most popular banking method in the United States.[14]

Future of Banking

LO 15-6

Investigate the challenges ahead for the banking industry.

Rapid advances and innovations in technology are challenging the banking industry and requiring it to change. As we said earlier, more and more banks, both large and small, are offering electronic access to their financial services. ATM technology is rapidly changing, with machines now dispensing more than just cash. Online finan-cial services, ATM technology, and bill presentation are just a few of the areas where rapidly changing technology is causing the banking industry to change as well.

Impact of Financial Crisis.   The premise that banks will get bigger over the next 10 years is uncertain. During 2007–2008, the financial markets collapsed under the weight of declining housing prices, subprime mortgages (mortgages with low-qualifying borrowers), and risky securities backed by these subprime mortgages. Because the value of bank assets declined dramatically, most large banks like CitiBank, Bank of America, and Wachovia had a shrinking capital base. That is, the amount of debt in relation to their equity was so high that they were below the minimum required capital requirements.

During this period, the Federal Reserve took unprecedented actions that included buying up troubled assets from the banks and lending money at the discount window to nonbanks such as investment banks and brokers. The Fed also entered into the financial markets by making markets in commercial paper and other securities where the markets had ceased to function in an orderly fashion. Additionally, the Fed began to pay interest on reserves banks kept at the Fed and finally, it kept interest rates low to stimulate the economy and to help the banks regain their health. Because banks make money by the spread between their borrowing and lending rates, the Fed managed the spread between long- and short-term rates to generate a fairly large spread for the banks.

Additionally, to keep interest rates low and stimulate the economy, the Fed bought $85 billion of mortgages and other financial assets on a monthly basis. By mid-2014, it had accumulated close to $4 trillion of securities on its balance sheet and in 2015 stopped its asset purchases as the economy improved. A major issue involves the impact this will have on the economy once the Fed begins to sell these securities.

Lastly, the future of the structure of the banking system is in the hands of the U.S. Congress. In reaction to the financial meltdown and severe recession, Congress passed the Dodd-Frank Wall Street Reform and Consumer Protection Act. The full name implies that the intent of the act is to eliminate the ability of banks to create this type of problem in the future.

Shadow Banking.   In broad general terms, shadow banking refers to companies performing banking functions of some sort that are not regulated by banking regula-tors. Shadow banking activities are increasing. In a letter to shareholders in its annual report, James Dimon, CEO and chairman of JPMorgan Chase, was quoted as saying to his shareholders that the bank will face tough competitors, including shadow banking. He may have said it best in the following quote.

> Many of these institutions are smart and sophisticated and will benefit as banks move out of certain products and services. Non-bank financial competitors will look at every product we price, and if they can do it cheaper with their set of capital providers, they will. There is nothing inherently wrong with this—it is a natural state of affairs and, in some cases, may benefit the clients who get the better price. But regulators should—and will—be looking at how all financial companies (including non-bank competitors) need to be regulated and will be evaluating what is better to be done by banks vs. non-banks and vice versa.[15]

In addition to shadow banks mentioned by Mr. Dimon, there are the peer-to-peer lenders like Prosper, a company that matches investors and borrowers with loans of between $2,000 and $35,000. There are other sources of funding by Internet websites such as GoFundMe, which helps people enhance their life skills, raise money for health care issues, and more. Another similar website is Kickstarter, which funds creative projects in the worlds of art, film, games, music, publishing, and so on. In many cases, funds provided for these projects replace loans that might have been used to develop the project. These forms of funding are growing rapidly. Kickstarter was formed in October 2009 and has already received a total of $2.3 billion to fund more than 104,000 projects.[16] There is also the budding use of virtual money and other futuristic ideas, so only time will tell how the world of banking changes over time and how bank regulators will deal with these nonbank institutions.

⊖ So You're Interested in Financial Systems or Banking

You think you might be interested in going into finance or banking, but it is so hard to tell when you are a full-time student. Classes that seem interesting when you take them might not translate into an interesting work experience after graduation. A great way to see if you would excel at a career in finance is to get some experience in the industry. Internships, whether they are paid or unpaid, not only help you figure out what you might really want to do after you graduate, but they are also a great way to build up your résumé, put your learning to use, and start generating connections within the field.

For example, Pennsylvania's Delaware County District Attorney's Office has been accepting business students from Villanova University for a six-month internship. The student works in the economic-crime division, analyzing documents of people under investigation for financial crimes ranging from fraud to money laundering. The students get actual experience in forensic accounting and have the chance to see whether this is the right career path. On top of that, the program has saved the county an average of $20,000 annually on consulting and accounting fees, not to mention that detectives now have more time to take on larger case-loads. One student who completed the program spent his six months investigating a case in which the owner of a sewage treatment company had embezzled a total of $1 million over the course of nine years. The student noted that the experience helped him gain an understanding about how different companies handle their financial statements, as well as how accounting can be applied in forensics and law enforcement.

Internship opportunities are plentiful all over the country, although you may need to do some research to find them. To start, talk to your program adviser and your professors about opportunities. Also, you can check company websites where you think you might like to work to see if they have any opportunities available. City, state, or federal government offices often provide student internships as well. No matter where you end up interning, the real-life skills you pick up, as well as the résumé boost you get, will be helpful in finding a job after you graduate. When you graduate, commercial banks and other financial institutions offer major employment opportunities. In 2008–2009, a major downturn in the financial industry resulted in mergers, acquisitions, and financial restructuring for many companies. While the immediate result was a decrease in job opportunities, as the industry recovers, there will be many challenging job opportunities available.[17]

Review Your Understanding

Define money, its functions, and its characteristics.

Money is anything generally accepted as a means of payment for goods and services. Money serves as a medium of exchange, a measure of value, and a store of wealth. To serve effectively in these functions, money must be acceptable, divisible, portable, durable, stable in value, and difficult to counterfeit.

Describe various types of money.

Money may take the form of currency, checking accounts, or other accounts. Checking accounts are funds left in an account in a financial institution that can be withdrawn (usually by writing a check) without advance notice. Other types of accounts include savings accounts (funds left in an interest-earning account that usually cannot be withdrawn without advance notice), money market accounts (an interest-bearing checking account that is invested in short-term debt instruments), certificates of deposit (deposits left in an institution for a specified period of time at a specified interest rate), credit cards (access to a preapproved line of credit granted by a bank or company), and debit cards (means of instant cash transfers between customer and merchant accounts), as well as traveler's checks, money orders, and cashier's checks.

Specify how the Federal Reserve Board manages the money supply and regulates the American banking system.

The Federal Reserve Board regulates the U.S. financial system. The Fed manages the money supply by buying and selling government securities, raising or lowering the discount rate (the rate of interest at which banks may borrow cash reserves from the Fed), raising or lowering bank reserve requirements (the percentage of funds on deposit at a bank that must be held to cover expected depositor withdrawals), and adjusting down payment and repayment terms for credit purchases. It also regulates banking practices, processes checks, and oversees federal depository insurance for institutions.

Compare and contrast commercial banks, savings and loan associations, credit unions, and mutual savings banks.

Commercial banks are financial institutions that take and hold deposits in accounts for and make loans to individuals and businesses. Savings and loan associations are financial institutions that primarily specialize in offering savings accounts and mortgage loans. Credit unions are financial institutions owned and controlled by their depositors. Mutual savings banks are similar to S&Ls except that they are owned by their depositors.

Distinguish among nonbanking institutions such as insurance companies, pension funds, mutual funds, and finance companies.

Insurance companies are businesses that protect their clients against financial losses due to certain circumstances, in exchange for a fee. Pension funds are investments set aside by organizations or individuals to meet retirement needs. Mutual funds pool investors' money and invest in large numbers of different types of securities. Brokerage firms buy and sell stocks and bonds for investors. Finance companies make short-term loans at higher interest rates than do banks.

Investigate the challenges ahead for the banking industry.

Future changes in financial regulations are likely to result in fewer but larger banks and other financial institutions.

Recommend the most appropriate financial institution for a hypothetical small business.

Using the information presented in this chapter, you should be able to answer the questions in the "Solve the Dilemma" feature at the end of this chapter and find the best institution for Hill Optometrics.

Revisit the World of Business

1. Why do you think student debt has become such a major problem in the United States?

2. What are some ways that lenders might act unscrupulously in trying to collect on student debt?

3. How much responsibility should the lender take in ensuring the student is likely to pay the debt back in the future? How much responsibility should the student take?

Learn the Terms

automated clearinghouses (ACHs) 485
automated teller machine (ATM) 485
brokerage firms 484
certificates of deposit (CDs) 473
checking account 472
commercial banks 479
credit cards 474
credit controls 478
credit union 481
debit card 475
discount rate 478

electronic funds transfer (EFT) 485
Federal Deposit Insurance Corporation (FDIC) 481
Federal Reserve Board 475
finance 468
finance companies 485
insurance companies 483
investment banker 485
monetary policy 476
money 468
money market accounts 473

mutual fund 484
mutual savings banks 481
National Credit Union Administration (NCUA) 482
open market operations 477
pension funds 483
reserve requirement 477
reward cards 474
savings accounts 473
savings and loan associations (S&Ls) 480

Check Your Progress

1. What are the six characteristics of money? Explain how the U.S. dollar has those six characteristics.

2. What is the difference between a credit card and a debit card? Why are credit cards considerably more popular with U.S. consumers?

3. Discuss the four economic goals the Federal Reserve must try to achieve with its monetary policy.

4. Explain how the Federal Reserve uses open market operations to expand and contract the money supply.

5. What are the basic differences between commercial banks and savings and loans?

6. Why do credit unions charge lower rates than commercial banks?

7. Why do finance companies charge higher interest rates than commercial banks?

8. How are mutual funds, money market funds, and pension funds similar? How are they different?

9. What are some of the advantages of electronic funds transfer systems?

Get Involved

1. Survey the banks, savings and loans, and credit unions in your area, and put together a list of interest rates paid on the various types of checking accounts. Find out what, if any, restrictions are in effect for NOW accounts and regular checking accounts. In which type of account and in what institution would you deposit your money? Why?

2. Survey the same institutions as in Question 1, this time inquiring as to the rates asked for each of their various loans. Where would you prefer to obtain a car loan? A home loan? Why?

Build Your Skills

Managing Money

Background

You have just graduated from college and have received an offer for your dream job (annual salary: $35,000). This premium salary is a reward for your hard work, perseverance, and good grades. It is also a reward for the social skills you developed in college doing service work as a tutor for high school students and interacting with the business community as the program chairman of the college business fraternity, Delta Sigma Pi. You are engaged and plan to be married this summer. You and your spouse will have a joint income of $60,000, and the two of you are trying to decide the best way to manage your money.

Task

Research available financial service institutions in your area, and answer the following questions.

1. What kinds of institutions and services can you use to help manage your money?

2. Do you want a full-service financial organization that can take care of your banking, insurance, and investing needs, or do you want to spread your business among individual specialists? Why have you made this choice?

3. What retirement alternatives do you have?

Solve the Dilemma

Seeing the Financial Side of Business

Dr. Stephen Hill, a successful optometrist in Indianapolis, Indiana, has tinkered with various inventions for years. Having finally developed what he believes is his first saleable product (a truly scratch-resistant and lightweight lens), Hill has decided to invest his life savings and open Hill Optometrics to manufacture and market his invention.

Unfortunately, despite possessing true genius in many areas, Hill is uncertain about the "finance side" of business and the various functions of different types of financial institutions in the economy. He is, however, fully aware that he will need financial services such as checking and savings accounts, various short-term investments that can easily and quickly be converted to cash as needs dictate, and sources of borrowing capacity—should the need for either short- or long-term

loans arise. Despite having read mounds of brochures from various local and national financial institutions, Hill is still somewhat unclear about the merits and capabilities of each type of financial institution. He has turned to you, his 11th patient of the day, for help.

LO 15-7

Recommend the most appropriate financial institution for a hypothetical small business.

Discussion Questions

1. List the various types of U.S. financial institutions and the primary function of each.

2. What services of each financial institution is Hill's new company likely to need?

3. Which single financial institution is likely to be best able to meet Hill's small company's needs now? Why?

Build Your Business Plan

Money and the Financial System

This chapter provides you with the opportunity to think about money and the financial system and just how many new businesses fail every year. In some industries, the failure rate is as high as 80 percent. One reason for such a high failure rate is the inability to manage the finances of the organization. From the start of the business, financial planning

plays a key role. Try getting a loan without an accompanying budget/forecast of earnings and cash flow.

While obtaining a loan from a family member may be the easiest way to fund your business, it may cause more problems for you later on if you are unable to pay the money back as scheduled. Before heading to a lending officer at a bank, contact your local SBA center to see what assistance it might provide.

See for Yourself Videocase

State Farm: Not Your Traditional Bank

Although State Farm is one of the nation's most well-known insurance companies, many do not realize that it also functions as a bank. Unlike most traditional banks, however, State Farm does not have physical bank locations. The company instead operates through its

network of independent insurance agents, its 24/7 call center, and the Internet. In fact, State Farm Bank owes much of its success to the explosion of online banking. And although it does not function like a typical bank, the company is quick to point out that it offers many of the same benefits at lower costs.

"With State Farm, you have direct deposit, you have an ATM debit card, so you can go to any ATM and have your services completed, much like most of the traditional banks but for a lesser fee," says State Farm representative Maylen Hernandez.

Other services State Farm Bank offers include Visa credit cards, money market accounts, CDs, and savings accounts. It also offers nonbanking services, including annuities, retirement savings, life insurance, and estate planning services. State Farm Bank is a savings and loan association (S&L). While S&Ls originally focused mainly on savings accounts, deregulation has allowed S&Ls like State Farm Bank to compete with traditional banks by offering a myriad of services. Like all banking institutions, the Federal Deposit Insurance Corporation (FDIC) insures State Farm Bank deposit accounts.

State Farm is unique because it acts as both a banking institution and a nonbanking institution in the form of an insurance company. A law passed in 1933 called the Home Owners Loan Act gives mutual insurance companies such as State Farm the ability to operate a financial services firm. Additionally, the 1999 Gramm-Leach-Bliley Act removed many of the barriers that existed between insurance and banking.

However, State Farm must be careful to maintain a delicate balance between its banking and nonbanking operations. Federal law prevents any one company from performing too many activities so as to prevent a financial firm from gaining too much control. Therefore, State Farm must operate two separate companies, one for insurance and the other for banking. Because State Farm operates as an S&L—also known as a thrift—it is regulated by both the Office of Thrift Supervision and the FDIC. This means that State Farm Bank has limitations that other banks might not have. For example, while it can provide car loans, it cannot do so directly through automobile dealerships.

Despite this fact, State Farm insurance agents often market the company's banking services as a way to increase value to their customers. Bernie Floriani, another State Farm representative, states, "It's very natural for us to not only do auto insurance on a customer, but also talk about auto financing, and that part of the whole State Farm Bank concept is very appealing to me as a business owner." Customers benefit because they can turn to State Farm for a variety of their financial needs, while State Farm is able to increase its share of the customer.

More recently, State Farm Bank has worked at adjusting its service offerings to take advantage of changing technology. For instance, it became one of the first banking firms to scan and deposit checks using mobile technology. The firm's Pocket Agent mobile app makes it easy for the bank's customers to deposit checks on-the-go through its MyTime Deposit service. State Farm's mobile banking technology also lets customers transfer funds among various accounts, pay bills, and view their balance.

By expanding into banking, State Farm has seized the opportunity to increase its presence in the financial services industry. This company, so well-known for its insurance, may someday rival the more traditional banking firms such as Bank of America or Wells Fargo. To compete in such a competitive environment, State Farm Bank must constantly monitor consumer banking practices, adapt to new technological trends, and be aware of new regulations that might help or hinder the industry.[18]

Discussion Questions

1. Describe State Farm Bank's banking and nonbanking services.

2. Why must State Farm keep its banking and nonbanking services separate? How does it accomplish this?

3. How is State Farm Bank adapting to changing technological trends in the banking industry?

You can find the related video in the Video Library in Connect. Ask your instructor how you can access Connect.

Team Exercise

Mutual funds pool individual investor dollars and invest them in a number of different securities. Go to http://finance.yahoo.com/ and select some top-performing funds using criteria such as sector, style, or strategy. Assume that your group has $100,000 to invest in mutual funds. Select five funds in which to invest, representing a balanced (varied industries, risk, etc.) portfolio, and defend your selections.

Endnotes

1. Natalie Kitroeff, "The Student Debt Collecton Mess," *Bloomberg Businessweek*, June 8–14, 2015, pp. 45–46; Aimee Picchi, "America's Skyrocketing Credit Card Debt," *CBS*, March 10, 2015, http://www.cbsnews.com/news/americas-skyrocketing-credit-card-debt/ (accessed July 16, 2015); Debt.org, "Types of Loans & Types of Credit," https://www.debt.org/credit/loans/ (accessed July 16, 2015); Danielle Douglas-Gabriel and Katie Zezima, "Obama Plans to Make It Easier to Pay Your Student Loans," *The Washington Post*, March 10, 2015, http://www.washingtonpost.com/news/get-there/wp/2015/03/10/obama-plans-to-make-it-easier-to-pay-your-student-loans/

(accessed July 16, 2015); Nancy Cook, "Confirmed: Millennials' Top Financial Concern Is Student-Loan Debt," *The Atlantic,* June 20, 2015, http://www.theatlantic.com/business/archive/2015/06/millennials-student-loan-debt-money/396275/ (accessed July 16, 2015).

2. Noelle Knox and Maxwell Murphy, "Some Big Firms Do Just Fine Without a CFO," *The Wall Street Journal,* October 13, 2014, http://www.wsj.com/articles/some-big-firms-do-just-fine-without-a-cfo-1413237258?cb=logged0.10800692904740572 (accessed December 18, 2015); Myles Corson, "The Evolving Role of Today's CFO," *Business Finance,* August 7, 2012, http://businessfinancemag.com/hr/evolving-role-todays-cfo (accessed December 18, 2015); Fred Destin, "If You Think Your Company Needs a CFO, Think Again," *Business Insider,* August 30, 2010, http://www.businessinsider.com/if-you-think-youre-startup-needs-a-cfo-think-again-2010-8 (accessed December 18, 2015).

3. Paul Krugman, "Why Is Deflation Bad?" *The New York Times,* August 2, 2010, http://krugman.blogs.nytimes.com/2010/08/02/why-is-deflation-bad/(accessed June 16, 2014).

4. Economic Research Federal Reserve Bank of St. Louis, "Currency in Circulation," June 4, 2014, http://research.stlouisfed.org/fred2/series/WCURCIR (accessed June 12, 2014).

5. "Why the Swiss Unpegged the Franc," January 18, 2015, *The Economist,* http://www.economist.com/blogs/economist-explains/2015/01/economist-explains-13 (accessed April 8, 2015); "Swiss-Made Products Become More Expensive as Franc Rises," *The Sydney Morning Herald,* January 16, 2015, http://www.smh.com.au/national/swissmade-products-become-more-expensive-asfranc-rises-20150116-12riei.html (accessed April 8, 2015).

6. "Weird and Wonderful Money Facts and Trivia," *Happy Worker,* www.happyworker.com/magazine/facts/weird-and-wonderful-money-facts (accessed April 25, 2016).

7. Ibid.

8. "About the Redesigned Currency," The Department of the Treasury Bureau of Engraving and Printing, www.newmoney.gov/newmoney/currency/aboutnotes.htm (accessed April 2, 2010).

9. Jessica Dickler, "Americans Still Relying on Credit Cards to Get By," *CNN Money,* May 23, 2012, http://money.cnn.com/2012/05/22/pf/credit-card/index.htm (accessed June 16, 2014); Martin Merzer, "Survey: Students Fail the Credit Card Test," *Fox Business,* April 16, 2012, www.creditcards.com/credit-card-news/survey-students-fail-credit-card-test-1279.php (accessed June 16, 2014).

10. Businesswire, "U.S. Bank Recognized by *Newsweek* for Its Environmental Sustainability," November 9, 2011, http://www.businesswire.com/news/home/20111109006367/en/U.S.-Bank-Recognized-Newsweek-Environmental-Sustainability-Efforts#.VZ2jLflViko (accessed July 9, 2015); U.S. Bancorp, *U.S. Bancorp Environmental Sustainability Policy,* March 2014, https://www.usbank.com/pdf/community/Environmental%20Policy%20March%202014-Final.pdf (accessed July 9, 2015); U.S. Bank, "Our Approach to Environmental Sustainability," 2015, https://www.usbank.com/community/environmental-sustainability.html (accessed July 9, 2015); Penny Crosman, "America's Greenest Banks,"*American Banker,* April 1, 2012, http://www.americanbanker.com/btn/25_4/green-banks-citi-huntington-1047907-1.html?zkPrintable=1&nopagination=1 (accessed July 9, 2015); U.S. Bancorp, "Good for You & the Environment," 2015, https://www.usbank.com/en/advertising/getGreen.cfm?redirect=getgreen (accessed July 9, 2015); U.S. Bancorp, *Leading by Serving: 2013 Corporate Citizenship Report,* 2014, https://www.usbank.com/pdf/community/2013_Corporate_Citizenship_Report.pdf (accessed July 9, 2015).

11. "Deposit Insurance Simplification Fact Sheet," FDIC website, www.unitedamericanbank.com/pdfs/FDIC-Insurance-Coverage-Fact-Sheet.pdf (accessed June 16, 2014).

12. Heather Jordan, "Meet the Michigan Native Who Just Sold His Mobile Payment Startup to PayPal," *MLive,* April 12, 2015, http://www.mlive.com/news/bay-city/index.ssf/2015/04/paypal_acquires_paydiant_co-fo.html (accessed July 23, 2015); Sara Castellanos, "Apple Pay Debacle Puts Paydiant Technology in Spotlight," *Boston Business Journal,* October 29, 2014, http://www.bizjournals.com/boston/blog/techflash/2014/10/apple-pay-debacle-puts-paydiant-technology-in.html (accessed July 23, 2015); Jacob Kastrenakes, "PayPal Is Buying Mobile Wallet Maker Paydiant to Take on Apple Pay," *The Verge,* March 2, 2015, http://www.theverge.com/2015/3/2/8135001/paypal-buying-paydiant-mobile-wallet (accessed July 23, 2015); Robin Wauters, "Paydiant Throws Its Hat Into the Mobile Payments Ring, Raises $7.6 Million," *Tech Crunch,* February 22, 2011, http://techcrunch.com/2011/02/22/paydiant-throws-hat-into-the-mobile-payments-ring-raises-7-6-million/ (accessed July 23, 2015); Paydiant, "Merchants," http://www.paydiant.com/merchants.html(accessed July 23, 2015); Dan Primack, "Why Paydiant Is Selling to PayPal,"*Fortune,* March 2, 2015, http://fortune.com/2015/03/02/why-paydiant-is-selling-to-paypal/ (accessed July 23, 2015); Steven Tweedie and Steve Kovach, "Now We Know the Truth About Why CVS and Rite Aid Blocked Apple Pay," *Business Insider,* October 29, 2014, http://www.businessinsider.com/why-rite-aid-and-cvs-blocked-apple-pay-2014-10 (accessed July 23, 2015); Robin Sidel, "Payments Network Takes on Google," *The Wall Street Journal,* August 15, 2012, http://www.wsj.com/articles/SB10000872396390444042704577589523094336872 (accessed July 23, 2015); Galen Moore, "This Boston Startup Hopes It Can Win Like Starbucks Vs. Apple Pay," *BostInno,* October 28, 2014, http://bostinno.streetwise.co/2014/10/28/who-is-mcx-can-it-win-like-starbucks-vs-apple-pay/ (accessed July 23, 2015); Greg Bensinger, "PayPal to Buy Mobile-Payments Firm Paydiant," *The Wall Street Journal,* March 2, 2015, http://www.wsj.com/articles/paypal-to-buy-mobile-payments-firm-paydiant-1425313818 (accessed July 23, 2015).

13. "NACHA Reports More Than 18 Billion ACH Payments in 2007," The Free Library, May 19, 2008, www.thefreelibrary.com/NACHA+Reports+More+Than+18+Billion+ACH+Payments+in+2007.-a0179156311 (accessed May 2, 2016).

14. "From the Vault . . ." Ohio Commerce Bank, Winter 2012, http://website-tools.net/google-keyword/site/www.ohiocommercebank.com (accessed June 16, 2014).

15. JPMorgan 2013 Annual Report, p. 10.

16. Kickstarter, "About," https://www.kickstarter.com/about (accessed May 2, 2016).

17. "CSI Pennsylvania," *CFO Magazine,* March 2008, p. 92.

18. State Farm Bank video, Viddler.com, http://www.viddler.com/embed/6dc42a21/?f=1&player=arpeggio&secret=80543757&make_responsive=0%22%20width=%22437%22%20height=%22399%22%20frameborder=%220%22 http://www.viddler.com/embed/6dc42a21/?f=1&player=arpeggio&secret=80543757&make_responsive=0%22%20 width=%22437%22%20height=%22399%22%20frameborder=%220%22 (accessed May 20, 2016); State Farm, "Mobile Banking," https://www.statefarm.com/finances/banking/manage-your-accounts/account-access/mobile (accessed May 20, 2016); Bloomberg LP, "Company Overview of State Farm Bank, F.S.B.," *Bloomberg,* 2016, http://www.bloomberg.com/research/stocks/private/snapshot.asp?privcapId=22653991 (accessed May 20, 2016); State Farm Bank, "Banking with State Farm Bank® as Easy as Point-and-Shoot," *PR Newswire,* August 3, 2010, http://www.prnewswire.com/news-releases/banking-with-state-farm-bank-as-easy-as-point-and-shoot-99816194.html (accessed May 20, 2016); State Farm, "Pocket Agent®," https://www.statefarm.com/customer-care/download-mobile-apps/pocket-agent (accessed May 20, 2016).

© Stockphoto/skodonnell

16

Financial Management and Securities Markets

Chapter Outline

Learning Objectives

After reading this chapter, you will be able to:

LO 16-1 Describe some common methods of managing current assets.

LO 16-2 Identify some sources of short-term financing (current liabilities).

LO 16-3 Summarize the importance of long-term assets and capital budgeting.

LO 16-4 Specify how companies finance their operations and manage fixed assets with long-term liabilities, particularly bonds.

LO 16-5 Discuss how corporations can use equity financing by issuing stock through an investment banker.

LO 16-6 Describe the various securities markets in the United States.

LO 16-7 Critique the position of short-term assets and liabilities of a small manufacturer and recommend corrective action.

Enter the World of Business ⊖——————————————

Marketing Digital Financial Products: No John Hancock Needed

Even financial services firms must invest in advertising to reach potential clients. As with any project, the company must first assess the risks involved, ensure that the costs will result in a sufficient return on investment, and budget the necessary funds. For financial services firm John Hancock, it wanted to engage consumers with entertaining content.

John Hancock offers financial services such as 401(k) plans, life insurance, investments, college savings, and long-term care. However, the average consumer is often not financially literate in these areas, so the company needed a campaign that would highlight these different products in ways the consumer could understand.

The firm decided to develop a digital campaign that could be experienced on several devices and across various social media platforms. The result was "Life Comes Next," a campaign that featured four different real-life situations that leave viewers on a cliffhanger and encourage them to visit Hancock's website to find out what happens next. Each video strives to create a relatable experience that highlights its product offerings. For instance, one of its videos deals with moving a parent into a nursing home, while another involves the challenges of paying for college. Each video can be followed up by three possible endings.

The videos also included financial statistics, such as the average cost of a college degree, which attempts to guide viewers to see themselves in each scenario. The campaign used the hashtag #LifeComesNext and encouraged viewers to tell their own financial stories. During the campaign's run, more than 1 million people visited the website, and there were almost 200,000 impressions across social media platforms. The increase in brand visibility seemed well worth the project's cost.[1]

Introduction

While it's certainly true that money makes the world go around, financial management is the discipline that makes the world turn more smoothly. Indeed, without effective management of assets, liabilities, and owners' equity, all business organizations are doomed to fail—regardless of the quality and innovativeness of their products. Financial management is the field that addresses the issues of obtaining and managing the funds and resources necessary to run a business successfully. It is not limited to business organizations: All organizations, from the corner store to the local nonprofit art museum, from giant corporations to county governments, must manage their resources effectively and efficiently if they are to achieve their objectives.

In this chapter, we look at both short- and long-term financial management. First, we discuss the management of short-term assets, which companies use to generate sales and conduct ordinary day-to-day business operations. Next, we turn our attention to the management of short-term liabilities, the sources of short-term funds used to finance the business. Then, we discuss the management of long-term assets such as plants, equipment, and the use of common stock (equity) and bonds (long-term liability) to finance these long-term corporate assets. Finally, we look at the securities markets, where stocks and bonds are traded.

Managing Current Assets and Liabilities

Describe some common methods of managing current assets.

Managing short-term assets and liabilities involves managing the current assets and liabilities on the balance sheet (discussed in Chapter 14). Current assets are short-term resources such as cash, investments, accounts receivable, and inventory. Current liabilities are short-term debts such as accounts payable, accrued salaries, accrued taxes, and short-term bank loans. We use the terms *current* and *short term* interchangeably because short-term assets and liabilities are usually replaced by new assets and liabilities within three or four months, and always within a year. Managing short-term assets and liabilities is sometimes called **working capital management** because short-term assets and liabilities continually flow through an organization and are thus said to be "working."

working capital management
the managing of short-term assets and liabilities.

Managing Current Assets

The chief goal of financial managers who focus on current assets and liabilities is to maximize the return to the business on cash, temporary investments of idle cash, accounts receivable, and inventory.

transaction balances
cash kept on hand by a firm to pay normal daily expenses, such as employee wages and bills for supplies and utilities.

Managing Cash.   A crucial element facing any financial manager is effectively managing the firm's cash flow. Remember that cash flow is the movement of money through an organization on a daily, weekly, monthly, or yearly basis. Ensuring that sufficient (but not excessive) funds are on hand to meet the company's obligations is one of the single most important facets of financial management.

Idle cash does not make money, and corporate checking accounts typically do not earn interest. As a result, astute money managers try to keep just enough cash on hand, called **transaction balances,** to pay bills—such as employee wages, supplies, and utilities—as they fall due. To manage the firm's cash and ensure that enough cash flows through the organization quickly and efficiently, companies try to speed up cash collections from customers.

lockbox
an address, usually a commercial bank, at which a company receives payments in order to speed collections from customers.

To facilitate collection, some companies have customers send their payments to a **lockbox,** which is simply an address for receiving payments, instead of directly to the

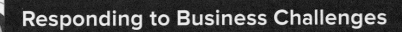

Is Too Much Disclosure Too Complicated?

Annual reports give investors a picture of a company's financial health. Regulators require companies to disclose certain information to ensure investors are given an accurate snapshot of the firm. However, investors and company officials claim that too many regulatory requirements have made financial reports so complex that investors will not even read them, let alone understand them. General Electric's annual report, for example, was nearly 110,000 words.

A major concern is that companies are creating reports that comply with legal requirements rather than doing what they are intended to do: inform investors about a firm's financial health. Companies often put in boilerplate information mandated by regulators. By putting in more information, CFOs protect themselves from claims they did not adequately disclose potential issues. Additionally, complex financial instruments such as derivatives add to the complexity of reporting.

The problem with too much disclosure is that it not only discourages investors from reading financial reports, but it also might hide unfavorable information in mountains of irrelevant data. A KPMG survey resulted in findings that might be helpful in addressing this issue. First, it is recommended that more graphic and tabular elements be used to visually depict data and prevent word overload. Another recommendation is to use technology to avoid repetition in the reports. Finally, firms could limit their risk factors to more company-specific risks.[2]

Discussion Questions

1. How can too much financial disclosure actually discourage investors from reading through financial information?
2. Why are financial reports so complex?
3. Why do CFOs seem to think that more information is always better?

---

company's main address. The manager of the lockbox, usually a commercial bank, collects payments directly from the lockbox several times a day and deposits them into the company's bank account. The bank can then start clearing the checks and get the money into the company's checking account much more quickly than if the payments had been submitted directly to the company. However, there is no free lunch: The costs associated with lockbox systems make them worthwhile only for those companies that receive thousands of checks from customers each business day.

Large firms with many stores or offices around the country, such as HSBC Finance Corporation, frequently use electronic funds transfer to speed up collections. HSBC Finance Corporation's local offices deposit checks received each business day into their local banks and, at the end of the day, HSBC Finance Corporation's corporate office initiates the transfer of all collected funds to its central bank for overnight investment. This technique is especially attractive for major international companies, which face slow and sometimes uncertain physical delivery of payments and/or less-than-efficient check-clearing procedures.

More and more companies are now using electronic funds transfer systems to pay and collect bills online. Companies generally want to collect cash quickly but pay out cash slowly. When companies use electronic funds transfers between buyers and suppliers, the speed of collections and disbursements increases to one day. Only with the use of checks can companies delay the payment of cash by three or four days until the check is presented to their bank and the cash leaves their account.

Investing Idle Cash.   As companies sell products, they generate cash on a daily basis, and sometimes cash comes in faster than it is needed to pay bills. Organizations often invest this "extra" cash, for periods as short as one day (overnight) or for as long as one year, until it is needed. Such temporary investments of cash are known as **marketable securities.** Examples include U.S. Treasury bills, certificates of deposit, commercial paper, and eurodollar deposits. Table 16-1 summarizes a number of different marketable securities used by businesses and some sample interest rates on

marketable securities temporary investment of "extra" cash by organizations for up to one year in U.S. Treasury bills, certificates of deposit, commercial paper, or eurodollar loans.

TABLE 16-1   Short-Term Investment Possibilities for Idle Cash

Type of Security	Maturity	Seller of Security	Interest Rate 6/23/2006	Interest Rate 4/18/2016	Safety Level
U.S. Treasury bills	90 days	U.S. government	4.80%	0.22%	Excellent
U.S. Treasury bills	180 days	U.S. government	5.05	0.35	Excellent
Commercial paper	30 days	Major corporations	5.14	0.46	Very good
Certificates of deposit	90 days	U.S. commercial banks	5.40	0.40	Very good
Certificates of deposit	180 days	U.S. commercial banks	5.43	0.45	Very good
Eurodollars	90 days	European commercial banks	5.48	0.65	Very good

Sources: Board of Governors of the Federal Reserve System, "Selected Interest Rates (Weekly)—H.15," April 18, 2016, www.federalreserve.gov/releases/H15/current/default. htm (accessed April 21, 2016); Fidelity, "Certificates of Deposit," www.fidelity.com/fixed-income-bonds/cds (accessed April 22, 2016).

these investments as of June 23, 2006, and April 18, 2016. The safety rankings are relative. While all of the listed securities are very low risk, the U.S. government securities are the safest. You can see from the table that interest rates have declined during the two periods presented.

The Fed used monetary policy to lower interest rates to stimulate borrowing and investment during the severe recession of 2007–2009 and continued to maintain low rates into 2016 in order to stimulate employment and economic growth. The Fed raised interest rates 25 basis points (1/4 of a percent) in December 2015 and is expected to raise rates again in the second half of 2016. Most economists agree that rates will rise over the next few years as the economy continues its slow growth recovery. But a return to 2006 rates is not expected during 2017.

Treasury bills (T-bills) short-term debt obligations the U.S. government sells to raise money.

Many large companies invest idle cash in U.S. **Treasury bills (T-bills),** which are short-term debt obligations the U.S. government sells to raise money. Issued weekly by the U.S. Treasury, T-bills carry maturities of between one week and one year. U.S. T-bills are generally considered to be the safest of all investments and are called risk free because the U.S. government will not default on its debt.

commercial certificates of deposit (CDs) certificates of deposit issued by commercial banks and brokerage companies, available in minimum amounts of $100,000, which may be traded prior to maturity.

Commercial certificates of deposit (CDs) are issued by commercial banks and brokerage companies. They are available in minimum amounts of $100,000 but are typically in units of $1 million for large corporations investing excess cash. Unlike consumer CDs (discussed in Chapter 15), which must be held until maturity, commercial CDs may be traded prior to maturity. Should a cash shortage occur, the organization can simply sell the CD on the open market and obtain needed funds.

One of the most popular short-term investments for the largest business organizations is **commercial paper**—a written promise from one company to another to pay a specific amount of money. Because commercial paper is backed only by the name and reputation of the issuing company, sales of commercial paper are restricted to only the largest and most financially stable companies. As commercial paper is frequently bought and sold for durations of as short as one business day, many "players" in the market find themselves buying commercial paper with excess cash on one day and selling it to gain extra money the following day.

commercial paper a written promise from one company to another to pay a specific amount of money.

During 2007 and 2008, the commercial paper market simply stopped functioning. Investors no longer trusted the IOUs of even the best companies. Companies that had relied on commercial paper to fund short-term cash needs had to turn to the banks for borrowing. Those companies who had existing lines of credit at their bank were able to draw on their line of credit. Others were in a tight spot. Eventually, the Federal Reserve entered the market to buy and sell commercial paper for its own portfolio. This is something the Fed was not in the habit of doing. But it rescued the market, and the commercial paper market is now standing on its own two feet without the Fed's help.

Some companies invest idle cash in international markets such as the **eurodollar market,** a market for trading U.S. dollars in foreign countries. Because the eurodollar market was originally developed by London banks, any dollar-denominated deposit in a non-U.S. bank is called a eurodollar deposit, regardless of whether the issuing bank is actually located in Europe, South America, or anyplace else. For example, if you travel overseas and deposit $1,000 in London, you will have "created" a eurodollar deposit in the amount of $1,000. Because the U.S. dollar is accepted by most countries for international trade, these dollar deposits can be used by international companies to settle their accounts. The market created for trading such investments offers firms with extra dollars a chance to earn a slightly higher rate of return with just a little more risk than they would face by investing in U.S. Treasury bills.

Individuals and companies can invest their idle cash in marketable securities such as U.S. Treasury bills, commercial paper, and eurodollar deposits.

© Tetra Images/Getty Images

eurodollar market
a market for trading U.S. dollars in foreign countries.

Maximizing Accounts Receivable.   After cash and marketable securities, the balance sheet lists accounts receivable and inventory. Remember that accounts receivable is money owed to a business by credit customers. For example, if you charge your Shell gasoline purchases, until you actually pay for them with cash or a check, they represent an account receivable to Shell. Many businesses make the vast majority of their sales on credit, so managing accounts receivable is an important task.

Each credit sale represents an account receivable for the company, the terms of which typically require customers to pay the full amount due within 30, 60, or even 90 days from the date of the sale. To encourage quick payment, some businesses offer some of their customers discounts of between 1 and 2 percent if they pay off their balance within a specified period of time (usually between 10 and 30 days). On the other hand, late payment charges of between 1 and 1.5 percent serve to discourage slow payers from sitting on their bills forever. The larger the early payment discount offered, the faster customers will tend to pay their accounts. Unfortunately, while discounts increase cash flow, they also reduce profitability. Finding the right balance between the added advantages of early cash receipt and the disadvantages of reduced profits is no simple matter. Similarly, determining the optimal balance between the higher sales likely to result from extending credit to customers with less than sterling credit ratings and the higher bad-debt losses likely to result from a more lenient credit policy is also challenging. Information on company credit ratings is provided by local credit bureaus, national credit-rating agencies such as Dun & Bradstreet, and industry trade groups.

Loans are important for most consumers purchasing a home or business. Interest rates have been at historic lows over the past few years but are expected to increase in the long run.

© Ryan McVay/Getty Images

Optimizing Inventory. While the inventory that a firm holds is controlled by both production needs and marketing considerations, the financial manager has to coordinate inventory purchases to manage cash flows. The object is to minimize the firm's investment in inventory without experiencing production cutbacks as a result of critical materials shortfalls or lost sales due to insufficient finished goods inventories. Every dollar invested in inventory is a dollar unavailable for investment in some other area of the organization. Optimal inventory levels are determined in large part by the method of production. If a firm attempts to produce its goods just in time to meet sales demand, the level of inventory will be relatively low. If, on the other hand, the firm produces materials in a constant, level pattern, inventory increases when sales decrease and decreases when sales increase. One way that companies are optimizing inventory is through the use of radio frequency identification (RFID) technology. Companies such as Walmart better manage their inventories by using RFID tags. An RFID tag, which contains a silicon chip and an antenna, allows a company to use radio waves to track and identify the products to which the tags are attached. These tags are primarily used to track inventory shipments from the manufacturer to the buyer's warehouses and then to the individual stores and also cut down on trucking theft because the delivery truck and its contents can be tracked.

The automobile industry is an excellent example of an industry driven almost solely by inventory levels. Because it is inefficient to continually lay off workers in slow times and call them back in better times, Ford, General Motors, and Toyota try to set and stick to quarterly production quotas. Automakers typically try to keep a 60-day supply of unsold cars. During particularly slow periods, however, it is not unusual for inventories to exceed 100 days of sales.

Although less publicized, inventory shortages can be as much of a drag on potential profits as too much inventory. Not having an item on hand may send the customer to a competitor—forever. Complex computer inventory models are frequently employed to determine the optimum level of inventory a firm should hold to support a given level of sales. Such models can indicate how and when parts inventories should be ordered so that they are available exactly when required—and not a day before. Developing and maintaining such an intricate production and inventory system is difficult, but it can often prove to be the difference between experiencing average profits and spectacular ones.

Managing Current Liabilities

While having extra cash on hand is a delightful surprise, the opposite situation—a temporary cash shortfall—can be a crisis. The good news is that there are several potential sources of short-term funds. Suppliers often serve as an important source through credit sales practices. Also, banks, finance companies, and other organizations offer short-term funds through loans and other business operations.

Accounts Payable. Remember from Chapter 14 that accounts payable is money an organization owes to suppliers for goods and services. Just as accounts receivable must be actively managed to ensure proper cash collections, so too must accounts payable be managed to make the best use of this important liability.

The most widely used source of short-term financing, and therefore the most important account payable, is **trade credit**—credit extended by suppliers for the purchase of their goods and services. While varying in formality, depending on both the organizations involved and the value of the items purchased, most trade credit agreements offer discounts to organizations that pay their bills early. A supplier, for example, may offer trade terms of "1/10 net 30," meaning that the purchasing organization may take a 1 percent discount from the invoice amount if it makes payment by the 10th day after receiving the bill. Otherwise, the entire amount is due within 30 days. For example, pretend that you are the financial manager in charge of payables. You owe Ajax Company $10,000, and it offers trade terms of 2/10 net 30. By paying the amount due within 10 days, you can save 2 percent of $10,000, or $200. Assume you place orders with Ajax once per month and have 12 bills of $10,000 each per year. By taking the discount every time, you will save 12 times $200, or $2,400, per year. Now assume you are the financial manager of Gigantic Corp., and it has monthly payables of $100 million per month. Two percent of $100 million is $2 million per month. Failure to take advantage of such trade discounts can add up to large opportunity losses over the span of a year.

Bank Loans. Virtually all organizations—large and small—obtain short-term funds for operations from banks. In most instances, the credit services granted these firms take the form of a line of credit or fixed dollar loan. A **line of credit** is an arrangement by which a bank agrees to lend a specified amount of money to the organization upon request—provided that the bank has the required funds to make the loan. In general, a business line of credit is very similar to a consumer credit card, with the exception that the preset credit limit can amount to millions of dollars.

LO 16-2

Identify some sources of short-term financing (current liabilities).

trade credit
credit extended by suppliers for the purchase of their goods and services.

line of credit
an arrangement by which a bank agrees to lend a specified amount of money to an organization upon request.

secured loans
loans backed by collateral that the bank can claim if the borrowers do not repay them.

In addition to credit lines, banks also make **secured loans**—loans backed by collateral that the bank can claim if the borrowers do not repay the loans—and **unsecured loans**—loans backed only by the borrower's good reputation and previous credit rating. Both individuals and businesses build their credit rating from their history of borrowing and repaying borrowed funds on time and in full. The three national credit-rating services are Equifax, TransUnion, and Experian. A lack of credit history or a poor credit history can make it difficult to get loans from financial institutions. The *principal* is the amount of money borrowed; *interest* is a percentage of the principal that the bank charges for use of its money. As we mentioned in Chapter 15, banks also pay depositors interest on savings accounts and some checking accounts. Thus, banks charge borrowers interest for loans and pay interest to depositors for the use of their money. In addition, these loans may include origination fees.

unsecured loans
loans backed only by the borrower's good reputation and previous credit rating.

One of the complaints from borrowers during the financial meltdown and recession was that banks weren't willing to lend. There were several causes. Banks were trying to rebuild their capital, and they didn't want to take the extra risk of making loans in an economic recession. They were drowning in bad debts and were not sure how future loan losses would affect their capital. Smaller regional banks did a better job of maintaining small business loans than the major money center banks who suffered most in the recession.

prime rate
the interest rate that commercial banks charge their best customers (usually large corporations) for short-term loans.

The **prime rate** is the interest rate commercial banks charge their best customers for short-term loans. For many years, loans at the prime rate represented funds at the lowest possible cost. For some companies other alternatives may be cheaper, such as borrowing at the London Interbank Offer Rate (LIBOR) or using commercial paper.

The interest rates on commercial loans may be either fixed or variable. A variable or floating-rate loan offers an advantage when interest rates are falling but represents a distinct disadvantage when interest rates are rising. Between 1999 and 2004, interest rates plummeted, and borrowers refinanced their loans with low-cost fixed-rate loans. Nowhere was this more visible than in the U.S. mortgage markets, where homeowners lined up to refinance their high-percentage home mortgages with lower-cost loans, in some cases as low as 5 percent on a 30-year loan. Mortgage rates rose to 6.5 percent by mid-2006 but fell again after 2012, and in April of 2016, homeowners could still get a fixed rate mortgage under 4 percent. Individuals and corporations have the same motivation: to minimize their borrowing costs. During this period of historically low interest rates, companies ramped up their borrowing, bought back stock, and locked in large amounts of debt at low rates. Think back to Chapter 14 and imagine what impact this behavior will have on the interest coverage ratio.

Nonbank Liabilities. Banks are not the only source of short-term funds for businesses. Indeed, virtually all financial institutions, from insurance companies to pension funds, from money market funds to finance companies, make short-term loans to many organizations. The largest U.S. companies also actively engage in borrowing money from the eurodollar and commercial paper markets. As noted earlier, both of these funds' sources are typically slightly less expensive than bank loans.

factor
a finance company to which businesses sell their accounts receivable—usually for a percentage of the total face value.

In some instances, businesses actually sell their accounts receivable to a finance company known as a **factor**, which gives the selling organizations cash and assumes responsibility for collecting the accounts. For example, a factor might pay $60,000 for receivables with a total face value of $100,000 (60 percent of the total). The factor profits if it can collect more than what it paid for the accounts. Because the selling organization's customers send their payments to a lockbox, they may have no idea that a factor has bought their receivables.

Additional nonbank liabilities that must be efficiently managed to ensure maximum profitability are taxes owed to the government and wages owed to employees. Clearly, businesses are responsible for many different types of taxes, including federal, state, and local income taxes, property taxes, mineral rights taxes, unemployment taxes, Social Security taxes, workers' compensation taxes, excise taxes, and more. While the public tends to think that the only relevant taxes are on income and sales, many industries must pay other taxes that far exceed those levied against their income. Taxes and employees' wages represent debt obligations of the firm, which the financial manager must plan to meet as they fall due.

Managing Fixed Assets

Up to this point, we have focused on the short-term aspects of financial management. While most business failures are the result of poor short-term planning, successful ventures must also consider the long-term financial consequences of their actions. Managing the long-term assets and liabilities and the owners' equity portion of the balance sheet is important for the long-term health of the business.

Long-term (fixed) assets are expected to last for many years—production facilities (plants), offices, equipment, heavy machinery, furniture, automobiles, and so on. In today's fast-paced world, companies need the most technologically advanced, modern facilities and equipment they can afford. Automobile, oil refining, and transportation companies are dependent on fixed assets.

Modern and high-tech equipment carry high price tags, and the financial arrangements required to support these investments are by no means trivial. Leasing is just one approach to financing. Obtaining major long-term financing can be challenging for even the most profitable organizations. For less successful firms, such challenges can prove nearly impossible. One approach is leasing assets such as equipment, machines, and buildings. Leasing involves paying a fee for usage rather than owning the asset. There are two kinds of leases: capital leases and operating leases. A capital lease is a long-term contract and shows up on the balance sheet as an asset and liability. The operating lease is a short-term cancelable lease and does not show up on the balance sheet. We'll take a closer look at long-term financing in a moment, but first let's address some issues associated with fixed assets, including capital budgeting, risk assessment, and the costs of financing fixed assets.

Capital Budgeting and Project Selection

One of the most important jobs performed by the financial manager is to decide what fixed assets, projects, and investments will earn profits for the firm beyond the costs necessary to fund them.

LO 16-3

Summarize the importance of long-term assets and capital budgeting.

long-term (fixed) assets production facilities (plants), offices, and equipment—all of which are expected to last for many years.

Pharmaceutical companies spend millions of dollars developing drugs such as Zyprexa without knowing if the drug will pass FDA approval and have a significant profit margin.

© Steve Allen/Brand X Pictures

capital budgeting
the process of analyzing the needs of the business and selecting the assets that will maximize its value.

The process of analyzing the needs of the business and selecting the assets that will maximize its value is called **capital budgeting,** and the capital budget is the amount of money budgeted for investment in such long-term assets. But capital budgeting does not end with the selection and purchase of a particular piece of land, equipment, or major investment. All assets and projects must be continually reevaluated to ensure their compatibility with the organization's needs. Financial executives believe most budgeting activities are occasionally or frequently unrealistic or irrelevant. If a particular asset does not live up to expectations, then management must determine why and take necessary corrective action. Budgeting is not an exact process, and managers must be flexible when new information is available.

Assessing Risk

Every investment carries some risk. Figure 16-1 ranks potential investment projects according to estimated risk. When considering investments overseas, risk assessments must include the political climate and economic stability of a region. The decision to introduce a product or build a manufacturing facility in England would be much less risky than a decision to build one in the Middle East, for example.

FIGURE 16-1
Qualitative Assessment of Capital Budgeting Risk

Highest Risk

Introduce a New Product in Foreign Markets (risk depends on stability of country)

Expand into a New Market

Introduce a New Product in a Familiar Area

Add to a Product Line

Buy New Equipment for an Established Market

Repair Old Machinery

Lowest Risk

The longer a project or asset is expected to last, the greater its potential risk because it is hard to predict whether a piece of equipment will wear out or become obsolete in 5 or 10 years. Predicting cash flows one year down the road is difficult, but projecting them over the span of a 10-year project is a gamble.

The level of a project's risk is also affected by the stability and competitive nature of the marketplace and the world economy as a whole. IBM's latest high-technology computer product is far more likely to become obsolete overnight than is a similar $10 million investment in a manufacturing plant. Dramatic changes in the marketplace are not uncommon. Indeed, uncertainty created by the rapid devaluation of Asian currencies in the late 1990s laid waste to the financial forecasts that hundreds of projects had relied on for their economic feasibility. Financial managers must constantly consider such issues when making long-term decisions about the purchase of fixed assets.

Pricing Long-Term Money

The ultimate profitability of any project depends not only on accurate assumptions of how much cash it will generate, but also on its financing costs. Because a business must pay interest on money it borrows, the returns from any project must cover not only the costs of operating the project but also the interest expenses for the debt used to finance its construction. Unless an organization can effectively cover all of its costs—both financial and operating—it will eventually fail.

Clearly, only a limited supply of funds is available for investment in any given enterprise. The most efficient and profitable companies can attract the lowest-cost funds because they typically offer reasonable financial returns at very low relative risks. Newer and less prosperous firms must pay higher costs to attract capital because these companies tend to be quite risky. One of the strongest motivations for companies to manage their financial resources wisely is that they will, over time, be able to reduce the costs of their funds and in so doing increase their overall profitability.

In our free-enterprise economy, new firms tend to enter industries that offer the greatest potential rewards for success. However, as more and more companies enter an industry, competition intensifies, eventually driving profits down to average levels. The digital music player market of the early 2000s provides an excellent example of the changes in profitability that typically accompany increasing competition. The sign of a successful capital budgeting program is that the new products create higher than normal profits and drive sales and the stock price up. This has certainly been true for Apple when it made the decision to enter the consumer electronics industry. In 2001, Apple introduced the first iPod. Since then, the iPod has undergone many enhancements in size, style, and different versions such as the small Nano. Sales of iPods have declined over time as iPhones took their place as music players. It was the iPod that made the iTunes Store possible, which now accounts for more than $16 billion in revenues. The iPhone, introduced in 2007, has now gone through many annual updates, with the latest being the iPhone 7 in 2016. During 2015, the iPhone sold 231 million units, accounting for $155 billion in sales, up 52 percent since 2014. Finally, the iPad tablet was introduced in 2010 and is now the third best product after the iPhone, selling 54 million units and generating almost $23 billion in sales. Interestingly, Apple did not appear to be negatively affected by the recession. In fact, its sales grew from $42.9 billion in 2009 to $233.7 billion in 2015. It is on track to keep up its growth as it expands into China, India, and other emerging markets. The ease of synchronization with all Apple computers caused the

Apple stock trades at approximately 100 times what it did nearly ten years ago.

© Bloomberg/Contributor

sale of iMacs and MacBooks to increase, selling 20.6 million units in 2015, accounting for $25.5 billion in sales, and making the computers the second best product behind the iPhone.

Even with a well-planned capital budgeting program, it may be difficult for Apple to stay ahead of the competition because the Google Android platform is being used by Apple's competitors. This intense competition may make it difficult to continue market dominance for any extended period. However, Apple is now the most valuable company in the world, valued at $586 billion on April 22, 2016. On June 9, 2014, Apple split its stock seven for one, meaning that for every share you owned, you would get six more for a total of seven shares. There is no real gain involved because the stock price is divided by 7, so stockholders still have the same value, just more shares at a lower price. An investor who bought $1,000 of Apple stock in 2003 for $0.91 would have had Apple stock worth $116,132 on April 22, 2016. The problem is having the patience to continue to hold such a winner without taking some profits along the way.[3]

Maintaining market dominance is also difficult in the personal computer industry, particularly because tablet computers are taking away market share. With increasing competition, prices have fallen dramatically since the 1990s. Weaker companies have failed, leaving the most efficient producers/marketers scrambling for market share. The expanded market for personal computers dramatically reduced the financial returns generated by each dollar invested in productive assets. The "glory days" of the personal computer industry—the time in which fortunes could be won and lost in the space of an average-sized garage—have long since passed into history. Personal computers have essentially become commodity items, and profit margins for companies in this industry have shrunk as the market matures and sales decline.

Financing with Long-Term Liabilities

Specify how companies finance their operations and manage fixed assets with long-term liabilities, particularly bonds.

As we said earlier, long-term assets do not come cheaply, and few companies have the cash on hand to open a new store across town, build a new manufacturing facility, research and develop a new life-saving drug, or launch a new product worldwide. To develop such fixed assets, companies need to raise low-cost long-term funds to finance them. Two common choices for raising these funds are attracting new owners *(equity financing),* which we'll look at in a moment, and taking on long-term liabilities *(debt financing),* which we'll look at now.

long-term liabilities
debts that will be repaid over a number of years, such as long-term loans and bond issues.

Long-term liabilities are debts that will be repaid over a number of years, such as long-term bank loans and bond issues. These take many different forms, but in the end, the key word is *debt.* Companies may raise money by borrowing it from commercial banks or other financial institutions in the form of lines of credit, short-term loans, or long-term loans. Many corporations acquire debt by borrowing money from pension funds, mutual funds, or life-insurance funds.

Companies that rely too heavily on debt can get into serious trouble should the economy falter; during these times, they may not earn enough operating income to make the required interest payments (remember the times interest earned ratio in Chapter 14). In severe cases when the problem persists too long, creditors will not restructure loans but will instead sue for the interest and principal owed and force the company into bankruptcy.

Bonds: Corporate IOUs

Much long-term debt takes the form of **bonds,** which are debt instruments that larger companies sell to raise long-term funds. In essence, the buyers of bonds (bondholders) loan the issuer of the bonds cash in exchange for regular interest payments until the loan is repaid on or before the specified maturity date. The bond itself is a certificate, much like an IOU, that represents the company's debt to the bondholder. Bonds are issued by a wide variety of entities, including corporations; national, state, and local governments; public utilities; and nonprofit corporations. Most bondholders need not hold their bonds until maturity; rather, the existence of active secondary markets of brokers and dealers allows for the quick and efficient transfer of bonds from owner to owner.

> **bonds**
> debt instruments that larger companies sell to raise long-term funds.

The bond contract, or *indenture,* specifies all of the terms of the agreement between the bondholders and the issuing organization. The indenture, which can run more than 100 pages, specifies the basic terms of the bond, such as its face value, maturity date, and the annual interest rate. Table 16-2 briefly explains how to determine these and more things about a bond from a bond quote, as it might appear in *Barron's* magazine. The face value of the bond, its initial sales price, is typically $1,000. After this, however, the price of the bond on the open market will fluctuate along with changes in the economy (particularly, changes in interest rates) and in the creditworthiness of the issuer. Bondholders receive the face value of the bond along

TABLE 16-2   U.S. Corporate Bond Quotes

For the week ending April 22, 2016

Company (Sticker)	Coupon	Maturity	Last Price	Last Yield	Est. Spread**	UST***	Est $ Vol (000s)
Wells Fargo (WFC)	3.000	Apr 22, 2026	99.368	3.074	119	10	712,864
Anheuser-Busch Inbev Finance (ABIBB)	3.650	Feb 1, 2026	105.495	2.982	110	10	509,341
Verizon Communications (VZ)	5.150	Sept 15, 2023	114.333	2.973	109	10	339,577

**Estimated spreads, in basis points (100 basis points is one percentage point), over the 2-, 5-, 10-, or 30-year hot run Treasury note/bond.

***Comparable U.S. Treasury issue.

Coupon—the percentage in interest payment that the bond pays based on a $1,000 bond

Maturity—the day on which the issuer will reissue the principal

Last Price—last price at which the security is traded

Last Yield—yield-to-maturity for the investor that buys the bond today and holds it until it matures

Est. Spread—amount of additional yield the investor will earn each year compared to a U.S. For example, the Wells Fargo bond would earn 1.19% more than a U.S. Treasury bond.

UST—U.S. Treasury bond

Est $ Vol (000s)—number of individual bonds that were bought and sold on the date indicated

Sources: MarketAxess Corporate BondTicker, www.bondticker.com; Barron's, "Corporate Bonds," April, 22, 2016, http://online.barrons.com/public/page/9_0210-corpbonds.html (accessed April 22, 2016).

with the final interest payment on the maturity date. The annual interest rate (often called the *coupon rate*) is the guaranteed percentage of face value that the company will pay to the bond owner every year. For example, a $1,000 bond with a coupon rate of 7 percent would pay $70 per year in interest. In most cases, bond indentures specify that interest payments be made every six months. In the example above, the $70 annual payment would be divided into two semiannual payments of $35.

In addition to the terms of interest payments and maturity date, the bond indenture typically covers other important topics, such as repayment methods, interest payment dates, procedures to be followed in case the organization fails to make the interest payments, conditions for the early repayment of the bonds, and any conditions requiring the pledging of assets as collateral.

Types of Bonds

unsecured bonds
debentures or bonds that are not backed by specific collateral.

secured bonds
bonds that are backed by specific collateral that must be forfeited in the event that the issuing firm defaults.

serial bonds
a sequence of small bond issues of progressively longer maturity.

floating-rate bonds
bonds with interest rates that change with current interest rates otherwise available in the economy.

junk bonds
a special type of high interest rate bond that carries higher inherent risks.

Not surprisingly, there are a great many different types of bonds. Most are **unsecured bonds**, meaning that they are not backed by collateral; such bonds are termed *debentures*. **Secured bonds**, on the other hand, are backed by specific collateral that must be forfeited in the event that the issuing firm defaults. Whether secured or unsecured, bonds may be repaid in one lump sum or with many payments spread out over a period of time. **Serial bonds**, which are different from secured bonds, are actually a sequence of small bond issues of progressively longer maturity. The firm pays off each of the serial bonds as they mature. **Floating-rate bonds** do not have fixed interest payments; instead, the interest rate changes with current interest rates otherwise available in the economy.

In recent years, a special type of high-interest-rate bond has attracted considerable attention (usually negative) in the financial press. High-interest bonds, or **junk bonds** as they are popularly known, offer relatively high rates of interest because they have higher inherent risks. Historically, junk bonds have been associated with companies in poor financial health and/or startup firms with limited track records. In the mid-1980s, however, junk bonds became a very attractive method of financing corporate mergers; they remain popular today with many investors as a result of their very high relative interest rates. But higher risks are associated with those higher returns (upward of 12 percent per year in some cases) and the average investor would be well-advised to heed those famous words: Look before you leap!

Financing with Owners' Equity

LO 16-5

Discuss how corporations can use equity financing by issuing stock through an investment banker.

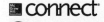

Need help understanding equity financing and debt financing? Visit your Connect ebook video tab for a brief animated explanation.

A second means of long-term financing is through equity. Remember from Chapter 14 that owners' equity refers to the owners' investment in an organization. Sole proprietors and partners own all or a part of their businesses outright, and their equity includes the money and assets they have brought into their ventures. Corporate owners, on the other hand, own stock or shares of their companies, which they hope will provide them with a return on their investment. Stockholders' equity includes common stock, preferred stock, and retained earnings.

Common stock (introduced in Chapter 4) is the single most important source of capital for most new companies. On the balance sheet, the common stock account is separated into two basic parts—common stock at par and capital in excess of par. The *par value* of a stock is simply the dollar amount printed on the stock certificate and has no relation to actual *market value*—the price at which the common stock is currently trading. The difference between a stock's par value and its offering price is called *capital in excess of par.* Except in the case of some very low-priced stocks,

TABLE 16-3   A Basic Stock Quote

Nike, Inc. (NKE) - NYSE   ★ Watchlist

59.43⬇ **0.65(1.08%)** 8:00PM EDT

After Hours: **59.40 ⬇ 0.03 (0.05%)** 7:51PM EDT

Prev Close:	**60.08**	Day's Range:	**58.97 - 60.22**
Open:	**60.18**	52wk Range:	**47.25 - 68.19**
Bid:	**59.20 x 500**	Volume:	**8,294,326**
Ask:	**59.58 x 500**	Avg Vol (3m):	**10,054,200**
1y Target Est:	**70.51**	Market Cap:	**100.12B**
Beta:	**0.513013**	P/E (ttm):	**28.86**
Earnings Date:	**Jun 23 - Jun 27 (Est.)**	EPS (ttm):	**2.06**
		Div & Yield:	**0.64 (1.07%)**

1. The **52-week high and low**—the highest and lowest prices, respectively, paid for the stock in the last year; for Nike stock, the highest was $68.19 and the lowest price, $47.25.

2. **Stock**—the name of the issuing company. When followed by the letters "pf," the stock is a preferred stock.

3. **Symbol**—the ticker tape symbol for the stock; NKE.

4. **Dividend**—the annual cash dividend paid to stockholders; Nike paid a dividend of $0.64 per share of stock outstanding.

5. **Dividend yield**—the dividend return on one share of common stock; 1.07 percent.

6. **Volume**—the number of shares traded on this day; Nike, 8,294,326 while the average volume over the last three months was 10,054,200 shares.

7. **Close**—Nike's last sale of the day was for $59.43 but after hours it traded down 3 cents.

8. **Net change**—the difference between the previous day's close and the close on the day being reported; Nike was down $0.65.

Source: Yahoo! Finance, http://finance.yahoo.com/q?s (accessed April 22, 2016).

the capital in excess of par account is significantly larger than the par value account. Table 16-3 briefly explains how to gather important information from a stock quote, as it appears on Yahoo!'s website. You should be familiar with EPS from Chapter 14. However, *beta* is a new term, and Nike's beta of 0.51 indicates that its stock price is 51 percent as volatile as the Standard & Poor's 500 Index. The market cap represents the total value of Nike's common stock, or the value of the company. The target price is the analysts' consensus of the potential stock price.

Preferred stock was defined in Chapter 14 as corporate ownership that gives the stockholder preference in the distribution of the company's profits but not the voting and control rights accorded to common stockholders. Thus, the primary advantage of owning preferred stock is that it is a safer investment than common stock.

All businesses exist to earn profits for their owners. Without the possibility of profit, there can be no incentive to risk investors' capital and succeed. When a corporation has profits left over after paying all of its expenses and taxes, it has the choice of retaining all or a portion of its earnings and/or paying them out to its shareholders in the form of dividends. **Retained earnings** are reinvested in the assets of the firm and belong to the owners in the form of equity. Retained earnings are an important source of funds and are, in fact, the only long-term funds that the company can generate internally.

retained earnings
earnings after expenses and taxes that are reinvested in the assets of the firm and belong to the owners in the form of equity.

Y Combinator: Y Not?

Y Combinator

Founders: Paul Graham, Jessica Livingston, Trevor Blackwell, and Robert Morris

Founded: 2005, in Mountain View, California

Success: Y Combinator is now recognized as Silicon Valley's most widely admired business incubator.

When tech incubator Y Combinator first started, it was viewed with skepticism. As an incubator, Y Combinator's founders wanted to provide assistance to help accelerate the growth of startups. Unlike more traditional firms in the industry that invest millions in startups for large stakes in the companies, Y Combinator provided smaller loans to meet basic needs so the startups could focus on developing products customers want.

Today, Y Combinator has a current investment portfolio of $1 billion. Tech startups that have received Y Combinator assistance include Reddit, Dropbox, and Airbnb and are valued at

more than $10 billion. Y Combinator gathers entrepreneurs for three-month periods, during which time it provides them with small loans, business insights, and coaching. Y Combinator also offers them access to its expertise, solid advice, and a creative environment. In exchange, it receives a 7 percent stake in their firms. Top graduates of the program have the opportunity to pitch their companies at Y Combinator's two annual Demo Days, which attract multimillion-dollar investors interested in these promising startups.[4]

Discussion Questions

1. How does Y Combinator differ from other incubators?
2. Why do you think Y Combinator chooses to provide small loans?
3. What are some of the advantages Y Combinator offers to entrepreneurs?

When the board of directors distributes some of a corporation's profits to the owners, it issues them as cash dividend payments. But not all firms pay dividends. Many fast-growing firms like Facebook retain all of their earnings because they can earn high rates of return on the earnings they reinvest. Companies with fewer growth opportunities like Campbell Soup or Verizon typically pay out large proportions of their earnings in the form of dividends, thereby allowing their stockholders to reinvest their dividend payments in higher-growth companies. Table 16-4 presents a sample of companies and the dividend each paid on a single share of stock. As shown in the table, when the dividend is divided by the price the result is the **dividend yield.** The dividend yield is the cash return as a percentage of the price but does not reflect the total return an investor earns on the individual stock. If the dividend yield is 2.06 percent on Campbell Soup and the stock price increases by 10 percent from $60.64 to $66.70, then the total return would be 12.06 percent. It is not clear that stocks with high dividend yields will be preferred by investors to those with little or no dividends. Most large companies pay their stockholders dividends on a quarterly basis.

dividend yield
the dividend per share divided by the stock price.

Investment Banking

A company that needs more money to expand or take advantage of opportunities may be able to obtain financing by issuing stock. The first-time sale of stocks and bonds directly to the public is called a *new issue.* Companies that already have stocks or bonds outstanding may offer a new issue of stock to raise additional funds for specific projects. When a company offers its stock to the public for the very first time, it is said to be "going public," and the sale is called an *initial public offering (IPO).*

New issues of stocks and bonds are sold directly to the public and to institutions in what is known as the

DID YOU KNOW? A single share of Coca-Cola stock purchased during its original 1919 IPO would be worth more than $5 million today.[5]

TABLE 16-4
Estimated Common Stock Price-Earnings Ratios and Dividends for Selected Companies

Ticker Symbol	Company Name	Price per Share	Dividend per Share	Dividend Yield	Earnings per Share (*)	Price Earnings Ratio
AEO	American Eagle	$ 15.90	$0.50	3.14%	$1.01	15.74
AXP	American Express	65.93	1.16	1.76%	5.05	13.06
AAPL	Apple	105.68	2.08	1.97%	9.40	11.24
CPB	Campbell Soup	60.64	1.25	2.06%	2.18	27.82
DIS	Disney	103.77	1.42	1.37%	5.35	19.40
F	Ford	13.61	0.60	4.41%	1.84	7.40
FB	Facebook	110.56	0.00	0.00%	1.29	85.71
GOOG	Alphabet	718.77	0.00	0.00%	23.59	30.47
HOG	Harley Davidson	48.57	1.40	2.88%	3.69	13.16
HD	Home Depot	135.66	2.76	2.03%	5.46	24.85
MCD	McDonald's	125.50	3.56	2.84%	4.80	26.15
PG	Procter & Gamble	80.95	2.68	3.31%	2.95	27.44
LUV	Southwest Airlines	47.25	0.30	0.63%	3.27	14.45
VZ	Verizon	50.55	2.26	4.47%	4.37	11.57

Source: Yahoo! Finance, http://finance.yahoo.com/ (April 22, 2016).

primary market—the market where firms raise financial capital. The primary market differs from **secondary markets**, which are stock exchanges and over-the-counter markets where investors can trade their securities with other investors rather than the company that issued the stock or bonds. Primary market transactions actually raise cash for the issuing corporations, while secondary market transactions do not. For example, when Facebook went public on May 18, 2012, its IPO raised $16 billion for the company and stockholders, who were cashing in on their success. Once the investment bankers distributed the stock to retail brokers, the brokers sold it to clients in the secondary market for $38 per share. The stock got off to a rocky start and hit a low of $17.73 in September 2012. However, by March 2014, it was at $71.97, and as you can see from Table 16-4, it was $110.56 on April 22, 2016. You might want to check out its current price for fun.

Investment banking, the sale of stocks and bonds for corporations, helps such companies raise funds by matching people and institutions who have money to invest with corporations in need of resources to exploit new opportunities. Corporations usually employ an investment banking firm to help sell their securities in the primary market. An investment banker helps firms establish appropriate offering prices for their securities. In addition, the investment banker takes care of the myriad details and securities regulations involved in any sale of securities to the public.

Just as large corporations such as IBM and Microsoft have a client relationship with a law firm and an accounting firm, they also have a client relationship with an investment banking firm. An investment banking firm such as Merrill Lynch, Goldman Sachs, or Morgan Stanley can provide advice about financing plans, dividend policy,

primary market
the market where firms raise financial capital.

secondary markets
stock exchanges and over-the-counter markets where investors can trade their securities with others.

investment banking
the sale of stocks and bonds for corporations

Going Green

Tesla's Green Play: Invest, Divest, or Protest

Many analysts consider Tesla to be a market disrupter. Although its vehicles sell for $100,000 or more, Tesla vehicles are well designed and 100 percent electric powered. This has caused investors to rapidly purchase Tesla stock.

However, it is widely believed that Tesla stock is overvalued. It has a $25 million market cap but has yet to post a profit. China, a market predicted to equal the U.S. market in 2015, has one-tenth the sales of the United States. This has caused Tesla's stock to fluctuate widely.

Supporters believe Tesla will pay off big and have scrambled to purchase stock when Tesla shares have plummeted. Lower gas prices have lowered Tesla's value, but many investors are not concerned because the customer base for Tesla's premium product will not likely be concerned with gas prices. Support for green vehicles and technology is growing worldwide, and Tesla develops a product that is admired for its quality.

On the other hand, UBS placed a "sell" rating on Tesla stock because it thinks that the challenges ahead will test Tesla significantly. It anticipates that costs will remain high for Tesla, affecting the bottom line. Also, it feels there will not be enough demand to meet Tesla's projections for its storage batteries. The debate over whether Tesla will become a blockbuster stock continues as consumer demand changes and competitors enter the market.[6]

Discussion Questions

1. Why do you think Tesla stock might be overvalued?
2. What are some of the arguments investors might have for supporting Tesla?
3. What are some arguments critics have for selling Tesla's stock?

---

or stock repurchases, as well as advice on mergers and acquisitions. Many now offer additional banking services, making them "one-stop shopping" banking centers. When Pixar merged with Disney, both companies used investment bankers to help them value the transaction. Each firm wanted an outside opinion about what it was worth to the other. Sometimes mergers fall apart because the companies cannot agree on the price each company is worth or the structure of management after the merger. The advising investment banker, working with management, often irons out these details. Of course, investment bankers do not provide these services for free. They usually charge a fee of between 1 and 1.5 percent of the transaction. A $20 billion merger can generate between $200 and $300 million in investment banking fees. The merger mania of the late 1990s allowed top investment bankers to earn huge sums. Unfortunately, this type of fee income is dependent on healthy stock markets, which seem to stimulate the merger fever among corporate executives.

LO 16-6

Describe the various securities markets in the United States.

securities markets
the mechanism for buying and selling securities.

The Securities Markets

Securities markets provide a mechanism for buying and selling securities. They make it possible for owners to sell their stocks and bonds to other investors. Thus, in the broadest sense, stocks and bonds markets may be thought of as providers of liquidity—the ability to turn security holdings into cash quickly and at minimal expense and effort. Without liquid securities markets, many potential investors would sit on the sidelines rather than invest their hard-earned savings in securities. Indeed, the ability to sell securities at well-established market prices is one of the very pillars of the capitalistic society that has developed over the years in the United States.

Unlike the primary market, in which corporations sell stocks directly to the public, secondary markets permit the trading of previously issued securities. There are many different secondary markets for both stocks and bonds. If you want to purchase 100 shares of Alphabet (formerly Google) common stock, for example, you must purchase this stock from another investor or institution. It is the active buying and selling by many thousands of investors that establishes the prices of all financial securities. Secondary market trades may take place on organized exchanges or in what is known as the over-the-counter market. Many brokerage houses exist to help investors with financial decisions, and many offer their services through the Internet. One such broker is Charles Schwab. Its site offers a wealth of information and provides educational material to individual investors.

Stock Markets

Stock markets exist around the world in New York, Tokyo, London, Frankfort, Paris, and other world locations. The two biggest stock markets in the United States are the New York Stock Exchange (NYSE) and the NASDAQ market.

Exchanges used to be divided into organized exchanges and over-the-counter markets, but during the past several years, dramatic changes have occurred in the markets. Both the NYSE and NASDAQ became publicly traded companies. They were previously not-for-profit organizations but are now for-profit companies. Additionally, both exchanges bought or merged with electronic exchanges. In an attempt to expand their markets, NASDAQ acquired the OMX, a Nordic stock exchange headquartered in Sweden, and the New York Stock Exchange merged with Euronext, a large European electronic exchange that trades options and futures contracts as well as common stock.

The New York Stock Exchange is the world's largest stock exchange by market capitalization.

© David R. Frazier Photolibrary, Inc./Alamy

Traditionally, the NASDAQ market has been an electronic market, and many of the large technology companies such as Microsoft, Google, Apple, and Facebook trade on the NASDAQ market. The NASDAQ operates through dealers who buy and sell common stock (inventory) for their own accounts. The NYSE used to be primarily a floor-traded market, where brokers meet at trading posts on the floor of the New York Stock Exchange to buy and sell common stock. The brokers act as agents for their clients and do not own their own inventory. Today, more than 80 percent of NYSE trading is electronic. This traditional division between the two markets is becoming less significant as the exchanges become electronic.

Electronic markets have grown quickly because of the speed, low cost, and efficiency of trading that they offer over floor trading. One of the fastest-growing electronic markets has been the Intercontinental Exchange (referred to as ICE). ICE, based in Atlanta, Georgia, primarily trades financial and commodity futures products. It started out as an energy futures exchange and has broadened its futures contracts into an array of commodities and derivative products. In December 2012, ICE made an offer to buy the New York Stock Exchange. When the NYSE became a public company and had common stock trading in the secondary market, rather than the hunter, it became the prey. On November 13, 2013, ICE completed its takeover of the NYSE. One condition of the takeover was that ICE had to divest itself of Euronext because international regulators thought the company would have a monopoly on European derivative markets. Also acquired as part of the NYSE family of exchanges was LIFFE, the London International Financial Futures Exchange. Many analysts thought that LIFFE was the major reason ICE bought the NYSE—not for its equity markets trading common stocks. What we are seeing is the globalization of securities markets and the increasing reliance on electronic trading.

The Over-the-Counter Market

Unlike the organized exchanges, the **over-the-counter (OTC) market** is a network of dealers all over the country linked by computers, telephones, and Teletype machines. It has no central location. Today, the OTC market consists of small stocks, illiquid bank stocks, penny stocks, and companies whose stocks trade on the "pink sheets." Once NASDAQ was classified as an exchange by the SEC, it was no longer part of the OTC market. Further, because most corporate bonds and all U.S. securities are traded over the counter, the OTC market regularly accounts for the largest total dollar value of all of the secondary markets.

Measuring Market Performance

Investors, especially professional money managers, want to know how well their investments are performing relative to the market as a whole. Financial managers also need to know how their companies' securities are performing when compared with their competitors'. Thus, performance measures—averages and indexes—are very important to many different people. They not only indicate the performance of a particular securities market but also provide a measure of the overall health of the economy.

Indexes and averages are used to measure stock prices. An *index* compares current stock prices with those in a specified base period, such as 1944, 1967, or 1977. An *average* is the average of certain stock prices. The averages used are usually not simple calculations, however. Some stock market averages (such as the Standard & Poor's Composite Index) are weighted averages, where the weights employed are the total market values of each stock in the index (in this case 500). The Dow Jones Industrial Average (DJIA) is a price-weighted average. Regardless of how they are constructed, all market averages of stocks move together closely over time. See Figure 16-2, which graphs the Dow Jones Industrial Average. Notice the sharp downturn in the market during the 2008–2009 time period and the recovery that started in 2010. Investors perform better by keeping an eye on the long-term trend line and not the short-term fluctuations. Contrarian investors buy when everyone else is panicked and prices are low because they play the long-term trends. However, for many, this is psychologically a tough way to play the market.

Many investors follow the activity of the Dow Jones Industrial Average to see whether the stock market has gone up or down. Table 16-5 lists the 30 companies that currently make up the Dow. Although these companies are only a small fraction of the total number of companies listed on the New York Stock Exchange, because of their size they account for about 25 percent of the total value of the NYSE.

The numbers listed in an index or average that tracks the performance of a stock market are expressed not as dollars but as a number on a fixed scale. If you know, for example, that the Dow Jones Industrial Average climbed from 860 in August 1982 to

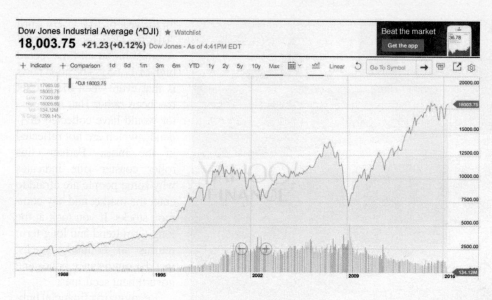

FIGURE 16-2

Recent Performance of Stock Market and Dow Jones Industrial Average (DJIA)

Source: "Dow Jones Industrial Average," Yahoo! Finance, http://finance.yahoo.com/q/bc?s=%5EDJI+Basic+Chart&t=my (accessed April 22, 2016).

a high of 11,497 at the beginning of 2000, you can see clearly that the value of the Dow Jones Average increased more than 10 times in this 19-year period, making it one of the highest rate of return periods in the history of the stock market.

Unfortunately, prosperity did not last long once the Internet bubble burst. Technology stocks and new Internet companies were responsible for the huge increase in stock prices. Even companies with few sales and no earnings were selling at prices that were totally unreasonable. It is always easier to realize that a bubble existed after it has popped. By September 2002, the Dow Jones Industrial Average hit 7,461. The markets stabilized and the economy kept growing; investors were euphoric when the Dow Jones Industrial Average hit an all-time high of 14,198 in October 2007. However, once the housing bubble burst, the economy and the stock market went into a free fall. The Dow Jones Industrial Average bottomed out at 6,470 in March 2009. The market entered a period of recovery, and by April 2010, it hit a new high

3M Co	General Electric	Nike
American Express Co	Goldman Sachs	Pfizer
Apple	Home Depot	Procter & Gamble
Boeing	Intel	Travelers Companies
Caterpiller	IBM	United Health Group
Chevron	Johnson & Johnson	United Technologies
Cisco Systems	JPMorgan Chase	Verizon
Coca-Cola	McDonald's	Visa
Du Pont	Merck	Walmart
ExxonMobil	Microsoft	Walt Disney

TABLE 16-5

The 30 Stocks in the Dow Jones Industrial Average

Source: "Dow Jones Industrial Average," http://finance.yahoo.com/q/cp?s=%5EDJI (accessed May 4, 2016).

During the housing bubble, banks provided loans to riskier subprime borrowers. Although these loans were highly profitable, it was only a matter of time before the bubble burst.

© Brian Bacardi/Getty Images

for the year of 10,975. By April 2016, the Dow Jones Industrial Average hit an all-time record high of 17,651. The good news is that even when the market has been rather flat, an investor would have collected dividends, which are not reflected in the index. Perhaps this roller coaster ride indicates why some people are afraid to enter the market and buy common stocks. If you look at the long-term trend and long-term returns in common stocks, they far outdistance bonds and government securities.

Recognizing financial bubbles can be difficult. It is too easy to get caught up in the enthusiasm that accompanies rising markets. Knowing what something is worth in economic terms is the test of true value. During the housing bubble, banks made loans to subprime borrowers to buy houses. (Remember that the prime rate is the rate for the highest quality borrowers and subprime loans are made to those who have low credit ratings.) As more money poured into the housing market, the obvious supply and demand relationship from economics would indicate that housing prices would rise. As prices rose, speculators entered the real estate market trying to make a fast buck. States such as Florida, Arizona, Nevada, and California were the favorite speculative spots and the states with the largest decline in house prices. To make matters worse, banks had created the home equity loan years ago so that borrowers could take out a second mortgage against their house and deduct the interest payment for tax purposes. Many homeowners no longer thought about paying off their mortgages but instead used the increase in the price of their houses to borrow more money. This behavior was unsustainable.

The bankers engaged in risky financial behavior packaged up billions of dollars of mortgages into securitized assets. In other words, an investor could buy a pool of assets and collect the interest income and eventually get a payment at the end of the life of the product. This technique allowed banks to make a mortgage, collect a fee, package the mortgage, and collect another fee. These securitized mortgages were sold to the market as asset-backed securities with a AAA credit rating off their books and replaced with cash to make more loans. In this case, when the bubble burst, it had extremely severe consequences for the economy, workers, and investors.

People defaulted on loans when they could no longer afford to pay the mortgage. Many of these subprime borrowers shouldn't have been able to borrow in the first place. The defaults caused housing prices to fall, and some people who had home equity loans no longer had any equity left in their house. Some homeowners owed the bank more than the house was worth, and they walked away from their mortgage. At the same time, investors realized that the mortgage-backed securities they owned were not worth their face value, and prices of these assets plummeted. Banks and other financial service firms that had these assets on their books suffered a double whammy. They had loan losses and losses on mortgage-backed securities that another division of the bank had bought for investment purposes. Soon, many banks were close to violating their capital requirement, and the U.S. Treasury and Federal Reserve stepped in—with the help of funding from Congress—to make bank loans, buy securities that were illiquid, and invest in the capital of the banks by buying preferred stocks.

The consensus of most economists is that through the actions of the U.S. Treasury and the Federal Reserve, the U.S. economy escaped what might have been another depression equal to or worse than the depression of the 1930s. The recession of 2007–2009 lasted 18 months and was the longest recession since the 1930s. Some worry that as the Federal Reserve becomes less accommodating and lets interest rates rise, the rising interest rates will have a negative effect on stock prices. This is always possible if corporate earnings do not increase enough to outweigh the impact of higher required returns motivated by higher rates and higher inflation.

For investors to make sound financial decisions, it is important that they stay in touch with business news, markets, and indexes. Of course, business and investment magazines, such as *Bloomberg Businessweek, Fortune,* and *Money,* offer this type of information. Many Internet sites, including CNN/*Money, Business Wire, USA Today,* other online newspapers, and *PR Newswire,* offer this information, as well. Many sites offer searchable databases of information by topic, company, or keyword. However investors choose to receive and review business news, doing so is a necessity in today's market.

⊖ So You Want to Work in Financial Management or Securities

Taking classes in financial and securities management can provide many career options, from managing a small firm's accounts receivable to handling charitable giving for a multinational to investment banking to stock brokerage. We have entered into a less certain period for finance and securities jobs, however. In the world of investment banking, the past few years have been especially challenging. Tens of thousands of employees from Wall Street firms have lost their jobs. This phenomenon is not confined to New York City either, leaving the industry with a lot fewer jobs around the country. This type of phenomenon is not isolated to the finance sector. In the early 2000s, the tech sector experienced a similar downturn, from which it has subsequently largely recovered. Undoubtedly, markets will bounce back and job creation in finance and securities will increase again—but until that happens, the atmosphere across finance and securities will be more competitive than it has been in the past. However, this does not mean that there are no jobs. All firms need financial analysts to determine whether a project should be implemented, when to issue stocks or bonds, or when to initiate loans. These and other forward-looking questions such as how to invest excess cash must be addressed by financial managers. Economic uncertainty in the financial and securities market has made for more difficulty in finding the most desirable jobs.

Why this sudden downturn in financial industry prospects? A lot of these job cuts came in response to the subprime lending fallout and subsequent bank failures such as Bear Stearns, which alone lost around 7,000 employees. All of these people had to look for new jobs in new organizations, increasing the competitive level in a lot of different employment areas. For young jobseekers with relatively little experience, this may result in a great deal of frustration. Uncertainty results in hiring freezes and layoffs but leaves firms lean and ready to grow when the cycle turns around, resulting in hiring from the bottom up.

Many different industries require people with finance skills. So do not despair if you have a difficult time finding a job in exactly the right firm. Most students switch companies a number of times over the course of their careers. Many organizations require individuals trained in forecasting, statistics, economics, and finance. Even unlikely places like museums, aquariums, and zoos need people who are good at numbers. It may require some creativity, but if you are committed to a career in finance, look to less obvious sources—not just the large financial firms.[7]

Review Your Understanding

Describe some common methods of managing current assets.

Current assets are short-term resources such as cash, investments, accounts receivable, and inventory, which can be converted to cash within a year. Financial managers focus on minimizing the amount of cash kept on hand and increasing the speed of collections through lockboxes and electronic funds transfer and investing in marketable securities. Marketable securities include U.S. Treasury bills, certificates of deposit, commercial paper, and money market funds. Managing accounts receivable requires judging customer creditworthiness and creating credit terms that encourage prompt payment. Inventory management focuses on determining optimum inventory levels that minimize the cost of storing and ordering inventory without sacrificing too many lost sales due to stockouts.

Identify some sources of short-term financing (current liabilities).

Current liabilities are short-term debt obligations that must be repaid within one year, such as accounts payable, taxes payable, and notes (loans) payable. Trade credit is extended by suppliers for the purchase of their goods and services. A line of credit is an arrangement by which a bank agrees to lend a specified amount of money to a business whenever the business needs it. Secured loans are backed by collateral; unsecured loans are backed only by the borrower's good reputation.

Summarize the importance of long-term assets and capital budgeting.

Long-term, or fixed, assets are expected to last for many years, such as production facilities (plants), offices, and equipment. Businesses need modern, up-to-date equipment to succeed in today's competitive environment. Capital budgeting is the process of analyzing company needs and selecting the assets that will maximize its value; a capital budget is the amount of money budgeted for the purchase of fixed assets. Every investment in fixed assets carries some risk.

Specify how companies finance their operations and manage fixed assets with long-term liabilities, particularly bonds.

Two common choices for financing are equity financing (attracting new owners) and debt financing (taking on long-term liabilities). Long-term liabilities are debts that will be repaid over a number of years, such as long-term bank loans and bond issues. A bond is a long-term debt security that an organization sells to raise money. The bond indenture specifies the provisions of the bond contract—maturity date, coupon rate, repayment methods, and others.

Discuss how corporations can use equity financing by issuing stock through an investment banker.

Owners' equity represents what owners have contributed to the company and includes common stock, preferred stock, and retained earnings (profits that have been reinvested in the assets of the firm). To finance operations, companies can issue new common and preferred stock through an investment banker that sells stocks and bonds for corporations.

Describe the various securities markets in the United States.

Securities markets provide the mechanism for buying and selling stocks and bonds. Primary markets allow companies to raise capital by selling new stock directly to investors through investment bankers. Secondary markets allow the buyers of previously issued shares of stock to sell them to other owners. The major secondary markets are the New York Stock Exchange, the American Stock Exchange, and the over-the-counter market. Investors measure stock market performance by watching stock market averages and indexes such as the Dow Jones Industrial Average and the Standard & Poor's (S&P) Composite Index.

Critique the position of short-term assets and liabilities of a small manufacturer and recommend corrective action.

Using the information presented in this chapter, you should be able to do the "Solve the Dilemma" feature at the end of the chapter presented by the current bleak working capital situation of Glasspray Corporation.

Revisit the World of Business

1. Describe the type of financial products John Hancock sells. How was it able to use promotion to make these financial products understandable and relatable to consumers?

2. Why must a company like John Hancock assess the risks and budget sufficient funds for projects such as advertising? What may happen if it fails to do so?

3. How can John Hancock evaluate the effectiveness of its digital campaign?

Learn the Terms

bonds 509 ✓
capital budgeting 506
commercial certificates of deposit (CDs) 500
commercial paper 500
dividend yield 512
eurodollar market 501
factor 504
floating-rate bonds 510
investment banking 513 ✓
junk bonds 510 ✓

line of credit 503 ✓
lockbox 498
long-term (fixed) assets 505
long-term liabilities 508
marketable securities 499
over-the-counter (OTC) market 516
primary market 513
prime rate 504 ✓
retained earnings 511
secondary markets 513 ✓

secured bonds 510
secured loans 504
securities markets 514
serial bonds 510
trade credit 503
transaction balances 498
Treasury bills (T-bills) 500
unsecured bonds 510
unsecured loans 504
working capital management 498

Check Your Progress

1. Define *working capital management.*
2. How can a company speed up cash flow? Why should it?
3. Describe the various types of marketable securities.
4. What does it mean to have a line of credit at a bank?
5. What are fixed assets? Why is assessing risk important in capital budgeting?

6. How can a company finance fixed assets?
7. What are bonds and what do companies do with them?
8. How can companies use equity to finance their operations and long-term growth?
9. What are the functions of securities markets?
10. What were some of the principal causes of the most recent recession?

Get Involved

1. Using your local newspaper or *The Wall Street Journal,* find the current rates of interest on the following marketable securities. If you were a financial manager for a large corporation, which would you invest extra cash in? Which would you invest in if you worked for a small business?
   a. Three-month T-bills
   b. Six-month T-bills
   c. Commercial certificates of deposit

   d. Commercial paper
   e. Eurodollar deposits
   f. Money market deposits

2. Select five of the Dow Jones Industrials from Table 16-5. Look up their earnings, dividends, and prices for the past five years. What kind of picture is presented by this information? Which stocks would you like to have owned over this past period? Do you think the next five years will present a similar picture?

Build Your Skills

Choosing among Projects

Background

As the senior executive in charge of exploration for High Octane Oil Co., you are constantly looking for projects that will add to the company's profitability—without increasing the company's risk. High Octane Oil is an international oil company with operations in Latin America, the Middle East, Africa, the United States, and Mexico. The company is one of the world's leading experts in deep-water exploration and drilling. High Octane currently produces 50 percent of its oil in the United States, 25 percent in the Middle East, 5 percent in Africa, 10 percent in Latin America, and 10 percent in Mexico. You are considering six projects from around the world.

Project 1—Your deep-water drilling platform in the Gulf of Mexico is producing at maximum capacity from the Valdez oil field, and High Octane's geological engineers think there is a high probability that there is oil in the Sanchez field, which is adjacent to Valdez. They recommend drilling a new series of wells. Once commercial quantities of oil have been discovered, it will take two more years to build the collection platform and pipelines. It will be four years before the discovered oil gets to the refineries.

Project 2—The Brazilian government has invited you to drill on some unexplored tracts in the middle of the central jungle region. There are roads to within 50 miles of the tract and BP has found oil 500 miles away from this tract. It would take about three years to develop this property and several more years to build pipelines and pumping stations to carry the oil to the refineries. The Brazilian government wants 20 percent of all production as its fee for giving High Octane Oil Co. the drilling rights or a $500 million up-front fee and 5 percent of the output.

Project 3—Your fields in Saudi Arabia have been producing oil for 50 years. Several wells are old, and the pressure has diminished. Your engineers are sure that if you were to initiate high-pressure secondary recovery procedures, you would increase the output of these existing wells by 20 percent. High-pressure recovery methods pump water at high pressure into the underground limestone formations to enhance the movement of petroleum toward the surface.

Project 4—Your largest oil fields in Alaska have been producing from only 50 percent of the known deposits. Your geological engineers estimate that you could open up 10 percent of the remaining fields every two years and offset your current declining production from existing wells. The pipeline capacity is available and, while you can only drill during six months of the year, the fields could be producing oil in three years.

Project 5—Some of High Octane's west Texas oil fields produce in shallow stripper wells of 2,000- to 4,000-foot depths. Stripper wells produce anywhere from 10 to 2,000 barrels per day and can last for six months or 40 years. Generally, once you find a shallow deposit, there is an 80 percent chance that offset wells will find more oil. Because these wells are shallow, they can be drilled quickly at a low cost. High Octane's engineers estimate that in your largest tract, which is closest to the company's Houston refinery, you could increase production by 30 percent for the next 10 years by increasing the density of the wells per square mile.

Project 6—The government of a republic in Russia has invited you to drill for oil in Siberia. Russian geologists think that this oil field might be the largest in the world, but there have been no wells drilled and no infrastructure exists to carry oil if it should be found. The republic has no money to help you build the infrastructure but if you find oil, it will let you keep the first five years' production before taking its 25 percent share. Knowing that oil fields do not start producing at full capacity for many years after initial production, your engineers are not sure that your portion of the first five years of production will pay for the infrastructure they must build to get the oil to market. The republic also has been known to have a rather unstable government, and the last international oil company that began this project left the country when a new government demanded a higher than originally agreed-upon percentage of the expected output. If this field is in fact the largest in the world, High Octane's supply of oil would be ensured well into the 21st century.

Task

1. Working in groups, rank the six projects from lowest risk to highest risk.

2. Given the information provided, do the best you can to rank the projects from lowest cost to highest cost.

3. What political considerations might affect your project choice?

4. If you could choose one project, which would it be and why?

5. If you could choose three projects, which ones would you choose? In making this decision, consider which projects might be highly correlated to High Octane Oil's existing production and which ones might diversify the company's production on a geographical basis.

Solve the Dilemma

Surviving Rapid Growth

Glasspray Corporation is a small firm that makes industrial fiberglass spray equipment. Despite its size, the company supplies a range of firms from small mom-and-pop boatmakers to major industrial giants, both overseas and here at home. Indeed, just about every molded fiberglass resin product, from bathroom sinks and counters to portable spas and racing yachts, is constructed with the help of one or more of the company's machines.

Despite global acceptance of its products, Glasspray has repeatedly run into trouble with regard to the management of its current assets and liabilities as a result of extremely rapid and consistent increases in year-to-year sales. The firm's president and founder, Stephen T. Rose, recently lamented the sad state of his firm's working capital position: "Our current assets aren't, and our current liabilities are!" Rose shouted in a recent meeting of the firm's top officers. "We can't afford any more increases in sales! We're selling our way into bankruptcy! Frankly, our *working* capital doesn't!"

Critique the position of short-term assets and liabilities of a small manufacturer and recommend corrective action.

Discussion Questions

1. Normally, rapidly increasing sales are a good thing. What seems to be the problem here?

2. List the important components of a firm's working capital. Include both current assets and current liabilities.

3. What are some management techniques applied to current liabilities that Glasspray might use to improve its working capital position?

Build Your Business Plan

Financial Management and Securities Market

This chapter helps you realize that once you are making money, you need to be careful in determining how to invest it. Meanwhile, your team should consider the pros and cons of establishing a line of credit at the bank.

Remember the key to building your business plan is to be realistic!!

See for Yourself Videocase

Tom and Eddie's: Fed through Nontraditional Channels

With the motto "We Put Good Taste in Everything We Do," Tom & Eddie's—a line of gourmet burger restaurants in the Chicago area—was launched in 2009. It was a difficult time to launch a new business because it was at the height of the recession and banks were not doing much lending to small startup businesses. The owners of Tom & Eddie's, former McDonald's executives Tom Dentice and Ed Rensi, both agree that access to cash was a major issue. However, they refused to be deterred. Today, the fast-food restaurant has three successful shops.

It began when Tom and Ed decided they wanted to create their own upscale burger restaurant. Both men had retired from McDonald's during the 1990s, but retirement was not for them. They conceived of a burger restaurant totally different from McDonald's, with unique menu items, great customer service, and comfortable seating. The men had researched the market and knew that there was a strong demand for gourmet burgers. To meet this demand, the men settled on fresh burgers of 100 percent beef with high-quality cheese such as smoked gouda and other toppings. For those who dislike hamburger, the restaurant also has Ahi tuna, edamame, and turkey options. Tom & Eddie's used the nearby College of DuPage as a test facility for its menu items.

Although the men were certain their idea would be a success, they knew banks at the time were reluctant to lend to small businesses. They ended up using their own money to finance the business and took on another partner. They also hired Brian Gordon, who they knew from McDonald's, to be the restaurant's CFO. They knew the restaurant needed someone skilled in financial management on board for things like operating expenditures, daily operational costs, and inventory management.

"In a small business, financial management is obviously very important. It's really the linchpin that holds everything together," says CFO Brian Gordon.

Immediate expenses for the restaurant included the cost for long-term assets, including the building, equipment, and furnishings and a sophisticated inventory management system. The restaurant uses trade credit to purchase its products in which it orders the products and is later invoiced for them.

One early decision they had to make was whether to build their own restaurant. Building a restaurant is tempting because the owners can customize it to meet their vision. However, it is also highly expensive. Tom and Eddie's made the decision to use buildings that already existed. As Brian Gordon explains, purchasing existing locations saves the company upfront costs. It also buys rather than leases its own equipment.

It was difficult to earn a profit initially. Tom and Eddie's struggled with the high cost of commodities, so it struggled to keep profit and loss under control. However, the restaurant proved popular among business people, who tend to eat there during the day, as well as couples who come in the evening. The longer the restaurant stays in business, the more access Tom and Eddie's will have to lines of credit because it will be able to prove to the banks that it can earn money and pay back loans.

This is not to say that Tom and Eddie's has everything figured out. Like all firms, it sometimes makes missteps that cost it financially. For instance, the restaurant chain had a fourth location in Deerfield, Illinois. After three years, however, the restaurant was not performing up to par, and the owners made the difficult decision to close it. The closure occurred before the lease expired, which meant the restaurant was still responsible for honoring its financial agreement. The restaurant did so and was able to maintain a good relationship with the landlords, which is crucial toward developing profitable business relationships in the future.

Tom and Eddie's has overcome a number of obstacles, including a recession when banks were not lending to small businesses. The restaurant is proof that strong financial management can help a business not only survive but thrive—even during periods of major economic contraction.[8]

Discussion Questions

1. Why was it difficult to open a new business in 2009? How did the owners of Tom and Eddie's overcome this obstacle?

2. Describe some ways the restaurant exhibited strong financial management in the early days of its operations.

3. What are some of the costs involved with closing a business location that does not earn enough money?

You can find the related video in the Video Library in Connect. Ask your instructor how you can access Connect.

Team Exercise

Compare and contrast financing with long-term liabilities, such as bonds versus financing with owner's equity, typically retained earnings, common stock, and preferred stock. Form groups and suggest a good mix of long-term liabilities and owner's equity for a new firm that makes wind turbines for generating alternative energy and would like to grow quickly.

Endnotes

1. Christine Birkner, "'Next' Steps," *Marketing News,* March 2015, pp. 12–13; Kaitlyn Smith, "John Hancock Ads Destroy the TV-Digital Divide," *Viral Gains,* September 9, 2014, http://www.viralgains.com/2014/09/john-hancock-ads-destroy-tv-digital-divide/ (accessed December 17, 2015); Amanda Walgrove, "John Hancock Puts on Their Storytelling Hat With 'Choose Your Own Adventure' Narratives," *Contently,* September 22, 2014,https://contently.com/strategist/2014/09/22/john-hancock-puts-on-their-storytelling-hat-with-choose-your-own-adventure-narratives/ (accessed December 17, 2015); John Hancock website,http://www.johnhancock.com/ (accessed December 17, 2015).

2. Vipal Monga and Emily Chasan, "The 109,894-Word Annual Report," *The Wall Street Journal,* June 2, 2015, pp. B1, B10; Justin Bachman, "Even the Accountants Think Financial Documents Are Too Long?" *Bloomberg Businessweek,* June 27, 2013, http://www.bloomberg.com/bw/articles/2013-06-27/even-the-accountants-think-financial-documents-are-too-long

(accessed July 6, 2015); KPMG, Disclosure Overload and Complexity: Hidden in Plain Sight, 2011,https://www.kpmg.com/US/en/IssuesAndInsights/ArticlesPublications/Documents/disclosure-overload-complexity.pdf (accessed July 6, 2015).

3. Calculated by Geoff Hirt from Apple's annual reports and website on June 16, 2014.

4. Y Combinator, http://ycombinator.com/ (accessed July 17, 2015); Sean Ellis, "Y Combinator Hatches Brilliant Entrepreneurs," *Start Up Marketing,* December 2, 2008, http://www.startup-marketing.com/y-combinator-hatches-brilliant-entrepreneurs/ (accessed July 17, 2015); Ryan Mac, "Top Startup Incubators and Accelerators: Y Combinator Tops with $7.8 Billion in Value," *Forbes,* April 30, 2012, http://www.forbes.com/sites/tomiogeron/2012/04/30/top-tech-incubators-as-ranked-by-forbes-y-combinator-tops-with-7-billion-in-value/ (accessed July 17, 2015);

Andy Louis-Charles. "Ignore Y Combinator at Your Own Risk," *The Motley Fool.* April 28, 2009; http://www.fool.com/investing/general/2009/04/28/ignore-y-combinator-at-your-own-risk.aspx (accessed July 17, 2015); Josh Quittner, "The New Internet Start-Up Boom: Get Rich Slow," *Time,* April 9, 2009, http://content.time.com/time/magazine/article/0,9171,1890387-1,00.html(accessed September 16, 2013); Max Chafkin, "Y Combinator President Sam Altman Is Dreaming Big," *Fast Company,* April 16, 2015,http://www.fastcompany.com/3044282/the-y-combinator-chronicles/california-dreamin (accessed July 17, 2015). John Rampton, "Top 10 Hot Incubators to Join in Silicon Valley," *Inc.,*November 26, 2015, http://www.inc.com/john-rampton/top-10-hot-incubators-to-join-in-silicon-valley.html (accessed July 17, 2015); "Business Incubator," *Entrepreneur,* 2015, http://www.entrepreneur.com/encyclopedia/business-incubator (accessed July 17, 2015).

5. Joshua Kennon, "Should You Invest in an IPO?"About.com,http://beginnersinvest.about.com/od/investmentbanking/a/aa073106a.htm (accessed May 4, 2016).

6. Jen Wieczner, "Tesla Investors Do the Electric Slide," *Fortune,* April 1, 2015, pp. 51–52; James R. Healey, "Tesla Loses Big, but Still Smiles," *USA Today,* February 12, 2015, p. 1B; Adam Hartung, "Why Now Is the Time to Buy Tesla Motor Stock," *Forbes,* January 6, 2015, http://www.forbes.com/sites/adamhartung/2015/01/06/why-now-is-the-time-to-buy-tesla-motors-stock/ (accessed July 24, 2015); "UBS Slams the Brakes on Tesla Stock," *CNN Money,* July 21, 2015, http://money.cnn.com/2015/07/21/investing/tesla-stock-downgrade/ (accessed July 24, 2015).

7. Vincent Ryan, "From Wall Street to Main Street," *CFO Magazine,* June 2008, pp. 85–86.

8. Tom and Eddie's website, http://www.tomandeddies.com/index.php (accessed May 10, 2016); Steve Sadin, "Burger Shop Tom & Eddie's Closes Its Doors in Deerfield," *Chicago Tribune,* September 12, 2014, http://www.chicagotribune.com/dining/chi-sp-burger-shop-tom-eddies-closes-its-doors-in-deerfield-20141210-story.html (accessed May 10, 2016); "Tom & Eddie Talk Burgers & Fries," *BurgerBusiness,* November 3, 2010, http://burgerbusiness.com/tom-eddie-talk-burgers-fries/ (accessed May 10, 2016).

BONUS CHAPTER

A The Legal and Regulatory Environment

Chapter Outline

© Africa Studio/Shutterstock

Learning Objectives

After reading this chapter, you will be able to:

LO A-1 Learn how the legal system resolves disputes.

LO A-2 Review regulatory agencies that oversee business conduct.

LO A-3 Examine the important elements that relate directly to business law.

LO A-4 Examine laws that determine parameters and requirements for business decision making.

LO A-5 Investigate legal issues related to the Internet.

LO A-6 Explore the Sarbanes-Oxley Act and its impact on business decisions.

LO A-7 Demonstrate the impact of the Dodd-Frank Wall Street Reform and Consumer Protection Act on business decisions.

Business law refers to the rules and regulations that govern the conduct of business. Problems in this area come from the failure to keep promises, misunderstandings, disagreements about expectations, or, in some cases, attempts to take advantage of others. The regulatory environment offers a framework and enforcement system in order to provide a fair playing field for all businesses. The regulatory environment is created based on inputs from competitors, customers, employees, special interest groups, and the public's elected representatives. Lobbying by pressure groups who try to influence legislation often shapes the legal and regulatory environment.

business law
refers to the rules and regulations that govern the conduct of business.

Sources of Law

Laws are classified as either criminal or civil. *Criminal law* not only prohibits a specific kind of action, such as unfair competition or mail fraud, but also imposes a fine or imprisonment as punishment for violating the law. A violation of a criminal law is thus called a crime. *Civil law* defines all the laws not classified as criminal, and it specifies the rights and duties of individuals and organizations (including businesses). Violations of civil law may result in fines but not imprisonment. The primary difference between criminal and civil law is that criminal laws are enforced by the state or nation, whereas civil laws are enforced through the court system by individuals or organizations.

Criminal and civil laws are derived from four sources: the Constitution (constitutional law), precedents established by judges (common law), federal and state statutes (statutory law), and federal and state administrative agencies (administrative law). Federal administrative agencies established by Congress control and influence business by enforcing laws and regulations to encourage competition and protect consumers, workers, and the environment. The Supreme Court is the ultimate authority on legal and regulatory decisions for appropriate conduct in business.

lawsuit
where one individual or organization takes another to court using civil laws.

Courts and the Resolution of Disputes

The primary method of resolving conflicts and business disputes is through lawsuits, where one individual or organization takes another to court using civil laws. The legal system, therefore, provides a forum for businesspeople to resolve disputes based on our legal foundations. The courts may decide when harm or damage results from the actions of others.

Learn how the legal system resolves disputes.

Because lawsuits are so frequent in the world of business, it is important to understand more about the court system where such disputes are resolved. Both financial restitution and specific actions to undo wrongdoing can result from going before a court to resolve a conflict. All decisions made in the courts are based on criminal and civil laws derived from the legal and regulatory system.

A businessperson may win a lawsuit in court and receive a judgment, or court order, requiring the loser of the suit to pay monetary damages. However, this does not guarantee the victor will be able to collect those damages. If the loser of the suit lacks the financial resources to pay the judgment—for example, if the loser is a bankrupt business—the winner of the suit may not be able to collect the award. Most business lawsuits involve a request for a sum of money,

When workers and management cannot come to an agreement, workers may choose to picket the organization and go on strike. Going on strike is usually reserved as a last resort if mediation and arbitration fail.

© McGraw-Hill Education/Andrew Resek

but some lawsuits request that a court specifically order a person or organization to do or to refrain from doing a certain act, such as slamming telephone customers.

The Court System

jurisdiction
the legal power of a court, through a judge, to interpret and apply the law and make a binding decision in a particular case.

Jurisdiction is the legal power of a court, through a judge, to interpret and apply the law and make a binding decision in a particular case. In some instances, other courts will not enforce the decision of a prior court because it lacked jurisdiction. Federal courts are granted jurisdiction by the Constitution or by Congress. State legislatures and constitutions determine which state courts hear certain types of cases. Courts of general jurisdiction hear all types of cases; those of limited jurisdiction hear only specific types of cases. The Federal Bankruptcy Court, for example, hears only cases involving bankruptcy. There is some combination of limited and general jurisdiction courts in every state.

trial court
when a court (acting through the judge or jury) must determine the facts of the case, decide which law or set of laws is pertinent to the case, and apply those laws to resolve the dispute.

In a **trial court** (whether in a court of general or limited jurisdiction and whether in the state or the federal system), two tasks must be completed. First, the court (acting through the judge or a jury) must determine the facts of the case. In other words, if there is conflicting evidence, the judge or jury must decide who to believe. Second, the judge must decide which law or set of laws is pertinent to the case and must then apply those laws to resolve the dispute.

appellate court
a court that deals solely with appeals relating to the interpretation of law.

An **appellate court,** on the other hand, deals solely with appeals relating to the interpretation of law. Thus, when you hear about a case being appealed, it is not retried, but rather reevaluated. Appellate judges do not hear witnesses but instead base their decisions on a written transcript of the original trial. Moreover, appellate courts do not draw factual conclusions; the appellate judge is limited to deciding whether the trial judge made a mistake in interpreting the law that probably affected the outcome of the trial. If the trial judge made no mistake (or if mistakes would not have changed the result of the trial), the appellate court will let the trial court's decision stand. If the appellate court finds a mistake, it usually sends the case back to the trial court so that the mistake can be corrected. Correction may involve the granting of a new trial. On occasion, appellate courts modify the verdict of the trial court without sending the case back to the trial court.

Alternative Dispute Resolution Methods

Although the main remedy for business disputes is a lawsuit, other dispute resolution methods are becoming popular. The schedules of state and federal trial courts are often crowded; long delays between the filing of a case and the trial date are common. Further, complex cases can become quite expensive to pursue. As a result, many businesspeople are turning to alternative methods of resolving business arguments: mediation and arbitration, the mini-trial, and litigation in a private court.

mediation
a method of outside resolution of labor and management differences in which the third party's role is to suggest or propose a solution to the problem.

Mediation is a form of negotiation to resolve a dispute by bringing in one or more third-party mediators, usually chosen by the disputing parties, to help reach a settlement. The mediator suggests different ways to resolve a dispute between the parties. The mediator's resolution is nonbinding—that is, the parties do not have to accept the mediator's suggestions; they are strictly voluntary.

arbitration
settlement of a labor/management dispute by a third party whose solution is legally binding and enforceable.

Arbitration involves submission of a dispute to one or more third-party arbitrators, usually chosen by the disputing parties, whose decision usually is final. Arbitration differs from mediation in that an arbitrator's decision must be followed, whereas a mediator merely offers suggestions and facilitates negotiations. Cases may be submitted to arbitration because a contract—such as a labor contract—requires it or because the parties agree to do so. Some consumers are barred from taking claims to court by agreements drafted by banks, brokers, health plans, and others. Instead, they are required to take complaints to mandatory arbitration. Arbitration can be an attractive alternative to a lawsuit because it is often cheaper and quicker, and the parties frequently can choose arbitrators who are knowledgeable about the particular area of business at issue.

A method of dispute resolution that may become increasingly important in settling complex disputes is the **mini-trial,** in which both parties agree to present a summarized version of their case to an independent third party. That person then advises them of his or her impression of the probable outcome if the case were to be tried. Representatives of both sides then attempt to negotiate a settlement based on the advisor's recommendations. For example, employees in a large corporation who believe they have muscular or skeletal stress injuries caused by the strain of repetitive motion in using a computer could agree to a mini-trial to address a dispute related to damages. Although the mini-trial itself does not resolve the dispute, it can help the parties resolve the case before going to court. Because the mini-trial is not subject to formal court rules, it can save companies a great deal of money, allowing them to recognize the weaknesses in a particular case.

In some areas of the country, disputes can be submitted to a private nongovernmental court for resolution. In a sense, a **private court system** is similar to arbitration in that an independent third party resolves the case after hearing both sides of the story. Trials in private courts may be either informal or highly formal, depending on the people involved. Businesses typically agree to have their disputes decided in private courts to save time and money.

mini-trial
a situation in which both parties agree to present a summarized version of their case to an independent third party; the third party advises them of his or her impression of the probable outcome if the case were to be tried.

private court system
similar to arbitration in that an independent third party resolves the case after hearing both sides of the story.

Regulatory Administrative Agencies

Federal and state administrative agencies (listed in Table A-1) also have some judicial powers. Many administrative agencies, such as the Federal Trade Commission, decide disputes that involve their regulations. In such disputes, the resolution process is usually called a "hearing" rather than a trial. In these cases, an administrative law judge decides all issues.

Federal regulatory agencies influence many business activities and cover product liability, safety, and the regulation or deregulation of public utilities. Usually, these bodies have the power to enforce specific laws, such as the Federal Trade Commission Act, and have some discretion in establishing operating rules and regulations to guide certain types of industry practices. Because of this discretion and overlapping areas of responsibility, confusion or conflict regarding which agencies have jurisdiction over which activities is common.

Of all the federal regulatory units, the **Federal Trade Commission (FTC)** most influences business activities related to questionable practices that create disputes between businesses and their customers. Although the FTC regulates a variety of business practices, it allocates a large portion of resources to curbing false advertising, misleading pricing, and deceptive packaging and labeling. When it receives a complaint or otherwise has reason to believe that a firm is violating a law, the FTC issues a complaint stating that the business is in violation.

If a company continues the questionable practice, the FTC can issue a cease-and-desist order, which is an order for the business to stop doing whatever has caused the complaint. In such cases, the charged firm can appeal to the federal courts to have the order rescinded. However, the FTC can seek civil penalties in court—up to a maximum

LO A-2

Review regulatory agencies that oversee business conduct.

Federal Trade Commission (FTC)
the federal regulatory unit that most influences business activities related to questionable practices that create disputes between businesses and their customers.

TABLE A-1   The Major Regulatory Agencies

Agency	Major Areas of Responsibility
Federal Trade Commission (FTC)	Enforces laws and guidelines regarding business practices; takes action to stop false and deceptive advertising and labeling.
Food and Drug Administration (FDA)	Enforces laws and regulations to prevent distribution of adulterated or misbranded foods, drugs, medical devices, cosmetics, veterinary products, and particularly hazardous consumer products.
Consumer Product Safety Commission (CPSC)	Ensures compliance with the Consumer Product Safety Act; protects the public from unreasonable risk of injury from any consumer product not covered by other regulatory agencies.
Interstate Commerce Commission (ICC)	Regulates franchises, rates, and finances of interstate rail, bus, truck, and water carriers.
Federal Communications Commission (FCC)	Regulates communication by wire, radio, and television in interstate and foreign commerce.
Environmental Protection Agency (EPA)	Develops and enforces environmental protection standards and conducts research into the adverse effects of pollution.
Federal Energy Regulatory Commission (FERC)	Regulates rates and sales of natural gas products, thereby affecting the supply and price of gas available to consumers; also regulates wholesale rates for electricity and gas, pipeline construction, and U.S. imports and exports of natural gas and electricity.
Equal Employment Opportunity Commission (EEOC)	Investigates and resolves discrimination in employment practices.
Federal Aviation Administration (FAA)	Oversees the policies and regulations of the airline industry.
Federal Highway Administration (FHA)	Regulates vehicle safety requirements.
Occupational Safety and Health Administration (OSHA)	Develops policy to promote worker safety and health and investigates infractions.
Securities and Exchange Commission (SEC)	Regulates corporate securities trading and develops protection from fraud and other abuses; provides an accounting oversight board.
Consumer Financial Protection Bureau	Regulates financial products and institutions to ensure consumer protection.

penalty of $10,000 a day for each infraction—if a cease-and-desist order is violated. In its battle against unfair pricing, the FTC has issued consent decrees alleging that corporate attempts to engage in price fixing or invitations to competitors to collude are violations even when the competitors in question refuse the invitations. The commission can also require companies to run corrective advertising in response to previous ads considered misleading.

The FTC also assists businesses in complying with laws. New marketing methods are evaluated every year. When general sets of guidelines are needed to improve business practices in a particular industry, the FTC sometimes encourages firms within that industry to establish a set of trade practices voluntarily. The FTC may even sponsor a conference bringing together industry leaders and consumers for the purpose of establishing acceptable trade practices.

Unlike the FTC, other regulatory units are limited to dealing with specific goods, services, or business activities. The Food and Drug Administration (FDA) enforces regulations prohibiting the sale and distribution of adulterated, misbranded, or hazardous food and drug products. For example, the FDA outlawed the sale and distribution of most over-the-counter hair-loss remedies after research indicated that few of the products were effective in restoring hair growth.

The Environmental Protection Agency (EPA) develops and enforces environmental protection standards and conducts research into the adverse effects of pollution. The Consumer Product Safety Commission recalls about 300 products a year, ranging from small, inexpensive toys to major appliances. The Consumer Product Safety Commission's website provides details regarding current recalls. The Consumer Product Safety Commission has fallen under increasing scrutiny in the wake of a number of product safety scandals involving children's toys. The most notable of these issues was lead paint discovered in toys produced in China. Some items are not even targeted to children but can be dangerous because children think they are food. Magnetic magnet desk toys and Tide Pods have both been mistaken as candy by children.

Important Elements of Business Law

To avoid violating criminal and civil laws, as well as discouraging lawsuits from consumers, employees, suppliers, and others, businesspeople need to be familiar with laws that address business practices.

Examine the important elements that relate directly to business law.

The Uniform Commercial Code

At one time, states had their own specific laws governing various business practices, and transacting business across state lines was difficult because of the variation in the laws from state to state. To simplify commerce, every state—except Louisiana—has enacted the Uniform Commercial Code (Louisiana has enacted portions of the code). The **Uniform Commercial Code (UCC)** is a set of statutory laws covering several business law topics. Article II of the Uniform Commercial Code, which is discussed in the following paragraphs, has a significant impact on business.

Uniform Commercial Code (UCC)
set of statutory laws covering several business law topics.

Sales Agreements.   Article II of the Uniform Commercial Code covers sales agreements for goods and services such as installation but does not cover the sale of stocks and bonds, personal services, or real estate. Among its many provisions, Article II stipulates that a sales agreement can be enforced even though it does not specify the selling price or the time or place of delivery. It also requires that a buyer pay a reasonable price for goods at the time of delivery if the buyer and seller have not reached an agreement on price. Specifically, Article II addresses the rights of buyers and sellers, transfers of ownership, warranties, and the legal placement of risk during manufacture and delivery.

Article II also deals with express and implied warranties. An **express warranty** stipulates the specific terms the seller will honor. Many automobile manufacturers, for example, provide three-year or 36,000-mile warranties on their vehicles, during which period they will fix any and all defects specified in the warranty. An **implied warranty** is imposed on the producer or seller by law, although it may not be a written document provided at the time of sale. Under Article II, a consumer may assume that the product for sale has a clear title (in other words, that it is not stolen) and that the product will serve the purpose for which it was made and sold as well as function as advertised.

express warranty
stipulates the specific terms the seller will honor.

implied warranty
imposed on the producer or seller by law, although it may not be a written document provided at the time of sale.

The Law of Torts and Fraud

tort
a private or civil wrong other than breach of contract.

A **tort** is a private or civil wrong other than a breach of contract. For example, a tort can result if the driver of a Domino's Pizza delivery car loses control of the vehicle and damages property or injures a person. In the case of the delivery car accident, the injured persons might sue the driver and the owner of the company—Domino's in this case—for damages resulting from the accident.

fraud
a purposefully unlawful act to deceive or manipulate in order to damage others.

Fraud is a purposefully unlawful act to deceive or manipulate in order to damage others. Thus, in some cases, a tort may also represent a violation of criminal law. Health care fraud has become a major issue in the courts.

product liability
businesses' legal responsibility for any negligence in the design, production, sale, and consumption of products.

An important aspect of tort law involves **product liability**—businesses' legal responsibility for any negligence in the design, production, sale, and consumption of products. Product liability laws have evolved from both common and statutory law. Some states have expanded the concept of product liability to include injuries by products whether or not the producer is proven negligent. Under this strict product liability, a consumer who files suit because of an injury has to prove only that the product was defective, that the defect caused the injury, and that the defect made the product unreasonably dangerous. For example, a carving knife is expected to be sharp and is not considered defective if you cut your finger using it. But an electric knife could be considered defective and unreasonably dangerous if it continued to operate after being switched off.

Reforming tort law, particularly in regard to product liability, has become a hot political issue as businesses look for relief from huge judgments in lawsuits. Although many lawsuits are warranted—few would disagree that a wrong has occurred when a patient dies because of negligence during a medical procedure or when a child is seriously injured by a defective toy and that the families deserve some compensation—many suits are not. Because of multimillion-dollar judgments, companies are trying to minimize their liability, and sometimes they pass on the costs of the damage awards to their customers in the form of higher prices. Some states have passed laws limiting damage awards and some tort reform is occurring at the federal level. Table A-2 lists the state courts systems the U.S. Chamber of Commerce's Institute for Legal Reform has identified as being "friendliest" and "least friendly" to business in terms of juries' fairness, judges' competence and impartiality, and other factors.

TABLE A-2   State Court Systems' Reputations for Supporting Business

Most Friendly to Business	Least Friendly to Business
Delaware	West Virginia
Vermont	Louisiana
Nebraska	Illinois
Iowa	California
New Hampshire	Alabama
Idaho	New Mexico
North Carolina	Florida
Wyoming	Mississippi
South Dakota	Missouri
Utah	Arkansas

Source: U.S. Chamber Institute for Legal Reform, "States," www.instituteforlegalreform.com/states (accessed February 25, 2016).

The Law of Contracts

Virtually every business transaction is carried out by means of a **contract,** a mutual agreement between two or more parties that can be enforced in a court if one party chooses not to comply with the terms of the contract. If you rent an apartment or house, for example, your lease is a contract. If you have borrowed money under a student loan program, you have a contractual agreement to repay the money. Many aspects of contract law are covered under the Uniform Commercial Code.

A "handshake deal" is, in most cases, as fully and completely binding as a written, signed contract agreement. Indeed, many oil-drilling and construction contractors have for years agreed to take on projects on the basis of such handshake deals. However, individual states require that some contracts be in writing to be enforceable. Most states require that at least some of the following contracts be in writing:

- Contracts involving the sale of land or an interest in land.
- Contracts to pay somebody else's debt.
- Contracts that cannot be fulfilled within one year.
- Contracts for the sale of goods that cost more than $500 (required by the Uniform Commercial Code).

Only those contracts that meet certain requirements—called *elements*—are enforceable by the courts. A person or business seeking to enforce a contract must show that it contains the following elements: voluntary agreement, consideration, contractual capacity of the parties, and legality.

For any agreement to be considered a legal contract, all persons involved must agree to be bound by the terms of the contract. *Voluntary agreement* typically comes about when one party makes an offer and the other accepts. If both the offer and the acceptance are freely, voluntarily, and knowingly made, the acceptance forms the basis for the contract. If, however, either the offer or the acceptance is the result of fraud or force, the individual or organization subject to the fraud or force can void, or invalidate, the resulting agreement or receive compensation for damages.

The second requirement for enforcement of a contract is that it must be supported by *consideration*—that is, money or something of value must be given in return for fulfilling a contract. As a general rule, a person cannot be forced to abide by the terms of a promise unless that person receives a consideration. The something of value could be money, goods, services, or even a promise to do or not to do something.

Contractual capacity is the legal ability to enter into a contract. As a general rule, a court cannot enforce a contract if either party to the agreement lacks contractual capacity. A person's contractual capacity may be limited or nonexistent if he or she is a minor (under the age of 18), mentally unstable, retarded, insane, or intoxicated.

Legality is the state or condition of being lawful. For an otherwise binding contract to be enforceable, both the purpose of and the consideration for the contract must be legal. A contract in which a bank loans money at a rate of interest prohibited by law, a practice known as usury, would be an illegal contract, for example. The fact that one of the parties may commit an illegal act while performing a contract does not render the contract itself illegal, however.

Breach of contract is the failure or refusal of a party to a contract to live up to his or her promises. In the case of an apartment lease, failure to pay rent would be considered breach of contract. The breaching party—the one who fails to comply—may be liable for monetary damages that he or she causes the other person.

contract
a mutual agreement between two or more parties that can be enforced in a court if one party chooses not to comply with the terms of the contract.

breach of contract
the failure or refusal of a party to a contract to live up to his or her promises.

The Law of Agency

agency
a common business relationship created when one person acts on behalf of another and under that person's control.

An **agency** is a common business relationship created when one person acts on behalf of another and under that person's control. Two parties are involved in an agency relationship: The **principal** is the one who wishes to have a specific task accomplished; the **agent** is the one who acts on behalf of the principal to accomplish the task. Authors, movie stars, and athletes often employ agents to help them obtain the best contract terms.

principal
the one in an agency relationship who wishes to have a specific task accomplished.

An agency relationship is created by the mutual agreement of the principal and the agent. It is usually not necessary that such an agreement be in writing, although putting it in writing is certainly advisable. An agency relationship continues as long as both the principal and the agent so desire. It can be terminated by mutual agreement, by fulfillment of the purpose of the agency, by the refusal of either party to continue in the relationship, or by the death of either the principal or the agent. In most cases, a principal grants authority to the agent through a formal *power of attorney,* which is a legal document authorizing a person to act as someone else's agent. The power of attorney can be used for any agency relationship, and its use is not limited to lawyers. For instance, in real estate transactions, often a lawyer or real estate agent is given power of attorney with the authority to purchase real estate for the buyer. Accounting firms often give employees agency relationships in making financial transactions.

agent
the one in an agency relationship who acts on behalf of the principal to accomplish the task.

Both officers and directors of corporations are fiduciaries, or people of trust, who use due care and loyalty as an agent in making decisions on behalf of the organization. This relationship creates a duty of care, also called duty of diligence, to make informed decisions. These agents of the corporation are not held responsible for negative outcomes if they are informed and diligent in their decisions. The duty of loyalty means that all decisions should be in the interests of the corporation and its stakeholders. Many people believe that executives at financial firms such as Countrywide Financial, Lehman Brothers, and Merrill Lynch failed to carry out their fiduciary duties. Lawsuits from shareholders called for the officers and directors to pay large sums of money from their own pockets.

The Law of Property

real property
consists of real estate and everything permanently attached to it.

Property law is extremely broad in scope because it covers the ownership and transfer of all kinds of real, personal, and intellectual property. **Real property** consists of real estate and everything permanently attached to it; **personal property** basically is everything else. Personal property can be further subdivided into tangible and intangible property. *Tangible property* refers to items that have a physical existence, such as automobiles, business inventory, and clothing. *Intangible property* consists of rights and duties; its existence may be represented by a document or by some other tangible item. For example, accounts receivable, stock in a corporation, goodwill, and trademarks are all examples of intangible personal property. **Intellectual property** refers to property, such as musical works, artwork, books, and computer software, that is generated by a person's creative activities.

personal property
all other property that is not real property.

intellectual property
refers to property, such as musical works, artwork, books, and computer software, that is generated by a person's creative activities.

Copyrights, patents, and trademarks provide protection to the owners of property by giving them the exclusive right to use it. *Copyrights* protect the ownership rights on material (often intellectual property) such as books, music, videos, photos, and computer software. The creators of such works, or their heirs, generally have exclusive rights to the published or unpublished works for the creator's lifetime, plus 50 years. *Patents* give inventors exclusive rights to their invention for 20 years. The most intense competition for patents is in the pharmaceutical industry. Most patents take a minimum of 18 months to secure.

A *trademark* is a brand (name, mark, or symbol) that is registered with the U.S. Patent and Trademark Office and is thus legally protected from use by any other firm. Among the symbols that have been so protected are McDonald's golden arches. It is estimated that large multinational firms may have as many as 15,000 conflicts related to trademarks. Companies are diligent about protecting their trademarks both to avoid confusion in consumers' minds and because a term that becomes part of everyday language can no longer be trademarked. The names *aspirin* and *nylon,* for example, were once the exclusive property of their creators but became so widely used as product names (rather than brand names) that now anyone can use them. A related term is *trade dress,* which refers to the visual appearance of a product or its packaging. Coca-Cola's contoured bottle and Hershey's 12 rectangular panels for its chocolate bars are examples of visual characteristics protected as intellectual property. In order for these visual characteristics to receive protection, consumers must strongly associate the shape or design with the product itself.[1]

Coca-Cola has received intellectual property protection for its contoured bottle because it has become so synonymous with the Coca-Cola product. This type of protection is known as trade dress.

© urbanbuzz/Alamy Stock Photo

As the trend toward globalization of trade continues, and more and more businesses trade across national boundaries, protecting property rights, particularly intellectual property such as computer software, has become an increasing challenge. While a company may be able to register as a trademark, a brand name, or a symbol in its home country, it may not be able to secure that protection abroad. Some countries have copyright and patent laws that are less strict than those of the United States; some countries will not enforce U.S. laws. China, for example, has often been criticized for permitting U.S. goods to be counterfeited there. Such counterfeiting harms not only the sales of U.S. companies, but also their reputations if the knockoffs are of poor quality. Thus, businesses engaging in foreign trade may have to take extra steps to protect their property because local laws may be insufficient to protect them.

The Law of Bankruptcy

Although few businesses and individuals intentionally fail to repay (or default on) their debts, sometimes they cannot fulfill their financial obligations. Individuals may charge goods and services beyond their ability to pay for them. Businesses may take on too much debt in order to finance growth, or business events such as an increase in the cost of commodities can bankrupt a company. An option of last resort in these cases is bankruptcy, or legal insolvency. Some well-known companies that have declared bankruptcy include Hostess, American Apparel, and RadioShack.

Individuals or companies may ask a bankruptcy court to declare them unable to pay their debts and thus release them from the obligation of repaying those debts. The debtor's assets may then be sold to pay off as much of the debt as possible. In the case of a personal bankruptcy, although the individual is released from repaying debts and can start over with a clean slate, obtaining credit after bankruptcy proceedings is very difficult. About 2 million households in the United States filed for bankruptcy in 2005, the most ever. However, a new, more restrictive law went into effect in late 2005, allowing fewer consumers to use bankruptcy to eliminate their debts. The law makes it harder for consumers to prove that they should be allowed to clear their debts for what is called a "fresh start" or Chapter 7 bankruptcy. Although the person or company in debt usually initiates bankruptcy proceedings, creditors may also initiate them. The subprime mortgage crisis caused a string of bankruptcies among individuals, and Chapter 7 and

TABLE A-3   Types of Bankruptcy

Chapter 7	Requires that the business be dissolved and its assets liquidated, or sold, to pay off the debts. Individuals declaring Chapter 7 retain a limited amount of exempt assets, the amount of which may be determined by state or federal law, at the debtor's option. Although the type and value of exempt assets vary from state to state, most states' laws allow a bankrupt individual to keep an automobile, some household goods, clothing, furnishings, and at least some of the value of the debtor's residence. All nonexempt assets must be sold to pay debts.
Chapter II	Temporarily frees a business from its financial obligations while it reorganizes and works out a payment plan with its creditors. The indebted company continues to operate its business during bankruptcy proceedings. Often, the business sells off assets and less-profitable subsidiaries to raise cash to pay off its immediate obligations.
Chapter 13	Similar to Chapter II but limited to individuals. This proceeding allows an individual to establish a three- to five-year plan for repaying his or her debt. Under this plan, an individual ultimately may repay as little as 10 percent of his or her debt.

Chapter 11 bankruptcies among banks and other businesses as well. Tougher bankruptcy laws and a slowing economy converged on the subprime crisis to create a situation in which bankruptcy filings skyrocketed. Table A-3 describes the various levels of bankruptcy protection a business or individual may seek.

LO A-4

Examine laws that determine parameters and requirements for business decision making.

Sherman Antitrust Act passed in 1890 to prevent businesses from restraining trade and monopolizing markets.

Laws Affecting Business Practices

One of the government's many roles is to act as a watchdog to ensure that businesses behave in accordance with the wishes of society. Congress has enacted a number of laws that affect business practices; some of the most important of these are summarized in Table A-4. Many state legislatures have enacted similar laws governing business within specific states.

The **Sherman Antitrust Act,** passed in 1890 to prevent businesses from restraining trade and monopolizing markets, condemns "every contract, combination, or conspiracy in restraint of trade." For example, a request that a competitor agree to fix prices or divide

TABLE A-4   Major Federal Laws Affecting Business Practices

Act (Date Enacted)	Purpose
Sherman Antitrust Act (1890)	Prohibits contracts, combinations, or conspiracies to restrain trade; establishes as a misdemeanor monopolizing or attempting to monopolize.
Clayton Act (1914)	Prohibits specific practices such as price discrimination, exclusive dealer arrangements, and stock acquisitions in which the effect may notably lessen competition or tend to create a monopoly.
Federal Trade Commission Act (1914)	Created the Federal Trade Commission; also gives the FTC investigatory powers to be used in preventing unfair methods of competition.
Robinson-Patman Act (1936)	Prohibits price discrimination that lessens competition among wholesalers or retailers; prohibits producers from giving disproportionate services of facilities to large buyers.
Wheeler-Lea Act (1938)	Prohibits unfair and deceptive acts and practices regardless of whether competition is injured; places advertising of foods and drugs under the jurisdiction of the FTC.

TABLE A-4   (Continued)

Act (Date Enacted)	Purpose
Lanham Act (1946)	Provides protections and regulation of brand names, brand marks, trade names, and trademarks.
Celler-Kefauver Act (1950)	Prohibits any corporation engaged in commerce from acquiring the whole or any part of the stock or other share of the capital assets of another corporation when the effect substantially lessens competition or tends to create a monopoly.
Fair Packaging and Labeling Act (1966)	Makes illegal the unfair or deceptive packaging or labeling of consumer products.
Magnuson-Moss Warranty (FTC) Act (1975)	Provides for minimum disclosure standards for written consumer product warranties; defines minimum consent standards for written warranties; allows the FTC to prescribe interpretive rules in policy statements regarding unfair or deceptive practices.
Consumer Goods Pricing Act (1975)	Prohibits the use of price maintenance agreements among manufacturers and resellers in interstate commerce.
Antitrust Improvements Act (1976)	Requires large corporations to inform federal regulators of prospective mergers or acquisitions so that they can be studied for any possible violations of the law.
Trademark Counterfeiting Act (1980)	Provides civil and criminal penalties against those who deal in counterfeit consumer goods or any counterfeit goods that can threaten health or safety.
Trademark Law Revision Act (1988)	Amends the Lanham Act to allow brands not yet introduced to be protected through registration with the Patent and Trademark Office.
Nutrition Labeling and Education Act (1990)	Prohibits exaggerated health claims and requires all processed foods to contain labels with nutritional information.
Telephone Consumer Protection Act (1991)	Establishes procedures to avoid unwanted telephone solicitations; prohibits marketers from using automated telephone dialing system or an artificial or prerecorded voice to certain telephone lines.
Federal Trademark Dilution Act (1995)	Provides trademark owners the right to protect trademarks and requires relinquishment of names that match or parallel existing trademarks.
Digital Millennium Copyright Act (1998)	Refined copyright laws to protect digital versions of copyrighted materials, including music and movies.
Children's Online Privacy Protection Act (2000)	Regulates the collection of personally identifiable information (name, address, e-mail address, hobbies, interests, or information collected through cookies) online from children under age 13.
Sarbanes-Oxley Act (2002)	Made securities fraud a criminal offense; stiffened penalties for corporate fraud; created an accounting oversight board; and instituted numerous other provisions designed to increase corporate transparency and compliance.
Do Not Call Implementation Act (2003)	Directs FCC and FTC to coordinate so their rules are consistent regarding telemarketing call practices, including the Do Not Call Registry.
Dodd-Frank Wall Street Reform and Consumer Protection Act (2010)	Increases accountability and transparency in the financial industry, protects consumers from deceptive financial practices, and establishes the Consumer Financial Protection Bureau.

markets would, if accepted, result in a violation of the Sherman Antitrust Act. The FTC challenged the proposed merger between Staples and Office Depot because it believed the merger could significantly reduce the competition in the "consumable" office supply market.[2] The Sherman Antitrust Act, still highly relevant 100 years after its passage, is being copied throughout the world as the basis for regulating fair competition.

Because the provisions of the Sherman Antitrust Act are rather vague, courts have not always interpreted it as its creators intended. The Clayton Act was passed in 1914 to limit specific activities that can reduce competition. The **Clayton Act** prohibits price discrimination, tying and exclusive agreements, and the acquisition of stock in another corporation where the effect may be to substantially lessen competition or tend to create a monopoly. In addition, the Clayton Act prohibits members of one company's board of directors from holding seats on the boards of competing corporations. The act also exempts farm cooperatives and labor organizations from antitrust laws.

In spite of these laws regulating business practices, there are still many questions about the regulation of business. For instance, it is difficult to determine what constitutes an acceptable degree of competition and whether a monopoly is harmful to a particular market. Many mergers were permitted that resulted in less competition in the banking, publishing, and automobile industries. In some industries, such as utilities, it is not cost effective to have too many competitors. For this reason, the government permits utility monopolies, although recently, the telephone, electricity, and communications industries have been deregulated. Furthermore, the antitrust laws are often rather vague and require interpretation, which may vary from judge to judge and court to court. Thus, what one judge defines as a monopoly or trust today may be permitted by another judge a few years from now. Businesspeople need to understand what the law says on these issues and try to conduct their affairs within the bounds of these laws.

Clayton Act
prohibits price discrimination, tying and exclusive agreements, and the acquisition of stock in another corporation where the effect may be to substantially lessen competition or tend to create a monopoly.

LO A-5

Investigate legal issues related to the Internet.

The Internet: Legal and Regulatory Issues

Our use and dependence on the Internet is increasingly creating a potential legal problem for businesses. With this growing use come questions of maintaining an acceptable level of privacy for consumers and proper competitive use of the medium. Some might consider that tracking individuals who visit or "hit" their website by attaching a "cookie" (identifying you as a website visitor for potential recontact and tracking your movement throughout the site) is an improper use of the Internet for business purposes. Others may find such practices acceptable and similar to the practices of non-Internet retailers who copy information from checks or ask customers for their name, address, or phone number before they will process a transaction. There are few specific laws that regulate business on the Internet, but the standards for acceptable behavior that are reflected in the basic laws and regulations designed for traditional businesses can be applied to business on the Internet as well. One law aimed specifically at advertising on the internet is the CAN-SPAM Act of 2004. The law restricts unsolicited e-mail advertisements by requiring the consent of the recipient. Furthermore, the CAN-SPAM Act follows the "opt-out" model wherein recipients can elect not to receive further e-mails from a sender simply by clicking on a link.[3]

The central focus for future legislation of business conducted on the Internet is the protection of personal privacy. The present basis of personal privacy protection is the U.S. Constitution, various Supreme Court rulings, and laws such as the 1971 Fair Credit Reporting Act, the 1978 Right to Financial Privacy Act, and the 1974 Privacy Act, which deals with the release of government records. With few regulations on the use of information by businesses, companies legally buy and sell information on customers to gain competitive advantage. Sometimes existing laws are not enough to protect people, and the ease with which information on customers can be obtained becomes a problem. For example, identity theft has increased due to the proliferation of the use of the Internet. A disturbing trend is how many children have had their identities stolen. One study of 40,000 children revealed that more than 10 percent have had their Social Security numbers stolen. The rates of child identity theft have risen since the advent of the Internet.[4] It has been suggested that the treatment of personal data as property will ensure privacy rights by recognizing that customers have a right to control the use of their personal data.

Internet use is different from traditional interaction with businesses in that it is readily accessible, and most online businesses are able to develop databases of information on customers. Congress has restricted the development of databases on children using the Internet. The Children's Online Privacy Protection Act (COPPA) of 2000 prohibits website and Internet providers from seeking personal information from children under age 13 without parental consent. Companies are still running afoul of COPPA. Two app developers paid $360,000 to settle charges from the FTC that they had allowed third-party advertisers to collect personal information from children under the age of 13.[5]

The Internet has also created a copyright dilemma for some organizations that have found that the web addresses of other online firms either match or are very similar to their company trademark. "Cybersquatters" attempt to sell back the registration of these matching sites to the trademark owner. Companies such as Taco Bell, MTC, and KFC have paid thousands of dollars to gain control of domain names that match or parallel company trademarks. The Federal Trademark Dilution Act of 1995 helps companies address this conflict. The act provides trademark owners the right to protect trademarks, prevents the use of trademark-protected entities, and requires the relinquishment of names that match or closely parallel company trademarks. The reduction of geographic barriers, speed of response, and memory capability of the Internet will continue to create new challenges for the legal and regulatory environment in the future.

Legal Pressure for Responsible Business Conduct

To ensure greater compliance with society's desires, both federal and state governments are moving toward increased organizational accountability for misconduct. Before 1991, laws mainly punished those employees directly responsible for an offense. Under new guidelines established by the Federal Sentencing Guidelines for Organizations (FSGO), however, both the responsible employees and the firms that employ them are held accountable for violations of federal law. Thus, the government now places responsibility for controlling and preventing misconduct squarely on the shoulders of top management. The main objectives of the federal guidelines are to train employees, self-monitor and supervise employee conduct, deter unethical acts, and punish those organizational members who engage in illegal acts.

A 2010 amendment to the FSGO directs ethics officers to report directly to the board of directors rather than simply the general counsel or top officers. This places the responsibility on the shoulders of the firm's leadership, usually the board of directors. The board must ensure that there is a high-ranking manager accountable for the day-to-day operational oversight of the ethics program. The board must provide for adequate authority, resources, and access to the board or an appropriate subcommittee of the board. The board must ensure that there are confidential mechanisms available so that the organization's employees and agents may report or seek guidance about potential or actual misconduct without fear of retaliation. Finally, the board is required to oversee the discovery of risks and to design, implement, and modify approaches to deal with those risks.

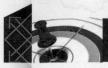
SEC Puts the Whistle Back in Whistleblowing

Whistleblowers may soon get new protections, thanks to a Securities and Exchange Commission (SEC) ruling limiting companies' abilities to censor and intimidate employees who report violations. The SEC offers financial incentives to some whistleblowers reporting large-scale misconduct. If a report results in a company receiving fines of more than $1 million, the SEC may award the whistleblower 10 to 30 percent of the fines or penalties levied against the company. The SEC's whistleblower program was created in 2010 as part of the Dodd-Frank Act. The intent of the program is to curb legal and ethical misconduct before it leads to disastrous consequences, such as the global financial crisis.

Some companies are suspected of forcing workers to sign nondisclosure agreements and harassing employees who voice concerns over misconduct. This includes clauses in employment contracts that limit the ability of whistleblowers to receive financial rewards for reporting misconduct, effectively neutralizing the incentive of employees to expose company violations. The Ethics Resource Center has found that 21 percent of employees experience retaliation after reporting misconduct. The SEC is fighting back and taking steps to protect the rights of whistleblowers. The government agency is requesting years of corporate training procedures, confidentiality agreements, and even lists of terminated employees from certain companies to see whether they engaged in illegal discrimination against whistleblowers. These steps demonstrate the SEC's commitment to whistleblower protection and could lead to fewer companies suppressing future reporting of misconduct.[6]

Discussion Questions

1. How is the SEC trying to prevent employers from silencing whistleblowers?
2. Why does the SEC feel that it is unfair for an employment contract to limit the ability of employees to receive financial rewards for blowing the whistle?
3. What is the SEC hoping to achieve by offering whistleblowers rewards for large misconduct convictions against firms?

If an organization's culture and policies reward or provide opportunities to engage in misconduct through lack of managerial concern or failure to comply with the seven minimum requirements of the FSGO (provided in Table A-5), then the organization may incur not only penalties but also the loss of customer trust, public confidence, and other intangible assets. For this reason, organizations cannot succeed solely through a legalistic approach to compliance with the sentencing guidelines; top management must cultivate high ethical standards that will serve as barriers to illegal conduct. The organization must want to be a good citizen and recognize the importance of compliance to

TABLE A-5 Seven Steps to Compliance

1. Develop standards and procedures to reduce the propensity for criminal conduct.

2. Designate a high-level compliance manager or ethics officer to oversee the compliance program.

3. Avoid delegating authority to people known to have a propensity to engage in misconduct.

4. Communicate standards and procedures to employees, other agents, and independent contractors through training programs and publications.

5. Establish systems to monitor and audit misconduct and to allow employees and agents to report criminal activity.

6. Enforce standards and punishments consistently across all employees in the organization.

7. Respond immediately to misconduct and take reasonable steps to prevent further criminal conduct.

Source: U.S. Sentencing Commission, Federal Sentencing Guidelines for Organizations, 1991.

successful workplace activities and relationships. In fact, the top concern of corporate lawyers is ethics and compliance. Implementing ethics and compliance ranks higher than any other concern, possibly due to the pressures placed on companies by the passage of Sarbanes-Oxley, the Dodd-Frank Act, and the Federal Sentencing Guidelines.[7]

The federal guidelines also require businesses to develop programs that can detect—and that will deter employees from engaging in—misconduct. To be considered effective, such compliance programs must include disclosure of any wrongdoing, cooperation with the government, and acceptance of responsibility for the misconduct. Codes of ethics, employee ethics training, hotlines (direct 800 phone numbers), compliance directors, newsletters, brochures, and other communication methods are typical components of a compliance program. The ethics component, discussed in Chapter 2, acts as a buffer, keeping firms away from the thin line that separates unethical and illegal conduct.

Despite the existing legislation, a number of ethics scandals in the early 2000s led Congress to pass—almost unanimously—the **Sarbanes-Oxley Act,** which criminalized securities fraud and strengthened penalties for corporate fraud. It also created an accounting oversight board that requires corporations to establish codes of ethics for financial reporting and to develop greater transparency in financial reports to investors and other interested parties. Additionally, the law requires top corporate executives to sign off on their firms' financial reports, and they risk fines and jail sentences if they misrepresent their companies' financial position. Table A-6 summarizes the major provisions of the Sarbanes-Oxley Act.

LO A-6

Explore the Sarbanes-Oxley Act and its impact on business decisions.

Sarbanes-Oxley Act
a law that criminalized securities fraud and strengthened penalties for corporate fraud.

TABLE A-6   Major Provisions of the Sarbanes-Oxley Act

1.	Requires the establishment of a Public Company Accounting Oversight Board in charge of regulations administered by the Securities and Exchange Commission.
2.	Requires CEOs and CFOs to certify that their companies' financial statements are true and without misleading statements.
3.	Requires that corporate boards of directors' audit committees consist of independent members who have no material interests in the company.
4.	Prohibits corporations from making or offering loans to officers and board members.
5.	Requires codes of ethics for senior financial officers; code must be registered with the SEC.
6.	Prohibits accounting firms from providing both auditing and consulting services to the same client without the approval of the client firm's audit committee.
7.	Requires company attorneys to report wrongdoing to top managers and, if necessary, to the board of directors; if managers and directors fail to respond to reports of wrongdoing, the attorney should stop representing the company.
8.	Mandates "whistleblower protection" for persons who disclose wrongdoing to authorities.
9.	Requires financial securities analysts to certify that their recommendations are based on objective reports.
10.	Requires mutual fund managers to disclose how they vote shareholder proxies, giving investors information about how their shares influence decisions.
11.	Establishes a 10-year penalty for mail/wire fraud.
12.	Prohibits the two senior auditors from working on a corporation's account for more than five years; other auditors are prohibited from working on an account for more than seven years. In other words, accounting firms must rotate individual auditors from one account to another from time to time.

Source: Pub. L. 107-204, 116 Stat. 745 (2002).

The Sarbanes-Oxley Act has created a number of concerns and is considered burdensome and expensive to corporations. Large corporations report spending more than $4 million each year to comply with the act, according to Financial Executives International. The act has caused more than 500 public companies a year to report problems in their accounting systems. Additionally, Sarbanes-Oxley failed to prevent and detect the widespread misconduct of financial institutions that led to the financial crisis.

On the other hand, there are many benefits, including greater accountability of top managers and boards of directors, that improve investor confidence and protect employees, especially their retirement plans. It is believed that the law has more benefits than drawbacks—with the greatest benefit being that boards of directors and top managers are better informed. Some companies such as Cisco and Pitney Bowes report improved efficiency and cost savings from better financial information.

LO A-7

Demonstrate the impact of the Dodd-Frank Wall Street Reform and Consumer Protection Act on business decisions

In spite of the benefits Sarbanes-Oxley offers, it did not prevent widespread corporate corruption from leading to the most recent recession. The resulting financial crisis prompted the Obama administration to create new regulation to reform Wall Street and the financial industry. In 2010, the Dodd-Frank Wall Street Reform and Consumer Protection Act was passed. In addition to new regulations for financial institutions, the legislation created a Consumer Financial Protection Bureau (CFPB) to protect consumers from complex or deceptive financial products. Table A-7 highlights some of the major provisions of the Dodd-Frank Act.

TABLE A-7   Major Provisions of the Dodd-Frank Wall Street Reform and Consumer Protection Act

1.	Enhances stability of the finance industry through the creation of two new financial agencies, the Financial Oversight Stability Council and the Office of Financial Research.
2.	Institutes an orderly liquidation procedure for the Federal Deposit Insurance Corporation to liquidate failing companies.
3.	Eliminates the Office of Thrift Supervision and transfers its powers to the Comptroller of the Currency.
4.	Creates stronger regulation and greater oversight of hedge funds.
5.	Establishes the Federal Insurance Agency to gather information and oversee the insurance industry for risks.
6.	Requires regulators to have regulations in place for banks. Also prohibits and/or limits proprietary trading, hedge fund sponsorship and private equity funds, and relationships with hedge funds and private equity funds.
7.	Regulates derivatives and complex financial instruments by limiting where they can be traded and ensuring that traders have the financial resources to meet their responsibilities.
8.	Provides a framework for creating risk-management standards for financial market utilities and the payment, clearing, and settlement activities performed by institutions.
9.	Improves investor protection through acts such as creating a whistleblower bounty program and increasing consumer access to their credit scores.
10.	Institutes the Bureau of Consumer Financial Protection to educate consumers and protect them from deceptive financial products.
11.	Attempts to reform the Federal Reserve in ways that include limiting the Federal Reserve's lending authority, reevaluating methods for Federal Reserve regulations and the appointment of Federal Reserve Bank directors, and instituting additional disclosure requirements.
12.	Reforms mortgage activities with new provisions that include increasing the lender's responsibility to ensure the borrower can pay back the loan, prohibiting unfair lending practices, requiring additional disclosure in the mortgage loan process, and imposing penalties against those found guilty of noncompliance with the new standards.

Source: Brief Summary of the Dodd-Frank Wall Street Reform and Consumer Protection Act, http://democrats.financialservices.house.gov/uploadedfiles/4173briefsummaryofd-f.pdf (accessed October 2, 2016).

The Dodd-Frank Act contains 16 titles meant to increase consumer protection, enhance transparency and accountability in the financial sector, and create new financial agencies. In some ways, Dodd-Frank is attempting to improve upon provisions laid out in the Sarbanes-Oxley Act. For instance, Dodd-Frank takes whistleblower protection a step further by offering additional incentives to whistleblowers for reporting misconduct. If whistleblowers report misconduct that results in penalties of more than $1 million, the whistleblower will be entitled to a percentage of the settlement.[8] Additionally, complex financial instruments must now be made more transparent so that consumers will have a better understanding of what these instruments involve.

The act also created three new agencies: the Consumer Financial Protection Bureau (CFPB), the Office of Financial Research, and the Financial Stability Oversight Council. While the CFPB was created to protect consumers, the other two agencies work to maintain stability in the financial industry so such a crisis will not recur in the future.[9] Although it is too early to tell whether these regulations will serve to create widescale positive financial reform, the Dodd-Frank Act is certainly leading to major changes on Wall Street and in the financial sector.

Review Your Understanding

Learn how the legal system resolves disputes.

The primary method of resolving conflicts and business disputes is through lawsuits, where one individual or organization takes another to court using civil laws. All decisions made in the courts are based on criminal and civil laws derived from the legal and regulatory system. Courts must have jurisdiction, or the legal power, through a judge, to interpret and apply the law and make a binding decision in a particular case. In a trial court, the court must determine the facts of the case and the judge must decide which law or set of laws is pertinent to the case and must then apply those laws to resolve the dispute. An appellate court deals solely with appeals relating to the interpretation of law.

There are alternative methods of resolving disputes. Mediation is a form of negotiation to resolve a dispute by bringing in one or more third-party mediators, usually chosen by the disputing parties, to help reach a settlement. Arbitration involves submission of a dispute to one or more third-party arbitrators, usually chosen by the disputing parties, whose decision usually is final. A mini-trial is when both parties agree to present a summarized version of their case to an independent third party. A private court system is similar to arbitration in that an independent third party resolves the case after hearing both sides of the story.

Review regulatory agencies that oversee business conduct.

The Federal Trade Commission (FTC) most influences business activities related to questionable practices that create disputes between businesses and their customers. If a company continues the questionable practice, the FTC can issue a cease-and-desist order, which is an order for the business to stop doing whatever has caused the complaint. The Food and

Drug Administration (FDA) enforces regulations prohibiting the sale and distribution of adulterated, misbranded, or hazardous food and drug products. The Environmental Protection Agency (EPA) develops and enforces environmental protection standards and conducts research into the adverse effects of pollution. The Consumer Product Safety Commission recalls about 300 products a year, ranging from small, inexpensive toys to major appliances.

Examine the important elements that relate directly to business law.

Important elements of business law include the Uniform Commercial Code (UCC), the law of torts and fraud, the law of contracts, the law of agency, the law of property, and the law of bankruptcy. The UCC is a set of statutory laws covering several business law topics. Article II of the UCC deals with express and implied warranties. An express warranty stipulates the specific terms the seller will honor. An implied warranty is imposed on the producer or seller by law, although it may not be a written document provided at the time of sale.

A tort is a private or civil wrong other than a breach of contract. An important part of tort law is product liability, businesses' legal responsibility for any negligence in the design, production, sale, and consumption of products. Fraud is a purposefully unlawful act to deceive or manipulate in order to damage others. A contract is a mutual agreement between two or more parties that can be enforced in a court if one party chooses not to comply with the terms of the contract.

An agency is a common business relationship created when one person acts on behalf of another and under that person's control. Property law is extremely broad in scope because it covers the ownership and transfer of all kinds of real, personal, and intellectual property. There are also laws dealing with bankruptcy, which occurs when individuals or companies ask a bankruptcy court to declare them unable to pay their debts and thus release them from the obligation of repaying those debts.

Examine laws that determine parameters and requirements for business decision making.

Laws that determine parameters and requirements for business decision making include the Sherman Antitrust Act, the Clayton Act, and a number of other laws. The Sherman Antitrust Act, passed in 1890, is meant to prevent businesses from restraining trade and monopolizing markets. The Clayton Act prohibits price discrimination, tying and exclusive agreements, and the acquisition of stock in another corporation where the effect may be to substantially lessen competition or tend to create a monopoly.

Investigate legal issues related to the Internet.

With the growing use of the Internet, privacy is becoming a major concern. Some consider that tracking individuals who visit or "hit" their website by attaching a cookie is an invasion of privacy. The CAN-SPAM Act of 2004 restricts unsolicited email advertisements. The Children's Online Privacy Protection Act (COPPA) prohibits website and Internet providers from seeking personal information from children under age 13 without parental consent.

Explore the Sarbanes-Oxley Act and its impact on business decisions.

The Sarbanes-Oxley Act criminalized securities fraud and strengthened penalties for corporate fraud. It created an accounting oversight board that requires corporations to establish codes of ethics for financial reporting and to develop greater transparency in financial reports to investors and other interested parties. Additionally, the law requires top corporate executives to sign off on their firms' financial reports, and they risk fines and jail sentences if they misrepresent their companies' financial position.

Demonstrate the impact of the Dodd-Frank Wall Street Reform and Consumer Protection Act on business decisions.

In 2010, the Dodd-Frank Wall Street Reform and Consumer Protection Act was passed. In addition to new regulations for financial institutions, the legislation created a Consumer Financial Protection Bureau (CFPB) to protect consumers from complex or deceptive financial products. The Dodd-Frank Act contains 16 titles meant to increase consumer protection, enhance transparency and accountability in the financial sector, and create new financial agencies. Dodd-Frank takes whistleblower protection a step further by offering additional incentives to whistleblowers for reporting misconduct. If whistleblowers report misconduct that results in penalties of more than $1 million, the whistleblower will be entitled to a percentage of the settlement. The act also created two other agencies: the Office of Financial Research and the Financial Stability Oversight Council.

Learn the Terms

agency 534	Federal Trade Commission (FTC) 529	principal 534
agent 534	fraud 532	private court system 529
appellate court 528	implied warranty 531	product liability 532
arbitration 528	intellectual property 534	real property 534
breach of contract 533	jurisdiction 528	Sarbanes-Oxley Act 541
business law 527	lawsuit 527	Sherman Antitrust Act 536
Clayton Act 538	mediation 528	tort 532
contract 533	mini-trial 529	trial court 528
express warranty 531	personal property 534	Uniform Commercial Code (UCC) 531

Check Your Progress

1. What are the sources of law relating to both criminal and civil actions?
2. How does the court system work to resolve business disputes?
3. Why is it important to understand how regulatory administrative agencies resolve disputes and protect the public?
4. What are the major elements of business law?
5. What are some of the most important laws that affect business practices?
6. Why is there the need for additional regulation to resolve issues related to the Internet?
7. What are the important steps to developing an ethics and compliance program?
8. What was the purpose of the Sarbanes-Oxley Act?
9. Why was the Dodd-Frank Act passed?

Build Your Skills

Developing an Ethics and Compliance Program

 The Federal Sentencing Guidelines for Organizations require a business's governing authority to develop an ethics and compliance program. This places responsibility for implementation on the firm's officers and board of directors. Organizations of all sizes can develop an ethics program. Below are the seven steps in developing an ethics and compliance program. After each step provide some activities that would help accomplish these steps.

I. Develop standards and procedures to reduce the propensity for criminal conduct.

_____

2. Designate a high-level compliance manager or ethics officer to oversee the compliance program.

_____

3. Avoid delegating authority to people known to have a propensity to engage in misconduct.

_____

4. Communicate standards and procedures to employees, other agents, and independent contractors through training programs and publications.

_____

5. Establish systems to monitor and audit misconduct and to allow employees and agents to report criminal activity.

_____

6. Enforce standards and punishments consistently across all employees in the organization.

_____

7. Respond immediately to misconduct and take reasonable steps to prevent further criminal conduct.

_____

Endnotes

1. Benjamin West Janke, "Hershey's Protects Candy Bar Design," August 6, 2012, http://www.bakerdonelson.com/hersheys-protects-candy-bar-design-08-06-2012/ (accessed March 2, 2016); International Trademark Association, "Trade Dress," November 2015, http://www.inta.org/TrademarkBasics/FactSheets/Pages/Trade-Dress.aspx (accessed March 2, 2016); Danielle Rubano, "Trade Dress: Who Should Bear the Burden of Proving or Disproving Functionality in a Section 43(a) Infringement Claim," *Fordham Intellectual Property, Media and Entertainment Law Journal* 6, 1 (1995), 345–367.

2. Federal Trade Commission, "FTC Challenges Proposed Merger of Staples, Inc. and Office Depot, Inc.," December 7, 2015, https://www.ftc.gov/news-events/press-releases/2015/12/ftc-challenges-proposed-merger-staples-inc-office-depot-inc(accessed February 26, 2016).

3. Maureen Dorney, "Congress Passes Federal Anti-Spam Law: Preempts Most State Anti-Spam Laws," *DLA Piper,* December 3, 2003, http://franchiseagreements.com/global/publications/detail.aspx?pub=622 (accessed April 7, 2014),

4. Elizabeth Alterman, "As Kids Go Online, Identity Theft Claims More Victims," *CNBC,* October 10, 2011, http://www.cnbc.com/id/44583556 (accessed February 26, 2016); Ron Lieber, "Identify Theft Poses Extra Troubles for Children," *The New York Times,* April 17, 2015, http://www.nytimes.com/2015/04/18/your-money/a-childs-vulnerability-to-identity-theft.html?_r=0 (accessed February 26, 2016).

5. Federal Trade Commission, "Two App Developers Settle FTC Charges THey Violated Children's Online Privacy Protection Act," Decemeber 17, 2015, https://www.ftc.gov/news-events/press-releases/2015/12/two-app-developers-settle-ftc-charges-they-violated-childrens (accessed February 26, 2016).

6. Rachel Louise Ensign, "SEC Bolsters Whistleblowers," *The Wall Street Journal,* April 2, 2015, p. C1; Rachel Louise Ensign, "Treatment of Tipsters Is Focus of SEC," *The Wall Street Journal,* February 26, 2015, p. C1; Steve Goldstein, "Whistleblower on Credit Suisse Dark Pool Says He'll Ask SEC for Millions," *MarketWatch,* September 22, 2015, http://www.marketwatch.com/story/whistleblower-on-credit-suisse-dark-pool-says-hell-ask-sec-for-millions-2015-09-22 (accessed September 29, 2015); Ethics Resource Center, *National Business Ethics Survey of the U.S. Workforce* (Arlington, VA: Ethics Resource Center, 2014), p. 24.

7. Ashby Jones, "Nation's In-House Counsel Are Worried about Ethics, Data and 'Trolls,'" *The Wall Street Journal,* February 2, 2015, http://blogs.wsj.com/law/2015/02/02/nations-in-housecounsel-are-worried-about-ethics-data-and-trolls/ (accessed February 25, 2016).

8. Jean Eaglesham and Ashby Jones, "Whistle-blower Bounties Pose Challenges," *The Wall Street Journal,* December 13, 2010, pp. C1, C3.

9. "Office of Financial Research," U.S. Department of Treasury, www.treasury.gov/initiatives/Pages/ofr.aspx (accessed February 26, 2016); "Initiatives: Financial Stability Oversight Council," U.S. Department of Treasury, www.treasury.gov/initiatives/Pages/FSOC-index.aspx (accessed February 26, 2016).

© Andrey_Popov/Shutterstock

BONUS CHAPTER

B Personal Financial Planning*

Chapter Outline

Learning Objectives

After reading this chapter, you will be able to:

LO B-1   Learn how to evaluate your financial situation.

LO B-2   Determine short-term and long-term personal financial goals.

LO B-3   Examine how to create and manage a personal financial budget.

LO B-4   Learn how to manage and use credit in your personal life.

LO B-5   Examine savings and investment choices.

LO B-6   Evaluate how insurance is a part of your personal financial planning.

LO B-7   Understand the concept of estate planning.

* This appendix was contributed by Dr. Vickie Bajtelsmit.

The Financial Planning Process

Personal financial planning is the process of managing your finances so that you can achieve your financial goals. By anticipating future needs and wants, you can take appropriate steps to prepare for them. Your needs and wants will undoubtedly change over time as you enter into various life circumstances. Although financial planning is not entirely about money management, a large part of this process is concerned with decisions related to expenditures, investments, and credit.

Although every person has unique needs, everyone can benefit from financial planning. Even if the entire financial plan is not implemented at once, the process itself will help you focus on what is important. With a little forethought and action, you may be able to achieve goals that you previously thought were unattainable.

The steps in development and implementation of an effective financial plan are:

- Evaluate your financial health.
- Set short-term and long-term financial goals.
- Create and adhere to a budget.
- Manage credit wisely.
- Develop a savings and investment plan.
- Evaluate and purchase insurance.
- Develop an estate plan.
- Adjust your financial plan to new circumstances.

LO B-1

Learn how to evaluate your financial situation.

personal financial planning
the process of managing your finances so that you can achieve your financial goals.

Evaluate Your Financial Health

Just as businesses make use of financial reports to track their performance, good personal financial planning requires that individuals keep track of their income and expenses and their overall financial condition. Several software packages are readily available to help track personal finances (for example, Quicken and Microsoft Money), but all that is really needed is a simple spreadsheet program. This bonus chapter includes some simple worksheets that can be reproduced to provide a starting point for personal financial planning. Comprehensive financial planning sites are also available on the Internet. For example, **http://money.msn.com/** and **www.smartmoney.com** both provide information and tools to simplify this process.

While it is possible to track all kinds of information over time, the two most critical elements of your finances are your personal net worth and your personal cash flow. The information necessary for these two measures is often required by lending institutions on loan applications, so keeping it up to date can save you time and effort later.

The Personal Balance Sheet

For businesses, net worth is usually defined as *assets minus liabilities*, and this is no different for individuals. **Personal net worth** is simply the total value of all personal assets less the total value of unpaid debts or liabilities. Although a business could not survive with a negative net worth since it would be technically insolvent, many students have negative net worth. As a student, you probably are not yet earning enough to have accumulated significant assets, such as a house or stock portfolio, but you are likely to have incurred various forms of debt, including student loans, car loans, and credit card debt.

At this stage in your life, negative net worth is not necessarily an indication of poor future financial prospects. Current investment in your "human capital" (education) is usually considered to have a resulting payoff in the form of better job opportunities and higher potential lifetime income, so this "upside-down" balance sheet should

personal net worth
the total value of all personal assets less the total value of unpaid debts or liabilities.

not stay that way forever. Unfortunately, there are many people in the United States who have negative net worth much later in their lives. This can result from unforeseen circumstances, like divorce, illness, or disability, but the easy availability of credit in the last couple of decades has also been blamed for the heavy debt loads of many American families. The most recent recession, caused partially by excessive risk-taking, has resulted in many bankruptcies and housing foreclosures. No matter the immediate trigger, it is usually poor financial planning—the failure to prepare in advance for those unforeseen circumstances—that makes the difference between those who fail and those who survive. It is interesting to note that we could say the exact same thing about business failures. Most are attributable to poor financial planning. If your net worth is negative, you should definitely include debt reduction on your list of short-and/or long-term goals.

You can use Table B-1 to estimate your net worth. On the left-hand side of the balance sheet, you should record the value of *assets*, all the things you own that have value. These include checking and savings account balances, investments, furniture, books, clothing, vehicles, houses, and the like. As with business balance sheets, assets are usually arranged from most liquid (easily convertible to cash) to least liquid. If you are a young student, it should not be surprising to find that you have little, if anything, to put

TABLE B-1   Personal Net Worth

Assets	$	Liabilities	$
Checking accounts	____	Credit cards balances (list)	____
Savings accounts	____	1 _____	____
Money market accounts	____	2 _____	____
Other short-term investment	____	3 _____	____
	____	Personal loans	____
Market value of investments (stocks, bonds, mutual funds)	____	Student loans	____
	____	Car loans	____
Value of retirement funds	____	Home mortgage balance	____
College savings plan	____	Home equity loans	____
Other savings plans	____	Other real estate loans	____
Market value of real estate	____	Alimony/child support owed	____
Cars	____	Taxes owed (above withholding)	____
Home furnishings	____	Other investment loans	____
Jewelry/art/collectibles	____	Other liabilities/debts	____
Clothing/personal assets	____		____
Other assets	____		____
TOTAL ASSETS	____	TOTAL LIABILITIES	____

PERSONAL NET WORTH = TOTAL ASSETS − TOTAL LIABILITIES = $ ____

on this side of your balance sheet. You should note that balance sheets are sensitive to the point in time chosen for evaluation. For example, if you always get paid on the first day of the month, your checking balance will be greatest at that point but will quickly be depleted as you pay for rent, food, and other needs. You may want to use your average daily balance in checking and savings accounts as a more accurate reflection of your financial condition. The right-hand side of the balance sheet is for recording *liabilities*, amounts of money that you owe to others. These include bank loans, mortgages, credit card debt, and other personal loans and are usually listed in order of how soon they must be paid back to the lender.

The Cash Flow Statement

Businesses forecast and track their regular inflows and outflows of cash with a cash budget and summarize annual cash flows on the statement of cash flows. Similarly, individuals should have a clear understanding of their flow of cash as they budget their expenditures and regularly check to be sure that they are sticking to their budget.

What is cash flow? Any time you receive cash or pay cash (including payments with checks), the dollar amount that is moving from one person to another is a cash flow. For students, the most likely cash inflows will be student loans, grants, and income from part-time jobs. Cash outflows will include rent, food, gas, car payments, books, tuition, and personal care expenses. Although it may seem obvious that you need to have enough inflows to cover the outflows, it is very common for people to estimate incorrectly and overspend. This may result in hefty bank overdraft charges or increasing debt as credit lines are used to make up the difference. Accurate forecasting of cash inflows and outflows allows you to make arrangements to cover estimated shortfalls before they occur. For students, this can be particularly valuable when cash inflows primarily occur at the beginning of the semester (for example, student loans) but outflows are spread over the semester.

How should you treat credit card purchases on your cash flow worksheet? Because credit purchases do not require payment of cash *now*, your cash flow statement should not reflect the value of the purchase as an outflow until you pay the bill. Take for example the purchase of a television set on credit. The $500 purchase will increase your assets and your liabilities by $500 but will only result in a negative cash flow of a few dollars per month because payments on credit cards are cash outflows when they are made. If you always pay your credit card balances in full each month, the purchases are really the same thing as cash, and your balance sheet will never reflect the debt. But if you purchase on credit and only pay minimum balances, you will be living beyond your means, and your balance sheet will get more and more "upside down." A further problem with using credit to purchase assets that decline in value is that the liability may still be there long after the asset you purchased has no value.

Table B-2 can be used to estimate your cash flow. The purpose of a cash flow worksheet for your financial plan is to heighten your awareness of where the cash is going. Many people are surprised to find that they are spending more than they make (by using too much credit) or that they have significant "cash leakage"—those little expenditures that add up to a lot without their even noticing. Examples include afternoon lattes or snacks, too many nights out at the local pub, eating lunch at the Student Center instead of packing a bag, and regularly paying for parking (or parking tickets) instead of biking or riding the bus to school. In many cases, plugging the little leaks can free up enough cash to make a significant contribution toward achieving long-term savings goals.

TABLE B-2 Personal Cash Flow

Cash Inflows	Monthly	Annual
Salary/wage income (gross)	$ _____	$ _____
Interest/dividend income	_____	_____
Other income (self-employment)	_____	_____
Rental income (after expenses)	_____	_____
Capital gains	_____	_____
Other income	_____	_____
Total income	_____	_____
Cash Outflows	**Monthly**	**Annual**
Groceries	$ _____	$ _____
Housing	_____	_____
Mortgage or rent	_____	_____
House repairs/expenses	_____	_____
Property taxes	_____	_____
Utilities	_____	_____
Heating	_____	_____
Electric	_____	_____
Water and sewer	_____	_____
Cable/phone/satellite/Internet	_____	_____
Car loan payments	_____	_____
Car maintenance/gas	_____	_____
Credit card payments	_____	_____
Other loan payments	_____	_____
Income and payroll taxes	_____	_____
Other taxes	_____	_____
Insurance	_____	_____
Life	_____	_____
Health	_____	_____
Auto	_____	_____
Disability	_____	_____
Other insurance	_____	_____
Clothing	_____	_____
Gifts	_____	_____

TABLE B-2 Continued

Cash Inflows	Monthly	Annual
Other consumables (TVs, etc.)	____	____
Child care expenses	____	____
Sports-related expenses	____	____
Health club dues	____	____
Uninsured medical expenses	____	____
Education	____	____
Vacations	____	____
Entertainment	____	____
Alimony/child support	____	____
Charitable contributions	____	____
Required pension contributions	____	____
Magazine subscriptions/books	____	____
Other payments/expenses	____	____
Total Expenses	$ ____	$ ____

NET PERSONAL CASH FLOW = TOTAL INCOME − TOTAL EXPENSES = $ ____

Set Short-Term and Long-Term Financial Goals

Just as a business develops its vision and strategic plan, individuals should have a clear set of financial goals. This component of your financial plan is the roadmap that will lead you to achieving your short-term and long-term financial goals.

Short-term goals are those that can be achieved in two years or less. They may include saving for particular short-term objectives, such as a new car, a down payment for a home, a vacation, or other major consumer purchases. For many people, short-term financial goals should include tightening up on household spending patterns and reducing outstanding credit.

Long-term goals are those that require substantial time to achieve. Nearly everyone should include retirement planning as a long-term objective. Those who have or anticipate having children will probably consider college savings a priority. Protection of loved ones from the financial hazards of your unexpected death, illness, or disability is also a long-term objective for many individuals. If you have a spouse or other dependents, having adequate insurance and an estate plan in place should be part of your long-term goals.

Create and Adhere to a Budget

Whereas the cash flow table you completed in the previous section tells you what you are doing with your money currently, a **budget** shows what you plan to do with it in the future. A budget can be for any period of time, but it is common to budget in monthly and/or annual intervals.

Determine short-term and long-term personal financial goals.

short-term goals
goals that can be achieved in two years or less.

long-term goals
goals that require substantial time to achieve.

Examine how to create and manage a personal financial budget.

budget
an internal financial plan that forecasts expenses and income over a set period of time.

Do you know whether your expenses are going up or going down? Use a budget to track them.

© Brand X/Jupiterimages/Getty Images

Developing a Budget

You can use the cash flow worksheet completed earlier to create a budget. Begin with the amount of income you have for the month. Enter your nondiscretionary expenditures (that is, bills you *must* pay, such as tuition, rent, and utilities) on the worksheet and determine the left-over amount. Next list your discretionary expenditures, such as entertainment and cable TV, in order of importance. You can then work down your discretionary list until your remaining available cash flow is zero.

An important component of your budget is the amount that you allocate to savings. If you put a high priority on saving and you do not use credit to spend beyond your income each month, you will be able to accumulate wealth that can be used to meet your short-term and long-term financial goals. In the bestseller *The Millionaire Next Door*, authors Thomas J. Stanley and William D. Danko point out that most millionaires have achieved financial success through hard work and thriftiness as opposed to luck or inheritance. You cannot achieve your financial goals unless your budget process places a high priority on saving and investing.

Tracking Your Budgeting Success

Businesses regularly identify budget items and track their variance from budget forecasts. People who follow a similar strategy in their personal finances are better able to meet their financial goals as well. If certain budgeted expenses routinely turn out to be under or over your previous estimates, then it is important to either revise the budget estimate or develop a strategy for reducing that expense.

College students commonly have trouble adhering to their budget for food and entertainment expenses. A strategy that works fairly well is to limit yourself to cash payments. At the beginning of the week, withdraw an amount from checking that will cover your weekly budgeted expenses. For the rest of the week, leave your checkbook, ATM card, and debit and credit cards at home. When the cash is gone, don't spend any more. While this is easier said than done, after a couple of weeks, you will learn to cut down on the cash leakage that inevitably occurs without careful cash management.

A debit card looks like a credit card but works like a check. For example, in the Netherlands almost no one writes a check, and everything is paid by debit card, which drafts directly from a checking account. You do not build up your credit rating when using a debit card. Figure B-1 indicates that the use of debit cards has become the predominant means of payment in the United States. On the other hand, credit cards allow you to promise to pay for something at a later date by using preapproved lines of credit granted by a bank or finance company. Credit cards are easy to use and are accepted by most retailers today.

Manage Credit Wisely

Learn how to manage and use credit in your personal life.

One of the cornerstones of your financial plan should be to keep credit usage to a minimum and to work at reducing outstanding debt. The use of credit for consumer and home purchases is well entrenched in our culture and has arguably fueled our economy and enabled Americans to better their standard of living as compared to earlier

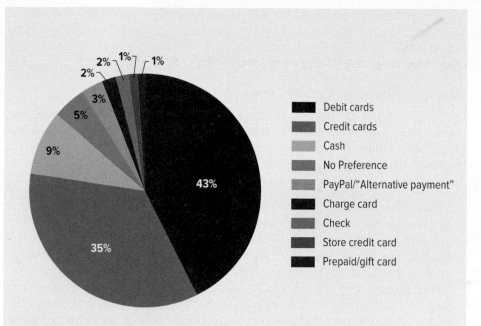

FIGURE B-1
Preferred Payment Type

Notes: Due to rounding, numbers do
not add up to 100.

Sources: TSYS 2014 Consumer
Payments Study; CreditCards.com

Pie chart legend:
- Debit cards
- Credit cards
- Cash
- No Preference
- PayPal/"Alternative payment"
- Charge card
- Check
- Store credit card
- Prepaid/gift card

generations. Nevertheless, credit abuse is a serious problem in this country, and the most recent economic downturn undoubtedly pushed many households over the edge into bankruptcy as a result.

To consider the pros and cons of credit usage, compare the following two scenarios. In the first case, Joel takes an 8 percent fixed-rate mortgage to purchase a house to live in while he is a college student. The mortgage payment is comparable to alternative monthly rental costs, and his house appreciates 20 percent in value over the four years he is in college. At the end of college, Joel will be able to sell his house and reap the return, having invested only a small amount of his own cash. For example, if he made an initial 5 percent down payment on a $100,000 home that is now worth $120,000 four years later, he has earned $12,800 (after a 6 percent commission to the real estate agent) on an investment of $5,000. This amounts to a sizable return on investment of more than 250 percent over four years. This example is oversimplified in that we did not take into account the principal that has been repaid over the four years, and we did not consider the mortgage payment costs or the tax deductibility of interest paid during that time. However, the point is still clear; borrowing money to buy an asset that appreciates in value by more than the cost of the debt is a terrific way to invest.

In the second case, Nicole uses her credit card to pay for some of her college expenses. Instead of paying off the balance each month, Nicole makes only the minimum payment and incurs 16 percent interest costs. Over the course of several years of college, Nicole's credit card debt is likely to amount to several thousand dollars, typical of college graduates in the United States. The beer and pizza Nicole purchased have long ago been digested, yet the debt remains, and the payments continue. If Nicole continues making minimum payments, it will take many years to pay back that original debt, and in the meantime the interest paid will far exceed the original amount borrowed. Credit card debt in the amount of $1,000 will usually require a minimum payment of at least $15 per month. At this payment level, it will take 166 months (almost 14 years) to pay the debt in full, and the total interest paid will be more than $1,400!

So when is borrowing a good financial strategy? A rule of thumb is that you should borrow only to buy assets that will appreciate in value or when your financing charges are less than what you are earning on the cash that you would otherwise use to make the purchase. This rule generally will limit your borrowing to home purchases and investments.

Use and Abuse of Credit Cards

Credit cards should be used only as a cash flow management tool. If you pay off your balance every month, you avoid financing charges (assuming no annual fee), you have proof of expenditures, which may be necessary for tax or business reasons, and you may be able to better match your cash inflows and outflows over the course of the month. There are several aspects of credit cards that you should be familiar with.

- *Finance charges.* Credit card companies make money by lending to you at a higher rate than it costs them to obtain financing. Because many of their customers don't pay back their debts in a timely fashion (default), they must charge enough to cover the risk of default as well. Interest is usually calculated on the average daily balance over the month, and payments are applied to old debts first. Although there are "teaser" rates that may be less than 5 percent, most credit cards regularly charge 13 to 24 percent annual interest. The low introductory rates are subject to time limitations (often six months or less), and they revert to the higher rates if you don't pay on time.
- *Annual fee.* Many credit cards assess an annual fee that may be as low as $15 or as much as $100 per year. If you regularly carry a very low balance, this amounts to the equivalent of a very high additional interest charge. For example, a $50 annual fee is the equivalent of an additional 5 percent on your annual interest rate if your balance is $1,000. Because the cards with fees do not generally provide you with different services, it is best to choose no-annual-fee credit cards.
- *Credit line.* The credit line is the maximum you are allowed to borrow. This may begin with a small amount for a new customer, perhaps as low as $300. As the customer shows the ability and intent to repay (by doing so in a timely fashion), the limit can increase to many thousands of dollars.
- *Grace period.* The grace period for most credit cards is 25 days. This may amount to twice as long a period of free credit depending on when your purchase date falls in the billing cycle. For example, if you used your card on January 1 and your billing cycle goes from the 1st to the 31st, then the bill for January purchases will arrive the first week in February and will be due on February 25. If you pay it in full on the last possible day, you will have had 55 days of free credit. Keep in mind that the lender considers the bill paid when the check is *received*, not when it is mailed.
- *Fees and penalties.* In addition to charging interest and annual fees, credit card companies charge extra for late payments and for going over the stated limit on the card. These fees have been on the rise in the past decade, and $25 or higher penalties are now fairly common.
- *ATM withdrawals.* Most credit cards can be used to obtain cash from ATMs. Although this may be convenient, it contributes to your increasing credit card balance and may result in extra expenditures that you would otherwise have avoided. In addition, these withdrawals may have hidden costs. Withdrawing cash from a machine that is not owned by your credit card lender will usually cause you to incur a fee of $1 or $1.50. The effective interest that this represents can be substantial if you are withdrawing small amounts of cash. A $1 charge on a withdrawal of $50 is the equivalent of 2 percent interest in addition to any interest you might pay to the credit card lender.
- *Perks.* Most credit cards provide a number of additional services. These may include a limitation on your potential liability in the event your card is lost or stolen

or trip insurance. Some cards promise "cash back" in the form of a small rebate based on dollar volume of credit purchases. Many credit card companies offer the opportunity to participate in airline mileage programs. The general rule of thumb is that none of these perks is worth the credit card interest that is charged. If, however, you use your credit card as a cash management tool only, paying off your balance every month, then these perks are truly free to you.

Student Loans

Student loans are fairly common in today's environment of rising college tuition and costs. These loans can be a great deal, offering lower interest rates than other loans and terms that allow deferral of repayment until graduation. Furthermore, the money is being borrowed to pay for an asset that is expected to increase in value—your human capital. Don't underestimate, however, the monthly payments that will be required upon graduation. Students today graduate with average student loan debt of approximately $35,000. This is the most debt to date that graduates are carrying after graduation, and it is triple the amount graduates carried 20 years ago. It is likely that next year's graduating class will have a higher average debt burden as the rate increases every year. The rate of student debt is increasing at a rate higher than inflation.[1] Table B-3 shows the

TABLE B-3   How Much Will It Take to Pay That Debt?

| Months to Pay | Interest Rate | Amount of Debt | | | |
		$1,000	$2,500	$5,000	$10,000
12	15%	$90.26	$225.65	$451.29	$902.58
	18%	$91.68	$229.20	$458.40	$916.80
	21%	$93.11	$232.78	$465.57	$931.14
24	15%	$48.49	$121.22	$242.43	$484.87
	18%	$49.92	$124.81	$249.62	$499.24
	21%	$51.39	$128.46	$256.93	$513.86
36	15%	$34.67	$86.66	$173.33	$346.65
	18%	$36.15	$90.38	$180.76	$361.52
	21%	$37.68	$94.19	$188.38	$376.75
48	15%	$27.83	$69.58	$139.15	$278.31
	18%	$29.37	$73.44	$146.87	$293.75
	21%	$30.97	$77.41	$154.83	$309.66
60	15%	$23.79	$59.47	$118.95	$237.90
	18%	$25.39	$63.48	$126.97	$253.93
	21%	$27.05	$67.63	$135.27	$270.53
72	15%	$21.15	$52.86	$105.73	$211.45
	18%	$22.81	$57.02	$114.04	$228.08
	21%	$24.54	$61.34	$122.68	$245.36

FIGURE B-2
Average Debt Per
Borrower in Each Year's
Graduating Class

Source: Mark Kantrowitz; wsj.com

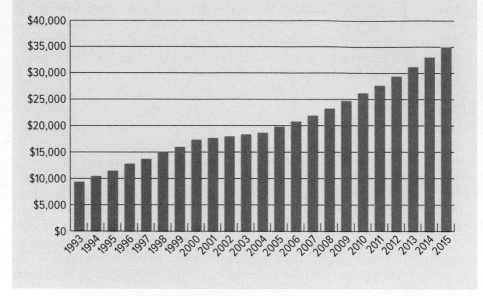

monthly payments required to repay the debt under various term and interest scenarios. For larger outstanding debt amounts, new college graduates in entry-level positions find that it is difficult to make the necessary payments without help.

Although the average student loan debt is $35,000, many students end up owing much more than that. In 2014, the amount of student loan debt among Americans reached $1.2 trillion, exceeding the amount of credit card debt they owe.[2] Figure B-2 shows how much the average debt per borrower has increased over the past 20 years. Both political parties agree that something must be done to curb this debt, although they appear split on how to do so. In 2013, Congress passed the Bipartisan Student Loan Certainty Act, which bases the interest rate on federal student loans according to market rate fluctuations. The year in which the loan is borrowed will determine the interest rate for the life of the loan. For example, the rate for the 2014–2015 school year was set at 4.29 percent. This will be the rate at which the loan generates interest until it is repaid.[3] In 2014, President Obama signed an executive order mandating that repayments not exceed 10 percent of the borrower's monthly income.[4]

Before borrowing for your education, check into federal student loans because they are less risky and less expensive than private loans. In order to see what kind of federal loans for which you qualify, fill out the Free Application for Federal Student Aid (FAFSA). It is important to keep track of the details of your loans, and keep your loan servicer updated on any changes in your information to avoid expensive late fees. For a list of all your federal student loans, frequently visit the National Student Loan Data System at www.nslds.ed.gov. Private loans can be accessed from your credit report, of which you can request a copy at www.annualcreditreport.com.

It is also helpful to understand your repayment plan options. The most common are standard repayment and income-driven repayment. Standard repayment is when the same sum is paid every month, and while the payment may be high, you will pay off your loans more quickly and pay fewer interest payments. Income-driven repayment bases your monthly payments on a percentage of income. They require annual income verification and other paperwork, and interest charges are high. Visit the Department of Education at www.studentaid.ed.gov/repay-loans for information and calculators regarding the different repayment options. Those who work in government, nonprofit, and other public service jobs may be eligible for student loan forgiveness after 10 years of faithful repayments. Other programs offer forgiveness of debt for teachers, military service members, or medical practitioners. More information can be found at www. studentloanborrowerassistance.org.[5]

Develop a Savings and Investment Plan

Examine savings and investment choices.

The next step to achieving your financial goals is to decide on a savings plan. A common recommendation of financial planners is to "pay yourself first." What this means is that you begin the month by setting aside an amount of money for your savings and investments, as compared to waiting until the end of the month and seeing what's left to save or invest. The budget is extremely important for deciding on a reasonable dollar amount to apply to this component of your financial plan.

As students, you might think that you cannot possibly find any extra dollars in your budget for saving, but, in fact, nearly everyone can stretch their budget a little. Some strategies for students might include taking public transportation several times a week and setting aside the gas or parking dollars you would have spent, buying regular coffees instead of Starbucks lattes, or eating at home one more night per week.

Understanding the Power of Compounded Returns

Even better, if you are a college student living on a typically small budget, you should be able to use this experience to help jump-start a viable savings program after graduation. If you currently live on $10,000 per year and your first job pays $30,000, it should be easy to "pay yourself" $2,000 or more per year. Putting the current maximum of $3,000 in an individual retirement account (IRA) will give you some tax advantages and can result in substantial wealth accumulation over time. An investment of only $2,000 per year from age 22 to retirement at 67 at 6 percent return per year will result in $425,487 at the retirement date. An annual contribution of $5,000 for 45 years will result in retirement wealth of about $1 million, not considering any additional tax benefits you might qualify for. If you invest that $5,000 per year for only 10 years and discontinue your contributions, you will still have about half a million dollars at age 67. And that assumes only a 6 percent return on investment!

What happens if you wait 10 years to start, beginning your $5,000 annual savings at age 32? By age 67, you will have only about a half million. Thirty-five years of investing instead of 45 doesn't sound like a big difference, but it cuts your retirement wealth in half. These examples illustrate an important point about long-term savings and wealth accumulation—the earlier you start, the better off you will be.

The Link between Investment Choice and Savings Goals

Once you have decided how much you can save, your choice of investment should be guided by your financial goals and the investment's risk and return and whether it will be long term or short term.

In general, investments differ in risk and return. The types of risk that you should be aware of are:

- *Liquidity risk*—How easy/costly is it to convert the investment to cash without loss of value?
- *Default risk*—How likely are you to receive the promised cash flows?

- *Inflation risk*—Will changes in purchasing power of the dollar over time erode the value of future cash flows your investment will generate?
- *Price risk*—How much might your investment fluctuate in value in the short run and the long run?

In general, the riskier an investment, the higher the return it will generate to you. Therefore, even though individuals differ in their willingness to take risk, it is important to invest in assets that expose you to at least moderate risk so that you can accumulate sufficient wealth to fund your long-term goals. To illustrate this more clearly, consider a $1 investment made in 1926. If this dollar had been invested in short-term Treasury bills, at the end of 2000 it would have grown to only $16.57. If the dollar had been invested in the S&P 500 index, which includes a diversified mix of stocks, the investment would be worth $2,586 in 2000 and about the same value in 2008, almost 200 times more than an investment in Treasury bills. But this gain was not without risk. In some of those 70 years, the stock market lost money and your investment would have actually declined in value.

Short-Term versus Long-Term Investment

Given the differences in risk exposure across investments, your investment time horizon plays an important role in choice of investment vehicle. For example, suppose you borrow $5,000 on a student loan today but the money will be needed to pay tuition six months from now. Because you cannot afford to lose *any* of this principal in the short run, your investment should be in a low-risk security such as a bank certificate of deposit. These types of accounts promise that the original $5,000 principal plus promised interest will be available to you when your tuition is due. During the bull market of the 1990s, many students were tempted to take student loans and invest in the stock market in the hopes of doubling their money (although this undoubtedly violated their lender's rules). However, in the recent bear market, this strategy might have reduced the tuition funds by 20 percent or more.

In contrast to money that you are saving for near-term goals, your retirement is likely to be many decades away, so you can afford to take more risk for greater return. The average return on stocks over the past 25 years has been around 17 percent. In contrast, the average return on long-term corporate bonds, which offer regular payments of interest to investors, has been around 10 percent. Short-term, low-risk debt securities have averaged 7 percent but were lower in 2010. The differences in investment returns between these three categories is explainable based on the difference in risk imposed on the owners. Stock is the most risky. Corporate bonds with their regular payments of interest are less risky to you since you do not have to wait until you sell your investment to get some of your return on the investment. Because they are less risky, investors expect a lower percentage return.

Investment Choices

There are numerous possible investments, both domestic and international. The difficulty lies in deciding which ones are most appropriate for your needs and risk tolerance.

Savings Accounts and Certificates of Deposit.   The easiest parking spot for your cash is in a savings account. Unfortunately, investments in these low-risk (FDIC-insured), low-return accounts will barely keep up with inflation. If you have a need for liquidity but not necessarily immediate access to cash, a certificate of deposit wherein you promise to leave the money in the bank for six months or more will give you a slightly higher rate of return.

Bonds. Corporations regularly borrow money from investors and issue bonds, which are securities that contain the firm's promise to pay regular interest and to repay principal at the end of the loan period, often 20 or more years in the future. These investments provide higher return to investors than short-term, interest-bearing accounts, but they also expose investors to price volatility, liquidity, and default risk.

A second group of bonds are those offered by government entities, commonly referred to as municipal bonds. These are typically issued to finance government projects, such as roads, airports, and bridges. Like corporate bonds, municipal bonds will pay interest on a regular basis, and the principal amount will be paid back to the investor at the end of a stated period of time, often 20 or more years. This type of bond has fewer interested investors and therefore has more liquidity risk.

Want to buy a car? How you have handled your debts will help determine if you get a loan.

Stocks. A share of stock represents proportionate ownership interest in a business. Stockholders are thus exposed to all the risks that impact the business environment—interest rates, competition from other firms, input and output price risk, and others. In return for being willing to bear this risk, shareholders may receive dividends and/or capital appreciation in the value of their share(s). In any given year, stocks may fare better or worse than other investments, but there is substantial evidence that for long holding periods (20-plus years) stocks tend to outperform other investment choices.

Mutual Funds. For the novice investor with a small amount of money to invest, the best choice is mutual funds. A mutual fund is a pool of funds from many investors that is managed by professionals who allocate the pooled dollars among various investments that meet the requirements of the mutual fund investors. There are literally thousands of these funds from which to choose, and they differ in type of investment (bonds, stocks, real estate, etc.), management style (active versus passive), and fee structure. Although even small investors have access to the market for individual securities, professional investors spend 100 percent of their time following the market and are likely to have more information at their disposal to aid in making buy and sell decisions.

Purchase of a Home. For many people, one of the best investments is the purchase of a home. With a small up-front investment (your down payment) and relatively low borrowing costs, modest appreciation in the home's value can generate a large return on investment. This return benefits from the tax deductibility of home mortgage interest and capital gains tax relief at the point of sale. And to top it off, you have a place to live and thus save any additional rental costs you would incur if you invested your money elsewhere. There are many sources of information about home ownership for investors on the Internet. What type of home can you afford? What mortgage can you qualify for? How much difference does investment choice make?

Everyone needs to have a place to live, and two-thirds of Americans own their own homes. Nevertheless, owning a home is not necessarily the best choice for everyone. The decision on when and how to buy a house and how much to spend must be made based on a careful examination of your ability to pay the mortgage and to cover the time and expense of maintenance and repair. A home is probably the largest purchase you will ever make in your life. It is also one of the best investments you can make. As in the example given earlier, the ability to buy with a small down payment and to deduct the cost of interest paid from your taxable income provides financial benefits that are not available with any other investment type.

Few people could afford to buy homes at young ages if they were required to pay the full purchase price on their own. Instead, it is common for people to borrow most of the money from a financial institution and pay it back over time. The process of buying a home can begin with your search for the perfect home or it can begin with a visit to your local lender, who can give you an estimate of the amount of mortgage for which you can qualify. Mortgage companies and banks have specific guidelines that help them determine your creditworthiness. These include consideration of your ability and willingness to repay the loan in a timely fashion, as well as an estimate of the value of the house that will be the basis for the loan.

A **mortgage** is a special type of loan that commonly requires that you make a constant payment over time to repay the lender the original money you borrowed (**principal**) together with **interest,** the amount that the lender charges for your use of its money. In the event that you do not make timely payments, the lender has the right to sell your property to get its money back (a process called **foreclosure**).

Mortgage interest rates in the past decade have ranged from 5 to 10 percent per year, depending on the terms and creditworthiness of the borrower. There are many variations on mortgages, some that lock in an interest rate for the full term of the loan, often 30 years, and others that allow the rate to vary with market rates of interest. In low-interest-rate economic circumstances, it makes sense to lock in the mortgage at favorable low rates.

Several measures are commonly applied to assess your *ability to repay* the loan. In addition to requiring some work history, most lenders will apply two ratio tests. First, the ratio of your total mortgage payment (including principal, interest, property taxes, and homeowners insurance) to your gross monthly income can be no more than a prespecified percentage that varies from lender to lender but is rarely greater than 28 percent. Second, the ratio of your credit payments (including credit cards, car loan or lease payments, and mortgage payment) to your gross monthly income is limited to no more than 36 percent. More restrictive lenders will have lower limits on both of these ratios.

Lenders also consider your *willingness to repay* the loan by looking at how you have managed debt obligations in the past. The primary source of information will be a credit report provided by one of the large credit reporting agencies. Late payments and defaulted loans will appear on that report and may result in denial of the mortgage loan. Most lenders, however, will overlook previously poor credit if more recent credit management shows a change in behavior. This can be helpful to college students who had trouble paying bills before they were gainfully employed.

The value of the home is important to the lender since it is the **collateral** for the loan; that is, in the event that you default on the loan (don't pay), the lender has the right to take the home in payment of the loan. To ensure that they are adequately covered, lenders will rarely lend more than 95 percent of the appraised value of the home. If you borrow more than 80 percent of the value, you will usually be required to pay a mortgage insurance premium with your regular payments. This will effectively increase the financing costs by ½ percent per year.

To illustrate the process of buying a home and qualifying for a mortgage, consider the following example. Jennifer graduated from college two years ago and has saved $7,000. She intends to use some of her savings as a down payment on a home. Her current salary is $36,000. She has a car payment of $250 per month and credit card debt that requires a minimum monthly payment of $100 per month. Suppose that Jennifer has found her dream home, which has a price of $105,000. She intends to make a down payment of $5,000 and borrow the rest. Can she qualify for the $100,000 loan at a rate of 7 percent?

---

mortgage
a special type of loan that commonly requires that you make a constant payment over time to repay the lender the original money you borrowed together with interest.

principal
The original money borrowed in the form of a loan.

interest
the amount that the lender charges for your use of the money.

foreclosure
when the lender gets the right to sell your property to get its money back if you cannot make timely payments.

collateral
assets pledged as security for a loan; if the loan is not repaid, the lender can use the assets pledged to settle the debt.

TABLE B-4   Calculating Monthly Mortgage Payments (30-year loan, principal and interest only)

Annual Interest %	Amount Borrowed			
	$75,000	$100,000	$125,000	$150,000
6.0	$450	$600	$ 749	$ 899
6.5	$474	$632	$ 790	$ 948
7.0	$499	$665	$ 832	$ 998
7.5	$524	$699	$ 874	$1,049
8.0	$550	$734	$ 917	$ 1,101
8.5	$577	$769	$ 961	$ 1,153
9.0	$603	$805	$1,006	$1,207
9.5	$631	$841	$ 1,051	$ 1,261
10.0	$658	$878	$1,097	$ 1,316

Using Table B-4, her payment of principal and interest on a loan of $100,000 at 7 percent annual interest will be $665. With an additional $150 per month for property taxes and insurance (which may vary substantially in different areas of the country), her total payment will be $815. Her gross monthly income is $3,000, so the ratio of her payment to her income is 27 percent. Unless her lender has fairly strict rules, this should be acceptable. Her ratio of total payments to income will be ($815 + $250 + $150)/$3,000 = 40.5 percent. Unfortunately, Jennifer will not be able to qualify for this loan in her current financial circumstances.

So what can she do? The simplest solution is to use some of her remaining savings to pay off her credit card debt. By doing this, her debt ratio will drop to 35.5 percent and she will be accomplishing another element of good financial planning—reducing credit card debt and investing in assets that increase in value.

Planning for a Comfortable Retirement

Although it may seem like it's too early to start thinking about retirement when you are still in college, this is actually the best time to do so. In the investment section, you learned about the power of compound interest over long periods of time. The earlier you start saving for long-term goals, the easier it will be to achieve them.

How Much to Save.   There is no "magic number" that will tell you how much to save. You must determine, based on budgeted income and expenses, what amount is realistic to set aside for this important goal. Several factors should help to guide this decision:

- Contributions to qualified retirement plans can be made before tax. This allows you to defer the payment of taxes until you retire many years from now.
- Earnings on retirement plan assets are tax deferred. If you have money in nonretirement vehicles, you will have to pay state and federal taxes on your earnings, which will significantly reduce your ending accumulation.
- If you need the money at some time before you reach age 59½, you will be subject to a withdrawal penalty of 10 percent, and the distribution will also be subject to taxes at the time of withdrawal.

In planning for your retirement needs, keep in mind that inflation will erode the purchasing power of your money. You should consider your ability to replace preretirement income as a measure of your success in retirement preparation. You can use the Social Security Administration website (**www.ssa.gov**) to estimate your future benefits from that program. In addition, most financial websites provide calculators to aid you in forecasting the future accumulations of your savings.

Employer Retirement Plans.   Many employers offer retirement plans as part of their employee benefits package. **Defined benefit plans** promise a specific benefit at retirement (for example, 60 percent of final salary). More commonly, firms offer **defined contribution plans,** where they promise to put a certain amount of money into the plan in your name every pay period. The plan may also allow you to make additional contributions or the employer may base its contribution on your contribution (for example, by matching the first 3 percent of salary that you put in). Employers also may make it possible for their employees to contribute additional amounts toward retirement on a tax-deferred basis. Many plans now allow employees to specify the investment allocation of their plan contributions and to shift account balances between different investment choices.

Some simple rules to follow with respect to employer plans include the following:

- If your employer offers you the opportunity to participate in a retirement plan, you should do so.
- If your employer offers to match your contributions, you should contribute as much as is necessary to get the maximum match, if you can afford to. Every dollar that the employer matches is like getting a 100 percent return on your investment in the first year.
- If your plan allows you to select your investment allocation, do not be too conservative in your choices if you still have many years until retirement.

Individual Retirement Accounts (IRAs).   Even if you do not have an employer-sponsored plan, you can contribute to retirement through an individual retirement account (IRA). There are two types of IRAs with distinctively different characteristics (which are summarized in Table B-5). Although previously subject to a $2,000 maximum annual contribution limit, tax reform in 2001 increased that limit gradually to $5,000 by 2008. The critical difference between Roth IRAs and traditional IRAs is the taxation of contributions and withdrawals. Roth IRA contributions are taxable, but

> **defined benefit plan**
> a type of retirement plan that promises a specific benefit at retirement.
>
> **defined contribution plan**
> a type of retirement plan firms offer where they promise to put a certain amount of money into the plan in your name every pay period.

TABLE B-5   Comparing Individual Retirement Account Options

	Roth IRA	Traditional IRA
2008–2010 allowable contribution	$5,000	$5,000
Contributions deductible from current taxable income	No	Yes
Current tax on annual investment earnings	No	No
Tax due on withdrawal in retirement	No	Yes
10% penalty for withdrawal before age 59½	Yes	Yes
Mandatory distribution before age 70½	No	Yes
Tax-free withdrawals allowed for first-time homebuyers	Yes	No

the withdrawals are tax-free. Traditional IRAs are deductible, but the withdrawals are taxable. Both types impose a penalty of 10 percent for withdrawal before the qualified retirement age of 59½, subject to a few exceptions.

Social Security. Social Security is a public pension plan sponsored by the federal government and paid for by payroll taxes equally split between employers and employees. In addition to funding the retirement portion of the plan, Social Security payroll taxes pay for Medicare insurance (an old-age health program), disability insurance, and survivors benefits for the families of those who die prematurely.

The aging of the U.S. population has created a problem for funding the current Social Security system. Whereas it has traditionally been a pay-as-you-go program, with current payroll taxes going out to pay current retiree benefits, the impending retirement of baby boomers is forecast to bankrupt the system early in this century if changes are not made in a timely fashion. To understand the problem, consider that when Social Security began, there were 17 workers for each retiree receiving benefits. There are currently fewer than four workers per beneficiary. After the baby boom retirement, there will be only two workers to pay for each retiree. Obviously, that equation cannot work.

Does that mean that Social Security will not be around when you retire? Contrary to popular belief, it is unlikely that this will happen. There are simply too many voters relying on the future of Social Security for Congress to ever take such a drastic action. Instead, it is likely that the current system will be revised to help it balance. Prior to the heavy declines in the stock market in 2008–2009 there was some general support for a plan that would divert some of the current payroll taxes to fund individual retirement accounts that could be invested in market assets. In addition, it seems likely that the retirement age will increase gradually to age 67. Other possible changes are to increase payroll taxes or to limit benefits payable to wealthier individuals. The proposed solutions are all complicated by the necessity of providing a transition program for those who are too old to save significant additional amounts toward their retirement. Figure B-3 indicates that most people are concerned about receiving fewer Social Security benefits when they retire.

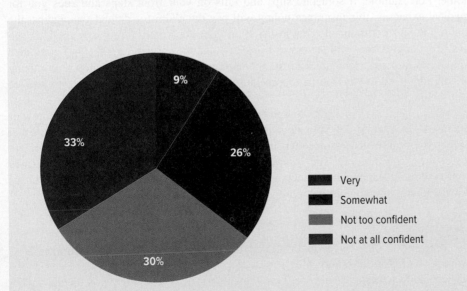

FIGURE B-3
Worker Confidence that Social Security Will Continue to Provide Benefits of at Least Equal Value to Benefits Received Today

Source: Employee Benefit Research Institute and Greenwald & Associates, 1993-2015 Retirement Confidence Surveys.

Evaluate and Purchase Insurance

The next step in personal financial planning is the evaluation and purchase of insurance. Insurance policies are contracts between you and an insurance company wherein the insurer promises to pay you money in the event that a particular event occurs. Insurance is important, not only to protect your own assets from claims but also to protect your loved ones and dependents. The most common types of insurance for individuals are identified and briefly described next.

Automobile Insurance

auto liability insurance
coverage that will pay claims against you for injuries to persons or property, up to a maximum per person and per accident.

In most states, drivers are required by law to carry a minimum amount of **auto liability insurance.** In the event that you are in a car accident, this coverage promises to pay claims against you for injuries to persons or property, up to a maximum per person and per accident. The basic liability policy will also cover your own medical costs. If you want to insure against damage to your own vehicle, you must purchase an additional type of coverage called **auto physical damage insurance.** If you have a car loan, the lender will require that you carry this type of insurance, since the value of the car is the collateral for that loan and the lender wants to be sure that you can afford to fix any damage to the vehicle following an accident. The minimum limits in most states are too low to cover typical claim levels. Good financial planning requires that you pay for insurance coverage with much higher limits.

auto physical damage insurance
coverage that will insure against damage to your own vehicle.

deductible
an amount that you must pay before the insurance company will pay.

Auto physical damage insurance coverage is always subject to a **deductible.** A deductible is an amount that you must pay before the insurance company will pay. To illustrate this, suppose your policy has a $250 deductible. You back into your garage door and damage your bumper, which will cost $750 to fix. The insurer will only pay $500, because you are responsible for the first $250. Once you receive the check from the insurer, you are free to try to get it fixed for less than the full $750.

Homeowners/Renters Insurance

homeowners insurance
coverage for liability and property damage for your home.

Homeowners insurance provides coverage for liability and property damage in your home. For example, if someone slips and falls on your front steps and sues you for medical expenses, this insurance policy will pay the claim (or defend you against the claim if the insurer thinks it is not justified). If your house and/or property are damaged in a fire, the insurance will pay for lost property and the costs of repair. It is a good idea to pay extra for replacement cost insurance because, otherwise, the insurance company is only obligated to pay you the depreciated value, which won't be enough to replace your belongings.

renters insurance
similar to homeowners insurance in that it covers you for liability on your premises and for damage to your personal property

Renters insurance is similar to homeowners in that it covers you for liability on your premises (for example, if your dog bites someone) and for damage to your personal property. Because you do not own the house, your landlord needs to carry separate insurance for his building. This insurance is very cheap and is well worth the cost, since your landlord's insurance will not pay anything to you in the event that the house burns down and you lose all your belongings.

Life Insurance

life insurance
insurance that pays a benefit to your designated beneficiary in the event that you die during a coverage period.

As compared to other types of insurance, the primary purpose of life insurance is to provide protection for others. **Life insurance** pays a benefit to your designated beneficiary (usually your spouse or other family members) in the event that you die during the coverage period. Life insurance premiums will depend on the face amount of the policy, your age and health, your habits (smoker versus nonsmoker), and the type of policy (whether it includes an investment component in addition to the death benefit).

The simplest type of life insurance is **term insurance.** This policy is usually for one year and the insurer promises to pay your designated beneficiary only the face amount of the policy in the event that you die during the year of coverage. Because the probability of dying at a young age is very small, the cost of providing this promise to people in their 20s and 30s is very inexpensive, and premiums are fairly low. Term insurance becomes more expensive at older ages, since the probability of dying is much higher and insurers must charge more.

Other types of life insurance usually fall into a category often called **permanent insurance,** because they are designed to provide you with insurance protection over your lifetime. To provide lifetime coverage at a reasonable cost, premiums will include an investment component. While there are many variations, typically in the early years of the policy you are paying a lot more than the actual cost of providing the death protection. The insurer takes that extra cost and invests it so that when you are older, the company has sufficient funds to cover your death risk. The primary difference between different types of permanent insurance is the way that they treat the investment component. Some policies allow the buyer to direct the investment choice and others do not.

term insurance
a type of life insurance that lasts usually for one year and the insurer promises to pay your designated beneficiary only the face amount of the policy in the event you die during the year of coverage.

permanent insurance
insurance designed to protect you with insurance protection over your lifetime.

Health Insurance

Health insurance pays the cost of covered medical expenses during the policy period, which is usually six months or one year. Most health insurance is provided under group policies through employers, but it is possible to purchase an individual policy. Because those who want to buy individual insurance are likely to be people who anticipate medical expenses, individual policies can be very expensive and are usually subject to exclusions, high coinsurance (the percentage of each dollar of expenses that you must pay out of pocket), and deductibles (the amount you must pay in full before the insurance pays).

From a financial-planning perspective, the type of health coverage that is most important is that which will protect you and your family from unexpected large medical costs. The usual checkups, shots, and prescription drugs are all budgetable expenses and need not be insured. At a minimum, you should have a policy that covers hospitalization and care for major disease or injury. This can be accomplished at relatively low cost by contracting for a large deductible (e.g., you pay the first $1,000 of costs per year).

health insurance
insurance that pays the cost of covered medical expenses during a policy period, which is usually six months to a year.

The two main types of health insurance plans are *fee-for-service* and *managed care*. In a fee-for-service arrangement, the insurer simply pays for whatever covered medical costs you incur, subject to the deductible and coinsurance. Blue Cross and Blue Shield plans are the best known of this type. Managed care includes health maintenance organizations (HMOs) and preferred provider organizations (PPOs). In these health insurance arrangements, your health insurer pays all your costs (subject sometimes to small co-pays for office visits), but the care you receive is determined by your physician, who has contracted with the health insurer and has incentives to control overall costs. You are often limited in your choice of physician and your ability to seek specialist care under these plans.

Medical costs can be astronomical. Part of keeping your finances in order is making sure you have health insurance.

Major changes in health insurance began to occur after the 2010 passage of the Patient Protection and Affordable Care Act. According to the law, individuals who are self-employed or who do not receive health insurance through their businesses can pay for insurance through state-based exchanges. Exchanges will also be created for small businesses to purchase health coverage, along with tax breaks for this purpose. All individuals who do not have insurance from their employers must pay for their own insurance or face penalties, but low-income people who cannot afford to pay can receive government subsidies. Employers with more than 50 employees must also pay for health care coverage. The purpose of this legislation is to provide health insurance for the more than 32 million Americans who were uninsured. The act also puts limits on insurers. For instance, insurers can no longer deny coverage or benefits based on a preexisting condition. The Patient Protection and Affordable Care Act will have a wide-ranging impact on the health care industry, including how much you will pay for future health care insurance.[6]

Disability Insurance

disability insurance
insurance which pays replacement income to you in the event you are disabled under the definition of your policy.

One of the most overlooked types of insurance is **disability insurance**, which pays replacement income to you in the event you are disabled under the definition in your policy. One in three people will be disabled for a period of three months or more during their lifetime, so disability insurance should be a component of the financial plan for anyone without sufficient financial resources to weather a period of loss of income.

Understand the concept of estate planning.

Develop an Estate Plan

As with retirement planning, it is difficult to think about estate planning when you are young. In fact, you probably don't need to think much about it yet. If you have no dependents, there is little point in doing so. However, if you are married or have other dependents, you should include this as a necessary part of your financial plan. The essential components of an **estate plan** are

estate plan
planning for the transfer of your wealth and assets after your death.

- Your will, including a plan for guardianship of your children.
- Minimization of taxes on your estate.
- Protection of estate assets.

Estate planning is a complicated subject that is mired in legal issues. As such, appropriate design and implementation of an estate plan requires the assistance of a qualified professional.

The Importance of Having a Will

There are several circumstances that necessitate having a will. If you have a spouse and/or dependent children, if you have substantial assets, or if you have specific assets that you would like to give to certain individuals in the event of your death, you *should* have a will. On the other hand, if you are single with no assets or obligations (like many students), a will is probably not necessary—yet.

Having a valid will makes the estate settlement simpler for your spouse. If your children are left parentless, will provisions specify who will take guardianship of the children and direct funds for their support. You might also like to include a *living will*, which gives your family directions for whether to keep you on life support in the event that an illness or injury makes it unlikely for you to survive without extraordinary interventions. Lastly, you may want to make a will so that you can give your iPad to your college roommate or Grandma's china to your daughter. Absent such provisions, relatives and friends have been known to take whatever they want without regard to your specific desires.

Gender Differences Create Special Financial Planning Concerns   Although most people would agree that there are some essential differences between men and women, it is not as clear why their financial planning needs should be different. After all, people of both sexes need to invest for future financial goals like college educations for their children and retirement income for themselves. In the past few years, professionals have written articles considering this subject. The results are both controversial and eye-opening.

- Even though 75 percent of women in the United States are working, they still have greater responsibility for household chores, child care, and care of aging parents than their husbands. This leaves less time for household finances.
- Women still earn much less than men, on average.
- Women are much less likely to have a pension sponsored through their employer. Only one-third of all working women have one at their current employer.
- Women are more conservative investors than men. Although there is evidence that women are gradually getting smart about taking a little more risk in their portfolios, on average they allocate half as much as men do to stocks.
- Most women will someday be on their own, either divorced or widowed.

Because women live an average of five years longer than men, they actually need to have saved more to provide a comparable retirement income. The combined impact of these research findings makes it difficult but not impossible for women to save adequately for retirement. Much of the problem lies in education. Women need to be better informed about investing in order to make choices early in life that will pay off in the end. If they don't take the time to become informed about their finances or can't due to other obligations, in the end they will join the ranks of many women over age 65 who are living in poverty. But when women earn less, they don't have access to an employer pension, and they invest too conservatively, it is no surprise that women have so little wealth accumulation.

In her book, *The Busy Woman's Guide to Financial Freedom*, Dr. Vickie Bajtelsmit, an associate professor at Colorado State University, provides a roadmap for women who are interested in taking charge of their financial future. With simple-to-follow instructions for all aspects of financial planning, from investing to insurance to home buying, the book provides information for women to get on the right financial track.

Avoiding Estate Taxes

As students, it will likely be many years before you will have accumulated a large enough estate (all your "worldly possessions") to have to worry about estate taxes. Although federal tax law changes eliminated the estate tax in 2010, the tax was reinstated and raised to 35 percent in 2011. Today, the estate tax is at a maximum of 40 percent of assets upon death.[7] This is an area of law that frequently changes. Because no one can predict the date of his or her death, this implies that estate tax planning should be done assuming the worst-case scenario. Current estate taxes can take a big bite out of your family's inheritance for wealthy taxpayers. Thus, much of estate planning is actually tax-avoidance planning. Professionals can help set up trust arrangements that allow all or part of your estate to pass to your heirs without incurring taxes.

Adjust Your Financial Plan to New Circumstances

Finally, to ensure the success of your overall financial plan, it is vital that you evaluate it on a periodic basis and adjust it to accommodate changes in your life, such as marriage, children, or the addition or deletion of a second income from your spouse. You may be preparing income tax returns now, but as your income increases, you may have to make a decision about professional assistance. Figure B-4 indicates that most Americans prepare their own taxes, but many taxpayers use a professional service. Your plan also must be adjusted as your financial goals change (for example, desires to own a home, make a large purchase, or retire at an early age). Whatever your goals may be, the information and worksheets provided here will help with your personal financial planning.

FIGURE B-4   How Do Americans File Their Taxes?

Source: GOBankingRates.com

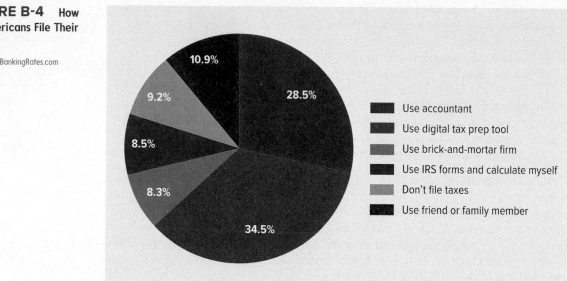

- Use accountant
- Use digital tax prep tool
- Use brick-and-mortar firm
- Use IRS forms and calculate myself
- Don't file taxes
- Use friend or family member

Review Your Understanding

Learn how to evaluate your financial situation.

Personal financial planning is the process of managing your finances so that you can achieve your financial goals. By anticipating future needs and wants, you can take appropriate steps to prepare for them. The two most critical elements of your finances you should track are your personal net worth, or the total value of all personal assets less the total value of unpaid debts or liabilities, and personal cash flow.

Determine short-term and long-term personal financial goals.

Short-term goals are those that can be achieved in two years or less. Long-term goals are those that require a substantial time to achieve. Short-term goals may include items such as a new car, a home, or a vacation. Long-term goals include retirement or college savings for children.

Examine how to create and manage a personal financial budget.

A budget shows what you plan to do with your cash in the future. It can be for any period of time but is most often done for monthly and/or annual intervals. A monthly budget would begin with the amount of income you have for the month. It is important to put high priority on investing and saving. It is also necessary to track how you are adhering to your budget.

Learn how to manage and use credit in your personal life.

Credit abuse is a serious problem in this country. A rule of thumb is that you should borrow only to buy assets that will appreciate in value or when your financing charges are less than what you are earning on the cash that you would otherwise use to make the purchase. It is important to be familiar with certain credit terms, such as finance charges, annual fees, credit lines, grace periods, fees and penalties, ATM withdrawals, and any perks associated with specific credit cards. An even bigger crisis than credit card debt, however, is student loans. Student loans are commonly used to pay for tuition costs, but it is important to manage student loan debt and look for favorable terms when selecting a loan. Students should also understand their repayment options.

Examine savings and investment choices.

Another major step is setting aside an amount of money for your savings and investments, as compared to waiting until the end of the month and seeing what's left to save or invest. Investing in individual retirement accounts gives you tax advantages and can result in substantial wealth accumulation over time. Once you have decided how much you can save, your choice of investment should be guided by your financial goals, the investment's risk and return, and whether it will be long term or short term. In general, the riskier an investment, the higher the return it will generate. Money invested for short-term needs should be invested in low-risk securities, while money invested for the long-term needs could be invested in riskier securities that offer a higher rate of return. Investment choices include savings accounts and certificates of deposit, bonds, stocks, mutual funds, and purchase of a home.

Purchasing a home requires a mortgage. A mortgage is a special type of loan that commonly requires that you make a constant payment over time to repay the lender the original money you borrowed (principal) together with interest. If you cannot make timely payments, the lender has the right to sell your property, known as a foreclosure. The value of the home is important to the lender because it can act as collateral for the loan.

In terms of saving for retirement, many employers offer defined benefit plans or defined contribution plans. Defined benefit plans promise a specific benefit at retirement. Defined contribution plans promise to put a certain amount of money into the plan in your name every pay period. For employees who do not have retirement benefit plans at their jobs, they can choose to contribute to retirement through a Roth IRA. Social security is a public pension plan sponsored by the federal government and paid for by payroll taxes equally split between employers and employees.

Evaluate how insurance is a part of your personal financial planning.

In most states, drivers are required by law to carry a minimum amount of auto liability insurance, which is coverage that promises to pay claims against you for injuries to persons or property, up to a maximum per person and per accident. Ensuring against damage to your own vehicle requires auto physical damage insurance. Auto physical damage insurance coverage is always subject to a deductible, meaning a certain amount you must pay before an insurance company will pay. Homeowners insurance provides coverage for liability and property damage in your home. Renters insurance is similar to homeowners in that it covers you for liability on your premises and to your personal property. Life insurance pays a benefit to your designated beneficiary in the event that you die during the coverage period. The simplest type is known as term insurance. It is usually for one year, and the insurer promises to pay your designated beneficiary only the face amount of the policy in the event that you die during the year of coverage. Permanent insurance is designed to provide you with insurance protection over your lifetime. Health insurance pays the cost of covered medical expenses during the policy period. Finally, disability insurance pays replacement income to you in the event that you are disabled under the definition in your policy.

Understand the concept of estate planning.

Estate plans involve your will, protection of estate assets, and minimization of taxes on your estate. If you have assets that you would like to leave to certain individuals in case of death, you should have a will. It is important to plan for estate taxes as they can take a big bite out of a family's inheritance.

Learn the Terms

auto liability insurance 564
auto physical damage insurance 564
budget 551
collateral 560
deductible 564
defined benefit plan 562
defined contribution plan 562
disability insurance 566

estate plan 566
foreclosure 560
health insurance 565
homeowners insurance 564
interest 560
life insurance 564
long-term goals 551
mortgage 560

permanent insurance 565
personal financial planning 547
personal net worth 547
principal 560
renters insurance 564
short-term goals 551
term insurance 565

Check Your Progress

1. How do you determine your personal net worth?

2. What is the difference between short-term and long-term financial goals?

3. Why should you develop a budget?

4. What are some of the dangers or abuses that occur when using credit cards?

5. Why is it important even for entry-level employees to develop a savings plan?

6. What should you know about investment choices in determining the best alternative for your risk tolerance?

7. Why is it important to learn as much as possible about retirement plans?

8. What are the different types of insurance decisions that you will have to make?

9. What are some of the gender differences that create special financial planning concerns?

10. What is an estate plan, and why is it important to have a will?

Build Your Skills

Determining Net Worth

Task

On a separate sheet of paper, write down the information from Table B-I. Fill out the information with details about your personal assets and your personal liabilities. Subtract your net liabilities from your net assets to determine your net worth.

Endnotes

1. Mark Kantrowitz, "Why the Student Loan Crisis Is Even Worse Than You Think," *Time,* January 11, 2016, http://time.com/money/4168510/why-student-loan-crisis-is-worse-than-people-think/ (accessed May 24, 2016).

2. Jillian Berman, "America's Growing Student-Loan-Debt Crisis, "*MarketWatch,* January 19, 2016, http://www.marketwatch.com/story/americas-growing-student-loan-debt-crisis-2016-01-15 (accessed May 24, 2016).

3. Federal Student Aid an Office of the U.S. Department of Education, "Interest Rates for New Direct Loans," July 1, 2014, https://studentaid.ed.gov/About/announcements/interest-rate (accessed May 24, 2016); Edvisors Network, Inc., "Interest Rates and Fees on Federal Student Loans," Edvisors, https://www.edvisors.com/college-loans/federal/stafford/interest-rates/ (accessed May 24, 2016).

4. Sam Frizzle, "Obama Looks to Reduce Student Loan Payments," *Time,* June 9, 2014, http://time.com/2847507/student-loan-debt-barack-obama/ (accessed June 16, 2014).

5. Maria Shriver, "Life Ed: How to Manage Student Loan Debt," *NBC News,* June 12, 2014, www.nbcnews.com/feature/maria-shriver/life-ed-how-manage-student-loan-debt-n129521 (accessed June 16, 2014).

6. Jill Jackson and John Nolen, "Health Care Reform Bill Summary: A Look at What's in the Bill," *CBS News,* March 21, 2010, www.cbsnews.com/8301-503544_162-20000846-503544.html (accessed May 30, 2012); "Patient Protection and Affordable Care Act," *Federal Register 75* (123), June 28, 2010, www.gpo.gov/fdsys/pkg/FR-2010-06-28/html/2010-15278.htm (accessed June 18, 2014).

7. Ashlea Ebeling, "IRS Announces 2016 Estate and Gift Tax Limits: The $10.9 Million Tax Break," *Forbes,* October 22, 2015, http://www.forbes.com/sites/ashleaebeling/2015/10/22/irs-announces-2016-estate-and-gift-tax-limits-the-10-9-million-tax-break/#a2e69916a7c3 (accessed June 30, 2016).

Glossary

A

absolute advantage a monopoly that exists when a country is the only source of an item, the only producer of an item, or the most efficient producer of an item.

accountability the principle that employees who accept an assignment and the authority to carry it out are answerable to a superior for the outcome.

accounting the recording, measurement, and interpretation of financial information.

accounting cycle the four-step procedure of an accounting system: examining source documents, recording transactions in an accounting journal, posting recorded transactions, and preparing financial statements.

accounting equation assets equal liabilities plus owners' equity.

accounts payable the amount a company owes to suppliers for goods and services purchased with credit.

accounts receivable money owed a company by its clients or customers who have promised to pay for the products at a later date.

accrued expenses all unpaid financial obligations incurred by an organization.

Personal financial planning the purchase of one company by another, usually by buying its stock.

administrative managers those who manage an entire business or a major segment of a business; they are not specialists but coordinate the activities of specialized managers.

advertising a paid form of nonpersonal communication transmitted through a mass medium, such as television commercials or magazine advertisements.

advertising campaign designing a series of advertisements and placing them in various media to reach a particular target market.

affirmative action programs legally mandated plans that try to increase job opportunities for minority groups by analyzing the current pool of workers, identifying areas where women and minorities are underrepresented, and establishing specific hiring and promotion goals, with target dates, for addressing the discrepancy.

agenda a calendar, containing both specific and vague items, that covers short-term goals and long-term objectives.

analytical skills the ability to identify relevant issues, recognize their importance, understand the relationships between them, and perceive the underlying causes of a situation.

annual report summary of a firm's financial information, products, and growth plans for owners and potential investors.

arbitration settlement of a labor/management dispute by a third party whose solution is legally binding and enforceable.

Personal net worth legal documents that set forth the basic agreement between partners.

Asia-Pacific Economic Cooperation (APEC) an international trade alliance that promotes open trade and economic and technical cooperation among member nations.

asset utilization ratios ratios that measure how well a firm uses its assets to generate each $1 of sales.

assets a firm's economic resources, or items of value that it owns, such as cash, inventory, land, equipment, buildings, and other tangible and intangible things.

Association of Southeast Asian Nations (ASEAN) a trade alliance that promotes trade and economic integration among member nations in Southeast Asia.

attitude knowledge and positive or negative feelings about something.

automated clearinghouses (ACHs) a system that permits payments such as deposits or withdrawals to be made to and from a bank account by magnetic computer tape.

automated teller machine (ATM) the most familiar form of electronic banking, which dispenses cash, accepts deposits, and allows balance inquiries and cash transfers from one account to another.

B

balance of payments the difference between the flow of money into and out of a country.

balance of trade the difference in value between a nation's exports and its imports.

balance sheet a "snapshot" of an organization's financial position at a given moment.

behavior modification changing behavior and encouraging appropriate actions by relating the consequences of behavior to the behavior itself.

benefits nonfinancial forms of compensation provided to employees, such as pension plans, health insurance, paid vacation and holidays, and the like.

blogs web-based journals in which writers can editorialize and interact with other Internet users.

board of directors a group of individuals, elected by the stockholders to oversee the general operation of the corporation, who set the corporation's long-range objectives.

bonds debt instruments that larger companies sell to raise long-term funds.

bonuses monetary rewards offered by companies for exceptional performance as incentives to further increase productivity.

boycott an attempt to keep people from purchasing the products of a company.

branding the process of naming and identifying products.

bribes payments, gifts, or special favors intended to influence the outcome of a decision.

brokerage firms firms that buy and sell stocks, bonds, and other securities for their customers and provide other financial services.

budget an internal financial plan that forecasts expenses and income over a set period of time.

budget deficit the condition in which a nation spends more than it takes in from taxes.

business individuals or organizations who try to earn a profit by providing products that satisfy people's needs.

business ethics principles and standards that determine acceptable conduct in business.

business plan a precise statement of the rationale for a business and a step-by-step explanation of how it will achieve its goals.

business products products that are used directly or indirectly in the operation or manufacturing processes of businesses.

buying behavior the decision processes and actions of people who purchase and use products.

C

capacity the maximum load that an organizational unit can carry or operate.

capital budgeting the process of analyzing the needs of the business and selecting the assets that will maximize its value.

capitalism (free enterprise) an economic system in which individuals own and operate the majority of businesses that provide goods and services.

cartel a group of firms or nations that agrees to act as a monopoly and not compete with each other, in order to generate a competitive advantage in world markets.

cash flow the movement of money through an organization over a daily, weekly, monthly, or yearly basis.

centralized organization a structure in which authority is concentrated at the top, and very little decision-making authority is delegated to lower levels.

certificates of deposit (CDs) savings accounts that guarantee a depositor a set interest rate over a specified interval as long as the funds are not withdrawn before the end of the period—six months or one year, for example.

certified management accountants (CMAs) private accountants who, after rigorous examination, are certified by the National Association of Accountants and who have some managerial responsibility.

certified public accountant (CPA) an individual who has been state certified to provide accounting services ranging from the preparation of financial records and the filing of tax returns to complex audits of corporate financial records.

checking account money stored in an account at a bank or other financial institution that can be withdrawn without advance notice; also called a demand deposit.

classical theory of motivation theory suggesting that money is the sole motivator for workers.

codes of ethics formalized rules and standards that describe what a company expects of its employees.

collective bargaining the negotiation process through which management and unions reach an agreement about compensation, working hours, and working conditions for the bargaining unit.

commercial banks the largest and oldest of all financial institutions, relying mainly on checking and savings accounts as sources of funds for loans to businesses and individuals.

commercial certificates of deposit (CDs) certificates of deposit issued by commercial banks and brokerage companies, available in minimum amounts of $100,000, which may be traded prior to maturity.

commercial paper a written promise from one company to another to pay a specific amount of money.

commercialization the full introduction of a complete marketing strategy and the launch of the product for commercial success.

commission an incentive system that pays a fixed amount or a percentage of the employee's sales.

commitee a permanent, formal group that performs a specific task.

common stock stock whose owners have voting rights in the corporation, yet do not receive preferential treatment regarding dividends.

communism first described by Karl Marx as a society in which the people, without regard to class, own all the nation's resources.

comparative advantage the basis of most international trade, when a country specializes in products that it can supply more efficiently or at a lower cost than it can produce other items.

competition the rivalry among businesses for consumers' dollars

compressed workweek a four-day (or shorter) period during which an employee works 40 hours.

computer-assisted design (CAD) the design of components, products, and processes on computers instead of on paper.

computer-assisted manufacturing (CAM) manufacturing that employs specialized computer systems to actually guide and control the transformation processes.

computer-integrated manufacturing (CIM) a complete system that designs products, manages machines and materials, and controls the operations function.

concentration approach a market segmentation approach whereby a company develops one marketing strategy for a single market segment.

conceptual skills the ability to think in abstract terms and to see how parts fit together to form the whole.

conciliation a method of outside resolution of labor and management differences in which a third party is brought in to keep the two sides talking.

consumer products products intended for household or family use.

consumerism the activities that independent individuals, groups, and organizations undertake to protect their rights as consumers.

continuous manufacturing organizations companies that use continuously running assembly lines, creating products with many similar characteristics.

contract manufacturing the hiring of a foreign company to produce a specified volume of the initiating company's product to specification; the final product carries the domestic firm's name.

controlling the process of evaluating and correcting activities to keep the organization on course.

cooperative (co-op) an organization composed of individuals or small businesses that have banded together to reap the benefits of belonging to a larger organization,

corporate charter a legal document that the state issues to a company based on information the company provides in the articles of incorporation.

corporate citizenship the extent to which businesses meet the legal, ethical, economic, and voluntary responsibilities placed on them by their stakeholders.

corporation a legal entity, created by the state, whose assets and liabilities are separate from its owners.

cost of goods sold the amount of money a firm spent to buy or produce the products it sold during the period to which the income statement applies.

countertrade agreements foreign trade agreements that involve bartering products for other products instead of for currency.

credit cards means of access to preapproved lines of credit granted by a bank or finance company.

credit controls the authority to establish and enforce credit rules for financial institutions and some private investors.

credit union a financial institution owned and controlled by its depositors, who usually have a common employer, profession, trade group, or religion.

crisis management (contingency planning) an element in planning that deals with potential disasters such as product tampering, oil spills, fire, earthquake, computer virus, or airplane crash.

culture the integrated, accepted pattern of human behavior, including thought, speech, beliefs, actions, and artifacts.

current assets assets that are used or converted into cash within the course of a calendar year.

current liabilities a firm's financial obligations to short-term creditors, which must be repaid within one year.

current ratio current assets divided by current liabilities.

customer departmentalization the arrangement of jobs around the needs of various types of customers.

customization making products to meet a particular customer's needs or wants.

D

debit card a card that looks like a credit card but works like a check; using it results in a direct, immediate, electronic payment from the cardholder's checking account to a merchant or third party.

debt to total assets ratio a ratio indicating how much of the firm is financed by debt and how much by owners' equity.

debt utilization ratios ratios that measure how much debt an organization is using relative to other sources of capital, such as owners' equity.

decentralized organization an organization in which decision-making authority is delegated as far down the chain of command as possible.

delegation of authority giving employees not only tasks, but also the power to make commitments, use resources, and take whatever actions are necessary to carry out those tasks.

demand the number of goods and services that consumers are willing to buy at different prices at a specific time.

departmentalization the grouping of jobs into working units usually called departments, units, groups, or divisions.

depreciation the process of spreading the costs of long-lived assets such as buildings and equipment over the total number of accounting periods in which they are expected to be used.

depression a condition of the economy in which unemployment is very high, consumer spending is low, and business output is sharply reduced.

development training that augments the skills and knowledge of managers and professionals.

digital marketing uses all digital media, including the Internet and mobile and interactive channels, to develop communication and exchanges with customers.

digital media electronic media that function using digital codes via computers, cellular phones, smartphones, and other digital devices that have been released in recent years.

direct investment the ownership of overseas facilities.

directing motivating and leading employees to achieve organizational objectives.

discount rate the rate of interest the Fed charges to loan money to any banking institution to meet reserve requirements.

discounts temporary price reductions, often employed to boost sales.

distribution making products available to customers in the quantities desired.

diversity the participation of different ages, genders, races, ethnicities, nationalities, and abilities in the workplace.

dividend yield the dividend per share divided by the stock price.

dividends profits of a corporation that are distributed in the form of cash payments to stockholders.

dividends per share the actual cash received for each share owned.

double-entry bookkeeping a system of recording and classifying business transactions that maintains the balance of the accounting equation.

downsizing the elimination of a significant number of employees from an organization.

dumping the act of a country or business selling products at less than what it costs to produce them.

E

e-business carrying out the goals of business through utilization of the Internet.

earnings per share net income or profit divided by the number of stock shares outstanding.

economic contraction a slowdown of the economy characterized by a decline in spending and during which businesses cut back on production and lay off workers.

economic expansion the situation that occurs when an economy is growing and people are spending more money; their purchases stimulate the production of goods and services, which in turn stimulates employment.

economic order quantity (EOQ) model a model that identifies the optimum number of items to order to minimize the costs of managing (ordering, storing, and using) them.

economic system a description of how a particular society distributes its resources to produce goods and services.

economics the study of how resources are distributed for the production of goods and services within a social system.

electronic funds transfer (EFT) any movement of funds by means of an electronic terminal, telephone, computer, or magnetic tape.

embargo a prohibition on trade in a particular product.

employee empowerment when employees are provided with the ability to take on responsibilities and make decisions about their jobs.

entrepreneur an individual who risks his or her wealth, time, and effort to develop for profit an innovative product or way of doing something.

entrepreneurship the process of creating and managing a business to achieve desired objectives.

equilibrium price the price at which the number of products that businesses are willing to supply equals the amount of products that consumers are willing to buy at a specific point in time.

equity theory an assumption that how much people are willing to contribute to an organization depends on their assessment of the fairness, or equity, of the rewards they will receive in exchange.

esteem needs the need for respect—both self-respect and respect from others.

ethical issue an identifiable problem, situation, or opportunity that requires a person to choose from among several actions that may be evaluated as right or wrong, ethical or unethical.

eurodollar market a market for trading U.S. dollars in foreign countries.

European Union (EU) a union of European nations established in 1958 to promote trade among its members; one of the largest single markets today.

exchange the act of giving up one thing (money, credit, labor, goods) in return for something else (goods, services, or ideas).

exchange controls regulations that restrict the amount of currency that can be bought or sold.

exchange rate the ratio at which one nation's currency can be exchanged for another nation's currency.

exclusive distribution the awarding by a manufacturer to an intermediary of the sole right to sell a product in a defined geographic territory.

expectancy theory the assumption that motivation depends not only on how much a person wants something but also on how likely he or she is to get it.

expenses the costs incurred in the day-to-day operations of an organization.

exporting the sale of goods and services to foreign markets.

extrinsic rewards benefits and/or recognition received from someone else.

F

factor a finance company to which businesses sell their accounts receivable—usually for a percentage of the total face value.

Federal Deposit Insurance Corporation (FDIC) an insurance fund established in 1933 that insures individual bank accounts.

Federal Reserve Board an independent agency of the federal government established in 1913 to regulate the nation's banking and financial industry.

Federal Trade Commission (FTC) the federal regulatory unit that most influences business activities related to questionable practices that create disputes between businesses and their customers.

finance the study of how money is managed by individuals, companies, and governments.

finance companies businesses that offer short-term loans at substantially higher rates of interest than banks.

financial managers those who focus on obtaining needed funds for the successful operation of an organization and using those funds to further organizational goals.

financial resources (capital) the funds used to acquire the natural and human resources needed to provide products; also called capital.

first-line managers those who supervise both workers and the daily operations of an organization.

fixed-position layout a layout that brings all resources required to create the product to a central location.

flexible manufacturing the direction of machinery by computers to adapt to different versions of similar operations.

flextime a program that allows employees to choose their starting and ending times, provided that they are at work during a specified core period.

floating-rate bonds bonds with interest rates that change with current interest rates otherwise available in the economy.

franchise a license to sell another's products or to use another's name in business, or both.

franchisee the purchaser of a franchise.

franchiser the company that sells a franchise.

franchising a form of licensing in which a company—the franchiser—agrees to provide a franchisee a name, logo, methods of operation, advertising, products, and other elements associated with a franchiser's business in return for a financial commitment and the agreement to conduct business in accordance with the franchiser's standard of operations.

free-market system pure capitalism, in which all economic decisions are made without government intervention.

functional departmentalization the grouping of jobs that perform similar functional activities, such as finance, manufacturing, marketing, and human resources.

G

General Agreement on Tariffs and Trade (GATT) a trade agreement, originally signed by 23 nations in 1947, that provided a forum for tariff negotiations and a place where international trade problems could be discussed and resolved.

general partnership a partnership that involves a complete sharing in both the management and the liability of the business.

generic products products with no brand name that often come in simple packages and carry only their generic name.

geographical departmentalization the grouping of jobs according to geographic location, such as state, region, country, or continent.

global strategy (globalization) a strategy that involves standardizing products (and, as much as possible, their promotion and distribution) for the whole world, as if it were a single entity.

grapevine an informal channel of communication, separate from management's formal, official communication channels.

gross domestic product (GDP) the sum of all goods and services produced in a country during a year.

gross income (or profit) revenues minus the cost of goods sold required to generate the revenues.

group two or more individuals who communicate with one another, share a common identity, and have a common goal.

H

human relations the study of the behavior of individuals and groups in organizational settings.

human relations skills the ability to deal with people, both inside and outside the organization.

human resources the physical and mental abilities that people use to produce goods and services; also called labor.

human resources management (HRM) all the activities involved in determining an organization's human resources needs, as well as acquiring, training, and compensating people to fill those needs.

human resources managers those who handle the staffing function and deal with employees in a formalized manner.

hygiene factors aspects of Herzberg's theory of motivation that focus on the work setting and not the content of the work; these aspects include adequate wages, comfortable and safe working conditions, fair company policies, and job security.

I

identity theft when criminals obtain personal information that allows them to impersonate someone else in order to use their credit to obtain financial accounts and make purchases.

import tariff a tax levied by a nation on goods imported into the country.

importing the purchase of goods and services from foreign sources.

income statement a financial report that shows an organization's profitability over a period of time—month, quarter, or year.

inflation a condition characterized by a continuing rise in prices

information technology (IT) managers those who are responsible for implementing, maintaining, and controlling technology applications in business, such as computer networks.

infrastructure the physical facilities that support a country's economic activities, such as railroads, highways, ports, airfields, utilities and power plants, schools, hospitals, communication systems, and commercial distribution systems.

initial public offering (IPO) selling a corporation's stock on public markets for the first time.

inputs the resources—such as labor, money, materials, and energy—that are converted into outputs.

insurance companies businesses that protect their clients against financial losses from certain specified risks (death, accident, and theft, for example).

integrated marketing communications coordinating the promotion mix elements and synchronizing promotion as a unified effort.

intensive distribution a form of market coverage whereby a product is made available in as many outlets as possible.

intermittent organizations organizations that deal with products of a lesser magnitude than do project organizations; their products are not necessarily unique but possess a significant number of differences.

international business the buying, selling, and trading of goods and services across national boundaries.

International Monetary Fund (IMF) organization established in 1947 to promote trade among member nations by eliminating trade barriers and fostering financial cooperation.

intrapreneurs individuals in large firms who take responsibility for the development of innovations within the organizations.

intrinsic rewards the personal satisfaction and enjoyment felt after attaining a goal.

inventory all raw materials, components, completed or partially completed products, and pieces of equipment a firm uses.

inventory control the process of determining how many supplies and goods are needed and keeping track of quantities on hand, where each item is, and who is responsible for it.

inventory turnover sales divided by total inventory.

investment banker underwrites new issues of securities for corporations, states, and municipalities.

investment banking the sale of stocks and bonds for corporations

ISO 9000 a series of quality assurance standards designed by the International Organization for Standardization (ISO) to ensure consistent product quality under many conditions.

ISO 14000 a comprehensive set of environmental standards that encourages a cleaner and safer world by promoting a more uniform approach to environmental management and helping companies attain and measure improvements in their environmental performance.

J

job analysis the determination, through observation and study, of pertinent information about a job—including specific tasks and necessary abilities, knowledge, and skills.

job description a formal, written explanation of a specific job, usually including job title, tasks, relationship with other jobs, physical and mental skills required, duties, responsibilities, and working conditions.

job enlargement the addition of more tasks to a job instead of treating each task as separate.

job enrichment the incorporation of motivational factors, such as opportunity for achievement, recognition, responsibility, and advancement, into a job.

job rotation movement of employees from one job to another in an effort to relieve the boredom often associated with job specialization.

job sharing performance of one full-time job by two people on part-time hours.

job specification a description of the qualifications necessary for a specific job, in terms of education, experience, and personal and physical characteristics.

joint venture a partnership established for a specific project or for a limited time.

journal a time-ordered list of account transactions.

junk bonds a special type of high interest rate bond that carries higher inherent risks.

just-in-time (JIT) inventory management a technique using smaller quantities of materials that arrive "just in time" for use in the transformation process and therefore require less storage space and other inventory management expense.

L

labeling the presentation of important information on a package.

labor contract the formal, written document that spells out the relationship between the union and management for a specified period of time—usually two or three years.

labor unions employee organizations formed to deal with employers for achieving better pay, hours, and working conditions.

leadership the ability to influence employees to work toward organizational goals.

learning changes in a person's behavior based on information and experience.

ledger a book or computer file with separate sections for each account.

leveraged buyout (LBO) a purchase in which a group of investors borrows money from banks and other institutions to acquire a company (or a division of one), using the assets of the purchased company to guarantee repayment of the loan.

liabilities debts that a firm owes to others.

licensing a trade agreement in which one company—the licensor—allows another company—the licensee—to use its company name, products, patents, brands, trademarks, raw materials, and/or production processes in exchange for a fee or royalty.

limited liability company (LLC) form of ownership that provides limited liability and taxation like a partnership but places fewer restrictions on members.

limited partnership a business organization that has at least one general partner, who assumes unlimited liability, and at least one limited partner, whose liability is limited to his or her investment in the business.

line of credit an arrangement by which a bank agrees to lend a specified amount of money to an organization upon request.

line-and-staff structure a structure having a traditional line relationship between superiors and subordinates and also specialized managers—called staff managers—who are available to assist line managers.

line structure the simplest organizational structure, in which direct lines of authority extend from the top manager to the lowest level of the organization.

liquidity ratios ratios that measure the speed with which a company can turn its assets into cash to meet short-term debt.

lockbox an address, usually a commercial bank, at which a company receives payments in order to speed collections from customers.

lockout management's version of a strike, wherein a work site is closed so that employees cannot go to work.

long-term (fixed) assets production facilities (plants), offices, and equipment—all of which are expected to last for many years.

long-term liabilities debts that will be repaid over a number of years, such as long-term loans and bond issues.

M

management a process designed to achieve an organization's objectives by using its resources effectively and efficiently in a changing environment.

managerial accounting the internal use of accounting statements by managers in planning and directing the organization's activities.

managers those individuals in organizations who make decisions about the use of resources and who are concerned with planning, organizing, staffing, directing, and controlling the organization's activities to reach its objectives.

manufacturer brands brands initiated and owned by the manufacturer to identify products from the point of production to the point of purchase.

manufacturing the activities and processes used in making tangible products; also called production.

market a group of people who have a need, purchasing power, and the desire and authority to spend money on goods, services, and ideas.

market orientation an approach requiring organizations to gather information about customer needs, share that information throughout the firm, and use that information to help build long-term relationships with customers.

market segment a collection of individuals, groups, or organizations who share one or more characteristics and thus have relatively similar product needs and desires.

market segmentation a strategy whereby a firm divides the total market into groups of people who have relatively similar product needs.

marketable securities temporary investment of "extra" cash by organizations for up to one year in U.S. Treasury bills, certificates of deposit, commercial paper, or eurodollar loans.

marketing a group of activities designed to expedite transactions by creating, distributing, pricing, and promoting goods, services, and ideas.

marketing channel a group of organizations that moves products from their producer to customers; also called a channel of distribution.

marketing concept the idea that an organization should try to satisfy customers' needs through coordinated activities that also allow it to achieve its own goals.

marketing managers those who are responsible for planning, pricing, and promoting products and making them available to customers.

marketing mix the four marketing activites—product, price, promotion, and distribution—that the firm can control to achieve specific goals within a dynamic marketing environment.

marketing research a systematic, objective process of getting information about potential customers to guide marketing decisions.

marketing strategy a plan of action for developing, pricing, distributing, and promoting products that meet the needs of specific customers.

Maslow's hierarchy a theory that arranges the five basic needs of people—physiological, security, social, esteem, and self-actualization—into the order in which people strive to satisfy them.

material-requirements planning (MRP) a planning system that schedules the precise quantity of materials needed to make the product.

materials handling the physical handling and movement of products in warehousing and transportation.

matrix structure a structure that sets up teams from different departments, thereby creating two or more intersecting lines of authority; also called a project- management structure.

mediation a method of outside resolution of labor and management differences in which the third party's role is to suggest or propose a solution to the problem.

merger the combination of two companies (usually corporations) to form a new company.

microentrepreneur entrepreneurs who develop businesses with five or fewer employees.

middle managers those members of an organization responsible for the tactical planning that implements the general guidelines established by top management.

mission the statement of an organization's fundamental purpose and basic philosophy.

mixed economies economies made up of elements from more than one economic system.

modular design the creation of an item in self-contained units, or modules, that can be combined or interchanged to create different products.

monetary policy means by which the Fed controls the amount of money available in the economy.

money anything generally accepted in exchange for goods and services.

money market accounts accounts that offer higher interest rates than standard bank rates but with greater restrictions.

monopolistic competition the market structure that exists when there are fewer businesses than in a pure-competition environment and the differences among the goods they sell are small.

monopoly the market structure that exists when there is only one business providing a product in a given market.

morale an employee's attitude toward his or her job, employer, and colleagues.

motivation an inner drive that directs a person's behavior toward goals.

motivational factors aspects of Herzberg's theory of motivation that focus on the content of the work itself; these aspects include achievement, recognition, involvement, responsibility, and advancement.

multidivisional structure a structure that organizes departments into larger groups called divisions.

multinational corporation (MNC) a corporation that operates on a worldwide scale, without significant ties to any one nation or region.

multinational strategy a plan, used by international companies, that involves customizing products, promotion, and distribution according to cultural, technological, regional, and national differences.

multisegment approach a market segmentation approach whereby the marketer aims its efforts at two or more segments, developing a marketing strategy for each.

mutual fund an investment company that pools individual investor dollars and invests them in large numbers of well-diversified securities.

mutual savings banks financial institutions that are similar to savings and loan associations but, like credit unions, are owned by their depositors.

N

National Credit Union Administration (NCUA) an agency that regulates and charters credit unions and insures their deposits through its National Credit Union Insurance Fund.

natural resources land, forests, minerals, water, and other things that are not made by people.

net income the total profit (or loss) after all expenses, including taxes, have been deducted from revenue; also called net earnings.

networking the building of relationships and sharing of information with colleagues who can help managers achieve the items on their agendas.

nonprofit corporations corporations that focus on providing a service rather than earning a profit but are not owned by a government entity.

nonprofit organizations organizations that may provide goods or services but do not have the fundamental purpose of earning profits.

North American Free Trade Agreement (NAFTA) agreement that eliminates most tariffs and trade restrictions on agricultural and manufactured products to encourage trade among Canada, the United States, and Mexico.

O

offshoring the relocation of business processes by a company or subsidiary to another country. Offshoring is different than outsourcing because the company retains control of the offshored processes.

oligopoly the market structure that exists when there are very few businesses selling a product.

online fraud any attempt to conduct fraudulent activities online.

open market operations decisions to buy or sell U.S. Treasury bills (short-term debt issued by the U.S. government) and other investments in the open market.

operational plans very short-term plans that specify what actions individuals, work groups, or departments need to accomplish in order to achieve the tactical plan and ultimately the strategic plan.

operations the activities and processes used in making both tangible and intangible products.

operations management (OM) the development and administration of the activities involved in transforming resources into goods and services.

organizational chart a visual display of the organizational structure, lines of authority (chain of command), staff relationships, permanent committee arrangements, and lines of communication.

organizational culture a firm's shared values, beliefs, traditions, philosophies, rules, and role models for behavior.

organizational layers the levels of management in an organization.

organizing the structuring of resources and activities to accomplish objectives in an efficient and effective manner.

orientation familiarizing newly hired employees with fellow workers, company procedures, and the physical properties of the company.

outputs the goods, services, and ideas that result from the conversion of inputs.

outsourcing the transferring of manufacturing or other tasks—such as data processing—to countries where labor and supplies are less expensive.

over-the-counter (OTC) market a network of dealers all over the country linked by computers, telephones, and Teletype machines.

owners' equity equals assets minus liabilities and reflects historical values.

P

packaging the external container that holds and describes the product.

partnership a form of business organization defined by the Uniform Partnership Act as "an association of two or more persons who carry on as co-owners of a business for profit."

penetration price a low price designed to help a product enter the market and gain market share rapidly.

pension funds managed investment pools set aside by individuals, corporations, unions, and some nonprofit organizations to provide retirement income for members.

per share data data used by investors to compare the performance of one company with another on an equal, per share basis.

perception the process by which a person selects, organizes, and interprets information received from his or her senses.

personal selling direct, two-way communication with buyers and potential buyers.

personality the organization of an individual's distinguishing character traits, attitudes, or habits.

physical distribution all the activities necessary to move products from producers to customers—inventory control, transportation, warehousing, and materials handling.

physiological needs the most basic human needs to be satisfied—water, food, shelter, and clothing.

picketing a public protest against management practices that involves union members marching and carrying antimanagement signs at the employer's plant.

plagiarism the act of taking someone else's work and presenting it as your own without mentioning the source.

planning the process of determining the organization's objectives and deciding how to accomplish them; the first function of management.

podcast audio or video file that can be downloaded from the Internet with a subscription that automatically delivers new content to listening devices or personal computers.

preferred stock a special type of stock whose owners, though not generally having a say in running the company, have a claim to profits before other stockholders do.

price a value placed on an object exchanged between a buyer and a seller.

price skimming charging the highest possible price that buyers who want the product will pay.

primary data marketing information that is observed, recorded, or collected directly from respondents.

primary market the market where firms raise financial capital.

prime rate the interest rate that commercial banks charge their best customers (usually large corporations) for short-term loans.

private accountants accountants employed by large corporations, government agencies, and other organizations to prepare and analyze their financial statements.

private corporation a corporation owned by just one or a few people who are closely involved in managing the business.

private distributor brands brands, which may cost less than manufacturer brands, that are owned and controlled by a wholesaler or retailer.

process layout a layout that organizes the transformation process into departments that group related processes.

product a good or service with tangible and intangible characteristics that provide satisfaction and benefits.

product departmentalization the organization of jobs in relation to the products of the firm.

product layout a layout requiring that production be broken down into relatively simple tasks assigned to workers, who are usually positioned along an assembly line.

product line a group of closely related products that are treated as a unit because of similar marketing strategy, production, or end-use considerations.

product mix all the products offered by an organization.

product-development teams a specific type of project team formed to devise, design, and implement a new product.

production the activities and processes used in making tangible products; also called manufacturing.

production and operations managers those who develop and administer the activities involved in transforming resources into goods, services, and ideas ready for the marketplace.

profit the difference between what it costs to make and sell a product and what a customer pays for it.

profit margin net income divided by sales.

profit sharing a form of compensation whereby a percentage of company profits is distributed to the employees whose work helped to generate them.

profitability ratios ratios that measure the amount of operating income or net income an organization is able to generate relative to its assets, owners' equity, and sales.

project organization a company using a fixed-position layout because it is typically involved in large, complex projects such as construction or exploration.

project teams groups similar to task forces that normally run their operation and have total control of a specific work project.

promotion a persuasive form of communication that attempts to expedite a marketing exchange by infl uencing individuals, groups, and organizations to accept goods, services, and ideas

promotional positioning the use of promotion to create and maintain an image of a product in buyers' minds.

psychological pricing encouraging purchases based on emotional rather than rational responses to the price.

public corporation a corporation whose stock anyone may buy, sell, or trade.

publicity nonpersonal communication transmitted through the mass media but not paid for directly by the firm.

pull strategy the use of promotion to create consumer demand for a product so that consumers exert pressure on marketing channel members to make it available.

purchasing the buying of all the materials needed by the organization; also called procurement.

pure competition the market structure that exists when there are many small businesses selling one standardized product.

push strategy an attempt to motivate intermediaries to push the product down to their customers.

Q

quality the degree to which a good, service, or idea meets the demands and requirements of customers.

quality control the processes an organization uses to maintain its established quality standards.

quality-assurance teams (or quality circles) small groups of workers brought together from throughout the organization to solve specific quality, productivity, or service problems.

quasi-public corporations corporations owned and operated by the federal, state, or local government.

quick ratio (acid test) a stringent measure of liquidity that eliminates inventory.

quota a restriction on the number of units of a particular product that can be imported into a country.

R

ratio analysis calculations that measure an organization's financial health.

receivables turnover sales divided by accounts receivable.

recession a decline in production, employment, and income.

recruiting forming a pool of qualified applicants from which management can select employees.

reference groups groups with whom buyers identify and whose values or attitudes they adopt.

reference pricing a type of psychological pricing in which a lower-priced item is compared to a more expensive brand in hopes that the consumer will use the higher price as a comparison price.

reinforcement theory states that behavior can be strenghtened or weakened through the use of rewards and punishment.

reserve requirement the percentage of deposits that banking institutions must hold in reserve.

responsibility the obligation, placed on employees through delegation, to perform assigned tasks satisfactorily and be held accountable for the proper execution of work.

retailers intermediaries who buy products from manufacturers (or other intermediaries) and sell them to consumers for home and household use rather than for resale or for use in producing other products.

retained earnings earnings after expenses and taxes that are reinvested in the assets of the firm and belong to the owners in the form of equity.

return on assets net income divided by assets.

return on equity net income divided by owners' equity; also called return on investment (ROI).

revenue the total amount of money received from the sale of goods or services, as well as from related business activities.

routing the sequence of operations through which the product must pass.

S

S corporation corporation taxed as though it were a partnership with restrictions on shareholders.

salary a financial reward calculated on a weekly, monthly, or annual basis.

sales promotion direct inducements offering added value or some other incentive for buyers to enter into an exchange.

savings accounts accounts with funds that usually cannot be withdrawn without advance notice; also known as time deposits.

savings and loan associations (S&Ls) financial institutions that primarily offer savings accounts and make long-term loans for residential mortgages; also called "thrifts."

scheduling the assignment of required tasks to departments or even specific machines, workers, or teams.

secondary data information that is compiled inside or outside an organization for some purpose other than changing the current situation.

secondary markets stock exchanges and over-the-counter markets where investors can trade their securities with others.

secured bonds bonds that are backed by specific collateral that must be forfeited in the event that the issuing firm defaults.

secured loans loans backed by collateral that the bank can claim if the borrowers do not repay them.

securities markets the mechanism for buying and selling securities.

security needs the need to protect oneself from physical and economic harm.

selection the process of collecting information about applicants and using that information to make hiring decisions.

selective distribution a form of market coverage whereby only a small number of all available outlets are used to expose products.

self-actualization needs the need to be the best one can be; at the top of Maslow's hierarchy.

self-directed work team (SDWT) a group of employees responsible for an entire work process or segment that delivers a product to an internal or external customer.

separations employment changes involving resignation, retirement, termination, or layoff.

serial bonds a sequence of small bond issues of progressively longer maturity.

sharing economy an economic model involving the sharing of underutilized resources.

small business any independently owned and operated business that is not dominant in its competitive area and does not employ more than 500 people.

Small Business Administration (SBA) an independent agency of the federal government that offers managerial and financial assistance to small businesses.

social classes a ranking of people into higher or lower positions of respect.

social entrepreneurs individuals who use entrepreneurship to address social problems.

social needs the need for love, companionship, and friendship—the desire for acceptance by others.

social network a web-based meeting place for friends, family, co-workers, and peers that lets users create a profile and connect with other users for a wide range of purposes.

social responsibility a business's obligation to maximize its positive impact and minimize its negative impact on society.

social roles a set of expectations for individuals based on some position they occupy.

socialism an economic system in which the government owns and operates basic industries but individuals own most businesses.

sole proprietorships businesses owned and operated by one individual; the most common form of business organization in the United States.

span of management the number of subordinates who report to a particular manager.

specialization the division of labor into small, specific tasks and the assignment of employees to do a single task.

staffing the hiring of people to carry out the work of the organization.

stakeholders groups that have a stake in the success and outcomes of a business.

standard of living refers to the level of wealth and material comfort that people have available to them.

standardization the making of identical interchangeable components or products.

statement of cash flows explains how the company's cash changed from the beginning of the accounting period to the end.

statistical process control a system in which management collects and analyzes information about the production process to pinpoint quality problems in the production system.

stock shares of a corporation that may be bought or sold.

strategic alliance a partnership formed to create competitive advantage on a worldwide basis.

strategic plans those plans that establish the long-range objectives and overall strategy or course of action by which a firm fulfills its mission.

strikebreakers people hired by management to replace striking employees; called "scabs" by striking union members.

strikes employee walkouts; one of the most effective weapons labor has.

structure the arrangement or relationship of positions within an organization.

supply the number of products—goods and services—that businesses are willing to sell at different prices at a specific time.

supply chain management connecting and integrating all parties or members of the distribution system in order to satisfy customers.

sustainability conducting activities in a way that allows for the long-term well-being of the natural environment, including all biological entities; involves the assessment and improvement of business strategies, economic sectors, work practices, technologies, and lifestyles so that they maintain the health of the natural environment.

T

tactical plans short-range plans designed to implement the activities and objectives specified in the strategic plan.

target market a specific group of consumers on whose needs and wants a company focuses its marketing efforts.

task force a temporary group of employees responsible for bringing about a particular change.

team a small group whose members have complementary skills; have a common purpose, goals, and approach; and hold themselves mutually accountable.

technical expertise the specialized knowledge and training needed to perform jobs that are related to particular areas of management.

test marketing a trial minilaunch of a product in limited areas that represent the potential market.

Theory X McGregor's traditional view of management whereby it is assumed that workers generally dislike work and must be forced to do their jobs.

Theory Y McGregor's humanistic view of management whereby it is assumed that workers like to work and that under proper conditions employees will seek out responsibility in an attempt to satisfy their social, esteem, and self-actualization needs.

Theory Z a management philosophy that stresses employee participation in all aspects of company decision making.

times interest earned ratio operating income divided by interest expense.

Title VII of the Civil Rights Act prohibits discrimination in employment and created the Equal Employment Opportunity Commission.

top managers the president and other top executives of a business, such as the chief executive officer (CEO), chief financial officer (CFO), and chief operations officer (COO), who have overall responsibility for the organization.

total asset turnover sales divided by total assets.

total quality management (TQM) a philosophy that uniform commitment to quality in all areas of an organization will promote a culture that meets customers' perceptions of quality.

total-market approach an approach whereby a firm tries to appeal to everyone and assumes that all buyers have similar needs.

trade credit credit extended by suppliers for the purchase of their goods and services.

trade deficit a nation's negative balance of trade, which exists when that country imports more products than it exports.

trademark a brand that is registered with the U.S. Patent and Trademark Office and is thus legally protected from use by any other firm.

trading company a firm that buys goods in one country and sells them to buyers in another country.

training teaching employees to do specific job tasks through either classroom development or on-the-job experience.

transaction balances cash kept on hand by a firm to pay normal daily expenses, such as employee wages and bills for supplies and utilities.

transfer a move to another job within the company at essentially the same level and wage.

transportation the shipment of products to buyers.

Treasury bills (T-bills) short-term debt obligations the U.S. government sells to raise money.

turnover occurs when employees quit or are fired and must be replaced by new employees.

U

unemployment the condition in which a percentage of the population wants to work but is unable to find jobs.

unsecured bonds debentures or bonds that are not backed by specific collateral.

unsecured loans loans backed only by the borrower's good reputation and previous credit rating.

V

value a customer's subjective assessment of benefits relative to costs in determining the worth of a product.

venture capitalists persons or organizations that agree to provide some funds for a new business in exchange for an ownership interest or stock.

viral marketing a marketing tool that uses a networking effect to spread a message and create brand awareness. The purpose of this marketing technique is to encourage the consumer to share the message with friends, family, co-workers, and peers.

W

wage/salary survey a study that tells a company how much compensation comparable firms are paying for specific jobs that the firms have in common.

wages financial rewards based on the number of hours the employee works or the level of output achieved.

warehousing the design and operation of facilities to receive, store, and ship products.

whistleblowing the act of an employee exposing an employer's wrongdoing to outsiders, such as the media or government regulatory agencies.

wholesalers intermediaries who buy from producers or from other wholesalers and sell to retailers.

wiki software that creates an interface that enables users to add or edit the content of some types of websites.

working capital management the managing of short-term assets and liabilities.

World Bank an organization established by the industrialized nations in 1946 to loan money to underdeveloped and developing countries; formally known as the International Bank for Reconstruction and Development.

World Trade Organization (WTO) international organization dealing with the rules of trade between nations.

Name Index

Note: Page numbers followed by n refer to notes.

Company Index

Subject Index

Note: **Boldface** entries denote key terms and the pages where they are defined.